ORANGEISM
THE MAKING OF A TRADITION

Orangeism

The Making of a Tradition

Kevin Haddick-Flynn

WOLFHOUND PRESS

Published in 1999 by
Wolfhound Press Ltd
68 Mountjoy Square
Dublin 1, Ireland
Tel: (353-1) 874 0354
Fax: (353-1) 872 0207

British Library Cataloguing in Publication Data
A catalogue record for this book is available from the British Library.

ISBN 0-86327-659-8

10 9 8 7 6 5 4 3 2 1

Cover Picture: Benjamin West, 'William III Crossing the Boyne, 1 July 1690'
    by kind permission of the Duke of Westminster
Cover Design: Slick Fish Design
Typesetting: Wolfhound Press
Printed in Scotland by Caledonian Book Manufacturing

Contents

Acknowledgements   7

Preface   9

Prologue   13

1. The Beginnings of Orangeism   15

2. The Coming of William   23

3. The Orange and the Green   32

4. The Siege of Derry   43

5. William in Ireland   53

6. The Green Grassy Slopes   61

7. Limerick, Athlone and Aughrim   69

8. The Glorious and Immortal Memory   85

9. Orangeism Without the Prince   92

10. The Protestant Nation   108

11. The Gathering Storm   120

12. The Battle of the Diamond   132

13. Orangeism Takes Root   147

14. A Land in Flames   162

15. 'Croppies Lie Down'   174

16. Aftermath and Union   191

17. The Spreading Orange Tree   202

18. The Ebbing Tide   215

19. Up, Protestants, Up!   228

20. Repeal and Reaction   242

21. The Years of the Great Test   257

22. Dolly's Brae and the Right to March   272

23. The Quaking Sod   288

24. The Orange Card   297

25. Home Rule is Rome Rule   312

26. The Orange State   326

27. The Discordant Drum   337

28. The Chosen Few   355

29. Under an Orange Arch   375

30. International Orangeism   393

Appendices:

   A   Maps: 401

        1.   The Route of William's Fleet — 1688   402
        2.   The Route to London — 1688   402
        3.   The Williamite Campaign in Ireland — 1689–1691   403
        4.   The Siege of Derry — 1689   404
        5.   The Battle of the Boyne — 1690   405
        6.   The Siege of Limerick — 1690   406
        7.   Sarsfield's Ride — 1690   407
        8.   Plan of Athlone — 1691   408
        9.   The Battle of Aughrim — 1691   409
       10. The Battle of the Diamond — 1795   410
       11. Orange Lodges in Ireland — 1798   411
       12. Orange Lodges in Ireland — 1990   412

   B   Leaders of Orangeism and Grand Masters in Ireland   413

   C   Grand Lodge of Ireland Office Holders 1998   414

   D   Addresses of Orange Grand Lodges   415

   E   The Orange Marching Season   416

   F   The House of Orange–Nassau   418

   G   Degree Structures in Loyalist Orders   419

Glossary   420

Notes   425

Bibliography   439

Index   443

Acknowledgements

I have incurred numerous debts in bringing this large ship into harbour. First of all, to the dozens of Orangemen in Northern Ireland who received me with courtesy and patiently helped me. Many of these gentlemen may disagree profoundly with much of what I have written, but I know they will accept that differences between us rest on sincerely held views. Throughout I have been mindful of the words of an aged Orangeman whom I encountered in Enniskillen. He said: 'If you do blacken us, take care to use a brush on which there is real tar.' I hope he will find that I have used neither tar nor whitewash.

I am indebted for general analytical comment to many friends in Ireland and Britain. Some of these are academics and some are journalists; some are a bit of both. I should like to thank them for their time, trouble, interest and support.

Numerous others have my deepest gratitude for lending material, giving advice and discussing many issues informally with me. Particular thanks in this regard are due to Bernard Canavan in London, Denis Hartnett in Tipperary, and Mrs Hilda Winter, Curator of the Dan Winter Museum, The Diamond, Loughgall, County Armagh. Special thanks are due to Maureen Kruger for her unfailing patience and the hard slog which she has put in, typing a poorly handwritten manuscript. At Wolfhound Press, Seamus Cashman and his staff have been a pleasure to work with, as have Helen Litton, who edited the manuscript, and Peter Costello (who deployed his unparalleled skills in picture research). The mistakes and other deficiencies are, as it is customary to say, all mine.

Finally, I want to say a big 'thank you' to my wife Una and my daughter Alexandra for patiently listening to me spouting about Orangeism for months on end. Their consideration and love, of course, know no bounds. The book is dedicated to the memory of my grandfather, Edward Haddick, at whose feet I first learnt of William, Sarsfield, Ballyneety, Aughrim, and all the other great personalities and places associated with the Williamite Wars.

Kevin Haddick-Flynn
London, 1999

This book is dedicated to the memory of
Edward Haddick

Preface

What is Orangeism? During the course of many visits to Northern Ireland I have put this question to numerous Orangemen and to those who oppose them. The answers which I received were trenchant and predictably partisan. In Portadown I was told: 'Put simply, Orangeism is Protestantism, patriotism, fraternalism and freedom.' And on the Falls Road in Belfast the reply was: 'Orangeism is bigotry, triumphalism, dysfunctional patriotism and a collusion to advance Protestants at the expense of Catholics.'

No matter how one views the phenomenon — as a religious institution, a political movement, or a religio-politico ideology — its controversial nature will not be denied. Perhaps no institution has been more bitterly maligned or more vigorously defended. Its central role in modern Irish history cannot be gainsaid. This role ought to be studied and this book attempts to do so in a straightforward and easily accessible fashion. It is written for the general reader who wishes to know more about a subject which, curiously, has received only sparse and spasmodic attention.

My account is highly personal, and necessarily so through the principle of selection involved. I have included only the things and people that seemed to me interesting or significant. I am especially conscious that I have concentrated on political narrative to the almost total exclusion of social and other matters. This was deliberate; otherwise an already lengthy manuscript would have been so long as to be unmanageable.

Whether one agrees with Henry Ford's dictum that history is bunk, or Napoleon's view that it is merely a fable agreed upon, there is little doubt that a trek through the reeds and bulrushes of Orange history will leave a mark. It may in fact, at times, put hairs standing on end. One thing is certain: no account of the subject will please everyone. I am almost painfully aware of the likelihood of ending up pleasing nobody. But, in truth, I have sought only to please myself. This will not, I hope, be seen as a brusque attitude but, given the nature of the subject, a judicious circumspection.

Although Orangeism, as we know it, dates only from 1795, its roots go back much further. It may, with propriety, be traced to the Dutch Revolt of 1568, when Protestants in the Low Countries began their long struggle against Spanish rule and the forces of the Counter-Reformation. It was this conflict which established the House of Orange as the great defenders of the Protestant cause and which disposed Protestants in the

Three Kingdoms to give allegiance to it. In Ireland the war which convulsed the country between 1688 and 1691 involved the presence of William III, Prince of Orange. It left behind a quartet of names — Derry, Aughrim, Enniskillen and the Boyne — which would forever have meaning for Irish Protestants, many of whom would later adopt the designation 'Orangemen'. The war bequeathed something more: a tradition of honouring William and celebrating the events associated with his coming — the Glorious Revolution, the Act of Settlement, the establishment of the Protestant Ascendancy and the military victories.

The vehicles used for celebrating those events were often brotherhoods. Some of these were open well-known societies, while others — adopting a trend of the period — were of a secret or semi-secret nature. In Britain, the best-known was probably the Loyal and Friendly Society of Blue and Orange, which had branches in Ireland. It is in Ireland, however, that we find the greatest number of societies — such as the Constitution Club of the Gentlemen of Kerry, and numerous Boyne and Aughrim clubs. Among the best-known was a small Dublin-based fraternity called the Aldermen of Skinners Alley, which met in the capital until the end of the nineteenth century; also well known was the Royal Boyne Society, which met in Drogheda until around 1850. Membership of these societies was confined largely to the well-heeled, and they exercised little or no influence over the infant Orange Order.

The Orange Order owes its immediate origin to sectarian feuds which broke out among the peasantry in County Armagh in 1784 and were to continue on and off for twelve years. These skirmishes gave rise to the Protestant and Catholic factions known as the 'Peep O'Day Boys' and 'The Defenders'. A number of writers hostile to Orangeism took the line that the early Orangemen were simply the 'Peep O'Day Boys' operating under a new guise. Orange apologists strenuously denied the charge. The Reverend Snowden Cupples, Rector of Lisburn (1796-1835) and Grand Master of the County Antrim Grand Lodge, wrote in 1799: 'The Orange Association should not be confounded as it has been with the disgraceful outrages which prevailed in County Armagh for several years.' Some historians have found Cupples' contention less than convincing. But Sir Richard Musgrave, himself a leading Orangeman, in his partisan *History of the Different Rebellions in Ireland* (published in 1800) echoed Cupples and included, in his list of those involved, 'the lower classes of Presbyterians'. Although a few Presbyterians and other Dissenters (like the publican Dan Winter, an ex-Quaker) were associated with early Orangeism, Musgrave was almost certainly incorrect. Presbyterians formed a small proportion of the population of County Armagh and were for many years a conspicuous minority in the Order.

The catalyst for the founding of the Order was the so-called 'Battle of the Diamond' on 21 September 1795, after which the victorious Protestants vowed to establish a society for their mutual protection. At least two of the early meetings were attended by Captain John Giffard, who commanded the Dublin Militia, then stationed at nearby Portadown. In 1810 Francis Plowden, in his *Historical Disquisition Concerning the Progress, Nature and Effects of the Orange Society in Ireland*, wrote of Giffard: 'To him are attributed the adoption of the title of Orangemen, their original oath and obligation and the first regulations by which they organised into a society.' The politically adept Giffard originally kept an apothecary's shop in College Green; he was a prominent Freemason, the editor of a newspaper, and held so many government sinecures that he was nicknamed 'The Dog in Office'. A few days after the founding of the Order he wrote to a friend, saying that 'he had founded in Loughgall a society that for generations would crib both Pope and Popery in Ireland'.

After an initial hesitancy, the Armagh gentry — the Blackers of Carrickblacker, the Atkinsons of Crow Hill, the Clarkes of Summer Island and the Maunsells of Drumcree — swung behind the Order. Among the first recruits were members of the recently formed yeomanry, a force which quickly took on an almost total Orange complexion. The early lodges expanded so rapidly that district and county jurisdictions were mapped out within months.

The first warrants to establish lodges were issued by James Sloan and his brother-in-law Wolsey Atkinson of Portadown, who was appointed Grand Secretary. It was soon recognised, however, that Portadown was an inappropriate base for a society with such potential, so the headquarters were moved to Dublin. The prime movers in this were the five sons of Colonel James Verner of Church Hill, who together established the first Dublin lodge in Harringtons Hotel in Grafton Street in 1797. Months later this lodge, No. 176, moved to the Verner town house at 6 Dawson Street, and rapidly became the lodge of the nobility and the gentry; it soon began to act as the ruling body.

By May 1798 Armagh had the greatest number of lodges — 78 — while warrants issued to other counties were: Tyrone 64; Down 45; Cavan 32; Monaghan 18; Fermanagh 16; Antrim 14; Carlow 11; Leitrim and Derry 10 each; Tipperary, Cork, Wicklow, Roscommon and Meath 3 each; Limerick, Dublin County, Sligo, Louth, Galway and Laois 2 each; Kildare, Wexford, Waterford and Kilkenny 1 each. Dublin City had 36 warrants.

The Order did not spring from a vacuum, but from old Williamite tradition which had long lain dormant among the Protestant weavers and tenant farmers along the Ulster borderlands. These staunch 'King's men' were caught in a continuing spiral of economic rivalry and sectarian bitterness with their Catholic neighbours, and had not forgotten that a few generations earlier their forefathers had defended the Walls of Derry and participated in William's campaigns. Their folk-memories had kept the Orange tradition alive, and its persistence was evidenced by the crude portraits of the king which hung in their homesteads, by the songs (many of which still survive) which they sang by their firesides, and by the innumerable hills, valleys and townlands which they named after their hero.

This tradition, as we know, lives on. Discussion and debate as to the manner of its contemporary expression has made names like the Garvaghy Road in Portadown and the Ormeau Road in Belfast reverberate around the world. And William is still at the heart of it. A freshly-painted gable mural in a Belfast housing estate, showing 'King Billy' crossing the Boyne, over the slogan 'Remember 1690', is not wholly about the past. It urges solidarity — today and tomorrow — to meet perceived threats to all those things which constitute the Orange tradition.

Prologue

Orangeism and History

Orangeism in Ireland takes its name from the historic figure who inspired it. This is William III, Prince of Orange, Count of Nassau, King of England, Scotland and Ireland and known historically to his devotees as The Great Deliverer. The portrait of this bewigged monarch crossing the River Boyne on a rearing white horse is the central icon around which Orangeism, as a popular phenomenon, has been concentrated.

To Ulster Protestants, William is the hero of the ages, stamped with imperishable fame. He is, as found in the pages of Macaulay,[1] a stalwart of gigantic proportions whose name and deeds are inscribed deeply on their history.

The Protestant love affair with William began early. When rumour of his impending invasion of England reached Irish Protestant communities in June 1688, it was greeted with rejoicing. He was seen as Providence's answer to the tyranny of the Catholic King James, who had threatened their power and tenure.

William had impeccable credentials. He was the scion of a princely dynasty which had championed the Protestant cause for three generations. His House had distinguished itself during the Dutch Revolt against Catholic Spain, and provided a shield behind which Protestant peoples sheltered from the forces of the Counter-Reformation. This background was relieving and encouraging to Irish Protestants, linking them with the early days of the reformed faith, and with those martyrs who, like William's ancestor, William the Silent, had died for religious and civil liberty.

Late seventeenth-century Irish Protestants had an abiding sense of history. The names which struck a chord were those of the Reformers who, as they put it, struggled against the errors and superstitions of Rome. They knew of the Waldenses and of the Albigenses who had fought the good fight for a purer faith. They remembered Hus, who was condemned because he denied the Pope's supremacy, and Wyclif, whose bones were dug up after sixty years and burned with his writings. And they saw themselves, in the land in which they had settled, as the children of those who in 1641 had survived a massacre at the hands of Catholic rebels.

The House of Orange was renowned as the established refuge of afflicted Protestants. The term 'Orangeism' itself had been coined by Dutch Calvinists as both a political slogan and a testimony to those sovereign princes who had rescued them from the 'vortex of perdition'. William, the latest of their line, had intervened to secure the affronted liberties of the people of England, and Irish Protestants were confident that he would be their succour too, and deliver them from their enemies.

This task he would surely accomplish, but only after a succession of the most bloody battles which Ireland has known. These, the Williamite Wars, established an Orange tradition which Protestants would forever celebrate. The invulnerable continuities of this tradition — with all their assonances and dissonances — are today evidenced by those Ulster gables which shriek: 'Remember 1690' and by the swaggering, confident steps of the brethren who march in William's honour on 12 July.

But this heritage has not been free of controversy. Is it, as its enemies aver, a self-deluding mythos emanating from the exigencies of a dynastic power struggle — which has seduced its adherents from a truer identity to be shared with their Catholic neighbours? Or is it an authentic, free-standing expression of the fortunes of their own singular history? These questions are academic and will not admit of answers which will please everyone. And maybe they are irrelevant. The Orange District Master who told his lodge: 'If William had not existed, then we should have to invent him' surely knew his brethren and how they had reached their historical consciousness.

In a sense, of course, they have invented William, if only to rival the competing hagiographical tradition where icons abound. Historian Eric Hobsbawm has shown how the invention of traditions has occupied political élites in Europe for much of modern history,[2] and in this regard the Orangeman is every bit as resourceful as his nationalist counterpart. Moreover, if history is — as some of its critical philosophers affirm — a selective record of the past to meet the needs of the present, the Orange-man is as competent at cherry-picking as anyone else. As the late Professor E.H. Carr might have said,[3] thousands of horsemen may have crossed the Boyne in history, but the writer on Orangeism is bound to say that only William's crossing had any significance.

—1—

The Beginnings of Orangeism

The French and Dutch Background

The Principality of Orange

The ancestry of the House of Orange can be traced to a tiny feudal principality in the south of France. The Principality of Orange was a medieval city state sited on the old Roman town of Arusio, twelve miles north of the papal enclave of Avignon. Its origin has not been clearly established but, according to tradition, its first prince was called, fittingly, William, and was given sovereignty of the Principality by Charlemagne in 793.[1]

The first prince of whom there is definite record was Gerald Ademar, who flourished around 1086. The succession devolved in 1393 to one John of Chavlons, whose line ruled for nearly 140 years until in 1530 its best known figure, Philibert, died. During Philibert's reign the House was granted extensive possessions in the Low Countries for services rendered to the Hapsburg Emperor Charles V.[2] The bequest was enormous. It included a quarter of Brabant, large stretches of Luxembourg, Flanders, French-Comte, and much else. Added to the Principality, these domains made the House of Orange one of the leading principates in Europe.

During Philibert's lifetime, a chain of political and religious events began in the Low Countries. The reformed faith spread from the German principalities, and the Emperor set his face sternly against it. He had actually met Martin Luther, at the Diet of Worms in 1521, and lived to regret his failure to deal with him then as decisively as he might have done later. Though Lutheranism was banned, it swept irrevocably on.

The authorities established a state-run inquisition and some 2,000 people were executed. It seemed that the 'heresy' might be crushed. Many fled to Germany and England, and fear stalked the land. But the forces which were to tear apart Hapsburg rule in the Netherlands were unstoppable.

Philibert, who was an Emperor's man, would have no truck with the new doctrines, and when he died he was succeeded by his nephew Rene, who became both Prince of Orange and Count of Nassau.[3] Rene was twenty-six years old, healthy, married and the father of at least one illegitimate child when he rode off to the wars in France. Before setting out he made a will in favour of a cousin many years his junior, the son of the Count of Nassau — Dillenburg, in Germany. Nobody thought much about it; it had been drawn up to ensure that in case of mishap his inheritance would not pass to a Lutheran uncle, because the Emperor would not countenance such vast possessions passing to a heretic. But tragedy struck. In July 1544 Rene was fatally hit by a bullet at St Dizer.[4]

William the Silent (1533–1584)

The eleven-year-old who came into this inheritance was also a heretic. But this, it was felt, could be changed. His father was a moderate man who had adopted the reformed faith a mere ten years earlier. Although his convictions were genuine and personal, they were not exactly passionate. The boy therefore converted to the older faith and was sent to the Netherlands to take possession of his new estates. His name was William.

A decade later his life took a serious turn when the Emperor's son, Philip II of Spain — a melancholy man who believed himself chosen by God to play an historic role — became ruler of the Netherlands. William held the office of Stadholder — the King's Lieutenant — of the provinces of Holland, Zeeland and Utrecht. He saw loyalty to his sovereign as his overriding duty, but this soon came into conflict with his sense of justice and growing sympathy with the plight of the people.

He and other nobles realised that the earlier spasmodic persecution of Protestants was to be stepped up, and that the King was determined to uproot the reformed faith at whatever cost. This policy, which included stripping recalcitrant nobles of their privileges, was ruthlessly implemented and led to renewed emigration — Norwich, in England, was almost forty per cent Dutch at this time.

In spite of the persecution there was an outburst of open-air religious gatherings everywhere. Huge crowds flocked to hear Calvinist ministers preaching in the safety of woods or on remote country roads. Then an event occurred which, to this day, accounts for the notably austere interiors of Dutch churches. This was the 'iconoclastic fury' in which places of worship were attacked by the populace and thousands of paintings and statues were destroyed. In one notorious instance a former hat-maker, Sebastian Matte, preached so effectively that twenty or so members of his congregation leapt up and smashed the images around them.

William and other nobles tried to defuse the agitation. They petitioned the King to take a more lenient line, but their efforts were ignored. The royal response was to send the notorious Duke of Alva, a man of merciless discipline, at the head of a large army. His Council of Troubles, a tribunal commissioned to deal with heresy and rebellion, soon became known as the Council of Blood. It implicated some of the nobles in the agitation and the Duke decreed that they be forcibly brought into line. Many were arrested and some executed. William was lucky to escape to his estates in Germany.

During this exile the Prince of Orange raised an army and tried, without success, to enlist foreign support. Although initially he saw the struggle exclusively in political terms, circumstances forced him to ally with the persecuted Protestants who, in the main, were Calvinists. Gradually he converted to Calvinism himself. He re-entered the Netherlands in 1572 with a force 20,000 strong, and by the end of the year he held two-thirds of Zeeland and Friesland. But the Spaniards rallied; by spring they had his most important strategic position, the city of Leiden, under siege. The heroic raising of the siege by the flooding of the surrounding countryside, and the transporting of food by barges to the besieged, are among the most renowned episodes of the conflict.

If fighting the Spaniards was William's greatest task, creating a unified country was hardly less formidable. The split between the Calvinist-dominated north and the Catholic south began to widen. The joining of most southern provinces in the Treaty of Arras (1579), and of the northern provinces in the Union of Utrecht shortly after, ended the prospect of unifying the Netherlands.[5]

The Assassination of William

In the summer of 1584, William and his wife Louisa took up residence at Delft where a son, Frederick Henry, was born to them. During the previous two years, with the connivance of the Spanish government, no fewer than five attempts had been made on William's life. A sixth was now made. On Sunday morning, July 8th, the Prince of Orange received a dispatch from the battle front. The courier who brought it was admitted to his bedroom. He called himself Francis Guign, the son of a martyred Calvinist, but he was really Balthazar Gerard, a Spanish agent and fanatical Catholic who for years had planned to murder the prince. He told the officer on duty that he wished to attend Divine Service in the church opposite, but that his clothes were too travel-stained to join the congregation, and William ordered that money be given to him. It was used to purchase a pair of pistols.

Two days later the Prince, his wife and others dined at midday. Following the meal they rose to go upstairs, but Gerard leaped from an alcove and fired point-blank. The Prince was carried to a couch in the dining room where, in a few minutes, he died.[6] Days later, his body was entombed at Delft amid the tears of his people. Never did a greater sorrow afflict them. On his tomb they wrote a simple inscription: 'To the glory of God and to the everlasting memory of William of Nassau — Father of the Fatherland.'

William had been named 'the Silent' for his ability to conceal high matters of state; notably he had remained tight-lipped when informed years before of French government plans to massacre the Huguenots. While not of a devout disposition, he had cultivated close links with Protestants. The Calvinists provided zealous troops, which served his purpose, and his overtures to the Huguenots would have borne fruit but for the Massacre of Saint Bartholomew (August 1572).

William's closeness to Protestants may be seen from his marriages. Three of his four wives were Protestant noblewomen. His second marriage, to Anna, daughter of the Elector of Saxony, brought him the disfavour of the King, who strongly opposed connections with heretics. The bond was a personal tragedy and ended in divorce when Anna was caught in an adulterous relationship with the father of the painter Peter Paul Rubens. His third wife, Charlotte de Burbon, had been forced to enter a convent as a girl. She renounced her vows and converted to Protestantism. She died of a fever shortly after restoring William to health following an assassination attempt. His last marriage was to Louise de Coligny, daughter of the martyred Huguenot leader Admiral de Coligny and widow of Sieur Tiligny; both her father and previous husband had been killed during the Massacre of Saint Bartholomew.

A further influence on William was the fate of his eldest son. The boy had been abducted while attending University at Louvain, and in Spain he was forcibly Catholicised and held prisoner until his fiftieth year.

These matters drove William, inexorably, towards Protestantism. So did his temperament. He cared little for dogma, and the imposition of revealed truths on minds which rejected them was abhorrent to him. He was a child of the new enlightenment; of an age of sharp antithesis and amazing contrasts, of great intellectual fervour and of fierce religious intolerance.

The foremost Netherlandish painter of the day, Pieter Breughel the Elder, in his famous tableau 'The Massacre of the Innocents', provides a stark image of the period. It shows an alien soldiery assaulting village folk and butchering their children. Mothers tug at the soldiers and turn away to weep. In the background a troop of cavalry is drawn up in the snow. Their commander, dressed in black, hunches on his horse, awesome and white-bearded. The work dates from one of the harsh winters of Alva's terror and is a striking evocation of the persecution of the Protestants.

Maurice (1567–1625)

William's second son, Maurice of Nassau, was a student at Leiden University when his father was struck down. He was immediately appointed stadholder of Holland and soon stadholder of the other provinces which made up the United Provinces of the Netherlands. He did not take the title Prince of Orange until the death of his older brother, the one-time hostage.

Maurice was one of the great soldiers of his age and a master of military strategy. Beginning in the 1590s, he won victory after victory over the Spaniards. Then, in 1609, a truce was signed which fixed the boundary between the United Provinces and the Spanish Netherlands, roughly where the Dutch-Belgian border runs today. But the constitution of the young republic was complex and cumbersome. Overlapping and conflicting powers were vested in the Provincial States and in the central legislative body, the Estates General.

An uneasy alliance emerged between Maurice and Johan van Oldenbarneveldt, advocate of the States of Holland and its delegate to the Estates General. When the alliance turned sour, a struggle for supremacy began. Van Oldenbarneveldt was drawn into theological disputes, but the crafty Maurice quietly consolidated his support in Zeeland and Amsterdam. Van Oldenbarneveldt became an advocate of Erastianism — the theory that the state should direct the affairs of the Church — and patron of the moderate Protestants, who sought toleration. Maurice supported the fundamentalists, who constituted the bedrock of Orange support.

When van Oldenbarneveldt obtained authority to raise levies of professional soldiers, Maurice saw the danger and acted quickly. His followers arrested van Oldenbarneveldt and accused him of plotting a coup d'état, and of secret dealings with the Spaniards. He denied the charges. The long political trial was marked by bias and injustice, and at its end, while Maurice did not himself pronounce the death sentence on his adversary, he ostentatiously refrained from exercising his prerogative of pardon. This execution of an old patriot and ally was to stain his character and his career. But the excited populace thought otherwise and, whipped up by the 'Orangists', they shouted the old slogan, 'Oranje Boven' (literally, 'Up Orange').

The truce expired in 1621 and, with the help of France, Maurice waged war until his death in 1625. The struggle with Spain continued for another twenty-three years.

Frederick Henry (1584–1647)

Maurice died unmarried and officially childless. He was succeeded by his half-brother Frederick Henry, youngest son of William the Silent. The new prince had been little over a year old when the fatal bullet struck his father. His godfathers were Frederick, the Lutheran King of Denmark, and Henry III of Navarre, the one-time Huguenot whose marriage had sparked the Massacre of Saint Bartholomew. Henry's flippant remark on his less than enthusiastic conversion to Catholicism, that 'Paris is worth a Mass', is often quoted as evidence of his cynicism.

The new Prince of Orange turned into a skilful politician and a renowned general. His successful conquest of enemy-held towns and fortresses earned him the sobriquet 'The Conqueror of Cities'. A remarkable run of successes made him a hero and he occupied an almost monarchical position in the young state. The Act of Survivance (1631) made his offices hereditary and he was given the title 'Highness' — an unusual distinction in a Republic. But with his beautiful and forceful wife, Amelia von Solms, he annoyed the Regents — those powerful oligarchs who wielded great political and commercial power — by maintaining a lavish court at The Hague and promoting a new Orange nobility. From a dynastic viewpoint his efforts were crowned by the marriage of his heir, William II, to the eldest daughter of Charles I of England. This began the fateful connection of the House of Orange with the House of Stuart.

The Dutch were at this time leaders in the commercial life of Europe. The country was not naturally wealthy, but was well placed to benefit from the enormous growth of Baltic trade with the rest of Europe. Its merchant fleet totalled more than that of its combined rivals. Overseas, the Dutch East India Company monopolised the profitable supply of eastern spices to Europe, and the West India Company wrested control of Brazil from the Portuguese and took possession of the Caribbean island of Curaçao. From there it supplied African slaves to the plantations of Brazil, the West Indies and America. Profits from these colonial adventures poured back to the Republic and it became the unquestioned financial centre of Europe, playing a crucial part in the development of industry and trade. The distinctive character of Dutch society was reflected in its arts. The sombre interiors of the Old Masters show the citizens to be dour, hard-working and frugal. The stern Calvinist Church did not support the arts, but merchants, artisans and farmers spent considerable sums on their collections of pictures and printed works.

Frederick Henry was himself a man of considerable erudition and patronised both the arts and the sciences. But his luxurious living was frowned on and he did not escape criticism from the pulpit. In 1647 he was succeeded by his son William II.

William II (1625–1650)

When Frederick Henry had arranged his son's marriage to Mary Stuart, he took full cognisance of her status as the daughter of a reigning monarch. He hoped that a marriage into the House of Stuart would boost his scheme for the establishment of an Orange monarchy. These ambitions were shared by his headstrong son. The new stadholder, in fact, saw himself as king already. He resented those oligarchs, particularly in the Estates of Holland, who sought to curb the House of Orange.

Shortly after his appointment, a peace was concluded with Spain which finally ended the war for Dutch independence. It failed to satisfy the young stadholder. He conspired with the French to resume hostilities and to win the portion of the Southern Netherlands still ruled by Spain. He was supported by his brother-in-law Charles Stuart, then in exile and hoping to be restored to the crown of England. But opposition came from within the Republic itself. The resentful oligarchs opposed Orange ambitions. Renewed conflict would, they maintained, increase taxation, interfere with trade and bring the rival Port of Antwerp into competition with the commercially vibrant Port of Amsterdam. Nor did they conceal their opposition to William's aggrandisement. In the Estates General they voted for the disbandment of the army and, when unsuccessful, withdrew their financial support for those regiments which they had funded.

The new Prince of Orange was not a man to take these matters lying down. On 30 July 1650 he moved swiftly against the Estates of Holland and imprisoned six of the leading oligarchs. He ordered his army to march on Amsterdam and to take power. The attempted coup failed, and a compromise was worked out. William had to promise to restrain his foreign policy. Few felt that this was the end of the matter and expected the Prince to strike again. This was not to be, for in October tragedy struck. William was staying at his hunting lodge in Dieren, near Arnhem, when after a few days of the chase, he suddenly felt ill. His doctors diagnosed smallpox and within the week he was dead.

For some time no one dared to tell Mary. She was well over eight months pregnant and it was feared that the shock might cause her to miscarry. As it was, her distress was increased by the fussy attentions of her mother-in-law Amelia, whose over-efficient secretary, Huygens, insisted that she should write in person to the rulers of Europe, informing them of her husband's death.[7]

Mary's confinement took place in a room hung with black mourning curtains. At 2.30 a.m. on 4 November she fell into labour; six hours later, a son was born. Mary wanted to call him Charles after her father the King of England, who had been executed the year before. But the dogmatic Amelia insisted that the child be given the good Orange name of William. After hours of argument, Amelia got her way. The boy became the tenth Prince of Orange to bear the name William.[8]

—2—

The Coming of William

The Young Prince

Born prematurely, and so delicate that his life was despaired of, William of Orange seemed to have a dismal prospect before him. As a result of his father's ill-judged audacity the office of stadholder had been abolished. The complicated affairs of the Republic were administered by an oligarchy, at the head of which was Johan de Witt, Grand Pensionary of the Province of Holland. By methods less than straightforward, he set in train legislation which excluded the House of Orange from power. But the infant Prince, shorn of his ancestral glories, was still regarded by his family's supporters, the Orangists, as their best hope for the future.

William was made a 'child of state' and brought up under the personal care of the Grand Pensionary. De Witt, a single-minded statesman, gave himself the task of creating a patriotic republican out of the young Prince, but failed miserably. The boy felt unhappy and isolated. As he grew, he harboured a bitter sense of wrong. But he showed remarkable signs of precocity and firmness of character that impressed all who met him. Even in his early teens he made it perfectly clear that he intended to fight, inch by inch, all who opposed a complete return of those powers and offices held by previous Princes of Orange, and which he considered his birthright.

His position was strengthened in 1660 by the restoration to the English throne of his uncle Charles II of England who, with his brothers James and Henry, had passed part of his exile in Holland. It was not, however, to the intrigues of the Orangists or the lazy efforts of his royal uncle that the young prince was to owe his reinstatement. War was the catalyst.

Downfall of de Witt

For years France had steadily grown in strength, and was now ruled by a third king of the House of Bourbon. Louis XIV had inherited the great power and organisation built by the renowned Cardinal Richelieu and his successor, the Italian Mazarin, but his vanity and bigotry led to the adoption of policies of extreme foolishness. In 1672 he sought to expand his borders and assert his prestige and so, invoking dubious legal claims that it was part of his wife's inheritance, he ordered his armies to invade the Netherlands.

The attack took de Witt by surprise. He had ruled for twenty years and had held his own among the statesmen of Europe; but he had made no provision for the catastrophe which now befell the Dutch people. There was an uproar against him. He was accused of incompetence and, in the popular anguish, as town after town fell to the invader, of selling out his country. In the feverish anti-de Witt demonstrations which ensued, his brother, Cornelis, was accused of treachery and of attempting to assassinate the Prince of Orange. The accusations were false, but Cornelis was arrested and thrown into prison. On 21 August 1672 when Johan, the fallen statesman, visited his brother, an Orange mob surrounded the prison and broke into the room where the brothers had met. They were both murdered in the most barbaric fashion.

William has been held responsible for this crime, or at least of approving of it when it was accomplished. The matter has been disputed, yet it is true that Orange agents — notably Michael Tichelear and companions — inflamed the mob, and at least one of them thereafter drew a life-long pension from William's estates.

The prince demanded full powers from the alarmed oligarchs, and received them. At the age of twenty-one he found himself Captain General of a small, miserably equipped and disorganised army which was falling back from positions held by the enemy. His task seemed hopeless. The Dutch had little spirit of resistance left and were willing to consider any humiliating terms which Louis might offer. It was suggested that William should surrender the few towns left to him and settle for a little duchy or princedom in the Netherlands under the sovereignty of Louis, together perhaps with the hand of one of Louis' bastard daughters.

William had different views. He would not accept compromise or defeat. He was determined, as he said, to die in the last ditch rather than yield to the invader. Bishop Burnet,[1] his chaplain, describes him at this time of speaking passionately 'to the amazement of all who heard him' to a packed assembly of the Estates General and persuading its members in an oration of 'nearly three hours' (probably an overstatement) that it was possible to defend the country and to defeat the enemy. These speeches were not mere bravura, as William was to prove. In a series of lightning campaigns, the young stadholder drove the enemy out of the country — he turned the sea itself against them by opening the dykes — and consolidated his position at the head of Dutch affairs. The war led to his entering into alliances with the Great Elector of Brandenburg, the Hapsburg Emperor and the King of Spain. The peace established by the Treaty of Nymwegen (1678) made him a considerable figure in European politics. And the alliances which he had negotiated would be utilised again in what he swore would be his life's work: the curbing of the expansionist ambitions of the King of France.

The Character of William

What manner of man was this young prince who had come to prominence so quickly? In appearance he was singularly unattractive. Small, hunched, hook-nosed, hollow-cheeked, he looked like some pallid bird of prey. With his long upper lip and acidulated gaze, he gave the impression of being egotistic, but he was not. His only showy gift was his superb horsemanship; for the rest, he was totally unaffected. Careless in dress and harshly brusque in manner, he possessed none of the condescension of seventeenth-century rulers. Nor did he have their voracious sexual appetites.

In fact, women seemed to interest him little. Throughout his life there were whispers that he was homosexual. Those aspersions rested largely on a veiled remark in Bishop Burnet's unreliable memoirs, and were never substantiated. Burnet wrote: 'He had no vice but one, in which he was very cautious and secret.' There is little doubt that William was attracted to handsome young men. For years his closest companion was a red-headed fellow called Hans Willem Bentinck, who had joined his service as a page. When William was thought to be dying of smallpox in 1675 and the doctors decided that the only cure was for a young man of his own age to lie in the bed with him, Bentinck unhesitatingly volunteered for the dangerous task. The warmth of Bentinck's body induced the sweat that helped to cure William.

But whether William was aware of a latent homosexuality is doubtful. It is more likely that he was simply happier in the company of men. A stern Calvinist upbringing had rendered him abstemious, priggish and parsimonious. 'His behaviour,' says Burnet, 'was solemn and serious, seldom cheerful, and but with a few.' The circumstances of his birth and background seemed to govern his whole life. He eagerly embraced the lot marked out for him, and made no effort to evade his responsibilities. Indeed, few figures of his era were so single-minded. He worked, as if driven, for the security of his country and to curb the power of France. This aim — essentially to achieve an equitable balance of power in Europe — may have been mingled, as his enemies aver, with personal ambition. But there is something poignant, almost painful, about the burning earnestness of the man, in a cynical age.

Marriage to Mary Stuart

Charles II was a clever politician, adept at handling the internal affairs of England. He was also a cynic and a bit of a rogue. He was the first to recognise that his continued lack of legitimate offspring would place on the throne his brother James, whom he knew was most unlikely to keep it.

Two of the most important aspects of Charles' reign were his dependence on financial aid from Louis XIV, which prevented him from entering alliances against France, and the marriage of his niece Mary Stuart, James' daughter, to William of Orange. Mary had been brought up in the Church of England. She was fifteen when she was informed that she was to marry her cousin, a complete stranger to her. On learning of her fate, she wept for days. William was twenty-six and, although something of a connoisseur of paintings and a good linguist, had not developed those talents requisite for wooing women. But it was to be a dynastic marriage, intended to draw together symbolically the Dutch and British peoples, and personal feelings hardly entered into the matter.

The ceremony took place in Saint James' Palace in London on 4 November 1677, and everyone was happy. Happiest of all was William. Not only would this English match strengthen his hand against Louis XIV of France, it would move him several steps closer to the British throne and advance the prestige of the House of Orange at home. If the ageing James did not provide the country with a Catholic heir, William and Mary might well provide a Protestant one.

At least the genially drunken Charles thought so. On the wedding night he had seen the newly-weds to their bedroom. Drawing the curtain, he had issued the strait-laced William with the injunction: 'Now, nephew, to work! Saint George for England!' The work, alas, turned out to be unsuccessful. Mary, although pregnant on several occasions in the coming years, failed to provide an heir.

The Glorious Revolution

The death of Charles II was neither dramatic nor unexpected. He had long lain ill, tormented by the measures which his doctors had devised to cure him. The last years of his life had certainly been the most contented, if not the happiest. For the final four he had ruled without a parliament, and the bickerings and strictures of politicians had ceased to trouble him. The English Court in these last years was a parasite of France, and Charles' advisers were sharply divided in their attitude towards this. Lord Halifax headed a group which disliked the French dependency, and he understood that French domination of the Low Countries would menace England's existence as a free power. He feared Louis' advancing armies on the Dutch and Flemish coasts more than supplies of French gold to Whitehall.

Halifax was justified in his anxieties. Consciously, for years, English foreign policy had concentrated on seeing that the Low Countries should remain in the hands of powers unable to threaten her command of the sea. Twice she had gone to war to maintain this state of affairs, and each time had not contemplated peace until her ends were achieved.

Opposed to Halifax and his colleagues stood James, the heir to the throne, and his Tory friends. On the day when Charles finally expired — after whispering his last pleasantry: 'Gentlemen: I am afraid that I am an unconscionable time in dying,' James inherited all the power and prestige which his elder brother had amassed during those last desperate years. In person, James was tall, elegant, fair-haired, with fine features marred only by a sneer of forbidding bitterness. 'A plain man in a nightgown' is how the diarist Pepys[2] described him. He grievously lacked a sense of humour, and both his portraits and personal lifestyle suggest that he may have been dyspeptic.

Almost as soon as he had buried his brother in Westminster Abbey and assumed the panoply of kingship, James summoned a parliament, composed chiefly of his Tory adherents. The Whigs, who not long before had tried to exclude him from the throne on account of his professed Catholicism, were removed from power. No sooner had this carefully selected body met than a stroke of luck established James more securely. The Duke of Monmouth, Charles' bastard son, landed at Lyme Regis and launched a pathetic attempt to wrest the crown from his uncle. The history of this episode need not concern us, save to note two men who played a part in turning the Battle of Sedgemoor into a crushing defeat for Monmouth's hopes. These were John Churchill, later to be renowned as the Duke of Marlborough, and a young Irish cavalry officer whose deeds in his own country, in a few years, would bring him fame: Patrick Sarsfield.

Having crushed Monmouth, James embarked on a series of policies seldom paralleled in the annals of kingly foolishness. His vindictive revenge on all who had taken part in Monmouth's rebellion alienated moderate men. He had been strong enough to afford mercy, and Monmouth's and half a dozen other heads would have satisfied the demands of contemporary convention. But a modest bloodletting would not satisfy James: he chose to unleash Judge Jeffreys and his 'Bloody Assizes'. The easy victory over his rebellious nephew had misled James into supposing that he could accomplish all his ambitions irrespective of the prejudices and determination of his subjects.

At his accession he had secretly resolved to devote his life to restoring to his realm its lost Catholic faith. Inflamed by his clerical advisers —

largely members of the Jesuit Order — and his French allies, he decided on the rapid conversion of England. He imagined that the fashionable doctrine of the Divine Right of Kings, with its concomitant prerogatives, would allow him to conduct his hapless subjects back to Rome without a protest. He was mistaken.

As a first step, and to prepare against possible resistance by his Whig enemies and the Anglican Establishment, he quartered a force of 30,000 men on Hounslow Heath, hoping, in the event of challenge, to render London docile. This force he officered illegally with Catholics, and he attempted, with the aid of numerous priests, to have the rank and file converted.

But the proselytising campaign proceeded too slowly to satisfy James; he imported squads of raw Irish recruits and incorporated them into the army. This action destroyed any chance which might have existed of transforming the army into an instrument of his will. The Irish were mainly Gaelic-speaking rustics and were regarded by their English associates as virtually wild barbarians from beyond the pale of civilisation.

The next step towards James' downfall was taken not by himself but by 'His Most Christian Majesty' Louis XIV, who elected, in a mood of exalted piety, to revoke the Edict of Nantes, which tolerated the Huguenots in France. The revocation was promptly followed by a persecution of such savage fanaticism that, in Trevelyan's words, 'the sum of human misery thus wantonly brought about is too horrible to contemplate.'[3]

This French persecution at once rebounded in England. Fleeing Huguenots arrived in thousands with tales of terror, murder and torture. It needed little perception to draw the obvious moral; the old cry of 'No Popery' rang out, and even James' Tory friends grew alarmed as their popularity wilted. Clergymen, who a year before had been preaching the doctrine of non-resistance and drawing on the Bible to justify the Divine Right of Kings, now changed their tunes. In Protestant pulpits up and down the land, James was denounced as another Nero, a new Antichrist. Fearful that he might lose all, James began to make concessions.

His bait consisted of a promise of civil equality and toleration for all his Christian subjects and was contained in a Declaration of Indulgence. Every parish parson was required to read from his pulpit this royal Declaration, which suspended all statutes against Catholics and Dissenters. The Anglican Establishment refused to tolerate this, and revolted. Seven bishops, led by William Sancroft, the Archbishop of Canterbury, approached the King with a petition that he should withdraw the Declaration, which they considered illegal. At once, and without legal advice, James prosecuted the bishops for seditious libel.

They stood trial in London. Every effort was made to secure a conviction. They were acquitted, and the people of London went wild with delight. On the same night, 30 June 1688, a messenger left for the Dutch Republic. Admiral Arthur Herbert (later the Earl of Torrington), disguised as an ordinary seaman, carried a letter signed by seven great leaders of political opinion, both Whig and Tory. It was addressed to the Prince of Orange, and invited him in unequivocal terms to bring an army to England, overthrow the popish monarch and restore for the people their outraged liberties.

That the letter was dispatched on the day of the bishops' acquittals was a mere coincidence. The immediate reason for the invitation was that almost three weeks earlier, one of James' dearest ambitions had been realised. His second wife, Mary of Modena, had given birth to a son who lived to be known in history as 'The Old Pretender'. This event killed all hope that James' reign was no more than a temporary affliction which would die with him. The news of the child's birth was conveyed to Thomas Osborne, Earl of Danby, one of the most powerful men in the land. With Danby's agreement, those men of weight and influence who hated James began to engineer a revolution to push him from the throne.

The Protestant Wind

From his wedding day onwards, William had kept a beady eye on English domestic affairs. He had apparently hoped that his father-in-law would join the League of Augsburg, a confederacy which William had formed against the aggressive rapacity of Louis XIV, but for some time he had realised that such a hope would not materialise. Practical in all things, he began to ingratiate himself with those people in England who hated James. As a first step he instructed his Chief Secretary to write a public letter denouncing James' religious policy. This was received in England with enthusiasm; Orange flags began to appear on private buildings and people whispered that William would be brought across to dispossess James. Protestants in Ireland, in the midst of their despair, began to reassess their position. Those who had resolved to flee the country hesitated, and decided to await developments.

It was not until 19 October that William sailed from the Netherlands. His fleet consisted of 52 men-of-war, 25 frigates, 25 fire-ships and nearly 400 transports for 3,600 horse and 10,692 foot soldiers. The prince's frigate could be identified by banners bearing the arms of Nassau and England, and by a flag inscribed with the motto: 'The liberties of England and the Protestant religion, I will maintain.' But a sudden gale swept the Orange ships back to port. William did not sail again until 1 November, when the famous 'Protestant Wind' took him across the channel to Yorkshire, where Danby was waiting for him. It was necessary, however, to avoid James' fleet and, favoured by changes of wind, William veered to the west and finally landed in Torbay on 5 November 1688.

He was not initially received with enthusiasm; the people of the West Country, remembering the Monmouth fiasco and the punishments dispensed by Jeffreys, were apathetic or afraid. They watched curiously while the magnificent Dutch army and the Danish, Prussian and Huguenot troops whom William had recruited disembarked and floundered over the rough country roads, but they made no effort to join them.

On learning of William's invasion, James dispatched John Churchill against him, at the head of an army of 5,000. Although his friends persistently warned that Churchill was untrustworthy, James did not doubt his loyalty. However, Churchill defected to the Orange side and many senior officers accompanied him. James' army seethed with confusion and disaffection. For once in his life James took a true measure of the situation. He prudently retired to London and attempted to negotiate. William did not pursue his quarry; he had everything to lose by shedding English blood on English soil. When James sent delegates to meet him, William received them politely but listened to their arguments with a cold, cynical smile.

The invader made his headquarters at Exeter, and attended Divine Service in the cathedral. The dean and chapter fled and Bishop Burnet, who accompanied the expedition, preached the sermon. It was here that the first Orange society in Britain was founded, for Burnet drew up a document entitled: 'An Engagement of the Noblemen, Knights and Gentlemen of Exeter, to assist the Prince of Orange in defence of the Protestant Religion'. Within a few days this document was signed by over 600 people, and became the constitution of the first association of William's supporters. The Prince spoke to his new adherents: 'Since God is pleased that we shall make preservation and happiness, let us not neglect this gracious opportunity; but with prudence and courage put into execution our honourable purposes. Therefore, gentlemen, friends and fellow Protestants, we bid you, and all your followers, most heartily welcome to our court and camp.'

Meanwhile, James hurried his wife and son to France and planned to follow them. Even in this comparatively simple endeavour, a cruel fate frustrated him. Fishermen at Faversham, near Rochester, detected his identity and stopped his flight; the miserable King was returned to London. The famous Dutch or Blue Guards, under Graf von Solms, had already displaced James' Watch at Whitehall and James submitted with incredible meekness to this insult. When William learned of the farcical escapade at Faversham, he immediately circulated the news that James had been caught in undignified flight from his realm. This proved the final blow. Those who remained loyal were now disgusted; those who, like Churchill, had joined the winning side, simply laughed. James, his kingdom lost by treachery and a bad joke, was quietly allowed to 'escape' to France. There, at the court of Versailles, with the sympathy of Louis and in a congenial atmosphere of loose living, not unmingled with piety, he managed to restore some of his self-esteem. So was effected 'The Glorious Revolution'.

—3—

The Orange and the Green

The Plantations

To the greater number of the King's subjects in Ireland, the revolution did not seem so glorious. These were the Catholics who had, not unnaturally, pinned their hopes on their co-religionist James. But to do justice to Irish Catholics meant depriving Irish Protestants of the fruits of their particular patrimony. And to Protestants the revolution was a deliverance from an anticipated hateful bondage.

This was a crucial period in Irish history and is rendered coherent only by reference to the country's past. The medieval conquest of Ireland had begun with the Anglo-Norman invasion of 1169, but had never been completed. It established an English colony and administration on Irish soil, and the claim of the English crown to the overlordship of Ireland, but it was not until the latter part of Elizabeth's reign that effective English rule began to extend beyond the area immediately around Dublin, known as The Pale. This extension brought the whole island, for the first time, under English rule. The great independent Irish lordships, both Gaelic and Anglo-Irish (that is, descendants of the Anglo-Normans), were finally destroyed, and the social structure of the old Gaelic world was fundamentally undermined. The last powerful Irish chieftain, Hugh O'Neill, Earl of Tyrone, submitted to James I at Mellifont in County Louth in 1603, and shortly afterwards fled the country with his principal retainers.

This 'Flight of the Earls' was followed by an unsuccessful rebellion by a minor chieftain, Sir Cahir O'Doherty of Inishowen, in 1608, which afforded the English government an opportunity for wholesale confiscation of lands in Ulster. These lands were assigned to English and Scottish 'undertakers' and the Plantation which followed was more systematic and thorough than the earlier confiscations in the midlands and Munster. It induced, from 1603 onwards, an influx of settlers from

England and Scotland whose religion, social customs and methods of working were very different from those of the Gaelic Irish.

Settlement in Ulster was not a new phenomenon. For centuries Scots and Irish had been criss-crossing the North Channel and settling in each other's territory. Many of the new settlements were private enterprise ventures; one of the most successful was the plantation of the Ards peninsula from 1606, as a result of a transaction between a local Gaelic lord and two Scots adventurers named Hamilton and Montgomery. This plantation acted as a bridgehead for smaller ones during the rest of the century. The newcomers fanned out over the counties of Down and Antrim and moved westward to fill the gaps left by the official plantations. The success of later plantations in the rest of the province meant that the overwhelming number of settlers in the region were Scots rather than English, and Presbyterian in religion rather than Anglican.

A number of different ethnic groups now shared the soil of Ireland: the new sixteenth-century settlers, known in Irish historiography as the 'New English' (Nua Ghaill); the 'Old English' (Sean Ghaill) — descendants of the eleventh-century Anglo-Normans; and the largest group, the 'Gaelic Irish' (Gaedhil) whose presence probably dated to Celtic migrations from Europe in the first and second centuries AD. Both of the latter groups were uniformly Catholic, with the 'Old English' having a traditional loyalty to the English crown. The 'New English' were wholly Protestant. This chronic division led to virtual paralysis. It was not until the Rebellion of 1641 that the two Catholic groupings coalesced and brought about the denominational bi-polarisation which exists to this day.

The 1641 Rebellion

The year 1641, when the dispossessed Catholics rose in an effort to regain their lands, was traumatic for Irish Protestants. The settlers had always lived in fear, as the dispossessed had not gone away but lurked in woods — the Protestants habitually referred to them as woodkerne — or on hillsides or lived homeless on the roads. There had been a prophecy that one day the Catholics would rise and cut the throats of the settlers. Contempt and hatred from the natives added to the uneasiness of the Protestants, and the date which they most feared turned out to be the 23 October.

In the early hours the leaders of the old Gaelic families in Ulster — Phelim O'Neill, Magennis, O'Hanlon, O'Hagan, Maguire, O'Reilly, and more — burst from the hills at the head of their cohorts and in a few hours overran the province. There was no wholesale massacre, but in the confusion which followed and in the willingness of the settlers to believe the worst, it became an established view that the Catholics had planned to exterminate the Protestants. Certain events lent credibility to the claim; one was the outrage which occurred on the bridge at Portadown, in County Armagh. Here, over one hundred Protestants — men, women and children — were dragged from their beds and thrown or driven over the parapet into the icy waters below. The insurgents took to boats and with heavy oars hit those who did not immediately drown until they stayed under. This barbarism gave rise to numerous legends, like that of the ghostly woman who for months afterwards was reputed to be seen rising from the waters and wailing: 'Revenge! Revenge!'

The Rebellion was not finally crushed until the intervention of Cromwell and his New Model Army in 1649. In the meantime a virulent propaganda literature flourished. Numerous piquant, salted tales — which included hair-raising narratives of killings and torture, of infants being ripped from their mothers' wombs, of children being boiled alive and old people slaughtered — fed the self-righteous vengeance which characterised Cromwell's campaign. His first action was to storm Drogheda and to put almost the entire population to the sword. 'A righteous judgement of God upon these poor wretches' is how he described it to parliament, adding that his measures would prevent a further 'effusion of blood'. Cromwell's claim that his methods prevented further bloodshed may have been true in the short term; in the long run, they created a hatred and bitterness which turned his name into a curse.

The settlement which followed begot the most extensive of the many plantations of Ireland. It embraced the entire country, with the exception of four counties west of the Shannon — Clare, Galway, Roscommon and Mayo. Those who benefited were the 'Adventurers' — people who advanced money to finance Cromwell — and the soldiers of his army, who numbered about 30,000 and whose pay was hopelessly in arrears. Catholic landowners who could not prove their innocence during the rebellion were deprived of their estates and ordered to move to 'Hell or to Connaught' by January 1654. The peasantry were not disturbed, as it was envisaged that they would be required as labourers for the new settlers.

The task of apportioning the land to its new owners was facilitated by the work of Sir William Petty, who conducted a land survey of the country in 1654. This — known as the 'Down Survey' because its details were 'set down' after calculation upon maps — is still extant. It provides the names of the displaced owners and of the settlers who supplanted them. Petty estimated that the area seized and planted came to eleven million acres, out of Ireland's total of twenty million.[1]

The settlement did not, however, make Ireland Protestant. The census of 1659 showed that even in Ulster, Catholics outnumbered Protestants by five to two, while in Connaught they formed ninety per cent of the population. Most of the land was, of course, now owned by Protestants and they were absolutely determined to retain it. The reign of James had threatened these arrangements and brought about changes which were designed to favour the Catholics, but which could only be sustained while a Catholic king remained on the throne.

The Rise of Tyrconnell

Shortly after his accession James had elevated a shrewd Catholic politician, Richard Talbot, to the peerage as Earl of Tyrone. Talbot was then fifty-five years of age (three years older than James), and a man of great energy, with a somewhat colourful past. He sprang from an old Anglo-Norman family and was the son of a successful lawyer who, despite his religion, had gained favour with the Protestant establishment. Talbot senior had been granted lands and a baronetcy, and Richard was brought up at the family seat at Carton, County Kildare. At an early age he received a commission in the Irish army of Charles I, and was one of a small number who survived Cromwell's massacre at Drogheda, where he was left for dead. In 1656 he joined Charles II in exile and struck up a friendship with James, then Duke of York, who formed a high opinion of him. This friendship was to last unbroken for thirty years.

In 1655 Talbot was in Ireland, where he hatched a plot to assassinate Cromwell and travelled to London to execute it. He was betrayed by a double-agent, arrested and brought before the Lord Protector himself. When he denied the plot, Cromwell threatened him with the rack and declared that he would spin the truth out of his bones. 'Spin me to a thread if you wish,' Talbot replied, 'I have nothing to confess and can invent only lies.' He received a prison sentence but somehow, en route to his incarceration, gave his guards the slip and escaped to Brussels. In Flanders he was soon commanding a French royalist regiment, and thereafter he went from strength to strength. Following the Restoration he was further promoted and in 1678 went back to Ireland where his brother Peter was Archbishop of Dublin.[2]

One of James' initial acts on becoming King was to recall the long-serving Irish Lord Lieutenant, the Duke of Ormond. This alarmed Protestants, who began to feel change in the air. Their fears were further increased when Talbot, who had become the most active of the Catholic leaders, was made a colonel in one of the elite regiments of horse. Clarendon, the King's brother-in-law and a staunch Protestant, was soon appointed to succeed Ormond. This was a disappointment to Catholics. They had hoped for Talbot who, as a coming man, had been tipped for the post. In fact it was Talbot — now newly created Earl of Tyrconnell — who was to dominate affairs during the period of Clarendon's weak tenure from 1686 to 1687. He was appointed to the rank of Lieutenant

General and put in charge of the army, which he rapidly re-modelled, getting rid of most Protestant officers and replacing them with Catholics. A similar policy was followed in other branches of the administration. Catholics were appointed judges, admitted to corporations, and even given seats on the Privy Council.

Clarendon offered little resistance to these measures. He believed that so long as the land settlement remained intact, the Protestant interest would be secure, putting his trust in James' assurances on this point. On his arrival in Dublin he had said: 'I have the King's command to declare upon all occasions that, whatever imaginary apprehensions any men may have, his Majesty hath no intention to altering the Act of Settlement.'

But whatever James' intentions might be, the new Earl of Tyrconnell made no secret of his own. 'By God, my Lord,' he exclaimed during an interview with the Lord Lieutenant, 'these Acts of Settlement are damned things.' Indeed, everything seemed to turn on the land settlement. Catholics, having gained a little, wanted more. Demands for repeal began to be heard. Judge Rice expressed the view that he could drive a coach and six through the appropriate Acts and Sir William Petty, the Cromwellian surveyor, compared them to Saint Sebastian, punctured with arrows.

Tyrconnell sensed that James' position was precarious. He knew that he had to act quickly if he were to swing the balance in favour of the Catholics. Two judges were sent to England to get the King's approval to a bill to alter the land legislation. In London they were met by an insulting mob who carried potatoes stuck on poles, yelling: 'Make way for the Irish ambassadors.'

Protestant alarm continued to increase. Some took fright and left for England. Others went to the Netherlands and offered their swords to William. These signs of Protestant panic had little effect on James, who was becoming more impatient than ever to effect his 'Catholic Design'. By January 1687, Clarendon had fallen by the wayside. To the utter despair of Protestants, Tyrconnell was appointed to succeed him. John Evelyn, the diarist, wrote: 'Lord Tyrconnell has gone to succeed the Lord Lieutenant in Ireland, to the astonishment of all sober men and to the evident ruin of Protestants in that Kingdom.'[3] Tyrconnell had made frequent visits to London, allegedly for the sake of his health, but had in fact been plotting with the King. He outmanoeuvred the hapless Clarendon and connived at his downfall.

While Clarendon's earlier assurances had carried little conviction, new ones given by Tyrconnell carried none at all. He was dubbed 'Lying Dick Talbot' and lampooned by a popular ditty called 'Liliburlero', written (or at least published) by the Whig politician Lord Thomas Wharton:

> Ho brother Teig, dost hear de decree
> Dat we shall have a new deputy;
> Ho by my soul, it is a Talbot
> And he will cut all de English troat.[4]

The song's words were a take-off of Irish peasant speech, and enraged Catholics. The last two verses were particularly insulting:

> Dare was an auld prophesy found in a bog
> That Ireland would be ruled by an ass and a dog
> And now the auld prophesy has come to pass
> For Talbot's a dog and James is an ass.

The First Irish Williamites

Tyrconnell realised that a Protestant backlash was inevitable and that time was running out. He moved to strengthen the army. In Ormond's day it had consisted of only eight regiments; Tyrconnell planned to increase this four times, and offered more than the going rate for recruits to join. There was a great number of unemployed Catholics, and young people literally flocked to the ranks. Soon he had an army approaching 40,000. True, it was untrained, ill-disciplined and badly armed, but it consisted of good material. The newcomers had an abiding hatred of Protestants, and would serve Tyrconnell's purpose well.

When news of James' overthrow reached Ireland (his flight from London was on 24 December 1688) there was great excitement. The Protestants declared for William immediately. Both in Dublin and the north large numbers of them were armed, and it was feared that they might strike against Tyrconnell. There was a plot, in fact, to seize Dublin Castle and to place him under house arrest. It was abandoned when the conspirators were informed that the Lord Deputy was wavering and may easily switch sides. But would Tyrconnell switch? It was impossible to discern the machinations of that astute political mind, but he had decided, in fact, to play a waiting game.

The Protestants in the north, feeling certain of where their interests lay, took action to meet the crisis. In January 1689 a meeting was held at Mountalexander, near Comber, County Down. A defensive organisation known as the Antrim Association (later to be called the North East Association) was founded to cover Antrim and Down. Its joint commanders were Hugh Montgomery, Earl of Mountalexander, and the Honourable Clotworthy Skeffington. Protestants in Armagh and Monaghan came together under Lord Blaney of Castleblaney; Londonderry, Donegal and Tyrone combined and elected Colonel Robert

Lundy and Major Gustavas Hamilton as their commanders. Sligo had already mobilised on 4 January, with Lord Kingston and the Honourable Chidley Coote in command.

A general council of these associations was formed, and established its headquarters at Hillsborough, County Down. A spirit of combat was in the air and one of the leaders, Sir Arthur Rawden, became so anxious for battle that he was nicknamed 'The Fighting Cock of the North'. An address to William was drafted by the parent association (Antrim) and its delivery entrusted to Captain Baldwin Leighton, who left for London on 10 January. It was essentially a supplication for men, money and materials to deprive James of a foothold in Ireland. Leighton returned in four weeks with a reply. In the convoluted prose of the period, William wrote:

> We are resolved to employ the most speedy means in our power to rescue you from the oppressions and terrors you lie under . . . In the meantime . . . We approve of the endeavours We understand you are using to put yourself into a position of defence . . . We are persuaded that there are even of the Roman communion many who are desirous to live peacefully, and do not approve of the violent and arbitrary proceedings of some who pretend to be in authority.

This letter was encouraging, but it only amounted to a promise. Leighton had news, however, of 15,000 men who were being held at Liverpool in readiness for deployment in Ireland. William was not, it would appear, yet ready to commit himself to intervention in Ireland. He sent a dispatch to Tyrconnell demanding that he surrender his authority. He also gave an undertaking that Catholics in Ireland would be permitted the same rights as they had enjoyed during the reign of Charles II, and assigned an influential Irish Catholic officer, Richard Hamilton, to bring these terms to Dublin. Hamilton had previously expressed the view that he could win over Tyrconnell but, to everyone's surprise, he turned his coat. On reaching Dublin he urged Tyrconnell to reject the terms. Tyrconnell, who had now definitely come off the fence, greeted him with delight. It was said that 'the papists lit bonfires when Dick Hamilton came over, and that he was worth ten thousand men.'[5]

The Comber Letter

The country was awash with rumour. Weeks before, on 3 December, an anonymous letter addressed to Lord Mountalexander had been found lying on the street of the village of Comber, County Down. Written in a semi-literate hand, it said:

To my Lord, this deliver with haste and care.
Good my Lord.

I have written to you, to let you know that all Irishmen through Ireland is sworn, that on the ninth of this month they are all to fall on, to kill and murder, man, wife and child, and I desire your Lordship to take care of yourself and all others that are judged by our men to be heads, for whosoever of them can kill any of you, they are to have a Captain's place. So my desire to your honour is to look to yourself, and give other noblemen warning, and go not out either night or day without a good guard with you, and let no Irishman near you, whatsoever he be. So that is all from him who was your father's friend, and is your friend, and will be, though I dare not be known as yet, for fear of my life.[6]

This document was unquestionably a hoax, but it raised the spectre of 1641, and created images of an Irish Saint Bartholomew's Day. News of the letter spread like wildfire through the north, and particularly to Derry where Protestants had begun flocking for protection. A few days later the city closed its gates to Lord Antrim's regiment of 'Redshanks' — a newly recruited and ill-disciplined force, whose name derived from the colour of the stockings which they wore.

As the temperature mounted, Tyrconnell issued a proclamation. He promised protection to all loyal subjects and denounced the rumour-mongering of King James' enemies, but he failed to stifle either the rumours or the fears. It was reported that an anti-Tyrconnell coup was being hatched in Trinity College. Three companies were ordered to occupy the buildings and to send the students to their homes. Many in the teaching faculty fled to England.

Following the Trinity incident the Marquis de Pontis, and an Irish officer named Michael Roth, arrived from France. They carried a letter from James, who had established a mini court-in-exile at Saint-Germain, near Paris. James told the loyal Tyrconnell to 'hold out until summer at least', but made no mention of imminent French support. Tyrconnell felt annoyed and frustrated, but showed his political skills when he replied. He stressed that military aid was urgently needed if he were to survive. Then he added: 'If, Sir, Your Majesty will in person come hither . . . I will be responsible to you, that you shall be entirely master of this Kingdom and of everything in it, and, Sir, I beg of you to consider whether you can with honour continue where you are when you may possess a kingdom of your own.'

It was an adroit call to the indolent James to accept his responsibilities. And it was timely, as James was being likewise pushed by his French hosts. De Pontis filed a report which emphatically stated that the Irish Jacobites had no hope of holding out without aid but added, 'that should sufficient men, money and arms be provided, they, so strengthened, could even carry the fight into England.' He seemed to sense a reluctance on James' part to come to Ireland, for he said: 'If Your Majesty would take a step here . . . to arrange affairs, you could return afterwards if you found it necessary.'

The Bandon Williamites

In the Bandon area of West Cork, a strong Protestant enclave had existed since the plantation of Munster in 1586. The town of Bandon had been founded by Richard Boyle, the First Earl of Cork, in 1608. It had successfully repelled assaults in 1641 and, although often in danger of being overwhelmed, contrived to hold out until Cromwell's arrival. Thereafter it was secure until James came to the throne. It was aggressively anti-Catholic. A notice on one of its gates is said to have borne the legend: 'Turk, Jew and Atheist may enter here, but not a Papist.' Not to be outdone, a Catholic wit scrawled underneath: 'Who wrote this, wrote it well, for the same is written on the gates of Hell.' In the present crisis it declared early for William. In February 1689 the townspeople disarmed the small Jacobite garrison and killed some of the soldiers.

Tyrconnell moved quickly, and dispatched a force under Lieutenant General Justin McCarthy to clear out what he called 'that nest of rebels'. But the Bandonians were strong-willed and courageous. They unfurled a banner which bore the words 'No surrender' (they were the first to use the phrase), but were caught napping. McCarthy marched his men through the gates while the Protestants were attending Divine Service, and effected a bloodless takeover. Two Jacobite pipers strode up the aisle of the church, sat themselves on the Communion Table and struck up such favourites as 'The Humours of Bandon' and 'The King Shall Enjoy His Own Again'.

But the Protestants were determined not to give up without a fight. Next day — 'Black Monday' — they rose again, killed eight solders and chased the new garrison away. McCarthy, who had left the town, was astonished by the news. He ordered his troops to return and, this time, the small group of insurgents had little hope. The ringleaders were rounded up and about to hang, when a young clergyman called Nicholas Brady caught the ear of McCarthy with a passionate plea for their lives.[7] This unexpected product of Westminster School and Oxford University must have been eloquent, for he persuaded McCarthy to hold his hand. The citizens, but not the ringleaders, were pardoned on payment of an indemnity of £1,500 and on giving a promise to make restitution to the families of the soldiers whom they had injured. McCarthy had a bright idea on how to deal with the leaders. He decided that they should petition James for their lives.

The Break of Dromore

Tyrconnell now turned his attention to Ulster, where there were numerous 'nests of rebels'. The Protestants had made an ineffective assault on the Jacobite garrison at Carrickfergus. A friar named O'Heggerty had witnessed the action and reported that the Protestants were, for the most part, short of arms, and that many were 'unfit for service'. Tyrconnell sent Lieutenant General Richard Hamilton, with 7,000 men, against them, and dispatched Lord Galmoy with a strong force to guard the passes to the west between Connaught and Ulster. He also sent a pliant Presbyterian clergyman, Alexander Osborne, to offer terms: in return for an immediate surrender and the handing over of all weapons and serviceable horses, he was prepared to grant a pardon. He made sure to stipulate the alternative: in the event of resistance, they would be crushed.

Osborne arrived to find the Hillsborough council in session. In an act of double-dealing, he urged the council not to accept the offer. The members had little difficulty in agreeing with him and sent Tyrconnell a defiant reply. They emphasised that they abhorred bloodshed and would try to avoid it, but as to surrendering — the answer was no. Their purpose, they stated, was to defend their civil and religious liberties, and they would not lay down their arms until these were secured.

Hamilton's army was now virtually upon them. Sir Arthur Rawden, determined to live up to his nickname of 'Fighting Cock', marshalled a local troop and prepared for battle. The clash came at the village of Dromore, but the Protestants were no match for Hamilton's superior numbers. They were cut to pieces and about a hundred lost their lives. The rest were humiliatingly chased through the streets and fled in disorder. This was the 'Break of Dromore'. By the end of the month Down and Antrim were in the hands of the Jacobites. Thousands of Protestants rushed to the seaports to escape. The port of Larne was said to be 'black' with people. Women and children sat huddled on the beach, waiting for any form of sea transport. The Earl of Mountalexander concluded that self-interest was the better part of valour, and took ship from Donaghadee to England.

Hamilton sacked every village and town before him, as he chased the fleeing Protestants. A good number took refuge in Coleraine, but soon the Jacobites were upon them and the town had to be abandoned, as were Omagh and Dungannon. By April, Hamilton's army had reached the banks of the River Finn. At Claudy Bridge and at Lifford they were met with stout resistance, but the Williamites were driven on remorselessly to Derry. Two days later a Catholic army was ranged before the walls of the Protestant city.

James in Ireland

On 12 March, James landed in Kinsale. He came not to rule his Irish kingdom but to utilise it as a stepping stone to Scotland, from where he planned to recover his throne. To him, Ireland was the pawn; England was the prize. He brought arms, ammunition and 2,000 men. He was accompanied by his illegitimate son, the Duke of Berwick, a boy of nineteen; and a group of experienced French officers. The party included such important figures as the Count d'Avaux (the French Ambassador) and Lieutenant General van Rosen, a Livonian with long service in the French army who had already acquired a daunting anti-Protestant reputation. Also with James was the Irishman Colonel Patrick Sarsfield. Tyrconnell and Lieutenant General McCarthy welcomed James at Cork. The humiliated Bandonians were presented and allowed to plead for mercy. James jumped at this opportunity of showing goodwill towards his Protestant subjects. He pardoned the prisoners, but made sure that his clemency did not go unnoticed. In the hearing of all, he announced that he had been lenient so that 'they may know that they had a generous King'. He used this to present himself in a favourable light at home. In a declaration to his English subjects, he said: 'The calumnies of our enemies are now shown to be false, for since our arrival in Ireland we have made it our chief concern to satisfy our Protestant subjects.'

The Bandonians were not convinced that James' goodwill would be permanent. Shortly afterwards about thirty of them took ship across the channel to Bristol and never returned. But James did arouse the enthusiasm of others. Along his processional route to Dublin he was greeted with acclamations of joy. Flowers were strewn before his coach, speeches were delivered and songs sung; young girls danced on the roadway, and in Carlow he 'was slobbered with the kisses of the rude Irish country-women, so that he was forced to have them kept from him'. In village after village there were shouts of 'God save the King' and a warm-hearted people, who had not seen a monarch since Richard II had come in 1394, were unrestrained in their welcome. On Palm Sunday, 24 March, he made a ceremonial entry into Dublin. Tyrconnell, pompously bearing the sword of state, preceded him. The Catholic gentry and their clergy came out in force. The city fathers were dressed up in their robes, and embroidered cloth, silks and tapestries hung from windows. Church bells rang and a succession of royal salutes pierced the air. It was a happy scene and symbolised the hopes of a downtrodden people. Next day James summoned a council and issued a number of proclamations. Then he marched against the City of Derry.

—4—

The Siege of Derry

With heart and hand
And sword and shield
We'll guard old Derry's Walls.

— from an Old Orange ballad

The siege of Derry is a great mythopoeic event in the history of Ulster Protestants, sometimes compared with the great anti-Protestant sieges of sixteenth-century Europe: Leiden, where the Dutch Calvinists held out against the Spaniards for four months, and La Rochelle, where the Huguenots resisted the armies of Richelieu for fifteen. Derry endured for three and a half months and suffered steady shelling and great privation. Yet it was not a classic siege, and when the full story is told it somehow lacks complete grandeur.

The besieging army did not possess either the training or the equipment for the task: it had only one gun (a 24-pounder) which was capable of breaching the walls, and many of its soldiers were armed with only primitive pikes — pointed sticks without even iron caps — as weapons. The gates of the city were frequently opened to admit refugees or to allow exit to those who wished to leave, and the military operation outside the walls could more accurately be described as a blockade than the Alamo-type which myth sometimes allows. This is not to diminish the importance of the siege or the heroism and steadfastness of the defenders, but to place these in perspective.

Like many such events, the 'siege' subsequently took on a life of its own and has owed much of its fame to poets, playwrights[1] and novelists. One of these, Mrs Cecil Francis Alexander,[2] a popular hymnologist and the wife of a nineteenth-century bishop of Derry, wrote some of the most memorable lines:

Twas the Lord who gave the word
When the people drew the sword
For the freedom of the present
And the future that awaits
O Child, thou must remember
That bleak day in December
When the Prentice Boys of Derry
Rose up and shut the gates.

The ancient name of Derry, Doire-Galach, is traced to Saint Columbcille. He is said to have fled Donegal fourteen hundred years ago to escape a plague and, by tradition, founded his first monastery in a grove ('doire' in Gaelic) on the west bank of the River Foyle. It was a holy place. The saint remarked that 'the angels of God sang in the glades of Doire and that every leaf had its angel.'[3] It was called Doire Columbcille until the English settled there under Sir Henry Docwra in 1600, its importance being mainly ecclesiastical. In the confiscations which followed the 'Flight of the Earls', the town and seven thousand adjoining acres were granted by King James I to a guild of London merchants called 'The Society of the Governor and Assistants, London, for the new Plantation of Ulster within the Kingdom of Ireland'. For over 300 years this body, which still exists, has been known as 'The Honourable Irish Society'. In compliment to the City of London, Derry was renamed Londonderry, but the old name still survives, and one name or the other is used according to political partisanship.

In 1641 Derry successfully repelled an attack by the Irish leader Sir Phelim O'Neill, and in 1649 was held for the parliament by Sir Charles Coote. By 1688 its population had increased to about 12,000[4] and was largely Protestant. The size of its Catholic citizenship is disputed, but it must have been significant. It consisted mainly of labourers and domestic servants and included 'a convent of Dominican friars'. In 1687 James withdrew the city's charter and replaced it with one amenable to Catholics. Under the new arrangements a number of Catholics sat on the Corporation, a matter which caused anxiety among Protestants. Their protection now lay with the Protestant garrison under Lord Mountjoy but Tyrconnell, perceiving his error in leaving the city in the hands of Protestant forces, recalled Mountjoy and his men to Dublin.

Arrangements were made to re-garrison the city with a troop under the Earl of Antrim. The fastidious Earl insisted that the replacements should be athletic six-footers, and had difficulty in finding suitable candidates. Eventually he gathered a mixed force of 1,200 Irish and Scots (Highlanders), all of whom were Catholics. The delay in recruitment meant that the new garrison was unavailable for duty when the old one quit, and the nervous citizens found themselves unprotected. At a time of unrest and mounting tension, this was more than a little unsettling.

The 'Redshanks'

On 16 December 1698 Antrim's regiment, en route to its new posting, stopped at Limavady. It was a motley and ill-disciplined crew, with a large camp-following of unsavoury women and unruly youths. It billeted on the property of the town's proprietor, Colonel George Phillips, who became greatly alarmed with its antics. He immediately wrote to an official in Derry, Alderman Samuel Norman, advising him of what to expect, and recommending that he 'should consult with the sober people of the town and set out the danger' before admitting the rabble. A courier was dispatched, riding through the night, to deliver the message.

On reaching Derry the horseman found one of the leading citizens, Alderman Alexander Tomkins, reading a document from the steps of the Market House to a large crowd. This was the Comber Letter [see p. 39] which had been received a little earlier. When the message from Colonel Phillips was read out, the crowd froze. The news that a force of semi-barbarians were about to descend upon them seemed to confirm their worst fears. Were they about to be massacred? Did not the Comber Letter predict their fate? The leading citizens went into immediate consultation.

What was to be done? Was the threat real? What would be the consequences of refusing entry to the King's troops? In the middle of their consultations a sentry from the walls shouted that the 'Redshanks' were approaching. This was only an advance party who had arrived on the east bank of the river. The citizens watched as two of them, a lieutenant and an ensign, rowed across the water. They had come, the lieutenant announced, to make arrangements for the reception of King James' new garrison.

A technical hitch in their warrants — they were unsigned — allowed the citizens to play for time. The leaders continued to confer, some arguing for the exclusion of the 'Redshanks', some not, and others wavering. It was decided to consult with the bishop, Dr Ezekiel Hopkins, but the old prelate, temperamentally cautious, and by vocation against resistance, preached peace and submission. By now, more 'Redshanks' had arrived and crossed the river. They were within a few hundred yards of the gate. At this critical moment, nine apprentice boys, tired of the argument and indecision going on around them, sprang to action. Led by young Henry Campsie they drew their swords, grabbed the key to the Ferryquay Gate, raised the drawbridge and slammed the heavy gates in the face of the advancing soldiery: then, instantly joined by four others, they secured all the gates to the city.[5] The people's relief was palpable, and a great cheer went up. A soldier, James Morrison, jumped on the walls and shouted to the stupefied 'Redshanks' to be off. They began to hector and hurl abuse, but when Morrison trained a gun on them they quickly fled. Not everyone was happy with the action taken. The deputy mayor and two sheriffs urged that the decision be reversed and upbraided Alderman Horace Kennedy for inciting the impetuous youths. But their views were ignored. The citizens had plainly opted to defend Derry against the forces of King James.

The citizens' numbers were quickly swollen by an influx of Protestants from the neighbouring districts, and a prominent citizen, David Cairns, set about organising the able-bodied into companies and arranging for the city's defence. The Earl of Antrim was sent a stern warning not to approach, and all Catholic citizens were expelled. A rumour had circulated prior to the closing of the gates that a few days earlier the Catholic clergy had asked their congregations to pray for a 'secret intention', and enjoined them to stand ready to obey orders. It was remembered that a friar from the convent had preached from the steps of the Market House with unusual energy on Saul's destruction of the Amalekites, and on the iniquity of saving those whom the Lord had marked for destruction. A wave of anti-Popish hysteria now swept through the swollen throng, and virulent abuse was roared at the departing Catholics.

A citizens' coup established an all-Protestant Corporation, and David Cairns was dispatched to London to solicit the help of the Prince of Orange. The new Corporation wrote to Lord Mountjoy and asked him to mediate with Tyrconnell. The letter was Machiavellian; it declared the inability of the leading citizens to restrain the people when terrified by the threat of massacre. It ascribed the closing of the gates to Providence, which had intervened and stirred the people up for their own safety. It pleaded that their action was one of self-defence and did not impinge on their allegiance. Tyrconnell was not deceived by these specious explanations. He instantly ordered Lord Mountjoy back to Derry to deal with the revolt. As a Protestant, Mountjoy was acceptable to the citizens, but his Catholic troops were not. After negotiations he was admitted on conditions, but his men were excluded. The citizens drove a hard bargain: they would only agree to give up the city if granted a pardon, and on condition that only two military companies were quartered in the city, and that one of these should be Protestant.

Tyrconnell was beside himself. These conditions were quite unacceptable and he was stung at being defied by the self-appointed protectors of a small out-of-the-way city. James was enraged too and, with the other Jacobite leaders, sat down to consider what strategy to apply. Some advocated sending a large irresistible force which would take the city by storm; others were for reducing it by starvation, and a few advocated a light siege which, in time, would bring the city under control. Fatally for James, this last measure was adopted and, to discourage the rebels, he resolved to lead his army to the walls of Derry in person.

Lundy — The Traitor

In the meantime two English colonels, Cunningham and Richards, had arrived in Lough Foyle with two regiments, sent as a result of David Cairns' audience with the Prince of Orange. They notified their arrival to the new governor, Lundy, whose orders they were instructed to obey, But Lundy declared that there was little hope of saving Derry, that provisions were low and that they should return at once to London. He informed the corporation of his views and recommended that terms of capitulation should be drawn up and sent to James, who was now approaching apace from the south. When the people learnt of this proposed surrender, they reacted with violent rage. In a frenzy they slew one of Lundy's men as he tried to escape the city, and wounded another. At this moment of distraction Captain Adam Murray, a local man of Scottish background, arrived at the head of a troop of irregulars. Murray was an inspirational figure, and the people gathered around him. He inveighed against Lundy and his foul design. Then someone shouted that King James and his army were in sight. A group of Murray's men rushed to the walls, loaded the cannon and fired at the advancing horsemen. The astonished James stopped in his tracks and retreated quickly when one of his aides, Captain Troy, fell dead at his side. Any hopes which he may have had of an easy victory were shattered. Yet this bewildered monarch stayed in the saddle all day in pouring rain and without food, hoping by his presence to bring his rebellious subjects to their senses. It was a forlorn hope. Next day, he quit and gave orders for the city to be invested.

The people of Derry chose two new governors to lead them, Major Henry Baker and the Reverend George Walker. Immediately the new men ordered the arrest of Lundy and instructed that he be kept under house-guard. But as they were unable to guarantee his safety from the wrath of the people, they connived at his 'escape'. He was last seen leaping over the wall disguised as a porter, bending under a bundle of sticks.

The Reverend George Walker

Eighteen Anglican clergymen and seven non-conformist ministers shared the dangers of the siege, taking turns in the use of the Cathedral for their different services. The Reverend George Walker preached trust in God and the necessity of unity, and was awesome in his denunciation of popery. A colourful figure, he was somewhat advanced in years, and little is known of him prior to the siege, save that originally he had come from Yorkshire and was appointed Rector of Lissan in County Londonderry in 1669. Later he received a living at Donoughmore, County Tyrone. Before the retreat to Derry he had raised a troop, and was determined to hold Dungannon until ordered to break the garrison by Lundy.

The forceful Walker (as depicted by Charlotte Elizabeth) inspired the garrison with his unflinching zeal, and in his unadorned writings left a description of the problems which beset it:

> A garrison we had composed of a number of poor people frightened from their homes, and who seemed more fit to hide themselves from the face of the enemy. When we considered that we had no persons of any experience in war among us, and those very persons who were sent to assist us, had so little confidence in the place that they no sooner saw it but they thought to leave it [he was obviously referring here to Cunningham and Richards]; that we had but few horses, with no forage; no engineers to instruct us in our works; no fireworks, not so much as a hand grenade to annoy the enemy; that they had so many opportunities to divide us, and so often endeavoured it . . . that they were so numerous, so powerful . . . that in all human probability we could not think ourselves in less danger than the Israelites at the Red Sea; when we consider all this, it is obvious enough what a dangerous undertaking we had ventured upon. But the resolution of our people, and the necessity we were under and the great confidence and dependence among us on God Almighty, that He would take care of us and preserve us, made us overlook all those difficulties.[6]

The defenders resisted all the pressures put upon them. They made sallies from the walls in a manner which defied all military rules. They successfully engaged the enemy on its own ground before returning to their fortress, and on each occasion the enemy was repulsed. Yet they could not gain relief from assault.

As the weeks passed they were threatened with more terrible enemies: disease, famine and pestilence struck during the hot months of summer. At the height of their affliction they looked from the walls and saw thirty ships which had been sent by the Prince of Orange for their relief. These were loaded with food, arms and men; yet their captains were too timid to venture past the wooden boom which their enemies had strung across the Foyle. Then one day they saw the ships set sail and disappear. Their hopes foundered, but at length a message was received from Captain Kirk, the commander of the fleet. He said that he had sailed around Lough Swilly and would now attempt to rescue them by land. They waited, but nothing happened.

The Stricken City

Each day the garrison was further reduced by disease, and the wretched survivors were more and more enfeebled by fatigue and hunger. On the seventy-fifth day Major Henry Baker, one of the governors, died of pneumonia, caught, it was said, by manning the walls in all weathers. Colonel John Mitchelburne was appointed in his place. From outside, General Hamilton sent messages of peace and tried to move them by gentle persuasion: they reminded him of his earlier treachery to the Prince of Orange and refused to listen. Van Rosen, the Livonian, thundered terrible menaces against them, and by convincing them that no mercy could be expected, steeled their resolution.

Maddened by their obstinacy, van Rosen warned that if they did not surrender by 1 July their co-religionists in the surrounding districts would be driven under the walls and allowed to perish. The appointed day arrived, but the people maintained their defence. On the next morning hundreds of Protestants — old, infirm, women and children — were herded before the walls. Some pleaded on their knees for their lives, but were kicked and goaded by the soldiers. With their arms raised to heaven they cried for mercy, but their tormentors scorned them.

The citizens of Derry looked on, helpless. But the new governor, Mitchelburne, resolved on an extreme measure. He erected a gallows in full view of the Jacobites and sent out word that all Catholic prisoners would be executed unless the Protestant captives were permitted, by a certain hour, to return to their homes. A war of nerves ensued, and Catholic priests were admitted to the city to administer the Last Sacraments; but van Rosen was unmoved. It was fortunate that news of his barbaric scheme travelled to Dublin. The Protestant Bishop of Meath, Dr Anthony Dropping, remonstrated with James, and the popish King did not conceal his anger and contempt for van Rosen's action. He described the Livonian as a 'wild animal' and immediately issued instructions that his Protestant subjects be allowed to go free. But before they left the walls some of the ablest were stolen into Derry and five hundred of the weakest were stolen out, passing undiscovered through the Jacobite lines.

The garrison continued its obstinate defence. The flesh of horses, dogs and vermin, hides, tallow and other nauseous substances were purchased at extravagant prices to fill empty stomachs. Even such miserable resources were not expected to last more than a few days. Still the sick and languid people hung on; still they listened to the exhortations of Walker; still he assured them that the Almighty would grant them deliverance. An empty shell containing a note offering surrender terms was fired over the walls. Walker took the note and went to the Cathedral to pray. On the altar his eyes fell on a passage in the open Bible. It was Psalm 37: 'Fret not thyself because of evildoers, neither thou be envious against the workers of iniquity. For they shall soon be cut down like the grass and wither as the green herb; trust in the Lord and do good, so thou shall dwell in the land verily, thou shall be fed.'

Outside, Walker gazed at the crimson flag flying from the roof of the Cathedral. It had been placed there by Mitchelburne in defiance of the enemy. Its distinctive colour, symbolic of blood and sacrifice, aptly depicted the spirit of Protestant resistance. The answer to the Jacobites was, again, no surrender.

With their heads reeling from the harangues of Walker, the garrison continued their watch from the walls. Suddenly they found that three ships were moving towards them up the Foyle. Captain Kirk and his fleet, which had abandoned them from 13 June to 30 July, had returned. Among the advancing ships were Ulster-owned vessels, the *Mountjoy* of Derry and the *Phoenix* of Coleraine. A terrible cannonade was opened against them but, favoured by the breeze, they ploughed on. The *Mountjoy* was the first to strike the barrier, but it recoiled, and briefly ran aground. There were jubilant cheers from their enemies.

Then a longboat from the third vessel, the *Swallow*, with nine ratings, led by a boatswain named Shelly, approached the boom. They began hacking at it fiercely with swords and hatchets. After what seemed an eternity it finally snapped, and the timbers drifted apart. The *Phoenix* sped quickly past the breach and was followed by the *Mountjoy*.

The daring captain of the *Mountjoy*, a native of the stricken city, Micriah Browning, was hit by a sniper's bullet. He did not live to enter Derry. Macaulay caught the terrible irony of the moment when he wrote: 'He died the most enviable of all deaths, in the sight of the city which was his birth place, which was his home and which had just been saved by his bravery and devotion from the most frightful destruction.' Today, Browning is remembered by a stone tablet set in the city walls near the spot where his body was brought ashore, and by the Browning Memorial Window in the city's Guildhall. Here, in beautiful stained glass, almost every episode in the city's history is illustrated.

The city was relieved, and Derry had not surrendered. The boom had been broken and Protestant Ulster had its epic, complete with Homeric heroes. Derry, the maiden city, was, in the words of one of its chroniclers, Charlotte Tonna, '. . . a maiden still'.[7]

For three days more the siege continued, but by the third night flames were seen rising from the Jacobite camp. On 1 August the people of

Derry watched the forces of their enemies march off in the direction of Strabane. To Ulster Protestants the name of Derry has a high emotional charge. Wherever their emigrants have scattered across the globe they have taken the name of Derry with them — often in old pictures and antique documents, occasionally as the name of a settlement or a small town which they have founded, but more often in their historical memories, and in their hearts. 'The Orange Minstrel', William Blacker, wrote a poem which has gained a special place in the Orange canon:[8]

> Behold the crimson banners float
> O'er yonder turrets hoary
> They tell of days of matchless note
> And Derry's deathless glory
> When her brave sons undaunted stood
> Embattled to defend her
> Indignant stemmed oppression's flood
> And sang out 'No Surrender.'
>
> Old Derry's walls were firm and strong
> Well fenced in every quarter
> Each frowning bastion grim along
> With culverin and mortar
> But Derry had a surer guard
> Than all that art could lend her
> Her 'prentice hearts the gates who barred
> And who sang out 'No Surrender.'
>
> Long may the crimson barrier wave
> A meteor streaming airy
> Portentous of the free and brave
> Who man the walls of Derry
> And Derry's sons alike defy
> Pope, traitor or pretender
> And peal to heaven their 'prentice cry
> Their patriot, 'No Surrender.'

Enniskillen

The second major centre of Protestant resistance was Enniskillen. Built on an island in Lough Erne, it consisted of about eighty buildings clustered around an old castle. Eight days after Derry had closed its gates, the Enniskilleners chose a local gentleman, Gustavus Hamilton, as their governor. He immediately resolved, as he said, 'to admit no popish garrison'. But Enniskillen was not, in fact, besieged; its role was to wage guerrilla war on the enemy. In a series of stunningly successful raids, it harried the Jacobite lines and extended its raids, on occasion, as far south as County Meath. It diverted forces from the attack on Derry and, on the very day that that city was relieved, it achieved a notable victory over Lord Mountcashel's forces at Newtownbutler. The Enniskilleners rode into battle bellowing a cry which would become a refrain: 'No popery'. During the battle a Jacobite order to retreat was misinterpreted, and hundreds of foot soldiers were driven to the shores of Lough Erne, where scores were either drowned or slaughtered. Mountcashel himself was captured, although he later escaped. The victory secured all areas west of the River Bann for William.[9]

William and Mary are Offered the Crown

On 13 February, the Prince and Princess of Orange met the 'Lords Spiritual and Temporal and Commons' in the splendour of Inigo Jones' masterpiece, the Banqueting House in Whitehall. With solemn ceremonial, the clerk of the House of Lords read aloud the Declaration of Rights. Then, in the name of all the estates of the realm, the Prince and Princess accepted the crown. William's reply was direct: 'We thankfully accept what you have offered . . . I shall do all in my power to advance the welfare and glory of the nation.'

Thus was concluded the central event in a historical drama when one king — James II, who claimed to rule by heredity, even divine right — was deposed in favour of two sovereigns, William III and Mary II, who occupied the throne by the will of the people as expressed through parliament. Protestants in the three kingdoms rejoiced, but none more than those in Ireland.[10]

—5—

William in Ireland

Marshal Schomberg's Campaign

Armand Friedrich Herman, Duke of Schomberg, was one of the great soldiers of his age. He was born in Schomberg Castle on the Rhine — between Coblenz and Bingen — in 1615, and was to die seventy-five years later amid the bloodstained waters of an Irish river. The son of a German father and an English mother, he enlisted in the service of Frederick Henry, William's grandfather, in 1632. During the Thirty Years' War he served on the Upper Rhine and was recruited for the French army by Cardinal Mazarin during the Wars of the Frondes. In 1675 he was on the staff of Louis XIV's army during the successful siege of Maastricht, and was one of the eight marshals of France appointed on Turenne's death.

He was a Protestant, and following the Revocation of the Edict of Nantes felt that he could not, in honour, continue to serve the French King. He relinquished his marshal's baton and returned home. Greeted warmly at the Court of the Great Elector of Brandenburg, he offered his sword to the Grand Alliance which had been formed against his old master. William was then recruiting an international force to frustrate James' designs in Ireland, and Schomberg was seconded to serve him. He did so with enthusiasm, and his reputation was so great, his qualities so impressive, that William immediately appointed him commander-in-chief of the new force, conferring on him the Order of the Garter and a Dukedom. The House of Commons showed its pleasure by voting an honorarium of £100,000. Everything seemed set for the great man to lead a successful campaign in Ireland.

When he arrived in Chester to take up his command, a number of problems awaited him. For one, there were too few trained officers; then, the army's newly manufactured rifles were found to be of poor quality, and the cannon was badly cast. Furthermore, many of the officers disliked the crusty old veteran, and soon he was accused of favouring Huguenots for senior positions. Criticism was made of his seemingly interminable delay in relieving the besieged Protestants in Ireland.

Despite these setbacks and delays, he arrived in Ireland on 16 August 1688, with 10,000 men. He disembarked without opposition at Grooms-port near Bangor, and within days was joined by Protestant corps from Derry and Enniskillen, which increased his numbers to 16,000. His first move was against the garrison at Carrickfergus, where General McCarthy Mor commanded about 600 men. The town was defended for ten days, after which the garrison ran out of powder. McCarthy surrendered on honourable terms, which were not adhered to. His men were disarmed and their womenfolk maltreated. Some sources say the women were driven, stark naked, through the town, and that the savagery shown by the Ulster corps was so fierce that it was a wonder anyone got away alive. Schomberg was forced to intervene to save a massacre and, with sword in hand, he expressed his fury at the vengeful Protestants.[1]

On securing Carrickfergus, Schomberg moved south by the coast road to Dundalk. The Jacobites were twenty miles away in Drogheda and reports from their spies hinted that not all was well in Schomberg's ranks: the reports suggested that many of his men could easily be induced to desert. To encourage them, the Jacobites issued a statement which promised any Williamite who transferred his allegiance a reward of forty shillings and fresh employment. The carrot was ineffective, but the discontent in the Orange ranks was real enough. Four hundred Huguenots had mutinied, and only returned to the ranks after the greatest persuasion.

James, in Dublin, learnt of Schomberg's location and ordered his army northwards, declaring that he would not be walked out of Ireland without striking a blow. On 25 September he concentrated 20,000 men in Ardee and challenged his opponent. But the foxy old marshal was cautious and, mindful of his inferior numbers, refused the challenge. He later attributed his refusal to the unfavourable terrain. 'What,' he said, 'with bogs to the right and to the left, such a country was never seen.' James was too irresolute to press his advantage, and his timidity angered a number of his commanders. Certainly, it is clear that he had a better chance of defeating Schomberg at this time (1 October) than later when the odds against him were greater. In fact, had James fought and won it is not improbable that William would have thought twice before venturing across the Irish Sea.

Having decided against attack, James felt it idle to go on watching his cautious opponent. He broke camp and placed his troops in winter quarters in the Boyne valley and elsewhere. Schomberg, having delayed to ensure that his enemy had withdrawn, acted likewise. He retired on a line from Newry to the sea. In the following months he was struck with unforeseen disaster. Typhus and other infections ravished his army, and his disease-stricken men literally died like flies. By the end of that terrible winter of 1689-90 he had lost, incredibly, 8,000 men due to illness.

The Winter Respite

On returning to Dublin, James ordered the disarmament of Protestants living in the city, an action which up to then had only partially been effected by Tyrconnell. He wrote a honeyed supplication to his French patron for more men, money and materials. Whilst awaiting a reply he sank into a strange lethargy and amused himself with 'disgraceful amours'. The Duchess of Orléans later recorded that 'there were two ugly creatures with whom he was on the most intimate terms.'[2] Occasional desultory raids were made on Ulster positions, but nothing was done which altered the strategic map. No attempt was made at further recruitment, nor were efforts taken to fortify vital points of communication. Virtually the entire Jacobite leadership became inactive. Patrick Sarsfield even found time to marry, to the fifteen-year-old Lady Honora Burke, twenty-five years his junior, the daughter of Lord Clanricard.

On the Williamite side matters were hardly more inspiring. Schomberg, a former marshal of France, at the head of 16,000 men, had achieved practically nothing, save to displace a modest Jacobite garrison at Carrickfergus. He had then remained inactive for three months, during which time he lost more men than if he had fought a major battle. At seventy-four he was too diffident, too fussy and too old to come to grips decisively with the enemy, never mind being able to bring the war to a successful conclusion.

William had second thoughts about the wisdom of Schomberg's appointment, and reluctantly announced that he would come to Ireland himself. It was noted that he treated the old marshal with a marked coldness, and that he pointedly ignored his advice. Later, at the Battle of the Boyne, when Schomberg urged an adroit flanking movement that would have caught the Jacobites in a pincer grip and destroyed them, William — who was an indifferent commander — opted for a frontal attack which, as it turned out, permitted the enemy to escape. The enmity between them deeply upset Schomberg and may even have encouraged him to seek an honourable death on the battlefield: certainly it is a mystery why he refused to wear his heavy armour when going into battle at the Boyne.[3]

The Williamites took care to increase their forces. Seven thousand Danish troops arrived under the command of the Duke of Württemburg;

a number of English and Dutch regiments landed, and the men who survived the winter epidemic recovered their health and spirits. Schomberg was strong again and by spring was ready to march. The Jacobites also bestirred themselves. In March, 7,000 well-armed French troops under the command of the Comte de Lauzun landed in Cork. The build-up on both sides intensified.

William Arrives

William crossed to Ireland on 14 June with a fleet of 300 transports and six warships. On board were 15,000 troops and a train of heavy artillery especially imported from Holland. He had 900 horses, 450 bread wagons and, in his purse, £200,000, which was like manna to Schomberg's unpaid men.

He had sailed from Hoylake in Cheshire on 11 June on board the yacht *Mary*, captained by the intrepid Edward Tarlton. The captain lost his bearings on the following day and hit a sandbank near the Point of Ayer, off the Isle of Man. This was a bad omen and the fatalistic William was perturbed, but nevertheless he arrived safely in Belfast Lough two days later. He was rowed ashore in the rear-admiral's barge and reached the Old Quay at Carrickfergus, under the shadow of the castle, in the early afternoon.

Although William spent only twelve days in Ulster — from June 14th to June 26th — his every move in the Province has been diligently recorded. Even the flagstone on which he took his first step on Irish soil has been preserved. Sibbet, the Orange historian, tells us that this relic is eight feet long, six feet broad and three feet thick, and then adds, rather sadly, that the imprint of the King's boot has not been retained on the granite.[4] The stone can still be seen on the steps leading from the water, inscribed with the legend: 'William III, June 14th 1690'. Nearby, the arrival is commemorated on a large blue plaque, and a few feet away a life-size statue of William broods over the quay. Strangely, he is shown in unheroic pose: slightly stooped, with a walking cane in his right hand and wearing a heavily plumed tricorne. Were it not for the inscription, he might be taken for an infirm Chelsea Pensioner out for a stroll.

On mounting the steps, William walked onto a red carpet and found a guard of honour drawn up to greet him. The town's dignitaries were present in their robes. William, wearing an orange sash 'of the finest watered silk', stood stiffly as they bowed before him. An aged Quaker had been chosen to give the formal address, but his religious scruples deterred him from doffing his hat or using royal titles. He shuffled forward, bare-headed, and said: 'William, thou art welcome to thy Kingdom.' This quaint greeting delighted the normally sullen William, who replied cheerfully: 'You are the best bred gentleman which I have met since I have come hither.' Then, without much further ado, he mounted and set off with his retinue.

For days prior to William's coming there had been expectant flutterings all over the north-east. Bonfires blazed around the coast and people kept watch, day and night, for a sighting of the royal flotilla. Belfast, then a small town with only five streets, was bustling with excitement. The main thoroughfare was swept daily and orange flags fluttered from every house. No one was allowed in the vicinity of the stable reserved for the King's horse.

Most of the Orange troops disembarked at the little port of Whitehouse, halfway along the shore. Schomberg and the other commanders waited at this spot for the King. The marshal introduced his son, Meinhard, Count Schomberg, who was followed by the Dutch and Danish commanders, General Godard Ginkel and the Duke of Württemberg. Then came Major General Kirk representing the English regiments, and Gustave Hamilton, the Governor of Enniskillen, on behalf of the Ulster corps. Local people cheered, and shouted: 'God save William' and 'Long live the Protestant King'. The spot where William stood acknowledging these cheers was marked for years by an old ash tree which grew out of the pavement; it is close to the old post office on the Belfast side of Whitehouse parish church.

William in Belfast

Belfast in those days had a population of only 2,000, and was wholly Protestant. It had two churches, the Anglican parish church, where Saint George's now stands on High Street, and the Presbyterian Meeting House in Rosemary Lane. These, with Lord Donegall's castle, were its only notable buildings. William and his army entered by the north gate, where a multitude had gathered to greet them. The Reverend George Story, a contemporary historian, says: 'The monarch was met without the town by a great concourse who at first could do nothing but stare, never having seen a king in this part of the world; but after a while some of them began to hurrah, and the rest took to it — like hounds to the scent — and followed his coach through several regiments of foot to His Majesty's lodgings, hoping that they could get a sight of him.'[5]

William was welcomed by the Sovereign, Captain Robert Leathes, and the Reverend George Walker, recently appointed Bishop Elect of Derry. The official reception was held in the castle, at that time the residence of Sir William Franklyn, husband of the Dowager Lady Donegall, who acted as a humble and deeply honoured host. In replying to the formal welcome, William commanded that a fast be kept throughout the Kingdom for his success in the coming conflict. A royal salute was fired, and Story says that there were 'great rejoicings'. At dusk bonfires blazed on the hillsides and Protestants took heart, for their Deliverer had come. William was relaxed among his most avowedly loving subjects. His spirits were high and he joked with his new aide-de-camp, Colonel Thomas Bellingham. He wrote a happy letter to Queen Mary, saying that he found the Irish air to his liking — probably a reference to his chronic asthma — and that he was pleased to see that his Irish Protestant subjects were of such good material.[6]

The next morning being Sunday, he attended Divine Service at the Corporation Church (now Saint George's) and heard the chaplain, the Reverend George Royce, preach from the text: 'Who through faith subdued kingdoms' (Hebrews 11.33). The preacher finished prophetically: 'When thou passest through the waters I shall be with thee' (Isaiah 43.2). When the King read the Lesson, some marvelled that his Dutch vowel sounds were not too dissimilar to their own. Tradition has it that he pronounced the word 'dog' as 'dug' — an intonation still heard across the channel in Renfrewshire, the ancestral home of many Ulster Protestants. But it was found that in ordinary conversation William's speech was more in line with that of the Gaelic Irish. His aspectural use of the word 'after', as in 'I am after eating', was seen as a case in point.[7]

On Monday, 16 June, addresses of loyalty were presented. The Reverend George Walker introduced an Anglican dignitary who read from a large parchment: 'To the King's Most Excellent Majesty, the humble address of the Church of Ireland, now in Ulster: Great Sir — We, Your Majesty's most loyal subjects, out of our deepest sense of the blessings of this day, with most joyful hearts congratulate Your Majesty's safe landing in this kingdom. As we must always praise God for the wonders which He has wrought by Your Majesty's hands, so we cannot but admire and applaud your remarkable zeal for the Protestant Religion and for the peace of these kingdoms. We owe all imaginable thanks to God, and acknowledgement to Your Majesty, for the calm and safety we have enjoyed by the success of your arms, under the happy and wise management of His Grace, the Duke of Schomberg. . . .'

A less saccharin address was read by the Reverend Patrick Adair, Minister of Belfast 'on behalf of the Presbyterian ministers and those of their persuasion in the North of Ireland'. This must have pleased William, for a few days later he issued a command to Christopher Corelton, Collector of Customs at Belfast, to pay £1,200 per annum to the clergy of the Presbyterian Church, being assured, as he said, 'of their constant labour to unite the hearts of others in zeal and loyalty towards us.' This may be taken as the real commencement of the Regium Donum, or Royal Bounty, previously granted to dissenting clergymen by Charles II, but irregularly paid, and scrapped altogether by James. The stipend was of great importance financially to its recipients. It gave the eighty clerics who were entitled to receive it the then considerable income of £15 each per year.

The interlude in Ulster was doubtless pleasant, but William announced that he had 'no intention of allowing grass to grow under his feet' and left Belfast on 19 June for the journey to Loughbrickland in County Down, where his troops were encamped. Tradition has preserved numerous stories of his ride: of people whom he met, incidents which occurred, and places which he passed — many of which were later named after him. For instance, there is the story of the King's cavalcade stopping to take shelter under trees from a downpour and William being invited by a local man, John Eccles, to take refreshment in his house — the spot was later called Orange Grove. Ulster historian Dr Nessa Robb says: 'A Huguenot blacksmith, Rene Bulmer, did William a service and asked, as a reward, that the King should embrace him, as French generals did when conferring an honour. Whereupon William said: "Mais oui, mon vieux; je te salueras voluntiers et ta femme aussi" (But yes, my old friend, I greet you gladly and your wife also) and kissed the blacksmith and his comely wife.'[8]

On 25 June William marched his army, which now numbered 36,000 men of various nationalities, to Newry. On the 27th they were beyond Dundalk. The Jacobites had failed to make a stand at the Moyra Pass — the traditional 'Gap of the North' — where a small force could have delayed the Orange army for a protracted period. The French Commander, Lauzun, felt, apparently, that the Jacobites could easily have been outflanked by an Orange force advancing from Armagh. He also held that the Jacobite army had moved too far from Dublin, which was largely unprotected, and urged James to pull back south. As the Boyne was the only major river between Dundalk and Dublin, James decided to take up a defensive position on its southern bank. County Louth, therefore, was surrendered to William without a fight.

On 30 June, the Orange army marched in two columns — singing 'Lilliburlero' as they went — from Ardee to the northern slopes of the Boyne. From Tullesker Hill outside Drogheda, William surveyed the surrounding countryside and is reputed to have made his famous remark: 'Gentlemen, this is a country well worth fighting for.' A troop of dragoons discovered about 200 old scythes in a farmhouse and brought them to him for inspection. William eyed them thoughtfully for a minute or two, and said dryly: 'These are very dangerous weapons,' winking knowingly to General Ginkel. His opponents, it was felt, would have to do better than fight with scythes.

It was sensational that two crowned monarchs, related by blood and through marriage, should face each other across an Irish river. The moment of high drama had arrived.

—6—

The Green Grassy Slopes

> July the first, on a morning clear
> One thousand six hundred and ninety
> King William and his men prepare —
> Of thousands he had thirty
> To fight King James and all his host
> Encamped near the Boyne Water.
>
> 'The Boyne Water'
> — *traditional Orange ballad*

William at the Boyne

The Boyne river rises in the Bog of Allen, near Edenderry on the Offaly–Kildare border, and flows north-east through Trim, Navan and Drogheda where it empties into the Irish Sea, its total length being 110 km. On its banks sit the magnificent Neolithic tombs of Newgrange, Knowth and Dowth, marvels older than Stonehenge and the Pyramids of Egypt. By its side is Tara, from where the High Kings of Ireland once ruled.

After Newgrange the river alters its course, turning northwards, and forms a deep curve between this point and Drogheda. Within the curve the ground rises in a succession of undulating slopes to the Hill of Donore, behind which lies a narrow road to Dublin. The northern bank, across from what was the hamlet of Oldbridge (now gone) is high and firm, while the southern bank is low and sedgy. On the northern bank, just before the curve, the Boyne is joined by the much smaller River Mattock, and on the left is the hill of Tullyallen.

When James had retreated to the Boyne, he turned and set his face against his enemies. Both Lauzun and Tyrconnell opposed his decision to fight a pitched battle. The Frenchman urged him to move westward and hold the line of the Shannon, where he could play cat and mouse with William for several months. This was sound advice, for time was not pressing on the Jacobites, and indeed James, if he cared to do so, could have spent the rest of his life in Ireland. But time was of the essence for William; every day which he spent in Ireland was keeping him from the real conflict in Europe. Moreover, a delay in Ireland would expose him to the threat of the French navy sweeping the Irish Sea of English shipping and pinning him down indefinitely. On the eve of the battle, in fact, Admiral de Tourville had won a major victory over the combined Dutch and English fleet at Beachy Head on the Sussex coast. So the danger for William was real.

James, however unwisely, had his own reasons for making a stand at the Boyne. For one, if he were to fight anywhere in the eastern zone, the Boyne was the place to do it. It was the only major defensive line between Dundalk and his headquarters in Dublin. If he did not make a stand here Dublin would fall, and, with Dublin gone, most of Ireland would also fall. For another, his heart was not in the campaign. With a characteristic sense of fatalism, he wanted to have done quickly. He regretted being in Ireland in the first place, and his letters to Mary of Modena, his queen, were full of forebodings about being stuck forever in an Irish bog. He disliked the Irish people, and found them artful, unreliable and vulgar. He pined for those personal comforts which were unavailable in a distressed and impoverished land.

Moreover, he lacked good advisers in Ireland, and he knew it. Lauzun was an adventurer rather than a serious soldier and his experience was negligible. The Duke of Berwick, James' natural son,[1] had observed that if Lauzun knew anything about war, he had forgotten it before setting foot in Ireland. La Hoguette, the other commander, lacked local knowledge and had little empathy with the Irish, and the most promising, d'Escots, had died suddenly. The ablest, Patrick Sarsfield, was confined to a minor role as James held, quite unreasonably, that he had 'no headpiece'.

Sarsfield's great defect in James' eyes was, in fact, being Irish. Certainly James wanted religious toleration for Irish Catholics, but he correctly saw that Tyrconnell, MacCarthy and the others wanted ultimately to break the connection with England. James was a unionist and believed in the inviolability of the empire. He would have no truck with inchoate Irish nationalism.

The Opposing Armies

Differing estimates have been given on the numerical strengths of the armies. The Jacobites are thought to have been about 25,000 strong and the Orange figures are usually given at 36,000.[2] A few thousand more on either side would seem the maximum variation. James' army consisted, in large part, of raw recruits who were poorly trained and ill-disciplined. They sided with him for their meagre wages and in the hope of achieving toleration for their faith. They gullibly accepted Jacobite rhetoric and had uncomplicated views on the conflict. Their commanders, drawn mostly from the 'Old English' class, had their eyes set on a favourable land settlement in the event of a victory; other aspirations could await the longer term.

The French were in the field at the command of their own King and saw the conflict in its wider context. Their particular misfortune was to be under the command of such an unconvincing soldier as Lauzun. On the Irish side, Tyrconnell had little experience in the field, but men like Lieutenant General Richard Hamilton and a few others could cause trouble for any opponents.

William's army was well trained and disciplined. Many of his soldiers were veterans of other campaigns. They were well equipped and had thirty field pieces to the Jacobites' six. Besides, most of his artillery was armed with the recently developed flintlock musket (which increased the range and speed of their firepower) whereas the Jacobites had to make do with the older matchlock type. The Orange army had large contingents of mercenaries whose only allegiance to William was the money which he paid them. Among the most motivated were the Huguenots, anxious to defeat an ally of the King who had dispossessed them and enforced their exile.

There are many accounts of the battle, mostly partisan and often contradictory on points of detail. One fable is that on the morning of the battle, when the Orange troops were asleep, James' army advanced silently to catch them by surprise, when a small bird — a wren — jumped onto a drum and began tapping. This awakened the drummer boy who sounded the alarm. Orange legend holds that this is why the wren is hunted down on Wren Day (26 December) in southern Ireland, in hateful revenge.

In those days the Boyne was tidal for a number of miles inland, but as the summer was dry it was fordable at many points during ebb tide. The main ford was at Oldbridge, with another a few miles downstream at Drybridge near Drogheda. Upstream there was a crossing at Rosnaree and further on, at Slane, a narrow bridge. On the eve of the battle, William and a few of his commanders rode down to inspect the crossings. They stood on the northern bank at Oldbridge, just within musket range of the Jacobites. While William sat on the ground making observations, he was spotted by enemy officers. They stealthily brought up a field gun and, just as he remounted, fired twice. The initial discharge killed two horses and a soldier standing nearby. The second grazed the river bank and, rising upwards, hit William on the right shoulder, taking away a piece of his leather jerkin and tearing the flesh. He leant forward heavily, and the Jacobites thought that they had killed him. But the wound was slight and he made little of it, his phlegmatic comment being: 'T'houbt niet naeder' (it need not have come nearer). A report that he had been killed quickly reached Dublin, and even Paris, and gave rise to premature Jacobite rejoicing, which included the lighting of bonfires. Next day, during the battle, he wore a plaster on his shoulder and carried his right arm in a sling. One historian has commented that the Jacobite gunner was not too many inches off solving the Irish problem![3]

Both sides held councils of war. In the Jacobite camp, Hamilton recommended that a strong force be detailed to defend the bridge at Slane and another to protect the crossing at Rosnaree; his advice was accepted only in part. Eight hundred dragoons, under Sir Neil O'Neill, were sent to Rosnaree, but Slane was ignored save for the destruction of the bridge. In the Orange camp, Schomberg outlined two strategies:[4] they might either attack and capture Drogheda, making their incursions there, or march up the river to Slane, repair the bridge and cross at that point, and at the ford at Rosnaree.

William rejected these recommendations and decided that his army should cross in three separate sectors: on the left, in the centre, and on the right. This, he felt, would enable him to take advantage of his numerical strength and force the turning of James' flanks both up and down the river. The initial crossing was to be in the right sector — at Slane and Rosnaree — and was assigned to Count Schomberg, the Duke's son. The Count was allocated 5,000 horse and 8,000 foot to cross the River Mattock and then force the Boyne at the designated points. The command of the centre was entrusted to the old Duke, and William was to take the left wing himself.

The bulk of James' army was drawn up on high ground at a distance of about half a mile from the river. Two regiments of infantry were placed in the hamlet of Oldbridge, and the rest — O'Neill's dragoons — were positioned at Rosnaree. Neither side had national colours. To distinguish themselves the Jacobites wore white paper in their hats, and the Orange army improvised with green sprigs.

Young Schomberg was the first to move. Before dawn he led the Orange right wing across the fields in an upstream direction. The Boyne Valley was shrouded in dense mist and visibility was bad. An hour or so later, as the sun rose, William and Old Schomberg scanned the Jacobite side of the river with their field glasses. To their surprise they saw that the Jacobites had broken camp and were in retreat. William became anxious that the enemy might escape and draw him into a prolonged struggle elsewhere. Although he intended deferring his thrusts until he had learnt of Young Schomberg's fortunes, the spectacle of his opponents retreating was too much for him. He immediately ordered the old Duke to attack through the centre — that is, at Oldbridge — and he himself, with his cavalry, moved to the left.

At Rosnaree, Young Schomberg found his way stubbornly disputed by O'Neill's dragoons, but by sheer weight of numbers he was able to force his way across. O'Neill was mortally wounded, and his men broke ranks and fled towards the village of Duleek. William's strategy on the right had worked, and the Jacobites could now be cut off on their left flank.

Lauzun knew that the road to Dublin from Duleek was so narrow that scarcely two wagons could pass each other and that, should it be taken, it would be impossible for the Jacobites to retreat. Disturbed by this possibility, and concerned for the personal safety of James, he made a fatal decision. He ordered his crack French troops — together with all the field guns and Sarsfield's cavalry — to Rosnaree to counter the Orange flanking movement. This fatally weakened the Jacobite centre and left the fords at Oldbridge to be defended by the inexperienced Irish infantry.

The Fight at Oldbridge

It was now ten o'clock. Old Schomberg gave the word for the Orange foot to make their thrust through the centre. William's beloved Dutch Blue Guard, under their commander Count Solmes, marched with drums beating to the edge of the water. Then suddenly the drums went silent and the men, ten abreast, waded into the river, holding their muskets high above their heads. The level of the tide was higher than expected and their bodies formed such a barrier that the water rose to their waists.

On the far side, the old houses of the hamlet were occupied by forces under Lords Antrim and Clanricard, and fortifications had been built to provide extra cover. As the Dutch reached the middle of the river, heavy musket fire opened on them. Much of it was inaccurate and they were able to press ahead. A Lieutenant of Grenadiers was the first to emerge, and he quickly drew up the men in two files. They returned several well-aimed volleys and succeeded in sending the Jacobites scampering up the hill to new positions. This gave the Dutch time to get further troops across and to establish a vital foothold.

Following this success the Huguenots, under their commander Colonel Callimotte, crossed a few hundred yards downstream. Next came the Enniskilleners and other Ulster units and then a little later the Danes, under the Duke of Württemberg, and the English, under Sir John

Hammer. Tyrconnell, from elevated ground half a mile away, saw what had happened and cursed Lauzun for weakening the centre. He now committed the Jacobite cavalry to stem the advancing tide. A fierce charge by Hamilton broke the Huguenot ranks and a number of their officers were killed. Callimotte himself was severely wounded in the thigh and died a few days later. As he was taken back across the river, he urged his men: 'À la gloire, mes enfants, à la gloire!' (on to glory, my children, on to glory!)

Schomberg, seeing the Huguenots in difficulty, could not restrain himself. He rushed impetuously into the river, shouting: 'Allons, messieurs, voilà vos persecuteurs' (Come on, gentlemen, these are your persecutors) — pointing his sword at the enemy. It was a rash venture. In the melee a lieutenant in Dorington's Irish Regiment, Charles O'Toole, struck the Duke in the neck with his sabre. It was not a fatal cut, but in the confusion a stray shot from Schomberg's own side hit him in the throat. The ball penetrated the windpipe, and he died within minutes without uttering a word.

The death of Schomberg maddened the Huguenots, who began firing wildly and roaring: 'Tue! tue! tue!' (kill! kill! kill!). They beat back Hamilton's horsemen, recovered Schomberg's body and carried it back across the river. It was a tragic end for the old veteran. William, when told the news by Schomberg's aide-de-camp, received it coldly. His displeasure with the dead man apparently still rankled. Yet it was surprising that Schomberg was not honoured with a military funeral; his body was quietly interred several days later in Saint Patrick's Cathedral in Dublin. For all his fame he was quickly forgotten. His tomb remained unmarked until, several decades later, Jonathan Swift and the Chapter of the Cathedral placed a plaque on it. This records Swift's criticism of Schomberg's relatives in neglecting the grave. It says: 'The fame of his valour was more effective with strangers than his closeness of blood was with his kinsmen.'

The Reverend George Walker of Derry fell shortly after Schomberg. William appeared indifferent to his loss also. On learning of Walker's fate, he said, with irritation, 'What took him there?' An eyewitness said that Walker's body was stripped of its clothing 'for the Scots-Irish . . . took most of the plunder.' He was buried near where he fell, and some time later his widow, Isabella, had the body disinterred. It was taken to Castle Caulfield, where it was reburied on the south side of the chancel in 1702.

Heavy fighting continued at the fords near Oldbridge. William was in despair as he watched his Dutch Blue Guards make vain attempts against the Jacobite cavalry. His Secretary of War, Sir George Clark, later remembered him mutter: 'My poor guards, my poor guards'; but when he saw them stand and form platoons 'he breathed out, as people do after holding their breath.'

A mile from Drogheda, at Drybridge, William crossed with his cavalry. Halfway across his horse became stuck in deep mud and he was forced to dismount while the animal was dragged to the bank (an incident not recorded on later Orange banners).[5] With his right arm in a sling, he carried his sword in his left hand (in some accounts he is mentioned as carrying a walking stick) and despite his discomfort, within minutes he was leading a cavalry charge. His crossing extended the Orange front by about half a mile and caused a predicament for the Jacobites, as they could not cover the lengthened line.

The heaviest clashes were still at Oldbridge. The Irish infantry initially fought well but really could not contend with the swarms of Orange troops sweeping across. The fighting had to be left to the cavalry. Tyrconnell, Parker, Sutherland and Berwick made repeated charges against the greater numbers. After each assault they wheeled back towards the Hill of Donore, regrouped and charged again. In one of the melees, Berwick's horse was shot from under him and he had to hide in a ditch until rescued by a trooper. But it was all to no avail; by mid-afternoon Tyrconnell saw that further resistance was impossible and gave orders for a retreat towards Duleek. The cavalry then did its best to protect the infantry until it was safely across the River Nanny in the rear.

In one of the last charges, Richard Hamilton sustained a head wound and was taken prisoner. He was brought before William, who asked whether the Irish were likely to charge again. He replied: 'Yes, your Majesty, on my honour, I believe they are, for they have a good body of horse still.' William looked him coldly in the eye and said: 'Your honour, Hamilton! Your honour!' He remembered how his captive had not too long ago turned his coat.

The Retreat

On the left the Jacobites were also falling back towards Duleek. There was great confusion as the retreating Irish infantry became mingled with the French cavalry arriving from Rosnaree. In the disorder, the French Colonel Zurlauben had to fire on the Irish to separate the foot from the horse. At this point the Jacobites were in greater danger from each other than from the Williamites. Shortly before, Lauzun had advised James — who had watched the battle from a church tower on the Hill of Donore — to make a run for it. The jittery monarch lost no time in making for Dublin, protected by a large cavalry escort.

Evening was now approaching and the Jacobites were everywhere in retreat. The infantry had scattered in many directions, but the cavalry kept reasonable shape as it disengaged. The Orange army was not, however, prepared to give up. It pursued its quarry for about six miles, as far as Naul, and any Jacobite taken was shot 'like a hare among the corn'.

The Battle of the Boyne was over, and the victors helped themselves to the spoils. The Dutch envoy, Jacob Hop, said: 'The enemy fled in considerable disorder, leaving behind guns and baggage, even gold watches and silver dinner services.' Among the papers found were plans against the life of William. An Orange soldier named Jones, who was in the pay of the Jacobites, was at the centre of a plot to assassinate him.

William had won, but in a military sense it was not a great victory.[6] Neither side had shown impressive generalship. It was not a glorious achievement for 36,000 well-armed Orange troops to oust 25,000 largely untrained men who had only six small cannon. As an armed encounter, the battle was later ridiculously overplayed for partisan purposes. James was ill-advised to have fought at all. His fatal decision not to move westward left him trying to defend an easily fordable river against overwhelming odds.

No account can be complete without mention of the conspicuous courage of William. That he exposed himself to great danger cannot be doubted: at Donore a musket ball shot the heel from his boot and, later, another shattered one of his pistols. At the end of the day, after sixteen hours in the saddle, with his painful arm in a sling, he expressed neither joy nor bravado but looked relieved. To him, the battle had been a duty and he had seen it through with characteristic determination. The date was 1 July 1690, and Te Deums were sung in Catholic cathedrals in Austria and Spain in celebration of the Protestant Victory.[7]

The Green Grassy Slopes of the Boyne

'The Green Grassy Slopes of the Boyne' is probably the most famous ballad on the Battle of the Boyne. There was mild disappointment among Orangemen in 1990 when, for the 300th anniversary of the battle, the Orange Order designated 'My Sweet Boyne Side' as the official tercentenary anthem. But 'The Green Grassy Slopes' retains its popularity.[8]

—7—

Limerick, Athlone and Aughrim

The Flight of James

James arrived in Dublin to be greeted at the castle gates by Lady Tyrconnell, the Lord Lieutenant's wife. She inquired what would he have for supper? He gave an account of what he had for breakfast and said that because of this, he had little stomach for supper. Then he added, acidly: ' Your countrymen can run well, madam.' No Irish partisan could listen to a crack like that without endeavouring to capsize it. She quickly retorted: 'Not so well as your Majesty, I see, for you have won the race.'

James summoned a council meeting, whose members advised him to leave for France immediately.[1] He said everything had gone against him. He vowed never again to lead an Irish army, and claimed that they had refused to stand by him. He would now seek safety for himself and advised those present to fend for themselves. They were not, he instructed, to wreak vengeance against the Protestants, or to do any injury to the city of Dublin, in which he still had an interest. He rode to Bray, ten miles away, and then to Arklow where he rested briefly. Next morning his group reached Duncannon in the Waterford estuary. There he boarded the vessel *Lauzun*. On board, he found that he had lost his hat. When General O'Farrel presented him with a new one, he remarked peevishly, 'If through the fault of the Irish I have lost my crown, at least they have given me a hat instead.' Sarsfield made a more incisive comment, when he later told the victors: 'Change kings and we will fight you over again.'

The hapless James arrived in Brest a week later and was the first to bring news of his defeat to the Continent. He was received coldly by Louis, for whom the outcome at the Boyne was a setback. The Orange victory was not greeted, as so often claimed, by the singing of Te Deums in the Vatican: these were sung, as mentioned earlier, in Catholic cathedrals in Austria and Spain, where the success of William, as the leader of the Grand Alliance, was received with delight.

William in Dublin

On 6 July, William made a triumphant entry into Dublin and was rapturously welcomed by the substantial Protestant population. The following day he issued a declaration demanding the unconditional surrender of all Jacobite forces in Ireland. The rank and file were offered a pardon, but the leaders were given no hope for the security of their estates. If William's intention was to bring the war to an early conclusion, he achieved the direct opposite. The Jacobites, still undefeated, stiffened their resistance, gathered their scattered forces, and retreated to Limerick. William hastened to follow them, and dispatched a separate force under Lieutenant General James Douglas to Athlone, County Westmeath, the gateway to the west.

But Athlone would not be easily taken. When Douglas called on the garrison to surrender the commander, Richard Grace, fired his pistol in the air and announced that he would hold the town until he had eaten his old boots. Confronted with such determined resistance and finding himself without adequate siege guns, Douglas raised the siege after a week. He had lost up to 400 men through sickness or battle before the walls.

William fared no better in Limerick. The Jacobites had decided to make a do-or-die stand. Limerick, the third largest city in the country, had a peacetime population of 12,000. Strategically it was of great importance, commanding the southern entrance to Clare and Connaught, and a port for large sea-going ships. The drawback was that its defences were poor. Moreover, the Jacobites had great problems: many soldiers were ill and others were losing heart. Lauzun and Tyrconnell favoured making terms with William, and the Frenchman announced — famously — that the city could be taken 'if bombarded with roasted apples'. He realised that no assistance could be expected from France. But the rank and file believed that their opponents would not honour terms and, besides, they were anxious to vindicate themselves from James' smears of cowardice. The most prominent of these diehards was Patrick Sarsfield.

Sarsfield

Sarsfield was to become one of the great figures in Irish history. Today, particularly in Limerick, streets, municipal buildings and sporting teams are named after him. He was descended on his father's side from an Anglo-Norman family who, during the religious upheavals of the Tudor period, had retained their Catholicism. Although the Sarsfields were 'gentlemen of the Pale' they had integrated with their Gaelic neighbours, and disliked the new 'upstart' gentry who were planted by Cromwell. This led to a marital connection with the renowned O'Mores of Laois, who traced their ancestry to the fabled Milesians. The O'Mores had risen nineteen times during the reign of Elizabeth, Sarsfield's grandfather was the legendary Rory O'More, one of the principal leaders of the Rebellion of 1641. His mother, Annie O'More, is reputed to have taught the young Sarsfield the legends of Gaelic Ireland and to have imbued him with a sense of his heritage.[2] The family certainly spoke Gaelic — as one of two languages — and burned with resentment that a portion of their lands had been confiscated by Cromwell.

In early manhood Sarsfield was involved in a series of duels, dismissed from the army, and took part in the abduction of two wealthy young women. His military career did not take off until he had served as a cavalry officer at Sedgemoor. In France, England and at home he was held in high esteem. His bravery and skill were much spoken of, and he enjoyed the respect, indeed the affection, of his compatriots. It was these, his fellow diehards, who would stick with him on the stormy paths which lay ahead.

The French wanted to go home, having no stomach for further fighting in Ireland. Lauzun left for Galway, from where he proposed to sail, and took many of the heavy artillery pieces with him. He appointed Tyrconnell Captain General and made Sarsfield second in command. The greatest authority was given to a senior French officer, Boisseleau, who became Governor of Limerick. Tyrconnell was not content. He felt in his bones that the writing was on the wall, and soon he followed Lauzun.

The Orange army arrived before the walls on 8 August. Its size was not as fearsome as had been expected; William's strength had been reduced. In response to requests from Whitehall he had been forced to transfer several regiments to England. Further, he was obliged to install garrisons in the towns which he had taken since the Boyne. The size of his army was now estimated at 25,000.

Ballyneety

William camped near the Ballysimon road on the outskirts of the city, and called on the garrison to surrender. A curt refusal was received from Boisseleau, and the Orange army was ordered to invest the city.

William did not anticipate the next event: a Huguenot deserter stole into Limerick and leaked the news that a convoy of heavy guns was on its way from Dublin and could be expected to arrive within days. Sarsfield recognised that little could be done to save Limerick if these were received. He determined at once to intercept the convoy and destroy it. With the Orange army encamped between Limerick and the approaching convoy (or siege train, as it was called), he realised that he would have to steal out of the city. He gathered 500 horsemen and slipped out by night. After stealing over Thomond Bridge, he rode north, crossed the Shannon at Killaloe and entered County Tipperary. A local rapparee named Galloping Hogan acted as his guide.

Hogan is said to have known every inch of the way, but this is disputed in the mountain villages of Tipperary,[3] where tradition holds that while Sarsfield was encamped on Keeper Hill, a message was sent to a local outlaw, Ned Ryan — the famous Eamonn An Cnoic (Ned of the Hill) — who was hiding on the Mother Mountain near Rearcross. The story goes that Ned led Sarsfield, Hogan and the others through Toor, Knockfine, Rearcross, around the shoulder of the Slieve Phelim Mountains, over Glengar, and down by the graveyard at Toem. From there they rode through the low country to Ballyneety. In County Limerick there are two places called Ballyneety; Sarsfield's destination was located in the parish of Templebraden, about fourteen miles south-east of the city.

The siege train was drawn up in a field near the ruins of an old castle. No attack was expected and it was lightly guarded. Most of the troopers and their camp-followers — who included a number of women and children — had settled for the night. As Sarsfield approached the townland of Derk, he learnt from a peasant woman (who had been selling apples in the Orange camp) that the password for that night was his own surname. The horsemen stole up, but a sentry was alerted by the undeadened hoofs, and challenged: 'Who goes there?' At this, Sarsfield sprang out, his horse rearing, and answered: 'Sarsfield is the word, and Patrick Sarsfield is the man.' In a flash the intruders overwhelmed the stupefied guards. Standing on their stirrups, they galloped through the camp, cutting down the half-awakened troopers. There was bedlam as the Jacobites wheeled their horses and charged again and again. Dozens of Orange soldiers were killed, and the rest ran like hares in all directions. In the heat of the fray a number of non-combatants, some of them women, fell victims to the onslaught. This was a serious blemish on what was otherwise a daringly executed operation.

Sarsfield instructed that everything be burnt. The cannons were stuffed with powder and their long barrels stuck into the ground. Fuses were lit, and the whole caboodle was blown sky-high. Today, one can still see the moonscape holes which were cut in the ground by the exploding cannon. The destruction of the siege train was a great morale booster to the garrison at Limerick. It raised Sarsfield's stature to new heights and provided further justification for continuing the war. In immediate terms, it delayed William's assault.

The Siege of Limerick

After a week of desultory exchanges, the siege of Limerick began in earnest. On 17 August the bugles rang at daybreak and the drums beat. William's cannon began hammering the walls. The defending army took up their positions, and the civilians fell in behind them; Limerick was prepared to die rather than yield.

The day was dull and cloudy; a thick mist lay on the Clare hills, but during the morning the sun broke through and the heat became intense. At two o'clock the guns ceased, and William called again on the city to surrender. There was no response. For over an hour a tense pause hung over the scene. Then the guns began again, and an Orange attacking column, 10,000 strong, moved forward. The Orange grenadiers in their piebald uniforms sprang from their trenches, firing and throwing grenades as they ran. A breach was made in the walls and the grenadiers began pouring through. Furious hand-to-hand fighting ensued. During the height of the combat an ammunition store known as the Black Battery exploded, inflicting great loss on William's Brandenburg Regiment, who took the weight of the blast.

The greatest fury was at the breach. For three hours the Irish infantry held the line, closing gap after gap as William hurled regiment after regiment against them. Slowly, the Irish began to push back the attackers. William called up his reserves, but the Irish still held them in check. The citizens rushed to defend the breach and deadly struggles ensued. Again, the Orange troops made a mighty thrust, but again the Irish, with dogged determination, forced them back. Then Sarsfield's cavalry, this time under Colonel Mark Talbot, came from the rear. It had been held in check all along. Now its turn had come. Galloping ferociously across Balls Bridge, it swept through the streets and onto the breach. William, seeing the danger, quickly ordered two troops of Danish horse to block its path, but the Irish cut through them, and swept on. Limerick had been saved.

William Leaves Ireland

The battle for Limerick was a turning point. William's losses were great; an estimate of 1,500 killed and wounded is probably not far out. Some of the Orange commanders urged that the assault be resumed next day, but most of the Orange ammunition and supplies had been expended and, besides, the weather had broken. Autumn was approaching and the ground was getting heavy. In these circumstances William thought it prudent to raise the siege.[4] The Orange army broke camp and withdrew wearily towards Tipperary. William had had enough of Ireland. A week or so later, early in September, he took ship to England. He was never to set foot in Ireland again.

Marlborough in Ireland

Before leaving, William appointed his Dutch general, Godard Ginkel, to take command. He also gave his consent to a daring scheme to disrupt Jacobite communications in the south-east. This was the Duke of Marlborough's plan to capture Cork and Kinsale, important landing points for fresh Jacobite forces coming from France. The Duke left England on 17 September, and a few days later was joined in Cork by about 5,000 Dutch, Danish and Huguenot troops under the Duke of Württemburg. The city's defences were weak and it fell easily. Within a few days Kinsale had fallen too. This short campaign, with few casualties, yielded the entire south-east to William. The loop was tightening on the remaining Jacobites. They were determined to make last stands in Limerick, Galway and Athlone. But winter had now drawn in, and the campaigning season closed.

The First Orange Anniversary

The country was in a dreadful condition. There was famine in many areas and the cost of food rose beyond the reach of the poor. Plundering was rife, and whole communities suffered from sickness and disease. But the Protestants suffered least. They were, in fact, reasonably content; William had delivered them and they believed that in a short while the victory would be complete. On 4 November, when they celebrated William's birthday, the first Orange parade to be held in Ireland took place in Dublin. The city's militia, 2,500 strong, marched through the streets to the sound of fife and drum. The Lord Justices Coningsby, Porter and Sidney, who had been appointed by William to conduct the civil administration, held a reception for senior Orange commanders at Dublin Castle, and Protestants throughout the land drank toasts to: 'Our new King', 'The Deliverer' and 'The Protestant King'.

Trinity College dismissed its Catholic Provost, Reverend Michael Moore,[5] and appointed a Protestant one. Members of its teaching faculty who had fled to England in the previous year returned to their duties. Protestant aldermen who had been dismissed by James were re-appointed, and established the first Orange Society in Ireland, known as The Aldermen of Skinners Alley. The administrative pattern which was to regulate the affairs of the country for years to come began to take shape. But the Jacobites were still undefeated and held a number of important strongholds.

St Ruth

Military operations did not resume until May 1691, and some Protestants had begun to question William's policy on grounds of slowness and adequacy. The Jacobites did not benefit from the delay, as there was acute division among their leaders. Tyrconnell and the Duke of Berwick resented the popularity of Sarsfield, and persistently misrepresented him at Versailles. Louis passed Sarsfield over and gave command to a French general. This was Charles de Claremont, the Marquis de St Ruth, a bigoted anti-Protestant, notorious for the cruel manner in which he had suppressed the Huguenots following the Revocation of Nantes. His name was linked with torture and burnings, and it was said that he now wished to continue his 'anti-heresy' crusade in Ireland. A big, paunchy, ugly-looking man, he had a harsh temper and menacing demeanour. He had successfully commanded Irish troops in Italy, and this was presumed to qualify him for command in Ireland. The Irish regretted that Sarsfield had not been appointed and in compensation James conferred on him the title 'Earl of Lucan'. Sarsfield thought this trivial and would have preferred tangible recognition.

Meanwhile the Orange forces, headed by Ginkel, assembled at Mullingar. Their first major point of attack was to be at Athlone.

The Bridge of Athlone

Athlone consisted of two walled towns, separated by the River Shannon. The previous year Colonel Richard Grace had defended the Irish town on the Connaught side. The new commander, Colonel Nicholas Fitzgerald, was determined to defend both towns so as to allow time for St Ruth to bring up the main body of his army from Ballinasloe.

Ginkel was fortunate in having under his command a clever Scot, General Hugh Mackay, who had recently crushed a Jacobite rebellion in the Highlands and who had come to Ireland to gain new laurels. Their plan was to take the English town by making a breach in the wall near the North Gate and pour men through in blitzkrieg fashion.

On 19 June a large cannon was mounted on the northern approach and it began pounding heavily. By mid-afternoon a gap thirty yards wide was opened and 4,000 men dashed through, firing rapidly as they went. The defenders were no more than 400, and could not stem the tide. They fell back and began tearing down the arches of the bridge to prevent further advance. It was deadly work, and dozens were shot to pieces. The bridge became a slaughterhouse as bodies fell upon bodies. Yet the defenders did not yield until two arches were broken.

The next day St Ruth arrived and immediately made arrangements for the defence of Irish Town. He placed heavy cannon on the ramparts of the castle, overlooking the bridge, and constructed breastworks along the river. His defensive position was strong, as it would be necessary for the enemy to neutralise the castle before moving forward. And the castle was exceptionally sturdy.

The Orange gunners set to work, opening the fiercest bombardment ever seen in Ireland. The castle was pounded heavily for days. Twelve thousand cannon balls, 600 bombs and many tons of stones were propelled across the river. The eastern wall was reduced to rubble, the breastworks flattened, and dozens of buildings set alight by mortars. In spite of it all, the Irish held on.

Ginkel was in a quandary. In the face of such stern opposition his options were limited. He sent a flanking party upstream, but it was unsuccessful. In desperation, he elected for a hazardous frontal assault, which meant that he would have to repair the bridge. It was a gambler's throw, but his need was great. Under heavy cover his men advanced to lay planks across the broken arches. Because of the hail of cannon fire, the Irish were powerless to stop the work, yet it took several hours to lay the timbers.

When the last plank was settled, a single man resolved to frustrate the scheme and save Athlone. His name was Custume, a sergeant in the dragoons. He called for ten men to join him in a bold attempt to topple the timbers. Dashing onto the bridge, they heaved at the heavy planks and sent several flying into the water. Their enemies raked the bridge with fire and, within a minute, all lay dead. Eleven others sprang up and ran onto the bridge. With hatchet and axe, they plied furiously at the planks. When the last timber fell, two men emerged from the dust and smoke and escaped by jumping into the water: twenty earned the martyr's crown.

The names of these men — unlike those who led the defence of Derry — are forgotten. No monument has been raised to their memory and no society or association has ever been founded to salute them. History forgets the men who held the bridge at Athlone, although it remembers those who defended the Pass at Thermopylae. But what history forgets, the poet — the unconscious voice of his people — remembers. The lines of the gentle Aubrey de Vere were once taught to Irish schoolchildren, and this may still be so:

> Does any man dream that a Gael can fear?
> Of a thousand deeds let him learn but one!
> The Shannon swept onwards broad and clear,
> Between the leaguers and brave Athlone.
>
> 'Break down the bridge!' six warriors rushed[6]
> Thro' the storm of shot and the storm of shell;
> With late, but certain victory flushed
> The grim, Dutch gunners eyed them well.

They wrenched at the planks, mid a hail of fire:
They fell in death, their work half done;
The bridge stood fast; and nigh and nigher
The foe swarmed darkly, densely on:

'Oh, Who for Erin will strike a stroke?
Who hurl yon planks where the waters roar?'
Six warriors forth from their comrades broke,
And flung themselves on the planks once more.

Again at the rocking planks they dashed;
Four dropped dead and two remained;
The huge beams groaned and the arch down-crashed;
Two stalwart swimmers the margin gained.

St Ruth in his stirrups stood up and cried
'I have seen no deed like this in France!'
With a toss of his head, Sarsfield replied,
'They had luck, the dogs! 'Twas a merry chance!'

Oh! many a year, on Shannon side,
They sang upon moor, and they sang upon heath,
Of the twain who breasted the raging tide,
And the ten who shook hands with death.

Athlone Falls

Ginkel summoned a meeting of his officers to consider whether to raise the siege. Time was running out, food and other supplies were low. Mackay was for quitting, Ginkel himself was unsure of what to do, and no decision had been reached when two deserters from St Ruth's camp were brought in. Their information flabbergasted Ginkel. The Jacobites, they confided, had inferred that Ginkel had abandoned hope of taking Athlone and had withdrawn towards Dublin. Further, St Ruth had himself left Athlone and withdrawn to the west, leaving only a light guard of untrained troops to hold the town. Ginkel was astonished, but quickly saw his opportunity. He ordered that a fresh assault be made on Athlone immediately.

The deserters had spoken the truth. The French commander had negligently left the defence of Athlone to raw levies. They were overrun without difficulty and the town was taken. An urgent message was dispatched, before the end, to St Ruth, but he pronounced it impossible that Ginkel could have resumed the siege. He was wrong. This is how, after a stubborn defence of over ten days, Athlone was lost in half an hour.

Aughrim

Aughrim is a small village three miles from Ballinasloe in County Galway. It was here that St Ruth sought to redeem his reputation following the disaster at Athlone. Sarsfield argued that he should withdraw further west and establish a base from which to launch guerrilla attacks behind Orange lines. St Ruth refused to listen. After his folly at Athlone he wanted a great victory, and this, he felt, could be achieved only by meeting the enemy face to face. Sarsfield was astonished by the decision. He argued that if they lost another pitched battle, it would be disastrous for the Jacobite cause. Why risk so much?

St Ruth would brook no objection. He dug his army in on Kilcommodon Hill (or, as it is sometimes called, Aughrim Hill) which rose some 400 feet and extended for about two miles from the ruined castle at Aughrim in the north to Kilcommodon Church in the south. This was an ideal position from which to fight a defensive battle. In front lay a red bog; to the south, beyond the hill, there was firm ground known as the Pass of Urrachree, and to the north, near the castle, a narrow causeway between two bogs. Thick hedges provided excellent cover for musketeers.

With the Orange army delayed at Athlone awaiting provisions, the Frenchman adroitly cut gaps in the hedges to allow his infantry an escape route and, importantly, to facilitate uninterrupted downhill cavalry charges. He strung his infantry (commanded by two competent officers, William Dorington and John Hamilton) out along the length of the slope and posted Colonel Walter Burke and a few hundred foot in the area around the castle. Burke was to receive, if required, back-up assistance from the dragoon and cavalry regiments of Colonel Henry Luttrell and Major Dominic Sheldon. On the right, Urrachree was to be protected by heavy guns supported by large battalions of horse. Sarsfield, because of St Ruth's envy of him, was confined to commanding the cavalry reserve, and positioned on the left wing at the rear of the hill. He was given the most frustrating instruction that can be issued to an enthusiastic soldier: 'Don't move until you receive further orders.'

Late on 11 July, the Orange army reached Ballinasloe. On learning of the strength of St Ruth's position, Ginkel was reluctant to offer battle, but Mackay dissuaded him. His plan was to advance against the Jacobite left and assault the castle; with luck, St Ruth might divert cavalry from his right to assist his left. Then, the Orange army should assault the weakened right with great strength; additionally, it should strike across the bog and engage the Jacobite infantry on the slope. It was an audacious scheme, and Ginkel was in two minds whether to accept it, but Mackay's views prevailed.

St Ruth's Appeal

At dawn on Sunday morning the Orange army filed over the bridge at Ballinasloe and advanced towards Aughrim. Visibility was poor and a heavy mist lay over the bog. Ginkel, despite Mackay's urgings, was still hesitant, but St Ruth was ready. All morning he had made great efforts to ignite the spirit of his men. From a makeshift platform he delivered a rousing speech:

> Gentlemen and Soldiers, I suppose that it is not unknown to you, what glory I have acquired and how successful and fortunate I have been in suppressing heresy in France, and in propagating the Holy Catholic Faith. I can without vanity boast of being the happy instrument in bringing over thousands of poor, deluded souls from their errors assisted by some members of our holy and unspotted church. It is for this reason that the most puissant King, my master, has chosen me to come hither. I am assured by my spies that the Prince of Orange's heretical army are resolved to give us battle and, as you see before you, are ready to do so. It is now, therefore, that you must recover your honour, your privileges and your forefathers' estates. You are not mercenary soldiers, you do not fight for your pay, but for your lives, your wives, your children, your liberties and your country, and to restore the most pious of kings to his throne. Stand by it therefore, my dears, and bear no longer the reproaches of the heretics who brand you as cowards, and you may be sure that King James will love and reward you; all good Catholics will applaud you; I myself will commend you; your posterity will bless you; God will make saints of all of you and his Holy Mother will lay you in her bosom.[7]

This toxic mixture of God and country was heady stuff. Eighty priests moved around the field stressing the importance of victory in the coming battle for the Catholic faith in Ireland. Macaulay says: 'The whole camp was in a ferment of religious excitement. In every regiment priests were praying, preaching, shriving, holding up the host and cup, while soldiers swore on the sacramental bread not to abandon their colours.'[8] This fervour was fortified by the liberal supply of French brandy provided to each company. The men, thus stimulated, were ready as never before to destroy the heretics.

The Battle

Across from Kilcommoden Hill, Ginkel made careful dispositions. The Duke of Württemburg, who was second in command, was given responsibility for the left wing, Mackay was placed in the centre and the

Huguenot, Ruvigny, on the right. Both armies were roughly equal in number, but in field guns the Jacobites were at a disadvantage, having only ten to Ginkel's twenty-five. The contest began in mid-afternoon at Urrachree when Danish dragoons tried to force the Pass, but were driven back. Next, the English tried, but were forced back too. Then there was a lull.

Ginkel was still uneasy and called a Council of War, which deliberated for two hours before deciding to press ahead. It was now five o'clock, and the Danes began a fresh advance to outflank the Irish who withdrew — as they had planned — from hedge to hedge and lured their opponents on. From behind the hedges the Irish musketeers opened fire and drove the attackers back in disorder. Then the Jacobite cavalry charged downwards and sent the Orange infantry scurrying across the bog. Ginkel ordered the Huguenots to attack on the right, but time and again they were driven back. Things were going well for the Jacobites, but still Ginkel maintained pressure on Urrachree.

Then, amazingly, St Ruth acted as Mackay had predicted. To fortify the Jacobite right, he weakened his left wing by ordering cavalry from near the castle to cross the hill and assist at Urrachree. Additionally, he moved some of his centre rightwards. The wily Scotsman, who had waited for this move, immediately ordered four infantry battalions to cross the bog. About 3,000 Orange troops advanced (up to their waists in mud and water) and the Irish were forced to retire up the hill. But halfway up, supported by cavalry, they turned and charged down again. The Orange infantry broke and were driven into the bog amid great slaughter.

The only progress which Ginkel could make was in the vicinity of the castle. A large body of English cavalry rushed the causeway, but Colonel Walter Burke saw them coming and opened fire. Then disaster struck. His ammunition ran low and the men smashed open fresh boxes, only to find that the new bullets would not fit their muskets. Incredibly, the ammunition was of English manufacture and could not be used in their French flintlocks. In desperation, they tore the brass buttons from their coats to use as ball, and even stuffed pebbles into the rifle muzzles. It was a ludicrous situation and, unsurprisingly, they were unable to prevent the English horse, under Ruvigny, from advancing.

St Ruth Falls

Henry Luttrell sat stiffly on his big black horse on the high ground beyond the causeway, with his dragoons at the ready. It was now up to him to drive the English back. He failed to do so. The charitable interpretation is that he was unable to act without cavalry; the less charitable is that he acted treacherously. Ruvigny watched him draw back and pressed his advantage. More and more English cavalry dashed across the causeway. Luttrell retreated further back.

St Ruth, watching this strange development through his field glasses, was confident that the advance could be checked, and called up a portion of Sarsfield's reserve to do the job. There was no doubt about the ability of Sarsfield's men to perform. Indeed, a single charge at the advancing English would likely have won the day for the Jacobites. But St Ruth did not want Sarsfield to share the glory, and the Irishman was ordered to remain behind with the remnant. St Ruth was determined to lead the final glorious charge himself. He raced across the field at full speed, shouting: 'La jour est à nous, mes enfants!' (the day is ours, my boys!) He was hit by a stray shot from the Orange battery below. A cannon ball carried off his head and for several minutes his horse ran wildly in circles about the slope. When it was caught, a cloak was thrown over the body and the animal was led over the summit. Some say that the corpse was interred hours later in Loughrea churchyard, about twelve miles away. Others maintain that it was buried locally, in the grounds of Kilcommodon church. The truth will probably never be known.

The death of its commander paralysed the Jacobite army. Luttrell and Sheldon rode, inexplicably, off the field.[9] The English cavalry was allowed without challenge to penetrate behind the Irish infantry and the rout commenced. Sarsfield realised that the day was lost when he saw the main body of the army break and run over the summit. He organised a retreat as best he could, leading the oddments of the defeated army on to Limerick.

The death toll was 7,000 — the greatest number ever slaughtered in battle on Irish soil. For weeks the dead remained unburied, and dogs and rats gnawed at the corpses. For years after, local people were reluctant to go near the site of the battle, calling it 'Áit Na Grainne' (The Ugly Place).

'The Last of the Brave'

The Jacobite defeat represented the destruction of the last vestiges of Catholic power. Colonel Charles O'Kelly, in his despairing account, said: 'The Irish lost the flower of their army and nation.'[10] Numerous poets wrote poignantly of the defeat. John Moore caught the mood of widespread anguish:

> Forget me not the field where they perished
> The truest, the last of the brave:
> All gone and the bright hopes we cherished
> Gone with them and quenched in the grave.

This reaction was to beget a lively sub-theme in Irish history: the concept of what did 'not' happen, and the tale of the missed chance. It was said that had St Ruth lived for a further twenty minutes, victory would have gone to the Jacobites. Tied to this thinking was the suggestion of treachery and betrayal. Why did Luttrell and Sheldon leave the field? In Luttrell's case the accusation seemed to be proven by his later conduct at Limerick, and his acceptance of a pension from William after the war. To this day, the spot at Aughrim where he let the Orange cavalry through is known as 'Luttrell's Pass' or the 'Traitor's Gate'. In later years, near the spot where St Ruth was struck down — a place called 'Bloody Hollow' — a bush was grown. Today it, or one of its successors, is marked with a plaque which says:

> The Jacobite General St. Ruth died here after a battle
> With the forces of King William on 12th July 1691.
> His defeat and death spelled an end for the hopes of
> James II and changed the course of Irish history.

At the bicentenary of the battle in 1891, a committee of local people made arrangements to erect a monument on the site. In that turbulent period of Irish history (the time of the Parnell split) the committee did not escape the pressures of the day and broke up. An incomplete Celtic cross of fine granite lay in a stonemason's yard in Ballinasloe for many years.

In more recent times, a local schoolmaster, Martin Joyce, reconstituted the committee, and it was responsible for erecting the cross near the old ruins of Aughrim castle, where the final stages of the battle were fought.[11] The inscription, in French, reads: 'A la Memoire du Lieutenant General Marquis de St. Ruth et des morts au Champs d'Honneur Aughrim 1691' and in English: 'To the Memory of Lt. General Marquis of St. Ruth and the dead on the Field of Honour Aughrim 1691.' Underneath is written: 'Stone presented by Jerry and Leo Beegan 1960, quarried by their father and grandfather.'

The Treaty of Limerick

Following the Orange victory at Aughrim, Galway opened its gates to Ginkel's army while the remnants of the defeated Jacobites, about 13,000 men, made their way to Limerick to make a final stand.

On 25 August, Ginkel invested Limerick on three sides. William was now impatient with the prolonged Irish imbroglio and empowered Ginkel to offer favourable terms: these included a free pardon to all, and a promise that the Catholic gentry would be restored to their estates. The offer split the Jacobites. Some wanted to accept it, others were opposed. Sarsfield said no, French aid might come. Sarsfield won the argument and the offer was refused.

Sixty big guns opened up on the city, and an English fleet bombarded it from the river. Unable to take Limerick by assault, Ginkel changed tactics and turned the assault into a blockade. Then Henry Luttrell, under a cloud since Aughrim, was found to be in correspondence with the enemy, and an officer called Clifford leaked information which enabled Ginkel to cross the Shannon and surround the city; finally, the loss of Thomond Bridge was a crushing blow. Again, Ginkel offered terms. Those who opposed Sarsfield said that it was folly to refuse. Yet Limerick made one more fight, on 23 September, from dawn to dusk. When the fighting ceased, both sides began to parley. For the third time Ginkel offered terms. With treachery and lack of resolve all around him, Sarsfield reluctantly accepted.

The surrender on 26 September 1691 was followed by the signing of the articles of a treaty.[12] The generosity of some of the terms reflects William's anxiety to free his army for service on the Continent. He instructed Ginkel to offer the utmost that was likely to be acceptable to parliament. The military articles of the treaty were straightforward — those who wished to go to France and to engage in military service there were free to do so. Arrangements were made for their transportation from Cork. The civil articles were more complicated; they promised Catholics such freedom of worship as was 'consistent with the laws of Ireland or as they did enjoy in the reign of Charles II'. This was an ambiguous phrase and could be variously interpreted.

The articles also provided indemnities for those who had fought for James and 'all such as are under their protection'. This last phrase was omitted from the final draft which was signed and taken to London. It was said that the Lord Chief Justice's lawyers, who arrived in Limerick while the negotiations were going on, found the phrase too sweeping and insisted on its exclusion. In London, William re-inserted it, but the 'missing clause' remained controversial and it was left out when the Irish parliament ratified the treaty. Whatever the reason, the Catholics felt betrayed and Limerick has since been called the 'City of the Broken Treaty'.

To the Jacobites the outcome was a compromise, not a surrender. This was, of course, a face-saving excuse. William had won; his victory in Ireland consolidated his seizure of power in Britain. His goal of denying Britain as an ally of Louis had been achieved, and he was able to bring his new resources into the Grand Alliance against France.

In Ireland itself, the 'Protestant Nation' was born. It would monopolise government, parliament, the army, the public service and land ownership for generations to come.

Protestant Ireland had a new hero in Ginkel. Following the surrender of Limerick, he returned to Dublin where he was hailed as a Caesar. The corporation and magistrates formally complimented him. When, at the end of the year, he went to London, the House of Commons voted him thanks and William created him Baron of Aughrim and Earl of Athlone. He was granted 26,400 acres of prime land from forfeited estates in Munster and Leinster.

As for Henry Luttrell, he opted not to accompany the Jacobites to France, received a handsome pension from William and was granted a forfeited estate. For many years he lived in great luxury, but was the object of great Catholic hatred. Several attempts were made on his life. On 3 November 1717, while in his sedan chair in Stafford Street in Dublin, he was shot dead. The assassins were never traced. Hatred followed him to the grave. His tombstone was many times desecrated, and the infamy which he incurred attached itself to his descendants.

The Wild Geese

The 11,000 or so who followed Sarsfield to France were remembered with great affection by their countrymen as 'The Wild Geese'. Whenever, as the Irish Brigade in the French army, they encountered the British — as at Blenheim (1704) or Fontenoy (1745) — they charged with the battle cry — 'Remember Limerick'.[13]

Sarsfield was made a Marshal of France, but died two years later fighting the British at the Battle of Landen in Flanders. Generations of Irish schoolchildren have been taught that his last words, as he tried to stem the blood from his wounds, were 'Oh, that this were for Ireland.' A fine life-size statue of him stands in Limerick (in the grounds of Saint John's Cathedral[14]). He is in heroic pose, with his left hand pointing towards the scene of one of his mighty deeds: Ballyneety.

—8—

The Glorious and Immortal Memory

The Aftermath

The Orange victory completed the conquest of Ireland which had begun so long before. Irish Protestants were confirmed in the ownership of the lands they held, and the English government in its power to rule Ireland without reference to its Catholic population. It remained only to take over much of the land still in Catholic hands — leaving them about one-seventh of the whole — and to protect the new Protestant supremacy by establishing a system of legal controls which would preclude all possibility of the recent Catholic challenge being repeated. Accordingly, there was enacted in the years following the Treaty of Limerick a large and intricate body of penal legislation designed to destroy Catholicism as a political force.

This legislation deprived Catholics of educational facilities, debarred them from the professions and from participating in public life, and imposed a number of other disabilities. It did not, however, include active religious persecution. Catholic worship was not suppressed, but only the barest minimum of activity was allowed. The penal laws were, in fact, intended to suppress the Catholics, not to convert them.

Glencoe

William's own interest in Ireland waned. He looked eastward towards Flanders and the Rhine and concentrated on the continental war against Louis. He pursued his purposes with his customary resolve and showed, on occasion, a streak of ruthlessness which surprised both his friends and enemies.

The darkest stain on his reputation was to come in Scotland, where a treacherous attack was made by his troops on the MacDonalds of Glencoe. In August 1691 the King had offered an indemnity to all chiefs who took the Oath of Allegiance by 1 January 1692. Alexander MacDonald postponed his submission until the last day — 31 December 1691. When he appeared before a military officer at Fort William for the purpose, he was told that the officer could not receive the oath. He then set out for Inverary to swear in the presence of the sheriff, but bad weather delayed him and it was not until 6 January that he was able to go through the formality.

This technical infringement suited the secret purposes of William's Scottish Under-Secretary, Sir John Dalrymple, Master of Stair, and such clans as the Campbells who were the hereditary enemies of the MacDonalds, since it offered an excuse for punitive action. Dalrymple persuaded the King to make an example of the MacDonalds, and William signed the authorising document. He later claimed not to have read it, for he often signed documents in haste. More than 100 troops were quartered among the MacDonalds, and for over a week accepted their crude hospitality. Suddenly, on a freezing winter's night, they turned on their hosts, and thirty-three men, two women and two children were put to the sword. It was clear that it was the troops' intention to murder the entire clan, but many were able to escape.

There was an outcry; although William had not specifically prescribed the methods employed, he bore responsibility for the crime, and the shame. His opponents detected shades of the callousness shown by his grand-uncle Maurice during the van Oldenbarneveldt Affair in 1619, and of his own unfeeling reaction towards the murder of the de Witt brothers in 1672.

William was a cold and calculating man. The admirable courage and tenacity which he showed when his own interests were at stake were seldom manifest in other causes. He had all the wiles, craft and slyness of a Machiavellian ruler, and took advantage of his opponents' weaknesses with an unerring sense of judgement. Yet, for all that, he was surprisingly tolerant of views which differed from his own. An austere Calvinist he was without personal religious prejudice. He dreaded and hated Catholicism less because of its theology than because of its political machinations. He employed Catholics in commanding positions when it suited him, and kept on good terms with the Pope, from whom he accepted money to fund his campaigns.

In Ireland he felt it expedient to acquiesce in anti-Catholic legislation, partly because it was supported by English opinion, but mainly because the co-operation of Irish Protestants was necessary if the country was to be kept in subjection. He was perturbed that a number of the civil articles in the Treaty of Limerick were either deviated from or broken, but he had much reason to dislike Irish Catholics, particularly when he found that those who had left with Sarsfield became an important section of the

French army — the famous Irish Brigade — and played a significant role in defeating his forces, and those of his allies, in Flanders, Italy, on the Rhine, and in the Pyrenees. Then the bulk of the thousand or so who had opted after Limerick to join him deserted while serving in France and Spain. He issued an order dismissing all remaining Irish Catholics from his army, and forbade their further recruitment.

The Continuing Threat

Despite their victory and the measures put in place to sustain it, Irish Protestants still felt insecure. True, the Jacobite army had been driven out of the country, but Sarsfield had pledged to return one day and renew the struggle, and James still claimed to be the rightful King and had the continuing support of the most powerful monarch in Europe. Moreover, James now had at his disposal an Irish army-in-exile, some 12,000 strong. Violence had not completely ceased for, following the war, bands of 'Rapparees' — armed gangs of ex-Jacobite soldiers — roamed the country terrorising Protestants and announcing the likelihood of fresh French intervention. Catholic priests had begun comforting their flocks with prophecies of the restoration of their lost estates.

To Protestants, these matters justified the new penal legislation, but their attitude also contained an element of revenge. They had a number of old scores to settle: the Rebellion of 1641, the humiliation at Dromore, and van Rosen's actions at Derry. They knew that they had escaped destruction by a narrow margin and were determined that their enemies should never threaten them again.

Many Protestants saw popery — as they termed it — as a great evil, an amalgam of error, superstition and unbiblical practices. It had, they believed, the effect of plunging the unfortunate aboriginals into a moral quagmire. It was a powerful and vigilant enemy, which sought time and again to wean Protestants from their purer faith. This great source of perdition was described, by their clergymen, with vivid Old Testament allusions: it was 'The Whore of Babylon', 'The Beast of the Apocalypse', 'The Scarlet Woman', and references were made to its 'pretentions' and 'presumptions'.

This hostility towards Catholicism was stiffened by the recent Huguenot strain which had entered Irish Protestantism. Migrations of Huguenots had followed the fall of La Rochelle and there were a number of later plantations such as that in Carrick-on-Suir where in 1667 the Duke of Ormond had settled 500 French and Walloon weavers. In all, up to 10,000 Huguenots settled in Ireland, and their ferocious anti-popery was stirred by recollections of the dragonnades in Poitou and Languedoc.

The New Ascendancy

William, when he troubled to bother himself with it, was supportive of the new Irish Ascendancy. It comprised in the main large landowners who belonged to the established Anglican Church, who built handsome houses on their estates and drew rents from their Catholic tenants. They were a Cromwellian and Williamite aristocracy, with new wealth rather than old blood, and they honoured William by mounting splendid portraits of him in their drawing rooms, drinking his health and naming locations after him. These powerful magnates were spread throughout the country, but only in Ulster and in the towns was there a sizeable population of Protestant working people.

Not all sections of the Reformed Faith were part of the Ascendancy. Dissenters, primarily Presbyterians, were excluded and discriminated against, but in a smaller measure than Catholics. In Ulster the Presbyterians had hoped that the courageous part which they had played in support of William might be rewarded, but such benefits as they received, like the *regium donum*, derived from William and Westminster rather than from the Dublin parliament. Moves to give them greater security were adroitly thwarted by an Ascendancy which feared a potential rival establishment, and one which might — as in Scotland — succeed in overthrowing the Established Church. Nor was William in a position to assist them; his powers as a constitutional monarch were limited and he could not do all he wished. Large numbers escaped their dilemma by migrating to America. Yet the Presbyterians continued to admire William and regarded him as the best friend whom they had ever had on the British throne.

The Death of Mary

During the early months of 1694 the dreaded smallpox virus raged in London. Thousands were struck down and died from it, including William's queen. Bishop Burnet later wrote:

> . . . he called me to his closet and gave free vent to the most tender passion; he burst into tears and cried out that there was no hope for the Queen, and that from being the most happy, he was now the most miserable creature on the earth. He said during the whole course of their marriage he had never known a single fault in her. . . .[1]

The day before Mary died she received the Sacrament, and had passages from scripture read to her. She tried to speak to William, who knelt at her bedside, but was unable to do so. She passed away quietly in the early hours of 28 December, at thirty-three years of age and in the sixth year of her reign. Her death was politically important, as it revived hopes in her father, James, that the British people might now feel justified in forswearing their allegiance to a Dutchman. But by this time the crown was securely on William's head.

Difficulties for William

The war with France continued, but in 1696 a number of factors had made both sides anxious for peace, and the Treaties of Rijswijk, which ended the conflict, were signed in 1697. William saw that this was really only a truce, as a new problem with France was looming over the problem of finding a successor to the childless King of Spain, Charles II. Louis intended putting forward a French claimant — a scheme which, if successful, would bring about the effectual unity of France and Spain, and have serious implications for the security of England and the Dutch Republic. In these circumstances William was prepared to go to war again, but the House of Commons took a different view. It was tired of expensive continental adventures and convinced that the new peace would hold. William entered into treaties with Louis on the partition of Spain — measures which involved him in serious friction with Parliament – but when the Spanish king died in November 1700, Louis ignored the treaties and accepted the crown of Spain for his grandson. For William, with his previous experience of Louis, this was scarcely a surprise. He castigated his English subjects for their apathy and set about rebuilding the Grand Alliance against France.

The following year James died at Saint-Germain, and Louis, breaking a condition of the Treaties of Rijswijk, recognised James' son, James Francis Edward Stuart, as the rightful King of England. There was an outcry in London and renewed enthusiasm for going to war with Louis. But William was at loggerheads with Parliament. Both sides of the House bitterly resented his granting of confiscated Irish land to his Dutch favourites; about 60 per cent of the forfeitures had been awarded to seven foreigners, including the Earl of Athlone (Ginkel) and Bentinck, while the remaining 40 per cent was shared among thirty-seven worthies. Most notorious of all was the granting of James' personal estates in Ireland to William's mistress, Elizabeth Villiers. Besides, Parliament did not see eye to eye with William on foreign policy.

He was so depressed that he considered abdicating and returning to Holland. The breaking point was Parliament's plan for cutting back on the size of the army. William saw this proposal as verging on criminal folly. He drafted a King's Speech to Parliament, which said: 'Seeing that you have so little regard for my advice; that you have no manner or care for your own security and expose yourself to evident ruin, by divesting yourself of your only means of defence, it would not be just or reasonable that I should witness your ruin.'[2] With these words he intended to bid Westminster a royal farewell. The Lord Chancellor, Sir John Somers, after much persuasion, induced him to stay.

William was not popular in England. He was not easy of access; he did not tolerate fools gladly and was, moreover, often surly and morose. Besides, with the death of Mary the English element in the joint crown had gone and, in truth, the English disliked being ruled by a Dutchman.

The Death of William

When the inevitable war came, it was too late for William. By 1701 his health was beginning to fail. For some time his legs had become progressively weaker and he had difficulty in riding. On 21 February 1702, he was cantering in Richmond Park on 'Sorrel', his favourite horse, when the animal stumbled on a molehill and threw him, and he broke his collarbone. He was taken immediately to Hampton Court and a doctor was called. He insisted, against all advice, on returning to Kensington Palace, and slept in his coach during the journey. He was in great pain, and that evening Dr Bedloo, his Dutch physician, was called. For a few days he was reasonably well. On 4 March he suddenly grew weaker and developed a high fever. Further doctors were called but could do little to improve him. He was plainly nearing his end, and asked for the Sacrament. Soon after, he said: 'Je tire vers ma fin' ('I draw towards my end'). Members of the Privy Council gathered outside and the Archbishop of Canterbury, Dr John Tillotson,[3] and Bishop Burnet led the prayers for the dying. Shortly after seven o'clock, the death rattle began and the commendatory prayers were hushed. In the end he sank into the arms of one of his pages, and died shortly after eight o'clock.

It was Sunday 8 March 1702, and the Great Deliverer was no more. He was aged fifty-two and had reigned for thirteen years and a few days.[4] England had lost a king, and Orange had lost its prince.

When William's body was opened, his lungs were found to be shrivelled and rotten. Around his neck he was wearing a black ribbon; attached to it were his wedding ring and a lock of Mary's hair.[5] He lay in state in Kensington Palace for three days; then his body was embalmed, and several weeks later it was interred, almost furtively, at midnight on 12 April in King Henry VIII's Chapel in Westminster Abbey. It had been argued that it would be wrong to expend large sums on a public funeral when the nation was about to go to war. William's death caused little sorrow in England. 'No king can be less lamented than this one has been,' noted a contemporary. Yet few in Europe doubted that William had been one of the great men of the age.

In Ireland the grief of the Protestant people was palpable. The King's passing was compared to the setting of the sun, or to a terrible eclipse passing over the earth. The Anglican Archbishop of Dublin, William King, referred to the extinction of a star, and told his congregation that 'the poetic mind will feel no impropriety in such comparisons, but will see rather a high truth, as standing by the grave of this child of genius it meditates on the loss which we, and the entire world, have sustained.'[6]

Dr Isaac Watts, whose great hymn 'Our God, Our Help in Ages Past' was later adopted by Ulster Protestants as an unofficial anthem, penned a noble elegy in twelve verses, beginning:

> Beneath these honours of a tomb
> Greatness in humble ruin lies
> (How earth confines in narrow room
> What heroes leave behind the skies).
>
> Preserve, O venerable pile
> Inviolate thy sacred trust;
> To thy cold arms the British Isle
> Weeping, commits her richest dust.
>
> Ye gentlest ministers of Fate
> Attend the Monarch as he lies:
> And bid the softest slumbers wait
> With silken cords to bind his eyes.[7]

Orangeism Without the Prince

The death of William ended the initial phase of Orangeism in Ireland, in which William and his army were direct participants in Irish affairs. In the new phase, that of Orangeism without the prince, we come to consider the religio-politico tradition which grew up around his name. This tradition began early and was grounded in the traumatic events of the years of war. Not all elements were crystallised until the Orange Order was founded three-quarters of a century later; yet from the start the aims of William's Irish campaign — the defeat of the Jacobites and the preservation of Protestant power — formed the basis of government policy. The connection between these aims made it easy to equate loyalty to the Protestant faith with loyalty to the Crown and Constitution, forming the bedrock of Orangeism.

A closer look at the events of 1688-1691, however, showed that there were inconveniences. History just about corresponded with the script. It had been expedient for William to 'deliver' the Protestants and he did not have to love them to do so. Indeed, had James and his French allies not transferred to Ireland it is likely that the Protestants would have been left, at least for a time, to fend for themselves. William saw the war in Ireland as an irritating sideshow, and was anxious to finish it quickly so that he could return to the real fighting in Europe. William's great contribution to the Protestant cause lay not, perhaps, in the achievements of his army in Ireland, important as these were, but in his successful invasion of England two years earlier, which had driven James into exile and provided the resources for the reconquest of Ireland. Once William made up his mind to challenge the Jacobite hold on Ireland, the issue could hardly be in doubt, although the story might have been different had Louis been willing to provide his Irish allies with sufficient resources to put up a stiffer fight. But to Louis, no less than to James, or to William, Ireland was an expendable pawn in a greater game.

William's enforced stay — no more than twelve weeks — in a land that was of little importance to him, and to which he never saw fit to return, may seem a tenuous basis on which to establish a tradition. Yet the shared memories of the years of struggle provided the Protestant people with more than enough material to raise an edifice in his name. Had James remained on the throne there would have been little to stop Tyrconnell and the Catholics from overrunning Derry and Enniskillen, and so seizing all of Ireland. It was thanks to William that the Protestants were able to maintain their dominance over the island for another two centuries. The seventeenth-century ancestry of Orangeism in Ireland is not, therefore, simply a peg on which the later Orange movement found it convenient to hang its historical credentials. It was the crucible in which these credentials were moulded.

The Aldermen of Skinners Alley

The first Orange Society formed in Ireland following the Williamite Wars was in Dublin. It was a small and fairly obscure body called, rather unoriginally, 'The Aldermen of Skinners Alley', for it consisted of Aldermen of the City of Dublin who had been dismissed by James and reinstated by William. It was little more than a drinking club and its members met in a coffee house-cum-tavern located in a narrow back street in the vicinity of Dublin Castle, an area originally inhabited by people who traded in hides and leather. The street ran between shops and small dwellings and was so narrow that two vehicles could hardly pass each other.

In this congested district Richard Pue, a printer and enterprising businessman, converted 'a fine building' into a fashionable coffee house which quickly became the most frequented establishment of its kind in the city, known as 'Dick's'. It was, however, no ordinary coffee house, and could best be described as a cross between a restaurant, a tavern and a casino. It was famous — as its handbills declared — for 'its sustaining ports, warming brandies and noble clarets', but its real reputation rested on the notoriety of its clientele. It was a rendezvous for politicians, literati, business people and 'men about town', all of whom gathered in its hospitable rooms to discuss the controversies which agitated society. Its ethos was well caught in a contemporary jingle:

> Ye citizens, gentlemen, lawyers and squires
> Who summer and winter surround our great fires
> Ye quidnuncs! who frequently came into Pue's
> To live upon politics, coffee and news;

Ye adepts, ye critics and orators nice
Ye grave connoisseurs at the drafts and the dice;
Who draw up your men like soldiers in battle
While the dice and the boxes like drums loudly rattle;

Like the Walpoles and Flourys demurely you sit
To practice politics, judgement and wit;
Now Kings ye set up, and with fury attack
Till one or the other is laid on his back.

'Dick's' was where the Orange Aldermen forgathered. They adopted the motto: 'Dum spiro spero' (while I breathe I hope) and were noted for the ribaldry of their drinking toasts. One of their milder lubrications ran:

> To the glorious, pious and immortal memory of the great and good King William, not forgetting Oliver Cromwell, who assisted in redeeming us from popery, slavery, arbitrary power, brass money and wooden shoes. May we never want a Williamite to kick the arse of a Jacobite! And a . . . for the Bishops of Cork! And all who drink this, whether he be priest or bishop, deacon, bellows-blower, grave digger or any other of the fraternity of clergy, may a north wind blow him to the south, and a west wind to the east, may he never have a dark night, a lee shore, a rank storm and a leaky vessel to carry him over the River Styx. May the dog Cerberus make a meal of his rump and Pluto a snuff box of his skull, and may the devil jump down his throat with a red hot harrow, and with every pin tear out his gut and blow him with a clean carcass to hell! Amen.

The reference to the Bishop of Cork was a riposte to the Very Reverend Peter Brown, who had written a pious tract attacking the custom of toasting William as a 'silly old popish practice'. The toast was, however, typical of the postprandial spouting of the period.

The Aldermen's Society remained in existence for over a hundred years. 'Dick's' was conveniently located near the Tholsel (City Hall), which meant that its often drink-sodden members did not have too far to stumble to perform their civic duties. The Tholsel itself was an impressive building, with a great air of civic authority. Built in 1683, it was almost a square in shape (62 ft x 68 ft), constructed in hewn stone and with eloquent arches at either end; in front — in the middle — two massive Tuscan columns supported a large vestibule, which was decorated with the city's arms. In the niches on either side stood statues of Charles II and James, as Duke of York (until the latter was replaced by William), and above these the royal arms, supported by scrolls, were formed into a kind of angular pediment. The overall impression was dour but dignified.

This was the beginning of the great age of the club. Members of the gentry and professional classes formed clubs up and down the country whose purpose, apart from providing a congenial setting for the intake of liquor, was to toast the good health of William. Much of this toasting was, however, less than jovial; in some instances it was deliberately provocative and used as a weapon to flush out political opponents. Real or imagined slights to William could cause great offence. In 1718 a Trinity College student named Forbes was expelled for a derisive reply to a toast in the King's honour, and from time to time a number of others were threatened with a similar fate.[1] In both England and Ireland it was common for Jacobite sympathisers to make crude jokes about the King, particularly his presumed sexual proclivities.

Jacobites drank also to the memory of 'Sorrel', the horse which threw William, and to the 'little gentleman in black velvet' — the mole who had done the damage in Richmond Park.

A Statue to William

From 1690, 4 November, William's birthday and the anniversary of his landing in England, was annually celebrated in Dublin. The first public tribute came in 1701 when the City Fathers commissioned a huge equestrian statue to their hero. The noted English sculptor Grinling Gibbons produced a virtuoso work in bronze and marble which showed the King dressed as an ancient Roman general with a laurel wreath on his head, riding a prancing horse, a fashionable pose for great men of the period. The tour de force was mounted on a high marble pedestal in College Green, and a white tablet bore the inscription:

> Guielmo Tertio
> Magnae Britanniae, Franciae, et Hiberniae Regi.
> Ob Religonem Conservatom, Restitutas Legas,
> Libertatem Assertam.

> (William, Third of Great Britain, France and Ireland, King.
> Preserver of Religion, Restorer of Laws, Upholder of Liberty.)

The statue was unveiled with great ceremony on 1 July, which was declared a public holiday. All the church bells of the city rang out and the shops were closed. Great crowds thronged the streets from early morning. The Lord Mayor, Aldermen, Sheriffs, Council Members and Wardens assembled at the Tholsel and walked in formal procession to College Green, preceded by military bands and the Grenadier companies of the Dublin militia. The Lord Justices then marched, bareheaded, three times round the statue. Following the second circuit the Recorder of the City, from a platform in front of the monument, delivered an address which expressed the attachment of the people of Dublin to the person of the monarch, and his lawful government. A volley was fired, and the cannon discharged. The dignitaries then made their third circuit of the statue, doffing their hats and bowing respectfully as they went. On being joined by the Provost and Fellows of Trinity College, everyone was conducted by the Lord Mayor to a 'great house' on College Green where refreshments were served. The cannon was discharged twice more, and cakes were distributed to the crowd. At nightfall, the celebrations were concluded with fireworks, illuminations and bonfires.

Not everyone, of course, was charmed. On the night of 25 June 1710, the statue was desecrated: the truncheon was removed from the King's hand and the entire figure was smeared with mud. There was an uproar. The following morning the members of the House of Lords, nearby, met in emergency session and resolved: 'That the Lord Chancellor, as Speaker of this House, forthwith attend His Excellency [the Lord Lieutenant, the Duke of Wharton] and acquaint him that the Lords being informed of the great indignities offered last night to the statue of his late Majesty King William, of glorious memory, erected on College Green to show the grateful sense of this whole kingdom, and particularly of the City of Dublin, of the great blessings accomplished for them by that glorious Prince, have made this unanimous resolution, that all persons concerned with that barbarous act are guilty of the greatest insolence, baseness and ingratitude; and desire his Excellency, the Lord Lieutenant, to issue a proclamation to discover the authors of this villainy, that they may be prosecuted and punished accordingly.'

The Lord Lieutenant immediately announced a reward of £100 for information leading to the arrests of the culprits. This was a huge sum at a time when a skilled workman would be lucky to earn a few shillings a day. It was promptly increased by the Lord Mayor, who offered a further £50. Within a fortnight, three Trinity College students were apprehended and charged. Two of them, Graffon and Vinicome, pleaded guilty and stated that they had been upset because the rear of the horse pointed towards the college gates. They were both expelled from the University, imprisoned for six months and fined £100 each. On 19 November, at 11 a.m., they were obliged to stand before the statue for half an hour, with placards hung around their necks which said: 'I stand here for defacing the statue of our glorious Deliverer, the late King William.' The third offender, Harvey, escaped and was not seen again.

Repairs to the statue were immediately put in hand and a new unveiling was arranged. The *Dublin Intelligence* reported: 'Thursday (the 17th) being the day of the franchise of the city, the truncheon was replaced to the said statue in the presence of the Lord Mayor, at the head of 24 Corporations, all of whom marched by the statue in good order, being well mounted on horseback and in general made a very gallant appearance.'² Virtually everyone who was anyone was present, and College Green was described as being 'thronged' with sedan chairs.

Assaults on the statue continued. Sometimes it was daubed in paint or excrement, on other occasions scarecrow figures — representing the Pope or King James — were seated on the horse behind the King. Finally, a lookout hut was built nearby and a permanent guard posted. Amazingly, there were further assaults. The statue became as much a focus of hate as of respect. It must be assumed that this was Catholic hate, although there is evidence that some Catholics participated in the celebrations. Virtually the entire Protestant population esteemed the statue and it is said that many 'visited it as if it were the shrine at Mecca'. They, in the words of a contemporary, 'saw it as a silent witness to the principles of the Glorious Revolution and to their deliverance from popish tyranny'.

The statue survived until 1929, when it was damaged in an explosion by the Irish Republican Army and never repaired. The Irish authorities refused a request from the Northern Ireland government to have it transferred to Belfast; instead it was removed to a builders' yard where the miscreants completed their task by stealing in one night and sawing off the King's head. All that now remains is the inscription tablet preserved in the Dublin Municipal Museum.

Orange Fervour

Celebrating the memory of William was not an obligation imposed from above. To Protestants of all classes, William was a potent icon. Some saw him as a liberating hero, some as a conservative champion, and others proclaimed him a radical figure. There was something in his persona for everyone. Enthusiasm for anything associated with William abounded. Orange emblems adorned Protestant homes and Orange songs entered the repertoire of the musical theatres. Flowers like the orange lily and sweet william were grown and distributed on commemorative occasions. Taverns displayed portraits of William on their signboards, and glass manufacturers, spotting the commercial possibilities, produced toasting glasses bearing royal insignia and inscribed with Williamite mottoes. Even house-building was influenced: certain buildings in Dublin and the provinces were conspicuous for their Dutch gables and high latticed windows. Dozens of streets and roadways were named after William. Even today, outside Ulster, major thoroughfares in Limerick, Waterford, Galway and Drogheda unconsciously honour him, and Dublin's Nassau Street is a discreet reminder of his German countship.

The College Green Tapestries

In 1733 two of the interior walls of the first great Irish public building of the period, the Parliament House (built by two of its members, Arthur Dobbs and R.L. Pearse), were decorated with rich tapestries depicting scenes from the Williamite war. An eminent landscape artist, William van der Hagen, was commissioned to produce designs highlighting the main Orange victories. Weavers were brought from Flanders to work under master weaver Jan van Bevan, and two magnificent tapestries were woven — 'The Battle of the Boyne' and 'The Defence of Londonderry'. These may still be seen in their original setting in the Bank of Ireland building on College Green. One interesting feature of the Boyne tapestry is that William is shown crossing the river on a chestnut horse, whereas he is usually depicted on Orange banners as riding a white one. The different renderings are not accidental. The white horse is the symbol of the House of Hanover and represents the Protestant succession. Contemporary paintings of the battle showed William on a brown horse as, for instance, in the work of his favourite court painter Jan Wych.

The tradition of the white horse began with a painting by the American artist Benjamin West, called 'William Crossing the Boyne', first shown in 1778. This well-known work depicts an idealised William, looking somewhat like a gay cavalier, sword in hand, and has inspired generations of Orange genre artists.[3] The depiction is, of course, fanciful; the artist was born over thirty years after William's death.[3]

The Boyne Obelisk

Although the defining battle of the Williamite War was fought at Aughrim, in Orange tradition the Battle of the Boyne takes pride of place. In the post-war fervour it was inevitable that the victory at the Boyne should be commemorated in some tangible fashion. This end was achieved by the erection in 1736 of a giant obelisk on the northern bank of the river at Oldbridge. The Williamite historian, George Story, had a hand in the project, and wrote: 'I have shown the spot of ground to some who design to erect a pillar where the King escaped so narrowly, to perpetuate so memorable an action.' The foundation stone was laid by the Lord Lieutenant, the Duke of Dorset, in a great ceremony attended by Protestant gentry from all over Ireland. The obelisk was raised on a huge rock some ten metres high and soared up a further thirty metres — its combined height being just a few metres short of Nelson's column in London's Trafalgar Square. The inscription read:

> Sacred to the memory of King William the Third, who of 1st July 1690, crossed the Boyne near this place to attack James the Second at the head of a popish army advantageously posted to the south of it, and

did on that day, by a successful battle, secure us and our posterity our liberty, laws and religion. In consequence of this action James the Second left this Kingdom and fled to France. This memorial to our deliverance was erected in the ninth year of the reign of King George the Second, the first stone laid by Lionel Sackville, Duke of Dorset, Lord Lieutenant of the Kingdom of Ireland MDCC XXXVI.

In perfectuam rei tam fortiter quam feliciter gastae memoriam, hic publicae gratitudinis monumenti. Fundamen manibus ipse suis posuit Lionellus Dux Dorsetiae 17 die Aprilis, Anno 1736.

This monument was erected by the contributions of several Protestants of Great Britain and Ireland.

Meinhard, Duke of Schomberg, in passing this river died bravely in defence of liberty.

The monument survived for 187 years until 1923, when it was blown up by the Drogheda brigade of the Irish Republican Army. Three powerful land mines were used to destroy the huge column, and the deafening explosion was spoken of locally for years afterwards. Until the mid-1970s, stones bearing pieces of the inscription were to be seen embedded in the nearby field; these disappeared in land improvements when a new layer of topsoil was spread. Today the site is a place of pilgrimage for members of the Orange Order, and Protestant families continue to picnic around what is now known as 'the stump'.

Bandon Remembers

The Protestants of Bandon were among the first to keep William's memory green, and began the tradition of ritualised ceremonies to commemorate the Boyne victory. On 1 July each year, crowds were on the streets of the town from early morning. The menfolk dressed in their best attire and wore orange cockades in their hats; the women pinned orange lilies to their bonnets. At eleven o'clock the gates of the market house were flung open and in marched a fife and drum band playing Orange tunes. The menfolk fell in and marched up and down the streets. Then, everyone attended Divine Service and listened to an edifying sermon on God's mercy and their providential 'deliverance'. Young and old then marched to the Fair Green where a pageant was enacted, a stock performance comprised of incidents from the Battle of the Boyne. The centrepiece was a 'sham fight', in which the orange-coated 'William' and a similarly-clad 'Duke of Schomberg' drove the green-attired 'James' and 'Patrick Sarsfield' into humiliating flight, to a succession of loud drum rolls. Following his 'victory' the 'King', mounted on a white horse called 'Billy Boyne', rode around the field raising his plumed hat in acknowledgement of the delirious cheering. This was the start of the sham fight tradition which, although it faded in Bandon, would continue in the County Armagh village of Scarva.

The Boyne Society

As the Orange tradition took root, groups of Orange ex-servicemen up and down the country came together to form old army comrade associations whose purpose was, initially, to commemorate the Orange victories.

At first these were little more than social clubs, and their membership was confined to professional officers; soon, however, they included members of the gentry, many of whom had military experience. In time they expanded to embrace rank-and-file soldiers who were expected to turn out and parade on the various anniversary dates. The landlords quickly perceived the usefulness of these associations and utilised them in putting down the periodic Catholic disturbances.

In time, many were brought under the control of a superintending body which was reputed to have been founded in Enniskillen as early as 1690.[4] This was the semi-secret Boyne Society, known variously as the Royal Boyne Society, the Orange Boyne Society and the Royal Orange Boyne Society. Around 1725 this society evolved into a kind of Orange Freemasonry and organised its members into orders or grades. Its first order was open to the general membership, known simply as 'Boynemen'. The second or higher order was confined to relatively few, and its members, mainly nobility and gentry, were designated 'The Knights of the Most Glorious Order of the Boyne'.

The Boyne Society plagiarised wholesale from the Masonic Order, developing an intricate system of secret signs, passwords, and ceremonial ritual. Its symbols and ceremonies were often connected with incidents from the Williamite War period such as, for instance, the signs adopted for mutual recognition: the placing of the left hand on the right shoulder, the spot where William was wounded at the Boyne, with the reply being the right arm held across the lower stomach, the position in which William held his arm in a sling during the battle.

That Irish Protestants should found a society based on Freemasonry is unsurprising. 'The Craft' had long taken root in Ireland and was identified, mainly, with Protestants. The Grand Lodge of Free and Accepted Masons of Ireland is the second oldest in existence, established in Dublin in 1729 following an initiative taken by the Grand Lodge of England eight years earlier. Although the first Irish lodges date from the period of the plantation, the earliest documentary evidence of Irish

Freemasonry comes from two manuscripts in Trinity College, Dublin, dated 1688 and 1711 respectively. These refer to a Masonic lodge in the college which included 'gentlemen, mechanics, and porters'. Trinity College in those days was, of course, exclusively Protestant.

That the Masonic trappings of the Boyne Society were developed by early Orangemen (although the term 'Orangemen' was not then in general use) who were Freemasons is indubitable. They wanted something which Freemasonry could not give them: a body which would be exclusively Protestant and dedicated to maintaining the Orange tradition. Freemasonry was not exclusive; then, as now, it did not canvass any particular religious belief, nor did it espouse a specific political viewpoint. Unlike later Orange organisations, it never barred prospective members on the basis of religion; its only requirements were that candidates should be without maim or defect, believe in God, and be over twenty-one years of age. In fact, Freemasonry in Ireland became predominantly Catholic in membership around 1800 and was to remain so until about 1840, when Daniel O'Connell, the Liberator, resigned his Dublin lodge on being informed that membership was incompatible with Catholic teaching.

Whether a subterranean link — tentative or otherwise — existed between the Boyne Society and Freemasonry is difficult to answer. A modern study of Freemasonry says that 'whenever Masons have common political aims but cannot pursue them through Masonry, they set up parallel public movements.'[5]

The rituals of the Boyne Society were firmly rooted in the Old Testament and based on such stories as the Exodus, the Crossing of the Red Sea, and the Wanderings in the Wilderness. That a Bible-loving people should adopt such scriptural themes as the basis of their ceremonial is hardly extraordinary. The themes chosen, besides, had conveniences for a people who felt themselves continually besieged. They could draw analogies between their plight as settlers in a hostile environment, and the Children of Israel cast into a strange land and surrounded by heathen worshippers. They saw themselves — the possessors of a purified faith — set among a spiritually corrupted people who despised their religion and culture.

And they could claim that their ancestors had perceived their plight similarly. Had not the Reverend George Walker written: 'The enemy were so numerous, so powerful and well-appointed an army, that in all human probability we could not think ourselves less in danger than the Israelites at the Red Sea'? Had not another Orange hero, the Reverend Andrew Hamilton, in his account of the campaigns of the Enniskilleners, written to William: 'We looked upon you as no other than a miracle; a Moses sent immediately from God, to deliver us from Egyptian serviture and idolatry'? Both Walker and Hamilton had met in March 1689 when the latter was dispatched from Enniskillen to make contact with the leaders in Derry before the net closed around the city. To facilitate contact between their groups, they took from Exodus 3: 4, a phrase to use as a password: 'Thus thou shall say unto the People of Israel,' with the reply being: 'I am, hath sent me unto you.' This was probably the first Orange password used in Ireland, and was later utilised by the Orange Order.

Boyne Society's Protective Role

Not much is known about the Boyne Society. References to it by Irish historians are rare, but two books written in 1825 and 1857, by the Wexford Orangeman Ogle Robert Gowan, provide information.[6] These are, however, late, and were published when the Society was in decline or even in extinction. In two chapters of his *Orangeism, its Origin and History* (1857), Gowan refers to the Boyne Society's role in protecting Protestants from Catholic violence. His remarks suggest that the Society was open and publicly known, but this was scarcely true. It had little public face and its protective role was carried out by auxiliary corps who acted in their own names. These bodies, like 'The Wicklow Orange Blazers', 'The Wexford True Blues' and 'The Bandon Williamites', were violently anti-Catholic. The very sound of their names was enough to terrify the Catholic peasantry.

Writing in the late 1850s, Gowan made no distinction between the Boyne Society and the Irish Volunteers (founded in 1775), but the distinction could easily have been blurred, for many volunteer companies had members who were initiated into the Boyne Society. Gowan says:

> The (Jacobite) Irish, being entirely subdued after the capitulation of Limerick, large guerilla parties of them, called 'Rapparees', spread themselves over different parts of the Kingdom and carried on a long and harassing warfare against the Protestant settlements. The nocturnal assassinations, the houghing of cattle, the burning of buildings and other dreadful atrocities which attended this desultory but sanguinary warfare, led to the extension of the Boyne Society into many neighbourhoods, where it was used by the persecuted colonists as a means of self-protection and mutual recognition. These Boyne Societies proved of the utmost importance to the peace of the country, the safety of Protestants, and the security of their settlements.

In another chapter, Gowan refers to the Boyne Society of thirty years later, in the reign of George II:

Many noblemen and gentlemen of property and standing lent their influence to the society and openly encouraged its extension. So effective and material were the exertions of the members of the Boyne Society in the protection and encouragement of all the Protestant settlements, that His Majesty, George II, openly supported them and declared that they were the great mainstay of the Church and English connection in that Kingdom (Ireland).

Gowan goes on to discuss the role of the Boyne Society in the next reign (George III, 1760-1820) and in the heightened atmosphere generated by the revolutions in America and France:

During the whole of this gloomy period, England was engaged in a sanguinary and protracted war, all her troops were employed abroad, not a man to spare for home service. The protection of Ireland was, therefore, necessarily dependent on the united services of Protestants enrolled in these clubs. The nobility and gentry of the Kingdom, seeing the effective services of those societies, applied to the government to have them enrolled and armed and placed on a more effective footing.

Gowan is referring to pressure which Protestants placed on the authorities in Dublin Castle for the establishment of a yeomanry force. This pressure bore fruit in September 1796, when the government announced that it proposed to enlist civilian volunteers in such a force. In the following month commissions were issued to local gentlemen and magistrates, empowering them to raise cavalry forces and infantry companies. Recruits took a 'yeomanry oath', and the new force was officered by the gentry, with the rank and file being paid, clothed, and armed by the government. Their remit was to free the regular army and militia from domestic peacekeeping and to assist with garrison duty. The yeomanry were quite distinct from the Boyne Society auxiliaries, although there was a considerable overlapping of individual membership. That the Boyne auxiliaries were active twenty years earlier can be seen from a return, which Gowan quotes, showing details of the first corps formed in County Cork:

Name of Association Formed		By Whom Commanded
'Boyne'	1776	Col. Bagwell, MP
'True Blues'	1776	Col. Morison
'Union'	1776	Capt. Hickman
'Culloden'	1777	Counsellor Bennet
'Enniskillen'	1777	Capt. J. Connor
'Aughrim'	1778	Major E. Jameson
'Independent'	1781	Lt. R. Hare, MP
'Muskey True Blues'	1781	Lt. Col. Hutchinson

The earliest associations founded in County Wexford, according to Gowan, were:

Name	Commanded By
'Ogle's Blues'	Capt. the Hon. George Ogle, MP (this was the godfather of the writer, Ogle Robert Gowan)
'The Ballaghkeene Blazers'	Capt. Hawtry White
'Wingfield Yeomanry'	Capt. John Hunter Gowan (the father of the writer)
'Branty Williamites'	Capt. Lord Loftus (later Marquis of Ely)
'Enniscorthy Rangers'	Capt. Archd. Hamilton Jacob
'Wexford True Blues'	Capt. James Boyd
'Newtown Barry Britons'	Capt. Hon. James Maxwell
'Saunders Court Defenders'	Capt. the Earl of Arran

Similar Boyne auxiliary corps existed in the Protestant districts of Limerick, Kerry, Sligo, Mayo and Galway. Each Ulster county had its corps, as did Dublin and most Leinster counties. In 1793, Colonel John Bagwell became Grand Master, and Colonel Richard Hare, who commanded the Cork 'Independents', was appointed his deputy. Bagwell had acquired a substantial estate at Marfield, Clonmel, from where his family controlled local politics and patronage until the late nineteenth century.[7]

Boyne Society Relics

The internal 'workings' of the Boyne Society remain a mystery. Its Masonic-like character may be seen from objects like the 22-year-old wall chart which has been preserved in the Armagh County Museum. Wall charts were used as visual aids to illustrate the principles taught in each degree of 'the system'. The Armagh chart depicts numerous emblems and scriptural scenes which were employed as motifs for ritual, and are similar to those used in the Holy Royal Arch degree in Freemasonry. The chart is a unique survival, and is described in the museum catalogue as:

> Framed exemplification of Orange symbols; painted on two sheets of parchment in colour, mounted in wooden cover on two leaves, hinged for closing, 3'8' x 2'8' when open. Each half 1'10' x 2'8' when closed. It was presented by Mrs Drummond of College St., Armagh in 1936. It owes its preservation to the late Mr Edward Rogers, County Librarian, author of 'The Revolution of 1688' and a number of books. It is probably the earliest relic of its class now surviving. Probably used on Lodge nights.

This particular chart belonged to the Loyal Orange Boyne Society in Armagh which was active in the 1790s. It confirms that many of the emblems utilised in later Orange ritual were not accretions but well-established accoutrements of older 'workings'.

It includes all the emblems found in the Royal Arch Purple Order, a body technically distinct from the Orange Order and which serves a purpose similar to that of the Royal Arch in Masonry; that is, a medium for the conferring of 'higher' degrees than those granted at primary level. In a history of The Royal Arch Purple Order, published in 1993,[9] the Biblical background to the symbols is explained:

> The bottom half of the chart is a stylised Biblical atlas in diagrammatic form divided into five panels depicting the Exodus: (1) The crossing of the Red Sea; (2) The wandering in the wilderness; (3) The wandering by day with a pillar of cloud; (4) Mount Sinai (the chart is crossed by a river, presumably the Jordan, with the letter 'G' on the left and the letter 'H' on the right. These letters may stand for Gilgal to the west and Heshbon, the capital of Amman, to the east); (5) Across the river is a walled city, presumably Jericho.
>
> In the bottom corners are wreathed figures of King George III and King William III. The top half of the chart is much more complicated and detailed. In the centre is an arch supported by two pillars adorned by three curtains of blue on each side, representing a stylised tabernacle. On the arch is inscribed 'Holiness to the Lord'. On the tops of the pillars are the letters 'A' and 'J' and on the bottom the letters 'G' and 'H'. If the supporting pillars had been intended to represent Solomon's Temple, it is probable that this would have been indicated by the letters 'B' and 'J', standing for Boaz and Jachin (Strength and Stability). II Chronicles 3:17. As they relate to the books of Moses and Joshua, the letters 'A' and 'J' at the head of the pillars probably stand for Aaron and Joshua. The letters 'G' and 'H' at the foot of the pillars are the same as those on the chart of the River Jordan, and may therefore mean the two banks in Gilgal and Heshbon. The floor of the archway is a checkerboard pavement, on which a coffin is placed. Also resting on the pavement is a representation of the Ark of the Covenant with two cherubims, Aaron's Rod and a three-branched candlestick.
>
> On either side is a paschal lamb and a heart with crossed swords. The lamb carries the blood red flag of a sacrificial victim and martyr, more usually depicted in Christian symbolism by a red cross on a white background, as in the Cross of St. George. This emblem is used as the badge of the 2nd Regiment of Foot (Kirke's Lambs) including the Red

Cross. This emblem is most significant, set as it is, surrounded by Old Testament imagery, where it provides and completes the New Testament interpretation and fulfilment.

The book also details the five biblical scenes which are shown down each side of the chart near its outer edges. It identifies these as: (1) Moses on Mount Nebo; (2) Elijah's cave on Mount Sinai; (3) Noah's Ark with a dove and olive branch;[4] the walls of Jericho falling down; and (5) Fiery serpents in the wilderness — all on the right side. Those on the left side are identified as: (A) Jezebel being thrown out of the window; (B) Moses and the Burning Bush; (C) Elijah on Mount Carmel and the cloud like unto a man's hand; (D) Joshua meets the captain of the Lord's Host with drawn sword; and (E) The return of the spies with a bunch of grapes.

The description continues:

> Other Biblical scenes have been fitted in, which are identified as Moses striking the Rock, Elijah's contest with the Priests of Baal and Elijah's Chariot of Fire with the mantle descending to Elisha. Fitted in between the central arch and the Biblical scenes are a great number of emblems. Above the arch is the All Seeing Eye, the sun, moon and seven stars, a key, a three-step ladder with the letter 'F', 'H' and 'C' (Faith, Hope and Charity), a five-pointed star, scales and a brazen serpent. To the left of the Arch are an anchor and the golden pot containing manna. To the right of the Arch are Gideon's trumpet and pitcher, a mallet and seven trumpets. Across the bottom of the chart are seven more emblems as follows: A beehive, a cock, seven candles in a triangle, three candles, skull and crossbones with the letters 'M.M.' (Memento Mori — Remember you must die), a small Biblical scene of Elijah under the juniper tree with the angel and, lastly, twelve candles in a triangle. Above the arch are the letters T.A.O.G., presumably The Ark of God. The letter 'L' is inscribed on the Ark itself, and may stand for the priestly tribe of Levi or the Book of Leviticus. It could, for example, refer to Chapter 26, Verses 11 and 12: 'I will set my tabernacle among you . . . and will be your God, and ye shall be my people.'

> A number of texts have been roughly written in pencil on the chart, which have assisted in the identification of the biblical scenes. Finally, between the pictures of Joshua and the spies there is a river, and in the river are twelve stones. This may appear to be an insignificant detail, but in fact it is the mark which makes a Marksman out of a wandering pilgrim about to enter the promised land, achieve his goal and win the prize.

Also held in the Armagh County Museum is a flag which belonged to the Killeavy Volunteers, who were either a branch of the Boyne Society in 1798 or were a regular company of Volunteers whose members had been initiated into the Boyne auxiliaries. It is described in the museum catalogue as 'a green flag with a profile of King William III surrounded by a wreath of Orange lilies and scrolls, above and below'. Above is inscribed 'Our King and Country' and below is embroidered 'And Great Williams Cause' and 'BOS 153' (the letters stand for 'Boyne Orange Society' and the figures indicated the Lodge number). The flag was presented to the Museum in 1957 by the Dean of Ossory, the late Very Reverend Dr Server, who could trace family connections with both the Boyne Society and the early Orange Order.

The symbols and rituals of the Boyne Society were of great importance to the later Orange Order, who adopted many of them. The founding fathers of the Order referred to the Boyne Society as 'a venerable body' and believed that they were acting in its tradition. When members of the Order first appeared in public — in Lurgan on 12 July 1796 — they issued a statement to the County Magistrates who were then sitting at the Armagh Assizes. It read: 'We are formed in imitation of that venerable body, the Boyne Society whose principles we act and adopt as our own. We therefore pray to be put on the same footing as the Boyne Society.'

The Protestant Nation

The Uneasy Peace

With the exception of occasional outbreaks of localised Catholic violence, Ireland was calm during the first half of the eighteenth century. But it was not the calm which results from a conscious sense of well-being; it was the torpor which follows exhaustion, the lethargy which is bred by prolonged despair. In 1729 and again in 1740, there was famine and thousands died of starvation. The malnutrition and disease which accompanied the poverty-stricken conditions made it impossible for Catholics to do much about their plight. Even the near-at-hand Jacobite rebellions in the Scottish Highlands — the Fifteen and the Forty-five — failed to arouse them. They had fought and suffered enough for the worthless King James, and now they spat upon his name. In the hapless 'hidden' Ireland of suffering and endurance he was known by the expletive 'Jim Dung'.

The plight of the masses related directly to the system of land-holding. The land of Ireland was, in the main, owned by Protestant landlords, some of whom were absentees. They were more concerned with making immediate profits than improving the prospects of their tenants. Their practice was to let the land on lease and to leave the tenants to do the best they could out of the deal. The rent which they charged was geared to agricultural prices at the time the lease was made; if prices rose tenants could survive, or even do reasonably well, but if they fell — as they sometimes did – the rent might become an impossible burden. The point of greatest difficulty was when the lease expired and the landlord availed of the opportunity to increase the rent and impose a renewal charge (known as a 'fine') prior to writing a new lease. It was not uncommon for a landlord to disregard the claims of an occupying tenant when a lease expired, in favour of another who offered to pay a higher rent or who could afford to remit a larger 'fine'.

Many landlords let their lands to 'middlemen' rather than directly to the cultivators of the soil. Before the cultivator secured an interest, there could be up to three or four (or more) 'middlemen' between himself and the head lessor. Each 'middleman' sought to maximise his investment by imposing the highest rent possible and letting the land for a shorter period than he had acquired it for. Acquisitiveness was the order of the day and, with so many taking a share of the fruits of his labour, the poor cultivator had to struggle all the harder just to make ends meet. But leaseholders were not the worst-off group in the system. Below them, and less secure, were the 'cottiers' — the farm labourers who lived in cabins on plots of ground given to them by their employers. They lost their tenure when they fell out of work, and survived on pitiful wages.

The wretchedness of this group made the strongest impression on travellers in Ireland during the period. One of the best known of these was Arthur Young, who went to Ireland in 1776 and later wrote that he found the cabins of the poor 'scarcely distinguishable from dunghills'.[1] These structures were crude habitations made of 'mud kneaded with straw' and the people, in many instances, lived under the same roof as their farm animals. The sum total of their furniture consisted of 'a pot, a stool, a few wooden vessels and a broken bottle'. In urban tenements, he said, one could find ten to sixteen persons, of all ages and sexes, 'stretched on a wad of filthy straw, swarming with vermin, and without covering, save for the wretched rags which constituted their wearing apparel'.

In sharp contrast to this squalor was the luxury of the houses of the new Protestant rich. The mansion of the Marquess of Downshire, at Hillsborough, County Down, for example, was described in 1780 as having a frontage of specially imported Bath stone, with Ionic columns supporting the pediment. White marble was imported from Italy; mahogany replaced oak as the most sought-after timber, and walnut was increasingly used. Fireplaces were designed in the style of Robert Adams and plaster mouldings were used to decorate the ceilings. In many of these mansions fashionable ladies played cards, painted in water colours and discoursed on art and music The menfolk spent their days hunting, gambling, duelling, travelling abroad and taking the waters at such fashionable spas as that at Mallow, County Cork. The Orange conquest of Ireland was yielding rich dividends.

The Tithes

A great burden on Catholics and on poor Protestant dissenters, who lived mainly in the north-east, was the payment of tithes for the maintenance of the established Anglican Church. Originally the tithe was payable to the Catholic clergy, but was transferred to the Anglican clergy at the time of the Reformation. It was not systematically collected, however, until the eighteenth century when it provided a major portion of the income of those who received it. Catholic and Presbyterian tenants were thus required by law to subsidise clergy whose ministry they rejected and, not unreasonably, they regarded this as an injustice. Their anger was directed, in particular, against the 'proctors' who actually collected the levy, but there was also considerable ill-feeling against the clergymen who benefited from it.

In the early part of the century, Catholic tenants did not dare protest against the tithe system, but as the century wore on they began to stir, aroused by another keenly felt grievance, 'enclosures'. From the days of old Gaelic Ireland, certain lands had been recognised as commonages, where people could put their smaller cattle without payment of rent. Around the middle of the century the landlords began to enclose these commons. Angry groups assembled and tore down the fences. Around 1761 tenants in County Tipperary combined to resist enclosures and to agitate against other grievances. The discontent spread to other parts of Munster, Leinster and Connaught, and those involved became known by the generic term of 'Whiteboys'.[2]

The Whiteboys

The Whiteboy movement was a natural result of the wretchedness and insecurity of the Catholic peasantry. It began in the Clogheen area of south Tipperary — Clogheen is a small village lying in a valley between the Galtee and Knockmealdown mountains, roughly halfway between Mitchelstown and Clonmel. It took its name from the white shirts which its members wore during their nocturnal activities against the landlords. Marching at night, their faces blackened, often in groups of up to 400, they levelled fences, houghed cattle (that is, deliberately maimed the animals by slashing their tendons) and dug up farmland. They felled trees, pasted threatening letters on landlords' hall doors, and gave their leaders fictitious military titles like 'Captain Rock' and 'Captain Right'. The spark which ignited this agitation appears to have been the removal in 1759 of restrictions on the importation of Irish cattle to Britain. This gave the landlords an incentive to extend their pastures, and numerous tenants were turned out of their farms; indeed, whole villages were swept away as commonages were enclosed.[3]

The authorities acted quickly to suppress the agitation. Punitive measures were rushed through the Irish parliament, and greater powers were given to local magistrates. The Marquis of Drogheda was sent to Clogheen with a large military force to (as the official euphemism put it) 'pacify the country around and about'. Whiteboy activities were made a capital offence and arrests, floggings and hangings became the order of the day. The agitation had direct implications for the growth of Protestant protection groupings, like the Boyne Society auxiliaries. In Tipperary, prominent landlords like Sir Thomas Maude and John Bagwell were Knights of the Most Glorious Order of the Boyne, and attempted to combat the Whiteboys by raising troops of horse from their most loyal tenants. The paranoia of the landlords ensured that the agitation was sucked into the wider political arena, and because of the involvement of a Catholic priest, Fr Nicholas Sheehy of Clogheen, some saw the disturbances as part of a 'popish insurrection' engineered, possibly, by French agent provocateurs to destabilise the country and subvert its Protestant constitution.

The Trials of Fr Sheehy

Fr Sheehy was a native of Fethard, a village seven miles north of Clonmel. He came from respectable Catholic stock (the Sheehys of Drumcollogher and, maternally, the Powers of Bawnfoun) and was educated on the Continent. According to the historian Dr Richard Madden, he had long been suspected of 'seditious operations' and was particularly vehement in his opposition to tithes. He had, in fact, advised the people of his adjoining parish of Newcastle not to pay, basing his argument on the fact that no Protestants lived in or near Newcastle and that therefore local Catholics had no liability. He also denounced a local tithe proctor named Dobbyn, who had demanded that Catholics pay a tithe of five pounds each when married in their own churches.

Sheehy had been indicted for being an unregistered priest and for administering 'unlawful oaths', and at the Spring 1764 Assizes in Clonmel he was charged with 'plotting insurrection and rebellion'. He thought it prudent to go into hiding, and the authorities declared him a fugitive from justice, offering £500 for his apprehension. Fr Sheehy agreed to give himself up on one condition: that he would not be tried before local magistrates in Clonmel, as he felt that he would not receive a fair trial. This condition was accepted and he was sent for trial in Dublin. The formal charge was: 'Inciting others to riot and rebellion.'

During a fourteen-hour hearing, three witnesses were heard. One was Miss Mary Butler, described in a contemporary account as being 'a lady of easy virtue, well known to the common soldiery'. Miss Butler was, in fact, a well-known prostitute whose activities had been denounced by Fr Sheehy. The other witnesses were John Toohy, a local man who a month previously had been sent to jail for horse stealing, and a vagrant youth named Lonergan who had been brought from Clonmel Jail to give testimony. The evidence of all three was discredited and Fr Sheehy was acquitted. But to everyone's surprise, he was re-arrested as he left the court and charged with the murder of a man called John Bridge.

Bridge was a Whiteboy who had been arrested months earlier, broke under questioning and turned King's Evidence, declaring that Sheehy and others whom he named were members of the Whiteboy conspiracy. Shortly after his release Bridge disappeared, and it was widely believed that he had been murdered, but his body was never found.

Despite the authorities' earlier promise, Fr Sheehy was brought before his enemies on the bench in Clonmel. He and his brother Edmund — known as 'Buck' Sheehy — who was also charged with the murder, were conveyed to court on 12 March 1766, on horseback under a strong military escort. The street was thronged with people protesting the brothers' innocence.

Fr Sheehy was accused of the murder of Bridge and with having proposed the murders of Lord Carrick, John Bagwell, William Bagwell and 'other people obnoxious to him' (Sheehy). The plot, the indictment said, took place at the house of Sheehy's sister, Mrs Green, at Shanbally, near Clogheen, during an assembly of the Whiteboys. Also included in the indictment was a charge of 'swearing all those present to secrecy, and to fidelity to the French King'.

The principal witness for the defence was Robert Keating, a member of a well-to-do Catholic family. He swore most emphatically that Sheehy had slept under his roof on the night of the alleged murder and therefore could not have killed Bridge. A Protestant clergyman, Reverend John Hewetson, stood up in court and informed the bench that to his knowledge Keating was a Whiteboy, and had recently been involved in a Whiteboy fracas — known as the 'Battle of Ballycastle' — when two soldiers had been killed. This disclosure created uproar. When things quietened, the arrest of Keating was ordered and he was carried off to jail in Kilkenny. His evidence was deemed useless, and dismissed.

At this point a number of other witnesses who had come to support Sheehy stood up and left the court in disgust, but it is not clear at whom their disgust was aimed. Sheehy, in despair, called his last remaining witness, Dr William Egan, parish priest of Clonmel (later to become Bishop of Waterford and Lismore). But Dr Egan refused to come forward; anything which he might say would make little difference to the outcome, and he perceived that the prosecution wanted to implicate him in a trumped-up 'popish plot'. Fr Sheehy's last chance vanished. He was found guilty, and hanged and quartered on 15 March 1766. His head was stuck on a pike over the porch of the old jail and remained there for twenty years, until his sister was permitted to take it away and bury it with the body. His grave at Shandangan became a place of pilgrimage.

Keating was tried at Kilkenny and acquitted; the principal witnesses were those who had given evidence against Fr Sheehy in Dublin. It was stated during the trial that John Bridge had not been murdered at all, but had simply fled the country. Lecky mentions a report which stated that Bridge was later seen in Newfoundland, and quotes from a letter, believed to be genuine, written by Fr Sheehy on the night before his execution to Major Sirr in Dublin, in which he confesses to knowing the identity of the man who murdered Bridges but says: 'I cannot make use of it for my own preservation.' This remark has been taken to mean that Sheehy was unable to reveal the name of the murderer because of the seal of the confession. Lecky sums up the case thus: 'He may not have been altogether the innocent martyr that he has been represented, but there can be little doubt that his trial was infamously partial, and it is probable that he was wholly guiltless of the murder of Bridge. The circumstances of the trial and the fact that Sheehy alone of the Whiteboy victims was in holy orders, left a deep and lasting resentment in the popular mind.'[4]

The Oakboys and the Steelboys

Although untouched by Whiteboyism, Ulster was soon to erupt with agrarian violence of its own. The first outbreak in 1763 was connected with the administration of grand juries under a new Act which empowered them to use compulsory labour in the repair and construction of roads. Hundreds of Presbyterian farmers and weavers banded together in an organisation called the 'Hearts of Oak' which took its name from oak sprigs worn on their hats. They tore up tollgates, felled trees, burned hayricks and maimed cattle. The disorders began in County Armagh and spread to Monaghan, Cavan, Tyrone and Londonderry. A few years later a similar organisation called the 'Hearts of Steel', named after the steel bars which its members carried as weapons, agitated against high rents and tithes. They compelled landlords and clergymen to moderate their demands and left a trail of destruction and violence.

The most serious disturbance occurred in 1770 when Lord Donegall, an absentee landlord and one of the largest proprietors in the country, began to disregard the claims of existing tenants, and granted leases to rich speculators from Belfast. He would advertise vacant holdings in the newspapers and invite bids from strangers. This had two implications for Protestant tenants: to retain their leases they must outbid the newcomers, and these could well be papists, their traditional enemies. Catholics, at this time, were desperately seeking tenancies and were prepared to bid — if they could scrape the money together — to the highest penny. The tenants' bile rose further when Lord Donegall's methods were adopted by other landlords.

The Steelboys attacked the property of landlords and speculators alike. A few days before Christmas 1770, 1,200 of them gathered at the Meeting House in Templepatrick and, with firelocks and pitchforks aloft, set out for Belfast. They set fire to a number of houses in Hercules Lane and other parts of the town before besieging a barracks to force the release of one of their comrades, held for maiming cattle. In the following weeks they created mayhem throughout the countryside. Crops were destroyed, hayricks set ablaze and threatening letters posted on landlords' doors. Gradually the landlords gave way and adopted more reasonable policies, and the agitation died down. Protestant tenants — for the first time since the Plantation of Ulster — had shown that when pushed to the limits of endurance they were prepared to use violence in defence of their interests.

Protestant Emigration

The suffering of the tenants was not over. There was a succession of bad harvests and a slump in the linen trade; thousands had no option but to flee the country. Many had already left. Discontent with the land-holding system, recurrent bad harvests and religious disabilities imposed by the Anglican Establishment had made life in Ireland singularly unattractive to Presbyterians, who made for the American colonies. During the worst phases of Lord Donegall's evictions, as many as 12,000 quit annually. In their new homeland they were known as the Scots-Irish and became renowned for their dogged ways and inflexible religious views. In Pennsylvania they were encouraged by the state authorities to settle in frontier areas as a barrier against Indian attack. By the 1750s there was a continuous chain of Scotch-Irish frontier settlements all the way from Pennsylvania to Georgia.[5]

They were an intensely religious and puritanical people, fiercely intolerant of the pockets of popery which they encountered. The formal establishment of Presbyterianism in America is credited to them. The Reverend Francis Makemie, born in Ramelton, County Donegal (circa 1658), travelled feverishly throughout the colonies, preaching and founding new churches. In 1706 he established the first American presbytery in Philadelphia, which became the unifying centre for churches scattered in Maryland, Pennsylvania, New York and New England.

The Ulster imprint on colonial America became marked as the settlers transplanted their culture. Traditional Scottish and Irish tunes — and the music derived from them — can still be heard in and around the Appalachian mountains. One commentator has said that 'Ireland's initial impact upon American music came predominantly from Ulster. . . .'[6] Another source provides an insight into their politics: 'They became . . . the most ardent supporters of colonial grievances against the home government, and when the war came, Washington paid tribute to their rebel qualities. "If I am defeated everywhere else," he said, "I will make my last stand among the Scotch-Irish of my native Virginia."'[7] No fewer than eight signatories of the American Declaration of Independence were of Irish Protestant extraction.

The College Green Parliament

Throughout the eighteenth century the Irish parliament was to remain the preserve of the minority Anglican ascendancy. It displayed as obviously as its sister parliament at Westminster the contemporary electoral phenomena of rotten boroughs and the buying and selling of seats. Many of these seats were in the patronage of the landlords. Elections were infrequent, since parliament might last until the death of the monarch; indeed one eighteenth-century Irish parliament sat for thirty-three years. The Irish parliament had no control over the executive in Dublin Castle; it was, in fact, a 'talking shop' — a clubby forum in which the ascendancy élite could let off steam and vent their grievances against the mother country. These were the inability of the Irish parliament to legislate on many primary matters, especially of a fiscal nature, the restrictions imposed on Irish manufactured goods and the curtailment of the country's right to trade freely. Campaigns to alleviate these grievances gave a sense of cohesion to Ascendancy politicians and, over time, an identity in opposition to Britain.

In the early part of the century, Irish administration was in the hands of English-born Lord Justices, one of whom was usually the Anglican Archbishop of either Armagh or Dublin. One of these, Archbishop George Stone, was so unpopular for his patent neglect of the country's interests that he was partly responsible for the growth of a 'patriot party' — an opposition grouping which became active towards the middle of the century. Because of his handsome appearance he was known as 'the beauty of holiness'[8] and was tolerant on religious questions, but to keep up appearances he had to beat the anti-popish drum occasionally. On the anniversary of the 1641 Rebellion each year, he availed of the opportunity to denounce the 'Whore of Babylon' and 'The Antichrist of Rome'.

But if his rhetoric did not upset his fellow politicians, his ineptitude on fiscal policy did. The leaders of 'the patriots', Anthony Malone, John Ponsonby, Henry Boyle and the Earl of Kildare, came into conflict with the Archbishop over a claim by the Privy Council in London to appropriate a surplus in revenue which had occurred in the fiscal years 1751 and 1753. At the instigation of Malone and Boyle, the Irish parliament rejected a money bill which had been submitted to it by Westminster. But the government in London — aided by its clients in Dublin Castle — overrode the will of the Irish Parliament and withdrew the disputed funds by issuing a special Royal Letter — effectively an injunction to remit the funds. The Irish parliament had to give way, but ever afterwards it took measures to ensure that no revenue surplus would be available for transfer, by ensuring that the expenditure for each fiscal year exactly balanced with the revenue.

Stone and his colleagues grew alarmed by the new opposition. They used a powerful solvent to win over the 'patriots': bribery. Boyle, the Speaker of the House, was given a pension and made Earl of Shannon; Malone became Chancellor of the Exchequer, and Kildare was made a Marquis and subsequently Duke of Leinster. From then on, the 'patriot party' co-operated whole-heartedly with Stone.

But within a decade a new 'patriot party' arose, led by men of sterner quality: Henry Flood, James Caulfeild, Earl of Charlemont, and a little later, Henry Grattan. Among the aims of this new opposition were the abolition of bribery within parliament, the reduction of the pension list, the winning of free trade for all Irish agricultural and manufactured products, and the obtaining of legislative independence for the Irish parliament.

For the most part, the new 'patriot party' was only concerned with the interests of Protestants. Its members gloried in the memory of William of Orange and went out of their way to celebrate the Orange tradition. Grattan, it is true, favoured the abolition of the penal laws against Catholics and advocated that the better-off among them should be granted the franchise, but Flood, Charlemont and the others opposed Catholic claims on the grounds that if they were admitted to parliament they would soon outnumber the Protestant members and subvert the constitution.

The Volunteers

In 1775 the prolonged quarrel between England and her American colonies came to a climax when the Westminster parliament declared war on the colonists. The main point at issue was Parliament's assertion of the right to legislate for the colonies. This was rigorously opposed by the Americans, who maintained that they were not bound by legislation passed by an assembly in which they were not represented. Their argument bore a striking similarity to that employed by 'the patriots' in Dublin. The struggle was watched with consuming interest in Ireland, and especially by the Presbyterians of the north whose kinfolk were in the forefront of the American cause. The radical clergyman William Steel Dickson told his congregation in Belfast: 'There is scarcely a family among us who does not have kindred with the inhabitants of that extensive continent.' Lord Harcourt, the Viceroy, informed London that the Ulster Presbyterians were 'Americans in their hearts'.

The position of the Catholics was different; if they had any sympathy with the Americans they kept it under their hats. Under the leadership of the Catholic Committee — a moderate, middle-class body founded in 1756 by Charles O'Connor of Balanagare and Thomas Wyse — they were content to keep their heads down and to accept what small favours came their way.

Despite its grievances with Westminster, the Irish parliament remained loyal too. When the largest military expedition to leave British shores was sent across the Atlantic to crush the Americans, this stripped Ireland and Britain of its defences and left both countries vulnerable to invasion. A critical situation arose in 1778 when France, Spain and Holland entered the conflict on the American side. This shook the support of Irish Presbyterians for the Americans. They had little difficulty in recognising the old popish enemy, and felt that combating the French was the more urgent task. As recently as 1760, during the Seven Years' War, the French Admiral Thurot had swept into Belfast Lough and held Carrickfergus for a week. In April 1778 the American privateer John Paul Jones had sailed brazenly into Belfast harbour in broad daylight and brought his vessel *Ranger* athwart the British ship *Drake*, raking her decks with grapeshot. In an hour-long engagement the English ship was set ablaze and a number of her crew were mortally wounded.

The citizens of Belfast became alarmed and applied to Dublin Castle for troops to protect them. For some time there was no response. Then a letter from the Chief Secretary, Sir Richard Heron, confessed to the inability of the authorities to send no more than 'a troop or two of horse and part of a company of invalids'. It urged the people to look to their own defence. And they did. Military associations were speedily formed, arms were procured and uniforms run up. Every effort was made to acquire the skills and discipline necessary to withstand invasion. The example of Belfast was followed all over the country as Protestants sprang to arms.

Volunteering became the fashion, and soon numerous corps of splendidly uniformed men could be seen everywhere. Reviews and parades became frequent, particularly in Dublin where each weekend gentlemen volunteers marched and clicked heels near the statue of William. These men wore orange cockades in their hats, carried orange flags and caparisoned their horses with orange ribbons. The greatest personages in the land took up positions of leadership, and Ireland soon abounded with captains and colonels. In the beginning no Catholics were permitted to join the corps, though some subscribed to the funds.

These corps were in no way revolutionary; a modern historian has said: 'They were more like the "B" Specials than anything else.'[9] The government looked askance at this new force, but was finally constrained to equip it, and handed over 16,000 rifles which had been earmarked for the regular army.

The threat of invasion did not materialise, and many wondered what to do with the force. Some of the politically astute saw it as a means of weakening the control of the governing oligarchy. Henry Flood, in particular, saw it as a weapon which might be deployed if political concessions from Westminster were denied. He felt that a British parliament, chastened by its experiences in America, could not ignore the implied threat. In a much quoted phrase, one of his 'patriot' colleagues, Walter Hussey Burgh,[10] declared: 'England has sown her laws in dragons' teeth, and they have now sprung up as armed men.'

Free Trade

At this time, the economic depression in Ireland was worsened by an embargo imposed by Westminster on Irish trade with the colonies; one of the reasons used to justify it was the facetious argument that the rebel Americans were kept going by means of Irish foodstuffs. The colonists retaliated with an embargo on Irish linens, and thousands of Irish textile workers were thrown out of employment. Protest marches were held in

Dublin and elsewhere, and when appeals to both the Irish and English parliaments went unheeded, a boycott of English goods was instituted, known as 'Non-Importation'. As a result, English exports to Ireland fell by over 70 per cent. English manufacturers, who had never hesitated to restrict Irish trade, now demanded that something be done to prevent their ruin.

In October 1779 the Irish parliament was almost unanimous in its support of an Address to the Lord Lieutenant which declared that 'by free trade alone the nation can be saved from impending ruin'. In the following month a large force of Volunteers paraded outside Parliament House and around the statue of King William. They tied placards on their artillery pieces, bearing the words 'Free Trade or Else' and 'Free Trade or This!' The Lord Lieutenant, alarmed by the show of force, informed the British government that large-scale concessions were necessary if an American-like situation was to be avoided. The British Prime Minister, Lord North, gave way and free trade was granted.

Legislative Independence

It soon became apparent that free trade was not enough. Measures to bring about the independence of the Irish parliament were demanded, as Westminster could at any time withdraw what it had so recently given. In February 1782, a great convention of the Ulster section of the Volunteers, held at Dungannon under the chairmanship of Lord Charlemont, passed resolutions demanding the repeal of both Poynings' Law (which prohibited the Irish parliament from legislating without the prior sanction of the King and his council, in London) and the Sixth of George I (legislation which affirmed that laws passed by the English parliament were binding on Ireland).

In the Irish parliament the demand for legislative independence was stepped up by Henry Grattan. Had England been successful in the American War, she might have resisted his eloquence but, as things were, she was in no mood for conflict. She repealed Poynings' Law and the Sixth of George I, but Flood was still not satisfied. He demanded a positive renunciation by England of all claims to legislate for Ireland. The English government again yielded, and these measures taken together became known as the 'Constitution of 1782'.

This 'Constitution' did not amount to self-government. The Irish executive was still in the hands of the Lord Lieutenant, appointed by the British Cabinet; the Irish parliament could not, if it so wished, bring him down. The new arrangements could best be described as 'self-legislation', although the Crown retained its power to veto Irish bills. Yet the new dispensation provided the best of all possible worlds to those of the Orange tradition. It gave Irish Protestants the right to legislate for themselves and yet retained a link with the British parliament and the connection with the Crown. It also had the virtue of keeping the papists in their place. No wonder that they all cheered when Grattan, in parliament, declared with characteristic flamboyance: 'I found Ireland on her knees . . . I traced her progress from injury to arms, and from arms to liberty. Spirit of Swift! Spirit of Molyneux! Your genius has prevailed. Ireland is now a nation. In her new character I hail her. And bowing in her august presence, I say: "esto perpetua" (may she be lasting).'[11] But Ireland was not a nation, and her new-found legislative independence was to be short-lived.

Parliamentary Reform

It became clear to 'the patriots' and the Volunteers that the loosening of the legislative ties with England would be of little value unless parliament itself was reformed. The problem was that those yielding power had no interest in seeing it relinquished completely. In November 1783 another great Volunteer convention was held in the Rotunda in Dublin. Volunteers from all over the country assembled, and appeared determined to force change. One of the matters debated was whether the franchise should be extended to Catholics, and the proposal was roundly defeated. A package of four other proposals was carried — that all male Protestants whose property yielded more than £20 a year should be entitled to vote; that 'rotten boroughs' should be reformed; that government pensioners should not be allowed to sit in parliament; and that an election should be called every third year.

The convention was stage-managed by Flood, by far its most dominant personality. Flushed with his success in persuading the Volunteers to adopt his views, he rushed to Parliament House, and there on the floor of the Chamber — still wearing his Volunteer uniform — he burst forth with a torrent of eloquence and asked leave to introduce a bill which incorporated the Resolutions. It was a theatrical and foolhardy act. Members of the House suspected that he had come to intimidate them. They were not to be compromised, so they refused him.

Flood's failure marked the death knell of the Volunteers. They had overplayed their hand and, having no wish to use force against a parliament representative of their own kind, they did the sensible thing: they went home. In the following year the American War ended, and the regular troops returned. Thereafter the Volunteers went into decline. Some corps disbanded, but others set off in a direction far removed from the movement's original aims.

The Gathering Storm

The times had altered. No matter how much the Irish parliament had set itself against its own reform, it could not for long resist the pressures for change which were coming from other areas of the body politic. Nor could it prevent the spread of those enlightenment ideas which were now seeping into the country from America and Europe, and most particularly from France.

Men like Jean-Jacques Rousseau and Thomas Paine were preaching the virtues of liberty, equality and fraternity, and with the decline of the Jacobite threat, the whole system of discrimination against Catholics was becoming, to some, increasingly distasteful. The 'Patriot' element in Parliament — while unhesitatingly professing loyalty to the British crown and Protestant constitution — had not only demanded the reform of Parliament, but also argued for concessions to Catholics. Yet even those of a decidedly 'patriotic' turn, like Henry Flood, while they condemned in the abstract the injustices of the penal laws and the oppressive conduct of the landlords, were very much against granting political concessions to Catholics. They viewed movements like the 'Whiteboys' with dread and outrage, and harboured suspicions that what Catholics wanted was not just relief but the destruction of the Protestant constitution and, most frighteningly, revenge.

The next initiative came from Westminster rather than from the Dublin parliament. The Irish government was pressed to pass a Relief Act (1771) which permitted Catholics to acquire bogland on a lease of sixty-one years, provided they were willing to reclaim it. This, of course, was a trivial and almost meaningless concession. Lord North, the Prime Minister in London, was convinced that more was required; he feared that the Catholics were less loyal than they pretended, and that unless further concessions were made he might have an insurrection on his hands. He told Parliament:

I have acquired a piece of information concerning a plot for revolt in the west of Ireland among Roman Catholics, with a view to over-turning the present Irish government, by the aid of the French and the Spaniards. . . . You may depend on its authenticity, and at this moment many friars are going secretly from France to Ireland to set it going; though the late Acts passed for the relief of the Roman Catholics will, it is to be hoped, prevent it from succeeding . . . my intelligence comes from Rome. . . .[1]

The Viceroy was instructed to urge the Administration in Dublin Castle to swallow its scruples and bring forward some measure of 'expedient relief'. Two bills were introduced by the Member for Dublin, Luke Gardiner, who afterwards as Lord Mountjoy was, in the words of Froude, 'to learn something of Catholic Emancipation when he was piked and hacked to death at New Ross'.[2] The first bill, which became law in 1778, allowed Catholics to take leases of 999 years and repealed the Gavelkind Act, which required a Catholic to divide his estate amongst all his sons. Gardiner's second Relief Bill permitted Catholic schools to be opened, subject to the permission of the local Protestant bishop, and allowed Catholics to purchase and sell freehold property.

Both these bills passed through the House without difficulty, but when political concessions to Catholics were proposed they were met with the most uncompromising opposition. North's government had indeed taken a more liberal attitude to Catholic claims than the Irish parliament. Its motives were to conciliate Catholics in face of the revolu-tionary doctrines emanating from Europe, and it felt that the disadvantage of alienating the ruling Irish elite would be compensated by securing a loyal and grateful Catholic population. These were not altogether naive calculations, but they were to backfire.

The Catholic Committee

The Catholic Committee had been the unofficial representative body of Irish Catholics since its foundation in 1756. At first it was led by timid aristocrats who held mild academic dreams of Catholic Relief by goodwill all round. It presented the Catholic case with much admired, but very little repaid, decorum. It was, in fact, a totally benign and ineffectual body. As a result of manoeuvres by an energetic Dublin businessman, John Keogh, the old leadership was ousted, and with a young barrister named Theobald Wolfe Tone as its assistant secretary, more aggressive policies were adopted. Tone's proposal in 1792 to hold a Catholic Convention in Dublin gave rise to a storm of Protestant indignation. The name 'convention' was ominous, for in September the National Convention had met in Paris, and its first act was the deposition of Louis XVI. At the beginning of December

Tone's Convention met in Tailor's Hall in Back Lane, Dublin, and was dubbed, derisively, 'The Back Lane Parliament'. It agreed to ignore the Irish parliament and to take its grievances to the King directly. The Protestant ultras were outraged. With a chorus of abuse ringing in their ears, the Catholic delegates crossed to London and presented their petition to the King in person. To the surprise of many, George III received them kindly, and his ministers were the personification of courtesy.

The result was the Catholic Relief Bill (1793) whose main provisions were passed by the Irish parliament with the utmost reluctance, and only after stern warnings from the new Prime Minister, William Pitt, on the consequences of its rejection. This bill enabled Catholics to vote as Forty-Shilling Freeholders, to become members of local corporations, to take university degrees and hold minor offices of state. They were also allowed commissions in the army below the rank of general, but were still debarred from parliament.

These measures failed to meet rising Catholic expectations, although they were not too dissatisfied with them. The Catholic Committee expressed its gratitude to Tone by presenting him with a gold medal and an honorarium of £1,500. Their hopes rose again with the appointment of Lord Fitzwilliam as Viceroy. He was a prominent English Whig, a friend of Henry Grattan, and was also known to strongly support Catholic Relief. When he arrived in Ireland on 4 January 1795, one of his first acts was to dismiss John Beresford, one of the most powerful men in the country, from the office of Chief Commissioner of the Revenue. No particular wrongdoing was attributed to Beresford, but he was the centre of an extensive network of family patronage and power; it was said that the Beresford family controlled a quarter of all public offices in Ireland. Beresford appealed directly to Pitt to be reinstated. It seems that the terms of Fitzwilliam's appointment were ill-defined or inexact, and he was deemed to have exceeded them. Moreover, since his arrival he had been stormed with Catholic petitions and had come to the view that relief was both necessary and imperative. This was his undoing. He was not supported by the British government and in March, after just two months as Viceroy, he was recalled, much to the disillusionment and frustration of Catholics.

There were two sides to the reform coin. The recent changes in favour of the Catholics had left Protestants — particularly the poorer ones, like the small farmers and cottage weavers in the north — feeling insecure and forgotten. They felt that a Catholic resurgence was in the air and that the fruits of their fathers' victory might be snatched from them. In much of east Ulster, economic rivalry between the poorer Protestants and Catholics had become intense, most particularly in the 'weaving triangle' which covered areas of Armagh and East Tyrone. Here, cottages of farmer-weavers lined the roadways, and their occupants competed fiercely for survival. The stage was being set for a venomous clash between them.

The First Republicans

The great convulsion which shook France in 1789 was vastly different from the revolutions that the world had seen before. In the previous century the 'Glorious Revolution' had brought about a shift in power between the Crown and the people; but the basic institutions of the state remained untouched. As yet there was no broadening of the franchise in the direction of popular democracy, and the liberties of ordinary people were neither asserted nor considered. No claims of human equality were heard, nor did their omission provide a serious sense of grievance. But with the American Revolution, things began to change. The Rights of Man were proclaimed and the new republic, across the Atlantic, glowed like a beacon of hope. People in the Old World who had never aspired to liberty before began to aspire now.

The new revolutionary explosion was detonated in France, but only a portion of its lofty expectations were to be fulfilled. Yet it was dissimilar to previous upheavals. The 'Glorious Revolution' had been a localised affair. So too, in the main, had been the American Revolution. But the French Revolution burst through its own boundaries and swept across the Continent. Its echoes were to reverberate in the ears of succeeding generations and its principles were to be invoked time and again.

In Ireland, it was viewed with mixed feelings. The Irish parliament, and even the 'Patriots', reflecting the mood of the Ascendancy at large, denounced the revolution. The attitude of the Catholic Church was similar. The Catholic bishops, educated in continental seminaries under the ancient regime, were imbued with traditional respect for monarchical authority, and were outraged by the excesses of the revolutionaries. They saw the Civil Constitution of the Clergy as the last straw, and an open challenge to the Christian tradition, and felt constrained to warn their congregations of the danger. But it is doubtful if political issues much appealed to the Catholic masses. Though hundreds of them now possessed the vote as Forty-Shilling Freeholders, they were no better off materially and had little interest in cosmetic reforms. Their main concerns were, as always, high rents, payment of tithes and security of tenure. The real danger to the Ascendancy lay in the possibility that, under French influence, Catholic grievances might be turned into revolutionary demands.

This danger was increased by the extent of anti-government feeling among Presbyterians in the north, who might well supply effective political leadership. It was they who provided the sturdy emigrants to North America, who were most active in the revolt against the mother country. They had given the cutting edge to the Volunteers and, most importantly, were the inheritors of a long-standing radicalism which could be traced to indigenous Presbyterian sources: to Calvin's Geneva, to the Dutch Republic, and to the utilitarian thinking of the Scottish Enlightenment. They were particularly influenced by the teachings of philosophers like Francis Hutcheson[3] and had drunk deeply of the Protestant republicanism of Oliver Cromwell. Like other sections of the community they contained conservative, even reactionary, elements, but what impressed and disturbed the authorities was the sheer rigour of their stubbornness and the depth of their nonconformity. These Presbyterians had seen in the overthrow of the ancient regime a new hope for the abolition of inherited privilege, and a fresh chance for the recasting of society on a more equitable basis. Acutely conscious of their status as second-class Protestants under the Anglican Ascendancy, and feeling particularly slighted by not being able to control the electoral politics of their own areas, they rejoiced in the news from France, which they hailed as 'a resurrection of the human spirit'.

The United Irishmen

A striking figure in the new drama now to be enacted in Ireland was a sallow-faced young man, with long lank hair and an enormous bridge on his nose. His name was Theobald Wolfe Tone and he was about twenty-six years of age. The son of a Dublin coach-maker, he had been born in Stafford Street in 1763. A brilliant, if erratic, student at Trinity College, at the age of twenty-three he eloped with the sixteen-year-old daughter of a clergyman and thereafter studied law in London. At one time he tried to enlist in the service of the East India Company and, at another, he devised a scheme for establishing a British military colony in the South Sea Islands. He carried his scheme to Downing Street, determined to convince William Pitt of the excellence of his proposal. The Prime Minister was unable to see him, and he vowed that one day he would force Mr Pitt to rue this act of discourtesy. He returned to Dublin and was admitted to the Irish bar, but practised little. Turning his mind to politics — when he became the paid assistant secretary of the Catholic Association — he wrote a popular pamphlet entitled *An Argument on behalf of the Catholics of Ireland*, which had a wide circulation. This greatly impressed a young officer of the 64th Regiment of Foot which was stationed in Belfast, and who became a life-long friend. This was Thomas Russell, later to go down in Irish history as 'The Man from God Knows Where'[4].

Belfast, a quintessential Presbyterian town, had long been a hotbed of political fervour, the first home of the Volunteers. Long after they had lost their strength elsewhere, they had continued in Belfast, ingeniously mixing martial enthusiasm with political ardour. Among the Volunteers was a company calling itself 'The Green Company', mainly composed of Presbyterian businessmen, which had formed among its members a political club called 'The Irish Brotherhood' whose affairs were directed by eleven people who sat on a 'secret committee'. They included a political livewire called Samuel McTier and a clever entrepreneur named Robert Simms, who owned a paper mill at Ballyclare. Among the membership were shipbrokers, linen drapers, booksellers, and one or two sons of the manse. They were all Freemasons, and Thomas Russell, sharing their views, was admitted to their company.

A young medical doctor with a poetic bent named William Drennan spent much of his spare time writing subversive letters to the Belfast newspapers under the pseudonym 'Orellana or an Irish Helot'. He had studied in Edinburgh, where he imbibed the philosophical legacy of Francis Hutcheson. In 1789 he transferred to Dublin and began to ponder revolution. He was a man of taste and culture, and is nowadays remembered as the author of the poem 'When Erin First Rose' and the inventor of the phrase 'The Emerald Isle'. He had raised the idea of a radical society in a letter to his Belfast brother-in-law Samuel McTier: 'I should much like that a society were instituted . . . having much of the secrecy and somewhat of the ceremonial of Freemasonry . . . a benevolent conspiracy — a plot for the people — no Whig Club — the Brotherhood its name — the Rights of Man and the Greatest Happiness of the Greatest Number its end — its general end, real independence to Ireland, and Republicanism its particular purpose.'[5] The proposal was taken up by 'The Green Company' and much of the initial planning was done by McTier, assisted by Simms, who became the Society's first secretary.

Intoxicated by the events in France, the Belfast radicals decided to celebrate the second anniversary of the Fall of the Bastille, in July 1791, with a procession through the town and a review of local Volunteer companies. Russell advised that they should prepare a manifesto setting out their objects, and added that the author of the pamphlet 'An Argument on behalf of the Catholics of Ireland' could assist. Dr Drennan, who had himself aspired to the intellectual leadership of the movement, was none too pleased, but the 'secret committee', impressed by Tone's writings, authorised Russell to contact him.

On 11 October 1791, Tone joined Russell in Belfast. He was delighted with the strong Jacobean spirit which prevailed. Thomas Paine's book *The Rights of Man*, Tone noted in his diary, 'is the Koran of Belfescu'. He had a strange and silly habit of calling places and people by their classical nicknames. Three days later, at 4 p.m. on 14 October 1791, he met the 'secret committee' in secret session in the back parlour of Betty Barclays Tavern[6] in Crown Entry, off High Street, a favourite drinking haunt of the Belfast radicals. It was at this meeting that the first Society of United Irishmen was founded. The title of the Society, suggested by Tone, described its aims, which were set out in three resolutions. These called for a union of all Irishmen to counter English influence, a radical reform of Parliament, and the inclusion in that reform of Irishmen of all religious persuasions.

Soon a branch of the new society was created in Dublin, at a meeting held in the Eagle Tavern in Eustace Street. Among its original members were Dr Drennan, James Napper Tandy and a strange young man who owned extensive estates in Counties Kildare and Down and who, for some obscure reason, reversed his surname with his first name. This was Hamilton Rowan, a prominent Freemason who, years before, had been initiated at Cambridge University, and was a member of the Grand Orient in France. He had also met Adam Weishaupt, the founder of the German 'Illuminati' and had become enrolled in that Order too.[7]

One of the first activities of the Belfast Society of United Irishmen was to launch a newspaper, *The Northern Star*, which was an instant success. Its columns carried a mixture of pungent comment and satire, and its polemicists spelled out the reforms required to the body politic. Its philosophy was nicely summed up by the only working man among the United leadership, the weaver-poet, Jemmy Hope:

> Och, Paddies, my hearties, have done with your parties
> Let min of all creeds and professins agree
> If Orange and Green min, no longer were seen min,
> Och, naboclis, how aisy auld Ireland we'd free.[8]

At first, the United Irishmen sought reform by working within the system, but it is certain that among the early leadership there were people who contemplated revolution. Among these were Tone and Napper Tandy. In his autobiography, Tone admits that a wish to break the connection with England was one of his first objects. Tandy had already given up hope of reform, but believed that it was necessary to 'play the constitutional game' until the time was ripe for a bold stroke. How much these aims were shared is unknown, but some, like Hamilton Rowan and Dr Drennan, believed that reform could come about by a 'gentle revolution'.

The times were not propitious for this. The outbreak of hostilities with France in 1793 hardened the government's attitude, and it set its face against all change. Early in that year, the Volunteers were suppressed, and the same fate befell the United Irishmen twelve months later. The downfall of Viceroy Fitz-william seems also to have been a turning point. Catholics felt that the door had been slammed in their faces, and the United Irishmen accepted this view.

A small inner circle in the movement, consisting of Tone, Rowan, Simms and others, set about reorganising the Society as an underground oath-bound body. Tone, after a run-in with the authorities, left Ireland, and in June 1796 went to France to seek aid from the French for the overthrow of the Irish government and the establishment of a republic. The organisation was tightened up considerably, and the Masonic backgrounds of the leadership may have proved useful when they set about establishing a system of signs and codes to facilitate secrecy. They identified one another by special handshakes and grips and used exchanges full of French revolutionary imagery:

> 'Are you consecrated?'
> 'I am.'
> 'To what?'
> 'To the National Convention.'
> 'For what reason?'
> 'To dethrone all kings, and to plant the liberty tree in our Irish land.'

As a badge, the Society adopted a harp surmounted by a cap of liberty bearing the words 'It is newly strung and shall be heard.' The close cropping of hair in the French style was also followed by some enthusiasts.

Rural Conflict

The United Irishmen were great idealists, but their idealism was little shared by the majority of Protestants at large. It was one thing for the more enlightened in Belfast and Dublin to stand on a common platform with their Catholic neighbours and to agitate for parliamentary reform, but it was quite another for the rural masses of both faiths — who still harboured ancient religious animosities — to do the same. The hewers of wood and drawers of water passed no resolutions about the inalienable rights of man. Imbued with their inbred hatreds, they looked to their own strengths. For years the tense relationship between them had been deteriorating and, in mid-Ulster, had reached boiling point.

A number of factors were involved. The Catholic Relief Acts had unsettled Protestants, and had been aggravated by Catholics making silly threats like: 'Our day is coming, and then we will deal with you.' Another was the manner in which the Volunteers had lost their strength. In some areas they disbanded in a piecemeal fashion and left their discarded weapons lying about. Catholics, who had not officially held weapons since the days of the Treaty of Limerick, were anxious to lay their hands on these. They attacked Volunteer homes at night and even ambushed parties of the militia in broad daylight to obtain their requirements.

Ireland had been rarely free from rural conflict, but in the past it had been sporadic. From the early 1790s it continually surged up. In mid-Ulster particularly, men were on the prowl, night after night, seeking to destroy the property of those they hated. Froude says:

> Houses were burnt, cattle were houghed with the peculiar ferocity which characterises the Irish peasant when aroused to violence; the udders of cows belonging to Protestants were sliced off. When arms were demanded and not delivered, death was the punishment. Barracks were surprised in the darkness . . . and by whom those deeds were done remained a mystery. In every cabin, men were sworn to secrecy. . . .'[9]

The most serious outbreaks surfaced in County Armagh. The long-held view has been that competition for land in this part of the 'linen triangle' was the main cause of the violence which lasted, on and off, for the best part of twenty years. Modern research has not disputed this view, but has shown that other complex causes were also involved. These included the knotty sectarian backdrop and distinct political circumstances. Armagh at this time was the most densely populated county in Ireland and supported a population of over 500 persons per square mile. Everywhere was humming with industry. Of the 49 million yards of linen manufactured in Ireland in the mid-1780s, about 15 million came from this zone.[10] Traditionally, weaving had been a Protestant preserve, but for some time Catholics had broken into it. Most of their operations were small and their looms were less sophisticated than those of the Protestants. They were also handicapped in having, unlike the Protestants, too little land for bleaching greens. As a consequence, the competition for land was fierce, and when new leases came on the market, Catholics sought to outbid Protestants. Nothing could be more calculated to fuel tension, and veritable riots occurred at land auctions.

There was also a general breakdown in social control. A destabilising factor was the rise of a new and independent class of wage earners. These tended to be young strapping fellows who could endure the long hours of spinning, weaving and bleaching. They turned up at the Portadown and Lurgan linen markets where 'nothing was accepted but for ready money', and cut hard deals with the linen drapers who depended on them for their supplies. Disporting themselves pugnaciously at markets, fairs and cockfights, they were a rowdy element who caused much disruption. In the tense, sectarian tinderbox that was Armagh, such hell-raisers could ignite enough sparks to set combustible material ablaze. Yet as an explanation for long-term violence — and for the proportions which it reached — such a category of mavericks appears insufficient.

More important was the fact that the three religious denominations — Anglican, Presbyterian and Catholic — were represented in equal proportions and that sectarian fault lines criss-crossed in places where each was strongest. The Anglicans were mostly settled in the northern reaches, the Presbyterians in the middle and the Catholics in the poorer south.[11] Different enclaves throughout the county meant that disturbances in one area could react in another.

There was also a three-way split in politics. On the one hand was the French radicalism of the United Irishmen; on the other was an unregenerate conservatism, sometimes expressed in the servile loyalty of Protestant tenants to their landlords. The middle ground was occupied by the Whiggish interests of Lord Charlemont and William Brownlow of

Lurgan. This in-between position was, however, quickly eroded in the run-up to the by-election of 1795, when Brownlow defected to the Conservative camp and won the seat by a handful of votes.[12] His narrow victory shook his landlord backers. A general election was due within a year and, if the voting pattern was maintained, the seat could well change hands. The stakes were high and the outcome depended on the Presbyterian 'swing' vote. Could Presbyterians be induced to follow their co-religionists in Belfast and opt for a programme of reform, which would mean, in the parlance of the radicals, entering into a 'brotherhood of affection' with their traditional enemies, the Catholics? Or would they continue to be swayed in the conservative interest by their high regard for the Orange tradition, and hatred of popery? An intensive propaganda war was waged on both sides, and the agrarian disturbances were used as counters on the political chequerboard. It cannot be assumed that those who sat near the seat of power in Dublin were neutral in this contest.

The Peep O'Day Boys and the Defenders

When the agrarian disturbances surfaced in Armagh, they followed the notorious faction-fight pattern familiar in other parts of Ireland. Strangely enough, in the beginning, the rival factions were not organised on sectarian lines. They were known as 'fleets' — the name being adopted because certain naval engagements during the recent war had caught the popular imagination. These fleets did not split on denominational lines until Protestant anger on the admission of Catholics to the Volunteers boiled over. The Reverend Mortimer O'Sullivan, in his evidence to the House of Commons Select Committee on Orangeism in 1835, had this to say:

> . . . after various encounters and outrages, associations were formed of a parochial nature, parish after parish, and were called fleets; the naval war was then in its pride. As yet there was no visible religious distinction; the associations formed were Presbyterian and Roman Catholic conjointly, but gradually one of the parties became subject to a great deal of Roman Catholic influence, and religious or sectarian acrimony gave a new character to the factions . . . one as the Bawn Fleet, one the Nappach, one — in which two districts were united and which certainly was not exclusively Roman Catholic — called its members 'Defenders'. Some alarm and suspicion appears to have been caused by a title given to one of those fleets, and which consisted exclusively of Roman Catholics . . . It was the Bawn Fleet . . . the name Bawn Fleet was given up and that of the Defenders adopted. . . .[13]

'The Defenders' became the generic title for groups who were exclusively Catholic and which were established, specifically, to protect Catholic homesteads from dawn raids by the Protestant Peep O'Day

Boys. This latter body was an amalgam of groups whose name was derived from the timing of their early-morning forays.

The Defenders and Peep O'Day Boys are reputed to have come into being following a minor incident at a cattle fair in Markethill. The story goes that two Presbyterians engaged in fisticuffs while haggling over the price of a cow, and that a Catholic bystander intervened on behalf of one of them. The fellow who came off worst blamed his humiliation on the Catholic and swore vengeance. He went away and organised a body of roughnecks who became known, in time, as the Nappach Fleet — as they came from the vicinity of the village of Nappach. This wild mob set about raiding Catholic homesteads and explained their activities by saying that in the absence of regular law enforcement they were simply carrying out a civic duty in dispossessing people of unlawfully held weapons. But their raiding parties did more than simply collect weapons. They used their early-morning swoops as a means of industrial sabotage, and smashed the weaving looms and webs of their victims. The Defender movement was formed as a response to this activity.

Under pressure of greater numbers, the Peep O'Day Boys came off badly. Both combinations became indistinguishable in their methods and drove fear into the hearts of many. The Peep O' Day Boys were perhaps the less sophisticated and were driven almost totally by primitive atavistic impulses. In time, the Defenders began to spread outside Armagh and became strong particularly in towns and places of rural industry. They developed a lodge system and a series of codes and handshakes to recognise each another. They also developed a rudimentary republican ideology, but this was never really coherent. In spite of their growth, their political development remained arrested, and their interests rarely rose above the correction of local grievances and faction fighting. Their methods, however, were to become embedded in later nationalist culture, and historians have traced the descent of organisations like the Ribbonmen, the Molly Maguires and the Ancient Order of Hibernians from them.[14] In Armagh, both the Defenders and the Peep O'Day Boys could mobilise huge forces. This is an index both of their wide influence, and of the depth of their antagonism.

The Forkhill Outrage

Early in 1791 an event at Mullaghbawn, near Forkhill on the Armagh–Louth border, sent waves of anger through the Protestant community. Alexander Barclay had established a school under the will of a deceased landlord named Richard Jackson. Under its terms, four vocational-type schools were to be established and a small colony of Protestants settled on waste ground on the Jackson estate. None of the existing tenants, either Protestant or Catholic, were to be disturbed, and all the schools were to be interdenominational. But the Catholics were perturbed that additional

Protestants were to be settled near them and that no provision was being made for the teaching of the Irish language. Incidents began to occur. The corn and turf on the glebe of the Reverend Edward Hudson, a trustee of the will, were set alight. He narrowly escaped assassination when his horse was shot from under him, and threatening notices were pasted to his door.

On the evening of 28 January, Barclay was visited at his home by about fifty men, led by one Terence Byrne. The schoolmaster was brutally attacked, and his tongue forced out of his mouth and cut off. His wife was violated and battered, and died as one of her breasts was being severed. Next, Barclay's brother-in-law was assaulted. His tongue was also cut out and the calves of his legs hacked away. This last attack, it would appear, was provoked by the part which the brother-in-law had played, not long before, in an assault on the Catholic parish priest of Forkhill. The assailants made no effort to conceal their identities. Following their crimes they marched away, four abreast, in a torchlight procession. Weeks later, a number were arrested. In court the mute brother-in-law identified a number of the assailants by nods of his head. One was found to be still carrying Barclay's watch, and another was wearing items of his clothing. Terence Byrne was not, however, seen again; the story was that he fled the country. In Protestant areas there were screams for revenge, and a new upsurge of violence followed. Catholics became so scared for their personal safety that many were afraid to be seen out of doors at any time of day.

Lisnagraed

The Protestant peasantry had never forgotten the events of the Williamite Wars. Crude paintings of William's crossing of the Boyne hung in every home and each twelfth of July was treated as a Day of Remembrance. When they gathered to commemorate the old victories, they were often known as 'William's Men' or sometimes as 'Orangemen'.

On 12 July 1791 a few hundred gathered at Aghaderg in County Down and marched along the road behind a fife and drum band. As they passed high ground near an old tree-covered fairy fort, at a place called Lisnagraed, they were attacked by a large number of Defenders, and they ran for cover. After a time, being better armed than their opponents, they decided to rush the fort, but waited their chance. The Defenders, during the lull, raised the white flag of the Stuarts and a banner bearing a portrait of the Virgin Mary. Suddenly the Protestants rushed, commando style, up the hill and took them by surprise. In a torrent of smoke and shot, the startled Defenders were forced from their cover, broke and fled. The incident was to go down in song and story, and began the Protestant custom of commemorating such skirmishes in verse, written with the type of venomous and, to Catholics, blasphemous spleen which would characterise much Orange invective in the future.

The Battle of the Diamond

> There Blacker, Sloan and Aiken's sons
> Stood true to the core
> With Sinclair and Dan Winter too
> And Verner evermore
> These were the sires that led the van
> And did true valour show
> At the Battle of the Diamond, boys
> One hundred years ago.
>
> *— from an Orange ballad commemorating those*
> *associated with the 'Battle of the Diamond'*

The Orange Boys

There lived in the Blackwater Valley, near the village of Dyan in County Tyrone, a substantial farmer named James Wilson. He was a large, florid and heavily bearded fellow who was nicknamed 'Buddra' by his friends and neighbours. His grandfather had fought with Walker and the others on the Walls of Derry and another of his name had been with William at the Boyne. As a boy he had sat at the feet of old men and listened to stories of the great Orange victories, and as he grew older he showed a strong pride in the achievements of his forefathers and a great love for the Orange tradition. In the Dyan he was a man of some substance: a Freemason, a hard-working and knowledgeable farmer, and it was said that he 'turned out a good horse and was a fine horseman'. His status as a Freemason has never been clearly established. In some accounts he is described as a 'hedge' or unwarranted Mason, others proclaim him as a free and accepted one.

He attended a meeting of his lodge in Benburb, County Tyrone, on 24 June 1794. On the same date the remains of a prominent Defender were interred in the old graveyard at Confeckle. The funeral was a large one, attended by Defenders from many parts of Tyrone and beyond. After burying their captain, a number retired to a public house in the village where they drowned their sorrows rather too freely, and began abusing and maltreating the Protestant villagers. Windows were smashed, doors kicked in and thatched roofs set ablaze. Villagers ran from their homes in terror.

News of the outrage spread to the surrounding countryside and Protestant farmers flocked to the village to defend their co-religionists; soon Benburb was clear of the intruders. Among those in the thick of it was 'Buddra' Wilson. He had pleaded with his Masonic brethren to join him in getting rid of the mob, but they steadfastly refused. As he mounted his horse for home, he shook his fist at his timorous friends and swore that 'he would light a star in the Dyan which would eclipse them forever.'

Next day he set about forming an organisation for the protection of Protestants with a number of like-minded colleagues, among whom were John and Abraham Dilly, who lived at Derryoughill, near Moy, and a local man named Isaac Jeffs. They were all agreed that something had to be done, and decided to form an organisation called 'The Orange Boys'. They proposed, in imitation of the Prince of Orange, to act as protectors of the Protestant people. Wilson, as their leader, recommended the adoption of a Masonic structure and accordingly they put together a series of codes and passwords, and devised a rudimentary ritual. To evade suspicion, they met again on a furze-topped or 'whinney hill' in Derryoughill and, clasping their hands together, swore on oath to protect their people, defend the Protestant constitution, and maintain a resolute loyalty to the Crown. In one account, they are said to have used a sprig of hyssop in their initiation ritual. If so, it is likely that they were acting out a dramatic passage from the Passover story which lent itself to their purpose:

> Then Moses called all the elders of Israel and said unto them: 'Go and procure lambs for your families, and slaughter them as Passover victims. Then take a bunch of hyssop and dipping it in the blood that is in the basin, sprinkle the lintel and the two doorposts with this blood.
>
> *Exodus 12:21 and 22.*

This version is disputed, as hyssop does not grow on 'whinney' hills. But the practice caught on and became part of later Orange ritual.

Although the formation of the Orange Boys represented a new initiative for 'Buddra' Wilson, he had been politically involved before. Two years earlier he had established an Orange Club in the Dyan with a view to raising Protestant political consciousness. On 1 February 1793, a notice appeared in the *Belfast News Letter* which read:

> At a meeting of 138 members of the Orange Club, near Dyan, County Tyrone. Resolved: at these alarming times, we collectively think it our duty to rouse from our lethargy, like bold Hibernians, in defence of our Sovereign, and venture life and fortune to maintain the Royal Order of His Majesty George III in person, Crown and dignity against all enemies and oppressions whatsoever.
>
> Signed: J. Wilson
> Master

Wilson's followers were tough, no-nonsense types, and their organisation quickly spread along both sides of the Blackwater River. It appealed to small farmers, weavers and landless labourers who were prepared to use their muscle in protection of their interests. By the end of 1789 about twelve Orange Boy lodges had sprung up, and their members — often indistinguishable from Peep O'Day Boys — began priming themselves for a crack at their enemies.

The Diamond

The Diamond crossroads — a hamlet a few miles from Loughgall in County Armagh — was an unlikely spot to achieve distinction. Yet it was the setting for a bloody encounter which would have a huge historical impact and become engraved forever on the hearts of Orangemen. In 1795 the Diamond consisted of six or seven whitewashed cottages which straddled the roads leading to Markethill, Verners Bridge, Loughgall and Portadown. It was the home of cottage weavers, who also worked the land as small tenant farmers. It was a hushed and lifeless place; now and again there might be a cockfight or a small rumpus as a few drunks made their way home from a wake. On the Loughgall side were a few terraced houses owned by a man called Dan Winter. His people had lived in the area (which formed part of the estate of the Copes of Loughgall) since 1665, and he was an assertive sort of fellow who was well known for miles around. A tall, handsome, rugged man, he wore his politics on his sleeve and bore two nicknames: 'Orange Dan' and 'Diamond Dan'. It was whispered that he was a Peep O'Day Boy, and the story was likely true. He had a number of irons in the fire: a farmer, a weaver, a Freemason and, importantly, the proprietor of a public house in the district. He was a relative of 'Buddra' Wilson and it was well known that both Orange Boys and Peep O'Day Boys met clandestinely on his premises. The Orange credentials of his pub were beyond doubt and, to emphasise the point, a large weathered signboard above the door showed a picture of King William crossing the Boyne.

On the evening of the May Fair Day in Loughgall, a cockfight was held at the crossroads and attended by a number of people returning from the fair. One ardent fellow, a Catholic, was foolhardy enough to loiter too long in this Protestant heartland and was set upon by a number of Peep O'Day Boys. Later, as he painfully limped home, he swore vengeance on his assailants. Soon it was reported that Dan Winter's pub had been earmarked for a Defender attack, and within a few days shots were fired at the premises by galloping horsemen.

The June Fair Day in Loughgall brought further trouble. From early morning a large number of strangers were seen in the village, passing signals to one another and showing little interest in the livestock. The Protestant farmers grew apprehensive. About ten o'clock they found themselves, quite suddenly, surrounded. Then, at the peep of a whistle they were jumped upon and assaulted. The strangers laid into them with ash plants and cudgels, and for half an hour Protestant blood flowed. Limbs were shattered, skulls broken and elderly people knocked to the ground. By half past ten the Protestants had been driven from the fair. Four hours later they rallied and, with reinforcements, re-entered the village; after a furious battle with sticks, stones and bottles, the tables were reversed on the intruders who were forced to flee.

From that day forward, things went out of control. The Sovereign of Armagh, McCann, grew alarmed and swooped into the area with companies of newly-raised militia. He arrested about fifty Defenders and a handful of Peep O'Day Boys, identified Dan Winter's pub as the epicentre of local Peep O'Day Boy activity and urged the authorities to revoke its licence. Nothing was done. A Defender attack on the pub was now inevitable, and Dan Winter did not propose to be caught unawares. He alerted 'Buddra' and the Orange Boys, and put the local Peep O'Day Boys on a ready footing.

The Battle

On 14 September, large numbers of Defenders began to assemble in the parish of Tartaraghan to the north of the Diamond. A few days later they took possession of Annaghmore gravel pit and hoisted a white flag with shamrocks running along its borders. Also raised was a large banner showing a picture of the Virgin Mary, which bore the inscription: 'Deliver us from these heretic dogs and set us free'. Their leader was a self-styled 'Captain' Quigley, who exercised dictatorial authority. When he bellowed they ran to him, touching their hats. Every few hours their numbers were increased by new contingents arriving from Cavan, Monaghan and Louth. Their numbers would have swollen further had not local landlord James Verner and his sons alerted the militia at Dungannon, and together they prevented new arrivals crossing the Blackwater River by confiscating the rowing boats and patrolling the banks.

The Defenders, in orderly formation, marched to traditional Irish airs. Their leaders were clad in green, with each man having a feather in his hat for identification. Some carried antique-looking muskets and others were armed with rusty old bayonets fixed to short poles. Quigley, the leader, had a quaint-looking blunderbuss which became an object of fun. Every time he used the weapon, the report was so loud that a cheer went up, 'There goes Quigley!'[1]

The local Peep O'Day Boys were not slow to take arms, aided by the eighteen-year-old William Blacker from Carrickblacker, near Portadown. His father, the Reverend Stewart Blacker, was re-roofing Carrickblacker House, and young William had the task of supervising the workmen. He later wrote:

> My father was adding to his dining room which occasioned the stripping of a considerable quantity of lead from the roof of the house. On the night of Thursday the 17th a carpenter's apprentice, Thomas Macan, and I made free with the best part of the lead and sat up nearly all night casting it into bullets of different sizes which Macan found means of having conveyed to our side next day.[2]

The Peep O'Day Boys, with their Orange Boy allies, gathered on Cranagill Hill and were joined by other Protestant groups, including the notorious Bleary Boys from Waringstown, County Down, whose reputation for rough-and-tumble fighting had gained them doubtful renown. Between the opposing sides lay the townland of Teagy, where the first clash occurred and a Defender lost his life. Both sides took to sniping at each other, but no harm was done, as the distance between them was too great. The sight of hundreds of people congregating on hilltops and firing shots at each other alarmed the local gentry, who came together in the local 'big house', 'Crowhill', the residence of landowner Joseph Atkinson, a Justice of the Peace. They were joined by three Catholic priests, and plans were made to broker a peace. Atkinson later gave his version of events:

> Sometime during the day (18th September) Mr Archdall Cope, and his brother Robert Camden Cope, Mr Hardy, Councillor Archdall, priests Taggart, McParland and Trainor, came to my house and we all went to where the Protestants were stationed on Cranagill Hill. Mr Archdall Cope and Taggart proposed to me to make the Protestants lay down their arms; in reply to which I declared that they should not do so until the others had laid down theirs first, as I considered that the Protestants were entitled to carry arms as the others were not. Upon this, Taggart said 'that they should fight it out', to which I replied, 'with all my heart.' We then rode to where the priests' party was

assembled, when a woman called out, 'There goes Atkinson the traitor!' Immediately one of the party presented a gun at me, when a woman, a tenant on my own property, said 'her landlord should not be shot.' We then went to my house where it was proposed that priest Taggart should go surety for the popish party, if I would go surety for the Protestants, in £500 each. I agreed to do so, the preliminaries were drawn up by councillor Archdall, and signed by me and priest Taggart, the money to be forfeited by the party who broke the treaty. I kept the priests to dinner. At night they proposed remaining until morning. Not having beds for all, I proposed that we sit up all night, which we did. . . .'[3]

With the signing of the treaty, both sides began to withdraw, but fresh contingents of Defenders began to arrive from Newtownhamilton and Keady. These did not feel bound by a treaty entered into in their absence and, besides, they were looking for action. They began to assemble on Faughart Hill, in the townland of Tullymore, just above the Diamond crossroads, and opened intermittent fire on the houses below. The Protestants firmly believed that they had come to drive them from their homes.

The Peep O'Day Boys were about to disperse when they heard the fresh firing, and quickly retraced their steps. With 'Buddra' Wilson at their head, they occupied Diamond Hill, which stands to the north at a place called Ruddocks Grange. Desultory firing continued for a time, then all went quiet. The next day, Sunday, continued quiet, and the Defenders took the opportunity to change their 'Captain'. Quigley, who was a Catholic priest, stepped down, and was replaced by a 'Captain' McGarry.

Just before daybreak on Monday, 21 September (a day which became known later as 'Running'[4] Monday because of the activity of the combatants) the Defenders launched an attack on Dan Winter's pub. Winter and his sons had barricaded the building and returned fire by shooting through the loopholed windows. For over an hour they kept the Defenders at bay, but through sheer weight of numbers the attackers managed to get closer. Two Defenders ran forward with blazing torches and set the thatched roof alight. Within minutes the old building was a blazing inferno. There was no door to the rear, so Dan and his sons had to make their escape by squeezing through narrow windows and running uphill through an orchard.

Meanwhile Quigley, now second in command, and a large party of Defenders tried to rush Diamond Hill. They were beaten back with heavy losses. Young William Blacker, accompanied by the carpenter Macan and others, arrived with supplies for the Peep O'Day Boys. They advanced over the Cranagill Road, which brought them to the rear of

Diamond Hill, but the action was almost over. The Loughgall Peep O'Day Boys had just driven off the Defenders with a number of well-aimed volleys. By now Dan Winter's pub was a smoking ruin. The contents, which included numerous barrels of beer, sacks of flour, quantities of tea and sugar, lay strewn along the roadway. The signboard with William's portrait had been torn down and smashed to frenzied cheering.

When the Winters scampered up the hill at the rear, their comrades were waiting on the brow, and they all lay low behind a thick blackthorn hedge. They waited until the Defenders had finished their ransacking, knowing that shortly they would pursue their quarry. Behind the hedge 'Buddra' Wilson had drawn up his Orange Boys in ranks of two or three, with those in front kneeling and ready to fire. As the disarranged Defenders made their way up the slope, he instructed: 'Wait until you see the whites of their eyes.' They held off until their foes were almost upon them, and then let loose. One volley quickly followed another and the Defenders reeled and fell like ninepins. Next came a furious downhill bayonet charge which overwhelmed the unfortunates who were still advancing. Many lay dead and wounded; others ran in all directions. William Blacker later recalled:

> The affair was of brief duration. The Defenders, completely entrapped, made off, leaving a number killed and wounded on the spot. The exact number who fell in the occurrence, I have never been able to ascertain; from those whom I saw carried off in cars that day and from the bodies found afterwards by reapers in the cornfields along the line of flight, I am inclined to think that not less than about thirty lost their lives.[4]

The victory was total. The Protestants — Peep O'Day Boys, Orange Boys and others — had driven off their opponents and frustrated what they saw as a Defender plan to drive them from the area.[5]

These extraordinary events were watched with mixed feelings by both the authorities in Dublin Castle and the United Irishmen. To the latter they were a source of great concern, as they threatened to destroy the very concept on which their organisation was based. Tone, in his correspondence, expressed his irritation by saying: 'Armagh has always been a plague on us.' Two senior United Irish leaders were dispatched to the scene, but their best efforts to reconcile the sides were in vain. The hostility of race and religion proved stronger than all the arguments of unity and a common cause.

The Founding of the Orange Order

The victors assembled in a field opposite the smoking ruins of Dan Winter's pub and, with their faces still blackened from gunshot powder, and sweat rolling down their cheeks, they clasped their hands and formed a circle around a small bush which grew near a spring well. They vowed a solemn oath to form a greater and more effective brotherhood than hitherto, and to take fresh measures for their mutual protection.

The leaders withdrew to a farmhouse — the ancestral home of the Winter family — about 200 yards from the Diamond crossroads. There they discussed the project in outline and agreed to hold a further meeting that evening in a pub in Loughgall owned by a man named James Sloan. They were a small group: 'Buddra' Wilson, Dan Winter, Sloan the publican, John Dilly from Derryoughill, Thomas Sinclair of Derryscallop, Robert Irwin from Kinnego and a man called Lockhart from Knocknacloy. Also present was Captain John Giffard of the Royal Dublin Militia. Some reports suggest that Giffard was the man who really laid the foundations of the new organisation, and this is very likely true. He later wrote to his friend Captain Willie Beresford in Dublin, saying that he had established at Loughgall 'a society that for generations would crib both pope and popery in Ireland'.

Giffard was already a well-known Protestant ultra, and the bête noire of radicals in Dublin. During the previous year he had been appointed Sheriff of the City, and combined this office with the position of editor of *Faulkners Dublin Journal* — a pro-Castle newspaper. Fitzpatrick, in his book *The Sham Squire*,[6] refers to him as 'an illiterate and illiberal alumnus of the Blue Coat Hospital' and says he:

> . . . began political life, like many a better contemporary, as an ardent patriot and Irish Volunteer . . . He practised as an apothecary . . . but soon forsook the pestle for the pen and acquired the sole editorial control of an influential newspaper . . . He at once prostituted the newspaper to the worst purposes of the venal party, which ruled supreme in Ireland . . . and it has been stated that the paper disclosed such violence, virulence, vulgarity and mendacity that at the present date its advocacy would be held detrimental to the cause of any party. . . . Yet its editor was preferred to places of honour and emolument.[7]

Giffard also held a lucrative place in the Revenue under Mr Beresford, and was called 'The Dog in Office' and his paper 'The Dog's Journal'.

Few of the surviving references to Giffard are flattering. Jonah Barrington speaks of his 'detestation of the Pope and his adoration of King William, on each subject of which he was occasionally delirious'. Henry Grattan once subjected Giffard to a devastating verbal attack, calling him 'the hired traducer of his country, the ex-communicated of his fellow citizens, the regal rebel, the unpunished ruffian, the bigoted agitator!' Giffard was so thunderstruck by this onslaught that he could find no rejoinder more apposite than 'I could spit upon you in the desert.' Giffard was a clever and forceful personality, who would have had little difficulty in influencing the views of the tenant farmers and weavers whom he met in James Sloan's pub.

Little was decided at that first meeting, save that the new body should be exclusively Protestant and more thoroughly organised than previous combinations. It was agreed that a number of 'soundings' should be taken on how the project should proceed. In due course a second meeting was held in Loughgall, and reports on the 'soundings' heard. With whom these were conducted is not known, but it was agreed to press ahead. Captain Giffard was accompanied by Colonel Sheldrake and Captain Cramp, members of an English regiment which may have been on a tour of inspection. The significance of their presence was twofold: Giffard was a government agent, as most likely were the others. Their purpose was to capitalise on the loyalty of the local Protestants and to utilise this as a counterweight to the propaganda of the United Irishmen which was beginning to sweep down the Lagan Valley. Secondly, like Wilson, Winter and Sloan, the military men were Freemasons and had little difficulty in persuading the farmers and weavers that the new brotherhood should be based on Masonry.

That this proposal should be attractive is unsurprising. Masonry was going through a period of growth in Ireland; already there were up to 100 Masonic lodges in County Antrim and about fifty in County Down; there was a heavy concentration in and around the Lagan Valley and in many of the Presbyterian belts. Moreover, organisations like the United Irishmen and even the Defenders already had quasi-Masonic structures. 'The Craft's' strong emphasis of collegiality and its elaborate system of codes, catechisms and passwords had an attraction for those who envisaged a body which could gain influence at different social levels. Clearly, Giffard and his colleagues were thinking beyond the immediate concerns of those whom they encountered in Sloan's pub. But the locals were themselves not unthinking; what they sought was an organisation which would offer protection from the Defenders and be sufficiently disciplined to attract the patronage of the gentry and to gain at least the benevolent neutrality of the authorities.

An early decision was taken that the new brotherhood should be called after the Royal House of 'The Great Deliverer', and that those initiated should be known as Orangemen. It would have been easy to adopt another name like, for instance, the 'Diamond Association'. But such a title would have been too localised and may have seemed to refer to a private feud between themselves and the Defenders. The name chosen — the Loyal Orange Society — more properly focused on their history and left no doubt as to their political colour. It also suited their self-image. They were, as their forefathers had been, 'William's Men' and accepted the constitutional settlement which William had won for them.

That tenant farmers, weavers and labourers — people who were not conspicuous beneficiaries of the existing social system — should form an organisation so ostensibly reactionary was a puzzle to contemporary liberal opinion. This was, after all, the high point of the Enlightenment, a time when everywhere men were shuffling off the shackles of ancient authority, and thinking anew on matters like personal liberty and democratic freedom. Why did the Protestant peasantry of south Ulster disregard the new ideas embraced by their co-religionists in other parts of the north-east, and opt for an association whose philosophy was tethered to the status quo?

The truth is that the contemporary liberal and radical analysis of the political propensities of the Protestant peasantry in areas like Armagh was wildly optimistic and therefore defective. The analysis failed crucially to take on board that reasonably well-to-do working people may not seek political or social change, and can have much to lose from it. This is evidently true where such people live among folk less well-off than themselves, whose numbers are threatening. The progressive ideologues were reminiscent of those French Jacobeans who were unable to fathom why the peasantry of the Vendée rejected revolutionary principles. A retort might be that the resistance of the Armagh peasantry was artificially induced, and the result of the Machiavellian skills of figures like Giffard. That there was manipulation is doubtless true, but there was much more to it.

Popular loyalism had deep roots in Protestant culture. The old Williamite tradition may, from time to time, have waxed and waned under the sterility of commemorative ceremonies, yet it lived on. For marginalised Protestants living on the borderlands of Ulster — who inhabited a seismic zone quite different from their co-religionists elsewhere — it remained a vibrant tradition, constantly stimulated by insecurity and rivalry, and by a reflex hatred of the religion of their neighbours. If one asks, for instance, why Presbyterians like 'Buddra' Wilson in Tyrone became Orangemen, while their fellow Presbyterians in Antrim and Down adopted Republicanism, the answer is surely that the politics of Presbyterianism depended more on local factors than on the ideological distinction between subversion and the acceptance of authority. The factors involved were more complex than those of simple economic rivalry with their Catholic neighbours; their whole approach to both history and religion was psychologically completely different.

The First Orange Warrants

James Sloan, the publican, became the nominal head of the new brotherhood and was given authority to issue warrants to enable the first

Orangemen to establish lodges. These documents, to begin with, were rough-and-ready slips of paper which bore the name of a person to whom, in time, a real warrant might be issued. They carried Sloan's signature and a crude seal showing William on horseback, surrounded by the words 'King and Constitution'. Sibbett provides an example:

> No. Eighty nine Timakeel July 7th 1796
> James Sloan
> To be renewed in the name of Daniel Balla
> Portadown District

Later, when Wolsey Atkinson (Sloan's brother-in-law) took over as Grand Secretary, the warrants became more sophisticated. Sibbett gives details of what became known as an 'Atkinson Warrant':

> (No. Six) hundred and seventy —
> To whom all these present shall come.
> Our well-beloved Brother John Hyde, of
> Ballymagerny in County Armagh, is hereby
> permitted to hold a Lodge or Orange Society
> at Ballymagerny, in said county — to act as
> Master, and perform the Requisites thereof.
> Given under my hand and Seal of Office at
> Portadown in the County of Armagh, this
> Third day of September 1798
>
> Wolsey Atkinson
> Grand Secretary of the
> Orange Societies of Ireland[8]

The price of the warrants was that of an old Irish guinea (£1.2s.9d.) — a cost sufficiently high to discourage lowly elements like the lumpen 'Peep O'Day Boys', from whom the new brotherhood now wanted to disassociate themselves. A new loyalist body could go far with official and landlord support; without it, the future would be bleak, so it was necessary to exclude any who might compromise the project.

There are at least three conflicting accounts of how the early warrants were allocated, and particularly on how the Dyan, in County Tyrone, secured the first one. The confusion is deepened by the tradition that 'Buddra' Wilson did not join the new brotherhood, but left Loughgall expressing hostility towards it. This may have been because he made a bid for the leadership and was rebuffed. His past may have been too murky for the respectable element who now took control and who, unlike himself, were mainly members of the Anglican communion. Yet it is interesting that Warrant No. 2 went to Derryscallop, and Nos. 3 and 4 to Derryoughill and Knocknacloy. These districts are close to one another and would have come within the catchment area of Wilson's Orange Boys. It is not improbable that Wilson was ejected from the leadership of the organisation which he had founded, and that it went on to re-invent itself under a new name and auspices. Whatever happened, Wilson, from this time, became less prominent.

Edward Rogers, of Armagh, who was well-versed in Orange lore, wrote:

> After the struggle at the Diamond some persons from that locality (i.e. the Dyan) came to Loughgall for the purpose of procuring from Sloan the necessary authority for admitting members into their lodge. Being in the garden at the time, Sloan directed them to the village to procure writing materials. During their absence, James Wilson on a similar errand arrived from the Dyan. On being informed that there was neither pen nor ink, he at once replied: 'If that be all, I can provide against that, and 'tis best; for the first Orange warrant should not be written by anything made by the hand of man.' Taking a sprig from a tree of hyssop, which grew in the garden, he handed it, together with the cover of a letter, to Sloan. Sloan, on being taken aback at the novelty of the proceeding, incautiously signed the paper, establishing the claim of the Dyan men to a number which, by right, should not have left the vicinity of the field of victory. When the men who had gone to the village returned and found what had been done, nothing could exceed their disappointment; and finally they refused to take a warrant. Others more fortunate were stepping in, and these poor fellows now rejoice in the possession of Number 118.[9]

There is also a tradition, unconnected with Rogers, which says that the Dyan men drew blood from their arms and, using a sprig of hyssop as a pen, signed the first warrant in their own blood. Sibbett, who examined the matter carefully, found Rogers' account implausible,[10] as he thought it unlikely that a pen and paper would have been unavailable in a public house which doubled as a general store. Moreover, he felt that the reference to Sloan directing the men to the village did not ring true, as the pub was situated on the main street. The reference to the sprig of hyssop may have had a connection with the ritual developed by Wilson and his men on the 'whinny hill' a few years before. And it could be that Rogers was simply spicing the story. The tradition that the initial warrants were signed in blood is more than a little dramatic, but it is not fantastic, given that Orangemen of a later generation used their blood when signing the Solemn League and Covenant against Irish Home Rule in 1912.

The second account came from a Mr Woods, a Loughgall Orangeman, who made no reference to a sprig of hyssop. He spoke of many men arriving at Sloan's pub for warrants and said that the Dyan men received No. 1 by mere chance. In his view, Dan Winter and his colleagues from the Diamond held back from pique, and therefore missed out on the early numbers.

The third version comes from James Verner Hart, a prominent nineteenth-century Orangeman, who related a story that he had learnt from his father who had fought at the Diamond. When giving a lecture to an Orange Lodge at Eldon, County Armagh, in 1875, he said:

> The tired Protestants, whose homeward road from the Diamond led through Loughgall, stopped for refreshments at the inn kept by James Sloan, whom I personally knew, and there they formed an Orange Lodge, after the model of the Freemasons.

He went on to explain:

> Every neighbourhood formed its own lodge; but it was soon found necessary to summon delegates to represent the lodges at large meetings, the members were obliged to number them. They summoned a meeting for the purpose, put the requisite numbers into a hat and drew them out one by one; and thus the Dyan, near Caledon, happened to get Number 1 instead of Loughgall where the first Orange Lodge was formed. My father, who was a clerk in Lord Hertford's office in Lisburn at the time, was delegated to go to Loughgall, and being there initiated, to bring the system to Lisburn. He did so and was energetically assisted by Thomas Verner (brother-in-law to Lord Donegall) who resided at Lisburn as Collector of Excise.

Details of the allocation of the early warrants have survived:

- No. 2 was received by Thomas Sinclair, who came from Derryscallop, County Armagh. He was a substantial farmer and linen merchant, and became a lieutenant in the Churchill corps of the Yeomanry which was shortly to be established. He had fought at the Diamond and held the position of Master of his Lodge until his death.
- No. 3 went to Derryoughill, not to Isaac Jeffs or the Dilly Brothers who were, significantly, friends of 'Buddra' Wilson's, but to a man named Bartley. He was a master tailor, and legend has it that he was so excited with his prize that he swam across the Blackwater River to take the short cut home.
- No. 4 was given to Lockhart from Knocknaclog. He had fought at the Diamond and was present at the first meeting in James Sloan's pub.

- No. 5 was obtained by Robert Irwin of Kinnego. Like many early Orangemen, he was initiated during a ceremony behind a ditch.
- No. 6 went to Killilea, County Armagh, but the name of the recipient has not survived.
- No. 7 was given to Thomas Lecky of Breagh, County Armagh. He was known for his quick temper and is said to have brandished his blackthorn stick over the heads of his brethren to obtain an early number. His lodge initially met in a lime kiln.
- No. 8 went to Richard Robinson of Timakeel, a man who had been involved in the fight at the Loughgall fair and who had played a leading part at the Diamond.
- No. 9 was given to a man from the Portadown area whose name has not survived.
- No. 10 fell to George Templeton, who led the assault against the Defenders at Faughart Hill.[11]

William Blacker was probably the first of the landed gentry to join. He later described the inaugural meeting of his lodge in the frame of a half-built house on the Carrickblacker estate: 'It was a scene not unworthy of the pen of a Scott or the pencil of Salvator Rosa to view the assemblage of men, young and old, some seated on heaps of sods or rude blocks of wood, some standing in various attitudes, most of them armed with guns of every age and calibre . . . inasmuch as rust and antiquity had blighted the spring of their days into utter incapacity to strike fire. There was a stern solemnity in the reading of the lesson from Scripture and administering the oath to the newly admitted brethren.'[12]

Sloan's House

So great was the anxiety of rank-and-file Orangemen to obtain early warrant numbers that James Sloan had to be satisfied with No. 28. In the beginning all lodges were of equal status, but Sloan's was *primus inter pares*, and a warrant was not a warrant unless signed either by him or by the Grand Secretary Wolsey Atkinson. Today 'Sloan's House' (as it is known to Orangemen) still stands on the main street in Loughgall but bears little resemblance to the building of 200 years ago. Then the front door opened in a hallway, which ran through to a small room overlooking a sizeable garden. Very often the house was unable to hold all who gathered there, and a summer house was used for Orange ceremonies. The room where 'Buddra' Wilson, Dan Winter and the others held their first meeting has today been turned into an Orange Museum. Among the many sashes, banners and other paraphernalia on display is the table on which Sloan signed the first warrant, and hanging on the wall is the blunderbuss used by 'Captain' Quigley at the Battle of the Diamond. Outside, over the door, a small tablet reads:

> This tablet was placed here by the Imperial
> Grand Orange Council of the World, 13th
> July 1937, to mark the birthplace of the
> First Lodge of the Loyal Orange Institution
> of Ireland, following the Battle of the
> Diamond, 21st September 1795.

> Fear God, Honour the King, Love the Brotherhood[13]

The Winters of the Diamond

Dan Winter and the men from the Diamond may have been peeved at not receiving warrant No. 1, but they settled for No. 118, which went on to become one of the most renowned lodge numbers. The Winter family themselves became enthusiastic members of the Order and have maintained, to this day, an unbroken connection. Nowadays the banner of Lodge 118 bears a beautifully painted picture of Dan Winter's cottage[14] — known as 'the birthplace of Orangeism' — and was unfurled in 1965 by the late Mrs J.R. Winter, wife of 'Diamond' Dan's great-great-grandson. Her grandson, Geoffrey Daniel Winter, is the lodge's current Worshipful Master. In fact, today Old 'Diamond' Dan has no less than six great-great-great-great-grandsons who are members of No. 118!

It is interesting to note that this lodge is one of the most traditional in the Order. Its members continue to wear the old-style sash, except for the officers who wear the modern collarettes when on parade, and the brethren have never marched behind a band, preferring to step it out to the sound of a single lambeg drum. For years the lodge met in a variety of places around the Diamond-Grange area until, in the years before the Great War, a Mrs Ruddock became so frustrated with the Orangemen using her parlour that she gave them a site for their first (and only) Orange Hall, which was completed just before the Great War. More recently an old warrant number — No. 85 — was awarded to another local lodge (known as the Diamond Memorial), which meets in a fine modern hall just north of Diamond Hill.

On 23 September 1995, a fine monument of black ebony stone was unveiled a little way from Dan Winter's cottage. Its inscription reads: 'This monument is erected by the Grand Lodge of Armagh to commemorate the bicentenary of the formation of the Orange Order after the Battle of the Diamond on 21st September 1795.'

—13—

Orangeism Takes Root

Now Armagh County still hold dear,
Grand secrets there were found . . .
Old Erin's shore we'll still adore,
And that grand spot you know
Where our true Order first saw light
One hundred years ago.

*— from a ballad written by an anonymous
member of Loyal Orange Lodge No. 124
to celebrate the centenary of the
Battle of the Diamond in 1895.*

The Armagh Outrages

Following the Battle of the Diamond, the Protestant peasantry went on the offensive and began a series of night raids against Catholics. These became known as the 'Armagh Outrages', and Lecky described them thus:

A terrible persecution of the Catholics immediately followed. The animosities between the lower orders of the two religions which had long been little bridled, burst out afresh and, after the Battle of the Diamond, the Protestant rabble of County Armagh, and of part of the adjoining counties, determined by continuous outrages to drive the Catholics from the country. Their cabins were placarded or, as it was termed, 'papered' with the words 'To Hell or Connaught', and if the occupants did not at once abandon them they were attacked at night by an armed mob. The webs and looms of the poor Catholic weavers were cut and destroyed. Every article of furniture was shattered and burnt. The houses were often set on fire, and the inmates were driven homeless into the world. The rioters met with scarcely any resistance or disturbance. Twelve or fourteen houses were sometimes wrecked in a single night. Several Catholic chapels were burnt and the persecution, which began in the County of Armagh, soon extended over a wide area in the counties of Tyrone, Down, Antrim and Derry.[1]

The Orangemen claimed that uncontrollable Peep O'Day Boy elements, who were not members of the Order, were responsible. They also claimed that the outrages were exaggerated and in some instances a hoax. It was suggested that the Catholics had themselves put their homes to the torch, so as to claim compensation under the Whiteboy Acts. It was also put about that they had left their properties to avail of cheaper land prices elsewhere. These arguments were specious and heard with disdain.

It cannot be established that Orangemen, acting as such, were responsible for the terror, but it is likely that a number wore two hats: one, as upright citizens when acting as Orangemen, and another when engaged in moonlight activities against Catholics. It strains credulity that Orange Boys or Peep O'Day Boys could be transformed overnight into subdued and disciplined members of a new organisation. Some apologists suggested that the outrages would have been worse but for the restraint imposed by the lodges. This may well be so, but it nourished the suspicion that Orangemen were responsible for the terror.

Thousands of Catholics sought refuge across the Shannon. Lord Altmont, the largest landowner in Connaught, wrote to the Under Secretary at Dublin Castle: 'The emigration from the northern counties to these parts still continues and I consider it the more alarming because the extent of it does not seem to be understood, nor the causes to have been sufficiently investigated by the Government.' Indeed, the Government seemed complacent. Thomas Pelham, the Chief Secretary, made a speech which tended to minimise what was happening, and provoked the Earl of Moira to respond (October 1796):

> The newspapers mention you as having said in your speech on the first day of the session, that the violence suffered by his Majesty's Catholic subjects in County Armagh had been much exaggerated. Lest false information should have been designedly given to you upon so serious a point, I cannot but feel it incumbent to assure you, Sir . . . that the outrages have gone on to a much greater extent than I have ever heard stated in Dublin, and the persecution is even now continuing with unabated activity . . . Upon reading your speech, I deemed it advisable to procure an authenticated account of the number of my tenantry who have been driven within the last year from four townlands within the parish of Tullylish. I have the honour to enclose a list of ninety-one persons who have been expelled from

their positions, and I have to add that most of them have had their property either destroyed or taken; many have been cruelly wounded . . . The place where this has happened is in the heart of the linen manufactures and in one of the most industrious parts of Ireland.[2]

Lord Gosford's Address

Three months after the Battle of the Diamond, on 28 December 1795, the Earl of Gosford, Governor of County Armagh, called an emergency meeting of magistrates and landowners to consider the state of the county. The most important people in the region assembled in his drawing-room, including William Brownlow, powerful grandee and Member of Parliament for Lurgan; Colonel James Verner, Member of Parliament for Dungannon and the owner of the estate at Churchill near Verners Bridge; A.J. Macan, the Sovereign of the Town of Armagh; Reverend Stewart Blacker, Archdeacon of Dromore and Rector of Seagoe (father of the young man who carried ammunition to the Diamond), and such notables as John Ogle, Sir Caple Molyneux, and Michael Obins. Among them were three clergymen who became bishops of the Established Church: Reverend C.M. Warburton, Reverend William Bisset, and Reverend Hugh Hamilton. A single Catholic turned up.

Gosford is reported to have given a speech which became controversial when quoted by Grattan and Philpott Curran in Parliament, and was to haunt Orangemen for years to come. It ran:

> Gentlemen, having requested your presence here today, it becomes my duty to state the grounds upon which I thought it advisable to propose this meeting . . . It is no secret that a persecution, accompanied by all the circumstances of ferocious cruelty, is now raging in this county. Neither age nor even acknowledged innocence as to the late disturbances, is sufficient to excite mercy, much less afford protection. The only crime which the wretched objects of this merciless persecution are charged with, is a crime of easy proof: It is simply a profession of the Roman Catholic faith. A lawless banditti have constituted themselves judges of this new species of delinquency, and the sentence they pronounce is equally concise and terrible; it is nothing less than a confiscation of all property, and immediate banishment. It would be extremely painful, and surely unnecessary, to detail the horrors of so wide and tremendous a proscription, that certainly exceeds, in the number of those it consigns to ruin and misery, every example that ancient and modern history can afford. For in what history of human cruelties have we read, of more than half the inhabitants of a populous country deprived at one blow of the fruits of their industry, and driven, in the midst of winter,

to seek shelter for themselves and their helpless families where
chance may guide them? . . . The spirit of impartial justice (without
which law is nothing better than tyranny) has disappeared in this
county, and the supineness of the magistracy is a topic of
conversation in every corner of the kingdom. It is said in reply that
the Roman Catholics are dangerous. They may be so; they may be
dangerous from their numbers, and still more for the unbounded
views they have been encouraged to entertain. But I will venture to
assert that upon these very grounds these terrible proceedings are not
more contrary to humanity than they are to sound policy. . . .[3]

Gosford's appraisal was beyond contradiction, and the meeting
passed resolutions that the Catholics were 'grievously oppressed by
lawless persons unknown, who attack and plunder their houses by night,
unless they immediately abandon their lands and habitations'. A
committee was formed 'to receive information on all persons of whatever
description who disturb the peace of this county' and measures were
taken to quell the disturbances. But the violence continued. In February,
Grattan quoted from Gosford's speech — which was printed as a
handbill and received wide circulation — when he spoke in Parliament:
'Much,' he claimed, 'has been said of the Defenders, nothing of the Irish
version of the Lord George Gordon riots in London, of the bigotry, of the
Protestant banditti who, being of the same religion as the state, have
committed the most horrid murders, massacred in the name of God, and
exercised despotic powers in the name of liberty.' Curran, following him,
claimed that 1,400 people had been driven from their homes. The
government benches were silent.

But the Orangemen were not undefended. Colonel James Verner rose,
and said:

The Orangemen were loyal to the King and well-disposed towards
the constitution. If they had come into collision with the Catholics in
Armagh, the Catholics were themselves to blame. They had been
robbing Protestants of their arms and assembling, to use their own
words 'to destroy man, woman and child of them.' Under the
pretence of making peace, they had fallen on the Protestants without
notice. They had been beaten as often as they tried the experiment. Of
those who left the county, many were involved in outrages and afraid
of arrest. Others had sold their farms and emigrated to cheap land in
Connaught. Orangemen had been accused of many crimes, but they
had not threatened the magistrates or destroyed cattle or burnt the
houses of those who attempted to enforce the law. In some instances
they had acted improperly, but not until they had been goaded
beyond the forbearance of human nature.[4]

It was a hot-blooded speech, and Verner sat down to mutterings of approval. The Orange tradition provided a bond between Protestants at all social levels, although some may have found the methods of the Orangemen a trifle rough. But whether the government, at this time, was sympathetic to the Orangemen is unclear. It had a dislike for 'popular' movements and was hesitant about them. A few weeks earlier an attempt had been made by a number of Dublin ultras, led by Lord Carhampton, to establish a 'Protestant Party' to 'aid the civil power in the face of seditious movements'. But there were few in the group who were not office holders or placemen and, with the history of the Volunteers of 1782 in mind, the Lord Lieutenant, the Earl of Camden, quickly stamped on the idea.

Rumours abounded. One was of an Orange conspiracy to exterminate Catholics which, it was said, involved the complicity of Dublin Castle itself; another asserted that Orangemen were required by their lodges to take extermination oaths. The Orangeman became, for the Catholic peasantry, a bogeyman whom they feared would come in the night. The United Irishmen were not slow to fan these fears in their recruitment drives. What better way to beat off the bogeyman than to take arms against him?

Orange apologists maintained that Gosford's speech could be taken with a pinch of salt. Textual analysis showed that nowhere did he mention the word 'Orangeman', nor did he suggest that the outrages were inspired by them. Colonel James Verner supported this view; he said that he had no recollection of Gosford giving any such address. Besides, Gosford was later found to be friendly enough towards the Orangemen. As to Grattan and Curran, it was noted that they had no direct knowledge of events in Armagh and had based their speeches on rumour and hearsay. This, it must be emphasised, was the case for the defence. To many people the activities of the Orangemen — or those associated with them — were beyond dispute and left an ill odour.

The violence continued until firm action was taken at the Spring Assizes by the Attorney General, John Wolfe. In Armagh, he declared 'that he would undertake to convince His Majesty's subjects, whatever their religious profession might be . . . that they could rely on receiving protection from every species of oppression.'[5] A number of terrorists on both sides were jailed, and two Defenders and two Orangemen were sentenced to death. Wolfe was seen to be impartial, and even the *Northern Star*, the organ of the United Irishmen, admitted:

> the Attorney General, on behalf of the Crown, evinced the utmost impartiality. Catholic witnesses who had been deterred from coming forward for fear of the Orange reprisals, were given a military guard to protect them.

By this time a reaction had set in, and the violence petered out. Some said that the canny Orangemen had cautiously turned down the heat, lest they alienate the gentry whose patronage they were canvassing.

The Marksman's Degree

The gentry at first did not know what to make of the Orange Order. They were reluctant to join an organisation in which they would have to rub shoulders with people of low rank. Like the government, they had no love of 'popular' movements. Yet the Order was different from other peasant organisations. It loudly proclaimed its loyalty, and its zeal for the Protestant faith. It also pledged itself to uphold lawful authority. These were dangerous times and the forces of law and order were prepared to accept allies wherever they could be found.

Defenderism had spread throughout the country and become mingled with the United Irishmen. Until recently a distinction could be made between these organisations — the Defenders had been primarily concerned with agrarian issues and the United Irishmen with parliamentary reform — but now both had become revolutionary, seeking to topple the government and break the connection with England. Seditious literature was being disseminated and sinister figures were administering unlawful oaths. It was also known that their leaders were in touch with the French.

The Orangemen were implacably opposed to all revolutionary groupings, and took an oath which left no doubt as to where they stood:

> I do sincerely promise and swear that I will be faithful and bear true allegiance to His Majesty King George the Third, and that I will faithfully support and maintain the laws and constitution of this Kingdom and the succession to the throne of His Majesty's Illustrious House. So help me God.

The gentry could not but look favourably on such an organisation. In spite of its unsavoury reputation and associations, its usefulness was obvious; the question was how to control it. The Orangemen themselves came up with the answer. They decided to introduce a new degree or second level of membership. This, they felt, would place more onerous obligations on their wilder spirits and bring greater control. It was a logical development, as it was customary for Masonic-type brotherhoods to operate a multi-degree system. Since the founding of the Order, the 'system' had consisted of one degree, 'The Orange'. This had been put together on the advice of John Giffard and was based, loosely, on the first degree of Craft Masonry, that of Entered Apprentice. Creating a second degree was not, however, an easy matter for unsophisticated men like Winter, Sloan and Wilson. They needed something different from

'The Craft', a 'working' which would be both functional and have a sound allegorical base. To be effective it would need to be tied to key Protestant beliefs or instincts. That a biblical theme would be well-suited was apparent, but which one?

The matter was resolved at the Summer Fair in Portadown, when Sloan, Wilson and Winter met up with John Templeton, a member of a local Masonic Lodge. Templeton was well versed in Masonic lore and much given to Biblical quotation. He invited the Orangemen into the lodge room, where a number of emblems and other paraphernalia were untouched following an earlier meeting. Here the second degree was formulated, largely by Templeton, and given the name 'Orange Marksman'. Its motif was taken from the Exodus story and the term 'Marksman' — which is also found in Freemasonry — adopted because of a scriptural reference. The Israelites, when crossing the Jordan, had left twelve memorial stones to mark the spot where the Ark of the Covenant stood when the waters were rolled back. In this sense they were 'marksmen' — that is, people who 'marked' at the behest of the Lord (Joshua 4: 1-8). In Freemasonry the term has a quite different meaning; it refers to the time-honoured practice of operative masons carving their marks on stone buildings.

It was agreed that initiates to the new degree should wear a ribbon of purple, blue and orange, and be required, for mutual recognition, to learn a password which ran:

Q — Why do you wear that?

A — Because I am free

Q — Free of what?

A — Of the Wilderness

Q — Whence come you?

A — From the Land of Moab

Q — Whither do you go?

A — To the plains of Jericho

Q — How do you get there?

A — By a password

Q — Have you that password?

A — I have

Q — Will you give it to me?

A — I will divide it with you; it is 'The Ark of God'

Q — Why do you make purple your colour?

A — Because the ornaments on the curtains of the Ark of God were purple, blue and red. I chose purple for mine.[6]

A number of Exodus passages were taken up, such as the giving of the Law on Mount Sinai and the wandering in the Wilderness, and these themes were acted out in episodic ritual dramas to give a sense of association with the Chosen People. It was a winning formula and would stand the test of time. Some of the details were leaked and the ritual had to be reformulated, but a few years later there were more leaks. By this time the brethren had perfected a format which could be adjusted to cope with the odd leak. The meeting with John Templeton is the last reported participation in the Order of 'Buddra' Wilson and Dan Winter. As they faded, new men came forward.

The Spread of Orangeism

With the establishment of greater control many landlords, who at first had stood aloof, began to take an interest. Some had been involved from early on — the Blackers of Carrickblacker, the Atkinsons of Crowhill, and the Verners of Churchill. These were now joined by the Maunsells of Drumcree, the Clarks of Summerisland, the Warings of Waringstown, and the Brownlows of Lurgan. From this time Orangeism became as much a 'top down' as a 'bottom up' movement. It represented a cohesive combination of landlords and tenants acting jointly, and stiffened Protestant resistance to the propaganda of the United Irishmen. The Order set about the political management of the areas in which it was strong. Waverers were brought into line, and those who had been passive or quiescent in the face of republicanism were emboldened to resist it. Protestants who had fled to the safety of the towns were given heart and encouraged to return. A new confidence arose as the faded fabric of the Orange tradition was taken out and refurbished. In the new atmosphere the Order grew beyond all expectations. Although its greatest strength lay in Armagh and in adjoining areas of Down and Tyrone, it soon began to seep into the Lagan Valley and, through the zeal of Anglican clergymen, took root among the tenants of landed estates. Lodges became numerous to the east and west of Lough Neagh, and it spread by way of Stewardstown into south Londonderry and parts of Donegal.

A most important figure was James Hart, an Armagh man who held a senior position on the Hertford estate in Lisburn. He had fought, with his brother-in-law, at the Diamond. On the founding of the Order, he was one of the first to make his way to Loughgall to be initiated. His enthusiasm impressed James Sloan, and he was appointed the Order's first organising agent. On returning to Lisburn he set to work among the Hertford tenants, and within a few weeks had established a dozen lodges in the area. Not far away was the large military camp at Blaris Moor. Here the persuasive Hart is credited with establishing the first military lodges; 'travelling' warrants were issued to regiments who transferred elsewhere. Soon Orangeism was found in the midlands and as far south as Limerick, Cork and Kerry.

Hart is also recognised as the man who took Orangeism to the republican stronghold of Belfast, although republicanism may not have been as deeply rooted there as commonly supposed. He was well received, indeed heartily welcomed, by a number of people prominent in the commercial life of the town. These are usually given as Henry Moore, William Ewart, Christopher Hudson, James Law and Stephen Daniel, and are significant in that their high social standing and willingness to financially support the lodges enabled the Order to take root in what was previously considered unpromising soil.

Demise of the Northern Star

The *Northern Star* lost no time in coming out against the new Belfast Orangemen. In its issue of 28 March 1796 it accused them of planning a massacre of known United Irishmen. It said: 'The Orangemen meditated an attack on the town of Belfast and were determined to destroy the persons and habitations of those who promoted a union of Irishmen.' In making such remarks in a period of heightened reaction, the paper was skating on thin ice, and, in fact, did not long survive.

In July 1796 there was a report that two republicans, Daniel Shanahan and Joseph Cuthbert, had driven out to Blaris Moor and distributed money among the soldiers camped there to gain their favour. Early in 1797 Colonel Charles Leslie uncovered a republican nest in the Monaghan Militia stationed at the camp; a large number of men had taken the United Irish oath. The regiment was paraded and told that it was in extreme danger unless the guilty confessed. Seventy did so. Of these, four — Daniel Gillan, Peter Carron, and the brothers Owen and William McKenna — were identified as ringleaders. A court martial was held and they were found guilty of 'exciting, causing, and joining in mutiny and sedition in the said regiment'. On the same day, they were made to kneel on their coffins before a firing squad.

The rest were pardoned and the humiliated regiment lost no time in refurbishing its reputation. To prove their loyalty the men became excessively aggressive towards suspected republicans. The privates and NCOs drew up a loyal declaration and submitted it to the *Northern Star* for publication. When the editor refused to print the document, the offices were broken into and sledgehammers used to smash the type and presses. The paper ceased publication and nothing was done to bring the perpetrators to justice. The authorities, in fact, acted as if a painful thorn had been removed from their side.[7]

Hart had by this time moved on to Larne, and was very successful in spreading Orangeism throughout Antrim. But the Order's rapid growth brought problems.[8] Many of the new Orangemen — who appear, in some instances, to have been initiated en masse — were similar to the

Peep O'Day Boy types of a year or so earlier. The tightened rules were ineffective in controlling them, and they frequently rampaged through Catholic areas, putting houses, barns and churches to the torch.

The Orange Order's First Public Appearance

By the summer of 1796 the Order was strong enough to make its first public appearance. It planned a number of demonstrations in areas near its home base for 12 July. Some, like General William Dalrymple, the army commander in Belfast, were apprehensive and felt that the demonstrations could lead to violence.

In the event, things passed off calmly. Marches were held at Portadown, Lurgan and Waringstown, and Lord Gosford was so impressed that he wrote to the Lord Lieutenant on the following day:

> I have the honour to acquaint Your Excellency that the meeting of Orangemen took place yesterday in different parts of the country. After parading through Portadown, Loughgall and Richfield they came towards this place. They halted about half a mile from my house and sent a courier to enquire whether I had any objection to allowing them to march through part of my demesne. My answer was that if they were sober and orderly I could have no objection . . . They accordingly came here about five o'clock in the evening, marching in regular files with orange cockades, and distinguished by their number of flags . . . The devices on the flags were chiefly portraits of King William, and on the reverse side of some of them I perceived a portrait of his present Majesty and the motto, 'God Save the King'. They were perfectly quiet and sober . . . The number who paraded amounted, I should imagine, to about fifteen hundred.[9]

This was a remarkable change of view for a man who a short time before was presumed to be hostile to Orangeism. General Dalrymple, too, adjusted his earlier impressions and wrote to the Chief Secretary, Thomas Pelham:

> The behaviour of the people at the Orange festival on the 12th was faultless. I received a great many assurances that in future no countenance will be given to any outrages, and I am inclined to believe them. In County Armagh they are chiefly over, but in Down and Antrim they still prevail.[10]

But not everyone was pleased. The *Northern Star* (which was still being published at this date) reported the 'Twelfth' by saying:

> The gentlemen called Orange Boys who have desolated the County of Armagh during the last year, paraded publicly in large numbers

through the towns of Lurgan, Waringstown and Portadown. This banditti . . . paraded in open day, under banners bearing the King's effigy and sanctioned by the magistrates. Irishmen! Is this not plain enough?[11]

A letter to the editor asked:

> Is it truth that higher powers have hired so-called Orangemen, at five guineas per man and one shilling per day to disturb, destroy and harass harmless inhabitants because they are Irishmen?

The Orangemen worked hard to gain acceptance by the powers-that-be. They drafted a 'humble petition' — really a policy statement — and submitted it to the magistrates who had met for the Summer Assizes in Armagh. It said:

> That at a time when disloyalty and disaffection pervades the land we should think ourselves wanting were we not to declare our sentiments . . . We declare that we are willing and ready at all times to step forward in support of our rightful sovereign King George III and his royal successors of the House of Brunswick, in support of the civil magistrates in the execution of their duty. Having learned with concern that every act of violence and outrage is imputed to us, we deny the charge with contempt. Our principles bind us in a most sacred and solemn manner to the contrary. We abhor and detest Defenders, Peep O'Day Boys or others and declare ourselves separate from them. Our principles are sacred and as distinct as that venerable body of Brotherhood called Freemasons. If our principles were thoroughly known, your Honours would cherish and support our Institution. We therefore pray that you may appoint one of your number to inspect our principles which can be obtained by observing certain solemn obligations. Having declared our loyal intentions to our King and Constitution; we humbly pray that you will take us under your protection; grant us favours agreeable to our merits, as we intend to assemble in a peaceful, quiet and orderly manner to celebrate the Glorious and Immortal Memory on 12th July.[12]

The Vicar of Derriaghy

Although a number of Presbyterians were associated with the Order from the beginning, it was essentially an Anglican movement. The parishes in which it originated were solidly Anglican, and Anglican clergymen adopted it quickly. Among the best known of these was Reverend Philip Johnson, the Vicar of Derriaghy. His parish lay astride the Antrim-Armagh border and directly in the path of the south-westerly sweep of United Irish propaganda. Johnson embraced Orangeism with open arms, although he took some time before joining the Order, being initiated in 1798 and later becoming Grand Chaplain.

To counteract what he called 'the progress of sedition' he organised the core parishes on the Hertford Estate — Derriaghy, Lambeg, Ballinderry, Glenavy and Lisburn — for the Order. So successful was he that when the government established a yeomanry force, the Hertford Estate was able to supply 1,500 Orange recruits. He became a great zealot and, being a magistrate as well as a clergyman, was to the fore in hunting down United Irishmen. His anti-Catholic preaching was such that he was accused of inciting Orangemen to burn down Catholic chapels. The accusation was strenuously denied. While admitting that chapels were burnt, he maintained that he was actually responsible for taking up a subscription to compensate Catholics for the loss of the chapels. The following resolution was passed at a meeting chaired by him in August 1798:

> We, members of the Royal Boyne Society, called Orangemen ... being informed that . . . Roman Catholic chapels in the parishes of Derriaghy, Ballinderry, Glenavy and Aughagallen have been set on fire by some wicked person or persons unknown; and being convinced that such atrocious acts have been committed by the enemies of our King and country with an intention of inciting the Roman Catholics of this neighbourhood to join in the Rebellion, or of supporting the groundless calumny that Orangemen are combined to persecute their Roman Catholic brethren . . . We therefore have contributed the sums annexed to our names towards the repair of the chapels, and we promise to pay double that sum for the discovery and convictions . . . of any person or persons who have committed these crimes.[13]

The sum amounted to almost £60, but did not save Johnson from incurring the wrath of Catholics. A number of unsuccessful attempts were made on his life, the best known being on 8 October 1796, when he rode into an ambush while riding from Lisburn to his home in Ballymacash. He was severely wounded and lucky to escape with his life. In 1803 he became Grand Master for County Antrim.

The Reverend Doctor Cupples

Another Anglican clergyman who played an important role in promoting the Order was the Reverend Snowden Cupples, Rector of Lisburn (1796-1835) and Vicar General of Down and Connor. Today he is best known for an eloquent sermon which he delivered in Lisburn on 12th July 1799 on the tenets of the Order, in which he said:

. . . few things have suffered more unjustly from misrepresentation than the Orange Institution . . . If a steady opposition to French principles and republican theories of government, which have deluged many nations of Europe with blood, be criminal, we plead guilty of the charge. If unshaken loyalty to our beloved and excellent sovereign be a crime, we confess to our guilt. If an inviolable attachment to the Protestant religion and a desire to secure the interest and prosperity of it by all fit and lawful means be reproachful, we certainly merit reproach. We reserve our present happy constitution and, disclaiming revolutionary projects, wish it to be perpetual.

We venerate the Protestant religion, with liberality of sentiment towards those who differ from us, and disavow every species and degree of persecution. These and these only are the principles of Orangemen, and we are neither afraid nor ashamed to acknowledge them. They are not the visionary ephemeral productions of metaphysical subtlety; but have been long tried and approved by the sure tests of reason and experience. They are the old Whig principles, and held by us in common with every good Protestant in these islands. They are handed to us from our ancestors, and we hope to transmit them unperverted and unimpaired, as a precious inheritance, to our posterity. They have been a source of abundant prosperity and comfort to the land of our nativity for more than a century; and in support of them we have declared our readiness 'to shed the last drop of our blood.' We have no secrets to conceal, except the marks and tokens by which we know one another . . . to divulge those would be to destroy their utility, and therefore the knowledge of them is strictly and properly confined to ourselves . . . I trust that you will scrupulously observe in all your meetings due order, sobriety and decorum. . . . By these means, and in these methods, we shall most effectively put to silence the ignorance of foolish and uninformed men, and extract the sting from the tongue of slander. We shall rescue our institution from the power of calumny to injure it, and render it truly and universally respected.[14]

Dr Cupples' words were uplifting, but the standards of which he spoke were, in many instances, observed in the breach rather than the practice. In spite of the best efforts of the leadership, outrages against Catholics continued, and the Catholic peasantry continued to believe that the Orangemen had taken an oath to exterminate them. This matter came to attention dramatically in 1813.

The Strange Case of the Pedlar's Wallet

Poleglass was a small village about a mile from Dunmurray, and less than a mile from Derriaghy. Its Orange Lodge, No. 170, consisted of about two dozen members, one of whom was Thomas Walker. He made his living going from village to village in his horse and trap, vending remnants of cloth which he had purchased from the textile factories in Belfast. He was well known in the countryside, and a familiar sight as he jogged along from place to place. One day, while showing his wares to a housewife in Drumbo, near Lisburn, he became ill and, within minutes, died. Sometime later *The Monthly Magazine*, published in Belfast, ran an article which said that an Orange certificate was found in his wallet, which read:

> We, the Master, Warden and Secretary of the Loyal Orange Association 170 held in Poleglass, in the Kingdom of Ireland, do certify that Thomas Walker did in June 1798 regularly receive the first, second and third degree of a true Orangeman; and that the said Thomas Walker was in June 1809 duly served notice to take the Extirpatory Oath which he, the said Thomas Walker, in the presence of us, refused to take, although duly admonished thereunto. These are, therefore, to caution all Loyal Associations not to recognise him as a Brother, under the present system.
>
> Entered 24 June 1798
> Drew off June 29 1809
> Given under the Hand and Seal of this Society
> this 29th day of June 1809.
> John Ducker, Master
> Jas. Rea, Secretary
> Wm. Martin, Warden.[15]

To some, this was proof positive that an extermination oath existed and a furious correspondence raged in the pages of the magazine and in sections of the press. For weeks there was a great hubbub which led to repeated Orange denials of such an oath, and even to a chemical examination of the seals on the certificate. In time the certificate was discounted as a forgery, but to many Catholic peasants, the story had a ring of truth. The matter has never been fully resolved: Cleary quotes ten 'authorities' to prove his contention that such an extermination oath existed in the early days of the Order,[16] but Sibbett, who was an Orangeman himself, and an official historian of the Order, denied the charge and called it a slander.[17]

Seventy-five years after the death of the pedlar, Timothy Healy, the Nationalist MP, found that there was still political mileage in the charge and gave the wording of the oath as: 'In the awful presence of Almighty God, I, A.B., do solemnly swear that I will do the utmost in my power to support the King and present government; and I do further swear that I will use my utmost exertions to exterminate the Catholics of Ireland.'[18] If such a fantastic and grisly oath ever existed, it may have been of the symbolic variety sometimes employed in Freemasonry, where phrases like 'having my throat cut across and my tongue torn from the root' are used figuratively rather than literally.

—14—

A Land in Flames

Oh the French are in the Bay
They will be there without delay
And the Orange will decay
Says the Sean Van Vocht.

— from an Irish revolutionary ballad

Bantry Bay

By 1796 Ireland was in a revolutionary ferment. The United Irishmen looked to the new French Republic — 'the Morning Star of Liberty' — to help them overthrow the Ascendancy regime, break the connection with England, and establish an Irish republic. Theobald Wolfe Tone, in exile in Paris, opened negotiations with Lazare Carnot, the French Minister of War, and pleaded for a large scale invasion of Ireland. His overtures were reinforced by those of two other envoys, Lord Edward Fitzgerald and Arthur O'Connor, unlikely revolutionaries. Fitzgerald was the brother of the Duke of Leinster, the grandson of the Duke of Richmond, a member of parliament, and heir to large estates. O'Connor was a nephew of Lord Longueville, sat in parliament for Philipstown, County Cork, and was a well-known figure in London drawing rooms. All three were persuasive, and presented the revolutionary situation in Ireland in the best possible light. The French were cautious but eager, and liked hearing that the arrival of troops in Ireland would cause tens of thousands of insurgents to rally to their side. 'To detach Ireland from England,' noted Carnot, 'is to reduce it as a major power and take from it much of its maritime superiority.'

On 15 December 1796, an expeditionary force of forty-three ships, with 15,000 men on board, sailed from Brest under the command of the brilliant young general, Lazare Hoche. From the beginning it was dogged with bad luck. Five ships were crippled in collisions at the time of departure; and when the main fleet reached the open seas it was enveloped in deep fog, with the result that less than half the force succeeded in reaching Bantry Bay. The ship carrying Hoche and the Admiral-in-Command got separated from the main body and made no contact thereafter. Tone, who had been given the rank of Adjutant-General in the French Army, was on board one of the ships, but neither Hoche nor the French Admiral de Galles ever approached the shores of Ireland. A fierce storm in Bantry Bay made a landing seem extremely hazardous. After waiting for a week in the hope that the wind would abate and that the remainder of the expedition would arrive, Grouchy, the second-in-command, began to have second thoughts about landing.

On Christmas Day, Tone, walking cold and disconsolate on the decks of the *Indomitable*, hugging his greatcoat and wrapped in 'gloomy reflections', heard through the storm orders being shouted for the seamen to cut their cables and return to France. But nothing happened. The next day brought disaster. The ships banged into each other in the narrow confines of the bay, and the leading ship, the *Immortalité*, became lost in darkness. Grouchy at last gave orders for all ships to weigh anchor and sail home. Slowly the heavy vessels pushed out into the Atlantic, and Tone gazed back in despair on his homeland as it melted into the mists. He later wrote that he did not wonder why Xerxes had the sea whipped when a storm had destroyed his bridge of boats; he felt like doing the same.

In Bantry the leading Protestant gentleman, Richard White of Seafield House, had watched the ships in the bay and quickly mobilised the local yeomanry. His vigilance did not go unrewarded; he was raised to the peerage as Lord Bantry. Later that morning, he gazed at the sky and watched the hurricane blow itself out, reflecting that it had been a close thing; but Ireland was safe. Providence had prevented it; it had been a Protestant Wind.

The Dragooning of Ulster

During the days that the French ships lay in the Bay there was no supportive stir in the Cork countryside. 'Poor Pat' (Tone's favourite condescending phrase for the Irish peasant) failed to rise to the occasion and refused the high destiny to which he had been called. Instead, as troops marched southwards to engage the French, peasants cleared snow from their pathways and supplied them with food. Yet the Protestant gentry became gripped with panic. Rumours of a landing led to a run on the banks in Dublin and Cork, and some made arrangements to flee the country.

That the French should have come so near to success alarmed Dublin Castle. Vigorous measures were taken against the United Irish conspiracy. The yeomanry, which had been set up under landlord control, sprang to life, and Orangemen rushed to join its corps. The Habeas Corpus Act was suspended and an Insurrection Act was quickly rushed through. This imposed a curfew on many districts, and extensive powers of search and arrest were given to the magistrates. General Gerard Lake, a heavy-handed soldier, was sent to the republican hotbed (or so it was deemed) of Belfast. He issued a proclamation calling for the surrender of illegally-held weapons, and sought information on where they might be concealed. In a short time, nearly 6,000 muskets and bayonets were given up, but Lake knew that a greater quantity remained hidden. He decided to act.

The result was a new paroxysm of terror which eclipsed virtually all previous violence. The conduct of the King's troops, urged on by fanatical Orange elements, put humanity to shame. The most disgusting outrages were perpetrated by a Welsh regiment called 'the Ancient Britons'. Men were murdered, tortured and maimed. They were half-hanged, taken down, and half-hanged again. Women were violated and unspeakable crimes committed against them. Lake's 'dragooning' burnt deeply into the consciousness of the people, and many of the seeds of hatred which would mar future generations were sown.

Orangeism in Dublin

By this time the Order had spread to Dublin. The first to embrace it were high-ranking office-holders; it had a natural constituency among the ultras who had supported Lord Carhampton's plan for a 'Protestant Party' a year or so before. Men like John Giffard had already promoted it in political circles, and figures like Thomas Verner, Archdale Hamilton and William Brownlow utilised their contacts to promote it further. They were pushing, largely, on an open door. The ultras saw the Order as a convenient vehicle to advance their views. They knew that it had been instrumental in driving a wedge between radicals and loyalists in Ulster and felt that it could be similarly deployed elsewhere. Moreover, some believed that they could control it.

On 4 June 1796, the first Orange lodge was established in Dublin. Its early meetings were held in Hannigans Hotel in Grafton Street, under Warrant No. 176. Thomas Verner (the eldest son of James Verner of Churchill, County Armagh) was installed as Worshipful Master and Captain Daniel Ryan, of the Saint Sepulchre Yeomanry Corps, became its secretary. It was Ryan who was responsible for the rather poorly written charter song:

Tell me friends, why are we met here?
Why thus assembled, ye Protestant boys?
Do mirth and good liquor, good humour,
Good cheer, call us to share the festivities joys?
Oh no! 'tis the Cause, of King, Freedom and Laws
That calls loyal Protestants to unite;
And Orange and Blue, ever faithful and true
Our King we support and sedition affright.

The impact of No. 176 was immediate. It became a lodge for high-ranking and socially powerful people, but not, as yet, a Grand Lodge. All lodges at this time were of equal status and there was no central authority, or uniformity of ritual or rules. It was to end such disparities that a special meeting was called for 2 July 1796 in Portadown. The brethren spent the day haggling but could not reach agreement. They decided to adjourn and did not reconvene for ten months. Eventually they sorted out their problems and established the Order's first Grand Lodge in Armagh. William Blacker, still a student at Trinity College but locally very much respected, was elected Grand Master. This lodge was given the status of *primus inter pares* (first among equals) and, at its first meeting, passed a resolution that all lodge members should remit three pence per annum to defray the expenses of Mr Wolsey Atkinson, the lodge secretary. It was further resolved that no lodge could sit anywhere in Ireland without a warrant bearing Atkinson's signature. By thus controlling the warrants, Armagh was able to maintain its position of primacy.

United Ireland Leaders Arrested

United Irishmen, desperately seeking foreign aid, succeeded in securing help from the Dutch republic in 1797, but the attempted invasion of Ireland which resulted was even more unsuccessful than the previous year's fiasco at Bantry Bay. In June, a fleet under Admiral de Winter assembled at Texel with 14,000 troops on board, but unfavourable weather delayed its departure and, when it eventually put to sea, it was intercepted by the British fleet under Admiral Duncan and destroyed at Camperdown.

A change of government in France drove Carnot from power, and in September General Hoche died. It became evident that France was turning away, at least temporarily, from the Irish cause, and Wolfe Tone and his friends had to abandon all hope of early French aid. But the United Irishmen could not stop now. They went ahead with plans for an uprising and nominated 23 May as the date when they would strike. In March they were hit with disaster. For some time the movement had been riddled with spies, and now at least three of these — Thomas Reynolds, Francis Higgins ('the Sham Squire') and Leonard McNally — leaked information to the government which practically destroyed the conspiracy. Members of the Leinster Directory were arrested in a swoop as they met in a house in Bridge Street. The information in this instance came from Reynolds, who was married to the sister of Mrs Wolfe Tone.

Lord Edward Fitzgerald, the effectual leader, managed to escape arrest by a last-minute tip-off. Before long his hiding place was disclosed (by Francis Higgins[1]) and he was arrested at a lodging house in Thomas Street. Three prominent Orangemen were responsible for his apprehension: Major Henry Sirr[2], Captain Daniel Ryan and Major Charles Sandyes. They crept upstairs to take Fitzgerald by surprise; Sirr broke the door and Lord Edward, quickly alert, rushed at him with a dagger. Sirr's pistol rang out and Lord Edward was hit in the arm. Ryan attacked him with a sword cane, and a fierce struggle ensued. In the next few minutes, Sandyes was wounded and Ryan fatally stabbed. Sirr used his pistol again and blasted another hole through Lord Edward's arm. He was then overpowered and taken to Newgate prison, where he died of his wounds several days later.

Rebellion in Wexford

Despite the Dublin arrests and the consequent disruption of their plans, the United Irishmen rose on the appointed day. Isolated risings occurred in Meath, Kildare and Carlow and were suppressed with great violence. At Tara, a body of soldiers put 4,000 badly armed insurgents to flight; and at the Curragh 2,000 surrendered to General Dunbar and were slaughtered while under arrest. Hundreds more were captured and a large number hanged without trial.

In Wexford the fight was long and bitter and, despite lack of arms and training, the insurgents proved more than a match for the regular troops. The county was relatively prosperous, with a large acreage under crops of wheat and barley. The Defenders had existed there for many years, and in 1793 a large bloodbath had occurred outside the town of Wexford itself, when a protest against compulsory military recruitment and tithes resulted in troops firing into a crowd and killing up to eighty people. In 1797 United Irish agents were active in the county, disseminating rumours that the Orangemen were about to descend on Catholics and slaughter them. Many landlords were steeped in the Orange tradition and had never bothered to hide their intolerance; among the most fanatical were the Loftuses of Loftus Hall (south of New Ross), the Rams of Gorey, the Boyds of Rosslare, the Hamilton-Jacobs of Enniscorthy, and smaller fry like the notorious John Hunter Gowan of Mount Nebo near Gorey, and Hawtrey White of Peppards Castle.

In March the authorities imposed martial law on selective areas and the military joined with the magistrates in searching for hidden arms. In the weeks that followed, intensive 'dragooning' took place. There were arrests, burnings and numerous cases of judicial torture. Three months earlier — on 10 January — the first Orange Lodge in Wexford had been established under warrant No. 406 at Mount Nebo, near Gorey, with Hunter Gowan as its Worshipful Master. In April three further lodges were formed, and when the North Cork Militia arrived they brought an officer's lodge with them.

The North Corks, with the Ancient Britons, set about 'roughing up' the Catholics further. When news of the slaughter in Kildare and Carlow reached Wexford, many peasants left their homes and slept in the fields at night for fear of attack. The methods employed by a fiendish sergeant in the Wicklow Militia named Hempenstall made people's blood run cold. He was nicknamed 'The Walking Gallows' for half-hanging his victims by slinging a rope over his tall shoulders and jerking on it as he walked away. They were also terrified of pitch capping, a technique perfected by a sadist in the North Corks known as 'Tom the Devil'. It involved filling a paper bag with pitch and planting it on the victim's head, then setting it alight. Employed too, was the triangle — three tall poles set up as a pyramid, on which victims were spreadeagled and flogged. There is an account of a man, with his flesh having been torn to shreds, begging to be shot and crying out, 'I'm cutting through.' Indeed, there are several reports of flesh being torn from the bone and of internal organs protruding.

Also notorious was a cavalry corps raised by Hunter Gowan, known as 'The Black Mob'. It earned a fearsome reputation and was responsible for numerous barbarous acts. Gowan had begun life as a professional outlaw hunter and was known throughout the countryside as a brutal tyrant whose main interest was casual violence. On one occasion he rode into Gorey with the amputated finger of one of his victims displayed on the point of his sword; the trophy was used as a spoon to stir punch at an Orange orgy in a public house. Some reports suggest that his irregulars were not official Orangemen but enrolled in 'black' or unauthorised lodges. With such heavy-handed methods employed by troops and partisans, the government virtually goaded the people into rebellion.

Boolavogue

On 25 May a group of men were cutting turf in a bog near the small village of Boolavogue, and their local priest, Father John Murphy,[3] was standing on a bank helping them to stack the sods. A troop of yeomanry — or 'yeos', as they were called — began shouting obscenities at the priest, but Murphy restrained his companions from being provoked. As the troops rode off, a number of the men swore to take arms in their own defence or hang their heads in shame. That evening, a beacon fire burst into flame on Corrigrua Hill, about ten miles from Ferns, immediately answered by a flame from the hill of Boolavogue, and soon smoke was seen rising from hilltops all around, signals to the men of Wexford that their hour had come. Father Murphy was to lead the men of Boolavogue. The rebellion, in fact, had begun two days earlier. The Wicklow United Irishmen had risen on the night of 22–23rd May, but had found, as they approached Dublin, that something had gone wrong with their plans; they had retreated to the hills, and were now defying every effort to dislodge them.

Rebel units began to gather at various rendezvous points. Their initial task was to secure arms, and throughout the night attacks were made on the homes of landlords, magistrates and others likely to hold weapons. The militia and the 'yeos' were taken by surprise, and rural Protestants began to make for the safety of the towns. Father Murphy and his men encountered a troop of 'yeos' under Lieutenant Bookey at The Harrow, whom they quickly dispatched, and then marched to the seat of Lord Mount Norris at Camolin Park. Here they came across a great prize — all the pikes and muskets which had been surrendered since 17 March and, with them, some sixty carbines and many sabres, intended for use by the Camolin yeomanry. The next day they took up a position on Oulart Hill, from where a large force of the North Corks tried to dislodge them, but were practically annihilated. Flushed with success, the rebel forces overran in quick succession Camolin, Ferns and Enniscorthy. The town of Wexford became a place of refuge for the Protestants but its garrison was weak, and Murphy's men took up a position at a place called Three Rocks on the outskirts. In spite of additional troops from the Fort at Duncannon, the garrison (aware of their inability to resist the rebels) abandoned the town and made for the safety of the Fort, burning houses and slaughtering peasants as they went. Murphy and his men simply walked in and took the town.

The Attack on Newtownbarry

The rebels established three encampments in different parts of Wexford: one at Three Rocks, one on Gorey Hill, and one on Vinegar Hill just outside Enniscorthy. They now had most of the county under their control, but knew that without help they must eventually fail. It became urgent to break out of Wexford and rouse the people in other counties. With this object they split their forces into three divisions. The first, a body of about 5,000 men, detached itself from the main force at Vinegar Hill and marched to attack the garrison at Newtownbarry (now Bunclody) with a view to opening communications with Carlow and

Kilkenny. The town's garrison was commanded by Colonel L'Estrange, who had a mixed force: 149 'yeos', virtually all Orangemen and led by the Worshipful Master of the Newtownbarry lodge, Captain Kirk:[4] 230 of the King's County Militia; and about forty troopers from the King's Dragoons. The numerical advantage was with the rebels, and the garrison was forced to abandon the town, but instead of consolidating their position the rebels took to the public houses. A number of Orangemen saw what was happening and sent messages to L'Estrange, entreating him to re-engage. He found the rebels completely disorganised and in an unfit condition to fight. About 400 rebels were killed, and their efforts to pass into Carlow and Kilkenny came to nought.

The Battle for New Ross

Three days later an attempt was made on New Ross, to clear the way to Waterford and the south. The rebels made their attack from an encampment on Carrigbyrne Hill, but first rounded up a large number of suspected Loyalists who lived inside a triangular area stretching from Foulkesmills to Adamstown to Fethard, and imprisoned them in a barn on the grounds of Scullabogue House, owned by a farmer named King. The rebels marched to New Ross under the command of Beauchamp Bagenel Harvey, a Protestant landowner who had embraced the radical cause. He had been clamped in jail — essentially to keep him out of the way — a few days prior to the Rebellion, but when Enniscorthy fell was released and asked to use his good offices with the rebels. Being unsuccessful in this, he was induced to join them. He did so reluctantly and — amazingly — they made him commander-in-chief of one of their divisions, although he had no knowledge of military affairs and little capacity for leadership. On the morning of 5 June he issued an ultimatum on New Ross to surrender; the only reply he received was to have his messenger shot dead.

About two in the morning, the rebels came on slowly and in enormous numbers. Scouts said that their number was not less than 20,000, but Major General Henry Johnson, who was in charge of the garrison, estimated it at half that. They marched in order of their baronies and, after sleeping rough for so many nights, presented a wild and savage appearance. Their tattered clothes were distinguished only by the green cockades which they wore in their hats. A number wore ladies' bonnets and female clothing which had been looted from country houses. They pulled up about a quarter of a mile from the town and clergymen were seen moving among them, wearing vestments and carrying crucifixes. Mass was said at the head of every column and for up to an hour they knelt, bareheaded, in prayer.

It was now well after three o'clock, and dawn was breaking. They rose and opened their lines so that a herd of cattle could come rushing through. Driving the cattle before them, they rushed at Lord Mountjoy's regiment; Mountjoy was fatally hit. Soon they penetrated the heart of New Ross, and a deadly battle raged up and down the streets for several hours. The garrison was forced to retreat bit by bit, over the river Barrow and into County Kilkenny. But two parties of troops, one under Major Vandeleur in Irishtown, and another at the Market House, maintained their positions. It seemed as if the rebels had won the day, but they took to plundering and again made for the public houses. Soon, many could be seen dancing in the streets and holding whiskey bottles to their mouths. Behind the river, General Johnson's men regrouped, stormed back into New Ross and with great determination pushed the surprised rebels back towards the main gate, where they re-organised beyond the gate and attacked again. Johnson's men were once more driven back to the Barrow.

One of the inspirational rebel leaders, John Kelly — known as the 'Boy from Killanne' — fell mortally wounded; Johnson seized his opportunity and charged into the town once more. This time he swept all in front of him, and the rebels scattered in all directions. After a battle which had lasted, in all, thirteen hours, the attack on New Ross failed. The number of men which the rebels lost cannot be accurately ascertained, but Musgrave says that Captain Tottenham, the proprietor of the town, 'employed six carts and a great many men for two entire days, in collecting the bodies. Most of those found were thrown into the river. The remainder were thrown into a fosse outside the town wall and buried there.'[5]

Scullabogue

Word went back to Scullabogue that the day was going badly, and orders arrived that the captives were to be killed. John Murphy of Loughnageer, who was in charge, refused to accept two orders on the grounds that they did not come from a sufficiently authoritative source, but when a third messenger arrived and stated that the orders were issued by a priest, Murphy told his men to proceed. Firstly, a number of Protestants held in Scullabogue House were taken onto the lawn and either shot or piked.[6] The doors of the barn were then nailed up and a torch applied to the thatched roof. As the flames rose, the rebels yelled with excitement and drowned the shrieks of those inside. One source[7] says that a child tried to crawl beneath the door of the burning barn, but a pike was stuck in its ribs and it was tossed back into the inferno 'as coolly as a farmer would put his fork into a sheaf of corn'.

Two hundred and twenty-four were held hostage at Scullabogue, the great majority Protestants. Twenty women and children were among the victims. Only three escaped — Richard Grundy, Loftus Fizzel and Benjamin Lett. The date, to be indelibly inscribed on the minds of Irish Protestants, was 15 June 1798.

Vinegar Hill

The rebels retreated to their main camp at Vinegar Hill. The locality all around was scoured, and all Protestants on whom hands could be laid were crowded into a windmill and a barn, and brought out in batches to be piked. Murder mingled with piety. Priests offered Mass at regular intervals in different parts of the camp, and a great tub of holy water was blessed daily so that the faithful could sprinkle themselves. Men were killing cattle, cutting bleeding carcasses to be roasted on the points of their pikes, women were busy boiling stews in great copper pans, everyone had plenty to eat and drink, and some took their meals from silver dinner services pillaged from Protestant homes. Pianos and fiddles had been brought up for those of a musical bent, and blind minstrels played their favourite tunes on stolen harps. Rising above everything was the great bell from the Protestant church in Enniscorthy, mounted between two beams and used for calling the devout to prayer and as an alarm in case of attack. Only a few tents could be seen; the rebels did not need them, as they had become used to lying in the open. Besides, the weather that summer was the best in living memory.

Wexford Bridge

A few days after the battle of New Ross the northern wing of the rebel army, aided by a contingent of Wicklow men, attacked Arklow, the gateway to Wicklow and Dublin. Led by Father Michael Murphy, the curate at Ballycanew, and by Anthony Perry of Inch, they made a fierce but poorly co-ordinated attack on the town. As in many other engagements, courage was insufficient against artillery and cavalry. They were defeated with heavy losses, and Father Murphy himself was killed.

By now large numbers of British troops had arrived in Ireland and a major assault on Wexford was getting under way. Wexford town — where a Republic of Ireland had been declared — was ruled by a Committee of Public Safety, headed by Matthew Keogh, who was appointed military governor. Mobs roamed the streets; about 160 persons, mostly Protestants, were held in jail for their own safety. To escape the fanaticism of the rebels, many Protestants sought conversion to Catholicism and ran to the priests requesting baptism. The priests knew that these were pseudo-conversions, but obliged in order to save lives.

On 9 June a proclamation was issued calling for the arrest of Hunter Gowan, Hawtrey White and two other magistrates who, as the document said, 'had committed the most horried acts of cruelty, violence and oppression against our peaceable and well-affected countrymen'. But they had escaped to the Fort at Duncannon.

On 19 June there was great panic. Gunboats were seen hovering in the harbour and it was believed that the British were about to crush them from the sea. News spread that the rebel camp at Vinegar Hill was being attacked and that Wexford town was being encircled. The mob was egged on by Thomas Dixon, a well-to-do publican and shipowner, and his fanatical wife Margery. In a scene that could have come from the French Revolution, Mrs Dixon appeared on the street holding aloft a pair of orange-coloured fire screens. She announced that she had made an important discovery: she had uncovered the place where the Orangemen held their lodge meetings, and here were their colours. A great cheer went up, and the lady explained that the embroidered allegorical figures on the screens were really Orange symbols. The anchor, shown below the figure of Hope, was a red-hot iron for burning Catholics. Then, she pointed to the blindfold on the figure of Justice and explained that this was a bandage covering the face of a Catholic whose eyes had been pulled out.[8] The mob demanded to know the location of the discovery, and she announced that the lodge was at the house of Colonel de Hunte, a yeoman captain who was already under house arrest. In a convulsion of anger, the mob rushed to where he was held and brutally assaulted him. But for the intervention of a priest, Father Broe, he would have lost his life.

At this time the authority of the Committee of Public Safety unravelled. Governor Keogh was suspected of treachery and had to go into hiding. Thomas Dixon seized his opportunity and gained control of the mob. He and his henchmen marched to the jail and dragged out the prisoners, a few at a time, and subjected them to drumhead trials. Two of the prisoners were forced to make 'full confessions' of their knowledge of an Orange plot to overrun the town. Mrs Dixon suggested that they be taken to the bridge, where large numbers would have an opportunity to see them die. This was agreed, and the first batch was hustled to the Customs House Quay beside the great wooden bridge, led by a man carrying a large black flag with a red cross painted on the centre; under the cross were the letters 'M.W.S.' which were taken to mean 'Murder Without Sin'.[9] Thomas Dixon acted as chief prosecutor, and in almost every case the sentence was death. The guilty were forced to kneel down, and were surrounded by pikemen who stuck their weapons into their victims' ribs, raised them from the ground and held them in the air until they were dead. The bodies were then tossed over the parapet into the water.

For two hours this ghastly ritual continued, and by eight o'clock about ninety had died, their bodies either lying on the parapet or in the water below. Then a messenger rode up shouting that the redcoats had converged on Vinegar Hill and that every available man was needed there. The prisoners who were awaiting execution were hurriedly taken to their cells, thanking God for their deliverance.

The Rout on Vinegar Hill

The next day, 21 June, the rebel camp at Vinegar Hill was attacked by General Lake. Following a bloody battle the pikemen were defeated, though some escaped through what became known as 'Needham's Gap', a line of escape named after the English general who failed to complete the encirclement. Lake's victory was followed by wholesale killings and destruction in and around Enniscorthy. A second army defeated more of the rebels at Foulksmills and went on to take Wexford town. Organised resistance collapsed, and when Father Philip Roche rode into Wexford to negotiate a surrender, he was beaten senseless, court-martialled and hanged. The rebellion in Wexford was over.

'Croppies Lie Down'

Poor Croppies, ye know that ye're sentence has come
When ye hear the sound of the Protestant drum;
In memory of William we hoisted the flag
And soon the bright Orange put down the Green Rag
Down, Down, Croppies lie down!

— *from a popular Orange ballad*

Rebellion in the North

During the conflict in Wexford and other parts of Leinster, most Protestants were deemed by the rebels to be Orangemen. This was not so, at least in a formal sense; there were about sixty lodges in Leinster, and the membership of each was less than a couple of dozen. If, however, we expand the term to include Protestants who felt themselves, instinctively, part of the Orange tradition, the picture is different. The great bulk of Protestants felt themselves as belonging to this tradition and held the memory of King William in high regard. To many the trappings and rituals of the Orange Order may have been outlandish, yet they could empathise with them. The traditions which the Order saluted were their traditions and the history which it revered was their history. And even if, on occasion, they felt embarrassed or compromised by these, it was still theirs and they were loath to deny it.

During the rebellion in Leinster, Orangemen were active in all the yeomanry corps sent from the North. Everywhere they were the fiercest opponents of the rebels. Robert Ogle Gowan tells of an incident involving lodge No. 406:

> Captain Gowan's yeomanry met in lodge, within the burnt walls of
> his mansion at Mount Nebo, and were in the act of initiating

Lieutenant George Smith of Cummer, when intelligence was brought in that about 200 of the King's troops had passed on the road from Gorey to Carnew to meet the rebels, then reported to be advancing from the hill of Killkevin. The lodge was immediately closed and the men, who attended without military uniform, but who carried muskets and bayonets . . . were ordered to fall in, and instantly marched off to support the royal forces. On reaching the village of Moneyseed, they could hear the fusillade in the direction of Carnew. They quickened their pace, but arrived at Ballyellis too late to assist Colonel Puleston, who had retreated with the remnant of his forces towards Carnew. On arriving at Ballyellis the rebels, on seeing the yeomanry dressed in ordinary costume, hailed them with cheers, conceiving that they were part of their own forces. The Orangemen did not open fire on the rebels till they were within ten or twelve yards of them, and then with such precision as to sweep down the dense mass that blocked the highway. After a few such discharges, the rebels retreated in great confusion.[1]

The Orangemen showed similar enthusiasm when revolt erupted in the North, and their strength was one of the reasons why the rebellion was confined to Antrim, Down and south Londonderry. In these counties the rebel turnout was partial and, in some respects, half-hearted. Lake's dragooning had greatly weakened the movement and many rebels (who were virtually all Presbyterian) had become disillusioned with republicanism. Besides, news of the atrocities at Scullabogue and Wexford Bridge had dampened their fervour. A number sensed the way the wind was blowing and quietly changed their allegiance by joining the lodges. In the event, barely half of those who had pledged to turn out did so. Those who did assemble were badly armed and completely without training; many carried hay forks, reaping hooks and scythes as their only weapons, and bags of oaten cakes as their frugal commissariat.

The first shots in the North were fired in Larne on 6 June, when the rebels drove the Tay Fencibles from their barracks. Later they forced the surrender of Ballymena by placing a blazing tar barrel against the Market House after a brisk encounter. Randalstown fell after a similar ploy, and the bridge at Toome was laboriously broken down to prevent the Orange yeomanry and the militia from crossing the River Bann. Henry Joy McCracken, the rebel leader, set out with his men from Craigarogan, near Roughfort. Two packhorses pulled their only cannon, a six-pounder which had been hidden under the floor at Templepatrick Meeting House. When they besieged Antrim town, the piece fell from its mounting after it had fired only two shots, and the combined forces of yeomanry and regulars poured into the narrow streets and put the rebels to flight. During the retreat the Governor of the county, Lord O'Neill, fell mortally wounded when a pike was thrust into his back. After hiding out on the recesses of Slemish Mountain for several days, McCracken was taken and hanged. His head was impaled on the gate of Belfast Market House. As he ascended the scaffold, he tried to address the watching crowd, but the noise of the redcoat drummers split the air and he could not be heard.

Munro's Men

The heaviest fighting was in County Down, where the rebels succeeded in occupying Saintfield, about a dozen miles from Belfast. Their success brought new recruits and the commander, Henry Munro (a linen draper from Lisburn), ordered his men south to Ballynahinch. If they could gain control of the town it would give them a commanding position in the centre of the county. Establishing themselves on Windmill Hill, a high point to the east, they awaited attack. Major George Nugent, the commander of the King's forces in Belfast, marched against them, burning all before him, and began pounding their position with heavy cannon. The rebels withdrew to the nearby estate of Lord Moira and set up camp in the woods. One poor fellow dallied too long on the hill and was apprehended; within the hour he was hanged from the sails of the windmill.

Meanwhile, Ballynahinch was occupied by Nugent's troops. The Monaghan militia, mostly Catholic, went on a drunken rampage and spent the night looting houses and molesting the womenfolk. Munro was advised to attack during darkness while the crown forces were running amok, but he rejected this advice and decided on a dawn raid. He struck at 3.00 a.m. and the next four hours saw heavy fighting as the battle swayed to and fro along the narrow streets. At 7.00 a.m. the rebels' ammunition began to run out, and in the face of a heavy cavalry charge they were forced to retreat. By this time most of Ballynahinch was a burning ruin — some sixty houses were destroyed and half that number badly damaged. About 150 rebels lay dead on the streets, and the Crown's casualties were not under seventy. Later, the remnant of Munro's army was overrun on Ednavady Hill and no quarter was given. The cavalry went in hot pursuit of fleeing rebels and cut them down viciously as they ran. Only one incident lived on in the popular memory. This was the fate of the rebel heroine, Betsy Gray.

Betsy Gray

Betsy Gray was a Presbyterian woman in her early twenties from the townland of Gransha, a little south-east of Six Road Ends, Ballygrainey,

County Down. She carried a green flag on Ednavady Hill and, during the battle, fought with a musket side by side with her brother George and fiancé Richard Boal. When the rout began, all three fled for their lives along the road towards Lisburn. Betsy, who was ahead of the others, was cut off by three yeomen at a low marshy spot called Ballycreen. They beat her savagely with horsewhips and had begun to molest her when her brother and fiancé came upon them. Instantly the yeos turned and shot both men, point blank, through the head. Then, one yeo — a brute named Jack Gill — lashed out with his sabre and cut Betsy's gloved hand clean off from the wrist. Following this, the other two, James Little and Thomas Nelson — both from the parish of Annahilt — raised their muskets and shot her through the back of the head. A local farmer, Matthew Armstrong, witnessed the young woman's fate, and later recovered the three bodies from a nearby swamp.

The story of Betsy Gray's violent death ran like wildfire through the countryside and, with each telling, a little more was added. She was portrayed as a young woman of remarkable beauty who led the rebels whilst mounted on a white horse and carrying a green flag. Pictures of an Irish Joan of Arc began to appear in every cabin and the ballad-makers strove to make her immortal. The parish of Annahilt was forever blackened with such lines as:

> Now woe be to you, Annahilt
> And woe be on the day
> When brother, lover, both were slain
> And with them, Betsy Gray.[2]

Years later a monument was raised 'on the lonely grave in the vale of Ballycreen' and it became a place of pilgrimage for Catholics on Sunday afternoons, but local Presbyterians claimed Betsy as one of their own and resented popish practices around her grave. When the centenary of the Rebellion was being commemorated, a Republican ceremony was arranged for Ballycreen, but on the evening before, a party of Orangemen appeared at the grave with sledgehammers and smashed the monument. The following day a bloody fracas broke out between the rival parties. The *Newry Standard* reported that 'many skulls were broken and that some of the injured had to be hauled away in carts.' Years after, one of the witnesses to the destruction, in old age, recalled: 'They meant no disrespect to the memory of Betsy Gray, sure wasn't she one of their own.'

The Grand Lodge of Ireland

Three months before the outbreak of the Rebellion in Leinster, on 8 March 1798, a number of leading Orangemen had gathered in Dublin to found a Grand Lodge of Ireland. Although they came from different parts of the country the hard core consisted of gentry from the North, particularly from Armagh. Some had, for some time, been operating behind the scenes, while others were more explicit in their Orangeism. These included the Corrys of Derrymore (the most noted of whom was Isaac Corry, who became Chancellor of the Exchequer later in the year); the Richards of Bessbrook; the Ensors of Ardress and, most prominently, Thomas Verner of Churchill and William Blacker of Carrickblacker, near Portadown. The militia and yeomanry were represented by Captain Hunter Gowan of the Wingfield Cavalry in Wexford, Sergeant Hughes, Quartermaster of the Cavan Militia, and John Claudius Beresford of the Dublin Militia. The chair was taken by Thomas Verner, a tall, handsome young man of sombre disposition. Twelve resolutions were put to the meeting which, in substance, were:

> That it is advisable that proper correspondence should be instituted forthwith between different Orange lodges in the Kingdom. That a Grand Lodge be formed for this purpose. That such a lodge be called the Grand Lodge of Ireland. To facilitate organisation and administration, each county should be divided into districts by the Grand Master and other Masters of the county. That each county should have a Grand County Lodge to be formed by District Masters.

A supplementary resolution said: 'That it is advisable that the first meeting of the Grand Lodge of Ireland be held on Monday 9th April 1798 at the house of Thomas Verner, Dawson Street, Dublin.'[3]

The main resolutions were submitted to all operating lodges for ratification. Some 471 warrants had been issued, but only 281 were registered with full details. Of these, a clear majority (167) approved, but a significant number in County Armagh said no. It is interesting that Lodge No. 1 in The Dyan in County Tyrone gave its approval, as did Lodge No. 36 in Loughgall, which had James Sloan as its Master.

The first meeting of the Grand Lodge of Ireland was an impressive affair, held in the upstairs drawing room of Verner's town house — nowadays the Graham O'Sullivan Coffee House — in Dawson Street. Among the forty-six men who attended were: The Right Honourable The Earl of Athlone; The Most Noble Marquis of Drogheda; The Right Honourable George Ogle MP; Lord Viscount (Isaac) Corry; The Right Honourable John Barry-Maxwell MP; Sir Richard Musgrave, Bart, Waterford; Major Henry Sirr, Dublin; The Honourable J.W. Cole (later Lord Enniskillen), Fermanagh; Captain John Claudius Beresford, Dublin Cavalry; Captain John 'Hunter' Gowan, Wexford; The Right Honourable Patrick Duigenan LLD, MP, Grand Master of the Aldermen of Skinners

Alley; and The Very Reverend Dean Keating, Chaplain to the Irish House of Commons.

The first person to speak was the bewigged George Ogle, the MP for Wexford. A tall graceful man, his accent formed by schools in England and Trinity College, he spoke the praises of Thomas Verner and recommended him for the position of Grand Master. William Blacker, who at twenty-two was a few years younger than Verner, rose to second the proposal. Approval was being nodded through when Verner himself rose. A countryman, unsophisticated in the ways of the grandees, he nervously fingered his eyeglass and said that he was sensible of the honour being done to him, but that in accepting it he should be usurping an award which belonged elsewhere. The most appropriate man to lead the Society, he said, was the last remaining descendant of General Ginkel, the hero of Athlone: the Earl of Athlone — Ginkel's grandson. The old Earl, crusty and overweight, muttered his thanks but tactfully declined. Someone proposed that The Marquis of Drogheda be appointed, but he too graciously declined and urged the brethren to again consider the merits of Thomas Verner who, he said, came, after all, from the county where the Society had been formed. With this, the pre-arranged courtesies were concluded and Verner was appointed.

Major Henry Sirr, a big, bluff, coarse Dubliner, then proposed that Sir Richard Musgrave, the MP for Lismore, be appointed Grand Treasurer, and added that there were few more dedicated to the ideals inspired by the Prince of Orange than Sir Richard. The appointment was agreed. Young William Blacker proposed that Captain John Claudius Beresford be appointed Grand Secretary. Beresford, a tall, thin man with bony features, had, through John Giffard, been an Orangeman for some time and, being a popular choice, was nodded through. A number of minor appointments followed and finally, The Very Reverend Dean Keating accepted the position of chaplain to the new Grand Lodge.

One item remained, the establishment of a committee to codify the rules and formulate a single set of ordinances which would apply to the Order as a whole. The task had to be approached with delicacy, given the sensitivities of some northern lodges. It was entrusted to two young men: Harding Giffard — the son of John Giffard, 'The Dog in Office' — and Samuel Montgomery. They could not report until November, for the long-anticipated rebellion broke out on 23 May. After final prayers, the Lodge broke up and the brethren moved to the downstairs parlour, where toasts of 'whiskey, wine and porter' were drunk to the 'Glorious and Immortal Memory'. Rumour was that some of the refreshments were the gift of Arthur Guinness, a Kildare man who twenty years before had established a brewery at Saint James' Gate for the production of a dark beer known as 'Guinness' black Protestant porter'.[4] The famous brewer was well-advanced in years, but his four sons — the eldest of whom was in holy orders — were among the early members of Lodge No. 176, and took their places, snugly, among the Orange elite.

Internal Orange Problems

With the establishment of the Grand Lodge of Ireland, the names of the Armagh weavers and tenant farmers who had fought at the Diamond and frequented Sloan's pub began to disappear from the Orange leadership. Wolsey Atkinson, the secretary of the Armagh Grand Lodge, lingered for some time and strove to preserve some of the prerogatives of his lodge. He resented receiving a letter from Dublin requesting the surrender of his books, and felt patronised when informed that a silver medal was to be given to him for his services. He and his brethren did not trust the grandees, and friction arose between them. Soon he was summoned to the Verner estate at Churchill where Thomas Verner and the Grand Secretary, Richard Carpenter Smith, demanded an explanation for the obstructive attitude which the Armagh Grand Lodge had taken on certain issues. The meeting was not a success and a few days later — on 15 January 1799 — a letter was dispatched to Atkinson in which he (and his brethren) were accused of acting in a manner which 'might possibly prove destructive to the Orange system'.[5] The dispute was not resolved until it was agreed that both the Grand Lodge of Ireland and the Grand Lodge of Armagh should jointly sign all new warrants.

In practice, this arrangement was unworkable. The Order was expanding rapidly and, in the conditions of the time, it was impossible to pass information quickly between Dublin and Armagh. In due course, Dublin grew impatient and began issuing warrants on its sole authority. This upset Armagh, and The Reverend Holt Waring, the Armagh Grand Secretary, wrote a number of bitter letters to Dublin. The problem was not, however, beyond the wit of the grandees. They devised a neat expedient:

> From the high respect which the Grand Lodge of Ireland have and will ever entertain for their brethren of the Grand Lodge of Armagh, in whose county our glorious Institution originated, they are of the opinion that all warrants issued in the province of Ulster shall be countersigned by the Grand Secretary, Armagh.[6]

This was a sensible solution and permitted Armagh to retain a special position. But there was no doubt where the greater authority now resided. Following this incident, Wolsey Atkinson bowed out quietly, and there are no further references to him. It was at this time that relationships between other lodges became troubled. Complaints were made that some rural lodges were initiating members too freely and that a variety of degrees (or 'higher orders') were being conferred. On 2 July 1799 the Grand Lodge of Ireland passed a resolution:

> That the Masters of Lodges be instructed not to admit any person into the Society of Orangemen under the age of eighteen, and not initiate an Orangeman into the Purple Order who does not belong to their own lodge without written recommendation from the Master of the lodge to which such an Orangeman may belong.[7]

As the purple degree (known, confusingly, as the Orange Marksman or Purpleman degree) had been devised in late 1796 as an instrument of control, it was vital for the Grand Lodge of Ireland to maintain its integrity. But its strictures were not universally accepted. Some lodges circumvented them by conferring totally new degrees which they called The Black, The Scarlet and The Blue. On 13 December the Grand Lodge decided to clamp down on these new degrees (or 'orders' as they were called) and issued a statement:

> [That] many persons have introduced various orders into the Orange Society which tend to injure the regularity of the Institution. The Grand Lodge disavows any orders but Orange and Purple and there can be no other unless issued and approved by them.

The controversy, however, continued and the issue of 'higher orders' was a source of rancour and disharmony for years to come.

The Grandees

It was the grandees — that is, the well-heeled Dublin Orangemen — who changed the face of the Order. Being men of power, money and influence, they included within themselves a circle known as the 'Castle Clique' which sought to manipulate the administration in Dublin Castle. Prominent in this 'clique' was Dr Patrick Duigenan, the Advocate General, a man of extreme anti-Catholic views, and Sir Richard Musgrave, the MP for Lismore, a truculent bigot who saw popish conspiracies behind every bush. Others were less intense, but opposed any suggestion that Catholics should have seats in Parliament or any real say in public affairs.

Among them were a number of southern landowners, such as Colonel John Rochford of Carlow and Sir Thomas Maude of Dundrum, County Tipperary, who had come in contact with Orangeism through their membership of Dublin clubs. On returning to their estates, these magnates introduced 'the system' to their Protestant tenants and established 'lodge rooms' in their big houses. In many areas Anglican clergymen were the shocktroops. Their congregations were largely drawn from estate workers, whom they were ideally placed to influence. They became chaplains of lodges and began (especially in the North) the tradition of conducting religious services for Orangemen on the great commemorative dates. From these evolved the custom of church parades, when the brethren would march from their lodge rooms by carefully planned routes to Divine Service. On 'The Twelfth' church bells would ring from early morning until noon, when the Orangemen would march, often headed by horsemen, to Union Jack-bedecked churches.

The Order was never free from controversy, but it was fortunate in always having in its ranks talented apologists who, because of their superior education or high social position, were able to deflect the attacks made upon it. Some of these are described below.

Thomas and William Verner

The first Grand Master of Ireland, Thomas Verner, did not carry as much weight as some around him. His family were substantial land owners, but a step down from the higher gentry. Thomas, however, was a shrewd, practical man and few doubted his competence or sincerity. He owed his position to the Armagh gentry who had endorsed the movement from early on, and to the fact that his father, the old Colonel, had sat in Parliament for Dungannon. Besides, he had grown up among the weavers and tenant farmers who had carried the fight to the Defenders, and had been on close terms with James Sloan, Dan Winter and the other grass-roots leaders. His estate at Churchill had been at the epicentre of early Peep O'Day Boy activities.

The Verner family hesitated before joining the Order; it was not until two years after its founding that a warrant — No. 162 — was obtained to establish a lodge on the estate. Once committed, the family took to Orangeism with fervour; all of the Colonel's five sons became senior Orangemen. The best known was not, in fact, Thomas, the Grand Master, but William, the war hero. He had been with Wellington during the Peninsular campaign and served in the 7th Hussars at Waterloo, where he was wounded. On returning to Ireland he became MP for Armagh and held the seat for over thirty years, establishing a record in being returned nine times without opposition.[8] He became Deputy Grand Master of the Order, and his breezy personality made him well liked in Dublin society. During a successful career, only a single shadow crossed his path: his dismissal from the magistracy in 1837 for proposing a toast to the 'Battle of the Diamond' (see p. 247).

Patrick Duigenan

Dr 'Paddy' Duigenan was one of the most curious men of his day, stuffed with enough learning to produce intellectual indigestion in an ordinary brain. Much of it was of an esoteric and antiquarian kind; for instance, he knew the theological dispositions of half the prelates who attended the Council of Orange in 529, when the church was concerned with refuting the Pelagian heresies, and drew on this lore when denouncing papal teaching and canvassing his own perspectives. A small, lively, rotund figure, he spoke with a womanish voice and was the butt of the Dublin wits. Born to a peasant family in County Leitrim, he had been baptised a Catholic, but as a schoolboy had been adopted by a Protestant clergyman attached to Saint Werburgh's Church in Dublin, and was sent to Trinity College, where he became an LL.B and LL.D without difficulty and was made a Fellow of the College.

He did not become well known until he led the opposition to the election of John Hely-Hutchinson as Provost of Trinity. At the time, the Provostship was a lucrative post, worth more than £2,000 a year, with a fine residence thrown in. It attracted Hely-Hutchinson, a Corkman, who had assumed his double-barrelled name when he married the daughter of Richard Hutchinson who had large estates at Knocklofty, near Clonmel. He was a very acquisitive type, and Lord North's quip about him bears repeating: 'If you were to give him the whole of Britain and Ireland as an estate, he would then ask for the Isle of Man for his potato garden.' The post was in the gift of the Viceroy, and in a piece of outrageous jobbery, Hely-Hutchinson was induced to resign as Prime Sergeant so that his position could be given to another claimant. Duigenan denounced this trickery in a series of celebrated pamphlets, published under the title *Lachrymae Academicae or The Present Deplorable State of the College*. He openly quarrelled with Hely-Hutchinson at a board meeting, and is recorded as having 'used improper and disrespectful language to the Provost'. Unable to prevent the appointment, Duigenan resigned his Fellowship and devoted himself to his practice at the bar. He became a King's Counsel and a bencher of King's Inns, and advocate-general of the High Court of Admiralty in Dublin.

He had long been an Orangeman and was 'Mayor' of the Alderman of Skinners Alley for many years. He entered Parliament in 1790 for the Borough of Old Leighlin, and used his great rhetorical skills to denounce the Catholic Bill in 1795. He was strongly in favour of the Union and was one of the main government spokesmen on the measure; when it was carried, he was appointed one of the Commissioners for distributing compensation for it. For his services he was given a place on the Privy Council and appointed Professor of Civil Law at Trinity. In the first united Parliament he sat for Armagh and continued to hold the seat until his death. He was bitterly opposed to all Catholic demands and hardly spoke on any other subject. Yet he married a Catholic lady, Miss Cusack, and permitted her to have an in-house chaplain. On his death, he left his fortune to her nephew, Sir William Cusack, who was a Catholic also.

Duigenan was famous in the House of Commons for his antiquated bob-wig and coarse Connemara stockings. Barrington, who knew him well, says:

> This eccentric person, whose celebrity originated from his crusades for Protestant supremacy . . . would have been a conspicuous character in whatever profession he adopted. Incapable of moderation on any subject, he possessed too vigorous and active an intellect to pass through life as an unsignalised spectator; and if he had not at an early period enlisted as a champion of Luther, it is more than probable that he would with equal zeal and courage have borne the standard of St Peter's followers. A hot, rough, intrepid, obstinate mind, strengthened by very considerable erudition and armed with a memory of the most extraordinary retention, contributed equally to his pen and his speeches. A partisan by his very nature . . . his intolerance was too unreasonable to be sincere; and whenever his Protestant extravagance appeared to have one lucid interval, it was immediately predicted that he would die a Catholic.[9]

The prediction failed. Duigenan died suddenly at his lodgings in Westminster in April 1816, after having been present at a debate in the House the night before. Pious, but apocryphal, legend had it that he expired after eating an orange!

George Ogle

George Ogle was less extreme than Duigenan. A Wexfordman, he was educated in England and at Trinity College, Dublin. From youth he excelled in literary studies and became an authority on the Italian Renaissance, publishing translations of Boccaccio and Petrarch. He wrote popular hunting and love songs (some of which were praised by Robert Burns) and a number of these appeared in nineteenth-century anthologies such as Crofton Croker's *Popular Songs of Ireland (1839)* and Samuel Lover's *Poems and Ballads* (1840). One of his best-known songs was 'Molly Astore', inspired by his unrequited love for a lady in the Midlands:

> As down by Banna's banks I strayed
> One evening in May
> The little birds in blithest notes made
> vocal every spray;
> They sang their songs of love
> They sang them o'er and o'er
> Ah, gra-mo-chree, mo colleen oge
> My Molly Astore.[10]

Ogle, a brilliant orator, was described *in The Review* of the Irish House of Commons as 'delighting in splendid superlatives and figurative diction, whilst the spirit and energy of his manner corresponded to the glowing warmth of his expressions'. He began as a Whig, and supported legislative independence, but was utterly opposed to Catholic emancipation. In 1778 he was challenged to a duel by a whiskey distiller named Barney Coyle, a member of the Catholic Board, on the grounds that he had publicly said 'that a papist could swallow a false oath as easily as a poached egg'. Ogle complained that he had been misreported and said that he had not referred to 'papists' but to 'rebels'. The duel went ahead, and eight shots were fired without the combatants coming to harm. Later, Ogle declared (reported in the *Hibernian Journal* of 1 June 1778) that he 'hated no man on account of his religious faith'. In 1779 he joined the parliamentary coterie known as 'The Monks of the Screw',[11] and in the 1780s raised a company of volunteers known as 'Ogle's Blues'. Many of these were both Orangemen and Boynemen, that is, initiates of the first degree of the Boyne Society. Ogle himself was almost certainly a Knight of the Most Glorious Order of Boyne. As a landlord he was considerate towards his tenants, and exceptional in that he denounced other landlords as 'great extortioners'.[12] In February 1795 he spoke strongly against the Catholic Relief Bill and prophesied that the admission of Catholics to Parliament would lead to either Ireland separating from Britain or to a legislative union between the countries. In the House he was a staunch defender of Orangeism, but took early retirement in 1796 and withdrew to his estate at Bellevue in Wexford.

When the 1798 Rebellion broke out he was staying at his town house in Dublin. He was persuaded to re-enter politics and was returned for the City of Dublin later that year (1798). He voted against the Union and encouraged Orange lodges in Dublin to declare against it. He sat in the united Parliament until 1806, but his active Orange career went on until his death ten years later. He is buried beside his wife in Ballycarnew churchyard, a few miles from Gorey.

After Ogle's death, a fine marble statue to him was placed in the north aisle of Saint Patrick's Cathedral in Dublin. On a tablet nearby, he is eulogised:

> This statue of the Right Honourable George Ogle is erected by his countrymen and friends as a tribute of affection and veneration for the man who by a combination of transcendent qualities shone conspicuous among the highest and purest of the age in which he lived. For 28 years he represented the county of Wexford in Parliament, during which period of incorruptible integrity the

brilliant talents and the ardent patriotism with which he discharged the duties of that sacred trust secured to him the unalterable attachment of his constituents. . . .[13]

The tribute continues, in similar vein, for a further three paragraphs.

The Two Beresfords

John Claudius Beresford, the first Grand Secretary of the Grand Lodge of Ireland, is less known to history than his formidable father, John Lucius (1738-1805), the Commissioner of Revenue and Member of Parliament for Waterford, who was also an Orangeman. The older Beresford, whose surviving portraits show a remarkable physical resemblance to George Washington, was notoriously called 'the King of Ireland', so extensive were his influence and patronage. His family held government sinecures estimated at the then enormous sum of £20,000 per annum. In a letter to Lord Auckland dated 9 January 1795 John Lucius repeated remarks which had been made about his influence:

> No Lord Lieutenant could exist with my powers; that I have been a Lord Chancellor, a Chief Justice of the Kings Bench, an Attorney General, nearly a Primate, and most certainly a Commander-in-Chief, it is impossible to doubt; that I was at the head of the Revenue and had the law, the army and a great deal of the Church at my beck and call, is equally impossible to doubt, and he also said expressly, that I was virtual King of Ireland.[14]

John Lucius did not actually hold all these offices, but the description was not too wide of the mark. John Lucius was not disliked: on occasion, the Dublin mob pulled his carriage through the streets and cheered him to the echo. He persuaded the great architect James Gandon to settle in Dublin, and at his behest the magnificent Customs House was built in 1781. John Lucius was also responsible for extending the quays and opening up Sackville Street (now O'Connell Street). He married one of the most celebrated beauties of the day, Barbara Montgomery, who had posed as one of the 'Three Graces' for Reynolds' famous painting.

His son, John Claudius, was a different kettle of fish. Whereas the older man was generous, expansive and outgoing, John Claudius was cruel, mean-spirited and arrogant. In politics, however, both father and son shared similar views. The younger one succeeded the older as a member of the 'Backstairs Parliament' — a name deridingly given to an inner power-broking circle of the Ascendancy. His hatred of Catholics bordered on the pathological, and with his friends, Major Henry Sirr and Lord Kingsborough, he had advocated — prior to 1798 — the goading of Catholics into rebellion. He privately employed a battalion of spies —

known as 'Beresford's Bloodhounds' — to keep their eyes peeled for seditious citizens. During the 1798 rebellion, the yeomanry riding school which he ran at Marlborough Street was used as a barracks for questioning and torturing rebels; so notorious was the place that one wag wrote above the door: 'Mangling done here by J.C. Beresford and Company.'[15]

For some years John Claudius was a successful banker, in partnership with a Mr Woodmason, at No. 2 Beresford Place. One day the bank went bust, and John Claudius lost every penny he had. People who had cringed before him now insulted him in the streets. Fitzpatrick paints a picture of him as an attenuated old man walking the footpaths with his back bent and muttering: *sic transit gloria mundi* (thus passes away the glory of the world).[16] But whatever about his personal fortunes, the demise of John Claudius' bank did not herald the downfall of the family dynasty. His modern descendant, the 8th Marquess of Waterford (also called John Beresford), resides on the family estates at Curraghmore, near Portlaw, in County Waterford.[17]

Sir Jonah Barrington

The great anecdotal chronicler of the Irish Ascendancy during the 1790s, Sir Jonah Barrington (1760-1834), became an Orangeman as soon as Lodge No. 176 was established and remained active until he withdrew to Paris in 1815. He practised at the bar for a number of years, took silk in 1790 and later became a judge of the Admiralty Court. Between 1798 and 1800 he sat in parliament for Tuam, and later had a longer tenure for Clogher. For years he occupied a house in Harcourt Street, adjacent to his great rival and fellow Orangeman, Lord Clonmel (John Scott). From 1815 he lived mostly abroad to escape his creditors, and in 1830 was formally removed from the bench after a parliamentary commission found that he had embezzled from the Admiralty Court several times during the previous years.

In his book, *Personal Sketches of His Own Times* (first published in 1827), Barrington gives vivid cameos of the leading figures of his day, and tells anecdote after anecdote of bibulous landlords, men-about-town, hacks and impostors of all kinds. He became a member of the Aldermen of Skinners Alley (at the invitation of 'Paddy' Duigenan) and relates a hilarious story of an 'Alderman' being thrown from a top window by his brethren for slighting the memory of King William. Sir Jonah was also good at tit-bits; he reveals, for instance, that the charter dish of the Aldermen's Society was 'pigs-trotters' — an allusion to King James' running away from Ireland in 1690.

Barrington was a humane and humorous rogue, but was no bigot and enjoyed the company of priests if they were witty and convivial. There was little doubt about where he stood politically. He bore the full weight of the Orange tradition and wrote: 'I followed up the principles my family had invariably pursued from their first settlement in Ireland.'

Sir Richard Musgrave

Sir Richard Musgrave was one of the most committed of Orangemen. Barrington's mischievous vignette captures him well:

> Sir Richard Musgrave, who except on abstract topics like politics, religion, martial law, his wife, the Pope, the Pretender, the Jesuits, Napper Tandy, and the whipping post, was generally in his senses and formed . . . a very entertaining company.[18]

He was the son of a minor landowner in Tourin, County Waterford, and entered Parliament for the Borough of Lismore in 1778. An early member of Lodge No. 176 in Dublin, he was active in promoting Orangeism among the rich merchant families. He was on good terms with the Castle; his loyalty was rewarded with a baronetcy (in 1782) and, following the Union, he received the lucrative post of Collector of the Dublin City Excise. During the Rebellion he showed great zeal in putting down the croppies and, on one occasion (in September 1786), personally flogged a Whiteboy when no one else could be found to execute the punishment. He warned of the coming Rebellion in a pamphlet entitled 'A Letter On The Present Situation of Public Affairs' in 1794, and after the bloodshed wrote an address 'To the Magistrates, Military and Yeomanry of Ireland' in which he exonerated them from accusations of having provoked it in the first place.

Musgrave's fame rests on his authorship of a single, highly successful book, entitled *Memoirs of the Different Rebellions in Ireland*, which first appeared in 1801 and became holy writ to Orangemen. Despite its high price of £1.7s.6d, the initial print run sold out in two weeks and further editions had to be rushed to the shops. It was extensively researched and contained a mass of detail – first-hand accounts, sworn affidavits, detailed battle plans and other material — which was unavailable elsewhere. Its message was straightforward: the Rebellion was a popish revolt, aided by Protestant dupes who should have known better. His critics, then and since, have castigated the book, describing it as part of an anti-Catholic genre, and have linked it with books, written after 1641 and 1689, which portray Irish Catholics as savages who hold inveterate blood lusts against Protestants. These works, written by Sir John Temple and Archbishop William King, were quoted by Protestant leaders in times of stress to remind the Protestant community of the dangers which would attend a loosening of Catholic chains.[19] In recent times there has been a revival of interest in Musgrave's book. This has arisen from a congruence of some of his arguments with modern re-interpretations.[20] A new edition in 1995 restored it to general circulation and it is now seen as an essential work for scholars. It is doubtful, however, whether the general reader will view it as other than a tainted version of the '98 Rebellion.

Musgrave was a man of considerable talent, warped by blind prejudices and a savage partisan spirit. He died at his home in Holles Street, Dublin in 1818.

John Hunter Gowan

John Hunter Gowan was the most notorious of the Orange yeomen who were active against the Wexford rebels in 1798, and his name was a byword for intransigence and cruelty. He liked hard riding, recreational violence, heavy drinking and fornication; when the rebellion broke out, he was seventy-one years of age, and had two broods of children, one by his wife and one by his mistress. One of the latter was Robert Ogle Gowan, who achieved fame in Canada, building the powerful Orange political machine which shaped Canadian history for more than a century.

The Gowans (originally McGowans) were not Ascendancy stock, but parvenues who entered the Wexford gentry almost by stealth. Hunter Gowan's father arrived as a penurious young lawyer and married the daughter of the Reverend William Hatton, Church of Ireland rector at Gorey. She was a niece of Colonel William Hatton, MP for Wexford, and brought with her the estate of Raheencullen, later named Mount Nebo after the height from which Moses viewed the Promised Land. This dowry established the Gowans among the landed families of north Wexford. The name 'Hunter' was believed locally to have come from 'priest hunter' – one who was paid a bounty during penal law times for turning in Catholic priests. In fact, it was derived from the surname of a great-grandfather from County Tipperary.

Early in 1798 Hunter Gowan took out the first warrant to establish an Orange lodge in Wexford, with himself as Master. It read:

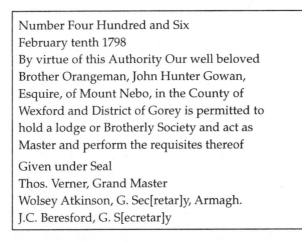

Number Four Hundred and Six
February tenth 1798
By virtue of this Authority Our well beloved
Brother Orangeman, John Hunter Gowan,
Esquire, of Mount Nebo, in the County of
Wexford and District of Gorey is permitted to
hold a lodge or Brotherly Society and act as
Master and perform the requisites thereof

Given under Seal
Thos. Verner, Grand Master
Wolsey Atkinson, G. Sec[retar]y, Armagh.
J.C. Beresford, G. S[ecretar]y

Hunter Gowan prized the warrant as if it were a trophy, and after each lodge meeting locked it away in a strongbox with another much-cherished prize, a silver coffee-urn which had been presented to him by Wexford notables who included the Marquis of Ely and the county's two MPs, George Ogle and Henry Hatton.

Both these accolades confirmed to Gowan that his methods of law enforcement had the blessing of those who mattered. He had assembled a corps of Horse and Foot known as the Wingfield Yeomanry, whose name brought fear to the Catholic population for miles around; they called it 'The Black Mob', and slept in fields at night, away from their homes, lest it descend upon them.

There is nothing on record to suggest that Gowan ever regretted his part in suppressing the rebellion. He lived for another twenty-two years, a bad-tempered old man, bickering with his children and feuding with his Protestant neighbours. His grave is still identifiable in the churchyard attached to Saint John's church at Hollyfort, near Mount Nebo. 'The Mount', as his mansion became known, was acquired in 1907 by the Benedictine Order, and became a prestigious school for boys, Mount Saint Benedict.

—16—

Aftermath and Union

To guard the faith which Luther preached —
The rights which William won
The Orangeman relies upon
His Bible and his gun
He prays for peace, yet war will face
Should rebels congregate;
Like the brave Orange yeomanry
Who fought in Ninety Eight.

— final stanza of an Orange poem on '98

The French in Killala

Late in 1798, when the uprisings in Wexford and the North had been crushed, two small but utterly inadequate French expeditions arrived in Ireland. The first consisted of three frigates and 1,036 men, with arms and equipment for a much larger number. It appeared, under the command of General Jean Joseph Humbert, in Killala, County Mayo, on 22 August.

The General was an experienced and skilful soldier and his troops, for the most part, were veterans who had served in several campaigns, but it was clear that so slender a force could achieve nothing without massive local support. This was not forthcoming. It was harvest time and the peasants were busily engaged in the fields. The French, who had expected to find Ireland still ablaze with revolution, soon found that they had been deceived as to the state of the country. When they began to distribute guns and uniforms, many ran to them, but it was found that on receiving supplies, a large number made off into the hills while others, disguising themselves, came back a second time to increase their spoils.

Over 500 agreed to join Humbert and declared that they were prepared to 'take arms for France and the Blessed Virgin'. One French officer said to Dr Stock, the local Protestant bishop: 'God help these poor simpletons, if they only knew how little we care for the Pope or his religion they would not be so hot in helping us.' The peasants were not to know that recently the French had driven the Pope from Rome, but they became suspicious when they saw how little respect was shown to the local Catholic clergy.

The English commanders, Lake and Hutchinson, lost no time in assembling forces to meet the invaders. Their numbers were sufficiently large, certainly double those of their enemies, but consisted mainly of militia whose quality was not up to the mark. Humbert marched to meet them, and the two forces encountered each other near Castlebar. The engagement, since known as 'The Races of Castlebar', lasted scarcely five minutes. On the government side, the artillery alone attempted resistance. The others broke before the charge of the French and fled in confusion, strewing the roads with their muskets which, for the most part, they had not even discharged.

The success of the French could only be temporary. Ireland was now full of British troops, most of whom were regulars of better quality than the runaways of Castlebar. No other French help came to support Humbert and, on 8 September, he surrendered to Lord Cornwallis at Ballinamuck, County Longford. The French were treated as prisoners of war, but their Irish allies were given no quarter. A few days later the little town of Killala was stormed, and the last embers of the revolt were quenched in blood.

The Capture and Death of Wolfe Tone

Shortly after the rout at Ballinamuck, the second French expedition appeared off the Irish coast. It consisted of one large battleship, *The Hoche*, and eight frigates under Admiral Bompart. Among the officers on *The Hoche* was Theobald Wolfe Tone. On reaching the coast, close to the entrance to Lough Swilly, they were attacked by a British squadron consisting of seven ships of war. *The Hoche* made a desperate resistance and only surrendered when almost sinking; some of the frigates succeeded in making their way back to France.

The prisoners were landed and the captured Frenchmen received the honourable treatment due to prisoners of war, but this was not given to Tone, who was taken to Dublin under an escort of dragoons. His rank in the French army was held to place him under military jurisdiction, and on 10 November he was brought before a court martial in the full dress of a French officer, wearing a tricolour cockade. From the dock he said that since his earliest youth he regarded the connection with Britain as being the misfortune of Ireland, and had laboured to break it.

'In a case like mine,' he continued, 'success is everything. Washington succeeded, Koschiusko failed.[1] I have forfeited my life. The Court will do its duty. I shall not be wanting in mine.'

Having been tried as a soldier, he requested a solder's death, but was sentenced to be hanged as a common criminal. He contrived to conceal a small knife in his boot and, with it, inflicted a wound in his throat, from which he died after lingering in pain for several days.

The Orangemen's Role

The Rebellion was now at an end, and the Orangemen could claim to have played a major role in its suppression. Under the favouring smile of the government, they had joined the yeomanry in large numbers and participated in virtually all the engagements, forming the cutting edge of the military operation. Their enthusiasm matched the anti-Catholic fanaticism of which they had stood accused during 1795, 1796 and 1797. They hit at their critics by saying that the disaffected had propagated malicious reports against them, and the Orangemen of Dublin published a lengthy declaration in the newspapers:

> To the loyal subjects of Ireland — From the various attempts that have been made to poison the public mind, and slander those who have had the spirit to adhere to their King and Constitution and to maintain the laws: We the Protestants of Dublin, assuming the name of Orangemen, feel ourselves called upon to vindicate our principles and to declare to the world the objects of our institution. . . .
>
> We have seen with pain the lower orders of our fellow subjects forced or seduced from their allegiance by the threats and machinations of traitors. And we have viewed with horror the successful exertions of miscreants to encourage a foreign enemy to invade this happy land, in hopes of rising into consequence on the downfall of their country.
>
> We therefore thought it high time to rally round the Constitution and pledge ourselves to each other, to maintain the laws and support our good King against all his enemies, whether rebels to their God or to their country; and by so doing, show to the world that there is a body of men in the island who are ready in the hour of danger to stand forward in the defence of that grand palladium of our liberties, the Constitution of Great Britain and Ireland, obtained and established by the courage and loyalty of our ancestors under the great King William.

Fellow-subjects, we are accused of being an institution, founded on principles too shocking to repeat, and bound together by oaths, at which human nature would shudder; but we caution you not to be led away by such malevolent falsehoods; for we solemnly assure you, in the presence of Almighty God, that the idea of injuring anyone, on account of his religious opinion, never entered our hearts; we regard every loyal subject as our friend, be his religion what it may. We have no enmity but to the enemies of our country.

We further declare that we are ready at all times to submit ourselves to the orders of those in authority under His Majesty, and that we will cheerfully undertake any duty which they shall think proper to point out for us, in case either a foreign enemy shall dare to invade our coasts or that a domestic foe shall presume to raise the standard of rebellion in the land. To these principles we are pledged, and in support of them we are ready to shed the last drop of our blood.

Thomas Verner, William James
Edward Ball, Isaac De Joncourt
John Claudius Beresford.[2]

Neither pious declarations nor flowery words could, however, conceal some of the dreadful methods which the Orangemen employed against defenceless civilians. They infiltrated the militia and regular forces and incited these services to adopt ruthless tactics; their influence on the behaviour of the notorious Ancient Britons and the North Cork Militia was particularly manifest. In 1797 the Ancient Britons had been stationed in Newry, where the local Orange yeomanry had its headquarters. The two forces fraternised and were involved in a combined attack, indeed a massacre, of the people of Ballyholan, County Down. This event, Lecky says, 'left an ineffable impression on the public mind'. It even disgusted no less a person than John Giffard, 'The Dog in Office', himself a leading Orangeman. Giffard and the Dublin Militia had been in the area searching for arms, so he was an eyewitness to the massacre and in a letter (dated 5 June 1797) to Edward Cooke, the Under Secretary at Dublin Castle, wrote:

The Welsh (Ancient Britons) burned a great number of houses and the object of emulation between them and the Orange yeomen seems to be, who shall do the most mischief to the wretches who certainly may have seditions in mind but who are at present quiet and incapable of resistance . . . I was directed by the smoke and flames of burning houses and by the bodies of boys and old men slain by the Britons, though no opposition whatever had been given by them, and, as I shall answer to Almighty God, I believe that a single gun was not fired, but by the Britons or yeomanry. I declare that there was nothing to fire at, old men, women and children excepted. From ten to twenty were killed outright; many wounded and eight houses burned.[3]

Giffard is a damning witness and may only have been induced to condemn the Britons because they had killed a member of his own militia. Later, the Britons — many of whom had been initiated into a lodge formed in their regiment — were placed at free quarters among the peasantry of Wicklow where, even before the outbreak of the Rebellion, they vied with the local yeomanry in goading the people into revolt.

The methods of the North Corks were no better.[4] Virtually all of the officer corps and a number of the rank and file were Orangemen, under the command of Lord Kingsborough, a friend of John Claudius Beresford. Both men were socially inseparable and Kingsborough was, in fact, present in Beresford's yeomanry riding school when two unfortunates, John Flemming and Francis Gough, were inhumanely flogged for information. It is known that Gough's flagellation was supervised by Kingsborough who, almost at every lash, enquired of his victim, 'how he liked it'.[5]

An interesting detail about the North Corks is that following the Battle of Oulart Hill, those of them who were taken captive were refused mercy by their fellow Catholics, though they pleaded for it in Irish. The Irish language, apparently, was not understood in Wexford at this time.[6]

The regiment which excited the greatest hatred and fear was the German Hessian Dragoons, a mercenary force who were recruited to the British army. These ruffians were notorious for their outrages against women and made a practice of cutting the petticoats off their victims with their sabres. Their officers boasted that in certain districts not a single woman was left undefiled. The Orange yeomanry were implicated in these outrages and at least one historian of Orangeism has quoted several sources which indict them.[7]

The Union

It is not known when the idea of a legislative union between Britain and Ireland first entered the mind of the Prime Minister, William Pitt, but his views were known to Dublin Castle prior to the Rebellion, although concealed from the country at large.

The idea was an old one. In the earlier part of the century — in 1703 and 1707 — the Irish House of Commons had actually petitioned for a union but the British government had refused it. A few generations later the views of the Ascendancy had changed and the project received no favour. In 1784 the Lord Lieutenant, the Duke of Rutland, declared that anyone making such a ridiculous proposal should be tarred and feathered; Irish officials advised the authorities in London that even the very mention of such a scheme would be ill-received in Ireland.

In the second half of 1798, both London and Dublin Castle became persuaded that a union of both parliaments was desirable and practicable. The rebellion had shown how unstable the Kingdom of Ireland really was; it could not have survived without British military support. The rebels had received French assistance and might do so again. For years the Catholic majority had been seeking the right to sit in Parliament, and their claims could not be deflected indefinitely. Supposing the Catholics (and their allies among the Presbyterians) achieved a majority in the Irish parliament, how long could the Ascendancy last? This question was not academic; some people in high places believed that the wolves were barking at the door.

Among them were the Lord Chancellor, Lord Clare, and the new Chief Secretary, Lord Castlereagh. Clare felt that a union was an imperial necessity; the remedy for Ireland was not additional liberty but firm government. The admission of Catholics to a united legislature, he thought, would be a great mischief, for it would unbalance the constitution. Castlereagh's views were a little different. He believed that the Constitution of 1782 was ill-conceived and fundamentally unworkable. To him, a parliament in Dublin professing to be representative and yet excluding four-fifths of the population was patent nonsense. He had seen that when the Irish parliament discovered its power to embarrass and extract confessions from Westminster, it had become a danger to harmonious relations between the two countries. Both men saw a union as the panacea, but Castlereagh, unlike Clare, accepted Pitt's view that a union would make it possible to emancipate the Catholics without disturbing Protestant control of a united parliament. The overwhelming majority of members would be Protestant and free to continue as before, with a small number of Catholics in their midst.

Yet many had a real fear of union. The Dublin business community, for instance, saw that the removal of Parliament would make their city a backwater and, besides, they did not trust the London government. They remembered only too well how British commercial jealousy had hampered the Irish wool trade, the glass industry, brewing, the export of livestock and efforts to develop shipping.

The legal profession was even more vociferous in its opposition. It saw the union as bringing Ireland's separate judiciary to an end, and had recently witnessed London's creeping domination. In the case of *Sherlock v. Annesley*, the English House of Lords had taken over from the Irish

House of Lords as the Supreme Court of Ireland. The profession was prepared to make a stand. On 9 September one of the country's most eminent barristers, a leading Orangeman, William Saurin, called a meeting of senior Irish lawyers in Dublin. The main resolution before the meeting was: 'That a legislative union would be highly dangerous and improper at the present juncture', and was carried by 166 votes to 32.

A few days later a meeting of Dublin bankers and merchants condemned the proposed union, while affirming their loyalty to the Crown. Amid the growing protests, a new newspaper appeared on the streets, called, simply, *Anti-Union*.

Castlereagh, who was responsible for carrying the measure, got down to business. In a meeting with the Catholic bishops, he pointed out that an extension of Catholic rights was more likely to come from a united Parliament than from the frightened and Orange-tainted assembly which sat in College Green. He hinted that a union would bring state funding for their clergy and that, shortly, they may be accorded the right to sit in Parliament. They took the bait, and after a meeting in Maynooth in January 1799, Castlereagh was advised that he could count on Catholic support. Whether the bishops were speaking for their entire flock is a moot point, for many Catholics later attended a great public meeting in Dublin to protest against the union, the first public appearance of Daniel O'Connell. His speech was remarkable for his declaration that, as a Catholic, he would rather lose all the privileges conceded by the Irish parliament and accept a return to the penal laws than give up the legislative independence of his country. Yet O'Connell was unlikely to be speaking for any great body of his co-religionists. With the crushing of the rebellion, most Catholics did not seem to care who ruled them, the English, the French or anybody else, so long as their grievances were attended to.

The Orange Response

The Orangemen, like the Protestant community at large, were divided on the issue. Many did not accept Pitt's argument that Ireland was an unstable kingdom which had just been saved from disaster by cross-channel intervention; Castlereagh and others were reminded that during the most dangerous period of the Rebellion, Irish loyalists had confronted and beaten the rebels unaided. Most of the hard fighting, it was pointed out, had been executed by the domestic militia and yeomanry, and when, after the Battle of New Ross, English troops poured into the country, the crisis had already well-nigh passed. Nor was it accepted that Ireland was a particularly troubled country. For most of the century, it was contended, Ireland had been less troublesome than some of the islands in the Pacific, and had been as free from sedition and rebellion as had, for instance, Devon or Cornwall. Orangemen generally attributed the recent disaffection to the fallout from the Westminster-imposed Catholic Relief Act of 1783 which, they claimed, had unreasonably raised Catholic expectations and opened the door to all kinds of revolutionary innovations. Irish Protestants could, they felt, continue to provide the country with effective government if left without interference.

As Orange opposition grew, the temperature began to rise. Senior Orange figures appealed to the yeomanry to step in, much as the old Volunteers had done in the agitation for free trade, and appeals were made for money to out-bribe the government. Some Orangemen even approached Catholics to join them in defence of the Irish parliament, but were rebuffed. They were reminded that recently they had been singing 'Croppies Lie Down', and, as a riposte, a new ditty appeared on the song sheets:

> Says Orange to Crop 'Let us quarrel no more
> But unite and shake hands and let discord be o'er
> Let Orange and Blue intermix with the Green
> In our hats and our bosoms hence forward be seen
> A union with Croppie for me!'

> 'I care not' says Croppie, 'not I by my soul
> Whether the English or Orange Ireland control
> If tyrants oppress this unfortunate land
> Tis the work of the Orangeman's hand
> No Orange alliance for me!'[8]

The Orange Order was now in mortal danger of splitting. To defuse the crisis the Grand Lodge of Ireland issued a statement counselling all brethren that they should 'strictly abstain from expressing any opinion, either pro or con, upon the question of legislative union because such expression of opinion and such discussion could only lead to disunion; that disunion would lead to disruption, and that disruption would promote the designs of the disaffected and in all probability lead to the destruction of the empire.'[9]

This statement only made matters worse. Several lodges came out in defiance of the Grand Lodge. Thomas Verner was accused of steering the Order, against the will of its members, in the direction of the union. Lodge No. 500 in Dublin stated: 'We have beheld with surprise and concern an address from the Grand Lodge to all Orangemen entreating them to be silent on a question whereby the loyalty of the most valuable part of our countrymen is shaken and endangered. We cannot think it our duty to submit implicitly . . . to the directions of a lodge composed of persons who are under a certain influence which is directed against the rights of Ireland. . . .'[10]

Verner was greatly shocked by this and other statements which flouted his authority and, in a huff, resigned his office. It was only after the greatest persuasion, and a specially convened meeting of the Grand Lodge, that he agreed to resume his position. But the divisions remained. On 1 March, thirty-one lodges met at the Maze, County Down, and passed a resolution stating: 'We consider a legislative union with Great Britain as the inevitable ruin to peace, prosperity and happiness in this kingdom.' A week later the Grand Lodge of Antrim, meeting in Belfast, took a pro-union stance and issued a statement appealing for restraint. In a resolution devised by Reverend Philip Johnson, it expressed regret at 'the appearance of division and discord among Orangemen on the proposed union, and called for adherence to the resolution issued by the Grand Lodge of Ireland that Orangemen should remain neutral on the question.' Four days later (on 12 March), the Masters of some thirty-six lodges, representing 2,100 Orangemen, met at the home of James McKean in Armagh city and adopted a series of strong resolutions against the union. Lodge No. 253, meeting at Charlemont, County Armagh, came out bitterly against Thomas Verner, proposing that he should step down as Grand Master and be replaced by George Ogle, who was against the union.

Orangemen in Parliament were also split. William Saurin was particularly angry and referred to the old concept of conditional allegiance. If Parliament persisted, he said, in making laws in direct opposition to the will of the people, such laws would not be binding and the right of resistance would reside with the people. He went on: 'If the powers of the legislature are transferred without constituent approval, the people will not be bound by any accompanying act, and their refusal will not be rebellion, but in accordance with the law.'[11]

He was strongly supported by Sir Jonah Barrington, George Ogle, Gustave Rochford, Arthur Dawson and others, but it was Orangemen like Sir John Parnell and the Speaker, Sir John Foster, who led the parliamentary struggle. Foster was a particularly formidable opponent of the measure, and his position as Speaker was quite different from that of the Speaker at Westminster, where the latter is supposed to have no politics and does not speak in debates. In the Irish Commons the Speaker could do so when the House was in Committee. It is interesting that a number of the grandees were split on the issue. John Claudius Beresford was against, mainly, it was said, to please his constituents, whereas his father John Lucius, the old Revenue Commissioner, was for the measure. Sir William Brownlow of Lurgan was strongly for, and a number of his family were against. Unsurprisingly, a strong pamphlet literature sprang up, and Orangemen such as Barrington, Richard Jebb and Charles Bushe wrote anonymous tracts against the union, while Dr 'Paddy' Duigenan and Sir Richard Musgrave wrote in its favour.

The definitive debate in Parliament took place on 15 January 1800, and the exchanges were heated. All night and into the morning the issue was tossed to and fro. At about 7.00 a.m. Henry Grattan entered the House, aided by two colleagues. Since his withdrawal from politics a few years earlier, he had been ill and suffering from severe depression. On the very day that Parliament met, his friends bought him a seat in Wicklow and rushed his election through. He appeared dressed in his old Volunteer uniform, and was so weak that he was unable to stand and had to obtain the permission of the House to speak while seated. His sharp features had become thinner and his face looked deadly pale. After taking the oath he went on to make one of the greatest speeches of his life. For two hours he assailed the advocates of union with invective, epithet and satire. In a final crescendo, his note was defiant:

> The Constitution may for a time be lost — but the character of the country cannot be lost. The Ministers of the Crown may at length find that it is not easy to put down forever an ancient and respectable nation by abilities however great, by power and corruption however irresistible. Liberty may repair her gold beams and with a redoubled heart re-animate the country . . . I do not give up the country. I see her in a swoon, but she is not dead; though in her tomb she lies helpless and motionless, still there is on her lips a spirit of life and on her cheeks a glow of beauty. . . .[12]

It was to no avail. The Ascendancy had unashamedly put itself up for sale, and Castlereagh had carefully marshalled the forces of bribery, jobbery and corruption. Leading figures traded their power and privileges for money, places and peerages as if they were buying and selling in an Oriental bazaar. Political power was seen as property and valued as such. Sixteen borough owners were given English peerages, twenty-eight new Irish peerages were created, and twenty existing peers were promoted. When the division bells rang, the result was predictable. The ayes were 158 and the noes 115, giving Castlereagh and the Government a majority of forty-three.

In the Lords the opposition was weaker, and the debate was enlivened by an ill-tempered speech from Lord Clare, in which he contrived to insult both the Catholics and his Ascendancy colleagues. He called the latter 'a puny and rapacious oligarchy' and the former 'deluded barbarians'. In the Commons there was a further debate towards the end of February, when a proposal for a general election on the issue was defeated. In March the measure was put before the Westminster parliament, where it was easily carried.

On 17 June the day came for the final step to be taken. Before the Report stage was reached, those against the union, unwilling to witness the ruin of their cause, withdrew as a body. Thus, although the galleries were crowded, there were a number of empty benches on the floor when Castlereagh moved the third and final reading of the bill. Amid dead silence, Sir John Foster, the Speaker, rose and asked the will of the House. The answer was given without enthusiasm, and Foster announced: 'The ayes have it.' Such was the end of the Irish parliament.

Among the senior Orangemen who voted against the union were Parnell, Barrington, Ogle, John Claudius Beresford, Rochford, Francis Knox, Arthur Dawson and Lord Cole. Among those who voted for the measure were Dr Patrick Duigenan and Sir Richard Musgrave. Some time later, when Orangemen were dressing the statue of King William in College Green, the Master of a Dublin lodge took a huge sash to which a large blue ribbon was tied, and hung it on the padlocked gate of the now defunct parliament building. The ribbon bore the words: 'Remember Me'.

In August the Act of Union received the Royal Assent and became law. On 1 January 1801, it came into operation. Guns were fired to mark the event and a new standard, on which for the first time the saltire of Saint Patrick — red on a white background — was joined with the crosses of Saint George and Saint Andrew, was flown throughout the United Kingdom. Ironically, to the pleasure of the descendants of many who then opposed it, it still flies in Ireland today.

The Spreading Orange Tree

When William to England came, the King of it to be
He brought a plant along with him, the Old Orange tree;
He planted it near London, so pleasant 'twas to see.
And when its branches sprung up, it frightened popery;
So let us join both heart and hand and lovingly agree,
For we are loyal branches of the Old Orange Tree.

— from an old Orange ballad

Dashed Expectations

The passing of the Union was received by the country at large with a tranquillity scarcely to be expected. Perhaps it was a weariness induced by the long and bitter arguments, or maybe — at least for Catholics — it was plain indifference. Catholics were sullen, but Protestants, although not jaunty, were more disposed to settle under the new arrangements.

Prior to the Union, Catholic expectations had been raised, and they almost universally believed that under the new dispensation their remaining disabilities would be removed. When the Union Parliament met in 1801 they held their breath for the King's Speech. Almost to their disbelief, they found nothing in it. It is true that no public or official assurance of their speedy emancipation had been given, but it was asserted that Pitt had made positive promises in his private correspondence and in interviews with individual Catholics, as was also rumoured of Castlereagh and the Lord Lieutenant, Cornwallis. Insult was added to injury when they learnt that the King, George III, was hostile to their claims. He had maintained since 1795 that placing Catholics on the same footing as Protestants would be a violation of his Coronation Oath, by which he promised to maintain the privileges of the Established Church.

Pitt's good-will on the matter was, however, generally accepted. In his famous defence of the Union in January 1799 he had broadly hinted that Catholic disabilities would probably soon be removed. He now realised that he had seriously underestimated the strength of the King's opposition, and his chagrin was shared by Castlereagh and still more by Cornwallis. In February 1801 he did the honourable thing and resigned, followed by other prominent members of the cabinet. In March he wrote to the King (whose mental stability was uncertain) and promised not to raise the matter again during the reign.

Three years later he returned to office, when England was in dire straits and faced with the threat of Napoleon. He announced that every other consideration must now be sacrificed to the country's safety. But he made little effort, either then or later, to redeem the faith which Catholics had placed in him. This left a stain on his reputation which history has not effaced.

The Orange Order in Britain

The anti-Catholic views of the King were representative of a large body of his subjects. Hostility towards Catholicism, in one form or another, had been a pervasive force in Britain since the days of the Reformation; indeed its centrality to British life could hardly be questioned. Nor could the fact that its resonance continued through the eighteenth and well into the nineteenth century. Popular history told how a steadfastly Protestant people had overcome the wiles of an untiring enemy, and certain incidents stood out: the Popish Armada of 1642, the Gunpowder Plot of 1605, and the Jesuitical policies of James in 1688. In 1708, 1715 and 1745 Popish-backed expeditions in support of the Pretender had landed in Scotland, seduced the people from their allegiance and on one occasion even marched south, intent on taking London. Apart from this, the British people learnt of the sufferings of European Protestants: of the massacre on Saint Bartholomew's Day; of the plight of the exiles from the Principality of Orange; of those who suffered in the dragonnades. These, and other Protestant persecutions, concentrated their minds in periods of crisis and made their fear of popery seem frighteningly relevant.

In more recent times a number of events had shattered their nerves: the loss of the American colonies was a bitter pill, and the French Revolution of 1789 had brought republicanism right to their back door. There was also, in the kingdom itself, a burgeoning cry for political reform, and working people had begun agitating for control of their affairs; in some areas workers had tried to form combinations to the detriment of their employers' interests; a growing challenge was being made to the Established Church, and voices were querying its official status. Most Anglicans were willing to make concessions, however grudgingly, to Dissenters as fellow Protestants, but drew the line at giving an inch to the Roman Church. In the past, papists could be tolerated as a puny minority, but since the Act of Union their numbers had increased, at a stroke, by four million. People who were happy to call themselves 'King and Country' loyalists were becoming alarmed. In this atmosphere of fear and confusion, shrewd heads in the Orange Order discerned an opportunity.

The first Orange lodge in England was formed in 1798, when the Lancashire Militia returned from Ireland with 'travelling' Warrant No. 220. This practice was adopted by other regiments, and in 1799 the Second Battalion of the Manchester and Salford Volunteers returned with Warrant No. 1128, and the notorious Ancient Britons came home with no fewer than three warrants. Soon Orange lodges were established in Bury, Stockport, Oldham, Ashton-under-Lyne, Rochdale and Wigan, as well as Manchester, which became the main stronghold.

These lodges were informal affairs and consisted of Irish Protestants who had taken the King's shilling as well as Englishmen. They were, in some respects, a cross between old comrades' associations, drinking clubs and 'King and Country' loyalist groupings. Their members believed that by participating in them, after their regiments had disbanded, they were serving a patriotic purpose. They were veterans who had quelled one rebellion and might well be called on to quell another. Besides, they hated the Catholic Irish and found, on returning home, that their adversaries were still under their feet. Large numbers of Irish had emigrated to Manchester and other English conurbations. They had brought with them not only their prejudices but their priests. These had established chapels in the numerous 'Little Irelands' which sprang up around the Midlands. To 'King and Country' Englishmen, these semi-vagrant and backward folk were not just a nuisance but a threat. They competed with indigenous workers for jobs, undercut wages, caused disturbances and, besides, their loyalty to the sovereign was suspect. English Orangemen felt that they had a role to play should these shifty intruders step out of line.

Domestic troublemakers needed to be encountered too. From the middle of the decade, textile workers in the East Midlands, South Lancashire and West Yorkshire had been meeting secretly in public houses and on the moors, taking treasonable oaths; they had smashed the machinery of mill-owners who refused their demands, and raised fears of a conspiracy to subvert lawful authority. Calling themselves after a mythical 'general' named Ned Ludd, they were reminiscent of the Irish Defender groupings. To English Orangemen — largely ex-soldiers and urban workers who had an instinctive hatred of rural labourers — these 'Luddites' were like a red flag to a bull. Their duty as Orangemen was clear: it was to assist the civil and military authorities in crushing would-be subversives.

The Leadership

The first public appearance of the Order in England was on 'The Twelfth' in 1803, when over a hundred Orangemen marched in Oldham. In the following years, marches were held regularly in a number of towns and invariably sparked off trouble, particularly in Manchester where the biggest marches were held. Sibbett says, erroneously, that the prime mover in Manchester was a clergyman named Reverend Robert or Richard Nixon, whom he associates with the collegiate church (nowadays, the cathedral).[1] In fact, the person involved was named Ralph Nixon and he was no clergyman, nor did he have a known connection with the collegiate church.[2]

It was a time of unrest in Manchester, and communal tensions were running high. Many of the Catholic Irish were living in poor accommodation in run-down areas of the town or near factory complexes on the outskirts, experiencing great economic hardship, and life was not made easier by Orangemen who painted 'no popery' slogans near their dwellings, or played anti-Irish tunes during celebratory marches.[3] A clash had been building up between both sides for months prior to 'The Twelfth' in 1807, when Nixon organised a parade of Manchester lodges to the collegiate church for a commemorative service. When the service ended the Orangemen, marching behind their band, were assailed by about fifty or sixty Irish working men yielding cudgels. A fierce brawl ensued and dozens of heads were cracked. The police were powerless to stop the fighting, which continued until the military was called out. It was clear that it was the workmen who had started the trouble, and Nixon denied that his followers had done anything to provoke them, but he referred to 'the overgrown power of an implacable enemy which had threatened to overwhelm Orangeism'. The confrontation quickly achieved celebrity status and English Orangemen came to regard it as their 'Battle of the Diamond'. For many years those who had participated were lionised by their fellows.

Nixon was a shady and reckless type, and it is difficult to understand how he acquired ascendancy over the Orangemen. There are few biographical details available, but at the time of the brawl in 1807 he was only nineteen years old and engaged in a small way as a fustian manufacturer. He lost his business and turned his hand to a number of things, including petty crime. In 1821 he was arrested for stealing a watch and other articles from a public house called the 'Turks Head' in Hanging Ditch, Manchester; when the police searched his lodgings, they came across a set of professional burglars' tools, a large stack of Bibles and quantities of fundamentalist Protestant literature. He was sentenced to seven years' transportation by a leading Tory magistrate, who might have been expected to be lenient on an Orangeman. By this time, however, it is likely that he had cut all ties with the brethren and that they were not too perturbed to see the back of him. Nothing further, it appears, was ever heard of him.[4]

Nixon's signal contribution to the Order in England cannot be gainsaid. He was the livewire who got things moving, and it is doubtful whether the Order would have grown so fast without him. On 2 December 1807 he wrote to Thomas Verner in Dublin, stating that a Grand Lodge had been established in Manchester for the purpose of 'co-ordinating Orange activities in the region'. Verner, who was anxious that control should be exercised from Dublin, was not happy with this news, but was unable to do much about it. In January 1808 the intrepid Nixon went to London for consultations with two Orange lodges which had been formed in the south, the Middlesex and Surrey lodges, who met jointly in a pub called the 'Moon and Seven Stars' in Holborn. The Grand Master of these was a former Irish yeomanry officer named Henry Staunton, a close friend of John Claudius Beresford in Dublin.

Nixon unveiled his plans for founding a Grand Lodge of England which would exercise control over all lodges in the country. Staunton had ideas of his own for a Home Counties Grand Lodge, although these were a bit far-fetched given that there were only two lodges in the south. Nixon was unimpressed by what he had found in London; Staunton's brethren were numerically small and were essentially low types who might be useful in fisticuffs with Catholics, but were otherwise of little note. He returned to Manchester convinced that if a Grand Lodge of England were to be established, it would have to be in the north.

Nixon saw that if the Order were to grow in England it would have to be led by people of good standing whom the rank and file could look up to. It is not known exactly how he met the two men on whom he counted to give the Order the required lustre, but both had already established reputations for themselves as 'King and Country' reactionaries. The first was Colonel Samuel Taylor, a blimpish type who lived on a landed estate at Moston Hall, near Moston, north-east of Manchester. He was the archetypal squire who rode to hounds two days a week, enjoyed shooting, and could, with propriety, be described as a 'King's man'. He had raised and financed the Manchester and Salford Volunteer Regiment, of which he was colonel; the regiment had served in Ireland during the rebellion and this probably was how he made his first contact with Orangeism. He was a cautious fellow and did not make decisions lightly; prior to making a commitment he requested details of the Order's rules, and these were dispatched from Dublin.[5]

The second notable was Colonel Ralph Fletcher from Bolton, about ten miles north-west of Manchester. He had acquired significant wealth through his father, John Fletcher who, with his partner Richard Guest, had purchased several coal pits in the vicinity of Altherton. Because of his wealth, and status as an employer, Fletcher became a magistrate, a commander of the yeomanry, and a significant figure in municipal politics. He was known to be bitterly opposed to workers' combinations and was active in hunting down Luddites.[6]

With these two, and a few others, Nixon was in a position to press ahead with his plans. A Grand Lodge of England was finally established in May 1808 at a meeting in the Star Hotel in Manchester. Taylor became the first Grand Master, Fletcher the Deputy Grand Master, and Nixon the Grand Secretary. The Grand Treasurer's position was given to a somewhat nondescript man named Woodburne, a solicitor in Deansgate who had acted for the lodges.

The new Grand Lodge got down to business immediately. Its initial task was to bring discipline to the unruly membership and ensure uniformity of ritual. In time, all the Irish warrants were called in and fresh ones issued. The first English warrant was made out to 'Mr Griffith Henderson of Manchester, in the County of Lancashire' and dated 28 October 1808. It was signed by Taylor, Fletcher and Woodburne but, strangely, not by Nixon. The successive numbers went to Oldham, Manchester, Stockport, Oldham (again), Bury and Ashton-under-Lyne.

Aiding the Civil Authority

The formation of the Grand Lodge of England did not pass unnoticed. From the start it drew the hostility of those aware of the Order's reputation for violence and sectarianism in Ireland, who had learnt of the numerous riots and disturbances associated with its marches in the midlands. It was generally scorned by liberal-minded people and viewed with the type of detestation shown towards Mosley's Blackshirt movement a hundred years later.

It attracted people who were fearful that their livelihoods would be endangered by the influx of Irish Catholic labour, and those who subscribed to the 'King and Country' jingoism prevalent in the years after Waterloo. It touched a chord in an age when bigoted forms of Protestantism still remained near the surface, easily aroused by suggestions that concessions to Catholics were looming. Orange leaders were able to draw on such anxieties and make analogies between the dispossessed and disaffected Catholics in Ireland and the ill-used and restless industrial population of the English Midlands. During the uncertainty of these years, the Order remained wedded to reactionary principles, and saw the King's enemies hiding behind every bush. When the Luddite troubles peaked in 1812, magistrates welcomed its support and swore in individual Orangemen as special constables and undercover agents.

Orangemen were active in 1817 when about 600 poor weavers known as 'The Blanketeers' (from the blankets which they carried on their backs) set off from Manchester in a forlorn attempt to present a petition to the Prince Regent in London. They participated in the arrest of about 200 'Blanketeers' in Stockport and aided the yeomanry in scattering the rest. At Macclesfield during the same year, members of the Order were involved when 'Oliver', a notorious spy, played Pied Piper on about 300 impoverished quarrymen and stocking-makers from the Derbyshire villages of Pentridge and Ripley, and led them into the none-too gentle arms of the cavalry at Nottingham.

More notoriously, Orangemen acted as special constables on 18 August 1819 when 60,000 men, women and children flocked to Saint Peter's Fields in Manchester to hear Henry 'The Orator' Hunt speak on political reform. While Hunt was expatiating, the magistrates (one of whom was Colonel Ralph Fletcher) decided to declare the meeting illegal and ordered the yeomanry to arrest the speaker. They had difficulty in forcing their way though the solidly packed crowd, and the military were called out. Within minutes, with sabres drawn, the troops charged into the crowd who, unsurprisingly, stampeded. Eleven were killed and over 400 injured. Colonel Fletcher must have been pleased when, a few days later, the Tory government congratulated the magistrates and rushed through the Six Acts — which, among other things, prohibited most meetings of over fifty people, gave magistrates power to search private dwellings, and curtailed the radical press. The events at St Peter's Fields were derisively dubbed 'The Peterloo Massacre' — a sarcastic comparison with the army's more august role on the field at Waterloo.

The role played by Orangemen in some of these incidents was relatively minor, because the Order's English membership was small and possibly not greater than ten or twelve thousand. This, however, did not restrain the Grand Lodge of Ireland from issuing a statement which claimed that the Orangemen had 'saved England'. It is difficult to assess the Order's political influence, if any, at this time. Small groups of predominantly working men, who did not have the vote, meeting once a month for their rituals in the upper rooms of public houses cannot have had much impact. Besides, the English movement was a provincial phenomenon and there is little evidence that senior politicians were interested in it. Certainly the Orange grandees from Ireland, Ogle, Foster, Duigenan and the others, who sat at Westminster, had little interest in their English offspring. If the Order was to grow, Nixon would have to put on his thinking cap again.

Objections to Lodges in the Army

Nixon saw a model for growth near to hand. The weavers and tenant farmers of Armagh had recognised from early days that the Order needed the support of the gentry, and it was this class, aided by military personnel, who carried the fledgling 'system' to Dublin and induced the grandees to join. Nixon and his friends were determined to follow a similar course; their immediate task was to attract English grandees, and they believed that the times were propitious to do so. The Catholic question was again to the fore in English politics, and there were aristocrats at Westminster and elsewhere who would not be adverse to a movement dedicated to fighting Catholic and 'popular' claims.

The majority of English lodges were civilian, with only about one-fifth being military, but voices were raised from the radical benches in Parliament complaining of soldiers being involved with a secret society. The matter came to a head when a magistrate in Worcester arrested a petty thief who was found in possession of a lodge membership certificate made out to a soldier called William Hall of the First West Yorks militia. The certificate was sent to Whitehall where the military secretary, Colonel Gordon, took a poor view of it and requested further information. He was informed that Hall was a man of excellent character and had probably lost the certificate while on a recruiting tour. It was confirmed that a lodge had existed in the West Yorks for ten years. Colonel Gordon became alarmed, and the matter was brought to the attention of the Home Secretary, Lord Liverpool. Information was sought on the prevalence of lodges in the army, and instructions issued to all commanding officers to inform the ranks that membership of oath-bound secret societies was contrary to military regulations.

Nixon realised that the interpretation of the Home Secretary could be applied to civil as well as military lodges, and moved quickly to revise the rules, particularly in regard to oath-taking. He went to great pains to discourage anything which might be conceived as being in defiance of authority. On 11 February 1811, he wrote to John Giffard, the Deputy Grand Master of Ireland:

> To shelter the societies (i.e. the lodges) from any persecution from the malevolent and to place them on a legal and permanent footing, the Grand Lodge (of England) has directed that the Rules and Regulations by which the societies be governed be revised so as to fall within the scope and meaning of proviso 33 GEO. 30 for regulating benefit societies. . . .[7]

Lodges continued to exist in the army under the guise of benefit societies, but from time to time regimental officers sought to curtail them.

Aristocratic Support

Meanwhile, the quest for English grandee support continued. The first important nobleman to join did so as early as 1808. This was George Tyrell Kenyon of Gredington, in Flintshire, known in the peerage as the Third Baron Kenyon or, more simply, as Lord Kenyon. He was introduced by Fletcher, who convinced him of the worthwhile part which the Order had played in Bolton during the period of industrial unrest. But Kenyon had other motivations. He was alarmed at the growing clamour for Catholic emancipation which he conceived — if granted — to be the beginning of a slippery slope to the destruction of the constitution. As a sincere Protestant, he held that Catholic worship was idolatrous and that the Pope was an enemy of freedom. On political grounds he believed that the bargain struck by Parliament and King William in 1688, the Bill of Rights, should be preserved inviolate. Besides, he hated compromise and expediency, and deplored the tendency of modern legislators to give way supinely to popular hullabaloos and to reverse legislation solemnly enacted.

Having made his commitment, Kenyon was prepared to give energy, time and money to build the Order into an effective force to meet the Catholic threat. He agreed with the Lancashire leadership that the Order should be built from the top down, and had already used his influence with like-minded peers. He persuaded Lords Winchelsea and Mansfield that the Order represented England's best chance, and his influence on the Duke of Gordon was particularly important, as Orangemen in Glasgow and elsewhere in Scotland saw the Duke's involvement as a stepping stone to greater things.

Orangeism in the Mall

In 1816, a suave and smooth-talking Dubliner named C. Eustace Chetwoode was made an Orangeman in his native city. The following year he transferred to London, but found the Orangemen whom he met in Holborn and Clerkenwell 'drawn mostly from the lower orders, and quite unappealing'. He founded a gentleman's lodge which met fortnightly at the British Coffee House in fashionable Cockspur Street, off the Mall. The Carlton Club had not yet come into being, but senior Tories met in clubs all around and Chetwoode moved easily in their circles. It is difficult to discern his status, but it is undoubtedly true that it was he (and Kenyon) who established the first links with High Toryism.

One of his most influential contacts was a man whom he intuitively understood, the grim and cunning Henry Addington, First Viscount Sidmouth, who was a trenchant spokesman for those back-bench Tory ultras who vehemently opposed Catholic relief. Sidmouth, whilst Home

Secretary, relied on informers and spies for his information about radical activists. Chetwoode's intimacy with him lends credence to the view that Orangemen acted as government spies. A number of Addington's friends also joined the lodges.

The Grand Old Duke of York

All of George III's seven sons were, in the description of Sir Winston Churchill, 'obnoxious'.[8] Two, however, had reputations more unenviable than the rest and these, for some reason, were the two who accepted high office in the Orange Order: Frederick Augustus, Duke of York, and Ernest Augustus, Duke of Cumberland. The Duke of York was intelligent, outgoing and boisterous, and Cumberland no less intelligent but hot-headed, impetuous and with a whiff of sulphur about him. Both were keen, courageous and efficient military men who would neither suffer fools gladly nor bridle their tongues. They were also wily politicians and active in the House of Lords, but frequently their caustic remarks made them enemies, and scandalous rumours continually circulated about them. As far as the Order was concerned, they were prime material. Apart from their prestige as Royal dukes, they were — like their father — Protestant ultras.

The first to be targeted was the Duke of York. He was known to have the ear of his father and that of his elder brother, George Augustus, the heir apparent. This Royal intimacy, it was felt, might be a valuable asset against the foreshadowed Catholic threat. If there was to be a change of attitude on the part of the King, his Majesty could be given a filial reminder of his Coronation oath, and who would have as good access to the royal person as the Duke of York?

He was a big, coarse man with a high-coloured face and an intimidating growl. In a throwback to an earlier age, he had been consecrated bishop of Osnabruck when six months old, not because of an infantile religious disposition but because of the vast revenues attached to the office. In 1793 he commanded an expedition against the French in Flanders and, after a courageous cavalry charge at Beaumont in April 1794, went on to an astonishing defeat the following month at Turgoing. After this he was recalled. In 1809 he became embroiled with Parliament when allegations were made against his mistress, Mary Ann Clarke, who had used her influence to sell army commissions. But despite his reputation for rudeness, boozing and whoring, the Duke had his admirers, and some regretted that he was caricatured in the nursery rhyme:

> The Grand Old Duke of York
> He had a thousand men
> He marched them up to the top of the hill
> And marched them down again.

When they were up, they were up
When they were down, they were down
But when they were half-way up,
They were neither up nor down.

He was responsible for a number of useful army reforms, and founded the Duke of York's Royal Military School (later Sandhurst Military Academy).

Contact with the Duke was initially made in 1813 through the young Marquis of Yarmouth, son of Lord Hertford, who sat in Parliament for the family's rotten borough in Antrim; the tenants on his father's estate had been among the first to join when organised by the legendary Reverend Philip Johnson. He had access to the Duke through his mother, who was well-established at court. In May 1813 he invited York to preside at a meeting of the Philanthropic Society (probably an Orange front organisation) at Saint Paul's Coffee House in the City. Afterwards they retired to Lord Kenyon's town house in Portman Square, where the Duke was initiated into the Order. A lodge was established for members of the nobility and a lodge room set up in Kenyon's library. Had all gone well, this would have replaced the Manchester lodge as the Grand Lodge of England and Colonel Taylor would have stepped down as Grand Master in favour of York. But the association of a Royal duke with the Order provoked an outcry from the Radicals in the Commons, and the Duke had to lie low as a rank-and-file member.

In January 1820, King George III died and was succeeded by the Prince Regent. Two weeks later the Grand Lodge convened a special meeting at the King's Head Tavern in Manchester and issued an Address of Loyalty to the new King. This was almost the last act which Taylor performed as Grand Master. He died in October, and the question of a new Grand Master engaged the brethren. The likely successors were either Fletcher or Kenyon, but someone suggested that the public mood had changed since 1813 and that the Duke of York should be invited to assume the office. It was agreed that the interests of the Order would be 'materially promoted' if it were led by the Duke, and an invitation was tendered. York readily accepted, on condition that Lord Kenyon would act as Deputy Master.

Following this, Manchester gave way to London as the seat of the Grand Lodge, and the relocation was announced in a letter from the Duke of York to all English lodges. But the tenure of the Duke was short. A new hubbub was raised in Parliament: the Order was described as a dark conspiracy, and instances were given of it being responsible for disorder on the streets. There was great comment on a clash with the Lord Mayor of Liverpool on 12 July 1819; the Mayor had banned the

Orangemen from marching, as they intended carrying effigies of the Pope and a Cardinal, and burning these in front of the doors of a Catholic church. The Orangemen were furious and took the matter to court, where they lost and had to pay hefty costs. These, it seems, were borne by Lord Kenyon.

The controversy over York's membership came to a head on 21 June, when Sir John Newport asked a question in the House concerning the legality of the Orange oath. Castlereagh replied for the government and said that York had agreed to serve as Grand Master on the understanding that the Order's objects were not of a political nature but merely rendered general support and loyalty to the Crown. He said: 'As soon as it was suggested to him (York) that there was some doubt as to the legality of the Association, he sent a communication to them in which, without imputing any intentional breach of law, he declined any connection with them.'

York's resignation letter to Lord Kenyon said:

> Your Lordship is perfectly aware of the grounds and principles upon which I accepted the Grand Mastership of the Orange Lodge in England. I have within these few days learnt that the Law Officers of the Crown and other eminent lawyers are decidedly of the opinion that the Orange Associations (i.e. lodges) under the Oath administered to their members are illegal . . . Under the circumstances . . . I could no longer be a member without violating those laws which it has ever been my duty to uphold and maintain.[9]

It must have been galling for York to resign. He loved the pomp and ceremony attached to the office of Grand Master and, besides, the tenets of Orangeism were close to his heart. In 1821, for instance, when William Conyngham Plunket, the Member for Dublin University, introduced a Bill for Catholic Relief, York displayed his anti-Catholic spleen. He said his views arose from principles 'which he had embraced ever since he had been able to judge for himself and which he hoped to cherish for the rest of his life'.[10] In 1825 he was particularly outspoken and, in the view of Lecky,[11] he made an indecent speech which showed his anti-Catholicism to be almost paranoid. Jumping from his seat in the House of Lords, he said that he felt forcibly on the Catholic question when he remembered that it had been responsible for the illness which clouded the final days of the late King. Waving his hands wildly, he declared that his principles were imbibed from his father and that he would maintain them until the last moment of his existence, 'so help me God'. It was remarked that few speeches had had such an electrifying effect on the House, and that the Relief Measure was thrown out largely under its influence. Following his resignation, York remained in contact with the Orangemen.

Some months before his death from dropsy (oedema) in 1827 he received an Orange delegation at his house in South Audley Street and was presented with a glowing address for his public service. He thanked the brethren by letter, saying:

> . . . I received with satisfaction the Address of the Members of the Grand Lodge of the Orange Institution of Great Britain which you have done me the honour of presenting to me; and I trust that you yourselves will accept and convey to other members of the Institution my thanks for the obliging and friendly terms in which the Address notices my public conduct, and my endeavour to discharge my duty as a Peer of the Realm in support of the religious rights and establishments of this country.
>
> I am, Lord and Gentlemen, yours
> Frederick.[12]

Enforced Rule Changes

With the Law Officers taking the view that the oath was illegal, it became imperative for the leadership to move quickly to bring the Order within the law. Chetwoode and Kenyon (who constituted the intellectual leadership) devised a scheme whereby no oath would be administered at all. Henceforward candidates were obliged to show in writing that they had taken an oath of allegiance before a public notary or similar official. The word 'lodge' was taken from use and members met under a warrant made out to an individual, and not, as hitherto, to a group. This gave the Order the appearance of being a devolved organisation rather than a federated one. The new scheme was cumbersome in that warrants were issued to specific brethren, who might be difficult to remove from office should the need arise. The overriding virtue of the arrangement was that it kept the Order, for the time being, within the law.

—18—

The Ebbing Tide

But fools there are plenty, and knaves are the same
So colours and orders into fashion came
This work, it was owing to Harry the Shaver
And him from Slievegullion, they call Tom Sayvor.

— Orange doggerel on those who sought
to preserve the 'Diamond System'

New Orders for Old

The years immediately after the Union were difficult for the Orange Order in Ireland, and the period is sometimes called the 'Ebb Tide of Orangeism'. It was convulsed with dissension and the membership went into decline, yet those at the top were working extremely hard. Thomas Verner introduced widespread changes and expended great energy in organisational matters. By 1800 he had appointed twenty-two Grand Masters, and in January of that year a committee produced new rules to replace those which had been adopted higgledy-piggledy over previous years. The Grand Lodge was itself reorganised, and a number of committees were formed to enquire into different aspects of the Order's affairs. One reported on the ritual for conferring the first degree, and its recommendations were adopted.

Other recommendations were so sweeping that, when adopted, they were called 'The New System'. To conform to the changes, existing memberships were cancelled and former members had to undergo a fresh initiation. The Grand Lodge appointed inspectors, known as 'Official Visitors', to visit, by rota, all lodges and supervise the adoption of 'The New System'. The new initiation ritual had similarities to that of the first degree ceremony in Craft Masonry. The candidate (known as 'a poor Israelite lost in the Wilderness'), accompanied by two sponsors and wand-bearing deacons, was taken before the throne of the Worshipful

Master, to hear an edifying address on the virtues of 'The System' and to partake in a simple catechism.

The innovations were not universally popular, and some demanded a return to the old forms known as the 'Diamond System'. They pined for the familiar rituals and prayers which, in some instances, could be traced to the Boyne Society. Verner's innovations were too drastic, and discontent with his leadership grew. Matters came to a head during 'The Twelfth' celebrations of 1801 when the Grand Lodge met to elect a new Grand Master. Verner was ousted by George Ogle, by a two-vote margin. Ogle was able and well respected, but as an MP was obliged to stay in London a great deal. To take some of the weight from him, a Deputy Grand Master was appointed. There was no surprise when this turned out to be John Giffard.

Meanwhile, the 'Official Visitors' found that a variety of practices — some esoteric, some not — were being employed in a number of lodges. In Armagh and elsewhere they discovered that Worshipful Masters were initiating Orangemen into so-called 'higher orders' which had names like 'Scarlet', 'Green', 'Arch Purple', 'Black' and 'Apron'. The ensuing controversy gave these 'orders' prominence and, in some instances, a new lease of life. They were particularly popular in Donegal. The Grand Lodge of Ireland was thoroughly against them, but some lodges were determined to retain them. The demand for retention was led by Thomas Server, the Grand Secretary for County Armagh, and Henry Sling, the Deputy District Master for Armagh Town. Server was a landed proprietor whose family had been associated with the Order from its early days, and Sling was a barber, popularly known as 'Harry the Shaver'.

The Grand Lodge of Ireland called a special meeting in November 1817 to 'consider the orders and alternatives lately introduced amongst brethren and to determine how far the same are or are not expedient to the well being of the Institution.' The meeting took place in Dublin with Giffard in the chair, and senior figures like Sir William Musgrave and J.H. Cottingham in attendance; Server and Sling were present to make their case. The issue was not resolved and a committee was set up to report on the purple degree, as (it was claimed) 'some confusion had crept into it.' It was hoped that a remodelled purple degree (which would include material from the older 'workings') would meet the objections of the traditionalists. It failed to do so, and they — tiring of the strictures of the Grand Lodge — decided to make their own arrangements, adopting a degree which deviant lodges had developed in 1802 to preserve elements of the 'Diamond System'.

This was called the 'Arch Purple' to distinguish it from the second or 'plain' purple degree, and it was based on a Biblical reference to a royal priesthood. Its initiates regarded themselves as being in holy orders and among God's anointed. The citation came from 1 Peter 2:9 : 'You however are a chosen race, a royal priesthood, a holy nation, a people He claims for His own to proclaim the glorious works of One who has called you from darkness into light.' The word 'royal', of course, does not refer to an earthly kingdom and the word 'arch' is used in the sense of 'chief' or 'higher' (as in archbishop or archangel) and indicates that the degree is more advanced than the two customary ones. Server and Sling tried to rally support for the royal arch purple degree, on the basis that it was part of the original 'system', and sent a circular to all lodges:

> We the undersigned, request that all Masters and Officers of lodges throughout Ireland who are determined to support and maintain the original Orange Institution, as formed in 1795, to meet in Armagh on Monday 10th July at the house of John Brown, Scotch Street, to enter into such regulations as may be deemed necessary for the further support of your glorious Institution.[1]

This was too much for the Grand Lodge in Dublin, and Server and Sling were expelled with a number of their supporters. In all, sixteen lodges were threatened with expulsion. Despite this, the Armagh meeting went ahead and is generally seen as the inaugural meeting of a separate and distinct body known as The Royal Arch Purple Order. Its founders were crusaders rather than rebels and did not see its creation as being opposed to the Orange Order; its purpose was merely to preserve the old traditions. It was agreed that membership should be open only to brethren who had taken the two established degrees (of the Orange Order) and that it should run, in every way, as a parallel Order. In time the powers-that-be accepted this arrangement and recognised the value of a body which kept the old traditions intact. The Royal Arch Purple Order was therefore accepted into the Orange family.

The Castle's Attitude Cools

The question of Catholic Emancipation had not died, but gone into slumber. After Waterloo the Papacy was seen to be as reactionary as any of the Great Powers. The Pope became an ally of Metternich, and the Catholic Church was recognised as a bulwark against revolution or political change. In England, Catholicism was no longer regarded as such a menace, except by a small section of ultras and by the new King, George IV, who adopted his father's views. George Canning, for example, a former disciple of Pitt, was now the leader of the liberal Tories and openly favoured Catholic Emancipation.[2] Orange opposition, however, remained virulent.

When the issue came to the fore in Ireland, Musgrave, Duigenan and others brought out pamphlets which stressed the part which popery had played in the Rebellion of 1798. Musgrave claimed that Catholic fanaticism had kept the country unsettled and asserted that two separate loyalties, to the King and to the Pope, would not co-exist without collision and discord. This aggressive Protestantism was not approved by Dublin Castle, which had nothing to gain from alienating Catholics. In fact, an English Catholic, Francis Plowden, was commissioned by the Castle to write a book to help reconcile the public mind to the Union, and Father Arthur O'Leary was engaged to pen a pamphlet showing that Catholic doctrines were not incompatible with loyalty to a Protestant constitution. Musgrave dedicated his own book, *Memoirs of the Different Rebellions in Ireland*, to the Lord Lieutenant, Cornwallis, and was slighted when that great figure requested that his name be deleted from future editions.[3] Dublin Castle was, in fact, seeking to disentangle itself from the Order, but had to act tentatively, as Orangemen had enmeshed themselves in virtually every area of the administration.

In 1801 the Earl of Hardwicke became Lord Lieutenant and adopted a cool attitude towards the brethren. Steps were taken to disband the yeomanry, which would have been a major blow as Orangemen constituted the force's backbone. Hardwicke's plans were overtaken by events when Emmet's rebellion scuppered any thought of change. In the event, the yeomanry received a new lease of life and were allowed to run amok. Five years later, the Duke of Bedford replaced Hardwicke and made fresh attempts to curtail Orange influence, but he, too, was balked. In 1807 the pendulum swung in the brethren's favour when the Duke of Richmond arrived and made a senior Orange figure, William Saurin, Attorney General. This appointment enabled Orangemen to dig themselves in, particularly as magistrates. But by now the Order's formal membership had slumped and its future looked bleak. Most of the founding fathers had ceased to be active, and attendances at lodge meetings were small and confined to diehards. Yet it was merely dormant, and under the joint challenges of a skilful Catholic leader, Daniel O'Connell, and the policies of a new and unfriendly Lord Lieutenant, it began to stir itself.

Richard, First Marquis Wellesley

The new Lord Lieutenant was the first Irishman to be appointed to the position since the seventeenth century. He was the former Lord Mornington, now Marquis Wellesley or, more simply, Richard Colley Wellesley. Born in Dangan Castle, near Summerhill, County Meath, as a young man he had sat in both Irish Houses of Parliament. By the time of his appointment he had gained a distinguished reputation. As Governor of Madras and Governor General of Bengal, he greatly enlarged British territory in India; at Westminster he had been a moderately liberal disciple of Pitt and his prominence gained him a place on the Privy Council.

Although in many ways an attractive figure, Wellesley had unfortunate defects. He was autocratic in manner and notoriously overbearing and self-important. Walter Scott described him as 'talking like a Roman Emperor' and it was said that he returned to Ireland 'boasting of his past victories over Indian cabals and anticipating further ones over the Irish'. He made a state entry to Dublin in December 1821, with his horses wreathed in shamrocks, and was heard to say: 'The Irish government, Sir! I am the Irish government!'[4]

On the positive side, Wellesley was a well-known emancipationist, and Catholics applauded his appointment. A decade earlier he had been among the first to invite Catholics to join the old Volunteers, and in 1809 had joined Spencer Perceval's cabinet only on condition that the Catholic question be kept open. Despite this, the terms under which he accepted his new appointment were unambiguous: he vowed to support the existing laws and not to change them. For Catholics he represented a breath of fresh air, but Protestants grew alarmed.

One of the Lord Lieutenant's first acts was to curtail Castle subsidies to the pro-Orange press. To combat this, a new Orange newspaper was launched, the *Dublin Evening Mail*,[5] which waged a sustained campaign against him. It found plenty of juicy tit-bits to print; Wellesley was a notorious womaniser, of whom it was said that 'neither the scullery maid nor the high born were safe'. When he married an American Catholic, Marianne Peterson, in a private ceremony at the Vice-Regal Lodge, the *Mail* could hardly restrain itself. 'At sixty-six,' it warned, 'love will make an old man who has lost more than toes, attempt more foolish things than dancing.'[6] A notice in the paper a few months later was even more cutting. It said: 'There will be a Rosary at the Lodge on the evening of Monday 20th. The ladies and gentlemen who attend are requested to bring their own beads.'[7]

'Dressing' the Statue

The first clash between Wellesley and the Order came with the dressing of William's statue for 'The Twelfth', in 1822. A few days before, he had received a letter from Daniel O'Connell, requesting an end to 'the disgusting practice'. Wellesley agreed, and took informal action to prevent it. The Orangemen ignored him and decorated the statue more elaborately than before. Things passed off calmly until late in the evening when the brethren were removing the decorations, and met a fusillade of stones and bottles from a Catholic mob. A riot ensued, and several were seriously injured. A few days later the matter was raised at Westminster by the pro-emancipationist, Henry Brougham, who denounced the Orangemen and insisted that they had provoked the disorder in the first place. He called them a despicable rabble.

This line pleased Wellesley, who was determined to take firm action should they step out of line on their next commemorative day — 4 November, King William's birthday. Tension mounted as the date approached, and instructions were given to the Lord Mayor, Alderman Fleming, to prevent the decorating of the statue. Fleming was in an invidious position. He was newly elected and the Corporation was top-heavy with Orangemen. No matter what he did he would be in the pillory, but he could not disobey the Lord Lieutenant. A few days prior to the anniversary he issued a proclamation stating: 'he would prevent by all legal means the decoration of the statue or the affixing thereto of any emblem, ornament or device.' This set the cat among the pigeons.

The Grand Lodge of Ireland could not openly defy lawful authority, yet it did not relish the brethren being prevented from engaging in traditional ritual. After some debate, it sat on the fence and advised Orangemen 'to use their discretion on whether or not to celebrate the day', adding: 'the decorating of the statue of King William in this city is a matter of local nature, and best left to the discretion of the authorities, the orders of whom must in every case be upheld by members of the Institution.'[8] This reduced the tension, but did not prevent the diehards from going ahead. In the early hours, under the cover of darkness, the usual emblems and ribbons were placed on the statue. From about 9.00 a.m. crowds began to gather in College Green, and on a few occasions were dispersed by the constabulary, but they kept returning. Around noon the scene turned ugly. There were cat-calls, and one or two bottles were thrown. A clash was prevented by the arrival of two Orange magistrates, Neville and Gabbett, who appealed for calm and engaged the rougher elements in dialogue. With a troop of horse ready to charge, the Orangemen saw that further protest would be useless. They heeded the magistrates, quietly removed the decorations, and went home. It had been a close call, for their blood was up.

The Bottle Riot

A riot in a Dublin theatre was not an unusual event, but this one was different. It was a gala occasion to mark the first public appearance of the Lord Lieutenant. Everyone who was anyone in Dublin society was drawn to the Theatre Royal, and a special performance of Goldsmith's *She Stoops to Conquer* was arranged. The prosperous city burghers and their ladies beamed from their boxes, and the scene was one of pomp and splendour.

The Lord Lieutenant's box was fitted with drapes of imperial blue, topped with a large escutcheon of the Wellesley arms, surmounted by the crown, lion and unicorn. In the centre stood a richly gilded chair, flanked by bewigged ushers resplendent in their white uniforms. His Excellency arrived at seven, accompanied by a brilliant entourage, and bowed to the applause of the patrons.

All was still as the curtain rose and the players came onto the stage. Then, suddenly from the pit, someone shouted: 'What about God Save the King!' This bolt stunned everyone, but the orchestra struck up. As the first Act proceeded, the gods became restless and there were shouts of 'No Popery' and 'A groan for the Lord Mayor'. Soon, the din became general and the shouting changed to 'A groan for Wellesley' and 'No Surrender'. The play continued. When Miss Gloria Graddon was singing the stanza 'Oh Lord our God arise', His Excellency rose, as if on cue, and moved to the front of his box. He glared defiantly at the rabble for several minutes, and went pale with anger. When the orchestra switched to 'Saint Patrick's Day', to show his scorn he waved his arms dramatically as if conducting the musicians. It was then that an orange labelled 'No Popery' was flung onto the stage. Next came a blade from a watchman's rattle, and then a bottle was hurled into the orchestra. The performance stopped, and Wellesley's private secretary rushed frantically downstairs, demanding the arrest of the culprits. Within minutes a few dozen Orangemen were frog-marched out, and the performance resumed. At the conclusion, as everyone stood for the national anthem, Wellesley was seen to be in a grim humour.

Seven Orangemen were taken to the constabulary station at College Street. The Attorney General, William Conyngham Plunket, attempted to have them convicted on conspiracy charges — Wellesley insisted that he had been the target of a full-scale murder attempt — but the Grand Jury, heavy with Orangemen, threw it out. Had the charges been more realistic and related to tumult, they might have succeeded. In the event, they provoked a huge display of Orange hostility towards the government. The whole affair was blown out of all proportion; had Wellesley been less concerned with his punctured dignity, he might have avoided the matter ending in fiasco.

The Catholic Revival

The first steps in a new demand for Catholic Emancipation came in February 1823 when Daniel O'Connell and another lawyer, Richard Lalor Shiel, met at the house of a mutual friend in the Dublin mountains, and formed a new political organisation which was to become more powerful than any previously known. This was the Catholic Association, and its purpose was 'to adopt all legal and constitutional measures as may be useful to obtain Catholic Emancipation.' Its other aims included its willingness to:

> . . . obtain legal redress for Catholics injured by Orange violence and oppression who were unable to obtain redress themselves. To prevent, legally, Orange processions, violence etc., and to bring the perpetrators to court. To prosecute Orange murderers. To procure for Catholics all rights to which they were entitled by law which for thirty years had been denied them.[9]

O'Connell was the power behind the new initiative. A man of almost superhuman energy and singular personality, no-one was a nobler incarnation of the aspirations of his people. With his powerful, ardent oratory he was able to articulate their wrongs and make their tormentors wince before him. He was from an old Gaelic family and educated in France, from where he fled the Revolution to complete his education in London. He was called to the Bar a few years later at Lincoln's Inn. O'Connell had little time for the United Irishmen and hated their deism; as to their efforts to raise the lot of the people, he saw them as blunderers who had brought untold suffering and paved the way for the Union. When Emmet made his forlorn attempt at rebellion in 1803, O'Connell was contemptuous of such futility and turned out with the Dublin yeomanry to bring the rebels to heel.

Initially, the progress of his new association was slow. Like earlier bodies, it drew its support from better-off Catholics, but his master stroke was to win the support of the clergy and the peasantry. By fixing the dues for membership at the rate of a farthing a week, he achieved important ends: he gave the peasants a sense of participation and roused their latent nationalism. At the same time he raised large sums from those who took out formal membership. The dues were dubbed the 'Catholic Rent' and, throughout the country, parish priests and curates used their pulpits to facilitate its efficient collection. Soon O'Connell had a formidable weapon in his hands: a resurgent peasantry organised for a definite purpose.

O'Connell, Peel and Saurin

Time and again O'Connell clashed with the judiciary and earned the animosity of Dublin Castle. One of his foremost antagonists was Robert Peel, the new Chief Secretary, with whom he was destined to battle for over thirty years. In 1812 Peel arrived as a new broom, and displayed all the characteristics which the Irish most detest. He was cocksure, supercilious and arrogant, and had an irritating habit of closing his eyes when arguing. He got O'Connell's back up because of his leaning towards Orangemen; O'Connell labelled him 'Orange Peel' and described his smile as 'like that on the breast plate of a coffin'. On learning that his father was a self-made cotton manufacturer from the Midlands, O'Connell snobbishly put the boot in:

> This youth squeezed out of the workings of I know what factory in England . . . sent here before he got over the foppery of perfumed handkerchiefs and thin shoes . . . a lad ready to vindicate anything and everything.[10]

This hostility nearly led to a shooting match which might have ended in serious consequences. The days of duelling were not over and O'Connell had recently been compelled to fight when an Orangeman named D'Esterre challenged him. They met, and D'Esterre was killed. In 1815 O'Connell accused Peel of traducing him in the House of Commons, where he could not be called to account. An engagement was scheduled to take place in Ostende. O'Connell left Dublin but was arrested in London and held on bail, and Peel was induced not to press the matter further.

A few years before, in 1813, Peel had had a chance of taking the measure of O'Connell when the Duke of Richmond retired from office. As Richmond packed his bags he was attacked by the editor of the *Dublin Evening Post*, John Magee, who took the opportunity to lash out at other former viceroys as well:

> They insulted, they oppressed, they murdered and they deceived . . . The profligate, unprincipled Westmoreland, the cold-hearted and cruel Camden, the treacherous Cornwallis, left Ireland more oppressed than they found her. . . .'[11]

A writ was issued against Magee for criminal libel and the prosecution was led by the Attorney General, William Saurin. O'Connell acted for the defence and the scene was set for high drama. The courtroom was crowded, the jury packed with several well-known Orangemen, and the illiberal Chief Justice, William Downes, was on the bench. O'Connell knew that there was little he could do for Magee and, with the probable agreement of his client, undertook to use the occasion for an attack on the Ascendancy system.

Saurin was a dangerous opponent. Black-eyed, lank-haired, with shining liquid eyes, he was one of the most feared members of the Irish Bar. The grandson of a Huguenot refugee, he was prominent among the Orange grandees. His purposes in life seemed to be to avenge the horrors of the dragonnades, and he saw the Irish law courts as a suitable field of battle. O'Connell's reply to the case made by Saurin should be read in its entirety; what follows are snippets.

O'Connell began by criticising his opponent's language:

> It was a farrago of helpless absurdity . . . violent and virulent, it was a confused and disjointed tissue of bigotry, amalgamated with congenital vulgarity . . . he called my client a malefactor, a Jacobin and a ruffian . . . he called him a brothel-keeper, a pander, a kind of bawd in breeches . . . I cannot repress my astonishment that the Attorney General could have preserved this diet in its native purity; he has for some years mixed among the highest orders of the state . . . He has had the honour to belong for thirty-five years to the Irish Bar . . . to that bar at which he has seen and heard a Burgh and a Duquery; at which he must have listened to a Burton, a Ponsonby, and a Curran; to a bar which still contains a Plunket, a Ball and, despite his politics, I would add a Bushe. With this galaxy of glory flinging its light around him, how can he alone have remained in the darkness? How has it happened that the twilight murkiness of his soul has not been illuminated with a single ray shot from their lustre? Devoid of taste and genius, how can he have had memory enough to preserve his original vulgarity? . . . As to his attack on the Catholic Board, I do here brand him an infamous and profligate liar.[12]

Saurin sat through it all with sweat running down his forehead, twiddling his pencil, and gazing blankly at a point on the ceiling.

Turning to the jury, O'Connell drove on:

> You are all, of course, Protestants. See what a compliment he pays to your religion and his own when he endeavours thus to procure a verdict on your oaths; when he endeavours to seduce you to what, if you were to be seduced, would be perjury, by indulging your prejudices . . . Will he succeed, Gentlemen? Will you allow him to draw you into a perjury out of zeal for your religion? And will you violate the pledge you have given to your God to do justice in order to gratify your anxiety for the ascendancy of what you believe to be His Church? . . . Gentlemen . . . reflect on the pious crime of violating your solemn oaths in aid of the designs of the Attorney General against popery. . . .[13]

He now cut at the quick of the Orangemen:

> Gentlemen, I sincerely respect and venerate your religion, but I despise your prejudices in the same proportion as the Attorney General has cultivated them. In plain truth, every religion is good — every religion is true to him who, in his conscience, believes it. There is but one bad religion — that of a man who professes a faith which he does not believe, but good religion may be, and often is, corrupted by the wretched and wicked prejudices which admit a difference of opinion to be a cause of hatred.[14]

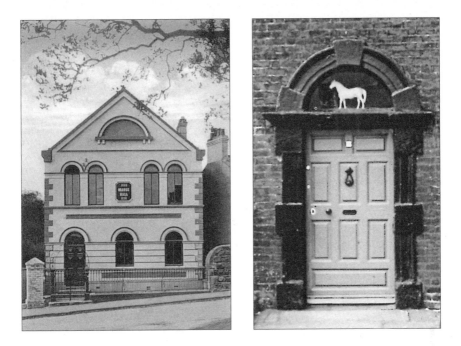

Above left: The Orange Hall at Limavady, 1890; typical of the almost Masonic appearance of lodges in towns across Ulster.

Above right: A white horse, the Williamite emblem, in the fanlight of a Protestant home in Erne Street, Dublin in the 1960s. *Courtesy: Ireland of the Welcomes.*

James Prinsep Beadle, The 36th Ulster Division going into action on the Somme, 1 July 1916: Ulster's bloody contribution to the First World War. *Courtesy: Belfast City Council.*

Above: Orangemen marching 'in the south' at Rossnowlagh, Donegal.
Courtesy: Colman Doyle.
Opposite: The Diamond Memorial Hall (Loyal Orange Lodge 85).
Below left: The Carleton Street Orange Hall (opened in 1873), Portadown, focus of parades by 32 lodges on 12 July every year.

Above: William III being received on landing in Ireland at Carrickfergus, 14 June 1690.

James II landing from France in Kinsale, 12 March 1689.

Clockwise from top left: William II of Holland; James II (contemporary painting from the City of Dublin Charter) *Courtesy: Dublin Corporation*; Medal struck in honour of the petitioning bishops — one of the incidents that brought about the call to William and Mary; Maurice of Nassau, son of William the Silent; John Gifford ('The Dog in Office'), hated by Dublin radicals; William of Orange as a young man; William III in the guise of a classical Roman hero; Frederick Henry.

Centre: Lord Tyrconnell, as the knave in a contemporary pack of playing cards, arming Catholics in Ireland

Far left: William Johnston of Ballykilbeg whose defiance of the marching ban at Bangor on 12 July 1867 made him a hero of the 1890's, as an exponent of resistance to Home Rule. He also became the subject of many banners. *Left:* Armand Friedrick Herman, Duke of Schomberg, killed at the Battle of the Boyne, 1690. *Courtesy: National Gallery of Ireland.*

Far left: Patrick Sarsfield, Earl of Lucan, James's most famous general. *Left:* Thomas Sloan, founder of the Independent Orange Order in 1902, and later MP for South Belfast.

Far left: Godart van Reede, Baron Ginkel, victor of Athlone, Aughrim and Limerick. *Left:* William Blacker, who witnessed the Battle of the Diamond, an important figure in the Orange Order in the early nineteenth century. *Courtesy: Dublin University Magazine. Board of Trinity College.*

Above: Derry in 1688, from 1887 edition of Rev. George Walker's account of the siege.

Limerick Castle, the redoubt held under siege for James, 1690—1691.

Right: William and Mary.
Below: Breaking the boom at
Derry — a symbolic moment
in orange history.
Bottom: Dan Winter's
Cottage, at the Diamond near
Portadown, scene of the so-
called 'Battle of the
Diamond' in 1795.

THE RELIEF OF DERRY. THE MOUNTJOY
BREAKING THE BOOM.

Benjamin West, William III crossing the Boyne, 1 July 1690.
By kind permission of the Duke of Westminster

Lady members of the Orange Order, photographed about 1911, the year after ladies' lodges were re-established.

Above: Orange Hall at Laghey, Co. Donegal, typical of local Orange lodges in rural Ireland.
Left: The former building of the Grand Orange Lodge of Ireland and the Fowler Memorial Hall, Parnell Square, Dublin — for half a century the centre of Orange activity in Ireland.

Below: The Apprentice Boys Memorial Hall in Derry, begun 1873, and opened on 13 August 1877.

Above: James II flees Ireland from Kinsale,
4 July 1690.
Right: Orange lodge members marching
with Carson banner. *Courtesy: Board of
Trinity College.*

Below: A political postcard from 1912. Carson recrossing the Boyne. *Courtesy: Board of
Trinity College.*

Above: The Ulster Volunteer Force, landing German guns in defiance of the law at Larne on 25 April 1914.

Left: Ulster 1914. 'Deserted! Well — I can stand alone.' A contemporary politcal postcard.
Courtesy: Board of Trnity College.
Below: Orangemen marching through Belfast to sign Ulster Solemn League and Covenant, on Ulster Day, 28 September 1912.

Above: Marching Orangemen triumphant in 1930s Belfast.

Orange Arch at Jervis Street, Portadown; the idea for which derives from an arch erected for William III's entry into the Hague in 1691.

Emblems of the Boyne Society, a precursor of the Orange Order, as shown on a tracing-board for the instruction of initiates. (The Biblical background to the emblems is given in Chapter 9). *Courtesy: Armagh County Museum.*

The author and his daughter at the Boyne crossing, with the remains of the monument (above) in the background.

At last he was finished, and in the view of Peel, who sat in the body of the court, he had uttered a greater libel than that of his client. He had publicly indicted the administration of justice in Ireland. The speech was reported in every newspaper, and over 100,000 printed copies were sold. It was translated into all the major European languages, and its sales abroad were as great as those at home. But the Orange jury remained unmoved: Magee was sentenced to two years in jail, fined £500 and ordered to find securities of £2,000 for seven years.

O'Connell was viewed by the Order with trepidation and, with the Pope and the Devil, entered its pantheon of hate figures. It was unsure of how to respond to him and, besides, it had more than enough on its plate. On 19 July 1823 the Unlawful Oaths Bill was passed, aimed at secret societies. To stay within the law, the Order had to be virtually reconstituted. Another 'New System' was adopted and, as in Britain, the lodges had to refrain from administering oaths. New members were required to satisfy their lodges that they had previously sworn oaths of allegiance, obduration and supremacy before a magistrate. But there were doubts as to whether even this was legal under the new Act. To avoid trouble, the Grand Lodge of Ireland cancelled all celebrations for the 1824 'Twelfth'. This angered the rank and file who saw it as weakness, but the Grand Lodge was in a dilemma. By cancelling the celebrations it was endangering the morale of the brethren and could easily drive its more combative spirits into the arms of Peep-O'Day-type organisations. It knew, equally, that its celebrations invariably led to violence and that further trouble could lead to a government ban.

The Unlawful Societies Act

O'Connell, too, had been skating on thin ice. His aggressive and abusive oratory was upsetting the authorities. The scurrility of his language may be seen in his treatment of Sugden, one of the most esteemed barristers of the day: O'Connell roguishly asked a jury, 'would you call a pig, now, by the name of Sugden?' For one who maintained that he was opposed to violence for political ends, O'Connell often seemed to be sailing close to the wind. In December 1824 he told an audience that Ireland would never have to resort to the methods used by the Greeks and the South Americans to obtain her rights, but then declared that if ever Ireland was driven to revolt, a 'new Bolivar' would emerge to lead her. Such language was playing with fire. The Irish peasant was easily aroused and the authorities knew it; already the Ribbonmen — the latter-day descendants of the Defenders — were burning and marauding in different parts of the country. The Castle sought an effective response to O'Connell, but legal opinion held that no existing law was being contravened, for O'Connell's threats were prudently hedged.

Throughout 1824 the authorities debated whether to suppress the Catholic Association. In the end they prosecuted O'Connell for his 'Bolivar' speech and, to show even-handedness, also indicted Harcourt Lees, an eccentric Orangeman, for a speech which he had made urging Ulster Protestants to take up arms against their Catholic neighbours. Both prosecutions were ill-advised, and failed.

The government had had enough. In February 1825 Henry Goulburn, the Chief Secretary, introduced the Unlawful Societies (Ireland) Act, which made it unlawful for any organisation which sought to redress grievances in either church or state to stay in existence for more than fourteen days. It was a draconian measure and an effective ban on political societies. Both the Orange Order and the Catholic Association came within its ambit. It became law on 9 March, and nine days later O'Connell dissolved the Catholic Association. On 18 March the Grand Lodge of Ireland held a final meeting in Dublin, and issued a statement:

> At no period was the Institution in a more flourishing condition or more highly respectable in the numbers added to its ranks. Notwithstanding this, the Parliament of the United Kingdom have considered it necessary that all political societies should be dissolved. Of course, our society is included. It therefore becomes our duty to remind you that any lodge meeting after this day becomes a breach of law.[15]

The opening sentence was hyperbole. The Order had been at a low ebb, but the banning did not kill it off. It went underground and awaited a new tonic.

Catholic Election Successes

O'Connell boasted that he could 'drive a coach and four through any Act of Parliament'. He now proceeded to do so, and established a new Catholic Association to replace the banned one. It was cleverly structured, and defeated the Act by being for charitable and educational objectives and 'all purposes not prohibited by law'. The new Association, it is true, could not demand changes in church or state, but it could defend Catholic doctrines and rebuff Orange attacks. The 'rent' continued to be collected, with such success that almost £500 per week entered its coffers.

At the parliamentary elections in 1827, Catholic voters (essentially the forty-shilling freeholders) voted for liberal Protestant candidates who supported emancipation. The most gripping contest was in Waterford, where the nominee of the Beresford family, Lord George Beresford, was defeated through the Catholic vote. Voting was by open ballot and tenants were expected to vote in accordance with their landlord's wishes, but in Waterford and elsewhere, the tenants — steeled by O'Connell's propaganda — ignored the instructions of their landlords and braved the risk of eviction.

In 1828, O'Connell's Association went a step further, and ran O'Connell himself as a candidate for Clare. He declared that if elected, he would not take the parliamentary oath as it was repugnant to his religious beliefs. His election would, therefore, bring the whole question of Catholic Emancipation to a head. From Loop Head to the Burren, from the Cliffs of Moher to the banks of the Shannon, the peasants flocked to support him. When the contest was over he had more than twice the votes of his opponent, and the tar barrels blazed on the hillsides in celebration. A few evenings later, he mounted a platform outside the Old Ground Hotel in Ennis and, with the torchlights blazing around him, told his frenzied supporters that: 'a blind man could see that it was the freeholders of Clare who had emancipated the Catholics of Ireland.'

Up, Protestants, Up!

By the blood of your fathers, the martyrs of old
By the honour and courage that never was sold
By the throne that we have and the faith we revere
Up, Protestants, Up! and in phalanx appear.

— *Orange verses to arouse Protestants against*
Catholic Emancipation in 1829

Problems for the Iron Duke

With the Orange Order in Ireland dissolved, loyalists had no mass organisation to counterbalance O'Connell and his Catholic Association. They organised meetings in many parts of the country, made fiery speeches, drafted resolutions against concessions to Catholics, but found that they were swimming against the tide.

Catholic Emancipation, although on the cards following O'Connell's victory in Clare, had yet to be enacted. The Returning Officer in Ennis had been placed in an invidious position. Catholics were perfectly entitled to give their votes to a co-religionist, yet the Returning Officer could not announce O'Connell as the new member, since no Catholic was allowed to sit at Westminster. On the other hand, if he declared O'Connell's election void the result could well be a rebellion, in which the opening shots would probably be fired at himself. His way out was to announce the result of the polling and transfer the problem to London.

The Prime Minister was an Irishman, but did not take any pride in the fact; Wellington had famously remarked that 'to be born in a stable did not make one a horse'. Yet the Iron Duke's mind had been moving, however reluctantly, towards emancipation. He was a realist, and the situation in Ireland convinced him that after the next election, Catholics would be returned in many constituencies; the electoral system would be seen as farcical if they were prevented from taking their seats. There was also a probability of violence, as they could not be expected to take their debarment lying down. Wellington told the Commons: 'I have probably passed a longer period of my life engaged in war than most and I must say this: if I could avoid by any sacrifice whatever even one month of civil war, I should give up my life to do it.'[1]

The Duke spent the winter months in negotiations with the King, the senior Anglican bishops, and Robert Peel, who was now Home Secretary. The King raged, and threatened to abdicate. The Archbishop of Canterbury and the Bishop of Durham made it known that they were opposed to Emancipation, and the Orangemen, both inside and outside Parliament, stirred up a rumpus. But the writing was on the wall.

The Benevolent and Loyal Orange Institution

Orangemen in Ireland felt that they could not allow themselves to be wrong-footed. If O'Connell could drive a 'coach and four' through the Unlawful Societies Act, so could they. On the initiative of Sir Harcourt Lees, 'The Benevolent and Loyal Orange Institution' was founded in Dublin on 2 December 1825. Its Grand Patron was the Duke of Gordon, and the Earl of Aldborough was installed as Grand Master. R. Ogle Gowan of Wexford was appointed Grand Secretary.[2] Its purpose was cleverly stated:

> This Association is formed by persons desirous of supporting the principles of the Christian religion; to support and relieve distressed members . . . and to afford assistance to such other religious and charitable purposes as may tend to the due ordering of religious and Christian charity. We associate also, in honour of King William the Third, the Prince of Orange, whose name we bear and whose immortal memory we hold in reverence.

The qualifications for membership were similar to those of the old Order and the new organisation was, in reality, the old dressed up as new. It was substantially pared down: there were no rituals, passwords or oaths. This may have been why it never really caught on; many missed the mystery, colour and Biblical foundations of the old Order. The new one served, for a time, as a stopgap; but its support was thin on the ground.

The Damnable Duke of Cumberland

It was at this time that Ernest Augustus, fifth son of King George III, made his mark as an Orangeman. In 1799 he had been created Duke of Cumberland in the peerage of Great Britain, and Earl of Armagh in that of Ireland. He is sometimes confused with William Augustus, an earlier Duke of Cumberland, who, after the Battle of Culloden, became known as 'Butcher Bill'.

Cumberland was the second Royal duke to join the Order, but did not accept office until after the death of the Duke of York, who had resigned following objections raised in the House by Sir John Newport in 1821. The position of Grand Master had been allowed to lapse during the last years of York's life and, following his death, was offered to Cumberland who accepted with the approval of the King. As there was no Irish Grand Lodge in existence, Cumberland became Grand Master of both Great Britain and Ireland.

Justin McCarthy, a temperate commentator, summed up his reputation as follows:

> His manners were rude, overbearing and sometimes even brutal. He had personal habits which seemed fitted for the days of Tiberius or the Court of Peter the Great, than for the time and sphere to which he belonged. Rumour not unnaturally exaggerated his defects, and in the mouths of many his name was the symbol of the darkest and fiercest passions, and even crimes. Some of the popular reports with regard to him had their foundations only in the common detestation of his character and the dread of his influence. But it was certain that he was profligate, selfish, overbearing and quarrelsome. A man of these qualities would usually be described in fiction as, at all events, bluntly honest and outspoken; but the Duke of Cumberland was deceitful and treacherous. He was outspoken in his abuse of those with whom he quarrelled, and in his style of anecdote and jocular conversation, but in no other sense.[3]

McCarthy's views are confirmed by numerous sources. Charles Grevell, the Clerk of the Privy Council, in his diary entry for 2 March 1829, wrote of Cumberland:

> There never was such a man, nor behaviour so atrocious as his — a mixture of narrow-mindedness, selfishness, truckling, blustering and duplicity with no object but self, his own ease and the gratification of his own fancies and prejudices.[4]

Cumberland gained an important influence over his milder-mannered brother, the Prince of Wales, and was able to mould him almost completely to his will. He constantly attended debates in the House of Lords and was a fierce Tory partisan. In 1805 he was elected Chancellor of Trinity College, Dublin, and a few years later presented a petition from Dublin Corporation to the Lords, in which he declared his undying opposition to any removal of Catholic disabilities.

He was said to have raped Lady Lyndhurst, driven Lord Graves to suicide, and committed incest with one of his sisters. The most notorious incident occurred on the night of 31 May 1810, when he was found in his apartments at Saint James's Palace with a terrible wound on his head, from a blow that would have been fatal had it fully met its target. Shortly afterwards his valet, Joseph Sellis, was found dead in his bed with his throat cut. The coroner's court returned the verdict that Sellis had committed suicide after attempting to assassinate the Duke. The absence of a reasonable motive, however, caused rumour, and some commentators hinted that Cumberland had really murdered Sellis. In 1813, a man named Henry White was sentenced to fifteen months' imprisonment and fined £200 for publishing such a rumour.

Cumberland was depicted as the wickedest of Queen Victoria's 'wicked uncles'.[5] Some people, however, took a different view. The Duke's friends in the Order, and among Tory ultras, saw him as a courageous man whose actions were based on patriotic principles and on a sound sense of public duty. He was certainly a brave cavalry commander: in a skirmish with the French at Tournai in May 1794, he showed high courage in an action which ultimately cost him the sight of his left eye. In November his cavalry squadron became embroiled with French dragoons and he broke his sword when parrying sabre thrusts, some of which got home and scarred him on the face; in the fury of battle he flung his arm around one of his adversaries and tore him from the saddle. His face was permanently marked and he suffered lifelong pains in his arm.

The accession of the Prince of Wales as George IV greatly increased Cumberland's influence, and the death of his sister, the Princess Charlotte, and brother, the Duke of York, brought him nearer the throne. He opposed the repeal of the Test Act with great vigour, and was angered by the rumour that Catholic Emancipation might be passed. He was, in fact, in Hanover when he learnt from Lord Kenyon that Wellington and Peel had softened. He received a warning about the Bill from his political mentor, Lord Eldon, who advised that his presence would be required in London at any moment. Lord Farnham, another Tory ultra, was more candid. In a hurried note he said: 'Every engine is set on foot to gain the consent, in a certain quarter, which his Royal Highness alone can perhaps prevent.'[6] It was thought that the Duke's strong mind could dominate the King's weak one, and that George would refuse to agree to Emancipation. Cumberland packed his bags and made for London.

The Brunswick Clubs

The Orangemen and Tory ultras did not rely solely on pressurising the King, but sought to excite the public with the slogan which had worked so often before: 'No Popery'. They established a high-powered organisation on both sides of the Irish Sea to push the message home.

Lord Kenyon took the initiative and wrote two open letters addressed to 'The Protestants of Great Britain and Ireland', urging them to maintain the Ascendancy, and went so far as to advocate that existing concessions to Catholics be withdrawn. He said:

> Protestants should petition the Throne and the Houses of Parliament to take from the papists privileges which experience has proved to be hurtful to the great mass of papists themselves, dangerous to the welfare of the state, the Protestant religion, and the civil and religious liberties of the people.[7]

On 14 August a banquet was held in Morrisons Hotel in Dublin in honour of one of the City's Members of Parliament, George Moore, attended by a number of noblemen and leading figures. After the function some of those present formed the first 'Brunswick Constitutional Club'. This was to be the parent of a new federated organisation established to oppose further concessions to Catholics, and was based on a plan devised by Lord Chandos in London. Lord Longford, the Duke of Wellington's brother-in-law, was elected the club's president.

Three weeks later, a large number of Tory ultras met in Maidstone, Kent, and established Brunswick Clubs in England. The executive consisted almost entirely of members of the peerage; Lord Guildford became president and the vice-presidents included Lords Kenyon, Farnham, Sidney, Abergaveny and Winchelsea. The name Brunswick was adopted at the suggestion of Lord Eldon, in deference to the Duke of Brunswick, and as a reference to, as he said, 'the illustrious Royal House which has sought to protect and cherish the Protestant Ascendancy since the days of The Glorious Revolution'. Clubs sprang up in many parts of the country, and often overlapped with Orange lodges. Patriotic calls were made to 'The Protestants of the Empire' to rally to the defence of the constitution. The government became apprehensive, and in November Peel made a speech in which he warned 'that clubs or combinations of any kind which resist or influence the deliberation of the legislature are dangerous instruments'.[8]

In Ireland the bulk of the Brunswickers were recruited from the former Orange lodges. Unlike the English Brunswickers, they had a strong evangelical streak and combined extreme reactionary views with burning anti-Catholicism. One intemperate activist was Thomas Langlois le Froy (a lawyer of Huguenot descent and friend of William Saurin), whose wild rhetoric agitated working-class audiences. O'Connell replied to one of his outbursts with this description: 'He is one of those persons who is seen on a Sunday morning walking through the streets of Dublin with three children walking before him and three following after, everyone carrying an enormous bible, giving fine material for an engraving of a religious family.'[9] By the end of 1828 there were over a hundred Brunswick Clubs in Ireland and a collection, modelled on O'Connell's 'rent', was set up. A newspaper called *The Star of Brunswick* was sold up and down the country. As the clubs grew, O'Connell began to plan against them.

His initial strategy was to whip up support from liberal Protestants. On 4 September he wrote to Lord Cloncurry, and urged him to use his influence with peers who agreed with Catholic Relief. He said:

> I think the Duke of Leinster and every other Protestant peer friendly to the principle of freedom of conscience should come forward and join the Catholic Association. There is in Ireland no neutral ground; whoever is not with us is against us. The time has come to take an active part in struggling to keep the country from bigots.[10]

Cloncurry and others made a positive response; an organisation called 'The Friends of Civil and Religious Liberty' was established and a dinner arranged at the home of the novelist Lady Morgan, where a declaration in favour of Catholic Emancipation was drawn up. This was an impressive testimony to liberal Protestantism in Ireland, signed by two Dukes, seven Marquesses, eleven Viscounts, twenty-two Baronets and fifty-two Members of Parliament.

The 'Invasion' of Ulster

O'Connell's next move was less happy. In 1826 he formed a brotherhood called the 'Order of Liberators'. Like its bête noire, it was modelled on Masonic lines and had three levels of membership: Knights of the Grand Cross, Knights Companion, and plain Liberators. Membership was confined to people who had performed a signal service for Ireland. An embarrassingly gaudy uniform — with a bright green sash, spattered with shamrocks — was designed for senior 'Liberators'. On 15 August one of the leaders, a former Belfast journalist named Jack Lawless, was mandated to go on a tour with a band of green-clad brethren to collect the 'rent' in areas where it had not previously been taken up. The North had always been poorly represented in the O'Connellite movement and there were new worlds to be conquered. O'Connell knew well that the Liberators would not be received with open arms in the Orange heartlands, but he wanted to raise the temperature.

Before Lawless set out, he issued a declaration of intent: his purpose was to appoint 'rent' collectors in every parish and build up an organisation for the regular collection of the levy. For a few weeks he hovered on the Ulster border, holding huge meetings in Meath and Louth.

At Drogheda he was cheered to the echo, and local Liberators entertained him to a public dinner. He then moved into Ulster and large numbers of Catholics turned out to greet him, often pulling his carriage through their villages. By 23 September he was in County Monaghan, making his way from Carrickmacross to Ballybay, when he was stopped in his tracks. He was told that thousands of armed Orangemen were gathered on the outskirts of Ballybay, and were intent on blocking his passage. They were led by their Worshipful Master, a publican named Sam Gray.

Lawless declared that he would not be intimidated and sent a message ahead saying that he had 250,000 men and would travel on the King's highway in spite of all opposition. His proclaimed strength was a gross exaggeration and the Orangemen (essentially yeomen out of uniform) knew it. They stood their ground and waited for him to arrive. The procession rolled on until General Thornton, with mounted lancers, intercepted and persuaded him to take a circuitous route towards Rockcorry chapel, about a mile and a half from the village. This prevented a direct clash, but some of Lawless's lieutenants advised him to rush the Orangemen, but he prudently halted at the chapel. Some Liberators went ahead and clashed with Orangemen on the Rockcorry Road. One was run through with an Orange bayonet and another had his leg shattered with a musket ball. The rest fled under fire. Lawless himself took fright and, mounted on a big grey horse, rode through the ranks behind him. He had a fortunate escape when a bullet fired by one of his angry followers narrowly missed him.

A few days later he attempted to enter the town of Armagh, but again the Orangemen turned out in great numbers against him and General Thornton, with a hopelessly outnumbered force, had little option but to stand by. Lawless thought it wise to retreat. O'Connell instructed him to give up the ghost, and the 'tour' was abandoned. The mobs on either side dissolved, and gradually the tension decreased. But the 'invasion' of Ulster could easily have ended in great tragedy. A major clash could have sparked a civil war, or so the Chief Secretary, Francis Leveson-Gower, thought. In a report to Wellington he said that Ireland had been 'on the eve of a civil war or rebellion, or both'.[11] The 'invasion' cast a long shadow. It was the first time in which the Ulster Protestant sense of territoriality manifested itself. No matter what success O'Connell might have elsewhere, the Orangemen showed that they would not (as they declared) 'give an inch' in Ulster. The concept of the 'separateness' of Ulster, and the Orange determination to remain supreme there, were markers for the future.

Emancipation

The Duke of Wellington and Peel bowed to the inevitable, and agreed to pass an Emancipation Bill. Once the decision was made, neither the

Brunswickers nor the Tory ultras could prevent it. When the King, in the Speech from the Throne (in February 1829), spoke of the 'government reviewing the disabilities of the Roman Catholics', it was apparent that Cumberland had failed to influence the royal mind. Peel, who had changed the views of a lifetime, resigned his seat for Oxford University and stood for re-election. The irate university Tories felt he had gone too far and threw him out, and to return to the House he had to hastily find a safe seat in a pocket borough. Wellington himself was the butt of foul language from Cumberland, whom he said he would horsewhip were he not a member of the Royal Family. He was inundated with insulting letters and even had to issue a challenge to the Orange Lord Winchelsea. The two men met on an early morning in Battersea Park, but without result.

On 6 March, Peel introduced the Bill. Every Orangeman in Parliament spoke or lobbied against it. The struggle to get it through lasted a month, and for a single day the country was without a government. The King announced that he would refuse to sign it if it were carried. Had he yielded at last to Cumberland? If so, the Iron Duke was in no mood for games. On learning of the King's attitude, he immediately announced the resignation of his government. In the dead of night the mercurial monarch, faced with alternatives which he could not stomach, changed his mind, and Wellington was recalled. The Bill (10 GEO IV C), entitled 'An Act for the Relief of His Majesty's Roman Catholic Subjects', was carried on the 30 April. Few Orangemen dared to consider its consequences, but one — who combined in his person and background the strongest traditions of Orangeism — made a remarkably accurate prophecy.

This was Lord George Beresford, the Protestant Archbishop of Armagh. Speaking in the Lords, he said that he saw Catholic Emancipation as the beginning, not the end, of a process which would overturn Ascendancy rule in Ireland. The Catholics, he believed, would use their newly acquired right to gain further rights, and he asked his fellow peers:

> Are you prepared to sacrifice the Irish church establishment and the Protestant institutions connected with it — to efface the Protestant character of the Empire — to transfer from Protestants to Roman Catholics the Ascendancy of Ireland?[12]

No one answered him. It was, however, clear to those for whom he spoke that neither the government nor public opinion could be relied upon to resist the onward march of the Catholics. The passing of the Bill was a historic turning point. Heretofore, the latent power of the Irish majority had been kept in check by their inability to use the franchise.

Now the floodgates were opened. The catalyst had been O'Connell's Catholic Association and the manner in which the Catholic clergy had swung behind it. O'Connell, the master politician, had also astutely made the Association an umbrella for a host of other grievances. This factor, and his popular rhetoric, enabled him to tap the embryonic nationalism of the masses. His success showed how electoral politics could be manipulated to threaten Protestant hegemony. It paid better dividends, in fact, than the methods employed by the United Irishmen a generation earlier.

The Orange Revival

Seven months prior to the enactment of the Emancipation Bill, the Orange Order was revived (25 September 1828) on the lapse of the Unlawful Societies legislation. It was too weak to participate in the final stages of the struggle against the Bill, and was content to leave the field to the Brunswickers. Eustace Chetwoode, the Grand Secretary of the Order in Britain, came to Ireland. He went on a tour of former strongholds and canvassed the return of men such as William Blacker and the Verners, who had gone into semi-retirement. Since the days of the Union, those at the top had been lacklustre; Giffard had been titular Grand Master since the death of George Ogle, although he never actually held the title. In his last years he was in indifferent health and unable to provide cogent leadership. In 1819 he was succeeded by Lieutenant General Mervyn Archdale of Castle Archdale, in County Fermanagh, a war hero who had been with Nelson in Egypt and participated in the night-time storming of the French ships in Aboukir Bay (22 March 1802). In this escapade he lost his right arm and very nearly his life.

He was invalided home and became a popular figure with the officers in the Phoenix Park. A tall, sociable man, he cut a dash with his waxed moustaches at Castle levees. In 1805 he was made an Orangeman, and around the same time married Jane Rochford-Hume, the daughter of the County Carlow Grand Master. Soon he entered Parliament and was kept active defending the Order from the attacks of Whigs and Radicals. He became Grand Master in 1819, although it was a difficult time to take over. The controversy over 'higher orders' was still raging, and a storm blew up concerning internal controls when one of the brethren in the Ballyhaise lodge in County Cavan leaked secrets to a notorious rebel. Archdale, who was not good in disputes, set up a Grand Lodge of Emergency and handed the problems over to it. He did not seek re-election in 1829 although he continued in Parliament as a doughty Orange champion for another fourteen years.

Lord O'Neill's Tenure

The next Grand Master of Ireland, Charles Henry St John O'Neill (2nd Viscount and 1st Earl) of Shanes Castle, County Antrim, had lost his father during the Battle of Antrim in 1798. The old man was piked in the back by a rebel who had been the family's lodge keeper for a number of years. Following the incident, O'Neill developed a loathing for Catholics which bordered on the pathological. His speeches in the House of Lords were unrestrained and, on occasion, he had to be brought under control by colleagues. He participated fully in the debates on the Union (which he supported) and when the rewards were distributed was given an earldom.

O'Neill's term as Grand Master was troublesome. The Order was embroiled in endless controversies over the 'dressing' of William's statue, and one 'New System' followed another. With the passing of the Unlawful Societies Act, he threw in the towel.[13] The Order in Ireland placed itself under the jurisdiction of the Grand Lodge of Great Britain, which was still legal. But in Britain there was a vacuum at the top. No Grand Master was appointed until Cumberland in 1827, and then the name changed to the Royal Orange Institution of Great Britain and Ireland. The word 'Royal' had been added during the Duke of York's brief tenure, but was later dropped. With the coming of a second Royal Duke, it seemed appropriate to re-adopt it.

New Structures

When the Order was re-launched in Ireland in 1828 it became necessary to build new operational structures. Negotiations were opened with the Benevolent and Loyal Orange Institution, with a view to merging the two bodies. A clash of personalities drew out the haggling, but eventually terms were agreed. A committee recommended, among other things, that the Duke of Cumberland's title be changed to Grand Master of the Empire, to reflect the fact that the Order had expanded to Canada and, to a lesser degree, to Australia. This was accepted, but in Ireland itself — where Orangeism was strongest — there was an anomaly in that there was no Grand Master. John Willoughby Cole, the 2nd Earl of Enniskillen, was recognised as the foremost Orangeman in the country but his title was that of Deputy Grand Master, and was shared with two others. In fact, the Irish Order was, led by a triumvirate consisting of Enniskillen, Colonel William Blacker, representing the Armagh gentry (who felt that they had almost proprietorial rights), and Robert Hedges Eyre from Cork, who looked after Orangeism in the south.

A notable development was that almost half the Order's executive were Anglican clergymen. This may have displeased the large numbers of Presbyterians who were joining, as their own clergymen were, as yet, standing aloof. The attitude of Presbyterians was summed up by one of their historians, W.T. Latimer, who said: 'Those who hated Catholics more than the landlords became Orangemen and those who hated the landlords more than the Catholics accepted either Republican or liberal principles.'[14] As the nineteenth century wore on there tended to be more of the former than of the latter.

Burgeoning Belfast

Continuing tensions and accompanying controversies provided the Order with a lifeline at a time when large numbers were fleeing the countryside and making their way to Belfast to provide manpower for its burgeoning industries. The influx disturbed the demographic balance of the fast-growing urban basin and created the Protestant and Catholic enclaves which exist to this day.

At the end of the eighteenth century Belfast was predominantly Presbyterian, but because of discriminatory legislation it was controlled by Anglicans, notably the nominees of Lord Donegall. The number of Catholics living there was less than 5 per cent and posed no threat. In fact, Catholics were looked on benevolently and their first church, Saint Mary's in Chapel Lane, was built with Protestant assistance. This cordiality changed as fresh Catholics were drawn in not only from the hinterland, but from the far west and south. By 1835 there were over 22,000 Catholics in Belfast, constituting over 33 per cent of the population as compared with 26,000 Presbyterians and 18,000 Anglicans. They settled largely in the Falls and Lower Falls areas which lead to the city from the west, and formed a wedge between the working-class Protestant areas of the Shankill Road and Sandy Row. One contemporary noted: 'Within a few years some four or five thousand raw, uneducated Catholic labourers from the south and west had poured into the town.'[15] But not all who came were Catholic. Protestants from the Orange heartlands also poured in, and among their preoccupations on arrival was the establishment of Orange lodges.

By 1835 the tendency of both communities to stay within their own territory was well-established. Sandy Row, for instance, was almost totally Protestant and the stretch which separated it from the Catholic district, The Pound, was already a perennial battleground. Thus the demographic conditions which existed in, say, rural Armagh were not only replicated but telescoped into the confines of narrow, urban streets. The first sectarian riots occurred in 1812, but those specifically associated with Orangeism date from 1834 when Orangemen returning from a 'Twelfth' march were caught in a crossfire between groups of stone-throwing Catholics. After about an hour of confrontation, the military intervened, including, it seems, the cavalry, as many of the injured were hauled away with sabre wounds. The *Northern Whig* reported:

> . . . one quarter of our town, including a part of Sandy Row and Barrack Street, has been the theatre of much excitement and rioting, the contending parties being Catholics and Protestants of low degree.[16]

A tradition was born, and 'flashpoints' developed around the city where fisticuffs, stone-throwing and the hurling of insults became the order of the day whenever the sides clashed.

The Rockites and the Ribbonmen

Politically, the gains which Catholics received from Emancipation were small, but psychologically, the effect was enormous as it represented a victory wrested from a grudging government. The legislation allowed them to return members to Parliament and to become eligible for positions previously denied, but in practical terms, it buttered few carrots. They still lived miserable, insecure lives as tenants-at-will under the heel of rapacious landlords, and were often on the verge of starvation and destitution.

When O'Connell took his seat at Westminster, the country was again being convulsed with agrarian violence. The Orangemen, and the Orange-dominated yeomanry, continued to clash with the Catholic peasantry. Catholic agrarian organisations sprang up as a defence against Orange marauders and to rectify local grievances. Two were of particular significance: the Rockites and the Ribbonmen.

The Rockites were named after the elusive 'Captain Rock' — the shadowy figure who inspired the 'Whiteboys'. They were based almost exclusively in Munster and south Leinster, and noted for their hostility towards the yeomanry. Their sectarianism was evidenced by their burning of Protestant churches and harassment of Protestant evangelicals. Historians often depict them as fitting into a millenarian tradition of peasant protest movements, as they believed in the fast-approaching doom of all Irish Protestants. These views were influenced by a wave of millenarian excitement which erupted around 1812, and which appears to have been sparked by a book from which prophecies were taken. This was *The General History of the*

Christian Church from her birth to her final Triumphant state in Heaven —
a pseudo-scholarly volume whose author signed himself 'Signor
Pastorini' ('the little pastor') and who, in fact, was an English
Benedictine named Charles Walmsley, titular Bishop of Rama in Italy
and, later, Bishop of York. The work was a reverie on the Book of
Revelation and its author's study of the Apocalypse led him to assert
that in the year 1825 the Protestant faith — described as the 'locust
from the bottomless pit which tormented the faithful for three
centuries since the Reformation'[17] — would finally be destroyed under
the Wrath of God. The volume went into several Irish editions and was
found in the cabins of the poor as well as on the shelves of the rich.
Copies were available in wayside hostelries as suitable reading for
travellers, and the more prophetic passages were printed as
broadsheets and sold by travelling schoolteachers and pedlars. A
senior Orangeman, Reverend Mortimer O'Sullivan, a curate in
Tipperary Town, recalled:

> . . . a considerable change began to take place in the nature of the
> little penny tracts of the itinerant pedlars. By one class of these
> productions the animosity of the Faithful was whetted against the
> b***dy Protestants, in another they learnt how heretics were to be
> treated.

The word went out that 24 December 1824 was to be the date of
Protestant destruction, and reports have survived of whole families
sitting in their homes, fully armed, with the doors and windows bolted
against their would-be exterminators.[18]

As the Pastorini fever increased, a number of Catholic bishops
began to denounce the prophecies. The much respected James Warren
Doyle of Kildare and Leighlin (who wrote under the pseudonym
'JKL'), wrote a pastoral denouncing the book, but advising his flock
that he understood why they were driven into secret agrarian
organisations: 'Your distress, your hatred of Orangemen, your love of
religion, your faith in prophecies, your hope of seeing your country
free and happy.'[19]

The aims of the Ribbonmen were very much akin to those of the
Rockites. They took their name from the red ribbons or ribands
which they wore as identification, and also deduced from the
Pastorini prophecies that Protestant doom was nigh.[20] The details of
the individual factors which led to their emergence were complicated
but doubtless related to the many and various confrontations with
Orangemen which had occurred around the Ulster borderlands.
Unlike most agrarian organisations, they expanded to urban areas
and became strong in Dublin.

O'Connell was of the view that the Rockites and the Ribbonmen fed off Orangeism, and said of Ribbonism:

> . . . in proportion as the Orange irritation increased. They act on each other; the existence of Ribbonism makes it necessary for one to become an Orangeman and the existence of Orangeism has certainly created many Ribbonmen'.[21]

—20—

Repeal and Reaction

Oh! friends be firm and gather to one head
Under our banner though a slender band
And the breach'd rampart rocks beneath our tread
Yet bold and loyal here we make our stand
For God's dear love and sacred Ireland
Against the leaguer and this subtle foe
Who, while he holds to heaven one impious hand
In mock appeal, works sinister below
To raise a purple throne on Britain's overthrow.

— from 'Inaugural Ode',
one of Sir Samuel Ferguson's
early Orange poems

Restraining the Brethren

The excitement aroused by Jack Lawless' 'invasion' of Ulster stirred
up the Protestant peasantry in the traditional heartlands and injected
a new and defiant spirit at a time when it was needed: the Order had
just emerged from its three-year period of dissolution and was still
racked with disputes over 'higher orders', while many in its
leadership had become sullen and frustrated with the passing of
Catholic Emancipation.

The brethren were prepared to show off their new vigour by
celebrating 'The Twelfth' and other Orange anniversaries with
greater gusto than before. But with the advent of Catholic
Emancipation they were no longer asserting an ascendancy which

existed in law. The Catholics now enjoyed similar rights to themselves and had, at least technically, access to the same privileges. Yet they felt superior and sought to assert an informal ascendancy. Their marches became larger and more militant and were, in fact, stylised acts of dominance. Their message to Catholics was clear. It was, as one historian has put it: 'We are your superiors: we dare you to do something about it; if you don't you confirm your own inferior status.'[1] That was the message of the drums.

But Orange rituals were not performed without fear of disruption. Catholics would not accept their inferior role and, as members of the Ribbon organisation and other groupings they sought to disrupt Orange activities. Several anti-procession laws were passed, but the marches and their concomitant disturbances continued. From time to time Orange leaders such as Lord Enniskillen, William Blacker and William Verner sought to discourage marching, but often their advice fell on deaf ears. It soon became apparent that the authorities in Dublin Castle and London had wearied of the Orangemen and there was a distinct possibility of a new dissolution. Cumberland, with his finger on the pulse in London, saw the danger and, conscious that the Order was unlikely to receive sympathy from Wellington or Peel, took steps to cool things down. On 28 May 1829 he wrote to Lord Enniskillen:

> Caution and vigilance are at the present crisis specially requisite for the prosperity and safety of our cause, particularly in respect of our public processions which, I think, ought by all means to be avoided . . . as leading to an infraction of the law, and a breach of the public peace . . . which would probably be followed by some legislative measures ruinous to the Orange Institution. I assure you that I feel an intense anxiety on this subject.[2]

The Grand Lodge in Dublin dared not risk upsetting the lodges who would resist too much dictation, and besides, it knew that marching (known in Orange jargon as 'walking') was the lifeblood of the Order. The remoteness of the Grand Lodge from rank-and-file brethren was apparent. The largely upper-class leadership saw the Order as a means of countering inroads to the constitution, whereas the brethren on the ground had joined their lodges to assert their traditional rights and to keep the papists in check. In the event, the Grand Lodge issued a statement designed to get itself off the hook should there be disturbances on the forthcoming 'Twelfth':

> Of the recommendation contained in the letter of our illustrious Grand Master, the Committee do not conceive it necessary to say

much. They merely declare their opinion that the utmost vigilance and caution be required to prevent the strength of Protestant Ireland from being broken and dispersed.[3]

This could have been interpreted as giving the brethren the all-clear and was, in fact, its effect. Up to 50,000 Orangemen 'walked' at several locations and crowds of several times that number watched them. Serious disturbances occurred in Armagh, Newry, Strabane and other urban areas, dozens were injured and a few killed. In the countryside there were numerous clashes with bands of Ribbonmen. A new dissolution was now clearly on the cards, but a fresh crisis erupted which played right into the hands of the Orangemen, at least in the short term. This was an outbreak of violence over tithes, which spurred the government to re-arm the yeomanry. With the compliments of Dublin Castle, firearms were placed in the hands of the Orangemen.

The Tithe War

There had been skirmishes over tithes for years; but real hostilities broke out in Graiguenamanagh, County Kilkenny, in 1830, when the Catholic peasantry declared to Colonel Harvey, the local magistrate: 'Let the parsons wait until parliament meets; maybe parliament will pay them; we won't, anyhow. Daniel O'Connell will get the tithes taken off us as he got Emancipation.'

Over the next three years there were frequent encounters between those who resisted payment, and the yeomanry and military who endeavoured to enforce it. In 1831, thirteen people were killed at Newtownbarry, County Wexford, in an attempt to resist collection. A few months later, eighteen policemen were killed in an affray at Carrickshock, County Kilkenny, and on 14 December 1831 one of the most infamous incidents occurred at Gortroe, near Fermoy, called 'The Massacre of Rathcormac'. The Reverend Archdeacon Ryder, known as 'Black Billy', left Fermoy to collect tithes from the Widow Ryan who lived at Gortroe. The amount due to him was four pounds, sixteen shillings. He was accompanied by two companies of foot, one of dragoons and a body of yeomanry. When they reached her house, they found about 150 of her neighbours, armed with sticks, pitchforks and slanes. The Archdeacon, present in his capacity as a magistrate, suggested to Begley, the Captain of the dragoons, that it might be prudent for his men to draw their sabres. The peasants had placed a farm cart on the boreen leading to the house, and Begley shouted at them to clear the way. The men answered: 'No tithes, no parson! You have no right to come.' Begley replied: 'We will use force, if you do not give way.' The men again retorted: 'No tithes, no parson!' Archdeacon Ryder read the Riot Act, then he climbed on the cart, cracking his whip at the peasants. They seized him by the neck and coat-tails and literally flung him back into the boreen. At this, a dragoon named Alves jumped on the barricade, waved his sword and called on the troop to follow. A local roared to his comrades: 'Now boys, at them' and a fierce conflict ensued, the peasants striking furiously at the soldiers as they tried to surmount the barricade. After about ten minutes, Major Waller of the dragoons instructed his men to open fire, and the peasants rushed for cover. When they emerged, twelve of their number lay dead and forty-two were wounded.

As the smoke cleared, Archdeacon Ryder appeared from around the back of the house and said to Waller: 'All right, Major, I have got my tithes'. While the battle was raging, he had slipped around the back of the widow's house and seized four stacks of her corn.

A month or so later an inquiry was held, which went on for fourteen days. The result was a mixed verdict; thirteen jurors being for the verdict of 'wilful murder', two for 'manslaughter' and eight for 'justifiable homicide'. Backed up by such examples of brutality, O'Connell instructed the people to resist the demands of the parsons and gave them a new slogan: 'No tithes! We want our rights!' In London, *The Times* newspaper accused him as being the cause of the trouble, and wrote:

> Scum, condensed of Irish bog
> Ruffian, coward, demagogue
> Boundless liar, base detractor
> Nurse of murderers, treason's factor.[4]

The tithe war lasted until 1838 when Lord Melbourne's government converted the levy into a rent charge. Tithes were to be lowered by a quarter; the tenant paid extra rent to his landlord, who in turn paid the parson. It was only a partial solution but it brought an end to the violence.

O'Connell's Agenda

O'Connell's success in winning Catholic Emancipation rested on his adroit manipulation of a mass movement in which the Catholic clergy, the rising Catholic middle class and the peasantry all had a part to play. But there was no such unity when he moved on to the next item on his agenda, which was repeal of the Union itself. The priorities of the Catholic clergy had shifted to the removal of the tithe burden and to the question of Catholic education; the middle classes had become preoccupied with the opportunities which emancipation had opened to them, and the peasant — as always — was concerned with security of tenure and warding off starvation.. O'Connell, although anxious to make progress on repeal, recognised that the time was not ripe. With a party of thirty-three members sitting behind him in the Commons (following the general election of 1835) he entered into a tactical alliance with Lord Melbourne's Whigs, known as the Lichfield House Compact. The useful things which emerged from it included a Poor Law Relief Act, a Municipal Reform Act and an informal understanding by which the government consulted him prior to making certain appointments.

The arrangement was eased by the appointment of an executive to administer the day-to-day affairs of the country in a more equitable manner, and by the appointment of three men who saw eye to eye with O'Connell. Those were the new Lord Lieutenant, Constantine Henry Phibbs, Lord Mulgrave; the Chief Secretary, Viscount George Morpeth and the most inspired appointment of all, that of the Under Secretary, a young Scotsman named Thomas Drummond.

Drummond and the Orangemen

Thomas Drummond was one of the most popular British officials to set foot in Ireland. He was from Edinburgh, and not quite forty when he arrived at Dublin Castle. His appointment was the brainchild of Perrin, the Attorney General, who suggested to Mulgrave that if there was to be a change of administrative style there ought to be a change of men. Drummond had previously worked in Ireland as an engineer attached to the Ordnance Survey Office. In this capacity he had written on Irish conditions and his account is a clear statement of the problems which faced him in office. In Ulster he found that, 'the people are frugal and industrious and intelligent . . . inhabiting a district for the most part of inferior fertility to that of the southern portion of Ireland, but cultivated better.' In the south the conditions were '. . . in every respect inferior to those of the north; their habitations are worse, their food inferior, consisting at best of potatoes and milk without meal.' The inhabitants of the western districts he found, '. . . are decidedly inferior to both, in condition and in experience; their food consists of potatoes alone, without meal, and in most cases without milk, their cabins are wretched hovels, their beds are of straw.'[5]

Drummond's moral sense was outraged by what he found, and he was indignant that every position of influence or power in the administration should be solely in the hands of Protestants who were often Orangemen. He was concerned with the manner in which justice was administered by Orange magistrates, who would not have surprised anyone had they sat on the bench in their regalia. In Ulster particularly, it was impossible to get a conviction against a member of the Order, no matter how blatant his guilt. Drummond was determined to do all in his power to clean the Augean stables.

His initial task was to ensure that the law was enforced impartially. He created a constabulary and insisted that Catholics should serve in it. He transferred the power of appointing chief constables from local magistrates to the Viceroy, thereby cutting off a slot which had been used for jobbery, and took the radical step of disallowing the forces of the Crown to assist in tithe collecting or evicting. A major problem was the increasing crime rate which he believed resulted from landlord injustices; evictions had led people who were thrown on the roadway to take the law into their own hands. This problem became acute in 1838 when a Tipperary landlord was murdered and the local magistrates demanded that punitive action be taken to protect life and property. In a letter which became famous, Drummond told them: 'Property has its duties as well as its rights'. The phrase flummoxed the recipients and was seen as downright seditious. In 1838 such a proposition seemed as paradoxical and provocative as Proudhon's remark: 'Property is theft', yet it hit home and was later carved on Drummond's statue. The Earl of Donoughmore, the Deputy Lord Lieutenant of Tipperary, felt that Drummond was impertinent and refused to publish the letter. Later, the phrase was taken up by Charles Gavan Duffy, and became the motto of the first Irish Tenant Protection Association.

Drummond, impervious to Orange pressure, censured or dismissed officials who engaged in Orange bluster and incurred great wrath when he dismissed Colonel William Verner from the magistracy for toasting 'The Battle of the Diamond'. Drummond declared that the Battle of the Diamond was an illegal affair and that a magistrate had no business in toasting it. The bile he incurred was similar to that shown in 1832 when, following the passing of the Party Processions Act, similar action was taken against Colonel William Blacker. On that occasion, Orangemen from Portadown had marched to Carrickblacker to pay their respects to the Colonel on 'The Twelfth'. As a dutiful magistrate, Blacker requested that they disperse and gave his instruction from a balcony. Although he wore no Orange insignia, his wife, and other ladies standing behind him, did. For this he lost the Commission of the Peace. The apparent injustice rankled with Orangemen for years, and the incident found its way into numerous ballads.

In 1840, after just four years as Under Secretary, Drummond died, it is said, from overwork. His doctor asked where he wished to be buried, and the dying man murmured: 'I wish to be buried in Ireland, the country of my adoption and a country which I have loved, which I have faithfully served, and for which I believe I have given my life.'⁶ A grateful people erected a sculptured image of him in the City Hall of their capital. Today he stands there alongside such tribunes as Grattan and O'Connell.

Repeal and the Orangemen

By the end of the 1830s, O'Connell had become disillusioned with the Whigs at Westminster and disappointed with the amount of reform the alliance had produced. He realised that the administration was in its death throes and most unlikely to be returned again. His policy had, by and large, diminished his popularity, a fact signalled by the sharp drop in the O'Connell Tribute — a voluntary collection taken up twice yearly at chapel gates to enable him to work full-time in politics. There were numerous criticisms of his political style, and voices were heard saying that he was living on past triumphs. He was going on 65 and had become corpulent and more than a little self-indulgent. The misgivings about him became pointed following the founding in 1842 of *The Nation* newspaper, a journal whose influence was immediate and surpassed anything previously seen. O'Connell's own newspapers, it should be said, were dull publications which rarely reached a circulation of four figures; *The Nation* reached five — twice — and within a few weeks of publication.

The Nation was the inspired handiwork of a ginger group which included Charles Gavan Duffy, John Blake Dillon and a man who was to become a nationalist icon, Thomas Davis. The group proposed a theory of cultural nationalism which was derived, ultimately, from Herder and the German Romantics. They saw the Irish people — in Bernard Shaw's words, 'that curious amalgam of Milesian, Danish, Norman, Scottish and Saxon blood'⁷ — as an organic whole, characterised by a distinctive culture, language and 'spirit'. Some of their contemporaries labelled them 'Young Ireland' and made sneering comparisons with Mazzini's 'Young Italy' — a tag which they repudiated. They attacked O'Connell's leadership as flaccid and ineffectual, hinting that he should make way for a new and more vigorous generation.

But O'Connell was not finished yet. With renewed energy, he flung himself into the campaign for the repeal of the Union. A new organisation called The Loyal National Repeal Association was run from Conciliation Hall on Burgh Quay in Dublin. O'Connell hoped to repeat the victory of Catholic Emancipation, and made overtures to the Orangemen to join him. He stressed that his organisation was 'loyal' as well as 'national', and made much play of his veneration for the new Queen, Victoria, who had come to the throne in 1837. He published a nine-point plan for the restoration of an Irish parliament and laid down its first principle: 'that the Irish people recognise, acknowledge and maintain and will continually preserve and uphold for the throne of Ireland, Her Majesty Queen Victoria, whom God protect.'[8] The last point ran: 'the connection between Great Britain and Ireland, by means of the power, authority and prerogatives of the Crown, to be perpetual and incapable of change or any severance or separation.' At a banquet in Drogheda, he went so far as to propose a toast to the 'Glorious and Immortal Memory' and ostentatiously drank a tumbler of water from the River Boyne.[9] He even lashed the Viceroy, the Duke of Northumberland, when Dublin Castle took measures to curtail Orange marches. 'Northumberland,' O'Connell said, 'had become odious to all parties.'

These overtures cut little ice with the Orangemen, who felt that O'Connell was up to his old strategic bluffs. Yet O'Connell took the surprising step of sending a second envoy to the North, this time not to collect 'the rent' but to win over the Orangemen directly. The man chosen for this unenviable task was a minor Dublin politician who had connections in the North, Counsellor James Costello, and he too had high hopes of the Orangemen.

Costello's relatives lived near Cookstown, County Tyrone, and he decided to begin his campaign there on market day. When he stood on a porter barrel and tried to harangue a group of Protestant farmers, he was heard for five minutes before being met with hisses and growls. A number of ash plants were waved in his face, and he quickly fled to his carriage before a volley of stones and debris. The same treatment was dished out in Dungannon, but this time Costello's coach was guarded by constabulary as he made his exit. Next came Belfast, where he established his headquarters at a public house in Rosemary Street. But local Orangemen learnt of his arrival and prepared a hot reception. Thomas White, the District

Orange Master, rushed out handbills to the brethren, calling on them 'to hold themselves in readiness to aid the magistry in case of disturbance.' In the event, Costello confined himself to a small indoor meeting which was attended mainly by Catholics; then he quietly returned to Dublin. The 'tour' had been a predictable failure.

The Reverend Holt Waring's Speech

In December 1831 a new association was founded in Dublin in reaction to O'Connell's efforts to win Orange support. Although called The Protestant Association, it was in fact an Orange front organisation. Many leading Orangemen attended the inaugural meeting, an event which would not have caused great interest but for a forceful speech delivered by a man who was high in the Orange hierarchy. This was the Very Reverend Dean Holt Waring, Rector of Shankill, near Lurgan, and Dean of Dromore. He had long been an Orange ideologue and had played a leading role in the development of ritual. His speech, although essentially a personal testimony, put into words views which were commonly held:

> The Protestants of Ireland were originally an advanced guard, or rather a forlorn hope of the army of civilisation thrown out of England to humanise this kingdom. They came over to this country and found that ignorance and barbarianism prevailed to such a degree that it was difficult for them to obtain a footing. In fact, the inhabitants of the South Sea Islands were in a state of civilisation compared with the native Irish. The Protestants came here under the promise of English support, and for some time the government of England did give all the assistance they required. Under the fostering auspices of England they established order and true religion where they had found outrage and superstition in full possession. They brought with them the religion of the Gospel. Through their energies, and by their care, manufactories, literal arts and agriculture flourished. In fact, everything beneficial followed in their train. But notwithstanding all their efforts to impart intelligence and humanise the country, they have been opposed from the very hour of their landing, up to the present period, by the obstinate and misguided race whom they sought to benefit. Everything was done by the Protestants to promote good feeling, nothing was left untried to conciliate the professors of the Romish religion; but all our attempts have proved failures.

Then the Dean turned to contemporary matters:

> With respect to processions of Orangemen, about which such an outcry has been raised, I will not argue whether they are right or wrong, wise or imprudent, but this I will say, that they were taught us by the government. I well remember the time when the Lord Lieutenant, accompanied by all the influential persons in the state, went on every 5th November in procession to College Green and paraded around the statue of King William . . . the whole formed such a noble display of high Protestant feeling as would satisfy the most zealous Orangeman in the kingdom. The Orangemen of Ireland have already suppressed one rebellion; and they may ere long be called upon to trample down another — they defended themselves, it is true, when attacked — and God forbid that they should not — but all attempts to fix the first aggression on them have failed. They are absolutely a defensive and conservative association and do not disturb any man in the exercise of his religion.'[10]

This type of outburst was likely to inflame sectarian passions and embroil the Order in charges of racism. But the Orangemen did not seem to mind. An article in a contemporary journal summed up their case succinctly:

> If popery were absent, there would be prosperity and peace. Wherever there is turbulence — wherever there is anarchy — wherever there is national excitement or civil war, popery is the sole author or agent.[11]

The Dublin Protestant Operatives Association

Popery was the target of a fiery cleric who exercised a powerful ascendancy over working-class Orangemen in Dublin for most of the 1830s. This was Reverend Tresham Dames Gregg, Rector of Saint Mary's Church in the parish of Saint Nicholas Within-the-Walls, and known in the rough backstreets as 'Trash 'em Gregg'. He was one of the most vituperative orators of his day and had what a rival called 'a dangerous gift of eloquence'. That a Bible-thumping divine should become the hero of sweated urban workers during a period of severe economic depression may seem peculiar, but not if one considers that economic upheaval may create conditions conducive to apocalyptic speculation. In the downturn which hit Ireland (and the rest of the

United Kingdom) between 1839 and 1842, the Protestant hand-loom weavers and textile workers of the Liberties area of Dublin came off badly. Many were forced to emigrate, while others were under-employed or pressed into destitution. The depression came at a time when poor Protestants felt vulnerable on a number of fronts: the Catholics, following Emancipation, were making inroads into Protestant privileges and were the beneficiaries of the reforms which resulted from the Whig alliance; the government — the traditional shield of the Protestants — had treacherously given way to the old enemy and now, on top of it all, Protestant livelihoods were in jeopardy.

Gregg caught the jittery mood when he formed the Dublin Protestant Operatives Association (DPOA) in April 1841. His message was two-fold: firstly, Protestants must not take recent Catholic advances lying down; they must object and agitate for their reversal so that Protestantism may be re-installed at the heart of national life; this, Gregg believed, could be achieved by putting consistent pressure on the powers-that-be and by utilising every form of lawful protest. Secondly, Protestants must feel secure in the belief that although they were downtrodden and depressed, God was on their side and the Antichrist (i.e. Church of Rome) was doomed and could not prevail. Sincere Protestants, Gregg preached, had a duty to arouse their fellows so that the Mother of Harlots would be destroyed. Only then would the wrath of God be alleviated and the people, aided by the pure truths of the Bible, be led to new and sunny uplands.

This message constituted the hub of the Order's teaching, and Gregg was the firebrand who would drive it home to the Protestant proletariat. It may be argued that working-class Protestants failed to identify the true causes of their plight and in their confusion were susceptible to oratorial sleight of hand; their evangelical conditioning made them prone to see their sufferings in an apocalyptic light, and as part of a personal struggle between good and evil. Gregg was not only their evangel but also their champion. The brethren from the large Dublin lodges crowded to hear him in 1839 when he engaged Father Tom Maguire, the Catholic theologian, in a five-day disputation. When Maguire prematurely retired from the marathon the Protestants claimed victory, and the brethren from the Schromberg Orange Lodge chaired Gregg shoulder-high and cheered him to the echo.

The success of Gregg's DPOA with the Protestant workers led O'Connell's repealers to woo the association. They argued that repeal would bring great benefits to Dublin workers and that an economic upsurge could be expected from the day of its enactment. The Young Irelanders added their voice and supportive articles appeared in *The Nation*. But it was all to no avail. Gregg and his followers were convinced that it was not Union with Britain which had caused Ireland's woes. They saw popery as the enemy and, before the DPOA was finally wound up in 1848, they issued a statement expressing the Operative's determination 'to maintain the Protestantism of the throne and the constitution which their fathers had died for,' adding: 'we are determined to join the Orange society and oppose revolution and popish aggression.'[12]

Orange Young Ireland

While Reverend Tresham Gregg was breathing fire and brimstone from the backstreet pulpits of Protestant Dublin, others were defending the cause of Protestant Ireland from inside the hallowed walls of Trinity College, a Protestant university founded to foster English culture in Ireland and to promote the reformed religion in its statutory form. Unlike Oxford or Cambridge, it had no pre-Reformation tradition. There were no Gothic windows for a Newman to dream under or the chant of priests or the swing of censers. It looked not to the Rome of the Popes but to the See of Canterbury for its inspiration. It was the showpiece of the Ascendancy, and from it had come such prototypes of the breed as Swift, Congreve, Farquhar (who, incidentally, witnessed the Siege of Derry and acted as a drummer boy at The Battle of the Boyne), Goldsmith and Berkeley; 'One of the finest stocks in Europe' as W.B. Yeats was to call them. An Orange lodge had been established in the college by William Blacker while he was a student there in the late 1790s, and nowhere in Ireland was the Williamite tradition so well rooted.

In the early 1830s a young Orangeman named Isaac Butt from Stranorlar, in County Donegal, founded a journal in Trinity called *The Dublin University Magazine* (or the DUM as it was jokingly known) and gathered together a number of Orange writers and intellectuals, who would later distinguish themselves in Irish life. Only a few were in fact formal members of the Order, but all were committed to the Orange tradition and saw the Williamite victories of olden days as the basis of their freedoms. Among the better known of those who actually wore the sash was Blacker himself, who wrote for the magazine under the name of 'Banville FitzSteward', and the poet Samuel Ferguson from Belfast. Another was the antiquarian Caesar Otway, from Tipperary (who in later years became obsessed with the imaginary sexual practices of priests and nuns and toured the country collecting anecdotes of 'beastly rites').[13] Others included the legal scholar and poet John Anster, from Cork, who made the first English translation of Goethe's *Faust* and became Regius Professor of Civil Law,[14] and John Frances Waller, from Limerick, who became Master of the Rolls and wrote large quantities of much admired satirical verse.

These young men boldly challenged the assumptions of Thomas Davis and the Young Irelanders that nationalism alone was the true repository of Irish patriotism, and they forthrightly asserted their Orange, unionist and Protestant convictions. Sometimes they were indignant at the way Britain failed to understand the sensitivities of Irish Protestants, and they did not hesitate to castigate those politicians who acceded to nationalist demands which they believed would undermine the stability of the country. Continually they claimed a moral and political ascendancy over their nationalist countrymen, and believed that their high civic position carried a responsibility to instruct as well as to lead. Although the term 'Orange Young Ireland' is of later coinage, it is apt, for the contributors to the *DUM* chose, in characteristic Orange fashion, to take the battle into enemy territory, putting the case, often aggressively, that Ireland was kept in turmoil by the machinations of popish priests, unthinking demagogues and, at the same time, mismanaged by English politicians who did not half-understand its plight.

As time went on, the Orange character of the magazine became less marked. One article, however, from its early days, written by Samuel Ferguson, caught its basic tone. This was called 'A Dialogue between the Head and the Heart of an Irish Protestant' and was published in 1833. The discussion begins with 'Heart' making a familiar moan:

> Here we are loyal Protestants and gentry of Ireland, by whose attachment to the Law, the Church, and the Crown, this island has for two hundred and fifty years (since the Conquest) been preserved to the British Empire. Whereby whom three dangerous rebellions have already been put down in this realm, and who would be ready to put down another in the same cause were it to burst out tomorrow. Here we are, I say, who are the controllers of popery; the safeguard of the British connection; the guardian of the Empire's integrity; the most respectful body of men for our members, in all Europe, whether we be

considered with regard to wealth, industry and intellect, position and absolute power; here we are, I say again, who are the arbiters of Britain's fate, deceived, insulted, spoilt and set at defiance.

'Head' agrees and says that O'Connell and his repealers are about to reverse the tables on the Protestants and shout: ''tis our turn now.' Then, he prognosticates that:

> . . . if emancipation produces repeal, so surely will repeal produce ultimate separation, so surely will there be a war levied, estates confiscated and the popish Church established.

'Heart' accepts that the outlook for Protestants is bleak and gives a description of their plight:

> Deserted by the Tories, insulted by the Whigs, threatened by the Radicals, hated by the Papists and envied by the Dissenters, plundered in our country seats, robbed of our town houses, driven abroad by violence, called back because of humanity and, after all, told that we are neither English nor Irish, neither fish nor flesh, but a peddling colony. . . .

Yet in spite of Protestant straits, 'Heart' is prepared to make allowances for those who would usurp them:

> . . . I love this land better than any other. I cannot believe that it is a hostile country. I love the people in it, in spite of themselves, and cannot feel them as enemies. I would not call them my countrymen if they could not remember or resent injury.

But 'Heart' loves his separated countrymen so much that he is willing to ill-treat them in avoidance of error:

> I would bear the pain of seeming their persecutor . . . for the sake of being able to love them as free, loyal and united Protestants.'[15]

'Head' concludes the dialogue by cautioning the more emollient 'Heart' against 'ill-judged' sympathy with Catholics, and warns that any apologetic wish to conciliate with them could undermine the Ascendancy '. . . on which the country must depend for its moral, intellectual and economic leadership.'

Ferguson's intellectual odyssey later took him some distance from these views. He set himself the task of stimulating, especially among Protestants, an interest in Irish antiquities as a means of fostering understanding between Irishmen of different faiths. The *DUM* went on to encourage Irish authors to dwell on Irish subjects, although it never quite lost its Orange streak.

—21—

The Years of the Great Test

When treason bared her bloody arm, and
maddened round the land
For King and laws and order fair, we drew the
ready band
Our gathering spell was William's name — our
word was 'Do or Die'
And still we put our trust in God, and kept
our powder dry.

*— from Colonel William Blacker's famous
Orange poem 'Oliver's Advice'*

The Light of Many Lamps

In the years which followed the rebellion of 1798, the radicalism which
had led large numbers of Presbyterians to take up arms weakened, and
many drifted towards Orangeism. Yet pockets of the old spirit lingered
and were in evidence up to the time of Gladstone's adoption of Home
Rule in 1886, when it was scuppered by the realisation that Irish self-
government would place Protestants in a permanent minority position.

Historically, the Presbyterians had received a raw deal. The
Anglican Ascendancy did not thank them for standing firm in support
of King William. Rather, after his death, they too, as non-conformists,
came under the constrictions of the penal laws, though to a lesser
extent than Catholics. The doors of their Meeting Houses were nailed
up during the reign of Queen Anne; their marriages were not officially
recognised and their offspring were deemed illegitimate; their clergyman
could not officiate at burial services and the burden of tithes weighed
heavily upon them. It was only with the arrival of the Hanoverians that
they began to enjoy some toleration and, even then, the Test Clause in

the legislation technically called 'An Act to Prevent the Further Growth of Popery', 1704, effectively excluded them from participation in local government.

In their own affairs Presbyterians had been prone to division. The 'New Lights' emphasised personal and civil liberties, while the 'Old Lights' stressed rigid, uncompromising Calvinism, and took their inspiration from Knox and the Scottish Covenanters. The 'New Lights' were drawn towards the radical thinking of Thomas Paine and that of the American and French revolutionaries, and were accused of taking some of their theological views from Arius — a second-century heretical priest who held that the Son was not eternal or equal with the Father. In 1815 an event occurred in Belfast which brought this arcane dispute to a head.

This was the opening of the new Academical Institute, a college supported by a number of public-spirited people which received an annual government grant of £15,000. The college was recognised by the Presbyterian Synod as being a proper body for awarding the General Certificate to ordinants. Earlier, such students had to travel to Scotland to earn the qualification. All went well until it was rumoured that Arianism had taken root among the teaching staff. There was a furore, and a new figure came forward to champion the 'Old Light' cause. This was the Reverend Henry Cooke, a spellbinding preacher whose brand of Protestant fundamentalism was in line with that of the Orangemen. Cooke never formally joined the Order, but became one of its great heroes. His ascendancy over Presbyterians and Orangemen alike made him known, derisively, to Catholics as 'The Presbyterian Pope'.

The Battle with the Arians

Cooke was the son of a tenant farmer who worked nine acres at Grillagh, a village between Maghera and Coleraine in County Londonderry. He has left a graphic description of the sort of schooling which was available to necessitous Presbyterians. The school building was a thatched cabin with a turf fire in the centre of the floor, a hole in the roof for a chimney, and blocks of wood from a neighbouring bog served as seats. He withdrew to a 'classical academy' which could boast of a decent roof and two window frames, but no glass, so that if there was light the students enjoyed a 'refreshing portion of rain and snow'. Stones were used as seats; and Cooke, who brought a stool, was deprived of it by the schoolmaster, who took it, as he remarked, 'to save himself from colic'.

Cooke claimed an illustrious ancestry; one of his forefathers was a hero of the Scottish Reformation, and another defended the Walls of Derry. Cooke described the latter with characteristic colour: 'At the first outbreak of the Rebellion all his family were murdered except for one little child. Driven from a distant part of County Down with thousands of starving Protestants, he carried the child in his arms to Derry and was, happily, one of those admitted to the city for its defence. When he mounted guard at night he had no nurse or caretaker for the little one, so he carried it with him to the walls and laid it between the embrasures where the cannon frowned defiance on James and slavery. Providence protected the boy in the midst of famine and death; and when, in after years, he was asked how he had fared for shelter, "Well enough," was the reply, "I had the shelter of my father's gun." Yes, God — the God of Battles — protected the motherless and homeless boy; and he who now addresses you is that boy's descendant.'[1]

At the age of fourteen Cooke was sent to Glasgow College and was ordained a Presbyterian minister in 1808. His fame as a preacher was well established by the time he accepted a call to Killyleagh on the shores of Strangford Lough, and began to engage in the kind of doctrinal controversy which would mark his whole life. His first encounter was with a Unitarian clergyman from England, the Reverend J. Smethurst, who was on a preaching tour. Cooke attended one of his services and, finding the views expressed too liberal, stood up and declared that he would refute each of the doctrines he had heard, one by one. On the following Sunday everyone assembled at Cooke's own Meeting House and sat rooted as they heard him destroy the 'Arian' tenets of Smethurst. There was great excitement when Cooke declared that he would follow the Englishman from village to village and denounce his 'unscriptural heresies' as they were uttered. The chase was as exciting as a fox hunt and established Cooke as an uncompromising upholder of Presbyterian orthodoxy. The Orangemen became inveterate Cooke supporters and saw him as a Protestant analogue to O'Connell.

The issue of the Arians in the Academical Institute came to a head when Cooke crossed swords with a new opponent, Dr Henry Montgomery, a man of stirring eloquence and head of the English School at the Institute. Montgomery had no time for Cooke's hard Calvinism or High Toryism, and might be called an early ecumenist. He disapproved of all forms of discrimination against fellow Christians and, like other latitudinarians, believed that subscription to the Westminster Confession, with its explicit anti-Catholic language and identification of the Pope with the Antichrist, should not be compulsory for Presbyterian clergymen on ordination. Cooke could not countenance what he felt was Montgomery's wishy-washy liberalism; at a meeting of the Synod of Ulster, he insisted that all members of the Synod be required to declare whether they believed in the doctrine of the Trinity as set forth in the Shorter Catechism. Montgomery opposed this move and both men debated the issue, with great erudition, for several days. At the end, the majority sided with Cooke.

This was in 1827 and, despite the debate, the issue was not resolved. It arose again in 1828 but, after further polemics, the result was still the same. Montgomery and his 'New Light' followers, now under considerable pressure, drew up a compendium of their grievances, which they called a 'Remonstrance', and advised the majority that if these were not met they should have little option but to withdraw from the Synod. In 1830 they were forced to quit, and went on to establish a separate body of their own, known as 'The Remonstrance of Ulster'. Cooke had won.

Hillsborough

Robert Jocelyn, 3rd Earl of Roden, was known for his love of 'The Good Book' and held every word of it to be literally true. So keen was the Earl that he held twice daily Bible readings for the workers on his estate at Tollymore near Castlewellan, County Down. Over the hall door of his mansion was emblazoned a quotation from Deuteronomy: 'Hear O Israel, the Lord is our God, the Lord Alone! . . . take to heart these words . . . drill them into your children . . . write them on your door posts and your gates. . . .' (Chapter 3, Verses 4–9).

This injunction to instruct the young was well heeded by Lord Roden, who was president of the Sunday School Society and believed it vital to implant the seeds of Truth from an early age. In September 1851 he went on a proselytising tour of Connemara, after which he recorded that scores of ragged Irish-speaking children flocked to him. He praised them for their ability to sing 'God Save the Queen' and rewarded them with soup and bread.[2] In one chapter of his remarkable book, *The Progress of the Reformation in Ireland* (London, 1851), the Earl recounts how he came across a farmer in Oughterard, County Galway, who had formerly been 'an active demagogue and great leader for Repeal in the district' but had turned Protestant and 'changed his political as well as his religious views'. As Lord Roden does not specify what led to the farmer's conversion, history can only speculate; was it the nutritional value of his Lordship's bounty; the ability of the convert to execute the anthem harmoniously; or, perhaps, the inscrutable workings of Providence?

Lord Roden, as a young man, had sat in Parliament for Dundalk and then, on the death of his father, succeeded to the peerage of the United Kingdom. No one questioned his evangelical zeal or the earnest manner in which he lived his life. There was, however, one smudge on the family escutcheon which he found disconcerting. This was the scandal in 1811 when his relative, Percy Jocelyn, the Anglican bishop of Clogher (a son of the 1st Earl), was caught 'in flagrante delicto' with a guardsman in the toilets of The White Hart public house in Westminster, London. The sensation rocked the Anglican establishment and became all the greater when it was revealed that the bishop, some years earlier, had denied making 'improper suggestions' to a manservant in Dublin, and was responsible for seeing the poor fellow flogged and jailed.[3]

The 3rd Earl, a public-spirited man, looked upon it as his duty to see to the welfare of his tenants and was known personally to tend the sick and poor. All he asked the recipients of his bounty was that at elections, parliamentary or local, they should vote for his candidate. He was the chairman of a number of local organisations and a loyal member of the Tory party. He did not become an Orangeman until 1831 when, following attendance at a meeting of the Protestant Association in Dublin, he became convinced that the policies of the Order represented his personal views. In the following year he was elected Grand Master for Louth, and it was then that he had a great vision of seeing Irish Protestants united under a single banner. To effect this purpose he organised a massive rally at Hillsborough, County Down, on 30 October 1834. Some 60,000 people attended, and Lord Roden himself arrived at the head of 15,000 men.

The occasion was a great show of Protestant strength, and among the dignitaries on the platform was Dr Henry Cooke who, as ever, was equal to the occasion. With white hair and clerical garb flowing in the wind, he launched a vituperative attack on O'Connell and the Repeal movement. 'Repeal,' he declared, 'is just a discreet word for Romish ascendancy and Protestant extermination.' When the applause had died, Cooke's voice — clear as a bell — rang out again, and he uttered the passage which is best remembered:

> Between the divided churches I publish the banns of a second marriage — the first, I would remind you, was consecrated behind the Walls of Derry when the Church and the Kirk did jointly in Columbus' Church most lovingly pray — a marriage, of Christian forbearance when they differ, of Christian love when they agree, and of Christian co-operation in all matters where their common safety is concerned. Who forbids the banns? None. Then I trust that our union for these holy purposes is indissoluble.[4]

Again, the crowd cheered. Crafty old Cooke — who knew his audience as a great musician knows his instrument — stood with tears in his eyes as they idolised him. To them he was poet, philosopher and sage rolled into one; and he knew it.

Some Presbyterians denied Cooke's right to propose such a union; others felt that it was high time for Protestants to unite against the rising tide of nationalism. Other large demonstrations quickly followed. In Cavan town some 30,000 Orangemen assembled, many carrying arms and at Dungannon, on 12 November 1834, some 75,000 filed past the reviewing platform. The Order was again on the march.

O'Connell in Belfast

O'Connell was prepared to beard the lion in its den. In November 1841 he accepted an invitation to speak in Belfast, as he had not ceased to hope that liberal Presbyterians would join him in his struggle for Repeal. When Dr Cooke learnt of his coming, he issued a challenge to debate the Repeal issue with him in public. He said: 'When you invade Ulster and unfurl the banner of Repeal, you will find that you are entering a new climate . . . I believe that you are a great bad man, engaged in a great bad cause.' O'Connell gave a flippant response and called the clergyman 'bully Cooke, the cock of the north' and 'a boxing buffoon of a divine'. The Orangemen quickly arranged to give O'Connell a hot welcome, but he arrived without notice. A few days later he tried to address a crowd from the balcony of the Royal Hotel, but hecklers interrupted his speech with cries of 'to hell with the Pope' and 'to hell with the Big Beggarman' — the favourite Orange epithet for O'Connell. When O'Connell attended a party for Saint Patrick's Orphan Society in Upper Arthur Street, an Orange mob went on the rampage and attacked Saint Patrick's chapel in Donegall Street and the homes of known Repealers. If O'Connell hoped — as he did — to awaken the radicalism of the Presbyterians, he was disappointed. The next morning he left Belfast under armed escort.

A few days later, Cooke spoke at another mass rally and, in a great peroration, told his audience:

> Look at the town of Belfast. When I was a youth I remember it almost as a village. But what a glorious sight does it now present — the masted grove within the harbour — (cheers) — our mighty warehouses teeming with the wealth of every climate — (cheers) — our giant manufactories lifting themselves on every side — (cheers) — All this, we owe to the Union. Yes, Mr O'Connell, we will guard the Union as we will guard our liberties . . . look at Belfast, and be a Repealer — if you can![5]

Enter Mr Fairman

In the years following Catholic Emancipation, the Order in England went into decline. Lodge meetings were poorly attended and the Grand Lodge itself did not meet between June 1829 and February 1831. In 1830,

George IV died and his brother, the uninspiring Duke of Clarence, came to the throne as William IV. The new King did not trouble himself with religious questions, but had been a mild supporter of Catholic Emancipation. The Duke of Cumberland did not always hit it off with the new monarch and lost much of his influence. Besides, with the Catholic question now settled, Cumberland found it expedient to find new fish to fry.

The issue of Reform was exciting the minds of the Duke's friends on the Tory Right. In 1832 the first parliamentary reform legislation since the days of Pitt the Younger had come before the Commons, and was carried in the face of fierce Tory opposition. The net effect was to release 143 parliamentary seats (out of a total of 658) for redistribution. The Act, according to one calculation, increased the electorate from 435,000 to 652,000. As a debating ploy, the Whigs represented it as a final settlement, but the Tory ultras were not deceived and saw the measure as the beginning of a slippery slope on which their interests would be forfeited. Some felt that the country was going to the dogs and that violent revolution was imminent. Cumberland, Lord Kenyon and others attempted to rally the forces of the Right through the agency of the Orange Order. To assist them they acquired the services of a colourful character who would later prove something of a Don Quixote.

This was an impressively moustachioed and monocled ex-soldier on half-pay named William Blennerhasset Fairman. He had been a captain in the Royal Irish Infantry and was given the rank of Lieutenant Colonel in the 4th Ceylon Foot. Little is known of his early career save that he became an Orangeman in 1814, when initiated into a London lodge. From the beginning of his connection with the Order, he sought to ingratiate himself with Cumberland and wrote a number of letters to the Duke describing the perilous state of the country. Among the matters he mentioned was his own earlier involvement in exposing a somewhat shadowy plot to overthrow the House of Brunswick. Self-confident and blimpish, he moved easily among the Tory ultras in their Mayfair drawing rooms. He was, in fact, a charming fellow, and with his flowing patter and man-of-the-world style he could be quite convincing, if a trifle flamboyant.

By 1831, Fairman shared the position of Deputy Grand Master in England with Eustace Chetwoode. But the position was not big enough to hold them both, and the powers-that-be determined that Chetwoode had to go. He was not disposed to fall on his sword and pretexts had to be found for his dismissal: firstly, he was accused of cooking the books of the Grand Lodge and then, amazingly, he was charged with being an undercover papist. In evidence given to the Parliamentary Enquiry on Orangeism in Britain (1835), it was stated that two tylers from the Grand Lodge (named Condell and Osborne) and another Orangeman (named Payne) broke into Chetwoode's apartment at Lyons Inn during his absence, and stole some of his papers. The complicity of the Grand Lodge was said to be evidenced by the fact that the thieves were in the pay of Fairman.[6] The break-in apparently deprived Chetwoode of the evidence which he needed to establish his innocence.

The year before, Fairman had written an extraordinary letter to Cumberland in which he suggested that a plot was afoot to make the Duke of Wellington Regent in the event of the King's early death, instead of allowing the Crown to pass to the lawful successor, the Princess Victoria, who was still a minor. There is no evidence that Cumberland treated this letter more seriously than the previous ones. But at the time there was some concern in the country about the King's indifferent health, and even suggestions — to avoid any possible crisis in the succession — that measures should be adopted to exclude Cumberland. Rumours began to circulate that the young princess was sympathetic towards Rome, and planned to convert on her succession. It was also reported that certain Orange figures were vigorously canvassing 'the paramount claims' of the Duke of Cumberland to the throne, in the event of a constitutional crisis.

Some who sat on the radical benches at Westminster, including O'Connell, got hold of these rumours and undertook to exploit them. The chief figure was an able Scots politician named Joseph Hume, who had originally entered Parliament as a Tory supporter but since had adopted the doctrines of James Mill and the Philosophical Radicals. A self-made man, he had acquired a fortune in India and returned to Britain to take up a string of good causes. Among his passions were Catholic Emancipation, the Repeal of the Test Act and Parliamentary Reform. One of his great hatreds was the Masonic Order and, in fact, he had no time for any secret society. The rumours which now reached his ears interested him a great deal, and particularly the one which suggested that the Duke of Cumberland had 'infiltrated' the army with Orange lodges. Hume and some of his friends (like Sir William Molesworth, the Editor of the *London and Westminster Review*) began making enquiries.

Meanwhile, the Grand Lodge of England had sent Lieutenant Colonel Fairman on a tour of the Midlands, the north, and Scotland, ostensibly to whip up support for the Order. He was given a 'travelling warrant' which authorised him to found lodges wherever he saw fit. He also carried introductions to certain members of the northern nobility, and part of his mission was to establish connections between aristocratic right-wing elements and the more plebeian Orangemen in the lodges. Hereward Senior observes:

> Many peers in the grand lodge may have imagined that there was a parallel between the Reform agitation and the activities of the United Irishmen. The difficulty was that the landed classes in Britain had no equivalent to the Armagh peasantry anxious to press upon them the leadership of the Orange societies. Moreover, as the landlords themselves were not threatened with anything like the Defender movement, they felt no immediate need to organise their tenants in Orange lodges. Even if such lodges had been created, it is difficult to see what could be done to counteract the urban Reform agitation.[7]

This pinpoints a contradiction at the heart of Orangeism in Britain: it was largely an urban phenomenon, and the Reform programme of the Whigs (which the Order's leadership vehemently opposed) could easily be shown to be in the objective interests of the rank-and-file membership. Indeed, it would require little perception to spot that the fondness of urban Orangemen for the Order lay less in matters concerning their welfare than in their atavistic hatred of Catholicism, and their delight in indulging themselves in the kind of 'King and Country' patriotism which was a speciality of the Order.

Whatever the rationale behind Fairman's tour, it does not appear to have been particularly successful. He seems to have spent most of his time 'sounding out' existing Orangemen on their likely reaction to a revolutionary situation (which he believed to be looming) rather than on promotional or recruitment work. Joseph Haywood, who was District Master of the Sheffield Lodge in 1832, later claimed that Fairman asked his lodge members whether they would rally to the Duke of Cumberland 'if a row took place'. This was dangerous talk, and when it got out (as it inevitably did) it led people to wonder whether the Order was planning something sinister.

But Fairman made a habit of being indiscreet. In a letter to the Marquis of Londonderry (dated June 1832) he wrote:

> By the rapid augmentation of our physical force we might be able to assume a boldness of attitude which should command the respect of our Jacobinical rulers . . . If we prove not too strong, for such a government as the present is, such a government will prove too strong for us . . . Hence the necessity of our laying aside that non-resistance and passive obedience which has hitherto been religiously enforced to our discomfiture.[8]

In another passage he commends Irish Orangemen who 'were resolved to resist all attempts on the part of the government to put them down'. In a letter dated 11 August 1833 to the Duke of Gordon (who had been appointed Deputy Grand Master for Scotland), Fairman was even more outspoken: 'Our institution is going prosperously . . . By our next meeting . . . we will be assuming an attitude of boldness which will strike the foe with awe.' Earlier he had written to Lord Longford: 'We shall speedily have such a moral and physical force, I trust, as will strike with terror and sore dismay the foes of our country.'

Hume Takes Action

Fairman received courteous replies and even expressions of sympathy from a number of the peers with whom he corresponded, but there is no evidence that they ever took any action as a result of his overtures. His speeches to rank-and-file Orangemen were also indiscreet, and he gave grounds for thinking that the Order was engaged in a move either to put Cumberland on the throne or to make him Regent. The cat was set among the pigeons when disaffected Orangemen leaked details of Fairman's speeches to Joseph Hume and Sir William Molesworth. Hume had already been trying to get information on the strength of Orangeism within the army; he had, in fact, uncovered evidence that Lodges existed in various units since the 1798 Rebellion, and claimed that the force had been so corrupted that there were up to fifty regiments whose fidelity could not be relied upon. Secret oath-bound societies in the army had been expressly banned. Hume and other Radicals now began pressing for a Parliamentary enquiry.

Their timing was propitious. The new Whig government under Lord Melbourne was without a majority and had to rely on Radical and Irish members for support. When Hume and W.F. Finn, MP for Waterford, brought the matter onto the floor of the House in the spring of 1835, a Select Committee was appointed to enquire into 'the nature, character, extent and tendency of Orange lodges, associations and societies in Ireland, Great Britain and the colonies.' The enemies of Orangeism hailed a victory and rubbed their hands with glee. The Order was to be turned inside out and exposed to the gaze of the public.

The Parliamentary Enquiry

A Select Committee consists of members of the House of Commons who are 'selected' by the entire House and appointed by it to act as a committee. Its members are nominated after having expressed a willingness to serve, and its prime function is to do work for which the House itself is not fitted — finding out the facts of a case, examining witnesses, sifting evidence and drawing reasoned conclusions. It is empowered to order the production of documents and the attendance of witnesses, but has no power to ensure the adoption of its recommendations. When it has concluded its business, its chairman — a member appointed by itself — produces a report of its findings. Its rules exclude the production of minority reports and it must act, therefore, with unanimity.[9]

The Select Committee on Orangeism was composed initially of twenty-seven members, eight of whom were known Orangemen; twelve were known to be hostile to the Order and the remaining seven had not previously expressed views either way. During its sittings, it interviewed dozens of witnesses, studied literally reams of documents and, it would appear, received the co-operation of both the Irish and British Orange bodies. The Grand Lodge of Ireland resolved:

> That an authority be granted under the Great Seal of the Institution to those Brethren who may be examined before the Committee of the House of Commons, now appointed to investigate the nature and tendency of the Orange Institution, to disclose all signs, passwords and secrets of the institution without any concealment whatever, and that the proper officer be instructed to prepare the same . . . The brethren therein alluded to shall have the power of laying before the Committee of the House of Commons all books and documents connected with the institution, and all such further information as may be required of them without reservation whatsoever.[10]

Testimony on the Irish Order was heard from such senior figures as Lieutenant Colonel William Verner (the Deputy Grand Master), Colonel William Blacker and his nephew, Stewart Blacker (Solicitor to the Grand Lodge), Henry Maxwell MP, the Very Reverend Holt Waring, Dean of Dromore, the Very Reverend Mortimer O'Sullivan (a Tipperary-born Catholic who had converted to Protestantism) and many others. Among those heard on behalf of the British Order were Lord Kenyon, Lieutenant Colonel William Fairman and C.E. Chetwoode.

In the end, four massive reports assembled in three volumes and containing 4,500 pages were produced. Two of the reports covered the testimony of those interviewed, and also gave information on the Order's early history, its rituals, signs and passwords. In one section Stewart Blacker, on being asked about the origin of the 'higher orders', replied:

> I have not the slightest idea but I imagine that they arose from the desire of the lower orders to have something more exciting or alarming in the initiation of members. I think that it may be a mixture of freemasonry with the Old Orange System, a species of mummery

innocent of itself and originating in the strong desire that vulgar minds in general manifest for awful mysteries and ridiculous pageantry.[11]

The third report dealt with the testimony of the hostile witnesses, who included Sir Frederick Stoven, Inspector General of the police; Randall Kernan, a Catholic barrister; Robert Millan, a medical doctor from County Meath; W.J. Hancock, a magistrate who acted as estate agent for William Brownlow, MP, of Lurgan; James Christie, a County Armagh Quaker; and the Liberal MP for Dundalk, William Sharman Crawford (a man who later played a significant role in the Irish Tenant League).

The fourth report was concerned exclusively with the Order in Britain and with its 'Achilles' heel' — the illicit army lodges. This report disposed Joseph Hume to move resolutions in the Commons on 4 August, declaring Orangeism illegal and alluding to its existence in the army. Hume also called for an address to the King, drawing attention to the incongruity of Cumberland's personal position, being on the one hand a Field Marshal and on the other Imperial Grand Master of the Order. The Duke seemed to be compromised, and all eyes turned upon him. As tension rose, Lord John Russell intervened and requested that further debate be postponed for a week. It was hoped that Cumberland would avail of the breathing space to reconsider his position as Grand Master, but he stuck to his guns, and on 24 August wrote to Hume (in the latter's capacity as Chairman of the Select Committee on British Orangeism) and acknowledged that he may have signed 'through the negligence or indiscretion of the officers of the Orange Institution' batches of military warrants without realising for whom they were being issued.

Hume replied with more than a little sarcasm: 'It is satisfying to know that one result of the enquiry of the Committee has been to bring to His Highness's knowledge, and convince His Royal Highness, that Orange lodges did and do exist in many regiments, and that he has presided as Imperial Grand Master over an institution which has for many years been acting in contravention of the orders of the army's officer corps.'[12]

Cumberland was in a cleft stick, but Hume was disposed to be gracious. When the debate resumed, he modified his resolutions so that they did not specifically accuse Cumberland of signing military warrants. A week later the Grand Lodge announced that all such warrants were cancelled.

Fairman Absconds

Hume then announced that, on giving evidence to the Committee, Fairman had persistently refused to furnish a letter-book dealing with military lodges. This counted as contempt of Parliament and a warrant was issued for his arrest. When the police arrived at his apartment, Fairman was not to be found. Events now took a bizarre turn. Joseph Haywood, who had been District Master in Sheffield in 1832, had since become disaffected, and wrote to the press stating that Fairman (during his tour of a few years before) had spent his time 'sounding out' Orangemen on the question of a coup d'état, to put Cumberland on the throne. This revelation hit the public like a bombshell and was enough to provoke Fairman, although still in hiding, to issue a writ for libel. The public were, however, denied seeing the denouement, for before the trial Haywood burst a blood vessel and died.

These matters raised a few questions: was there an Orange conspiracy to alter the succession to the throne? Was Fairman, in his speeches and correspondence, outlining Orange policy, or were the views he expressed simply the machinations of an over-heated imagination?

At least one respected figure opted for acceptance of the conspiracy theory. Elie Halévy, the French historian, widely regarded as having written the most detailed history of England in the nineteenth century, wrote: 'Incredible though it may seem, there can be little doubt that their [the Orangemen's] leader, the Duke of Cumberland, the King's brother, believed it possible to set aside by a military coup his little niece, the Princess Victoria, who was a devoted Whig, and seize the succession to William IV.'[13] But Halévy provides no hard evidence to substantiate this view, and appears to have based it on an article which he found in Sir William Molesworth's less than detached *London and Westminster Review* and upon a book called *The Early Court of Queen Victoria*, in which the author sketches a conversation between Cumberland and his aide-de-camp, but fails to provide the source of her information.[14] Similar views are found in Miss Harriet Martineau's book *The Thirty Years' Peace*, but again without a reference source.[15]

Those works have been quoted frequently by writers and pundits hostile to Orangeism; for instance, Cleary, a firm advocate of the conspiracy theory, quotes Martineau no less than twenty-four times. Outside of these writers, very little information has ever come to light on the subject of an Orange conspiracy. There were probably fewer than 10,000 Orangemen in Britain during the mid-1830s, and nothing has been unearthed about them gearing up for a coup. No arms depots or dumps — like those, for instance, found in Dublin during the Emmet rebellion of 1803 — have ever been discovered. The number of military warrants issued at the time was thirty-one. The average size of an army lodge was not more than twelve, which would bring the total number of military Orangemen to less than 400 in total and these would, of course, be scattered in barracks in several different parts of the country. Although Cumberland was known to be an accomplished intriguer, and some felt him capable of conjuring up some rather sinister designs, nobody marked him down as a fool. The Reverend John Brown, an official Orange historian, was not far off the mark when he commented: 'Whatever else Cumberland, Kenyon, the Duke of Gordon, the Marquis of Chandos and the Bishop of Salisbury may have been, they were never thought to be lunatics.'[16]

Cumberland Dissolves the Order

The parliamentary reports were damaging, as were the shenanigans over Fairman's letter-book and the revelations in the press. When Parliament resumed in 1836 there were hot debates and, in February, Hume pressed for the dismissal of all Orangemen from civil and military office. The Government was, at this time, more dependent on the Radicals and O'Connell than ever, and it felt obliged to act. The climax came when the Home Secretary, Lord John Russell, proposed that an address be presented to the King which would suggest the advisability of discouraging political societies which excluded people of different religions and which used secret signs and symbols. The King replied in a manner which virtually repeated the terms of the Address:

> I willingly assent to the Address of my faithful Commons, that I will be pleased to take such measures as may seen to be advisable for the effectual discouragement of Orange lodges and generally of all political societies, excluding persons of a different religious faith, using secret signs and symbols and acting by means of associated branches. It is my firm intention to discourage all such societies in my dominions, and I rely with confidence on the fidelity of my loyal subjects to support me in this determination.
>
> William Rex[17]

The next day, the Home Secretary received Cumberland's assurance that he would 'take immediate steps to dissolve the Loyal Orange Institution of Britain'.

In Ireland, many Orangemen were inclined to resist the King's wishes, and heated arguments occurred over whether the Grand Lodge of Ireland should be dissolved on the basis of 'the novel doctrine that the mere wish of the Sovereign expressed through his Ministers in answer to an Address from the House of Commons has the force of law or can restrain the subject in the legal exercise of constitutional rights.'

The temper of many Orangemen was again up, and for several weeks the Order was in danger of splitting between those who were for and against dissolution. But on 14 April the Grand Lodge resolved by 79 votes to 59 that, 'the end for which the Orange Association was originally framed will no longer be served by the further continuance of that Institution and is hereby dissolved.'

—22—

Dolly's Brae and the Right to March

> 'Twas on the twelfth day of July in the year of forty-nine
> Ten hundred of our Orangemen did together combine
> In memory of King William on that bright and glorious day
> To march around Lord Roden's park and right over Dolly's
> Brae.
>
> — *first verse of ballad in commemoration of the*
> *'Battle of Dolly's Brae', 12 July 1849*

Armagh Assumes Control

It was with misgiving that the Grand Lodge of Ireland voted itself out of existence and announced the dissolution of the Order in Ireland. Thousands of Orangemen up and down the country — and particularly those in Ulster — believed that the Order had been ambushed by its enemies and that gross calumnies had been perpetrated against it. Instinctively, the old cry of 'No Surrender' went up. The mood was caught by Lodge No. 365 in Roscrea, County Tipperary, which resolved:

> We cannot avoid expressing the regret and astonishment we feel at the premature and perceptive surrender of our glorious Institution . . . everyday experience tends to convince us of the absolute necessity of some association for the protection of our lives and property. We consider the Orange Society, being based purely on defensive principles, best calculated to that object . . . we cheerfully respond to the heart-stirring appeal of 'No Surrender' and will rally under the unsullied banner at the usual time until suppressed by a legal enactment.[1]

As the Order had not been outlawed by legislation, Orangemen were quite entitled to meet in their lodges and conduct their lawful business. The Roscrea resolution was echoed by nine lodges in County Cork, two in Westmeath, one in Waterford, one in Offaly, six in Dublin City, two in Dublin County, sixteen in Tyrone, ten in Fermanagh, ten in Monaghan, and practically all in County Armagh. The wishes of these brethren could not be ignored, and at a meeting of the Armagh Grand Lodge on 13 June 1836 it was resolved: 'That the business of the Institution in this country be entrusted, as in the early days, to the Grand Lodge of the same until the Grand Lodge of Ireland resumes its function.' The man who took over as Grand Master was the veteran Colonel William Blacker who, with his nephew Stewart Blacker, had participated in the last meeting of the Grand Lodge of Ireland, and had voted against dissolution.

Armagh's new ascendancy was as brief as intended. The Grand Lodge of Ireland was reconstructed at a meeting in Tim's Club, Grafton Street, Dublin in November 1837. But many in the old aristocratic leadership failed to return to the ranks. In their view, the Grand Lodge had been abolished and the Order dissolved forever. Lord Roden, who had been entrusted with the books and records of the old Grand Lodge, failed to attend the meeting but was elected Grand Master of Ireland in his absence. The new Grand Lodge never really got off the ground and was relaunched in Enniskillen town hall in August 1845, this time with the 3rd Earl of Enniskillen in the Chair. The Earl was provisionally appointed Grand Master of Ireland and, in the following year, this was ratified at a meeting in Dublin.

Famine and Revolt

The Famine which devastated Ireland between 1845 and 1851 left almost a million dead and caused another million to emigrate. This appalling disaster was caused by the failure of the potato crop on which a substantial portion of the population depended for their food. It shocked Europe and North America and left an enduring scar on the consciousness of the Catholic population, who suffered most. It did not hit the North, or Orangeism, to the same extent because the grain and flax crops were good, and the linen industry was still running at a sufficient level to provide subsistence. Not all Orange families, however, escaped its horrors and it is recorded that Orangemen in Clogher, County Tyrone, marched to the house of the local Catholic priest, Father James McDonnell, to thank him for his efforts in helping the less fortunate of their brethren.

Some, like the Reverend Samuel Marcus Dill of Cookstown, County Tyrone, saw the hand of God in the Famine. It was, he believed,

Providence's way of punishing the unrighteous Catholics. In an extraordinary work entitled *The Problem Solved*, Dr Dill wrote:

> It is a matter of easy calculation that if things go on for some years, as, by all appearances, they intend to, Popery in Ireland is doomed. It would seem as if God has resolved to clear the country and replenish it anew. The land is rapidly passing into English hands. With the emigration of the Irish, there has commenced the immigration of the Scotch and English; and the numbers are only awaiting the adjustment of the land question to settle among us. Thus, God is renovating the country by the double process of driving Popery beyond the ocean, and bringing Protestantism from across the Channel.[2]

In 1847 John Mitchell broke with the Young Ireland group who had founded *The Nation* newspaper and established his own publication called *The United Irishman*. This paper advanced the view that only an independent republic could solve Ireland's problems. It thus brought Republicanism – forgotten since the days of Tone — back into Irish politics. The government grew alarmed at some of Mitchel's editorials and, in May, he was arrested and sentenced to fourteen years' transportation. His arrest forced his more conservative colleagues to consider rebellion.

The Orangemen, aware of what was transpiring, sent loyal addresses to the Crown and Lord Lieutenant, and the government was informed that members of the Order were prepared to assist the armed forces in the event of insurrection. There were no direct dealings, but Dublin Castle, through its emissaries Captain Kennedy, Major Turner and Colonel Phaire, made known its willingness to accept the offer. In certain areas, Orangemen were either provided with arms or given arms licences. They were also invited to act as intelligence agents, but spying was not one of their traits, so they refused.

The rebellion, when it came, was little more than an affray in a Tipperary village and was put down without difficulty. When the ringleaders were shipped out of the country and all was safe, the Lord Lieutenant, Lord Clarendon, publicly thanked Lord Roden for his advice and assistance. Although the Orangemen were not specifically named, they took Clarendon's remarks as a pat on the back.

The March to Tollymore

During these years the main opponents of the Order were the Ribbonmen, members of a Catholic agrarian terrorist organisation which traced its descent from the Defenders. They operated in various parts of the country but were particularly strong in the Ulster border regions. In February 1848 they killed a young Orangeman named David McDowell at Katesbridge in south Down, and a month later terrorised Protestants in Downpatrick by going on the rampage and firing their guns into Protestant houses. On the same day (Saint Patrick's Day, 17 March) they paraded through Crossgar and clashed with the police; one constable was killed and two seriously injured. By the time 'The Twelfth' came around, tension between both sides had reached fever pitch in south Down.

At this time it was common for Orange lodges to group on 'The Twelfth' and link up with brethren from other districts for joint celebrations. In 1848, lodges in the Castlewellan area marched to Ballyward to join brethren from Rathfriland. In doing so they made their way along the 'new road' so as to avoid the Catholic townland of Maheramayo. Word was spread that the Orangemen had been afraid to take the 'old road', which was shorter, and at fairs and markets they were taunted for their cowardice. Before the 1849 'Twelfth' the Rathfriland lodges announced that they were unafraid, and that they now intended to march to Castlewellan by the 'old road'.

The authorities grew alarmed and hoped that if enough troops were poured into the area, a clash would be avoided. On 10 July, Major Wilkinson was sent to Castlewellan with the 13th Light Dragoons and two companies of the 9th Foot Regiment. With him was Captain Skinner, a Justice of the Peace, and two resident magistrates representing the civil authorities.

Early on 'The Twelfth' the lodges from Rathfriland assembled at Ballyward, in the demesne of Francis Beers, a local JP and brother of their County Grand Master, William Beers. There were about 1,200 brethren present, and a similar number of women and children. Many bore arms. Looking through a telescope, their leaders saw a large number of Ribbonmen assembling in the distance on Maheramayo Hill. They were unperturbed, as the police and military had arrived to escort them and, besides, they had their weapons. The march set off with the magistrates riding in front accompanied by mounted police, and the rear made up by a troop of cavalry. In the middle, forming the bulk of the procession, were the Orangemen, stepping it out behind their band and wearing their regalia. A few weeks before, Lord Roden had agreed to host the brethren in his demesne at Tollymore, not far from Castlewellan. He had arranged for a large tent to be erected in the grounds and had laid on refreshments.

The march progressed along the 'old road' and approached a steep defile just beyond Maheramayo Hill, known as Dolly's Brae. The name was derived from a man named O'Hara who had once lived in the vicinity and, for some reason, had been nicknamed 'Dolly'. The word 'Brae' is of Scottish derivation, defined in the Oxford Dictionary as 'sloping ground'. This was thought by the marchers to be the danger spot; it was low, curved and an ideal place for an ambush. As the brethren advanced towards it, the police and dragoons lined both sides of the roadway to protect them. Nothing happened save that some Catholic women and children shouted abuse from the ditches. The Ribbonmen remained on Maheramayo Hill.

The Rathfriland lodges had been joined by lodges from Kilkeel, Newcastle and Mourne, and thus strengthened, the march was now led by William Beers. The total brethren at this point numbered about 6,000 (representing fifty lodges), and the camp followers may have constituted half as many more. Lord Roden came out to meet them, mounted on a white horse, wearing the regalia of Deputy Grand Master, and accompanied by a retinue of local gentry. The Orangemen saluted him, swung into the demesne, broke ranks and made for the refreshments. After an hour a bugle was blown, and the brethren were marshalled in front of a platform where William Beers and Lord Roden stood to address them.

Roden's speech was bland and pious:

> Much as I thank you for this visit, I feel the honour was not so much intended to me personally as to those Protestant principles which I hold, and which I have endeavoured to maintain for a period of thirty years' residence amongst you . . . It is true Protestant principles held up and maintained in this land that can alone prove a guarantee for the liberties of all classes and denominations of the people. . . .

> We have seen heavy blows and great discouragement given to Protestantism; but still you maintain your loyalty. You have never forgot, I trust, that your motto is unchanged — 'Semper Eadem' (always the same) — involving the preservation of your rights, the promotion of peace, and the welfare of all denominations of our fellow-subjects. I trust that you will rather take evil than provoke it; that nothing will induce you, in returning to your homes today, to resent even any insult you may receive. May God bless you and uphold you, keeping you firm in your principles, determined to support the laws of your country, and enabling you by well doing to put to silence the ignorance of foolish men. . . .[3]

At Maheramayo Hill, the Ribbonmen spent their time drilling and firing their weapons. They were closely watched by Major Wilkinson's cavalry, but no attempt was made to disperse them. Two Catholic clergymen, Father Patrick Morgan, the local parish priest, and Father John Mooney spent several hours on the Hill arguing with them to return to their homes. Their leader, 'Captain' Lennon — an activist who a short time before had been discharged from police custody — was adamant that they should remain.

The Battle of Dolly's Brae

When the proceedings at Tollymore were concluded, the lodges regrouped for the return march. The Castlewellan Orangemen went their way and the Rathfriland brethren began to retrace their steps on the 'old road'. Around 5.30 they approached Dolly's Brae, and at Maheramayo the police again lined the roadway. When they were twenty yards or so beyond the danger zone, someone threw a squib and all hell broke loose. It has never been firmly established who was responsible for this malicious act. Walter Berwick, the Queen's Counsel who conducted the official investigation, wrote: 'Several trustworthy witnesses stated that it came from the rear of the Orange party, and others, equally credible, stated that it came from the Hill.'

Everyone panicked. The Ribbonmen on the Hill began firing indiscriminately at the Orangemen and the police, and they returned fire equally indiscriminately. Who began the shooting is anybody's guess, but the police quickly took the decision to dislodge the Ribbonmen from the heights. Led by Sub-Inspector Hill, they leaped the ditch and charged up the hill, firing as they ascended. Some of the Ribbonmen fled, and others were captured. At this point, Berwick's report says: 'In the meantime a body of about 100 to 200 of the Orange party dashed up the hill transversely towards the same quarter, firing shots at the retreating body on the Hill, and the police were in considerable danger, being placed between two fires.' Berwick continues:

> While this was going on I lament to say that the work of retaliation both on life and property by the Orange party was proceeding lower down the hill, and along the side of the road in a most brutal and wanton manner . . . One little boy, ten years old, was deliberately fired at and shot while running across a field. Mr Fitzmaurice stopped a man in the act of firing at a girl who was rushing from her father's house. An old woman of seventy was murdered and the skull of an idiot was beaten in with the butts of muskets. Another old woman was severely beaten in her house, while another, who was saved by the police, was much injured and left in her house which had been set on fire. An inoffensive man was taken from his house, dragged to his garden and stabbed to death by three men with bayonets in the sight of his family. The Roman Catholic Chapel, the house of the Roman Catholic Curate, and the Schoolhouse were fired into and the windows broken, and a number of the surrounding houses of Roman Catholic inhabitants were set on fire and burned, every article of

furniture having been first wantonly destroyed therein; and had it not been for the active interference of magistrates and troops, much more loss of life and property would undoubtedly have taken place. It was alleged by the Orange party that shots had been fired at them from the cover of some of these houses. By the exertions of the troops, the Orange body on the road and in the fields was, after some delay, pressed forward and removed from the scene of the action, but no prisoners were made of that party — a matter both of surprise and regret.

The number of lives lost at Dolly's Brae has never been established, but there were no Protestant casualties.[4] Two months later, a pro-Orange pamphlet published by the *Newry Telegraph* said: 'From information obtained from authentic sources it is calculated that no less than thirty in all were killed and a great many wounded.'

The Aftermath

There was uproar among the Catholic population, and heated debates were held in the House of Commons and the House of Lords. The government ordered an inquiry, and Walter Berwick QC of Newry was appointed to conduct it. He and his team sat for a week at Castlewellan National School and heard evidence from military witnesses, the magistrates who accompanied the march, Lord Roden, William and Francis Beers, and a large number of residents from the Maheramayo area who had suffered injury or arson, or who were related to the victims. For some reason, none of the rank-and-file Orangemen who participated in the march were called.

In the end, no one was convicted of any of the crimes committed, but Berwick's Report blackened the Orangemen. He castigated William and Francis Beers and Lord Roden, who were magistrates:

> The magistrates who took part in the transactions of that day could have adopted a line of conduct which would have prevented the outrages then perpetrated, and which the information they possessed ought to have suggested to their minds. I cannot avoid noticing the grievous error thus committed, where the consequences have been so formidable to the public peace . . . they appear to have acted with a great misunderstanding of the nature of their duties — some of them to such an extent as actually to give countenance and protection to persons engaged in proceeding at variance with the law.[5]

Berwick's last remark is thought to refer to a speech which William Beers delivered at an Orange function a few days after the outrage. He was reported as saying: 'They [the Orangemen] had only lately celebrated the Twelfth of July, and such an anniversary it would have been, only for a little blot — if blot it could be called — no! it was a treacherous attempt to betray the innocent Protestants of the district . . . there was nothing contemplated by their enemies but murder and treachery. What could have saved them [the Orangemen]? . . . only that God had directed them. They had the blessings of many clergy and brethren with them at Dolly's Brae . . . but it was no longer 'Dolly's Brae', as it had been re- christened 'King William's Hill'. . . .'[6] In fact, the renaming of the hill took place during the outrage. Brethren from two lodges — Benraw and Laganny — rushed to the summit, planted their banners and, as their drummers and fifers played 'The Protestant Boys', their leaders pronounced the new name.

The Lord Lieutenant, Clarendon, accepted Berwick's Report and made recommendations to the Lord Chancellor that William and Francis Beers and Lord Roden be dismissed as Commissioners of the Peace. When the Lord Chancellor announced the dismissals, Berwick was accused of bias and hostility towards Orangeism. The Lord Chancellor was castigated for accepting the recommendations, and doubts were cast on his right to do so. It was declared that the executive had no right to proffer advice to the judiciary;[7] it was said that Berwick was merely an agent of the Lord Lieutenant, and that anything which he reported had no legal status.

Hundreds of letters of support and sympathy were received by Lord Roden and the Beers brothers, and Orange lodges passed resolutions condemning the treatment they had received. The *Down Recorder*, in its issue of 1 December 1849, reported that one of the Addresses received by Roden had 8,000 signatures on it. Roden himself took the matter coolly and defended himself with dignity in the House of Lords. Afterwards he participated little in Orange affairs. He died in 1870 in Edinburgh, where he had gone for health reasons, and was buried in the family vault at Bryansford, County Down.

On 8 February 1850 Sir William Meredith, the Chief Secretary for Ireland, brought in a bill outlawing Party Processions. He made it obvious that the legislation was aimed at the Orangemen, and on 12 March it became law. It differed from previous legislation in that it was intended to be permanent. But the memory of what had occurred at Dolly's Brae lived on, and a new ditty entered the Orange repertoire which extolled the virtues of Lord Roden:

> Lord Roden was Grand Master of our Orangemen just then,
> A better chieftain could not be found from all the sons of men,
> He sent an invitation to Rathfriland corps
> To come and spend the day with him in sylvan Tollymore.

> The Orangemen of late increased, and bold and violent grew
> And, as I say, would cross the Brae, hostilities to renew
> Lord Roden did them all invite to see his Lordly Hall
> And into the park at Tollymore where they assembled all.

In the years following the passing of the Party Processions Act, the Order went into decline, and was avoided by many Protestant dignitaries. That it was in bad odour with the authorities is shown by the manner in which one of its loyal addresses to Queen Victoria was rejected. In 1850 the Grand Master, Lord Enniskillen, wrote:

> To the Queen's Most Excellent Majesty, We, the members of the Loyal Order Institution in Ireland, beg permission to approach Your Majesty . . . and to tender the expression of our unswerving attachment to Your Majesty's Royal person, as well as to those great principles of constitutional government and religious liberty which gave to your ancestors the throne of this mighty Kingdom, and which still maintain, as we earnestly pray that they will long maintain, Your Majesty thereon.

> We further dutiously and respectfully pray Your Majesty to remember that should any necessity arise from passing events for the service of faithful men, there exist in Ireland 1,800 lodges of Loyal Orangemen, every one of whom will be ready, in God's name, and at Your Majesty's call, to peril life and fortune, as our forefathers under like circumstances have done, in defence of Your Majesty's crown and dignity, as well as of our common Religion and liberty.

> (Signed on behalf of the Orangemen of Ireland) Enniskillen, G.M.

The Home Secretary replied:

> My Lord, I have the honour to acknowledge receipt of your Lordship's letter of the 14th inst., enclosing an address to Her Majesty from members of the Loyal Orange Institution of Ireland, purporting to be signed by your Lordship, as Grand Master, and I beg to inform your Lordship that I do not feel it to be consistent with my duty to present this address to Her Majesty.

> I have the honour to be, Your Lordship's obedient servant G. Gray.[8]

Lord Enniskillen pressed the Home Secretary to state his reasons for rejecting the address, and was informed that 'it was owing to the attitude the late King had assumed towards the Orangemen in 1836.

Johnston of Ballykilbeg

The Party Processions Act was a great bane to the Orangemen. Their hatred of this type of legislation was compounded in 1860 when, following a serious riot at Derrymacash, near Lurgan, County Armagh, a Party Emblems Act was passed. The displaying of party flags, banners or emblems from buildings (or other public places) was prohibited; so, too, was the ceremonial discharge of cannon or firearms. Even the playing of traditional party tunes in public was outlawed. Orange leaders denounced both Acts as tyrannical, unconstitutional and an infringement of British liberties, yet they insisted that all brethren should obey them. The rise of Fenianism after 1856 and the contravention of the law by nationalist groupings increased their indignation further. This boiled over in July 1863 when a large nationalist demonstration took place in Dublin for the laying of the foundation stone of the O'Connell monument in Sackville Street. Those who participated wore, openly, green emblems, carried ''98' pikes and marched behind saffron-kilted pipers. The police turned a blind eye.

For years, Orangemen had criticised the timidity of their leaders on the marching issue. They wanted something more than rhetorical denunciations and called for positive action, as one of their number stepped forward to pick up the cudgel. This man, who would become an Orange legend, was William Johnston, a stormy petrel from Ballykilbeg, a townland outside Downpatrick. He was a small landowner, articulate and well-educated, and had already shown himself to be a tough customer. He had trod on sensitive toes in the Grand Lodge of Ireland on the issue of 'higher orders', and was an untiring agitator and political scribbler. A low-sized fellow, with a long bushy beard, he had the bright eyes of the fanatic and tended to dominate all who came near him. He was the product of a strongly committed Church of Ireland evangelical family, and his dislike of Rome was ingrained. At twenty he was made an Orangeman when initiated into a small lodge on the family estate, and from that day forward Orangeism became his credo. He spent a spirited few years in Dublin and took a degree at Trinity College. In 1839, on the death of his father, he returned to Ballykilbeg, and inherited the property. He was temperamentally unsuited to estate management and ran into financial difficulties which were to curse him throughout his life and, on occasion, force him into compromises.

In 1854 he founded the Down Protestant Association, whose aims included the abolition of Catholic convents, the withdrawal of government grants from Saint Patrick's College, Maynooth, and the recovery of all ground lost by the Protestant Ascendancy. In July 1855 he began publishing a local newspaper, *The Downshire Protestant*, 'to advocate the view that enlightened Protestantism is the true foundation of individual happiness, national prosperity and glory'. However, he needed to make substantial sums quickly, so he tried his hand at novel-writing. A few of his books are still mentioned by literary historians, the best of which is *Nightshades* — a forthright exercise in crude anti-Catholicism. The work contains a full cast of intriguing Jesuits, unchaste nuns and secretly Romanisng High Churchmen, in the best tradition of Charles Kingsley's *Westward Ho!*; the action ranges through Ireland, England, Scotland and France to the seat of 'The Beast' in Rome. Johnston was fascinated by contemporary events in Italy and blended his study of Garibaldi's campaigns with material found in the Book of Revelations. The resultant brew convinced him that the Church of Rome was about to collapse. To give it a final push, he felt he needed to break into politics. But Ulster politics were dominated by powerful landowning magnates, and he needed a major issue which would propel him to the forefront. He found it in the discontent aroused by the Party Processions Act.

The March to Bangor

Johnston began by going on a tour of Orange Halls and holding the brethren enraptured with his spellbinding oratory. He followed this up with a resolution from the County Down Grand Lodge to the Grand Lodge of Ireland, recommending that a major demonstration be organised on the coming 'Twelfth' (1864) for the repeal of the hated Act. When the Grand Lodge turned down his proposal, saying that 'such a measure would be undesirable and injudicious', he set about organising a demonstration of his own. Without the Grand Lodge's backing, he was unable to entice lodges outside his own part of Ulster; none the less, he got significant support, and on the 12 July, 1867, he took over 14,000 Orangemen from 117 lodges onto the public highway.

With banners hoisted, Johnston marched his brethren from Newtownards to Bangor and, on arrival, held a large open-air meeting in the town's square. From the platform, dressed in full regalia, he told the brethren that it was insufferable that they should be prohibited from lawfully 'walking' on 12 July; that they should be told not to display their banners in honour of King William, while the government itself had recently permitted a parade in honour of Daniel O'Connell. They were tired, he said, of 'hole-in-the-corner' meetings and would stand oppression and tyranny no longer.

The authorities realised that by enforcing the law against Johnston at a time when Protestant feeling was running high, they would likely make a martyr of him, but if legal action was not taken the floodgates would open and further illegal parades would follow. They decided to prosecute, and Johnston and twenty-three others were summoned to appear at Bangor Petty Sessions on 4 September; the matter later went for trial at the Spring Assizes in Downpatrick in February 1868. The case was heard before Mr Justice Morris (later Lord Killanin), and the

Attorney General travelled to Downpatrick to prosecute. A number of the accused pleaded guilty and were bound over, but Johnston and two others refused. Some of the charges were dropped, yet Johnston was jailed for a month, at the end of which time he was to enter bail for £500, with two securities. He was incarcerated in Downpatrick amid widespread Orange indignation.

In jail, Johnston's health broke down and the authorities, fearing his death, tried to arrange his early release on humanitarian grounds. But Johnston knew that his popularity was soaring in the Orange world outside, and that a general election was imminent. In fact, a few days after his imprisonment it was agreed, at a protest meeting in the Ulster Hall in Belfast, to nominate him as an independent Orange candidate. The authorities offered him early release again, but still Johnston refused. As news of his illness grew, his popularity rocketed to new heights. At last, on 22 April, he was released and a deputation from the Belfast Protestant Working Men's Association travelled by special train to greet him as he stepped through the prison gates. He was carried shoulder-high up and down the streets of Downpatrick and later conveyed to Ballykilbeg in a flag-bedecked horse and trap, preceded by a band playing 'The Protestant Boys'. One of the banners carried by his Belfast supporters bore the slogan: 'William Johnston, our future Member, Defender of our Rights and Liberties'. Orangeism had found its first modern hero.

Johnston in Parliament

The 1868 general election was bitterly fought, particularly in Belfast. Johnston threw himself into the campaign with relish. With the halo of an Orange martyr glowing around his head, he was warmly received in Protestant working-class areas. Acutely aware of working-class hardship and endowed with a radical temperament, he touched the right note when he said that the capital would always have its defenders, but 'it is more necessary that the particular interests of Labour should be watched over.'[9] To get the candidate's message across, Johnston's supporters launched a daily broadsheet, *The Belfast Election Circular*, and a group of Orange workers hired the Ulster Hall and staged a great 'Welcome Back Rally'. Johnston told the packed auditorium to beware of ultramontane Catholicism which, he claimed, was rapidly asserting itself in Ireland under the evil hand of Cardinal Cullen. He also fiercely attacked the proposals then in train for the disestablishment of the Church of Ireland.

Johnston's problem was that there were several other popular candidates. Craftily, he formed an alliance with the pseudo-liberal Thomas McClure, and together they outflanked and defeated the two Tory candidates, Sir Charles Lanyon, a well-known architect, and Jack

Mulholland, a wealthy linen manufacturer. When the results came in, the tar barrels blazed on the hillsides, and in Downpatrick a torchlight procession formed up outside the market house and went through the streets, preceded by an Orange band. In front was a huge banner which said: 'Long live the gallant Johnston and the artisans of Belfast, an honour to the nation!'

At Westminster, Johnston set to work immediately to repeal the Party Processions Act, but it was not until 1870 that he was able to introduce a Bill on the matter. In a tangled controversy with the Liberal government, the Bill ran into trouble, and the Orangemen's anger ran so high that the Omagh District Lodge passed a resolution calling for Repeal:

> We call on our countrymen of all breeds to join us in adopting all legal means to obtain a repeal of the Union.

Sixmilecross District Orange Lodge struck a similar note, and Crommelin Irwin, an Orange leader, announced at a Twelfth of July rally:

> If England does not give us justice, I would not care if there were repeal of the Union tomorrow, because we might as well be under any other country in that case . . . We would be far better under America if we are obliged to submit to the thraldom that is imposed on us.[10]

Johnston raised the matter at every opportunity and eventually, on 27 June 1872, the Liberal government repealed the Act. There was great Orange rejoicing, and it was thought a bonus that the legislation was removed from the statute book a few weeks before 'The Twelfth'.

Johnston's Last Days

Johnston of Ballykilbeg was instrumental in establishing the Grand Black Chapter of Ireland (in 1846) and the Imperial Grand Orange Council of the World (in 1867). He retained his Belfast seat — save for a brief period when he took up a government appointment as Inspector of Fisheries — until his death in 1902. In his last years he was invited by lodges everywhere to attend their functions, often as a special guest. His proficiency as a popular orator never diminished, and up to the end he could coin a witty phrase or make a cutting remark. His independence as a Member of Parliament was undermined when, near the end, he had to rely on Tory funding to keep the wolf from the door; Members at the time were unpaid. In all his difficulties, he never lost the support or affection of the Belfast craftsmen, artisans or small shopkeepers who put their trust in him. Time and again, when he attended their lodges, his biting forays against the Pope and the Catholic Church set the brethren in a roar.

Johnston's final years were sad. As his own and his wife's health declined, his youngest daughter Ada came home to look after them. Soon she was attending Mass at the Catholic chapel in Ballykilbeg, and then it was reported that she was taking instruction in the Catholic faith. On Easter Sunday 1898 she was received into the Catholic Church. It was a great blow to Johnston, but he was a man of strong moral fibre. Thereafter, he dutifully escorted his daughter, Sunday after Sunday, to her chosen place of worship and made no attempt to interfere with her beliefs. Indeed, woe betide anyone who would slight Ada's views in the presence of her father. A few years after the old man's death she returned to the faith of her birth.

Today, a full-length biography of Johnston is in print; his portrait appears on the banners of Orange Lodges[11] and at least one lodge – 'Johnston's Golden Star' (LOL 1934) — is named after him. On the banner of the Ballykilbeg Lodge (LOL 1040) he is shown as he must have looked near the end — an old, frail man with a long beard. Underneath is a caption which reads: 'When shall we see his like again?'

Disestablishment

In 1868, William Ewart Gladstone, shortly after becoming Prime Minister for the first time, invited the Reverend Doctor Richard Trent, Archbishop of Dublin, and other leading prelates of the Church of Ireland to Downing Street to discuss his proposals for the disestablishment and disendowment of their Church.[12]

That the matter should come up was inevitable, for all the world knew that the Church of Ireland was not favoured by the great majority of the Irish people, and that for some time an alliance of leading nationalists and Catholic churchmen had been campaigning for its privileged status to be removed. The census of 1861 had provided, for the first time, reliable figures relating to the various denominations in Ireland. Out of a population of 5.7 million there were 4.5 million Catholics, while the Established Church had only 700,000, more than half of which were concentrated in Ulster. Gladstone had an invincible faith in common sense, and this led him to believe that he might be able to obtain from the Protestant bishops their voluntary agreement to his proposals. Robert Lowe, a Liberal member of the Commons, had already provided the House with a blistering critique of the Church of Ireland:

> You call it a missionary church. If so, its mission is unfulfilled. As a missionary church it has failed utterly. Like some exotic thing brought from a far country, with infinite pains and useless trouble, it is kept alive with difficulty and expense in an ungrateful climate and

ungenial soil. The curse of barrenness is upon it; it has no leaves; it bears no blossoms; it yields no fruit: cut it down! Why cumbereth it the ground?[13]

But the Protestant bishops saw things differently. The Prime Minister was dismayed to find that they thought him an enemy of God, and a brigand; they returned to Ireland in an agitated mood and their pulpits rocked with denunciations of the proposals. Most Orangemen were of the Church of Ireland Communion, and agreed with their bishops. They, too, were vehement in their denunciation of the proposals, claiming that they constituted a fundamental breach of the Union, Article 5 of which united the Church of Ireland with the Church of England, and stated that the combined church 'shall be deemed to be an essential and fundamental part of the Union.' If the status of the Church of Ireland were to be compromised, they argued, the precedent would endanger other institutions. Would rights connected with property, for instance, be respected if those linked with the church were to be disrespected and invaded? Orange spokesmen came out strongly against the proposal and one of them, the Reverend John Flanagan, Rector of Killevan, told an audience of Orangemen at Newbliss, County Cavan, that the Queen should refuse to sign Gladstone's legislation:

> She should be reminded that one of her ancestors who swore to maintain the Protestant religion forgot his oath, and his crown was kicked into the River Boyne. We must speak out and tell our gracious Queen that if she breaks her oath, she has no longer any claim to the crown.[14]

Flanagan was castigated for gross impertinence and told to watch his tongue, yet some Orangemen believed that Queen Victoria would resist signing the Disestablishment Bill. In December 1868, the Grand Lodge of Ireland passed a resolution:

> That in the event of our beloved Sovereign being placed in the trying and difficult position of being called upon to refuse assent to any measure brought before her, we hereby pledge ourselves to afford Her Majesty every aid and support in our power.

The resolution was moved by J.H. Nunn, a Wexford Orangeman, but it changed nothing. The Bill to disestablish the Church of Ireland became law on 26 July 1869. Henceforth the Church would be a voluntary body, without state aid and having its finances and property invested in a Temporalities Commission.

The Orangemen were crestfallen. Nunn took the matter to heart and moved another resolution: 'That the members of the Orange Institution shall not henceforth be bound as Orangemen to maintain the Union.' But the Wexfordman spoke only for a small number of his brethren, a few of whom began to take an interest in a new movement which was founded in May 1870, in the Bilton Hotel in Dublin. This was the Home Government Association. Its founder was an able lawyer and Freemason who had once sat on the Committee of the Grand Lodge of Ireland, and had been one of the leading lights in 'Orange Young Ireland'. His name was Isaac Butt.

—23—

The Quaking Sod

O Lord our God, arise
Scatter our enemies
And make them fall;
Confound their politics;
Frustrate their Fenian tricks
On Thee our hopes we fix;
God save us all.

— *an Orange prayer*

Land War

As dawn was breaking on 3 April 1878, a crusty, seventy-two-year-old Orangeman, William Sidney Clements, 3rd Earl of Leitrim, was driving on a deserted roadway near his estate, adjacent to Mulroy Bay in County Donegal. A number of armed men brought him to a halt, and pointed their weapons directly at him.

For years he had rent-racked and evicted his tenants, and forced himself upon their daughters, shot their goats and pigs before their eyes and lashed them with his horsewhip as he rode by. His name had become a byword for severity and intransigence, and several attempts had been made on his life. Now the men of Fanad had caught him by surprise. The first shot killed his driver, who had sought to shield him, and two more mortally wounded his clerk. Mickey Rua MacElwee jumped upon the trap and threw him to the ground. The others moved in, and clubbed him with their musket butts. His features were scarcely recognisable when the body was found. The assassins escaped by boat; they were never brought to trial, although their identity was an open secret. The police, it was believed, took the view that the world was a better place without the Earl of Leitrim.

The killing was one of the first incidents in a new wave of violence which swept the country, due to a combination of catastrophic circumstances: falling prices, crop failures and atrocious weather which had continued almost uninterruptedly for two years. Thousands of tenants faced starvation, eviction and bankruptcy. In Mayo, in particular, the tenants searched desperately for a solution, but none appeared. While official Ireland had turned its back on them, a concerned, serious young man, with an accent not found locally, stepped forward to help them. He was, in fact, one of their own, called Michael Davitt. A tall, gaunt fellow with an earnest look, there was a sense of purpose about him. His family had been forced to emigrate to Lancashire when he was a child, and there, at the age of ten, he lost his right arm whilst working on unguarded machinery in a cotton mill. From early manhood he had been an active Fenian, and in 1870 was caught gun-running and sentenced to fifteen years' hard labour. In a succession of British prisons — Dartmoor, Newgate, Portland and Millbank — with shaven head and broad-arrow clothing, he broke the stones and picked the oakum, and managed to survive the harsh treatment.

In 1877 he was released on ticket-of-leave and went to America, where he rejoined the movement. In 1879 he moved to Mayo and involved himself in the land agitation. His methods were uncomplicated but innovative: a universal withholding of rent and a shunning of the landlords. His purpose was to end rent-racking, evictions and landlord oppression, and to give every tenant, on fair terms, control of the land on which he worked.

In 1879 he formed the Land League in Daly's Hotel in Castlebar, and soon another determined man — the rising star in the Home Rule movement, Charles Stewart Parnell — accepted the presidency of it. Within a year the League claimed 200,000 members, scattered throughout Ireland in 1,000 branches. Nothing to equal its fervour had been seen since the days of O'Connell, over fifty years before.

But as the agitation against the landlords was stepped up, violence, murder and mayhem became the order of the day. These outrages were disapproved of by the League but were, perhaps, the inevitable concomitant of so murky an agitation. Parnell recommended a better way. At a meeting in Ennis he spelt out to the tenants what their policy should be:

> When a man takes a farm from which another has been evicted, you must shun him on the roadway when you meet him. You must shun him in the streets of the town. You must shun him in the shop. You must shun him on the fair-green . . . by isolating him, as if he were a leper of old, you must show him your detestation of the crime he has committed.[1]

Although the 1880 harvest showed a marked improvement on that of the three previous years, much of Connaught continued to be a distressed area. The League decided to adopt a policy of 'holding the harvest'. Parnell's sister, Fanny, caught the mood in her poetry:

> Hold the rent and hold the crops, boys
> Pass the word from town to town
> Pull away the props, boys
> So you'll pull coercion down.[2]

The 'coercion' was the strong-armed methods employed by the Chief Secretary, W.E. Foster (known as 'Buckshot' Foster), and the Royal Irish Constabulary, and was rooted in two Acts, passed in February and March 1881, which empowered them to imprison anyone whom they viewed with a reasonable amount of suspicion. One of those Acts, called the Protection of Persons and Property Act, obviously referred only to the landlords and to their property.

The Land League and the Orangemen

Most of the landlords and their agents were Protestants, and some were Orangemen. The violence against them caused widespread resentment, particularly within the higher echelons of the Order. The attitudes of the rank-and-file brethren were less certain. When the landlords sought the Order's support, there was some hesitancy in rural lodges. Many brethren were themselves tenants and could see virtue in the Land League's campaign to reduce rents and obtain security of tenure. Besides, they did not like the airs of the landlords and were reluctant to see the Order turned into a rich man's poodle. A small populist wing emerged which indicated its support for the tenants' struggle. In County Tyrone, one lodge announced that it would assist the tenants but keep at arm's length from the Land League. In County Monaghan, a little later, another lodge made a similar declaration and helped Tenant-Right candidates in the 1880 general election.

Davitt was not slow to see the possibilities of Orange support and took his campaign to Ulster, addressing meetings in the Orange heartlands. The first Land League meeting held in the North was at Belcoo, County Fermanagh, in December 1879, and Orangemen were among those who attended. Bit by bit Davitt ingratiated himself with the rural brethren. In Kinnegoe, County Armagh, a large meeting was organised by the Loughgall branch of the League, showing that it had support in the very cradle of Orangeism. At this meeting the chair was taken by James Weir, the Worshipful Master of the local lodge. In pouring rain, hundreds of Orangemen assembled in a field, and Davitt told them:

You are no longer the tame and superstitious fools who fought for amusement and profit with your equally foolish and superstitious Catholic fellow workers, and allowed the landlords to pick both your pockets during the encounter. Did you ever hear tell of a Catholic landlord who gave a reduction of rent to a tenant who had his hand broken in a fight for the honour of the Pope? Or a Protestant gentleman . . . who would refuse to evict an Orangeman who drank to the memory of the vanquisher of that miserable coward, King James, at the Boyne? No, my friends, the landlords of Ireland are all of one religion — their God is mammon, and rack-rents and evictions their only morality, while the toilers of the soil, whether Orangemen, Catholics, Presbyterians or Methodists are the victims whom they desire to see fling themselves beneath the juggernaut of landlordism.[3]

There was more of the same from John Dillon, who told a huge gathering in Armagh in April 1881:

I tell you that the dispute between Orangemen and Catholics has been maintained by the landlords and magistrates of Ulster lest people might agree, for they know that those who see the Orange farmer and the Catholic farmer unite in one organisation will see the downfall of landlordism.[4]

For a time the Order was placed in an untenable position as a result of conflicting pressures. At 'The Twelfth' celebrations in July 1881, the usual ritual attacks were made on Catholicism, but this time they were mingled with calls for 'a just settlement' to the land question. The truth was that the majority of Orangemen disliked Catholicism more than they disliked the landlords. Their natural reaction to any movement perceived to be in conflict with the constitution was one of hostility and to most brethren the Land League, led by the Fenian Davitt and the Nationalist Parnell, could not — despite some sympathy with its aims — have their support. When the League won over a small number of lodges, the Grand Lodge of Ireland withdrew the warrants of two lodges in Fermanagh and issued final warnings to others. Its policy was spelled out in unequivocal terms: the Land League was part of a new and devious conspiracy to subvert the constitution and cut the connection between Ireland and England.

The Emergency Relief Committee

In October 1880 the Order decided to take direct action against the Land League. An Emergency Committee was established to 'aid those of Her Majesty's subjects who are suffering persecution at the hands of an illegal organisation known as the Land League', i.e. to organise groups of scab Orange labourers to relieve landlords who were in conflict with the League. The first 'Relief Expedition' (as they were termed) was dispatched to the estate of Colonel John O'Callaghan at Mayfort, Tulla, County Clare, and thereafter numerous others were sent to various parts of the country. At one time up to 300 Orangemen were engaged in assisting landlords in nineteen counties. The Emergency Committee, however, went further: it employed men to issue writs against tenants and arranged for purchasing agents to attend auctions where sequestered cattle were being sold. It also employed armed caretakers, usually retired policemen or ex-soldiers, to occupy vacant farms and drive away those who tried to return to their holdings.

In all, the Emergency Committee was the bane of the Land League and sought to frustrate its purpose at every turn. The most notorious clash between these inveterate opponents (and one which was to achieve enduring fame) occurred on the estate of the Earl of Erne, on the shores of Lough Mask in County Mayo. This highly-charged encounter brought the attention of the world to a man whose career and character are now almost totally forgotten, but whose name lives on in every dictionary of the English language: Captain Charles Cunningham Boycott.

Captain Boycott and the Orangemen

John Crichton, 3rd Earl of Erne, was one of the most prominent Orangemen in Ireland. His wife, the strikingly beautiful Selina Griseld, was also of high Orange provenance, being the daughter of the Reverend Charles Crabbe Beresford. His son John Henry (at this time Viscount Crichton) was Member of Parliament for Enniskillen and was in 1886 to become Grand Master of the Orange Order in Ireland. The family's main seat was at Crom Castle, on the 31,000-acre estate at Newtownbutler, County Fermanagh, but they had a smaller estate — 2,184 acres — in the vicinity of Lough Mask, some four miles from Ballinrobe, County Mayo.

The Earl's agent on this estate was an ex-officer of the 39th Regiment of the Line, Charles Cunningham Boycott, the son of a vicar from Bury Saint Peter in Norfolk. Boycott had been farming in Ireland for over twenty-five years and had married an Irish Protestant, Miss Annie Dunn from Queen's County (County Laois). He had a lease on Lough Mask House and on a number of the surrounding acres, and acted as Lord Erne's agent in collecting the rents of thirty-eight small tenant farmers. The annual value of these rents was under £500, and Boycott received £50 commission for collecting them. The first intimation he received of impending trouble with the Land League was when, on 1 August 1879, he found a threatening notice pinned to the wrought-iron gate of Lough Mask House. This informed him that he must reduce his rents by 25 per cent on account of the poor harvest and pending famine in the district;

underneath the notice was a crude drawing of a coffin. He ignored the notice and, a few weeks later, served notices to quit on tenants who had defaulted in their payments.

The Land League responded by instructing the tenants to avoid all contact with Boycott, and by urging them to remain calm. The word was passed around and everyone, whether tenant or not, was included in the instruction. Boycott's labourers and servants refused to work for him; the local shopkeepers refused to serve him; no one would drive his trap or handle his farm machinery; the blacksmith slammed the door in his face and the postman refused to carry his mail. Worst of all, nobody would assist him in taking in his harvest, and if help did not come shortly, the crops would perish in the ground.

For some days there was complete stalemate. The tenants were the first to blink, deciding to make a direct appeal to Lord Erne himself. They sent a delicately-worded letter to Crom Castle which outlined their plight, and added that they were prepared to pay a fair rent (which they defined as being one which they could afford to pay). They also gave details of their grievances against Boycott: his refusal to allow them to collect wood, his imposition of petty fines and his general tyranny. On 1 October, Lord Erne said that he had found most of their complaints of a frivolous nature and, therefore, could not countenance them; he insisted that his rents were fair, and could only conclude that they were the recipients of bad advice. On 13 October the tenants wrote to Lord Erne again; they re-emphasised their plight and expanded on their complaints against Boycott. This time, his Lordship's reply was brief: he said that the complaints against Captain Boycott were unjustified and that he had nothing further to say.[5]

By this time Boycott's position in relation to the harvest had become even worse. Erne's dismissive replies had further angered the tenants and made them more determined to dig their heels in. Stones with death threats attached began to smash through the windows of Lough Mask House on a daily basis. The Captain, fearful for the safety of his wife and family, applied to the constabulary for increased protection. In his frustration, isolation and anger he wrote a letter to *The Times*, and said that it was the avowed intention of the Land League to bring about his ruination. *The Times* printed the letter and also carried an editorial on it: 'A more frightful picture of triumphant anarchy has never been presented in any community which pretended to be civilised and subject to law.'[6] It openly wondered what the government intended to do about the situation (18 October 1880).

At this juncture Mr Bernard Becker, a special correspondent for the *London Daily News*, arrived in Ballinrobe. After several days in the locality, he wrote a lengthy, punchy piece entitled 'The Isolation of

Captain Boycott', and alerted the world to the drama at Lough Mask. Within days the article was reprinted in the staunchly Orange *Belfast News Letter* and the pro-landlord Dublin *Daily Express*. Instantly, the focus of Orangemen throughout Ireland was on the plight of Captain Boycott. The first to move was a Dublin Orangeman named William Manning, who had once been a land agent himself. In letters to the *Daily Express* he called for the immediate establishment of a fund to relieve the beleaguered Captain. In Ulster, the idea was instantly taken up and developed. The Reverend William Stewart Ross, a Belfast Orangeman, called for volunteers to go to Mayo, and began to stir up the lodges. He hurriedly established a Relief Expedition to be led by himself and other prominent Orangemen. Excited brethren flocked to Ross's vicarage to enrol for what was called 'The Invasion of Mayo'. The hackles of the Orangemen were up, and special trains were ordered from the Midland and Great Western Railway to convey hundreds of volunteers to Mayo. The old cry of 'No Surrender' gave way to a new slogan: 'On to Mayo, boys!'

Smoke Along the Track

'Buckshot' Foster, the Chief Secretary, learnt of the Orangemen's relief scheme with more than a little trepidation. Urgent telegrams passed between himself and the Prime Minister, Gladstone, in London, and he received instructions to call a press conference. He told the assembled newsmen that the government would not permit an expedition to Mayo in excess of fifty men. He dispatched three train loads of infantry and cavalry to Ballinrobe, bringing the number of uniformed men in the town to 900. Elsewhere in Connaught, 7,000 more were put on alert.

The lodges had no difficulty in gathering fifty men. They were drawn from Cavan and Monaghan, and left Clones by rail on 11 November. Each one of them was given a revolver and instructed in how to use it. The train was preceded by a pilot engine in case the Land Leaguers had interfered with the track. At various points the route was patrolled by the Royal Irish Constabulary, and at one location there was great anxiety when a cloud of smoke was seen rising from under a railway bridge. As it turned out, it was only a peasant woman burning nettles. At stations along the line, crowds gathered to hiss and boo the Orangemen. When they arrived at Claremorris, a large scramble of reporters and photographers were waiting to meet them. As they alighted from the train, a *Times* correspondent later reported that a local wag approached him and said: 'Bedad, Sur, it is the queerest menagerie that ever came into Connaught' (15 October 1880).

There was no transport available to take the Orangemen to Lough Mask House. They left the station precincts under an escort of dragoons with sabres drawn, and were met with an outburst of hissing, booing and spitting from the people of Claremorris who lined the footpaths and roared from their top windows. They trudged in biting rain to Ballinrobe, only to be met with a similar reception, and then footslogged it on to Lough Mask House. As they plodded through Hollymount, with some miles still to go, they were met with shouts of 'ye're late for breakfast', 'the turnips are boiling' and 'where is ye're Lambeg drums?' For the next two weeks the Orangemen, guarded by the military and police, slept in tents, sang Orange songs around their campfires, and worked in drenching rain, successfully harvesting Captain Boycott's crops. They were, however, hard done by: Boycott charged them nine pence a stone for the potatoes which they ate. They got their own back by killing some of his geese and ducks and putting them into their pots. In the end, the entire exercise was seen as a fiasco. Davitt estimated that it cost £3,500 to harvest crops valued at £300, or, as Parnell put it, with a peal of laughter: 'One shilling for every turnip dug.'[6]

When the Orangemen left on 26 November, Captain Boycott quit too, but the wrath of the Land League followed him. His host in Dublin, the proprietor of Hammond's Hotel, was warned not to keep him under his roof. In fact, it was on this gentleman's advice that the Captain hurriedly took ship to England. He left on the Holyhead boat, and was heard to say, as he went on board, that he was glad to get away from 'the blasted Irish'.

Shortly after the Boycott affair had blown up, an American reporter, James Redpath, spoke to the local Catholic parish priest, Father John O'Malley, who was President of the Land League branch involved. He wanted to depict for his readers what had occurred at Lough Mask, but felt that the word 'ostracism' was inadequate. The locals, he said, had never used such a word and were unlikely to do so. O'Malley came up with 'boycott'; recent events, he insisted, could not be better described, and the word could be used as both a verb and a noun. Redpath grabbed the idea and, a few days later, used the word several times in an article for the American paper *Inter-Ocean*. It caught on almost immediately, and within weeks had made its way into the French, German, Russian and English languages. The former master of Lough Mask was thus immortalised.

The tenants' land agitation went on, but amid all the ferment there was much amused comment on how 'Buckshot' Foster sent hundreds of his crack troops to protect a few dozen Orangemen as they gathered mangolds and turnips in Mayo. *The Nation* contributed to the gaiety when it published some light-hearted lines which were recited at social gatherings up and down the country:

> To Crichton of Fermanagh, thus 'twas Buckshot Foster spoke:
> I find, my Lord, upon my word, this business is no joke.
> To gather in your agents' crops bring Orange Ulster down,
> And we'll defend the diggers with the army of the Crown.

> Thus from Monaghan and Cavan the valiant Volunteers
> protected by revolvers from the country people's jeers,
> With spade and sned, with mate and bread,
> and knives and forks and spoons
> Surrounded by the bhould infantry and the peelers and dhragoons.

> Hail, champions of the loyal North, hail warriors of the Queen
> To you a long afflicted man now welcome bids serene
> Long may your praise in trilling lays to time unborn go down.
> Brave sons of Orange Ulster, brave defenders of the Crown.

> They dug out all the praties, and they thrashed out all his corn
> His turnips and his mangels saved, that long had laid, forelorn:
> And nothing interrupted their enterprising work
> But all the rain from Heaven and the wind from Maam Turk.

> But 'tis said that his purtectors have put Bycutt to great cost;
> with trampled lawns and trees cut down, and much good substance
> lost: The troopers of Her Majesty made free with his young lambs
> And ate his mutton and his ducks, and thanked him with God damns. . . .[7]

—24—

The Orange Card

Sail on, O ship of State
Sail on, O Union Great
Shall Ulster from Britain sever?
By the God Who made us — never!

— Lord Randolph Churchill, the Ulster Hall, Belfast,
22 February 1886

Enter Mr Gladstone

In August 1885 William Ewart Gladstone, the most outstanding statesman of the age, was recovering from illness and taking a holiday amid the Norwegian fjords aboard the vessel *Sunbeam* owned by his friend Sir Thomas Bassey.

For years he had brooded over the puzzle that was Ireland and discerned in it the great unsolved moral issue in British politics: how Ireland could be justly governed in the interests of all its people. As he sailed through those placid waters he reflected on the Norwegian example. It interested him that a small people could prosper and yet remain constitutionally tied to a larger neighbour. Could it be, he wondered, because the Norwegians enjoyed a large measure of self-government? This thought was not at variance with liberal thinking in other parts of Europe, where it was held that devolved government could effectively conciliate growing nationalist pressures without weakening national sovereignty. Yet Mr Gladstone's vision of a devolved or 'Home Rule' assembly for Ireland did not spring from a single movement's rumination. Years before he had written, prophetically, to his wife:

Ireland! Ireland! That cloud in the West! That coming storm! That minister of God's retribution upon cruel, inveterate, but half-intoned justice! God grant us the courage to look them in the face!

During an earlier period of office, the Grand Old Man, as he was now styled, had sought to grapple with elements of the Irish problem. He had focused on the ecclesiastical question, and disestablished and dis-endowed the Church of Ireland; with the Land Acts of 1870 and 1881, he had attempted to resolve the land question, but his efforts, he knew, were invariably too late or insufficient to satisfy the increasing demands of the Land Leaguers or Home Rulers at Westminster. Gradually he found himself forced into coercion — a veritable policy of martial law enforced by 'Buckshot' Foster. Between 1881 and 1882, this entailed putting Parnell and a number of Land Leaguers behind bars in Kilmainham Jail.

When he plumped for Home Rule, Gladstone at first kept his views to himself. He was anxious that an Irish settlement should not, as he put it, 'fall into the lines of party conflict'. He genuinely thought that the matter ought to be settled by the Conservatives for, among other things, with their control of the House of Lords, they had the greater chance of settling it. But if they refused the poisoned chalice, Gladstone was not adverse to draining it himself.

For some time the Tory opposition had been making the kind of noises which the Home Rulers wanted to hear. A small ginger group within the party led by Lord Randolph Churchill had been especially cordial towards Parnell and had, on occasion, supported him. They disagreed with Gladstone's coercion policy and vigorously attacked it. On a number of issues Gladstone's government was tardy and out of touch, particularly when it misjudged the public mood and failed to send a timely expeditionary force to relieve General Gordon at Khartoum. It surprised nobody when on 8 June 1885 the Home Rulers combined with the Tories to turn Gladstone out.

When the result of the division was known, Lord Randolph Churchill jumped from his seat like a schoolboy and flung his hat in the air. The young, ambitious MP for Woodstock felt that his hour had come. Parnell and his Home Rulers felt that they had something to cheer about too; by joining with the Tories in the lobby, they believed that they had given coercion a knock-out blow.

Parnell Makes his Choice

Gladstone immediately resigned and Lord Salisbury formed a caretaker Conservative administration until a general election could be held. The

Tories immediately dropped the Irish Coercion Acts and introduced the Property of Land (Ireland) Act — a generous scheme of loans, at very low interest, to enable tenants to purchase their holdings. Parnell felt that he had received an adequate down payment for his support; the question was, how much more could he get?

For months Irish loyalists had been smelling a rat. Home Rule was in the air, and they knew it. During the dying days of Gladstone's government, when the Tories and Parnell were coquetting, they established an organisation called the Irish Loyal and Patriotic Union. It was principally the brainchild of Southern unionists and its purpose was to solicit all Irish unionists, liberal as well as conservative, to support unionist candidates at the election which was looming. The new association was led by high-ranking unionists such as Lord Castletown, Lord Longford, Lord De Vesci, Lord Neath, Colonel A.L. Tottenham and Arthur Patton, and drew support from Protestant landowners, businessmen and academics who undertook to underwrite its finances. It quickly got off the mark, and by polling time had distributed 14,000 pamphlets and 27,000 leaflets.[1]

The political manoeuvring, at this point, became intense. Each of the parties initiated probing exercises to discern who would support whom in the event of a hung parliament. Many held that the political arithmetic would allow the Home Rulers to hold the balance of power; it therefore became incumbent on the Westminster parties to discover what exactly Parnell wanted for his support or, to put it more accurately, how little he could be induced to accept. When he opened his campaign in Dublin on 24 August, Parnell set out his stall in the plainest fashion. His party would support whoever undertook to introduce a Home Rule Bill: this was his bottom line.

Political flirtation now began in earnest. Lord Carnarvon, the Irish Lord Lieutenant, and Parnell met (with Salisbury's leave) in a house in Mayfair, from which the Home Rule leader emerged with the impression that the Tories were prepared to offer some form of self-government to Ireland. During the autumn Parnell was enmeshed in numerous behind-the-scene meetings, in which he tried to play one party off against the other. Gladstone himself, although knowing exactly where he stood, was a stumbling block; he would not be drawn, partly because he found political auctioneering distasteful, but also because he was unsure whether the extreme left and right wings of his party could be made to swallow Home Rule.

As the dates for polling approached, tension mounted. This was the first election to follow the Third Reform Act (1884), the Redistribution Act (1885), the extension of the franchise, and the redrawing of constituency boundaries. In Ireland, the changes were thought to benefit the Home Rulers, particularly in Ulster where small boroughs, once the preserve of the old ascendancy, lost their separate representation and were merged with revised county divisions. Many Catholics had been given the vote for the first time. For weeks Parnell juggled with the odds, and at last, on 21 November (two days before polling) he called on the Irish in Britain to vote Conservative. His tactics were obvious: he wanted a result which would bring the two large parties as close as possible, and to achieve this he had to throw his strength onto the weaker side. If the weaker side were to gain office with his support, he would be in a position to extract the maximum concessions from it.[2]

The Liberals won 335 seats, and the Tories and the Home Rulers together took a similar number. Parnell, with 86 MPs, held the balance of power. The punters estimated that in Britain, Parnell's advice to Irish voters cost the Liberals between 20 and 40 seats: enough to damage the Liberals, but not enough to give the Tories a majority. Parnell's strategy had worked, but too well.

In Ireland the results were remarkable. Not a single Liberal was returned. Previously they had held fourteen seats, but now they were out bag and baggage. Out of the 89 contestants in Ireland, the Home Rulers won no fewer than 85, most with overwhelming majorities. In two divisions of Cork, the Home Rulers polled nearly 10,000, to 300 votes for the Tories; in Mayo they polled 10,000 to 200 votes for the Tories, and in Kilkenny they received 4,000 against 170 for the Tories. Antrim was the single county where the vote was solidly against Home Rule and, even there, in one contest the Home Ruler was only beaten by 35 votes. Many seats, however, were uncontested, and the overall result for the Home Rulers was 85 out of 103, leaving the Tories with 18 seats. There was little doubt that the overwhelming majority of the electorate voted for Home Rule, and that they purged the party which had been responsible for coercion.

The 'Hawarden Kite'

The Tories realised that support from the Home Rulers would be insufficient to keep them in office. Even if such support was forthcoming, they would be too insecure to contemplate a Home Rule measure; their Ulster MPs would very likely defect, as would others who could not stomach Home Rule. It was a cheerless situation for them; yet one man saw possibilities in it. This was Lord Randolph Churchill, and what he saw was a gap opening up in the Liberal Party which he proposed to exploit. He remarked to the Home Rule supporter, Justin McCarthy: 'We have done our best for you, and now we shall do our worst against you.'[3]

But Gladstone had not declared his hand. It distressed him to see the Irish question made into a plaything, and he still strove to have it settled by mutual party consent. He made overtones to the Tories, urging them to settle the issue and indicating that he was prepared to curtail party rivalry to allow them to do so. His approaches were rejected. Churchill's view of Gladstone's accommodating hints to the Prime Minister's nephew, Arthur Balfour, were summed up in a letter to a colleague which he wrote on Christmas day:

> Very Private. G.O.M. has written what is described to me as a 'marvellous letter' to Arthur Balfour, to the effect that he thinks it will be a public calamity should the Irish question fall into the lines of 'party conflict' and saying that he desires that the question be settled by the present government. He be damned![4]

Gladstone's every move was closely watched. His public reticence annoyed no one more than his son Herbert, who was also a Member of Parliament. The younger Gladstone, not fully appreciating the manoeuvring which was going on, was fearful that the Tories would outbid his father for the Home Rulers' affections. On 16 December he impetuously went to the National Press Agency and broke the news that his father had converted to Home Rule. It was a bombshell, and the incident became known as the 'Hawarden Kite', after the name of Gladstone's country home. Some pundits, then and since, have felt that the leak was inspired by the Grand Old Man himself, but this view is surely ill-founded.[5] Indeed, considering the shattering impact which the revelation had on his party, a leader concerned with party advantage would surely have dropped the Home Rule issue like a hot potato.

The fallout was immediate; the Liberal Party began to crumble. The Whigs on the Right, led by Lord Hartingdon, would not hear of Home Rule and prepared to jump ship; the Radicals on the Left, under Joseph Chamberlain — noted for his ribboned monocle and the orchid in his buttonhole — also threatened to defect. All the factors calculated to ferment a bitter struggle over Home Rule came into play.

Colonel Edward Saunderson

The election result had gone down badly with the Orangemen. They attributed the poor unionist showing, particularly in Ulster, to lack of organisation. The loyalist vote had split between Liberals, Conservatives and Orange candidates, with the result that the Home Rulers did well in normally staunchly loyalist constituencies. The shock of the setback, taken with Gladstone's conversion to Home Rule, spurred all anti-Home Rulers to unite. On 8 January 1886, the North-West Loyal Registration and Electoral Association was founded at a meeting in Omagh, County Tyrone, with Lord Abercorn at its helm.[6] Its function was to ensure that there would be no further slip-ups in loyalist voting. Almost immediately the new association teamed up with the Orange Order and arrangements were made to pool the unionist strength. One of the men involved in this project was a wealthy County Cavan landowner who was to play an important role in unionist and Orange politics for some years to come, Colonel Edward Saunderson.

A big, bluff red-faced man, with a handlebar moustache, Saunderson was a curious blend of bucolic charm, evangelical zeal, and political guile. He was also an exception to the rule that anyone educated by the Jesuits at an early age is likely to be theirs for life.[7] His early education was in Nice, where Saunderson senior had removed his family so that they may be spared the sight of a country bedevilled by famine. When the patriarch died, the household left France and settled in Torquay in Devon and, later, on the Isle of Wight. By this time Edward was circulating among the moneyed classes of the English south coast, and preparing for the day when he would return to his inheritance at Castle Saunderson, near Belturbet.

When he did eventually return with his bride Helena, daughter of Lord Ventry, his interests focused on two rather dissimilar preoccupations: yachting on the Lough Erne, and evangelical preaching. The first of these obsessions was acquired when he lived at Cowes, where he made the acquaintance of such enthusiasts as Kaiser Wilhelm II and the Prince of Wales. The second came with his mother's milk: the Saundersons always held a strong Christian witness and partook of the more exuberant forms of Protestantism. Indeed, the wonder is that Edward was ever allowed near any Jesuits. From an early period he maintained a small chapel at Castle Saunderson and declaimed regularly to his tenants.

In 1865 he entered Parliament for County Cavan as a Whig and held the seat until, in a surprise result, he was defeated in 1874. His downfall was imputed to his annoying his Catholic constituents by an attack on transubstantiation at a meeting of the General Synod of the Church of Ireland. Thereafter he retired from politics until 1881, when he became alarmed by the rise of the Home Rulers and felt that he should play a part in opposing them. He quickly developed into a lively and aggressive opponent of Parnell. It was not, however, until after the Phoenix Park murders in Dublin in May 1882 — when the newly arrived Chief Secretary, Lord Frederick Cavendish, and his Under Secretary T.H. Burke, were assassinated — that Saunderson donned the Orange sash. He did so, he said, in response to the anarchy which he saw all around. His first speech as an Orangeman was at 'The Twelfth' in 1882 at

Ballykilbeg. He told the brethren: 'When the very foundations of society are shaken and about to crumble to the dust, I ask myself, is there an organisation capable of dealing with this condition of anarchy and rebellion? There is only one answer. . . .'[8]

In the same speech, Saunderson called for direct action against the Land Leaguers and proposed that the Order be turned into 'a disciplined body' to 'resist rebellion and treason'. This was effectively a call to arms, and made the powers-that-be in the Order prick up their ears and take notice. At Ballykilbeg he shared the platform with the intrepid Lord Rossmore, who became a firm friend. In the succeeding months the two men met at several dinner parties, and drew up Orange strategies over their port and cigars. Within twelve months, Rossmore entered Orange martyrology when he was dismissed from the magistracy for making a rabble-rousing and anti-Catholic speech at an Orange rally in the village of Roslea, County Monaghan. Standing beside him on that day was Edward Saunderson, who nodded approval at everything his lordship uttered.

During the fevered time when the Tories were coquetting with the Home Rulers, Saunderson came up with the idea of forming an independent unionist grouping in Parliament. He spent a number of months promoting the concept and, in December 1885 and January 1886, made several speeches in Dublin and Ulster on the subject. In these, he made heavy allusions to the possibility of military resistance in Ireland to any enactment of a Home Rule bill. These speeches, and his growing influence within Orangeism, brought him to the attention of powerful people in Dublin who had the ear of Lord Randolph Churchill, who himself had announced in London his intention, as he put it, to 'agitate Ulster'. This connection between the Orange firebrand and Churchill foreshadowed things to come.

The Orange Card

Lord Randolph Churchill had pushed himself forward as the Tory party's 'expert' on Ireland. He had some reason to be so considered, for he had spent several of his early years in the country and had made a study of its affairs. His mother was the daughter of the Marquess of Londonderry and his father was the Duke of Marlborough. In 1874 he became Member of Parliament for the family borough of Woodstock, but being little interested in politics at the time, he took himself off to Ireland where he acted as unpaid secretary to his father, now Lord Lieutenant. He was taken up by a number of powerful Irish Tories and semi-Orangemen, wealthy, well-connected, professional people who held political salons at their fashionable town houses and 'long weekends' at their suburban or seaside villas.

The particular circle which Churchill was associated with became known as the 'Howth Set'. Among its members was the legendary John Pentland Mahaffey, scholar, don, diner-out, controversialist and conversationalist, and future Provost of Trinity College. Also included were Thomas Ball, a scholar nowadays best remembered for his book *The Reformed Church in Ireland* (Dublin, 1886) who became Lord Chancellor of Ireland in 1880; Michael Morris, MP for Galway in 1865, later Lord of Appeal, and future Lord Killanin; and David Robert Plunkett, Legal Adviser to Dublin Castle, MP for Trinity College, Solicitor General, and future 1st Baron Rathmore. But the man who made the greatest impression on Churchill, and who was to remain intimate with him for the rest of his life, was Gerald Fitzgibbon, Solicitor General in 1877, Lord Justice of Appeal in 1878, whose intellectual prowess had made him a 'golden boy' at Trinity College a few decades earlier. Fitzgibbon was robustly Tory, intractably unionist and implicitly Orange, and was one of the most influential Freemasons in Dublin.[9] He became Churchill's political mentor and the person to whom Churchill later wrote, famously:

> I decided some time ago that if the G.O.M. went for Home Rule, the Orange Card would be the one to play. Please God it may turn out to be the Ace of Trumps and not the Two.[10]

Churchill spent Christmas 1885 in Dublin with his Howth cronies. He came out openly in support of the unionist cause, and made arrangements with Saunderson to speak in Belfast, but first he spoke to his new constituents in South Paddington by way of 'warming up'. Foster describes this speech as 'a violent Orange tirade', during which he unleashed a volley of backs-to-the-wall Protestant clichés and, to the surprise and delight of die-hard Ulster opinion, called up images of civil war brought about by Gladstone's 'monstrous and unparalleled combination of verbosity and senility' and repeatedly offered the assistance of English 'hearts and hands to their beleaguered co-Religionists'.[11] Many were scandalised by the intemperate tone of Churchill's remarks and there were even calls for his arrest, on the grounds that he was inflaming one section of Her Majesty's subjects against another. Churchill scoffed at his critics and left London on 21 February with Colonel Saunderson, Lord Rossmore and a few others to catch the mailboat to Larne.

Ulster will Fight, Ulster will be Right

Ulster was already alert, and preparing to stifle any Home Rule move by the government as a matter of life and death. The doors of Orange Halls were flung open for men to drill in, and every available weapon which

Orangemen and other loyalists could lay their hands on was requisitioned. In Belfast the mood was piping hot. There were over one hundred Orange lodges in the City, with about 4,000 brethren organised in six districts. Every man stood on alert. On 22 December the Grand Lodge of Ireland met in Dublin and resolved to work with all parties, whatever their complexion, against Home Rule. Lord Enniskillen sent a memo to all lodges, urging them to demonstrate against the establishment of a government in Dublin. The leaders of the business community in Dublin, Belfast and Cork sent deputations to Lord Salisbury protesting against any measure which would weaken the links between Ireland and the rest of the United Kingdom, and the Belfast Chamber of Commerce passed a resolution which said:

> that the commercial prosperity which has blessed peaceable parts of this country will receive a sudden shock and lasting injury from any legislation which would have a tendency to imperil the connection between this country and Great Britain.[12]

The Reverend Hugh 'Roaring' Hanna, the minister at St Enoch's, the largest Presbyterian church in Belfast — a firebrand whose sermons had frequently incited violence against the Catholic population — sought to raise Protestant fears of Home Rule to a new pitch. In January 1886 he painted a picture of what Home Rule would mean:

> . . . there is a little ragged urchin selling newspapers and crying every morning, *The Morning News*. That ragged urchin under the new code is to be Marquis of Donegal. There is a nationalist riveter on Queens Island and he is to be successor to W.J. Perrie (the Managing Director of Harland and Wolff shipyards), and Mr Perrie, for some service he has shown to the Nationalists, is to be regulated to the superintendence of a little smithy in Connemara; and Paddy O'Rafferty, a ragman resident in the slums of Smithfield, is to succeed Sir Edward Harland as Lord Mayor of Belfast. . . .[13]

Drill instructors were appointed in practically every district, and night after night young and old turned out to master the skills of guerrilla warfare. One rumour said that the Grand Lodge of Ireland hoped to raise an army of 100,000; another said that Viscount Wolseley, who had won fame in Egypt and the Sudan, would come and support the Protestants with 1,000 British troops; yet another rumour held that Lord Charles Beresford, a southern unionist, had threatened to resign as Lord of the Admiralty rather than coerce the Protestants. The *Belfast News Letter* began to carry advertisements for firearms and drill instructors. Some lodges, on their own initiative, ordered arms from abroad and declared that every means, legal and illegal, would be used to throttle Home Rule.

At a rally of 20,000 Orangemen in Belfast on Easter Monday 1886, a resolution was passed which stated: 'We shall not acknowledge that (Home Rule) government . . . we will refuse to pay taxes imposed by it; and . . . we will resist to the utmost all attempts to enforce such payments.'[14]

This was the atmosphere which Churchill entered when he stepped off the ferry at Larne on 22 February, to be greeted by a crowd whose ecstasy bordered on hysteria. Local lodges presented him with an address of welcome. En route to Belfast, his train stopped at Carrickfergus, where he received similar homage, and when it pulled into the Northern Counties Station in Belfast, the welcome was even more euphoric.

That evening he sat on the huge stage of the Ulster Hall with William Johnston, Saunderson, Rossmore and other Orange and Unionist leaders by his side. Above his head a great banner read: 'England Cannot Desert the Protestants of Ulster'. When Churchill rose to speak, he had to wait several minutes before the applause subsided. Then, with the hall hushed, he began to speak slowly and with great precision in his high-pitched upper-class accent. Soon he warmed to it, and in a bout of free-flowing rhetoric which lasted over an hour, he told his audience what they wanted to hear. He said that their fate was in their own hands and that they should remember the old slogan of 'No Surrender!' He told them to 'give practical meaning to the forms and ceremonies of Orangeism'. It was a barely concealed call to insurrection and it was cheered to the echo. Then he continued:

> I believe that this storm will blow over and that the vessel of the Union will emerge with her Loyalist crew stronger than before; but . . . if the struggle should continue . . . then I am of the opinion that it is not likely to remain within the lines of what we are accustomed to look upon as constitutional action . . . if it should turn out that the parliament of the United Kingdom was so recreant from all its high duties . . . as to hand over the Loyalists of Ireland to the domination of an Assembly in Dublin which must be to them a foreign and alien assembly . . . in that dark hour there will not be wanting to you those of position and influence in England who would be willing to cast in their lot with you.

He wound up to delirious cheering when he said:

> . . . those who at the exact moment, when the time is fully come — if that time should come — will address you in words which are best expressed by one of our greatest English poets:

'The combat deepens; on ye brave
Who rush to glory or the grave
Wave, Ulster, all thy banners wave
And charge with all thy chivalry.'[15]

Succeeding speakers fanned the flames: Saunderson called for a new Battle of the Boyne, and Johnston announced the triumph of the Orange cause now that it was hitched to the greatest party in the United Kingdom. The consequences were immediate. As Churchill drove through the streets of Belfast that evening, serious rioting broke out and several people were injured. The next day he left for London, and was never to return to Ireland.

When Churchill next entered the House of Commons he was booed by the Irish members, and some of the Liberals called for his censure. It was even suggested that he should be indicted for high treason. But he was wholly unrepentant. In an open letter to a Liberal Unionist member, he used a phrase which caught the imagination and which would forever become an Orange clarion:

> If political parties and political leaders . . . should be so lost to every feeling and dictate of honour and courage as to hand over coldly . . . the lives and liberties of the Loyalists of Ireland to their hereditary and most bitter foes, make no doubt on this point — Ulster will not be a consenting party; Ulster at the proper moment will resort to the supreme arbitrament of force; Ulster will fight, Ulster will be right.[16]

There can be no doubt as to Ulster's willingness to fight. In March, *The Pall Mall Gazette* interviewed William Johnston, who said:

> The other day, when I was at Ballykilbeg, a hundred men assembled to confer as to the best kind of arms they should secure, and I was to confer with some military men in England on the best means of Defence.[17]

That evening Johnston presided over a lecture given in Dungannon Orange Hall by a local rector, who spoke on the life of Governor George Walker of Derry. In his introduction, Johnston compared the events of 1688 with those of 1886 and, in a hot-tempered outburst, said:

> We must inform the people of England better before a general election comes . . . they must be told that we are prepared to take the Bible in one hand and the sword in the other . . . We will defend the Protestant religion and our liberties won at the Boyne with rifles in our hands.[18]

The First Unionist Grouping

When members of the new House of Commons were sworn in on 14 January 1886, Colonel Edward Saunderson immediately threw himself into the task of organising an independent unionist grouping from among those members elected on anti-Home Rule tickets. Many were prepared to join him, but there was the question of who should lead such a grouping, and some jockeying for position took place behind the scenes. Finally, at a meeting in the Saint Stephen's Green Club it was decided that initially the grouping should have a chairman, and that the position should rotate. William Johnston was appointed, although he had few leadership skills in a parliamentary sense. Soon Saunderson was seen as the best man available, and Johnston was nudged aside. Johnston had earlier led a parliamentary delegation to see the Prime Minister. He urged Salisbury to reintroduce coercion, as terrorism in Ireland was still flaring up. Salisbury consolidated his hold on Unionist affections by readily agreeing, and the following week the Leader of the Commons, Michael Hicks-Beach, made the relevant announcement. This move ignited the indignation of the Home Rulers, and a few days later they combined with the Liberals to vote down the government. Salisbury was out.

The First Home Rule Bill

During the general election campaign Gladstone stood for South-West Lancashire and, in a series of resounding speeches, lashed the Protestant Ascendancy in Ireland. He compared it to 'some tall tree of noxious growth . . . but now at last the day has come when, as we hope, the axe has been laid to the root.' Symbolically, he was in the process of cutting down a tree at Hawarden when he received news that the Queen was going to ask him to form a government. At first he continued swinging his axe and then, turning to a companion, announced with great solemnity: 'My mission is to pacify Ireland.'[19]

After kissing hands with the Queen, Gladstone, with the support of the Home Rulers, formed his third administration. There were rumours that he had already drafted a Home Rule Bill, but beyond those reports nothing definite was known. In the formation of his government he found that some of his colleagues would not acquiesce in a Home Rule measure. Lord Hartington declined office and Sir Henry James, to whom the Lord Chancellorship was offered, also declined. Joseph Chamberlain and Sir George Trevelyan accepted, only to withdraw a few weeks later when Gladstone's designs were known. It was a time of great excitement, and curiosity was at a high pitch. Gladstone's age — seventy-seven — seemed prohibitory for the effort which would be required to carry

Home Rule, but on 8 April he asked the House for permission to introduce the Bill, and there seemed to be no waning of his powers.

That morning he drove from Downing Street to the Commons amid the thunderous cheers of those who had gathered to see him. The scene inside had never been witnessed before; every inch of floor space from the mace to the bar was crowded with chairs and extra benches. Not for years had so great and brilliant an audience filled the House — peers and ambassadors, ladies of high rank, foreign princes and business magnates, together with the full complement of members, were all present. When the Prime Minister arrived, accompanied by his wife and three daughters, a splendid reception awaited them. The Liberal members rose as a body and there was tremendous cheering and clapping as he took his seat. At 4.30 p.m. he rose to speak and the House fell silent. For the next three and a half hours he gave a virtuoso performance. The breadth of his arguments and the richness of his vocabulary held the House in rapt attention.[20] In a peroration of great eloquence, he abjured his listeners to 'go into the length and breadth of the world, ransack the literature of all countries, find if you can a single voice, a single book, in which the conduct of England towards Ireland is anywhere treated except with profound and bitter condemnation. Are these the traditions by which we are exhorted to stand? No, they are a sad exception to the glory of our country. They are a broad, black stain on the pages of its history.' Then, raising his voice and sweeping his hand at the benches opposite, he said: 'Think, I beseech you; think well, think wisely, think not for the moment but for years that are to come, before you reject this Bill.'[21]

But reject it they did, amid scenes of wild enthusiasm. And at the ensuing General Election, the British people endorsed their verdict. The once great Liberal Party was split from top to bottom and the fate of Ireland seemed settled for years to come. But as his cab rumbled over the cobblestones of Palace Yard that evening, Edward Saunderson was not so sanguine. He scribbled a note to his wife Helena, which said: 'Home Rule is dead, but not yet buried.'

Trouble in Belfast

Nowhere was the result of the Commons vote greeted with more jubilation than in Belfast. Bonfires were lit on the hills all around, and Orangemen and their families danced in the streets. Orange bands paraded up and down and swaggering band leaders threw their batons in the air. The rattle of the lambegs could be heard in the side streets late into the night, punctuated only by rapturous whoops of joy. But the celebrations were not universal. On the Catholic Falls Road, people set their chimneys on fire in the traditional symbol of lamentation. Their mood was bitter, sharpened by the great wave of violence which had occurred a few days earlier. This had been sparked by a trivial incident: a Catholic overseer on the Alexandra Dock became embroiled in a dispute with a Protestant workman and was crass enough to taunt him, saying that once Home Rule was carried, neither he nor people like him would be allowed to earn a crust on the docks. News of the taunt spread like wildfire, and the following day (4 June) around lunchtime, hundreds of Orange shipyard workers from Harland and Wolff descended on the Alexandra Docks, wielding cudgels.

The Catholic workers were hopelessly outnumbered and took flight. To escape, some jumped into the Lagan River, but one poor fellow, Jimmy Curran, from the Short Strand district, was unable to swim and drowned. A few days later, hundreds of Catholics turned out to attend his funeral, but as the cortège made its way to Milltown cemetery it was showered with stones and bottles by Orange mobs. Following this outrage, the violence eased for a few weeks, but on 'The Twelfth', when the Orangemen found their marches disrupted by stone-throwing Catholics, it resumed with a dire intensity, and continued sporadically until September. The death and destruction which occurred far exceeded anything known since the rebellion of 1798.

Throughout this unsettled period, the Order seemed to thrive. The number of lodges everywhere increased, and in Belfast certain of them began to control entry into skilled trades; their writ ran in the shipyards, the docks, the mills and in countless small-scale work places. The Order became a conduit for massive Protestant jobbery and, with its system of signs and codes, had little difficulty in looking after its own.

The Home Rule scare brought more and more middle-class Protestants within the Order's ambit, and although not all unionists were Orangemen, certainly all Orangemen were unionist. In Parliament, twelve of the pro-unionists elected in 1885 were formal members of the Order and Saunderson, their leader, quickly moved up the Orange ladder. Within two years of donning the sash he became Deputy Grand Master of the Order in Ireland. His status appears to have been noted in London, for around this time he became a member of Queen Victoria's Privy Council.

The Second Home Rule Bill

The pattern of riot and violence seen in 1886 was repeated in 1893 when Gladstone, again briefly in power and dependent on the Irish nationalist vote, introduced a second Home Rule Bill. The Orangemen prepared for battle again and worked in tandem with the newly-formed Unionist Clubs, set up by Lord Templetown. A number of the more spirited joined an organisation called Young Ulster, founded by an indefatigable organiser named Fred Crawford, who worked in Harland and Wolff as an electrical engineer. This was an underground army; each member had to own a revolver, a Martini-Henry rifle or a Winchester carbine, and possess 100 rounds of ammunition.

The second Home Rule Bill got through the Commons, but was assuredly and reliably defeated by the House of Lords. Gladstone, still undaunted and now aged eighty-four, was prepared to plough on. He reeled off to his cabinet a number of reasons for an immediate appeal to the country. But his colleagues had had enough. They did not wish to lose office a second time because of Irish Home Rule, and the Grand Old Man, seeing things going completely against him, gave up. Within a few months he retired honourably, acknowledging that he had failed in his mission to pacify Ireland.

Home Rule is Rome Rule

A Rope, a Rope, to hang the Pope
A pennyworth o'Cheeze tae choke him
A pint o'lamp oil tae wash it down
A big hot coal tae roast him.

— a children's street rhyme from Sandy Row

The Bible-Thumpers

Evangelical Protestantism is a loose doctrinal disposition which has always been favoured by Orangemen. It is cross-denominational, centred on the assumption that Scriptural Truth is all that is needed for salvation. In the closing years of the nineteenth century this doctrine was preached passionately in Belfast by dozens of fundamentalist clergymen who habitually garnished their tirades with strident criticisms of 'Popery'. They disrespectfully disparaged such Catholic precepts as the primacy of Rome, transubstantiation, purgatory, mediators and intercessors — everything they felt to be unscriptural. Belfast was the capital city of revivalism; evangelical sandwich men, bedecked front and rear with biblical texts splashed across canvas aprons, could be seen everywhere. Freelancers harangued tram queues or imprecated passing shoppers. The more respectable confined their preaching to the dozens of little gospel halls which dotted the city.

Many of the preachers were Orangemen, as were their more zealous followers. The content of their outpourings was no different from that uttered on official Orange platforms, and the Order turned a blind eye to their excesses. Some became Orange heroes, like Thomas Roe, who had the Roe Memorial Orange Lodge named after him, and whose portrait appeared on silken banners on 'The Twelfth'. Roe's favourite open-air pitch was at the rear of Belfast's neo-classical Customs House — a place where a variety of preachers and political orators drew crowds on Sunday afternoons and which was known locally as 'The Steps'. So venomous were Roe's outpourings that on several occasions irate Catholics rushed his platform to pull him off. On such occasions the constabulary, who were Protestant to a man, gave him support; they usually remained concealed behind the Customs House until trouble broke out, and then emerged to make numerous arrests. These events eventually led the Protestant newspaper *The Northern Whig* to urge restraint: '... We address ourselves to the good sense of the ministers of religion and ask them if they think that the cause of religion is promoted by street preaching in Belfast.'[1]

This view was too much for one of the more rabid preachers, the Reverend Hugh 'Roaring' Hanna, a Presbyterian cleric whose loud voice and agitated manner earned him his enduring nickname. Hanna defiantly announced that he would continue preaching from 'The Steps' despite 'Romish mobs or magistrates'. His stance was widely supported; the *Belfast News Letter* came out in his favour, saying:

> The Romish mobs have triumphed in our town. The preaching of the gospel in our streets to the destitute, ragged, and poor, is put down. Belfast now ranks with Kilkenny, Cork or Limerick. In these Romish cities, where priests are regnant and their mobs omnipotent and the authorities bow to their behest, no Protestant minister dare lift his voice in the streets or highways to proclaim the peaceful message of the Cross.[2]

Following a particularly brutal confrontation between Hanna's followers and a Catholic crowd on Sunday 6 September 1857, in which crowbars, marlinspikes, oars and cudgels were used, the Reverend wrote an open letter to the Protestants of Belfast:

> Men and Brethren — your blood bought and cherished rights have been imperilled by the audacious and savage outrages of a Romish mob . . . but you were not to be bullied or cajoled out of your rights. They are not to be surrendered, and they are to be strenuously maintained. That you have unmistakenly shown on the past Sabbath. Then you arose, calm but powerful, as the thunder reposing in the cloud . . . A few more Sabbaths like the last will achieve a permanent good.[3]

Hanna, born in the village of Dromara, County Down, was violently anti-Catholic from an early age. Those in his flock who knew him well spoke not only of his righteous wrath but of his warm and friendly personality when not in the pulpit. He founded a number of elementary schools and, apparently, believed that preaching was not enough: he spent much of his time traversing the poorer districts of Belfast tending the 'decent poor' and discouraging the 'demon drink'. He built Saint

Enoch's Church in Carlisle Circus, the largest of Belfast's Presbyterian churches; a massive statue to him now stands nearby. Hanna's fame was equalled only by that of the Limerick-born Reverend Thomas Drew, who arrived in Belfast in 1833 as the first Rector of the newly-built Christ Church in Durham Street. Boyd, in his seminal study *Holy War in Belfast* (Tralee, 1969) describes him as a well-known 'denouncer of popery' and says:

> He had sermons for every Protestant centenary and celebration. He could preach as easily on the birth of Luther as on the death of Latimer, and could talk for hours on the massacre of St Bartholomew or the Battle of the Boyne. He built chapels of prayer in many parts of Belfast and dedicated them to the great Protestants of history — Wycliffe, Luther and Hus.

In an impassioned sermon on 12 July 1857 at Christ Church, Drew told a congregation of Orangemen:

> The Sermon on the Mount is an everlasting rebuke to all intolerance, and all legislative and ecclesiastical cruelty. Of old time, lords of high degree with their own hands, strained on the rack the delicate limbs of Protestant women, prelates dabbled in the gore of helpless victims; and the cells of the Pope's prisons were paved with calcined bones of men and cemented with gore and human hair . . . at this hour, the world has its record of existing wrong. Austria crushes the throbbing hearts of Italy. France basely upholds the Pontiff's detested throne; and America has not yet regarded the cry of millions she calls 'chattels' and not men . . . He who lives, labours, plans and gives for the posterity of his own church alone is a narrow-minded Christian. He may be a believer; he may be, to some extent, a good Christian . . . Let him, however, not dream of taking to himself the time honoured name of Protestant. That glorious and eloquent name is reserved for those only who can rise above congregational littleness; who can unite on broad and evangelical principles against the common foe . . . To the honour of Orangemen, they have always discouraged these internecine clamours which gladden the hearts of Rome's children and subserve the aggression of the ever-watchful Papacy.[4]

Drew wrote numerous Orange songs and pamphlets. His 'Twenty Reasons for being an Orangeman' contains such nuggets as:

> I learn from the doctrines, history, and daily practices of the Church of Rome, that the lives of Protestants are endangered, that the laws of England are set at nought and that the Crown of England is subordinated to the dictates of an Italian bishop.

He saw conspiracies everywhere. He refused to accept the official census of 1841 which showed that Catholics constituted the largest religious grouping in Ireland, claiming that the figures were altered to play down the strength of the Protestant churches, as a prelude to a shift in government policy towards Catholics. Much of this sort of thinking was, so to speak, in the family. One of his daughters was married to William Johnston of Ballykilbeg and, like his son-in-law, Drew believed that the British people had (as he repeatedly asserted) 'a God-given mission to Protestantize the world.'

The Independent Orange Order

It was from the preaching on 'The Steps' that the most serious challenge to the authority of the Order was to emerge. This arose from the founding of a schismatic body called 'The Independent Loyal Orange Institution of Ireland', known variously as the 'I Double O' or 'The Independents'. The events which led to its formation can be traced to the exploits of a well-known evangelist named Arthur Trew, an irrepressible zealot who gyrated wildly each Sunday on his soapbox. He held his audiences spellbound with torrents of wit, sarcasm, and fiery denunciations of popery. For years he lived in Dublin and travelled by train each Sunday morning to Belfast. He had three great hatreds: Catholicism, Ritualism in the Anglican Church, and Socialism. His antipathy towards the latter led to brawls between his followers and members of the newly formed Independent Labour Party, who also spoke from 'The Steps'.

From these punch-ups sprang a politico-religio organisation whose brand of muscular Christianity soon became notorious. This was the Belfast Protestant Association or 'BPA', which was led by Trew and an Orange lay-preacher named Richard Braithwaite. In June 1901 both men were prosecuted for attacking a Catholic Corpus Christi procession. Trew was imprisoned for a year and Braithwaite for six months.[5] During Trew's incarceration, his place on 'The Steps' was taken by Thomas Sloan, a young semi-skilled shipyard worker who had a talent for public speaking. Sloan was actually a Bible-thumping veteran who held lunch-time evangelical meetings in the platers' shed at Harland and Wolff's.[6]

At 'The Twelfth' field in Castlereagh in 1902, Sloan led a group of hecklers against Colonel Edward Saunderson, who was addressing the brethren in his capacity as Belfast Grand Master. Their complaint was that Saunderson had failed in Parliament to support a Bill providing for the inspection of convent laundries. The evangelicals and Orangemen had long been fascinated by the imagined sexual exploits of Catholic nuns and priests, and had the deepest suspicions of what might be going on behind convent walls. This prurient curiosity is often traced to a rage of anti-Catholic (and anti-Irish) hysteria which erupted in Boston, Massachusetts in 1831, when a Protestant mob burned down a Catholic convent. Not long afterwards, a book appeared entitled *Maria Monk's Awful Disclosures* which purported to be the true story of a young woman's fate in a Montreal convent. The volume became an international best-seller and was, in fact, a lewd catalogue of liaisons between nuns and priests, replete with the grisly details of the murder of the offspring of such couplings. It was a prime piece of filth and went into scores of printings, with most readers ignoring its dubious (and proven) origins. Everyone knew that it was fabricated by fundamentalist fanatics, and that its heroine was well known to the Montreal police as a prostitute and pickpocket, but this did not quench the insatiable thirst for the book. Quotations from it became staple fare for many fundamentalist preachers and, in Belfast, some of the more eccentric of the breed carried around specially-bound copies. Thomas Sloan and his companions took the book seriously, and were in no doubt that the purported goings-on in Montreal were being repeated nearer home.

Saunderson was unable to outshout his hecklers, and the disturbance continued until he sat down. Due to its cumbersome rules the Order was unable to discipline Sloan until it received a formal complaint, and this was not received for several months. In the meantime, on 17 July, William Johnston of Ballykilbeg died, and his Belfast South seat became vacant. As Johnston had been a working-class hero, the BPA felt that it had a right to the seat. Sloan's ascendancy during Trew's absence made him a popular choice as a candidate. He stood in opposition to the official Unionist Charles W. Dunbar-Buller, a fellow of All Souls College, Oxford, and Master of a Belfast Orange lodge.

A tricky situation arose when it became known that the Unionist nomination was denied to W.J. (afterwards Lord) Pirrie, senior partner in Harland and Wolff and a man who had accomplished great things for Belfast. Pirrie took his rejection badly (he had been deemed too liberal by the Orangemen who controlled the Unionist/Conservative caucus) and he covertly supported the candidature of Sloan with money and influence. Sloan's followers accused the Unionist and Orange leaders of being a wealthy elite, more concerned with their own interests than with helping the workers. His supporters were no respecters of the toffee-nosed Dunbar-Buller, whom they enjoyed shouting down at meetings. In some districts they smashed the furniture on his platforms and forced him to abandon canvassing in certain areas. Sloan, in contrast, canvassed everywhere. His energetic campaign team was led by Thomas Galbraith, a big, bald-headed man nicknamed 'The Bubble Buster' (this tag came from his frequent declarations that he had a bubble up his sleeve which he was going to burst!)

Support was received from a number of quarters: temperance societies like the Rachibites came on side, as did workers' organisations like the Municipal Employees' Association. An activist in this latter organisation was Alex Boyd, an influential grassroots Orangeman who was Master of the Donegal Road Temperance Lodge. With Boyd's support, many Orange working-class votes were likely to swing in Sloan's favour. This, in fact, is what happened, for when the result became known on 18 August, it was no surprise that Sloan had 826 votes more than his rival. The victory was seen as a snub to the Orange Order by the Belfast Protestant working class.

Sloan was now very much in the Order's bad books. He sought to ingratiate himself by offering a verbal apology to Saunderson, but this was unacceptable to the Grand Lodge in Belfast, who insisted that it must be in writing. Sloan appealed to the Grand Lodge of Ireland, but was turned down. The Grand Lodge also revoked the warrants of three Belfast lodges who had supported him. One of these was Alex Boyd's lodge at Donegall Road. This was too much for Boyd, and it was he who suggested that an independent body be established. Sloan was hesitant and would have preferred to stay with the old Order; when it was pointed out that he was being slighted, his new-found dignity as a Member of Parliament would not allow him to eat further humble pie. He threw in his lot with the new Order, as did a number of lodges in and around Belfast.

The Magheramorne Manifesto

The first public appearance of the Independent Orange Order was at 'The Twelfth' in 1903 at Dundonald, outside Belfast. Five hundred people attended and eight lodges marched. Over the next few years the number of independent lodges increased and peaked at fifty-five, mainly due to the addition of newly-formed ones. The 'I Double Os' 'Twelfth' demonstration of Ballymoney in 1904 attracted 10,000 people, and provided firm evidence of its appeal. Its defining characteristic was its social radicalism, and the hostility which it showed towards the old Order's links with the Unionist and Conservative parties. Not much of its early success can, however, be attributed to Sloan. He was a man of limited ability and soon offended his plebeian supporters by wearing a fur-trimmed overcoat and smoking small cigars. Inspired leadership came from a new figure on the Belfast scene, Robert Lindsay Crawford, a Lisburn-born businessman and journalist who had lived in Dublin for a number of years, where he founded a journal called *The Irish Protestant*. His growing interest in political affairs led him back to the North, where he became editor of *The Ulster Guardian*, a liberal weekly. In 1905 his brand of radicalism was shown when he drafted the famous

Magheramorne Manifesto; this denounced unionism as a 'discredited creed' and proclaimed that the members of the 'I Double O' stood 'once more on the banks of the Boyne, not as victors in the fight nor to applaud the noble deeds of our ancestors . . . but to . . . hold out the right hand of fellowship to those who, while worshipping at other shrines, are yet our countrymen — bone of our bone and flesh of our flesh'. The Manifesto went on to attack clericalism in Irish politics and attributed the 'lamentable condition of Ireland to the false conception of nationalism that prevails among rulers and people; to the fact that our country has been governed not on national, but on sectarian lines'. The document was a long screed of almost 3,000 words and was signed by Crawford (as Grand Master), Sloan (as Deputy Grand Chaplain), by Reverend D.D. Boyle (Grand Chaplain) and James Mateer (Belfast Grand Master).

When its contents sank into the collective minds of unionists, it was thoroughly denounced. The main unionist newspapers in the Province – *The Northern Whig*, the *News Letter* and *The Belfast Evening Telegraph* — thundered against it, and all the signatories, especially Lindsay Crawford, were rounded on. Sloan took fright and beat a hasty retreat. He announced that the Manifesto was misunderstood, and made awkward attempts to defend it; he also vehemently reaffirmed his unionism and Protestantism.

Crawford stuck to his guns, but developed an increasingly uneasy relationship with other members of the 'I Double O'. Over the next two years he made several efforts to blend working-class Orangeism with nationalism and advocated a policy which, in its main thrust, was virtually indistinguishable from Home Rule. But it was all no good; the rank and file refused to go along with him. Finally, in May 1908, he was expelled from the 'I Double O', ostensibly because of his pro-Home Rule speeches and letters to newspapers. Years later, he looked back on the brief flirtation of the 'I Double O' with non-sectarian politics:

> The old Orange bottle could not hold the new wine of twentieth century democracy . . . (the Independents) had earned for themselves a definite place in Irish history as the vanguard of Protestant democracy, whose lips had been touched with fire from the altar of national freedom. The old Order was the last bastion of class rule in Ireland and the open foe of the people.[7]

The 'I Double O' continued without Crawford. In his later career he went full circle from Orangeman to Nationalist, and ended his working life as trade representative of the Irish Free State in New York. Since his day the 'I Double O' has been unashamedly sectarian and unionist, although some claim to discern a shade of the old social radicalism in its philosophy. North Antrim remains its heartland, and its membership (based on estimates of its 'turnouts' at annual parades) may be up to 1,000 strong. In 1996/97 its members participated in a picket on the Catholic Church at Harryville, Ballymena, when Orangemen sought to intimidate Mass-goers as part of a protest against Catholic opposition to Orange parades.

The Third Home Rule Bill

After the death of Gladstone in 1898, many held the view that Home Rule had accompanied him to the grave. Even when the Grand Old Man was still alive, Henry Herbert Asquith, the future Liberal Prime Minister, described Home Rule as a policy of 'ploughing the sands'. This ignored the underground currents which were coming to the fore in Irish life, and the more vibrant forms of nationalism which were developing. These forces began to manifest themselves in a plethora of organisations and movements whose members felt that Home Rule was not enough. A major crisis was developing at Westminster over Lloyd George's budget of 1909, and in the stalemate thrown up by the two general elections of 1910 the Home Rulers, under the leadership of John Redmond, found themselves again holding the balance of power. If Asquith was to complete his programme of social reform, he needed the help of Irish votes. These would be available only if he took up, however reluctantly, Home Rule.

He bit the bullet and, with Irish support, carried through the Parliament Act which curbed the absolute veto of the House of Lords and limited it to a two-year period. Since it was the Lords alone who had saved the previous Home Rule Bill from being carried, the Unionists and Orangemen became worried. The Ulster peer, Lord Cushenden, voiced their fears when he characterised the bridling of the Lords as 'the forethought of a careful burglar who poisons the dog before breaking into the house'.[8] Asquith introduced the Third Home Rule Bill in 1912. Under the terms of the Parliament Act 1911, it would come into effect with or without the approval of the Lords within two years, provided it passed three successive sessions of the House of Commons.

This was the context in which Orangemen and Unionists began to organise their fiercest resistance yet to Home Rule. They found a new champion to lead them who, although not an Orangeman, would go on to become their greatest hero since King William himself.

Carson

Sir Edward Carson became the 'Uncrowned King of Ulster' during the height of the campaign against the third Home Rule Bill. Rarely had a more suitable man been found for a leadership role. His brilliant and lucid oratory, his uncompromising forthright air, his great theatrical sense, his drive and energy, all marked him out as a spellbinder.

Born in Dublin in 1854, Carson completed an arts degree at Trinity College and entered on a legal career which would span half a century. Initially his views were liberal and he supported Gladstone's disestablishment of the Church of Ireland in 1869 but, with the Grand Old Man's espousal of Home Rule in 1886, he burned his boats on liberalism. The union of Ireland and Britain was to him, as he said, 'a guiding star'. In July 1892 he became Solicitor General for Ireland, and the same month was returned to Parliament as the Member for Trinity College. A man of Carson's obvious talents might reasonably have expected a government post during the long reign of Lord Salisbury, but his opposition to the Conservative policy of 'Killing Home Rule with Kindness' ensured his exclusion. This virtual blackballing gave him time to build up a successful legal career in England, and he joined the English Bar in 1893. His involvement in a series of famous trials such as the Oscar Wilde libel case helped to establish his reputation, and by 1900 he was seen as one of the highest earners in his profession.

In 1906 Colonel Edward Saunderson died, and his place as leader of the Unionist Party fell to an Englishman, Walter Long, who sat for Dublin South. In 1910, Long switched to a London constituency and the Unionists felt obliged to seek a new leader. One of their leading figures was Captain James Craig, an Orangeman and Member for East Down. He, and those around him, knew that a major battle lay ahead and that if they were to fight it effectively, a dynamic leader would be required. In February 1910, J.B. Lonsdale, the Secretary of the Unionist Party, carried a letter to Carson's chambers in London, inviting him to assume the leadership.[9] Carson knew what the fateful invitation implied, and pondered before accepting it. He was fifty-six, in indifferent health, and not really desirous of a new adventure. Yet a still, small voice told him that his prime reason for being in politics was to save the union. That evening he broke the news to his wife by telling her that he had accepted his most difficult brief yet.

The Solemn League and Covenant

Carson was determined to use the two-year breathing space, between the introduction of the third Home Rule Bill and its passing, in purposeful opposition to the measure. As unionist support was strongest in Ulster, he naturally centred his campaign there. He was introduced to the Protestants of the province in September 1911 when he spoke to a huge rally at Craigavon, the home of James Craig on the southern shore of Belfast Lough. The impressive turn-out of 50,000 Orangemen and

Unionists convinced him that opposition to Home Rule was massive and serious. He told his listeners:

> I know the responsibility you are putting on me today. In your presence, I thereby accept it, grave as it is, and I now enter a compact with you and every one of you, and with the help of God, you and I are joined together . . . and will yet defeat the most nefarious conspiracy that has ever been hatched against a free people.

Then he revealed the implications of their designs:

> We must be prepared the morning that Home Rule passes, ourselves to become responsible for the government of the Protestant Province of Ulster.[10]

From 18 September 1912, a series of mass rallies took place, beginning in Enniskillen and culminating in a province-wide signing of the Solemn League and Covenant on 'Ulster Day' (28 September) in Belfast. On that morning, Protestants went to their places of worship and sang 'Oh! God, Our Help in Ages Past' more fervently than before. Shops, shipyards, factories and offices were silent as a huge procession, headed by Carson (marching under a faded Orange banner said to have been flown at the Boyne), made its way to the City Hall. Inside, under the great baroque dome, the magnificent ceilings and stained glass provided a pageant of the founding of Belfast over three hundred years before. Scenes of heroic workers labouring at spinning, weaving and shipbuilding (the great industries of the city) threw their lustre down on the marble floors and walls. In this setting, Carson, with a silver pen, was the first to sign the Covenant. For hours, tens of thousands streamed into the building, where a line of desks ran down the great corridors, while a bevy of bowler-hatted stewards struggled to keep the vast concourse moving.

The Covenant, drafted by Carson, condemned Home Rule as being 'disastrous to the material well-being of Ulster as well as the whole of Ireland . . . and perilous to the unity of the Empire'. Those who signed pledged themselves to 'stand by one another in defending for ourselves and our children our cherished position as equal citizens in the United Kingdom, and in using all means which may be found necessary to defeat the present conspiracy to set up a Home Rule parliament'. As unionists were against female suffrage, women signed a separate declaration; altogether 471,414 persons of Ulster birth signed either the Covenant or the Declaration. All were given a copy, and this cherished token was to be hung prominently in their homes, often adorned with a sash, for the edification of generations to come.

As dusk descended on the city, Carson was saluted by a fusillade at Donegall Quay as he boarded the vessel *Patriot* which was to take him to

Scotland to address huge rallies in the Unionist cause. As the little vessel steamed away, a great flame on Cave Hill leaped towards the sky. It was one of the sixty bonfires lit around Belfast that night to mark the fatal date. Was 'King' Carson (as they called him) the new William, the new deliverer, come to rescue his people from a hateful bondage?

The Ulster Volunteer Force

In December the phrase in the Covenant which referred to its signatories 'using all means which may be found necessary to defeat the present conspiracy' took on an ominous meaning when Carson and Craig decided to establish a paramilitary force. This body would be known as the Ulster Volunteer Force (UVF), composed of all adult males who had signed the Covenant. Once again the doors of the Orange Halls were thrown open and the brethren began to drill and train in large numbers. Carson justified the force on the basis that the mass demonstrations had made little impression on the British government. The Home Rule Bill was continuing its slow but unamended progress through the Commons, and nothing was done to meet the fears of the Unionists. He believed this new move would show that he meant business.

By June 1914, 91,000 men had enlisted and the services of Lieutenant General Sir George Richardson, a retired army officer and veteran of the Afghan Wars, were acquired to supervise training. Richardson drilled his men several evenings a week at venues throughout Ulster, and introduced a tight discipline. Soon the force began to look professional: it had a signals battalion, a motorcycle corps and an intelligence section which was able to both formulate and break codes. But the very existence of the force meant that Carson, Craig and senior Orangemen like Colonel Robert Wallace were engaged in treasonable activity. It also meant that official British forces had every right, under the law, to fire on the volunteers. But the die was cast, and Carson and the others let it be known that they were prepared to accept responsibility for their actions.

The Larne Gunrunning

On Friday night, 24 April 1914, an eerie atmosphere hung over Belfast. Shoppers passed each other in the streets in grim silence and hurried along under the light mist. An air of expectancy hung over the city, and none could say why. The UVF had been marching that evening and had taken up positions inside the Midland Railway Station which served the small towns along the Antrim coast. Another battalion of the force had lined up near the landing berths in Belfast harbour. The authorities appeared to be as baffled as everyone else with the posturings of these amateur soldiers. Could it be that Carson's men were about to receive a shipment of arms?

Those who were curious may have sighted a darkened ship, showing only her navigation lights, cautiously slipping up Belfast Lough. They may also have noticed that she appeared to be flashing signals to someone on the shore. The military and the police saw the ship too, and watched her carefully as she berthed. Then, in a swoop, accompanied by customs officials, they went to board her. They found that she was the *SS Balmarino* and instructed her master to open the hatches. He refused to do so. When asked to state the nature of his cargo, he remained silent. As a mild confrontation developed, a by-stander may have grown suspicious of it all. Both sides appeared to be stalling, and the police seemed unofficious in their approach. In fact, the *SS Balmarino* was a decoy ship and her presence in Belfast Lough was meant to divert attention from what was happening elsewhere.[11]

'Elsewhere' was the little town of Larne, some twenty miles up the Antrim coast. At 8.00 p.m. the UVF had taken control of the town and its harbour and posted lookouts on the hills all around. Their commanders scanned the sea with binoculars until, at last, a small ship was sighted. It was the *Mountjoy*, and at 10.30 p.m., after flashing an agreed signal, she crept slowly into the harbour. She was quickly made fast, and men rushed to her and began removing the long crates of rifles which she held in her hold. They loaded them into the score of motor cars and lorries which were standing by, their engines running impatiently. As one car was loaded and sped into the darkness, another moved up to take its place. When the final crate was carried away the *Mountjoy* battened down her hatches and made her way once again to the open sea. The operation was repeated further down the coast at the little harbours of Bangor and Donaghadee. Hours later, as the sky lightened and gold streaks appeared on the horizon, the men were still at work: they were unloading the crates at Orange halls, old churches, at hillside farm houses and at the seats of country squires. The hero of the hour was Major Fred Crawford, the Order's swashbuckling gunrunner who, without compunction, had purchased arms in German territory and had the audacity to smuggle them home under the very noses of the authorities.

The government's authority had been demonstrably flouted. The message was clear: if it attempted to impose Home Rule on the North, the result would almost certainly be massive bloodshed.

'Ulster 1912'

As the crisis deepened, many people of power and influence in Britain gave their support to the Unionists. One was the writer Rudyard Kipling, whose angry poem 'Ulster 1912' appeared in the *Morning Post*:

The dark eleventh hour
Draws on and see us sold
To every evil power
We fought against of old
Rebellion, rapine, hate
Oppression, wrong and greed
Are loosened to rule our fate
By England's act and deed.

The faith is where we stand
The laws we made and guard
Our honour, lives and land
Are given for reward.
To murder done by night
To treason done by day
To folly, sloth and spite
And we are thrust away.

Believe, we dare not boast
Believe, we dare not fear —
We stand to pay the cost
In all that men hold dear.
What answer from the North?
One law, one land, one throne
If England drive us forth
We shall not fall alone.[12]

The Curragh Incident

The impact of events like the signing of the Covenant, the formation of
the UVF and the Larne gunrunning was dramatic. They injected the
Unionists with confidence and improved their morale. In England, the
Conservative party came out openly in their favour and its leader,
Andrew Bonar Law, did not mince his words in their support. He was
the son of an Ulster Presbyterian minister who, from the age of twelve,
had been reared in Scotland with cousins who were members of the
Order. Ulster was almost the only subject in which he had an interest,
and his views were inflexible. In July 1912 he told a large rally at
Blenheim Palace, Woodstock, Oxfordshire: 'I can imagine no length of
resistance to which Ulster will go, which I shall not be ready to
support.'[13] He fervently believed that a Home Rule Parliament would
mean the destruction of Irish Protestantism, and was ready to sanction
any intrigue, however hazardous, to prevent its establishment. His party
was prepared to use its majority in the House of Lords to reject the

annual Army Bill, thereby putting military discipline at risk and making army involvement in Ulster problematic.

In the event, the step proved unnecessary. The head of military operations at the War Office was County Longford-born Sir Henry Wilson, a staunch unionist and Orange supporter, and a born intriguer who was not above passing to Carson and Bonar Law confidential military information which might be useful against Home Rule. In March 1914, a dramatic incident occurred. The Commander-in-Chief of the British forces in Ireland, Sir Arthur Paget, was summoned to the War Office in London and told to prepare for a mass movement of troops from the Curragh army base, in County Kildare, into Ulster. When he returned and conveyed these instructions to the officers of the 3rd Cavalry, fifty-eight of the men, led by Brigadier General Hubert Gough, announced their intention of resigning their commissions rather than march against their kith and kin in the North. This was not, as often suggested, a mutiny; no direct orders were disobeyed, but it was clear that the army could not be relied upon to coerce the Protestants, and that any move against Ulster would be fraught with peril.

The upshot was that the War Office refused to accept the resignations, and Gough and his colleagues were informed that the government did not intend to take offensive action against Ulster. This assurance was given without government authority and later repudiated by the Prime Minister, but the damage was done. It was plain for all to see that the government lacked the resolve to stand up to Carson. The incident also helped to scotch rumours that Carson and Craig would be arrested and charged with high treason, although it was known that the government had toyed with the idea months before. Such action would, apart from the practical difficulties, have likely sparked a civil war. Besides, British public opinion may have reacted adversely. Certainly it would have been difficult to find a jury to convict men who claimed that their only purpose was to maintain the unity of the United Kingdom.

—26—

The Orange State

> The thunder clouds are driving
> At'ward the lurid sky
> But put your trust in God, my boys
> And keep your powder dry.

> *—from 'Oliver's Advice' by Colonel William Blacker*

The Men who Marched Away

The political crisis now deepened. King George V became concerned lest matters should spin out of control, and at his suggestion a last-ditch conference was held at Buckingham Palace in late July as a desperate effort to reach an agreement between Carson and Redmond. It failed, and there was every indication that there would be an Irish bloodbath. Then a strange Providence intervened. The shots fired by a terrorist gunman in Sarajevo a few weeks before echoed around the world and, amazingly, Britain found herself at war with Germany. In Ireland there was palpable relief as both sides agreed to postpone a resolution to their conflict until the war was over.

The Larne gunrunning would be the only significant incident to involve the UVF. Instead of defending their constitutional position in the United Kingdom, the men found themselves defending Britain against the Central Powers. Anxious to show Ulster's loyalty to King and Country, Carson and Craig pledged an Ulster Division of 35,000 men to be drawn from the Volunteers. Within weeks, 21,000 had flocked to the recruiting offices and Lord Kitchener agreed to the inclusion of the word 'Ulster' in the names of all units to be formed. Craig made arrangements with Moss Brothers to supply the uniforms needed and, shortly, one of the most cohesive divisions in the British army had been forged. Orangemen from the same Belfast lodges found themselves together in battalions; members of companies from small towns and villages found themselves rubbing shoulders with lads whose hands they held on lodge nights; their homogeneity was emphasised by each man holding similar religious beliefs, similar political views, and a similar unswerving loyalty to the Crown.[1]

The Division received its formal training at Finner Army Camp in County Donegal and at Malone on the outskirts of Belfast and, much to the annoyance of those who believed that the war would be over before an Orange shot was fired, were brought to the peak of their fitness slowly. During these months rumours circulated that they were being held back whilst other Irish Divisions were shedding their blood, but this was untrue. By 8 May 1915 they were ready. Bands played and crowds cheered as they marched through Belfast, their rifles at a slope, their bearing high, and their faces flushed with pride. As cries of farewell rang in their ears, a strain of sadness could be heard in the cheering. Wives, children, aged parents and loved ones had leaden hearts as they watched the men march past and disappear from view.

General Douglas Haig, the new commander of the British forces in France, had a fresh offensive planned, to be launched at a point where the British and French lines crossed in the region of the River Somme. Among the units which he brought forward on 1 July 1916 was the 36th (Ulster) Division, who had held a section of the line from north-east of Thiepval Wood to the River Ancre.

The Ulstermen advanced towards enemy lines; many were mindful that it was the anniversary of the Battle of the Boyne, and some wore their Orange sashes over their khaki jackets. On their lips and in their hearts were those rallying cries they had known from childhood: 'No Surrender' and 'Remember 1690'. Then a mighty blast shattered the air, a heavy bombardment was opened against them, and the heavens were ripped asunder. When it stopped, the whistles blew to indicate who had survived. The German gunners emerged from their nests to do their deadly work, and wave after wave of the young men of Ulster — carpenters, riveters, farmhands, shopboys and lads who had not learnt a trade — rushed at them, their bayonets glistening in the morning sunshine. And then, as the battle waged, they fell and died.

The Covenant had been sealed; the full price of loyalty had been paid.

A City in Mourning

A heavy pall hung over Belfast; it seemed as if every family was bereaved. Day after day the casualty lists in the newspapers grew longer and the people stood, stupefied, as they read the familiar names. The Order went into mourning and all lodge meetings were cancelled. The Lord Mayor requested that a five-minute silence be held at noon. As the rain pounded down, people stopped in their tracks and stood bare-headed in great solemnity. On a rampart of earth near Mac Art's Fort, on the summit of Cave Hill, a lone Orangeman stood. At the stroke of twelve he drew a flute from his jacket and played a lament. The lonely notes appeared to flutter in the breeze, before being lost in the pall that enveloped the city.

Months later it was found that a survivor from Derry had written of the bravery of his comrades. While lying in a field-hospital, he had scratched on a card:

> And onward they dashed, from trench to trench,
> As streams in a rushing tide
> The Fountain, Dark Lane, Rosemont and the lads from Waterside
> Yet onwards, ever onwards, their progress none could stay
> They weren't out 'goose stepping' nor singing 'Dolly's Brae'.[2]

The Birth of Northern Ireland

When the King signed the Home Rule Bill on 18 September 1914, he also appended his signature to the Suspensory Act. This deferred the operation of the Home Rule Bill until the passage of an Amendment Bill, which would modify it so that it might secure greater consent; in fact, it meant that the government had backed down on its repeated resolve to introduce Home Rule in its original form. Carson's show of force had paid off. During the debate in the Commons, Asquith said:

> The employment of force of any kind, for what is called the coercion of Ulster, is an absolutely unthinkable thing and, so far as I and my colleagues are concerned, it is a thing which we would never countenance or consider.[3]

Although the Bill was suspended for the duration of the conflict, the four years which followed did not pass without incident in Ireland. During the early days of the war the republican movement in the South grew in magnitude, and in 1916 a rebellion broke out in Dublin, followed by executions which inflamed republican emotions among the population. An attempt was made by Lloyd George, who became Prime Minister at the end of 1916, to break the deadlock by calling a Convention of representative opinion from all over Ireland. After deliberating for months under the chairmanship of Sir Horace Plunkett, the delegates found the difficulties too great, and no solution emerged. It remained for parliament to come up with an answer.

Late in 1919 the Cabinet produced a plan for the establishment of two parliaments, one in Dublin, the other in Belfast. This policy formed the basis of the Government of Ireland Act (1920) which became law on 20 December.

The six counties of Antrim, Armagh, Down, Fermanagh, Londonderry and Tyrone were to have their own legislature, and this came into being in the City Hall, Belfast, on 7 June 1921. King George V attended the state opening and called for peace and reconciliation in Ireland.

Sir James Craig became the first Prime Minister of Northern Ireland, and his speeches at the time suggest that he felt that the best way forward was to break down the sectarian barriers which divided the population.[4] But violence broke out all over Ireland and the Irish Republican Army (which had developed from the Irish Volunteers of the 1916 Rebellion) made a distinct attempt to undermine the fledgling state in the North. The bomb, the gun and the sniper's bullet were heard day after day in Belfast, and Craig's government formed a Special Constabulary to deal with security, comprised predominantly of Orangemen and divided into three categories. The 'A' Specials were full-time men mobilised as police constables within the Royal Irish Constabulary; the 'B' Specials were part-time and received an allowance; the 'C' Specials were an unpaid reserve. The Catholic population became alarmed, and the new Under-Secretary, Sir Ernest Clark, took pains to assure them that the 'Specials' would be kept under proper control. He urged that Catholics should join in sufficient numbers to keep order in their own areas. The Catholics did not listen; from the beginning they hated the force.

When the worst of the violence of these years subsided, a new source of friction arose with the establishment of a Boundary Commission to review the frontier between Northern Ireland and the Irish Free State. The promise of this Commission had been part of the Anglo-Irish Treaty, signed in December 1921, which had led to the establishment of the Irish Free State. The Commission had elicited from Craig the phrase which became an Orange mantra: 'Not an Inch'. It did not, in the end, result in frontier changes, but so alarmed the government of the new Free State that it entered into immediate arrangements for a settlement, signed on 3 December 1925 by the three governments. Under Article One, the territory of Northern Ireland as defined in the Government of Ireland Act (1920) was confirmed, and the whole of the six counties was definitely secured to Northern Ireland. This arrangement was ratified by an Act of the Westminster parliament, and also by an Act of the Dublin parliament which became No. 40 on its statute book for the year 1925.[5] In the Northern Ireland parliament, Craig moved on 10 December 1925:

> that this House approves of the agreement dated 3rd December 1925, entered between the governments of Great Britain, the Irish Free State and Northern Ireland.[6]

As this resolution was accepted by all three parliaments, it was thought that the question had been definitely settled, but later, when Eamon de

Valera came to power in Dublin in 1932, he spoke of the 'outrage of partition' and protested against the 'alienation of the most sacred part of our national territory, with all the cultural and material loss this unnatural separation entails.'[7]

Stormont — the Largest Orange Lodge in the World

The Orangemen always denied the validity of Irish nationalism, and wanted to retain the whole of Ireland for the Union. Yet they were realists and recognised that unionists could not sustain an electoral majority in more than the six north-eastern counties. They grieved to lose Cavan, Donegal and Monaghan, which became known as 'The Three Lost Counties', and Orangemen in these counties did not take their exclusion lightly. They vehemently opposed being cut off from their brethren, and for months passed resolutions in their lodges denouncing their treatment, although they knew that protest was futile.

In June 1922, a civil war had broken out in the South over the signing of the Anglo-Irish Treaty. As anti-government Irregulars retreated from their cover in the Dublin's Four Courts, they took up defensive positions in buildings in and around Rutland Square, including the Fowler Memorial Orange Hall, the headquarters of the Grand Lodge of Ireland. Large quantities of incunabula were removed from the library for use as breastworks, and in the ensuing bombardment, dozens of volumes bearing information on the old Williamite societies were destroyed. When the Irregulars finally withdrew, an old van drew up outside the building, and the books and documents which survived were taken to Belfast. For over forty years they remained stored in the vaults of a bank, completely forgotten. Then an enterprising clerk stumbled across them and notified the Grand Lodge of Ireland, which had years before itself transferred to Belfast. The treasure chest is today housed in the library of the Grand Lodge and includes the Minute Book of the first meetings held in Thomas Verner's house in Dawson Street, Dublin, in 1798.[8]

The Orangemen quickly identified themselves with their new state, which they regarded as their own creation. An opportunity for an expression of their pride came on 16 November 1932, when a great new neoclassical parliament building was opened at Stormont on the eastern outskirts of Belfast. It was a magnificent pile, standing imposingly at the end of a long drive, the final approaches being dominated by a huge statue of Carson in full oratorical flight.

The working assembly consisted of two Houses, a forty-two-member Commons and an Upper House or 'Senate' which had twenty-four members elected by the Commons and two ex-officio nominees. Although only a legislature with limited powers, many of its procedures replicated those of Westminster, one of the differences being that it sat for only a couple of months each year. It attracted fierce criticism from nationalists, who often refused to take up their seats, stigmatising it as 'The Largest Orange Lodge in the World'.

Between 1921 and 1968, 138 out of the 149 Unionist MPs who sat in Stormont were members of the Order, as were all the Prime Ministers. In those years the Order's influence over government policy was often remarked on: 'There is clear evidence in the Public Records Office in Belfast in the 1920s and 1930s that Sir Charles Blackmore, who was Cabinet Secretary, was essentially a messenger boy for the Orange Order. He would go to Sir James Craig, the Prime Minister, and Sir Wilfred Spender, the head of the Civil Service, and convey the Orange Order's fears about this or that civil servant who was either a Catholic or believed to be a Catholic,' says historian Henry Patterson. This paranoia reached its height in 1934 when the Order interfered to have a Catholic gardener at Stormont sacked because of his religion. 'This Catholic,' says Patterson, 'had volunteered in the First World War. He had a magnificent army record — and a reference from the Prince of Wales!'[9] The Order's closeness to the government was unquestionable and indicated, famously, in 1934, when Craig told parliament: 'I have always maintained that I am an Orangeman first and a politician and Member of Parliament afterwards . . . All I boast of is that we are a Protestant parliament for a Protestant people.'[10]

The Orange Heyday

The heyday of the Order was between 1921 and 1968 when it ruled the roost in Northern Ireland. Its power was first demonstrated when it opposed the 1923 Education Act introduced by the Minister for Education, the Marquess of Londonderry. The Marquess was something of an antique figure, known for his Victorian frock-coats and high butterfly collars; he spoke to his civil servants as if they were his stable hands, and emphasised each instruction by banging a riding crop on his desk. Yet his Education Act was surprisingly liberal and a rare example of Unionist vision. It proposed to establish a non-sectarian democratically accountable educational system under which Protestant and Catholic children would be educated together, with no provision for religious teaching during school hours. This provision was strictly in accord with the Government of Ireland Act (1920), Section 5, which made it illegal for any religion to be endowed.

The Bill created an uproar, particularly among Orangemen. Any educational system which failed to include Bible instruction was totally unacceptable to the Order, and to the Protestant churches. Sir Joseph Davidson, the Belfast Grand Master and a senior Grand Lodge member, denounced what he called 'the secularisation of education', and made vigorous protests to the Prime Minister. He was a prime mover in forming a United Committee of Protestant Churches to arouse public opinion against the Bill, and circulated hysterically worded handbills headed: 'Protestants Beware!' The popular reaction frightened the government and, during a week when Londonderry was away in London, Craig capitulated and an Amending Act was rushed through. Henceforward, religious education (innocuously labelled 'Biblical instruction') became compulsory in state schools. In practice, it was imbued with a Protestant ethos and thus unacceptable to Catholics, who opted out of the state system and established their own schools. The measure, in fact, meant that the state had endowed Protestant education. But it had a further drawback for Catholics: as ratepayers, they were forced to pay for the upkeep of a system which they could not use. Although the Act was contrary to the Government of Ireland Act (1920), it remained on the statute book until after the Second World War, when a new Education Act opened up greater opportunities for Catholic secondary education.

The issue alerted the Order to the importance of educational policy. Following a resolution from the County Tyrone Grand Lodge, an Orange Education Committee was established in 1928, to monitor teaching in schools and colleges, and to ensure that it was in line with Protestant principles. On numerous occasions the Committee sought 'clarifications' and 'explanations' from school managements and, on occasion, took its complaints to the highest authority.

Orangeism and the Unionist Party

Getting the ear of the government was never a problem for the Order during the years of unionist hegemony. Through its ex-officio representation on the Ulster Unionist Council, the governing body of the Unionist Party, it had a channel to the top. But this formal link with the party made it impossible for Catholics to consider joining the party, and exposed it to charges of sectarianism. In 1959 Sir Clarence Graham, a member of the party's standing committee, daringly suggested that Catholics should be invited to join and be selected as prospective parliamentary candidates. Immediately, the Order intervened and shot down the proposal. When it was pointed out that one of the objects of the party was to protect civil and religious liberties, Sir George Clark, Grand Master for Ireland, intervened and said: 'I would draw your attention to the words 'civil and religious liberty'. This liberty, as we know it, is the liberty of the Protestant religion . . . in view of this it is difficult to see how a Roman Catholic, with the vast difference in our religious outlook, could be either acceptable within the Unionist Party as a member or, for that matter, bring himself unconditionally to support its ideals.

Furthermore, an Orangeman is pledged to resist by all lawful means the ascendancy of the Church of Rome. . . .'[11] Sir George's views were held by the rank and file of party members. A few years later an election leaflet issued by the party was circulated in the Saint George district of Belfast. It informed voters that the party's three candidates 'employ over 70 people, and have never employed a Roman Catholic'.[12]

The Special Powers Act

It is not disputed that from the inception of the Northern Ireland state, up to one-third of its population gave it no allegiance. The security situation was thus inherently unstable. In 1922 one of the most draconian pieces of legislation found in the western world was placed on the statute book, the Civil Authorities (Special Powers) Act. One of its admirers was Dr Hendrik Verwoerd, Prime Minister of South Africa (1958-1966) who declared that his own powers were puny in comparison.[13] Two sentences from the legislation became notorious: 'The Civil Authority shall have power in respect of all persons and things within the jurisdiction to take all such steps and issue all such orders as may be necessary for preserving peace and maintaining order,' and 'if any person does any act of such a nature as to be calculated to be prejudicial to the preservation of peace and maintenance of order in Northern Ireland and not specifically provided for in the regulations, he shall be deemed to be guilty of an offence against the regulations.' With these sweeping powers, further controls hardly seemed necessary, yet other legislation provided the police with the right to intern without trial, to arrest without warrant, to declare curfews and to prohibit inquests. This last measure was seen as particularly obnoxious, as it effectively blocked investigations of illegal killings by the security forces. Other legislation was introduced to deal with non-violent forms of protest, such as the Public Order Act (1951) and the Flags and Emblems Act (1954).

It would be disingenuous to suggest that all these measures were not aimed at the nationalist community or that they were not enforced with vigour by the Royal Ulster Constabulary (RUC), which was predominantly Orange. In fact, some police divisions had their own Orange lodges. One was the notorious Sir Robert Peel Lodge (LOL 1334) whose first Worshipful Master was a hardliner named John William Nixon. This hothead was dismissed from his position as Inspector during the period of the Boundary Commission for inciting Orangemen to defend the border physically. His record was dubious; he had previously been implicated in the killing of a number of Catholics, one of whom was an influential nationalist named Owen McMahon.[14] None of this burdened the brethren. Following his sacking, Nixon was hailed as an Orange martyr and went on to a successful career as an independent unionist politician.

Orangemen made few apologies for the Special Powers legislation. They argued that it was necessary to meet the ongoing subversive threat, and asserted that every government in the South had used similar measures to arrest and intern (and, in some instances, to execute) the same type of people who were bent on destabilising the North. In comparison with the South, they pointed out that no special court or tribunal in the North had ever executed anyone or even imposed a sentence in excess of three years' penal detention.[15] In the South there had been numerous executions (and long periods of penal servitude) ordered by special courts other than the ordinary courts of justice.

This was the case for the defence made by Orange and unionist apologists following the fall of Stormont in 1972. They reminded critics that at all times the Province had been a parliamentary democracy, in which the executive was subject to the scrutiny of Parliament; there was no question which could not be aired by elected representatives, nor were there curbs on free speech or on the free expression of political views.

Yet all the world knew that these appurtenances of democracy concealed tight hegemonic control. Northern Ireland was a one-party state designed for Protestants, not for Catholics. Opposition parties could never reasonably hope for power and, besides, there was proven gerrymandering of electoral boundaries. Derry City Council is often cited as a glaring example: in a blatant manipulation of wards, 14,000 Catholics could elect only eight councillors, while 9,000 Protestants could end up with twelve. This pattern was repeated elsewhere and led to wholesale discrimination in such matters as the allocation of public housing. But there was widespread discrimination in other areas too, particularly in employment. Most employers were Protestants, and often Orangemen, and felt no inhibitions in looking after their own. Catholics were recognised by their names and addresses, which were enough to ensure their rejection. One of the biggest employers in the province, the Harland and Wolff shipyard, was notorious for job discrimination. At one period, out of a workforce of 10,000, it employed only 400 Catholics.

The Order, with its system of secret grips and codes, was the invisible hand which pulled strings in many areas of employment. It fingered not only Catholics, but also suspect lukewarm Protestants who showed liberal tendencies. The man whose Orange fervour was doubted walked in fear, lest his livelihood was taken away.

The Troubles

The day-to-day policies of the Unionist government were directed towards securing a level of financial subvention from Westminster which would enable Northern Ireland's health and welfare services to march in line with those in Britain. In this it was largely successful, as it was in some of the economic initiatives which it took in the sixties. But Catholics contended that to preserve Protestant dominance, employment and other opportunities were kept from their areas. In 1971, for example, Catholic unemployment was almost 14 per cent and Protestant 5.6 per cent, and the quality of jobs held by Catholics was much inferior to those held by Protestants. This had little to do with educational achievement; the Catholic middle classes, for instance, were disproportionately employed in the liberal professions, where entry is determined by examination success. In the end, the straw which broke the camel's back was the unfair allocation of housing. This, coupled with the long-term decline of traditional industries and the rise of a new, post-war educated Catholic population who were not prepared to be cowed, led to large-scale discontent. The lid finally came off the powder keg in 1968.

Westminster took little interest until things got out of hand, by which time a civil rights movement had emerged to agitate for some of the more obvious reforms. The campaign attracted hostility and resistance, particularly from Orangemen. Some brethren were prominent among extremist groups who attacked civil rights meetings and Catholic homes during 1969. The government of Captain Terence O'Neill responded (under pressure from London) by calling in the British army. Although initially welcomed by the Catholics, the troops were gradually seen as another unionist instrument of control, acting under Stormont's direction. This situation was exploited by the IRA, which opened a campaign of violence against the security forces. This was met with counter-violence from Protestant paramilitary groups, and by 1978 the mayhem had claimed 1,800 lives. Eventually the inability of the Stormont government to restore order, and the increased alienation of the nationalist community, led to the suspension of the Northern Ireland parliament and to direct rule from London. To Orangemen this was a major blow. The loss of Stormont rocked their confidence and swept away one of their greatest achievements.

Sunningdale

In an effort to resolve the problem the British government called a high-level conference at Sunningdale in Berkshire, in 1973. It was attended by the British and Irish prime ministers, senior cabinet ministers on both sides, and by representatives of the main political parties in Northern Ireland. The outcome appeared hopeful. New governmental structures were agreed: there was to be a new assembly headed by an Executive consisting of members of the main political parties in each community. Agreement was reached on a Council of Ireland to co-ordinate matters of common interest between the Republic and Northern Ireland. The Executive took office in January 1974 but was brought down five months later by a general strike. The Order had opposed it from the start, and Orangemen were involved with the groups which toppled it. Direct Rule from Westminster was re-introduced, and in the years which followed a number of fresh attempts were made to find an agreement. One was a Constitutional Convention which met for nine months in 1975-76, but failed to produce a report likely to attract widespread support. Following this, a political stand-off developed.

The Discordant Drum

It was a quiet Sunday
As the Brethren left prayer
But one thousand RUC men
Were waiting for them there.

Freddie Hall[1] he had the choice
That day in Portadown
He told his men to go to Drumcree
And face the Orange down.

*— opening lines of a ballad in celebration of the Orange
march on the Garvaghy Road in Portadown following
the 'stand-off' at Drumcree, July 1995*

'Sold Down the River'

The Anglo-Irish Agreement signed by the British and Irish prime ministers, Margaret Thatcher and Dr Garret FitzGerald, at Hillsborough Castle, County Down on 15 November 1985 was the most important political initiative taken on Northern Ireland since the collapse of the power-sharing executive in 1974. From the brethren's standpoint, it represented the most serious blow to their position since Asquith's Home Rule initiative in 1912. It created the unthinkable — a role for the Irish government in the internal affairs of Northern Ireland. An innovation was the establishment of an Intergovernmental Conference headed by British and Irish ministers and served by a secretariat drawn from civil servants north and south of the border. In a key departure from previous policy, the British government accepted that an internal settlement to 'The Troubles' was unlikely and that the Irish government should act as a guarantor to the nationalist community, monitoring the performance of the administration and pressing for whatever reforms it considered necessary. Because the Conference had no powers, Britain could claim that there was no diminution in sovereignty, but the Agreement unquestionably changed the context of the problem.

The Order and the Unionist parties reacted with shock and fury. They would not countenance Southern involvement in Northern Ireland's affairs and were determined to either abort or undermine the Agreement. That a British government, particularly one headed by the 'Iron Lady', Margaret Thatcher, should strike a deal with the 'Old Enemy' was seen as a gross act of treachery. James Molyneaux, the leader of the Unionist Party and Sovereign Grand Master of the Royal Black Preceptory, gave vent to his feelings in no uncertain manner. He told a meeting of the Northern Ireland Assembly: 'We are going to be delivered, bound and trussed like a turkey prepared for the oven, from one nation to another.'[2] The *Belfast News Letter*, the morning after the signing, was almost apocalyptic: 'At Hillsborough yesterday the ghosts of Cromwell and Lundy walked hand in hand to produce a recipe for bloodshed that has few parallels in modern history.'

On 18 November the Reverend Ian Paisley placed an advertisement in the *News Letter* headed 'For God and Ulster':

> Dr Ian Paisley MP, as an elected representative, calls on all Bible-believing Protestants to set aside the next Lord's Day, 24th November 1985, as a special day of prayer for our beloved Province. A base betrayal has taken place. The right of the majority to have any say in the Dublin/London joint rule of our Province has been denied and the use of the ballot box stopped. We must now turn to the God of our Fathers. The word of God promises that when we are at our wit's end and cry unto the Lord in our trouble, He will bring us out of distress (see Psalm 107:27:28). Let us, next Lord's Day, at our bedsides, with our families, in our churches and in our halls, fervently, simply and sincerely call on God. For without faith it is impossible to please Him: for he who cometh to God must believe that He is a rewarder of them that diligently seek Him (Hebrews 11-6).

Numerous forms of protest were undertaken, including the relatively novel spectacle of unionist violence against the RUC, but they came to nothing. The old slogans of 'No Surrender' and 'Ulster Says No' lost their potency. The Agreement held, and both governments set about implementing it.

The Bowler and the Balaclava

If the Agreement's short-term aim was to bring about peace, it failed abysmally. The tit-for-tat killings between the rival paramilitary groups continued. Innocent people on both sides lost their lives in the most horrendous circumstances. On Sunday, 8 November 1987, eleven people were killed and sixty-three injured at a wreath-laying ceremony at the Enniskillen War Memorial. The Provisional IRA had placed a bomb at the gable end of Saint Michael's Reading Room, which crashed down and buried the victims beneath the rubble. On 17 January 1992, a mini-bus was bombed at Teebane Cross, near Cookstown, County Tyrone, and eight Protestants were killed and six injured. In a direct response the Ulster Freedom Fighters, a wildcat loyalist terrorist organisation, burst into Sean Graham's betting shop on the Ormeau Road in Belfast and opened fire indiscriminately, killing five Catholics and wounding seven more. A few months later members of the Ballynafeigh Orange Lodge marched past the site of the killings, giving five-fingered salutes (one finger for each of the dead) in mockery, and Orangewomen danced on the roadway. The total number killed between 1969 (the year in which 'The Troubles' began) and 1989 was 2,781.

Orangemen felt that they were among the prime targets of republican gunmen and bombers. In February 1997 the *Orange Standard* published a roll of honour which listed 157 members of the Order as having lost their lives violently. Of those killed, 39 were members of the RUC (that is, 13 per cent of all police victims), 50 were members of the Ulster Defence Regiment, a part-time armed force set up to replace the discredited 'B' Specials, and four were serving prison officers.[3]

There were numerous concerted arson attacks on Orange halls. In July-August 1995, halls in Keady, Beleek, Augher, Toombridge, Dungannon and Whitewell Road in North Belfast were damaged at an estimated repair cost of half a million pounds. Because of the continuing danger to the halls, the Order found it next to impossible to arrange insurance cover. The attacks were seen as more than an attempt to put the Order out of business: as most of the properties served rural Protestant communities, they were construed as part of an IRA campaign of ethnic cleansing.[4]

During the years of violence, the Order's connection with the security forces, particularly with the RUC, was raised on several occasions from within the nationalist community. It was a standard republican canard that the RUC were only Orangemen in uniform. It would, however, have been odd if sympathy did not exist within the force for Orangeism, as most policemen were drawn from the same section of the community as rank-and-file Orangemen. The importance of the question could not be ignored: whether it was proper for members *Irish News* of secret brotherhoods to serve as policemen. According to the (4 November 1996), Ronnie Flanagan, the Chief Constable, resigned from the Masonic

Order on assuming his position 'so that people would trust him to act impartially'. When the Pat Finucane Centre, an independent human rights organisation in Derry, wrote to the Police Authority requesting information on cross-membership of both the Authority and the RUC with the Orange and other loyalist Orders, it was informed that members of the Authority were not required 'to declare their membership of the organisations referred to'.[5] The second part of the question was ignored. Owing to the manner in which the RUC stood up to the Order on the re-routing of contentious marches (following the Anglo-Irish Agreement), the matter was shelved, but it remained a vexed question. In July 1998 a Select Committee on policing in Northern Ireland recommended that new recruits to the force should not be members of the Order or other marching organisations.[6]

The Downing Street Declaration

The Orange anger generated by the Anglo-Irish Agreement was compounded when the Downing Street Declaration (officially known as the Joint Declaration for Peace) was signed by the British and Irish prime ministers, John Major and Albert Reynolds, on 15 December 1993. The Declaration was designed to bring Sinn Féin into democratic politics and was a masterpiece of the draftsman's art. It cleverly balanced the rival claims of unionists and nationalists and gave the impression that the British government was a neutral and honest broker standing in the middle. Article 4 was a direct sop to the republicans and stated that Britain had 'no selfish strategic or economic interest in Northern Ireland'. It also 'affirmed that the government would uphold the democratic wish of the people of Northern Ireland should they prefer to support the union or a sovereign united Ireland'.

Orangemen saw the text as a sophist undermining of the Union, part of a 'softening-up' process designed to slide them into a united Ireland. The Ulster Unionist Party who, in this instance, had been consulted, was initially hesitant in its criticism. Dr Ian Paisley's Democratic Unionist Party more accurately reflected grassroots Orange opinion when it denounced the Declaration and accused the British government of engaging in a sell-out of Ulster. But the government had given little. When some of the more astute analysts got hold of the document they noticed that the absence of a comma after the word 'selfish', in the phrase that Britain had 'no selfish strategic or economic interest in Northern Ireland', was significant. On a closer reading, the phrase could be interpreted as meaning that Britain could have another selfish interest (if not a strategic one) in Northern Ireland, although this could not be economic.[7] The matter of a comma did not, however, reassure the Orangemen that their constitutional position was secure.

The Framework Document

By the time of the IRA and Loyalist ceasefires in 1994-96, it had become clear that the British and Irish governments had worked out a blueprint for a settlement based not only on Protestants and Catholics sharing power, but on a cross-border 'Irish dimension'. This concept built on the Anglo-Irish Agreement and gave recognition to the sense of Irish identity felt by most Northern nationalists. Orangemen saw it as a further sop to the republicans, as the Sinn Féin leader, Gerry Adams, had been calling for 'parity of esteem'. In fact, both governments were trying hard to get a talks process under way and, to facilitate this, they set out the parameters for a possible agreement in the 'Framework Document' (officially, *A New Framework for Agreement*) signed by John Major and the new Taoiseach (Irish prime minister), John Bruton, on 22 February 1995. The guiding principles were outlined in paragraph 10 and were based on the principle of consent, with agreement to be reached exclusively through democratic and peaceful methods, and any new arrangements affording parity of esteem to both traditions.

Again, the Order thought it smelled a rat. Numerous lodges came out against the document. The County Armagh Grand Lodge, for instance, at its half-yearly meeting at Bessbrook, expressed its 'total opposition to the Framework Document as a basis for constructing a just society for the greater number of citizens of Northern Ireland, as part of the United Kingdom'. It said that it considered the document to be 'an agenda which could lead to a United Ireland' and that the evidence for this was 'in the duplicity of the Westminster government in that it continued to undermine the unionist position in meeting with apologists for terrorism in advance of any sign of them laying down their weapons.'[8] There was a definite feeling that the British government was dancing to an Irish tune, and great dismay as the brethren watched Sinn Féin and the IRA reap gains from the ceasefires: there were prisoner releases (particularly in the Republic), daytime army patrols were reduced and some troops were transferred back to the UK. Visas were issued to Sinn Féin leaders to travel to the US, and the broadcasting ban against Sinn Féin was lifted in both Britain and the Republic.

Orangemen did not believe, however, that the IRA ceasefire would hold; they saw it as a tactical ruse and noted that the word 'permanent' was not used, and that the IRA were unwilling to decommission their weapons. They pressurised Unionist politicians, in these circumstances, not to enter into negotiations and, once again, a deadlock developed. In November 1995, United States Congressman George Mitchell was brought in to study the decommissioning issue and to advise on how new momentum could be injected into the peace process. In the meantime an old issue, now appearing in new garb, came to the forefront: the right to march. Few Orangemen foresaw that this would spark a great upheaval in the Order.

The Order on the March

As the guns and bombs fell silent, however intermittently, a new strategy was developed and covertly implemented by Sinn Féin. This was the ploy of sending political operatives into certain Catholic housing estates to stir up the residents to oppose Orange marches which either went through or adjacent to their areas. It was an old issue which dated back to the days of Johnston of Ballykilbeg and beyond. To resurrect it now was an astute move by the Sinn Féin leadership, whose objectives were twofold: to test the British government's commitment to 'parity of esteem', and at the same time provoke the anger of the Orangemen, whom they knew to be irked by the concessions to the nationalist agenda. The strategy was also designed to pit the brethren against the police and army whilst Sinn Féin sat back and watched the fun.

Sinn Féin laid its trap cleverly and felt that the Orange leadership was stubborn and foolhardy enough to walk into it. The issue was a difficult one for the Order. Marching was at the core of its existence; to curtail it meant giving way to the enemy. But for all that could be said of marching being the kernel of Orange culture, the world knew that it was an old-fashioned stylised act of dominance which carried a subliminal message to Catholics. This message was: 'We are the masters here and you are Fenian scum — we will march where we wish and you are powerless to stop us.' The swaggering braggadocio of the bandsmen made sure that the message got through. Not prepared to bow to the none-too-subtle machinations of Sinn Féin, the Order continued to march on its traditional routes and, as before, relied on its strength of numbers and dogged determination to see it through.

Catholics had learned to live with the marches, usually by staying indoors and ignoring them. Occasionally there would be flare-ups; the notorious Battle of the Bogside in Derry in 1969 was, for instance, ignited by an Apprentice Boys march and led to the worst rioting across the Province for fifty years. By the mid-1990s, in a changing political climate, the Order recognised that it needed to get a tighter grip on the marches and make them more congenial. The old 'blood-and-thunder' bands were bridled, only hymn tunes were played on church parades, and bands remained silent when passing places of worship. Slogan-shouting and unseemly language were prohibited, as was the use of intoxicating liquor.[9] In 1995 a band in the Armagh District was prevented from marching with a UVF flag, and the following year the Royal Black Preceptory sent a band home for a similar reason. But as far as Catholics were concerned, these changes were meaningless. Many in the housing estates were prepared to listen to the *agents provocateurs* and to serve on the 'Resident Rights' Committees' which sprang up.

Drumcree (Mark I)

Throughout Northern Ireland there were numerous flashpoints at which local residents could clash with Orangemen, Blackmen and Apprentice Boys over marching routes. Two were to achieve particular prominence: the Lower Ormeau Road in south Belfast, and the Garvaghy Road in Portadown. On the Lower Ormeau Road the protests developed from the notorious march which passed through the area on 8 July 1992, when Orangemen made their obscene salutes outside Sean Graham's betting shop. This act upset many people, and The Secretary of State, Sir Patrick Mayhew, said that it 'would have disgraced a tribe of cannibals'. The residents came together in a body called the Lower Ormeau Road Concerned Community and resolved to oppose further marches.

In Portadown the marching issue had been bubbling for years and there had been many re-routings away from the largely Catholic Obin Street and the Garvaghy Road. In early 1995 the Garvaghy Road Residents' Coalition was formed under the chairmanship of Breandán MacCionnaith (Brendan MacKenna), a Sinn Féin member who had spent time as a convicted terrorist. To Orangemen, Portadown was virtually holy ground. It was the scene of the most commemorated massacre of Protestants during the Rebellion of 1641, and the Battle of the Diamond had taken place a few miles west of the town in 1795. In 1893 Colonel Edward Saunderson, whose statue stands in front of Saint Mark's Church in Portadown, had told the Commons that a Home Rule Bill may pass through the House but 'it will never pass the bridge at Portadown'. With intransigent attitudes on both sides, the stage was now set for a clash, and the RUC was the piggy in the middle.

On Sunday, 9 July 1995, the sun shone brightly as 6,500 Orangemen made their way from Carleton Street Orange Hall in Portadown via a non-controversial route to Drumcree Church, less than two miles away, accompanied by two accordion bands. Elderly folk stood on the pavements watching as they set off, as did noisy clusters of children and their dogs. One old lady, who knew what lay ahead, waved her prayer book and said that the behaviour of the residents on the Garvaghy Road was a disgrace. 'What sort of people are they, trying to stop good Christian men from walking to church?' she said.

Four Union Jacks fluttered outside Drumcree church and the bells rang as the Orangemen arrived. From high up in his pulpit the rector, the

Reverend John Pickering, gave a tasteful sermon and everyone rose and sang. A collection plate was passed round and some threw a handful of small change, while others parted with larger sums. After the service they regrouped outside the church, this time to march back to Portadown along the disputed Garvaghy Road route. They set off in unison, their furled umbrellas by their sides, as the march leader shouted: 'Left, Right, Left, Right.'[10]

A few hundred yards down the road they found their way blocked by Land Rovers and a strong force of RUC men, in riot gear. Harold Gracey, the Worshipful Master of the Portadown District Lodge, approached the constable in charge and demanded that he and his brethren be permitted to continue along the Queen's highway. He was told that the march would not be permitted to go down the Garvaghy Road and was asked to disperse the brethren and withdraw. But Gracey and the Orangemen refused to budge. Incensed, they told the police that they intended to stay put until they were allowed to continue; then they installed themselves in front of the barricades and in the surrounding fields. Hours passed and the stand-off became more bitter. Hundreds of fresh Orangemen descended on Drumcree, to be followed by literally thousands. They declared that their civil liberties were being infringed and hurled the most virulent abuse at the police. Over the next twenty-four hours ugly confrontations developed and, on several occasions, the Orangemen attempted to outflank the police lines by skirting the surrounding fields, only to be driven back by heavy baton charges and the firing of plastic bullets. Several running battles broke out, and time and again fusillades of stones, debris and bottles were directed at the police, who continued to respond with plastic bullets.

During the intermittent periods of calm, several fiery speeches were made by Orange leaders and, on 10 July at a massive rally near the church, a formal resolution was put to the crowd and carried amid great cheering. It said:

> We the Orangemen assembled at Drumcree, loyal subjects of Her Majesty Queen Elizabeth, do hereby resolve that we will maintain and defend our religious and civil liberty.

> We do not accept a ghetto system. As free-born Britons we demand equal treatment with every other British citizen. We repudiate the slander of those who accuse us of triumphalism and intimidation in the expression of our cultural and religious identity. We totally condemn the tyrannous and unnecessary interference with the peaceful procession returning from a Protestant place of worship on the Sabbath Day.

We re-assert that the Queen's highway belongs to all law-abiding citizens. No faction under any pretence whatsoever can claim it as their own exclusive territory. We call upon the police to uphold this fundamental principle. That is their duty to the people of this land.[11]

On 11 July the Reverend Ian Paisley appeared and, although not an Orangeman, addressed the huge crowds. With characteristic hyperbole, he told them:

. . . There can be no turning back on this issue — we will die if necessary rather than surrender, if we don't win this battle all is lost, it is a matter of life and death. It is a matter of Ulster or the Irish Republic, it is a matter of freedom or slavery.[12]

The next evening, he turned up again and said:

We have the resolution, strength and determination to win through. And we will, because you can't beat the Ulster people . . . All across the Province tonight there are protests — here, there and everywhere. Across Ulster people have made up their minds that this is the crisis hour, but it is also the hour in which we can win back what we have lost.[13]

David Trimble, the local Unionist MP, shared a platform with Dr Paisley and assured the Orangemen that eventually they would be allowed to continue their march. But things grew nastier. Heavy plant-hire machinery appeared on the hill above the barricades and it looked as if the brethren intended to ram their way through. Frantic efforts were made behind the scenes to find an accommodation between the Orangemen and the residents, made more difficult by the unwillingness of the Orangemen to engage directly with the residents. Senior clergymen such as the Catholic and Protestant primates, Cardinal Cahal Daly and Archbishop Robert Eames, strove manfully to broker a deal. The services of a voluntary conciliation service, the Northern Ireland Mediation Network, were utilised. Eventually, when everyone was on the point of exhaustion, a compromise was hammered out. The residents agreed to permit the Orangemen to march past their homes on condition that they did so in silence, flew a single banner, and undertook to re-route one of their marches on the following day – 'The Twelfth'. The Orangemen accepted.

Trimble, who was involved in the negotiations, became, with Paisley, a hero of the hour. Both men were filmed with hands clasped, swaggering through the ranks of applauding Orangemen. The ending of the three day 'siege' was hailed as a victory and entered the Orange pantheon alongside the Siege of Derry and the Battle of the Boyne. The Grand Lodge of Ireland saluted the Portadown brethren on 'their steadfast stand for faith and freedom' and struck a commemorative medal for those who played leading roles. Trimble subsequently denied that the Orangemen compromised with the residents, and the part which he played was widely believed to have catapulted him to the leadership of the Unionist party a few months later.

The residents felt let down. The triumphalism shown by the Orangemen was contrary to the spirit of the deal. They resolved that the brethren would not be allowed to pull such a fast one the next time round.

Drumcree (Mark II)

The 'siege' of Drumcree returned to haunt everyone twelve months later. In the meantime, the Chief Constable, Hugh Annesley, and others had tried to persuade the Orangemen to forgo what they termed 'their right' to march on the Garvaghy Road. To show restraint in the matter, Annesley believed, would be a victory for common sense. But compromise was not on the cards. The Orangemen, alarmed at the growth of Catholic assertiveness, refused to back down, and the residents likewise held firm. As the day of the 1996 march approached, Annesley issued an order banning it on the grounds of preserving public order. But according to *The Sunday Times* (14 July 1996) he did not know that the Reverend Martin Smyth, the Grand Master of the Grand Lodge of Ireland, had spent months preparing to paralyse the province in the event of a ban. Smyth, the paper said, told reporters that Orangemen may have to break the law and take the consequences.[14] Extremist elements were not slow to take advantage of the situation. Loyalist gangs began to roam the streets of north Belfast, throwing stones at Catholic houses, attacking the police and generally creating a climate of fear. In towns across the Province — Coleraine, Derry, Ballymena, Ballymoney, Newtownards, and Portadown itself — barricades sprang up, shops and showrooms were attacked, and the resources of the police were fully stretched.

But the RUC still held the line at Drumcree. Thousands of Orangemen again turned up, and the pressure on the police became close to breaking point. Disorder continued night after night throughout the province; the International Airport was blocked off, and a Catholic taxi-man was murdered near Lurgan. On the fifth day of 'the siege', Annesley buckled and did a U-turn. He let the march through, and again Orangemen 'walked' on the Garvaghy Road.

The U-turn provoked a fierce Catholic backlash. In Derry a man was killed in clashes with the army. Militants hijacked cars, vans and buses and set them alight. The Taoiseach, John Bruton, and the Catholic Primate, Cardinal Daly, condemned the British government for giving in to intimidation, and for failing to handle the matter impartially. The Sinn Féin leader, Gerry Adams, gave his verdict: 'I want to say clearly that the peace process is in ruins.'

Curfew and Cages

The residents of the Lower Ormeau Road were no more fortunate that same year than their counterparts in Portadown. The 2,500 of them who lived in side streets off the Road were put under a fifteen-hour curfew before the Orangemen walked through the area at their scheduled time on 'The Twelfth'. Police and soldiers had saturated the area to prevent residents engaging in a sit-down protest, then a ring of steel had sealed them off from the rest of the city — the streets were blocked with Saracens and Land Rovers, and entry or exit became impossible.[15] One old lady commented: 'They treat us like animals, they'll put us in cages next.' Another said: 'There are no rights in Northern Ireland but Orange rights.'

At 9.30 a.m. on 'The Twelfth' the residents banged their bin lids and saucepans as they heard the Orange bands approach — six lodges and five bands came past, with the brethren sporting red carnations in their bowlers. They wore tight smiles as they passed the fenced-in Catholics and made their way to the city centre to join up with the main parade.

At the 'Field' outside Belfast that afternoon, Robert Saulters, the new Grand Master of Ireland, addressed the brethren for the first time in his new capacity. He had earlier hit the headlines in Britain for comments which he had made about Tony Blair, the leader of the Labour Party: 'it was a bleak prospect,' he said, 'that the future Prime Minister had married a Roman Catholic.' He continued: 'He has sold his birthright by marrying a Romanist and by receiving communion in a Roman Catholic church; he would sell his soul to the devil himself. He is not loyal to his religion. He is a turncoat. The future looks bleak.'[16] However, this bleak future ultimately had less to do with Blair's marriage than with his enormous Commons majority after the general election of May 1997; Unionists no longer held the balance of power.

Adams is Caught Out

Sinn Féin now had an additional reason for keeping the marching protests going. The IRA ceasefire had broken down with the Docklands bombing in London on 9 February 1996, and the party was anxious to divert attention from 'the active service units'. They were also coming under strong pressure to restore the ceasefire. The evidence of the Sinn Féin strategy came from, of all places, an Irish television broadcast. The Irish station, RTÉ, acquired a tape of a speech which Gerry Adams had delivered to a 'closed' session of a Sinn Féin conference. He had told his audience:

> Ask any activist in the North, did Drumcree happen by accident, and he will tell you 'no'. Three years of work on the Ormeau Road, Portadown, and parts of Fermanagh and Newry, Armagh and in Bellaghy, and up in Derry. Three years of work went into creating that situation and fair play to those who put the work in. They are the type of scene changes we have to focus on and develop and exploit.[17]

Adams did not like being caught out and reacted angrily, but he did not disown the material on the tape.

Drumcree (Mark III)

To many people's amazement, a further twelve months brought no solution to the annual scrimmage at Drumcree. The new Labour Party Secretary of State, Mo Mowlam, searched for a solution with both parties, and several mediators used their good offices, but to no effect. In 1997 it was uncertain up to the last minute whether the RUC would ban the march. The residents planned to hold a community festival by the roadside on the marching day, but the RUC prevented it going ahead. Some residents began holding overnight vigils and an alarm system was installed to alert them in case the RUC swooped to seal off the area. As the countdown began, tension increased dramatically throughout the province and sixty families were evacuated from the Garvaghy Road following a loyalist bomb scare.

Before dawn on 6 June the RUC struck, and caught the residents by surprise. They entered the area around the Ballyoran section of the road with a massive show of force, and literally batoned the residents into their homes. An unusual feature of the operation was that the RUC wore fireproof balaclavas, thereby making it impossible for the residents to identify them. Later that morning, five priests celebrated Mass behind a line of Saracens as the residents were not permitted to leave for their places of worship. It was the first occasion since Penal times that British soldiers prevented Irish Catholics from attending Mass.

At noon, almost 1,200 Orangemen marched down the Garvaghy Road in full regalia. The Catholics remained hemmed in behind rows of Land Rovers. They protested as best they could; bin lids and saucepans were banged, and every type of missile was hurled in the direction of the marchers. But the Orangemen looked straight ahead, their faces immobile. It was not until they reached the Shillington Bridge at the edge of Portadown and received the greetings of well-wishers that they broke into a smile. As they entered the Orange Hall in Carleton Street, one wizened old fellow, whose collarette and bowler seemed much too large, scribbled a note and passed it to a reporter. It said: 'The Orange: 3, The Green: Nil.'

The Bell Tolls at Drumcree (Mark IV)

In February 1922, Sir Winston Churchill, speaking in the House of Commons about the return to peace after the Great War, referred to 'the dreary steeples of Tyrone and Fermanagh rising above the receding waters of worldwide carnage, locked forever in the integrity of their ancient quarrel'. He was alluding to intransigence and the spire of Drumcree church now came to symbolise a late twentieth-century version of Ulster intransigence. Inside the church a solitary Union Jack hangs over a plaque on the wall near the door, listing the names of young men from the parish who died in the war of which Churchill spoke. Ninety-five went out to fight for King and Country, less than fifty returned.[18] Some fell on Flanders fields, others on the Somme. The memory of these young men is etched on the souls of the local Orange community. After the war they built a fine British Legion Hall in Portadown to perpetuate their memory. On 5 August 1981, Breandán MacCionnaith, later the leader of the Garvaghy Road Residents' Coalition, tried to blow it up with all who were inside. No one was killed. The following year MacCionnaith was jailed for five years in connection with the crime, and also convicted of holding a family hostage while using their car in the bombing, and given six years for firearms offences, all to run concurrently. He served only four years. This helps to explain why the Orangemen refused to speak to him or accept him as a suitable negotiator to break the stand-off deadlock.

In 1997 a new element was introduced. A Parades Commission was set up by the government to monitor contentious marches and adjudicate on which ones should go ahead, be re-routed or banned outright. Its rulings were given the force of law. The Order was unsympathetic to the idea and felt that the Commission was established to provide a smokescreen for the banning of its marches. It criticised it on the grounds that its rulings would curtail the right of free assembly and other civil liberties. The Executive Officer of the Grand Lodge of Ireland, George Patton, disliked the guidelines which the Commission laid down, saying:

> It is insulting to those people taking part in a parade and also to any protesters . . . the idea that we need any guidelines on how to behave is ridiculous . . . while I believe in a right to protest, I also understand that parades can provide passion and people may get excited and say things. If I'm walking in the middle of someone's road, they may well call me names, but how can you legislate against that? Are we going

to approach a policeman and say, 'excuse me officer, but that guy over there was rude and abusive to me, and under Section 45 I would like him arrested!'[19]

The Order refused to acknowledge the authority of the Commission and decided to ignore its rulings.

The Commission deliberated long on whether the 1998 Drumcree march should go ahead and, in the end, came down against it. All sections of the loyalist community castigated the decision and described it as 'unwise'. But the government stood over the ruling, and both the Secretary of State and the Prime Minister left no doubt that it would be upheld. This march was to take place in the more hopeful atmosphere generated by the 'Good Friday Agreement' of April 1998, and the subsequent North/South referendums which had overwhelmingly endorsed peace.

Up to the eleventh hour it was hoped that an accommodation could be reached. Some commentators were sharp in their criticism of the Orangemen for their refusal to enter dialogue with the residents. They said that it was hypocritical to refuse to speak with MacCionnaith when Orangemen had previously shown few qualms about conversing with the loyalist terrorist Billy Wright, who was responsible for several serious crimes before being gunned down himself in prison in late 1997.[20] It became clear that compromise could only be reached through recognition of mutual rights of representation. In its absence the Garvaghy Road residents expected the government to enforce the Commission's ruling.

Another stand-off took place. This time there was no weakening on the part of the authorities; the police and army mounted heavy steel barricades across the road, dug trenches in the surrounding fields and used large quantities of razor wire to ensure that the Orangemen would not pass. Again hundreds and, later, thousands of Orangemen descended on Drumcree. The scenes around the barricades turned ugly. Obscenities of the most vile sectarian nature were used by the protesters and rocks, smoke bombs and even live ammunition were deployed against the police and army. It was noted that the more well-heeled Orangemen seemed to be engaged in plotting the mayhem, whilst the rougher types — their beer bellies spilling out of their jeans and their arms bearing loyalist tattoos — were preoccupied with the dirty work: throwing Molotov cocktails, smoke bombs and other missiles. After dark on Friday (day six of 'the Siege') the mob showed increased determination to break through, and the police were forced to fire greater quantities of plastic bullets. In the barrage of missiles, about twenty people were injured. Orange leaders challenged the Secretary of

State to launch an inquiry into the 'misuse' of plastic bullets; but some who watched the film footage of these events on television were of the view that the police and army acted with commendable restraint.

Earlier, the Reverend Ian Paisley had put in an appearance and said that the 'Twelfth' (which was but a few days away) would be 'the settling day', predicting dire consequences if the Orangemen were not permitted to complete their march before then. It was said that boatloads of Orangemen were on their way from Liverpool and Scotland to assist their beleaguered brethren. Over 50,000 Orangemen were expected to arrive at Drumcree following their local 'Twelfth' marches. Sympathetic protests were anticipated in other parts of the province which would likely bring industrial and commercial life to a standstill, in repetition of the loyalist strike of May 1974 (when the power-sharing executive was brought down).

Horror in Ballymoney

Then a horrendous thing happened. At 4.30 a.m. on 12 July, arsonists threw incendiary devices into the home of a Catholic woman living in a loyalist housing estate in Ballymoney, County Antrim. Mrs Chrissie Quinn and her Protestant partner managed to escape, but Mrs Quinn's three sons, Richard (aged 11), Mark (9) and Jason (7) were trapped and lost their lives in the fire. Ronnie Flanagan, the Chief Constable, appeared on early-morning television and said that the police were convinced that the attack was sectarian. Within the hour, the Order was put in the dock and accused of creating the tensions which led to the outrage. The triple murder caused shock and revulsion everywhere. In the United States a White House spokesman said: 'President Clinton is deeply saddened by the deaths of three children in a sectarian attack.'[21] In Paris, President Chirac broke off celebrating his country's victory in the World Cup to express his horror, and both the British and Irish prime ministers expressed their rage. David Trimble, the new First Minister in the recently-elected Northern Ireland Assembly, and the Reverend William Bingham, the Order's influential County Armagh chaplain, were the first Orangemen to reverse their previous support for their brethren at Drumcree.

Bingham, a thirty-five-year-old rising star in the Order, told his Sunday morning congregation at Pomeroy, County Tyrone:

> I am not ashamed to say that I wept when I heard of the loss of three little boys in Ballymoney . . . I have to say this: that after last night's atrocious act a fifteen-minute walk down the Garvaghy Road by the Orange Order would be a very hollow victory, because it would be in the shadow of three coffins of little boys who wouldn't even know what the Orange Order is.[22]

Over the next few days impassioned appeals from across the political and religious spectrums were made for the protest at Drumcree to be called off. It was then learnt that there were splits in the Orange leadership and that a number of the Order's chaplains had resigned. Things appeared to be spiralling out of control as different Orange voices were heard, one contradicting the other. The protest at Drumcree began to crumble and the crowds melted away. But a hard core of Orangemen from the Portadown District Lodge stuck to their guns and re-stated their defiance. They found themselves isolated, and in the media and elsewhere abhorrence was expressed at their attitudes. But they declared that they would not be made scapegoats for a crime which had taken place seventy miles away, and which had no connection with their principled protest. The murder of the little boys, they said, was being used cynically to discredit them, and they resolved to 'maintain a presence' at the barriers. This seemed at variance with the mood of most of their fellow Orangemen who felt that it was now time to draw a line.

The 'Spirit of Drumcree' Faction

On the day of the funeral of the Quinn children, the image which Northern Ireland presented to the world was doleful — a sobbing father stroking the white coffin of his dead child, and a heartbroken mother standing by the graveside of her sons, saying: 'That is what Drumcree has done for me.' A few days earlier 'The Twelfth' had been celebrated. In Ballymoney the Orange bands marched passed the house where the three white coffins of the children were lying. They remained silent for twenty yards before and after the house. Forty yards of respect were deemed adequate for the bereaved.[23]

On the Lower Ormeau Road in Belfast, the Catholics decided on a silent protest. They hung out black flags and carried placards which were raised as the Orangemen marched past. Their message was stinging: it was: 'Shame on you.' It was amazing how quickly the public mood changed against the Orangemen. In the days prior to the Ballymoney tragedy, they had been building up to 'the settling day' and the air was thick with threats. David McNarry, one of their leaders, had claimed that they had the ability to 'paralyse the country in a number of hours' and the Portadown brethren had warned that 'The Twelfth' would be Tony Blair's 'Bloody Sunday'. But now, all that was felt for the protesters was disgust.

The violence had lasted a full week, and the police released statistics to show the price which had been paid. There were 12 shooting incidents, 25 blast bombs thrown, 412 petrol bombs, 136 vehicles hijacked, 93 properties damaged and 92 people arrested.[24] The police also revealed that their intelligence showed that the two main loyalist paramilitary organisations, the Ulster Volunteer Force (UVF) and the Ulster Defence Association (UDA), had orchestrated some of the violence in support of the brethren. It also emerged that a new group, using the name of The Protestant Association, was involved.

Press reports said that this was a cover name for a dissident Orange faction called 'The Spirit of Drumcree'. This splinter group was believed to be responsible for egging-on the blast bombers and stone throwers on Drumcree hill, and for much of the mayhem which occurred around the Province. The group first came to light following the stand-off in 1995, and was reputed to be led by Joel Patten, a hardliner from Dungannon. Its aim was to prevent the Order from entering agreements with residents' groups, and it denounced all compromise as appeasement. Patten held that the Order was growing soft under the leadership of Robert Saulters, the Belfast accountant, who had taken over as Grand Master in November 1996. So opposed were the group to Saulters that it forcibly occupied the premises of the Grand Lodge of Ireland (known as the 'House of Orange') at 65 Dublin Road, Belfast, to prevent his election for a second term. The seizure of the building made it impossible to hold the Annual Meeting, which had to be transferred to an Orange Hall on the Shankill Road.

In the days following the collapse of the Drumcree protest, the 'Spirit of Drumcree' faction — known by the disparaging acronym 'SODs' — was particularly active. Its members turned up on 'The Twelfth' at Pomeroy and heckled the Reverend William Bingham as he spoke. Violent scuffles broke out and television viewers (later that evening) were treated to a spectacle of bowler-hatted Orangemen wading into each other with their furled umbrellas. Prior to leaving 'The Field' Bingham was assaulted and flung into a ditch.[25]

The Precept and the Practice

It was now quite clear that the Order was an ailing organisation, at war with itself and alienated from large sections of the public. Its basic problem lay, perhaps, in the glaring contradiction between what it purported to stand for and what it was actually seen to be. It claims to be based on Christian principles and on a premise of tolerance towards Catholics, although opposed to Catholic doctrine. Yet it has a well-attested reputation for bigotry, intolerance and inciting sectarian passions. This is no pettifogging criticism but a widely-held view. Its known contempt for the views of others would seem to reduce the meritorious features of 'The Qualifications of an Orangeman' (see p.381) to a list of pious banalities, having little bearing on how Orangemen behave in the real world. And its references to 'popery' must be seen as crudely insulting, not just to the Catholic religion but to neighbours and fellow citizens who espouse that religion. Its attempts to conflate the right of its members to march with Protestant culture and civil and religious liberty are surely disingenuous and widely off the mark. Orange or Protestant identity is patently not endangered if marches are forbidden through Catholic neighbourhoods where, entirely reasonably, they are seen as triumphal enactments of past military victories, and thus resented.

Whatever its conceits, the truth is that there is no requirement for the public to respect or tolerate the Order, its paraphernalia, its caperings or its ethos. If it seeks public respect it must, like other bodies, be deserving. Public perceptions are unlikely to change while its precepts and practice are seen to be so far apart.

—28—

The Chosen Few

We won't give up the Bible
Let men say what they will
We've learned to love its precious truths
And mean to love them still.
We won't give up God's holy Word
For we know it true;
The bulwark of our brotherhood
The Orange and Purple too.

— *hymn sung at Orange Lodge meetings in Scotland*

The 'Blackmen'

On 12 August 1996, Robert Overend, known as 'Black Bob', marched up the main street of the village of Bellaghy, County Londonderry at the head of a procession of members of the Royal Black Institution. It was the end of a nineteen-hour stand-off between about 150 'Blackmen', as they were known, and up to 300 nationalists who had protested against their presence and blocked the roadway. Afterwards, in the local Orange Hall, 'Black Bob' folded his collarette and spoke to the press about the origins of his Order:

> For the benefit of those who do not know the Royal Black Preceptory is a Christian institution dating back to the crusades. And for those who do not know what the crusades were, they were when the crusaders tried to regain the Promised Land for the Christian people.[1]

This was the first that most of those present had heard of the origins of 'The Blackmen' or, to give the Order its official title, 'The Imperial Grand Black Chapter of the British Commonwealth'. Everyone had, however, some familiarity with it. 'The Black' or 'RBP', by which names it was also known, had been holding 'processions' (as opposed to 'marches') through villages and towns in Northern Ireland as long as anyone could remember. It was recognised as one of three inter-related loyalist Orders — the others being the Orange and Royal Arch Purple Orders — devoted to upholding Protestantism and maintaining Northern Ireland's position in the United Kingdom. The propriety and dignity of its processions had often been remarked on: its members were always impeccably turned out; they wore distinctive black regalia, bowler hats and white gloves, and trod gravely behind a large banner showing a red cross over the Constantinian motto 'In hoc signe vinces' ('In this cross we conquer').

Where 'Black Bob' acquired his historical information is not known, and it is difficult to establish whether his version is accurate. 'The Black' has never produced an official history and refuses to make its records available to researchers. But the history of any society claiming direct descent from the Crusades must be treated with caution, particularly if it is Protestant. The Crusades were military expeditions called by Pope Urban II in 1095, to recapture the Holy Sepulchre from the Saracens. The Reformation did not occur until over 400 years later. A number of the Crusading armies were formed as religious military Orders, but there is no reliable record indicating that any of their lineal descendants converted to Protestantism. It is known that 'non-operative' Protestant military Orders were much later founded, and that these sometimes claimed Crusader origin, but could not seriously profess to be in strict descent. The matter is complicated in that a number of these Orders evolved into secret brotherhoods, and such bodies are notorious for giving themselves grandiose titles and bogus histories. Some were established in the late eighteenth century, and thereafter they proliferated. The great exemplar was the Masonic Order, many of whose degrees were modelled on those of the old Crusading Orders, and whose rituals were widely copied.

Dr Anthony Buckley, Curator of the Ulster Folk and Transport Museum at Cultra, County Down, is an authority on fraternal societies and brotherhoods in Ireland. He says:

> My belief is that several groups in the 18th and 19th (and indeed the 20th) centuries borrowed images, symbols and traditions associated with the crusading Orders of Chivalry, but that there was no clear direct historical connection with them. In much the same way, the Odd Fellows claimed to be descended from the Jews of the Babylonian exile and the Freemasons from the builders of Solomon's temple. But I do not believe these legends to be historically accurate either. . . .

Of course one should not forget that the real Order of Malta continued to exist into the Napoleonic period, not only in Malta but also in other Catholic countries such as France, but whether there was any Protestant version of this Order in Scotland with any lineal link to the present, I do not know.[2]

The mention of Scotland is apposite for another authority, the late Aiken McCelland, believed that 'The Black' (of which he was a member) transferred from there to Ireland:

The Grand Black Chapter apparently owes its origin to the Imperial Grand Black Lodge of Knights of Malta and Parent Lodge of the Universe — later known as the Imperial Grand Encampment of the Universe and the Grand Black Lodge of Scotland of the Most Ancient, Illustrious and Knightly Order of the Knights Hospitallers of St John of Jerusalem. [McClelland adds: 'not to be confused with the Sovereign and Military Order of St Johns of Jerusalem, of Rhodes, and of Malta, usually referred to today as the Knights of Malta'.] Founded in Scotland, presumably about the middle of the 18th century, and supposed to be based on the famous order of chivalry, it soon spread to Ireland. The Knights of Malta was, I assume, something similar to the Masonic Order, with this important difference, no Roman Catholics were admitted, and its members were the clandestine, unwarranted, or hedge masons to whom reference was sometimes made in the *Belfast News Letter* of the late 1780s and early 1790s.[3]

Whatever 'The Black's' early history, it is known that Black Lodges were operating in Ireland as early as 1797 and that a Grand Black Orange Lodge of Ireland was established in 1802. It seems that in its early days 'The Black' was poorly organised and not quite respectable, and the Orange Order was reluctant to associate with it. Yet Orangemen who found that the two-degree system of their Order was too restrictive for them were attracted by 'The Black' and began to take out membership of this institution. The Orange Order's views were summarised by the Secretary of the Grand Lodge of Ireland, Stewart Blacker, when he gave evidence before the Royal Commission on Orange Lodges, in 1835:

The Grand [Orange] Lodge was always desirous of keeping its two Orders [i.e. degrees] of Orange and Purple perfectly unshackled and unconnected with any other Order whatsoever. They had reason to believe that those Black lodges, over which they did not have the slightest control nor the slightest connection, had indeed induced some of their members to join that body.[4]

The Degree System

In 1834, the Loyal Black Association of Scotland began to issue warrants in Ireland, but Irish 'Blackmen' preferred to 'work' under a local body. In 1844 they established a Grand Priory of Ireland, and two years later, following a meeting in Portadown, went further and formally instituted the Grand Black Chapter of Ireland. To preserve links with the earlier Black Lodges, the new body was designated 're-constituted'. Its first warrant was issued to Tandragee, County Armagh, whose Preceptory was named 'Erin's First Royal Black Preceptory'.

Like its companion Orders, 'The Black' is a secret society in the sense that its rituals and signs of recognition are known only to members who are sworn not to reveal them. 'Blackmen', however, reject the term 'secret society' and affirm that their institution is a 'society with secrets'. Its 'system' consists of eleven degrees, named: Royal Black, Royal Scarlet, Royal Mark, Apron and Blue, Royal White, Royal Green, Royal Gold Star and Garter, Crimson Arrow, Link and Chain, and Red Cross. All eleven may be taken at successive monthly Preceptory meetings, but are confined to those who already hold the Royal Arch Purple degree (which, itself, is restricted to holders of the two Orange Order degrees). The system is thus interlocking, and its security is fastened by rules which state that members expelled from one Order are automatically expelled from the others. This is largely academic for many Orangemen do not aspire to achieving 'higher degrees'.

Being a chivalric Order, the rites and ceremonies of 'The Black' are different from those of the other Orders. The basic ritual is derived from the old feudal theory of knighthood. 'Blackmen' are raised to the status of Knighthood by the Sovereign Grand Knight tapping them on both shoulders with a sword and saying: 'Arise Sir (first name)!' This dubbing follows an 'investing' of the prospective knight with a white tunic, stretched to the knees, and adorned with a large red cross. He also dons a medieval belt, spurs and helmet and is given a shield and broadsword. Thus attired, he undertakes an obligation to defend the Holy Christian Faith (which is understood to mean Protestantism) and is informed of the 'mysteries' associated with the royal black degree. Henceforward, he will be known among his brethren as 'Sir Knight'.

The Grand Masters of 'The Black' since its re-constitution have been:

Thomas Irwin	1846	W. H. H. Lyons	1914
Morris W. Knox	1849	Sir William Allen	1924
Thomas H. Johnson	1850	Sir Norman Stronge	1947
William Johnson	1857	Sir James Molyneaux	1972
Hunt W. Cambre	1902	William Logan	1999

Brownlow House

The Headquarters of 'The Black' are at Brownlow House, a large neo-Gothic mansion set in parkland (with an enormous artificial lake) at the end of Windsor Avenue in Lurgan. The mansion is the former seat of the Brownlow family, pillars of the old Anglo-Irish Ascendancy who became Earls of Lurgan. It has been described as the most sumptuous Orange building in the world; the walls of the Octagon Room, for example, were covered in marble panelling executed by Italian artists, and there was a large collection of paintings. It was firebombed in August 1996 and half destroyed. During the struggle to save it, the level of the artificial lake was said, improbably, to have gone down two feet, so great was the quantity of water poured on the flames. Priceless artefacts, valuable memorabilia, documentation and relics were destroyed, as was much of the ornate woodwork, fine carpets and chandeliers. The 'Blackmen' were sickened and angry, but when the fire crews withdrew, Sam Gardiner, the Worshipful District Master, and a colleague, Clive Higginson, entered the building and, through the smoke and burning embers, made their way to the lantern tower and unfurled a large Union Jack.[5] As it opened to the breeze, they defiantly shouted: 'No Surrender.' Within hours a team of architects was on the site drawing up plans to restore the mansion to its former glory, at an estimated repair cost of £5 million. The local brethren have accepted a heavy burden, but their aim is to rehabilitate the House not only for the use of loyalist Orders, but for the enjoyment of all the people of Lurgan and beyond.

Brownlow House continues to function as the home of several local preceptories and lodges. Among the quarters occupied by 'The Black' is the exquisitely furnished Cushnie Room, called after Alex Cushnie who worked for years in Brownlow House as Imperial Grand Registrar (1936-1978) of the Grand Black Chapter. Among the duties of the present Imperial Grand Registrar is the issuing of warrants to the 970 preceptories which come within the jurisdiction of Brownlow House. Geographically, the numbers are: Ireland 536; England 27; Scotland 62; Australia 20; Canada (called British America) 230; New Zealand 20; Togo one; Ghana one. All are issued on paper which shows the crest of the Order, the skull and crossbones. The skull stresses the impermanence of life and the pointless vanity of worldly matters, and the bones signify death, 'of which all should be reminded'.

The word 'Black' in the Order's name denotes that it is in mourning. The object of its lamentation is Joseph, the son of the Old Testament patriarch Jacob, who was sold into slavery in Egypt by his brothers. This story, with its motif of betrayal and wrongdoing, has great significance for 'Blackmen'. It enjoins them to be wary of false friends who might ensnare them into the arms of their enemies. The story is one of many chosen to provide allegorical messages, such as that of the Children of Israel in Canaan, overcoming corrupt and heathenish foes who seek to destroy them. These chronicles provide easily understood metaphors on the existential plight of Ulster Protestants and convey concepts of steadfastness, loyalty and religious purity — qualities which 'Blackmen' believe will be needed in a forthcoming apocalyptic struggle between the forces of Light and Darkness.

'Master McGrath'

No reference to Brownlow House would be complete without mention of 'Master McGrath', the world-renowned greyhound owned by Charles Brownlow, second Baron Lurgan, a noted track-racing enthusiast. Stories of this remarkable hound, who achieved fame by winning the Waterloo Cup in 1866, 1869 and 1871, abound, and there is a stone obelisk to his memory on the front lawn of Brownlow House.

He died of pneumonia shortly before Christmas, 1871. A newspaper account of his burial said:

> . . . When the dog was buried the tenants and retainers of the estate gathered together, each with a greyhound on the leash. Slowly they passed through the little gate, circled the lawn and around the little coffin, pausing for a moment before it. Then, out by the same gate an old retainer carried the oaken coffin to be buried amid the laurels some yards away.

There are monuments to 'Master McGrath' in Bury St Edmunds in Suffolk (where the Brownlows also had an estate) and in his native Dungarvan, and the Borough of Craigavon has given him pride of place in its armorial bearings.

The Sham Fight at Scarva

'The Blackmen' play a prominent role in the annual 'marching season' in Northern Ireland, which runs from late spring until the last Saturday in August. Virtually every weekend some Preceptory is on the march. 'The Black' does not, however, appear in full strength until the last day of the season, known as 'The Last Saturday'. They then meet at rallying points in the main towns and villages, and hold their biggest processions. But the greatest day in the calendar is 13 July when a popular spectacle is held in Scarva, a County Down village with a population of less than three hundred. Sham Fights were once held all over Ireland, but Scarva's is the sole survivor. Some say the Fight dates from a nearby clash between Peep O'Day Boys and Defenders in 1783, others date it further back. The sleepy village comes alive each year as 30,000 Orangemen (and not a few tourists) descend upon it. The tiny streets are hung with bunting, and the very kerbstones are painted red, white and blue. Vendors do a brisk trade in Orange souvenirs — everything from King William dolls to toytown replicas of Dan Winter's cottage is on offer — and local Protestant churches erect marquees in their grounds for the serving of refreshments. A 'must' for every child is to be photographed under 'King William's Tree' — a sprawling Spanish chestnut in the grounds of Scarva House, under which (as legend has it) King William rested on his way to the Boyne.

The day begins with a procession of over seventy Preceptories along a mile-long route to Scarva House, whose owners, the Buller family, lend their demesne for the day. The brethren look extremely respectable as they step along in their dark suits, bowler hats, black collarettes and Masonic-like aprons. The crowds swarm after them into the courtyard of Scarva House to hear the routine speeches, and then the stage is set for the Sham Fight.

To an explosion of loud drum rolls, 'King William', astride a white charger, leads his Protestant heroes against the cowardly 'King James' and his papist hordes. After about twenty minutes of scuffling with wooden swords, the Jacobean flag is thrown to the ground and 'James' flees with his head hung in shame. Then, to loud cheering, a triumphant 'King Billy' acknowledges the homage of the crowd before riding to the rear of Scarva House and oblivion. Protestant Ireland has been saved, and for the rest of the afternoon the crowds are free to picnic on the grass, or to stroll and listen to the soapbox preaching which is on offer every few hundred yards. It is a good Orange day out, and a carnival spirit prevails whatever the state of the weather.[6]

Royal Arch Purple Chapter

It was related earlier how Thomas Server and Harry 'The Shaver' Sling and others met in Armagh on 10 July 1820, to determine how the old Orange rituals (known as 'The Diamond System') could best be preserved. This gathering was seen as the beginning of the Royal Arch Purple Order, as it agreed that the Arch Purple degree should continue to be 'worked'. The structures set up at the time, however, were not formally endorsed by the Orange Order. In practice, the degree was 'worked' as a third Orange degree, but technically it was outside the Orange system. The arrangement was unsatisfactory, for without formal supervision a number of abuses crept in. It was not until 1911 that a recognised body was created to take responsibility for the degree. On 30 November of that year, the Grand Royal Arch Purple Chapter of Ireland was founded in the Orange Hall, Clifton Street, Belfast, and Lieutenant Colonel Sir William Allen, of Lurgan, installed as the first Worshipful

Grand Master. 'Purplemen', however, trace the true birth of their Order to the earlier date.

'The Purple', as it is known, has the lowest public profile among the Loyalist Orders. In the degree sequence it is sandwiched between 'The Orange' and 'The Black', and few outsiders are aware of its existence. Its members meet in 'Chapters' which are drawn from Orange lodges, and it is said that its initiation ritual is the most daunting of all the Orange ceremonies. In the past the ordeal which initiates had to undergo was so unnerving that a number of fatalities occurred. In 1893 a candidate named David Blair, while being initiated, was blindfolded and put standing on a table or chair; he fell over backwards, struck a sharp object, and lost his life. In 1927 a 'Purpleman' named Samuel Tweedie was charged by the police after accidentally discharging a loaded pistol at a candidate. In 1923 and 1930 the Grand Chapter appealed for subscriptions to benevolent funds to aid candidates who received injuries. It is unlikely that such mishaps could occur nowadays as lecturers, who are responsible for preparing candidates, are better trained, and candidates receive better tutoring in advance. In 1955 W.J. Moorhead, the then Grand Lecturer, introduced a Lecturer's Code to codify procedure; yet there are still rumours of candidates having to engage in tomfoolery around the Chapter floor, and of 'riding a billygoat' during initiation.[6]

The Royal Arch Purple ritual is the most 'Masonic-like' in the Orange system, but its theology is distinctly different from the comparable degree (the Holy Royal Arch) in Masonry. In the Arch Purple, the candidate is required to act out certain dramatic passages from the Exodus story. All the material is scriptural, and the prayers have a particular Christian orientation. In contrast, the Masonic degree mixes biblical references with what Masons call 'traditional history' or, in less varnished terms, with mythology. For instance, in the Book of Kings, when Solomon built his Temple in Jerusalem, he sent for a man called Hiram from Tyre to complete the decorations. Hiram was neither a mason nor an architect, but a worker in brass. A man of similar name did not enter Masonic ritual until the 1720s, when he was given the surname 'Abif' and styled 'the most accomplished mason who ever existed'. In fact, the latter character is a fabrication and unknown outside Masonry. No such constructs exist in the Arch Purple.

In other areas, the Arch Purple ritual is similar to that of Masonry. Candidates are blindfolded prior to entering the Chapter. Their left trouser leg is rolled above the knee and a slipper placed on the foot. Unbeknown to the candidate, a hangman's noose is placed around his neck and dropped down his back. Then, wearing a rough smock, he is made to look like a medieval heretic appearing before the Inquisition. All this is to denote that the candidate is entering the Chapter humbly and in a condition of poverty and that, irrespective of his social status, his standing in the lodge is similar to that of other brethren. The ritual corresponds in detail with Masonry.

There are stringent requirements on secrecy and the candidate must undertake to uphold Protestantism and adhere to the principles of the 'Glorious Revolution'. These obligations are set out in the 'Qualifications of a Purpleman':

> No person shall become a member of the Royal Arch Purple Chapter unless duly qualified, and of his own free will and accord; he shall voluntarily, solemnly and sincerely declare that he will never reveal unlawfully, but will ever conceal the proceedings of his Brother Royal Arch Purplemen in Chapter assembled, nor will he disclose any matter or thing therein communicated to him unless to a Brother Royal Arch Purpleman . . . He will to the utmost in his power support and maintain the Protestant Religion and Glorious Constitution of 1688, against all foes, foreign or domestic; that he will aid and assist all true and faithful Royal Arch Purplemen in all just and lawful actions, and will not wrong nor see any of them wronged nor defaulted, if in his power to prevent it . . . He shall further promise and declare never to marry a Papist, nor stand sponsor for a child of a Roman Catholic or Papist when receiving baptism from a Romish priest, nor allow a Papist to stand sponsor for his child when being baptised... He shall always obey, without scruple or reserve, in all things lawful, the bye-laws of his Chapter and the rules and regulations drawn up and published by the Grand Royal Arch Purple Chapter of Ireland.[7]

Ten main symbols connected with the Arch Purple degree are meant to convey the Morals and Dogma on which it is based. The word 'Dogma' is used in its old-fashioned sense, meaning 'doctrine' or 'teaching':

- The Open Bible — this is a fundamental symbol and stands for the truths on which the Order is based.

- The Ark of the Covenant — to serve as a reminder of God's promise to guide his children through the wilderness, that is, through life.

- The Anchor — to show that although life is a stormy voyage, with the anchor of truth man can safely reach the shore.

- The Ladder — this is based on Jacob's dream, and the letters CHF on the rungs stand for (backwards) Faith, Hope and Charity, which are virtues to be encouraged in everyday dealings.

- Noah's Ark — to recall the Flood and the Deluge; the means by which God purified His Creation and regenerated life on earth.

- The Five-Pointed Star — this is a symbol of fellowship with the equal points denoting that all men are dependent on each other.

- The Three-branched Candlestick and Candles — the branches stand for the Father, Son and Holy Spirit and the candles signify the light which assists men in their daily lives.

- The Coffin — this is a sombre reminder that no man knows when he will be called from his labour.

- The Sword pointed at the Heart — the sword represents Justice and the heart that this should be tempered with mercy.

- The Arch — also a basic symbol in Freemasonry where it refers to the building of Solomon's Temple. In the Arch Purple it means 'big' or 'great' as in 'archenemy' or 'Archbishop'. Thus the Arch Purple Degree is greater than the 'Plain Purple Degree'.

The Grand Masters of the Royal Arch Purple Order since its 're-construction' in 1911 have been:

Lieutenant Colonel Sir William Allen 1911

Right Honourable W.H.H. Lyons 1923

Sir Joseph Davidson 1924

James A. Barlow 1947

John McFall Hood 1955

J.A. Anderson 1972

Kenneth S. Watson 1985

Lieutenant Colonel Sir William Allen

While not as well known in national terms as Johnston of Ballykilbeg or Colonel Edward Saunderson, Sir William Allen was nevertheless an important figure who commanded great respect in County Armagh and represented the county at Westminster for thirty years. He served with the 36th (Ulster) Division, ending the Great War as a battalion commander. He was the son of Joseph Allen, one of the founders of Johnston, Allen & Co., linen manufacturers. In 1906 he launched out on his own and built a substantial linen-making business. Like many businessmen of his time, he believed that Ireland's well-being depended on maintaining the Union with Britain, and threw himself whole-heartedly into Unionist politics.

In 1902 Allen was instrumental in acquiring Brownlow House for the Orange Order, and was later prominent in the formation and training of the Ulster Volunteer Force. As the third Home Rule crisis unfolded, he served on the Ulster Unionist Council and became one of its Honorary Secretaries. At the General Election in December 1918 he was opposed by Ernest Blythe, a leading member of Sinn Féin and later Vice-President of the Executive Council of the Irish Free State. Allen polled nearly 80 per cent of the valid poll and had a majority of 7,379 over his opponent. On a number of subsequent occasions he was opposed by Republicans and Liberals, but secured overwhelming and convincing majorities. In 1923, 1931 and 1945 he was returned unopposed. In 1938, at a meeting to mark his completion of twenty-one years in Parliament, his constituents presented him with a motor car and a substantial cheque as a measure of their esteem. In December 1947, Sir William was knocked down by a lorry as he was getting off a tram in Belfast. He died a fortnight later and was buried in his native Lurgan. At eighty-one, he was the second-oldest member of the House of Commons.

The Association of Loyal Orangewomen

Women have never been given leave to join the Orange Order in Ireland, or any of its associate Orders, and there are no tantalising stories of them gaining admission by default as there are in Freemasonry (the most famous example in Masonry is that of Elizabeth St Leger, who stumbled on a lodge in her father's house at Doneraile, County Cork, in 1713 and was promptly initiated so that the 'secrets' which she learnt would remain intact). In Orangeism, female entry has never been an issue, primarily because women did not seem concerned to join. This did not mean that they felt less passionately about Orange principles than their brethren. In fact, of the 447,197 Ulster Protestants who signed the Covenant in 1912, a majority were women (228,991 women and 218,206 men), and a preponderance of these can be presumed to be Orangewomen. The best-known Orangewoman of all is, perhaps, the nineteenth-century novelist Charlotte Elizabeth Tonna (1790-1846), the daughter of a Norfolk clergyman who came to Ireland with her husband, an army officer, and later settled in Ulster. She wrote over thirty novels and numerous Orange ballads, like 'The Orangeman's Submission' — a protest against the suppression of the Order under the Unlawful Societies Act (1825).

The first Association of Loyal Orangewomen was founded in Dublin in the mid-nineteenth-century, based at Orange headquarters in the Fowler Memorial Hall. Its membership was comprised of middle-class women who enjoyed decorating King William's statue prior to Orange holidays and participating in charity work for poor Protestants. It developed many of the trappings of the male Order; its members met in 'lodges' and wore sashes during their meetings. It became dormant around 1887 and may have remained so had not

Papal policy provoked one of its former members to revive it. This was the promulgation by Pope Pius X of the 'Ne Temere' (literally, 'Not Rashly') decree on mixed marriages in 1908. The decree's main provision forbade marriages between Catholics and non-Catholics, but stated that dispensations may be obtained if certain written promises were provided. The non-Catholic party had to undertake to raise the children of the marriage in the Catholic faith alone. This requirement was objectionable to Protestants, and seen as insulting: a mixed marriage in a Protestant church, although valid in the eyes of the law, was declared no marriage, and the wife of such a marriage was said to be living in concubinage. On the other hand, if the parties opted for a marriage in a Catholic church, they could not be married before the altar but in a less sacred part of the church, and a nuptial mass was forbidden.

The decree caused great anger among Protestants, and meetings were held in Belfast and Dublin in protest. Protestant pulpits fulminated for months, and Orange polemicists depicted the decree as evidence of Catholic intolerance and spiritual tyranny. What upset many was the intimation by the Papacy that its Canon Law took precedence over the law of the land. This led to Orange claims that the Pope was seeking to undermine the Protestant constitution.

One person who was deeply upset was Mrs R.H. Johnstone of Bawnboy, County Cavan, wife of the Senior Deputy Grand Master. She had been a member of the old Association of Loyal Orangewomen and wished to revive it to run a campaign to discourage young Protestants from marrying Catholics. She applied to the Grand Lodge of Ireland for permission, and was helped by the case of a young Presbyterian girl, in Belfast, who had married a Catholic named McCann and had two children by him. The marriage was performed in a Registry Office and the girl, despite pressure from Catholic clergymen, refused to have the ceremony repeated in a Catholic church. The matter boiled over when McCann took the children from the family home to have them brought up by his parents. There was an immediate Protestant uproar and claims that the children were kidnapped. Protest meetings were held in various parts of Belfast, including a large one in the Assembly Hall where the Church of Ireland Primate, John Baptist Crozier, added his voice to the condemnations.

In December 1911, the Grand Lodge of Ireland gave the green light to Mrs Johnstone. The initial meeting of the new Association was held in the Fowler Memorial Hall, and Warrant No. 1 was issued to Mrs William Bridgett, who founded the first ladies' lodge in Sandy Row Orange Hall in Belfast. Warrant No. 2 went to Ballymacarret, and No. 3 to Kingstown (now Dún Laoghaire), County Dublin.

In the years following the hubbub over the 'Ne Temere' decree, the Association became less active. The 'Sisters', as they were called, did not go on parade unless invited to do so by specific Orange lodges; such invitations were few, and the 'Sisters' were left to do the domestic chores in the Orange Halls whilst the menfolk marched. In recent years, things have been changing. An increasing number of parades nowadays include ladies' lodges, and new lodges have been opened in the Irish Republic and in Northern Ireland. The most recent is the Aughlish Loyal Orangewomen's Lodge No. 148, founded in May 1998, in Aughlish, near Tandragee, County Armagh.[8]

The Loyal Orangewomen engage in fund-raising for the upkeep of Orange Halls and for the Lord Enniskillen Memorial Orphan Society. This charity was established in 1888 and is administered from the Grand Lodge of Ireland in Belfast. It is funded by donations from individual Orangemen, participatory fees from lodges, and the activities of the Orangewomen. It provides financial assistance to necessitous orphans of Orangemen whose widows are members of ladies' lodges. The assistance is often in the form of direct payment, but may include grants for specific purposes, such as medical treatment and bursaries for college or university. Its role became of particular importance during 'The Troubles' because of the number of fatalities to Orangemen.

The ladies' lodges operate under their own Grand Lodge and are independent of the Orange Order, although a close working relationship exists. The present officers of the Grand Lodge of Orangewomen are: Sister Doreen Williamson, Grand Mistress of Ireland; Sister Margaret Lewis, Grand Secretary; Sister Kathleen Weathers, Grand Chaplain.

The Junior Orange Association

In most Protestant communities in Northern Ireland, involvement with Orangeism begins at an early age and is considered a rite of passage. Young boys become eligible for membership of the Junior Orange Association at eight, and remain in its ranks until they are sixteen. The function of the Junior Orange Association is to inculcate in the young the principles of the Reformed Faith and to generally improve the moral climate in which they live.

Juvenile lodges first appeared in Belfast in the 1880s, but were not organised on a formal basis until after the First World War, by Tommy Henderson, a popular politician who represented the Shankill Ward in Stormont for nearly thirty years. Henderson and a colleague, Robert Hamilton, are also credited with leading the first Junior Orange parade at Holywood, County Down, in 1919. It was not until the 1930s that the Association really got off the ground, but much of its work was

undone by the disruption of the Second World War. In 1974 a Junior
Grand Lodge was founded on initiatives taken by the Grand Master of
the senior Order, Sir George Clark, and the Grand Secretary Walter
Williams.

The Junior Association organises youth programmes and runs a
residential hostel called Warren House, in Donaghadee, County Down,
where members spend weekends and holiday periods. The Association
is not without its critics. Some say that it is divisive in a society where
young Protestants should be allowed to integrate with youth of other
religions. Also, the Association has been accused of inculcating anti-
Catholic bigotry. One result of this is said to be the custom, beloved of
Orange youth, of painting the word 'Pope' on a football and ritually
kicking it around a field.

The Apprentice Boys of Derry

Thirteenth August 1873 was a great day for the Protestants of Derry.
From early morning they began to gather on the Walls, and in the
bright sunshine were entertained by Orange musicians from the
Fountain district on the west bank of the River Foyle. Around 11
o'clock they made way for a procession of smartly dressed
Apprentice Boys, which swung its way past the Royal Bastion and
into a nearby space known as Blair's Corner. Their Governor, John
Guy Ferguson, laid the foundation stone of a building which would
always have a special place in their affections, the Apprentice Boys
Memorial Hall.

The stone-laying ceremony was a colourful one, and thronging
around the Governor stood Apprentice Boys carrying banners which
depicted scenes from the famous Siege. Each man wore a crimson
sash in commemoration of the blood-red flag which had flown from
Saint Columb's Cathedral 185 years before. Ferguson had a keen
sense of history, and laid beneath the foundation stone a copper
casket containing objects of interest to posterity: a volume of
Hampton's *Siege of Londonderry*, coins of 1873, and a parchment
which had been inscribed with the names of the current leaders of
the Apprentice Boys. When the stone had been put in place, Ferguson
held his trowel aloft and said that the laying of the stone represented
years of hard work for a great and patriotic purpose, but soon the
Apprentice Boys would have a home of their own of which they
could be justly proud.

The building, in fact, took four years to complete and cost the then
princely sum of £3,250. Designed by Ferguson himself, it blended a
variety of styles, Tudor, Neo-Gothic and Scottish baronial. 'The

Mem', as it would be known, would go on to provide not only a seat for the Apprentice Boys, but a home for members of other Loyalist Orders who would establish lodge rooms within its hospitable walls.

The Apprentice Boys movement, the oldest in the Loyalist family, had been founded to honour the 'Brave 13' — the term used for the youths who closed the gates in 1688 — and to commemorate, twice annually, the great events of the Siege. Its purpose was celebratory, and it was conscious that the first celebration had taken place at the time of the Siege itself — on Sunday evening, 28 July 1689 — when the boom was broken and the starving citizens rejoiced in their deliverance. From the earliest days, the resident garrison had annually celebrated the Relief of the City. Infantry battalions marched on the Walls to martial airs, and gunners discharged the cannon. But the celebrations were always contingent on which regiments occupied the garrison and on the whim of the commanding officer. The Apprentice Boys movement represented the civilian community and was desirous that the celebrations be put on a permanent basis, irrespective of which regiment happened to be in town.

Their first club was founded by two Siege heroes, John Mitchelburn and Benjamin J. Daris, in 1714. These men began the yearly ritual of hoisting a crimson flag on the cathedral steeple, and discharging musket fire over the city gates. Their first celebrations went on for three days and included dining with their fellows at Bradley's Hotel in Gracious Street (now Ferryquay Street) and attending a gala dance in the Town Hall. The first club did not survive the death of Mitchelburn in 1721, but his own fame endured. For years after his passing, local Protestants assembled annually at the tomb in Glendermott Churchyard where he lay next to his old comrade in arms, Adam Murray.[8]

In the years which followed, a number of Apprentice Boys clubs were founded, named usually after Siege heroes. It was not until 1859 that they came under the supervision of a single ruling body. This was the Grand Committee of the Apprentice Boys of Derry, and the brain-child of Ferguson. But the early days of the movement were lean. The foundation of today's organisation was not laid until the 100th anniversary of the Shutting of the Gates on 8 December 1788. This was a notable event. The Reverend John Graham, in his book *The Siege of Derry and the Defence of Enniskillen* (Dublin, 1829), has left a vivid account:

> The dawn was announced by the beating of drums, the ringing of bells and the discharge of cannon, and a crimson flag, the symbol of the virgin city, was displayed on the cathedral. . . .

At 10.30 a.m. an impressive procession formed up on the Ship Quay, led by members of the Corporation, the Clergy, Royal Navy officers, the Army and the Londonderry Volunteers, merchants and principal citizens, and then the Apprentices. Preceded by Mr Murray (the great grandson of Colonel Adam Murray and carrying the sword with which his ancestor slew the French General Maumont!), this procession marched to the cathedral to listen to a fine sermon from Dean Hume. Meanwhile, 'HMS Porcupine', with cannon booming, turned up in the Foyle to do honour to the celebrations. The lower orders produced an effigy of Lundy, which they burned in the market place.

A significant feature of these celebrations was Catholic participation. The Catholic bishop of Derry, Dr Peter McDavitt, and a number of his clergy were present at the Thanksgiving Service in Saint Columb's Cathedral. Graham added:

At 4.00 p.m. all citizens, including the Roman Catholic clergy, sat down to a fine banquet in the Town hall. The guest of honour was an aged man who had been born just before the Siege and had survived within the Walls with his parents.

This harmony did not, unfortunately, long endure; later anniversaries were often marred by violence. It is not easy to pinpoint when the murder and mayhem began, or which side was responsible, but Catholics at some stage began a practice of shouting abusive language at the Apprentice Boys, and they, in turn, started to fling small coins from the walls at their impoverished opponents quartered below. Some of the Apprentice Boys clubs became increasingly aggressive and took to firing heavy musketry over the gates, and elsewhere. This behaviour led to clashes between the Apprentice Boys and the Town Constabulary.

The Walker Memorial

By the 1820s the Apprentice Boys movement was strong in numbers and, correspondingly, confident. A fresh 'Apprentice Boys of Derry' club was set up in 1814, and a 'No Surrender' club (called after the old watchword) came into being in 1824. Around this time plans were made to erect a monument to ex-governor Reverend George Walker. Among the larger subscribers was the Honourable Irish Society who presented a cheque for 50 guineas, and Londonderry Corporation who gave £50. In December 1826 the foundation stone of a fine 81-foot pillar, surmounted with a statue of Walker, was set in the Royal Bastion on the West Wall. It cost £4,200; its diameter was 6 feet 9 inches and it could be ascended on the inside by a staircase of 100 steps. Walker was shown in heroic pose, with his left hand pointing down the River Foyle to where the ships relieved the city. Huge marble tablets on the base of the monument gave the names of the principal Siege heroes, and the inscription read:

> This monument was erected to perpetuate the memory of Reverend George Walker who, aided by the garrison and brave inhabitants of this city, most gallantly defended it through a protracted siege from 7th December 1688 to the 1st August following, against an arbitrary and bigoted monarch, headed by an army of upwards of 20,000 men, many of whom were foreign mercenaries, and by such valiant conduct in numerous sorties and by patiently enduring extreme privations and sufferings, successfully resisted the besiegers and preserved for their posterity blessings of civil and religious liberty.[9]

In 1832 the tradition of burning the effigy of Lundy from the pillar began. At the time, passions were running high and the Party Processions Act was in force. The burning was regarded as a serious offence and a squad of police were assigned to prevent it. The Apprentice Boys duped them by concealing the effigy until the last minute and then igniting it as it swung from the pillar. The police arrested a number of Apprentice Boys and arraigned them before the local court.

Incidents of this sort continued for years, but the August 1860 celebrations were particularly troublesome. Because of the growth of the railways (particularly the opening of the Londonderry-Belfast line), greater numbers were able to enter Derry than before. The day prior to the celebrations, the Party Emblems Act received its second reading in the Commons and was likely to be carried soon. Because of this, the Protestant bishop, Dr Higgin, felt obliged to ban the crimson flag from the cathedral precincts and refused to permit the ringing of bells. The Apprentice Boys protested that they were not acting in a party spirit, but engaging in a civic activity. Besides, they asserted, the Emblems Act was not yet law. Dr Higgin, an Englishman, with perhaps an incomplete understanding of the mind-set of the Apprentice Boys, stuck to his guns. During the night 'The Boys' commandeered the cathedral and hoisted the flag. To the delight of their well-wishers it was fluttering from the steeple at sunrise. At 10.00 a.m. the infuriated bishop instructed the sexton to haul it down, but the Apprentice Boys intervened, took possession of the belfry, and ran the flag up again. The police were called, and when they failed to censure the culprits, word spread that they were in collusion with the Apprentice Boys.

The following year the police, at least initially, showed a different attitude towards the Apprentice Boys. A massive security presence was brought into the city, and the atmosphere became tense. The Apprentice Boys announced that they would forgo firing their muskets over the gates. Discipline, however, broke down and a number of die-hards insisted on firing their customary volleys. Despite the military and police presence, there was no move against them. They flew their flag from the cathedral, rang the bells and marched in a swaggering fashion along the circuit of the Walls. The only police activity was a baton charge against a few hundred residents of the Catholic Bogside who had shouted abuse and flung stones at the marchers.

In April 1869, Queen Victoria's youngest son, Arthur, Duke of Connaught, arrived in Londonderry for a brief stay. His presence inflamed partisan feeling, and serious rioting broke out. The police fired into a Catholic crowd, and killed three. A Catholic organisation, the Liberal Workingmen's Association, appealed to the Lord Lieutenant, John Poyntz, 3rd Earl Spencer, for protection against both the police and Apprentice Boy mobs. The Lord Lieutenant replied 'that all proper steps would be taken in the preservation of the peace'. The December celebrations of that year were quieter than usual and passed off without incident, although the Apprentice Boys were given a rousing speech by William Johnston of Ballykilbeg.

Johnston was also present at the August 1871 celebrations. As he led the Apprentice Boys to the cathedral, he was wearing a large crimson sash. The police stopped the march and asked him to remove the sash, but he refused. There was a hot exchange, and Johnston challenged a policeman to forcibly remove his sash. The Chief Constable arrived and, wary of arresting an MP while the House was sitting, prudently sent for a magistrate. The magistrate allowed the march to proceed, but in Bishop Street it was stormed by the cavalry and a pitched battle ensued. Time and again the Apprentice Boys showered the cavalry with stones and bottles. Desperate one-to-one tussles took place as the cavalry tried to grab the Apprentice Boys' sashes and tear them from their shoulders. In the following months, Johnston stepped up his agitation against the Party Processions Act.

The Later Apprentice Boys Movement

The twice-yearly celebrations of the Apprentice Boys have become an accepted feature of life in Derry, although the Catholics continue to resent them. Each celebration is heralded by the firing of cannon from a replica of an old siege gun, 'Roaring Meg'. Then visitations are made by members of the General Committee of the Apprentice Boys to the four historic gates — Bishop, Butcher, Ferryquay and Shipquay. Before setting off, they initiate new members at the Memorial Hall; a strict rule is that all initiations must take place within the Walls. Each new 'Boy' solemnly vows to honour the two annual days of commemoration (7 December and 12 August) and to keep evergreen the spirit of the 'Brave Thirteen'. Following a Thanksgiving Service in the cathedral, a wreath is laid on the Apprentice Boys' Mound — a grave in the precincts which contains the bones of former citizens (and among whom, it is presumed, are the remains of the original Apprentices). The mound is surmounted by a ten-foot pillar, whose base is inscribed with biblical quotations:

> This sacred spot shall remind us of duty well done in the past.
> May the God that stood by them still guide us in safety through the Tempest and Blast.
> Go search through the annals of story, on the bright scroll of flame it will be found.
> That the heroes most covered with glory are those that sleep in the Mound.
>
> Revelations 7: 14–17

Saint Columb's Cathedral

Today the cathedral holds a number of artefacts which are dear to the Apprentice Boys. In the porch is a large mortar shell weighing 270 pounds, which was fired into the city by the Jacobites containing their terms of surrender; on the north aisle are memorial tablets showing the names of past luminaries, including that of the Reverend George Walker; in the chancel are three flags captured from the French during the Siege (although their silk panels have been renewed a number of times, the flag poles and the wirework are original); above the choristers' vestry is beautiful stained glass depicting the Closing of the Gates (on the left), the Relief of the City (in the middle) and the Centenary Celebrations of 1789 (on the right). The corbels in the nave show the heads of bishops, including Dr Ezekiel Hopkins who held the See at the beginning of the Siege. In the baptistry is the Alexander Chapel, dedicated to the memory of Mrs Cecil Francis Alexander (1818–1895) who wrote some of the most poignant lines on the Siege. There is also a museum in the Apprentice Boys Memorial Hall which contains a number of artefacts dating to the Siege. A special room is set aside for the making of the Lundy effigy each year; this privilege rotates between the senior Apprentice Boys' Clubs.

Organisationally, the Apprentice Boys movement has a federal structure, with eight parent clubs grouped around the Central Committee. Each club has numerous branch clubs, of which there is an estimated 225. The total membership is somewhere between 10,000 and 12,000, with the true figure probably being nearer to the former. The structure is such that the senior membership in Londonderry has ultimate control.

—29—

Under an Orange Arch

Slaughter, slaughter, Holy Water
We will kill the Papists one by one
We will tear them asunder
Until they lie under
The Protestant boys who follow the drum.

— Derry street rhyme

The Brethren and their Lodges

The Loyal Orange Institution of Ireland (to give the Order its official designation) is, as its name suggests, an all-Ireland body. At its head is the Grand Orange Lodge of Ireland, located at 65 Dublin Road, Belfast, which superintends all subordinate lodges. The Order is, however, governed as much from the bottom up as the top down. The basic unit is the Private Lodge to which all Orangemen must belong; then comes the District and County Lodges. Each Private Lodge elects six representatives to a District Lodge, of which there are 126 in Ireland. District Lodges send delegates to one of twelve County Lodges, which control Orange affairs at county level. At the apex is the Grand Lodge, which is made up of 250 representatives from the county lodges and has a total membership of 373. From the Grand Lodge is drawn the powerful Grand Committee, which supervises internal discipline. There are also a number of authoritative sub-committees dealing with finance, education, press relations and the Order's monthly newspaper, *The Orange Standard*.

There are about 1,400 Private Lodges, each operating under its own warrant and with its own distinctive traditions, banners and names. Lodge names tend to be heroic-sounding and flamboyant: 'The Grange True Blues', 'The Derryadd Loyal Sons of Joshua', 'The Ballinary Chosen

Few'. Average lodge membership is around thirty, and they convene at Orange Halls, of which there are about 1,000 in Ireland. The overall membership is about 80,000, but the Order may be considered three or four times stronger if one takes account of family and kinfolk who may not be members but who share Orange principles. Lodges may be based at workplaces, social clubs, colleges or wherever a sizeable number of Protestants foregather (there is, for instance, a lodge in the House of Commons in London, founded by Sir James Craig in 1919). The main source of a lodge's income is subscription and initiation fees, and some lodges fare better than others, depending on the occupational profile of members. In urban areas, middle-class brethren tend to gravitate towards lodges consisting of their own kind. In the countryside things tend to be more democratic, and a wealthy farmer, for instance, may find himself on lodge evenings holding hands with one of his workmen and referring to him as 'brother'.

A lodge can have up to nine or ten officers: The Worshipful Master, two Wardens, a Treasurer, Secretary, two Deacons, Inner Guard and Tyler. A Master may also appoint a Chaplain, who most often is a clergyman. His function is to give prayers at the opening and closing of the lodge and at set times during ceremonies. If no Chaplain is appointed, the Master may instruct one of the brethren to act.

The Worshipful Master is the most important man in the lodge, and his office is the highest honour which his brethren can confer on him. He is elected by a ballot of members present at a specific meeting each year. He has a casting vote when any matter results in a draw. Second in seniority is the Senior Warden, who assists the Master and acts in his absence. Next comes the Junior Warden. He also assists the Master and is responsible for the admission of visitors and should, in theory, examine them. In practice, this is done by the Tyler. The Treasurer is elected by ballot and is responsible for finances, although most expenditure is voted on, as are proposed increases in lodge fees. The Secretary takes the minutes and issues summonses to convene meetings. Next come the Deacons, who act as messengers and bear commands from the Master to the Wardens. They carry wands denoting their office. The Inner Guard stands by the inner door and attends to knocks and signals. He also collects the password and forbids entry and exit without the permission of the Master. Then there is the Tyler, who is responsible for guarding the outside door against 'the profane' (known as 'cowans'). Among his manifold duties is the task of preparing candidates for entry to the lodge.

Orange and Masonic lodges are 'opened' in a similar fashion. A comparison of a Masonic opening (in the first degree of Craft Masonry) with a Royal Arch opening shows this similarity.

The Masons are assembled, and the Worshipful Master begins by asking a question of the Junior Warden:

W.M: What is the first care of every true Mason?

J.W: To see that the lodge is properly tyled. (The Junior Warden orders the Inner Guard to see that the lodge is properly tyled. The Inner Guard then gives one knock which is answered by the Tyler, and informs the Junior Warden that the lodge is properly tyled. The Junior Warden then gives three knocks and reports to the Worshipful Master.)

W.M: (to Senior Warden): What is the next care?

S.W: To see that none but Masons are present.

W.M: How many principal officers are there?

J.W: Three, namely the Worshipful Master, Senior Warden and Junior Warden.

W.M: How many assistant officers are there?

S.W: Three besides the Tyler, namely the Senior Deacon, Junior Deacon and Inner Guard.

The Purplemen are assembled, and the Worshipful Master begins the dialogue:

W.M: What is the first duty of a Royal Arch Purpleman in the Chapter assembled?

Deputy
Master: To ascertain that the door is guarded inside and outside by members of our Ancient Order, Worshipful Master.

W.M: Discharge that duty.

D.M: The door is properly guarded, Worshipful Master.

W.M: Brethren, stand while the Lecturers collect the annual, and report to me.

Lecturers: Worshipful Master, all correct on the Right; all correct on the Left. (The knocks of the degree are then given by the Worshipful Master and repeated by the Inner Board, and answered by the outside Tyler.)

W.M: Deputy Master and Brethren, stand to order and assist me in opening the Chapter.

Ritual of the 'Orange' Degree

It is not intended to trespass on the privacy to which Orangemen are entitled by describing their rituals in any detail. Suffice it to say that they hold these rituals in high regard and believe them to have a beauty and rhythm which allows them to tap into the wellsprings of their faith. Through the floor-work of the lodge these rituals give corporal

expression to passages from Scripture which illuminate concepts like
brotherhood, fidelity and integrity — all of which underlie their
obligations to one another, and to God.

The passages which follow detail the initiation ritual of the 'Orange'
degree as shown in Cleary's book *The Orange Society* (1897).[1] Over the
years this ritual has remained, by and large, unaltered, and it has
appeared, in one form or another, in many popular Orange publications.

The candidate is introduced between two sponsors — the brethren
who proposed and seconded his admission — carrying a Bible and a
copy of the Rules and Regulations. The Chaplain begins the dialogue:

Chaplain: Who will ascend the hill of the Lord or who shall stand in this
Holy Place? He that had clean hands and a pure heart, who
had not lifted up his soul to vanity nor sworn deceitfully. He
shall receive the blessing from the Lord, and righteousness
from the God of his salvation. (Psalm XXIV, 3–5)

(During this reading the candidate sits at the foot of a table, with the
brethren all standing in their places.)

Master: Friend, is it of your own free will and accord that you seek
admission into the Orange Institution?

Candidate: It is.

Master: Who will answer for this friend, that he is a true Protestant
and a loyal subject? (The sponsors bow to the Master and
signify the same, each mentioning his own name.)

Master: Have you duly considered the responsibility you have
incurred to the Institution at large, and this Lodge in
particular, in thus becoming a guarantor to us for this friend?

Sponsors: We have.

Master: It is required of you, in order to be a true Orangeman, that
you shall be faithful and bear true allegiance to Her Majesty
the Queen; that you shall support and maintain to the utmost
of your power the Laws and Constitution of Great Britain and
her colonies, and the rightful succession to the Throne of Her
Majesty's illustrious house, being Protestant, and that you
will always be ready and willing to aid and assist when
called upon, the Magistrates and Civil Authorities in the
lawful execution of their duties.

Chaplain: Let every soul be subject unto the higher powers, for there is
no power but the powers that are ordained by God; for rulers
are not a terror to good works, but to evil. Wilt thou, then, not
be afraid of the power? Do that which is good and thou shall
have praise of the same. Wherefore ye must needs be subject

not only for wrath, but also for conscience sake (Romans XIII, 1, 2, 3).

Master: Friend, it is required of you that you avoid, discountenance and repudiate all societies and associations which are composed of persons who seek to subvert the just prerogative of the Crown, the established rights of property, and the connection between the United Kingdom of Great Britain and Ireland.

Chaplain: (Quotes from Proverbs 1, 10-16)

Master: Friend, it is required of you that you be true and faithful to every brother Orangeman in all just actions, and never know him to be wronged without giving him due notice thereof. And it is also required of you that, should you now or at any future period be in possession of the electoral franchise, you will support by your vote and interest Orange and Protestant candidates only, and in no way refrain from voting remembering our motto: 'He who is not with us is against us.' Your neglecting to fulfil those conditions will render you liable to expulsion.

Chaplain: A new commandment, I give unto you, that you love one another (John XIII, 34). And this commandment have we from Him, that he who loveth God, loveth his brother also (I John IV, 21). I will not be ashamed to defend a friend, neither will I hide myself from him; and if any evil happens unto me by him, every man that heareth it will be aware of him.

Master: Friend, if it is not your determination to perform the duty and fulfil the expectation that I have now laid before you, you are at liberty to withdraw, rather than bring disgrace on your proposer, dishonour and expulsion on yourself, discredit on the Institution, and consequent injury on the cause we espouse. Friend, what do you carry in your hand?

Candidate: The Word of God.

Master: Under the assurance of your worthy Brothers who introduced you, we will trust that you also carry it in your heart. What is that other Book?

Candidate: The Book of Rules and Regulations. Master: With the like assurance we will further trust that you will study them well, and obey them in all lawful matters. Therefore, we gladly receive you into our Institution. Brethren, bring forward your friend.

(The Candidate is then brought to the right hand of the Master and kneels down to take the obligation:)

Candidate: I do solemnly and sincerely declare that I will be faithful and bear true allegiance to Her Majesty Queen Victoria; that I will to the utmost of my power support and maintain the Protestant Religion and the succession to the Throne in Her Majesty's illustrious house being Protestant, and that I will ever hold sacred the name of our Glorious Deliverer, William The Third, Prince of Orange; that I am not, nor never was, and never will be, a Roman Catholic, and that I am not married to one, nor will I marry one, or willingly permit any child of mine to marry one; that I am not, nor ever was, nor ever will become a member of any treasonable society or any body of men who are enemies to the lawful Sovereign or the Protestant Religion, and that I never took oath of secrecy to any treasonable society; that I will, as far as in me lies, assist magistrates and civil authorities in lawful execution of their duties, when called upon to do so; that I will be true and faithful to every Brother Orangeman in all just actions, that I will not wrong, nor know him to be wronged or injured, without giving him due notice thereof, if in my power so to do; and that I will not in any manner communicate or reveal, by word, act or deed, any of the proceedings of any Brother Orangeman in Lodge assembled, nor any matter or thing therein communicated to me, unless to a Brother Orangeman, well knowing him to be such, or until I shall have been authorised to do so by the Grand Lodge, that I have not to my knowledge or belief been proposed in or rejected by, nor suspended or expelled from any other Orange Lodge, and that I now become an Orangeman without fear, bribery or corruption, steadfastly resolving by God's help to observe and abide by all rules made by the government of the Orange Institution. . . .

Chaplain: (Quotes from Ephesians VI, 10–13.)

Master: We receive thee, dear Brother, into the Religious and Loyal Institution of Orangemen, trusting that thou wilt abide a devoted servant of God and a true believer in His son Jesus Christ, a faithful subject of our Queen and supporter of our Constitution. Keep thou firm in the Protestant faith, holding its pure doctrine and observing its holy precepts, make thyself the friend of all pious and peaceful men, avoiding strife, and seeking benevolence; slow to take offence, and offering none, thereby as far as in thee lieth, turning the injustice of our adversaries into their own reproof and confusion.

(Here the Master invests the newly made Orangeman with the insignia of the Order, and raises him by the hand, which he will hold while he repeats:)

> In the name of the Brotherhood, I bid thee welcome, and pray that thou mayest long continue a worthy Orangeman — namely fearing God, honouring the Queen and maintaining the Law.

Qualifications of an Orangeman

Prior to a candidate's initiation, his sponsors will have presented him with a booklet containing the Laws and Ordinances of the Institution, which says:

> The Institution is composed of Protestants, united and resolved to the utmost of their power to support and defend the Rightful Sovereign, the Protestant Religion, the Laws of the Realm and the succession to the throne of the House of Windsor, BEING PROTESTANT and united further for the defence of their own Persons and Properties, and the maintenance of Public Peace. It is exclusively an association of those who are attached to the Religion of the Reformation, and will not admit into its Brotherhood persons whom an intolerant spirit leads to persecute, injure and upbraid any man on account of his religious opinions. They associate also in honour of KING WILLIAM III, Prince of Orange, whose name they bear, as supporters of his glorious memory.

Elsewhere are listed the qualifications which a candidate must satisfy prior to joining a lodge:

> An Orangeman must have a sincere love and veneration for his Heavenly Father; a humble and steadfast faith in Jesus Christ, the Saviour of Mankind, believing in Him as the only mediator between God and man. He should cultivate truth and justice, brotherly love, kindness and charity, devotion and piety, concord and unity, and obedience to the laws; his deportment should be gentle and compassionate, kind and courteous; he should seek the society of the virtuous and avoid that of evil; he should honour and diligently study the Holy Scriptures, and make them the rule of his fate and practice; he should love, uphold and defend the Protestant Religion, and sincerely desire and endeavour to propagate its doctrines and precepts; he should strenuously oppose the fatal errors of the Church of Rome, and scrupulously avoid countenancing (by his presence or otherwise) any act or ceremony of Popish Worship; he should by all

lawful means resist the ascendancy of that Church, its encroachments and the extension of its power, ever abstaining from all uncharitable words, actions or sentiments towards his Roman Catholic brethren; he should remember to keep holy the Sabbath day and attend the public worship of God, and diligently train up his offspring and all under his control, in the fear of God, and in the Protestant faith; He should never take the name of God in vain, but abstain from all cursing and profane language, and use every opportunity of discouraging those, and all other sinful practices, in others; his conduct should be guided by wisdom and prudence, and marked by honesty, temperance and sobriety; the glory of God and the welfare of man, the honour of his Sovereign and the good of his country, should be the motives of his actions.

Some remarks may be made about these ordinances. Firstly, they suggest a candidate for membership should either be a saint or have a capacity for sainthood. Next, the requirements bear little relationship to Orangemen as known to the real world, where they are often seen as bigots, intolerant towards those who disagree with them. Thirdly, although an Orangeman is expected to act charitably towards Catholics he is forbidden, on pain of expulsion, from attending even minor Catholic ceremonies. This is a high-handed prerequisite, but expulsions for it have occurred. One of the most notorious accidents arose in 1966 when a Stormont MP, Phelim O'Neill (a cousin of the then Prime Minister) and the Deputy Lieutenant of County Antrim, Colonel Crammie, were arraigned before a Grand Lodge tribunal for attending a Catholic service during a civic-week festival in Ballymoney. Neither man attended the tribunal. The Central Committee took two years to reach its decision to expel the culprits.[2] But expel it did, although its decision was largely academic, for long before both men had lost interest in the Order.

A similar case involved another Stormont MP, Nat Minford, who attended the opening and blessing of a Catholic school in his constituency. He consented, however, to appear in the Orange dock and was let off with a caution. These incidents caused minor stirs. The leader of the Nationalist Party at Stormont, Eddie McAteer, felt that he was on to something and asked the Speaker, Sir Norman Stronge, whether 'dictation by the Orange and Black Orders to Unionist MPs infringed the privilege of the House'. Without much adjudication, Sir Norman ruled in the negative. At the time he was Sovereign Grand Master of the Royal Black Preceptory.

Romish Rigmarole

The Grand Lodge did not take the adverse publicity from the church attendance incidents lying down. It stated that the Order, like all organisations, had a right to expect its members to obey its rules. Its views on such matters were in line with the teachings of most Reformed Churches — that Catholic ceremonies are unscriptural and therefore a peril to the pure strain of Christianity, embedded in Protestantism.

These points, of course, have some validity but, like the lofty language of the Ordinances, would carry greater weight if Orangemen did not habitually assail the religious beliefs of Catholics. An example is found in the official brochure of the County Armagh Grand Lodge published in July 1995, to commemorate the 305th anniversary of the Battle of the Boyne. Page one shows the laudable 'Qualifications of an Orangeman' but a later page has a poem entitled 'Romish Rigmarole', which reads:

> Holy fathers and holy mothers, Holy sisters and holy brothers,
> Holy daughters and holy sons, Holy wafers and holy nuns.
> Holy scapulars, holy beads, Holy water and holy creeds,
> Holy mortar and holy stones, Holy rags and holy bones.
> Holy pictures, holy bells, Holy sounds and holy smells,
> Holy visions and holy signs, Holy mounts and holy shrines.
> Holy lamps and holy altars, Holy albs and holy halters,
> Holy statues, holy copes, Holy city and holy popes.
> Holy wells and holy grottos, Holy 'stations' and holy motto's,
> Holy oils, unholy scandals. Holy smoke, both black and white,
> Holy days and holy light, Holy crozier and holy ring,
> Holy every kind of thing —
> Masses, transubstantiation, Intention, penance, and vocation.
> Novenas, decades, Mariolatry, Patron saints and foul idolatry,
> Concommitance and prayers for the dead, Peter's pence, Saint
> Anthony's bread.
> Pardons, bulls and dispensation, Celibacy, unction, veneration,
> Seven sacraments, fast in Lent, Forged Decretals and Council
> of Trent.
> Pilgrimages, incantation, Octaves, retreats, and invocation,
> 'Nummy Dummys' and absolutions, genuflections and convolutions.
> Indulgence and 'True Church' boasts, The Adoration of the 'Host',
> Infallibility, supererogation, Interdicts and excommunication.
> Anathemas, auricular confession, Complines, aves, intercession.
> Beautification and hagiology, Polytheism from old mythology,
> Never was seen such an unholy brew — A seething, reeking nephritic
> stew.

Now blind belief in this rigmarole
Does not save the devotee's soul,
And all his faith is rendered nugatory
When at the last he enters Purgatory,
There to roast mid fire and curses
Till all his friends have empty purses.

Through Ecumenists would in this nonsense join,
Yet WE are as those who won the Boyne,
And he who once has 'ridden the goat'[3]
Should never want to turn his coat.
WE trust in God, our Great Defender,
And our watchword still is 'NO SURRENDER'.

— Daisy Hill

Orangeism and Freemasonry

Orangeism and Freemasonry are frequently compared, and the former is sometimes held to be a development within the latter. Both Orders, in fact, deny any connection. An article in *The Freemason's Pocket Reference Book* (revised, 1965 edition) describes the Orange Order as 'A militant anti-Catholic society' and goes on to say:

> Some of the early ritual and symbolism is believed to have been 'borrowed' from Freemasonry, but it need hardly be stated that there has never been the slightest connection with the Craft, in fact in the early 19th century private Masonic lodges not infrequently forbade their members to have anything to do with certain organisations, including the Orange.[4]

It is, of course, true that Freemasons were among the founders of the Orange Order and that the Masonic model was readily adopted. This, however, tells us little. Freemasons were among the founders of many contemporary societies which were the very antithesis of Orangeism, such as the republican Society of United Irishmen. Besides, it was commonplace in the late eighteenth and early nineteenth centuries for new societies to imitate Masonry.

The most significant and, indeed, fundamental difference between the two Orders is that one is unequivocally Christian (and forthrightly Protestant) and the other is Deist. As we have seen, the Laws and Ordinances of the Orange Order state

> the Institution is composed of Protestants, united and resolved to the utmost of their power to support and defend . . . the Protestant religion. It is exclusively an association attached to the religion of the Reformation.

Freemasonry admits to membership candidates who believe in a 'Supreme Being' whom it styles 'The Great Architect of the Universe'. This Being is not necessarily the Christian God and can be interpreted variously. It may be the Jewish or Muslim God, or the god of any monotheistic religion. Orangeism holds that the godhead is reached exclusively through Jesus Christ, whom it terms the Saviour of Mankind. Another difference is that Masonry draws on pre-Christian mysticism, Gnosticism, and even elements of paganism in its workings. Orange ritual, by contrast, is based exclusively on biblical material, and excludes what Masons call 'traditional history'.

The Eleventh Night

The greatest date in the Orange calendar is 12 July, and many Orangemen like to arrange their holidays to coincide with it. In Belfast there is a general flutter for weeks before. Orange arches are thrown across streets in Protestant areas, and Union Jacks are hung from upstairs windows. On gable ends, murals show King William, on his white steed, victoriously crossing the Boyne; the kerbstones are picked out in red, white and blue paint.

Traditionally, the celebrations begin with 'The Eleventh Night' (11 July) when dozens of streets compete with each other in making massive bonfires. From as early as March, youths scour all around for combustible material to put on the blaze. By early July the rubbish pile may be as high as fifty or sixty feet. Then, as the countdown begins, an Irish tricolour and an effigy of the Pope are placed on top. By 11.30 p.m. on the night, the 'Billy Boys' — the toughs with the tattoos on their arms and rings in their ear lobes — roll out of the pubs and make their way towards the fun, singing and swilling from their beer cans. The air is full of excitement and the 'auld ones' are on their doorsteps waving their Union Jacks. The street comes alive with merriment and children run around wildly, chanting: 'We are, We are, We are the Billy Boys!', or 'Yippie, Yippie, Yippie, the Pope is a bloody hippie.'

On the stroke of twelve, Molotov cocktails are flung on the pile and, to a gathering roar, the flames shoot into the sky. All around there is cheering and dancing. When 'old red socks' (the effigy of the Pope) catches fire there is a visceral roar, and this is repeated when the tricolour falls from its perch. The party continues until, little by little, everyone drifts away to their beds to be ready for the serious business on the morrow.

'The Glorious Twelfth'

It is old and it is beautiful, and its colours they are fine
It was worn at Derry, Aughrim, Enniskillen and the Boyne

My father wore it as a youth in the bygone days of yore:
So on the 'Twelfth' I'll always wear the sash my father wore.

The words and the tune of 'The Sash' — the most famous of all Orange
songs — are well known. So, too, are the images which they suggest:
men in bowler hats, with ornamental cuffs on their serge suits; rolled
umbrellas; fanatical youths, blue in the face from hammering on large
lambeg drums; swaggering marchers — proud as peacocks — stepping it
out on their way to The Field to hear the old harangues of paralysing
boredom about the wiles and conspiracies of Rome.

This is a scene from an Irish Mardi Gras; it is also something else: a
ritual which takes place all over Northern Ireland as the brethren
celebrate the Orange victory at the Boyne, and pledge their loyalty to
Queen and country.

The biggest parade is held in Belfast, where over 300 lodges and
innumerable bands assemble and set off from Carlisle Circus. The show
begins with the evangelical sandwich men who march ahead of the
parade, their placards splattered with biblical texts. Their message is
sombre: 'Repent, the wages of sin are death' and 'The end is nigh'. Then
the smartly dressed brethren come into view, headed by the Miller
Memorial Flute Band followed by officials from the Grand Lodge and
dignitaries from abroad. Next come the forty lodges (each led by its own
band) of the large Ballymacarret District (LOL No. 6) who are given
pride of place, with the other nine Belfast Districts following in their
wake.[5]

They march down Clifton Street, into Royal Avenue, around City
Hall, then out along the Lisburn Road towards The Field at Edenderry,
seven miles away. Each man is wearing his best attire, has white gloves,
an Orange collarette and a black bowler — evoking a kind of foreman's
respectability. All the lodges march as units under their distinctive
banners which provide a sort of moving cartoon on the great events in
Orange history. Some banners show portraits of Protestant divines, and
others evoke images of the days of British imperial splendour, like that of
Queen Victoria and Prince Albert graciously receiving the Bible from an
African youth, over the caption:

The secret of England's greatness.

Marching with each lodge is its band; sometimes it is part of the lodge
itself, but more often it is hired for the day. The uniform of the musicians
varies from the full Highland dress to the more modern cutaway jacket
and striped trouser leg. In front is a young baton twirler; the manner in
which he tosses his staff into the air and deftly catches it is a sight to
behold. Also accompanying the marchers are groups of middle-aged

women, who trip along close to the pavements. They are dressed in costumes made entirely of Union Jacks and have great fun waving their red, white and blue parasols.

Nowadays the bands have abandoned the old sectarian tunes like 'Croppies lie down' and 'Kick the Pope', and harmless numbers like 'The Fields of Athenry' and 'You are my Sunshine' have entered the repertoire. The lambeg drum is no longer carried in Belfast, as its great weight tended to slow things down. It is, however, alive and well and found on rural parades. The lambeg is seen as a weapon of psychological warfare, as its great cannonade can drive fear and trembling into the hearts of the disaffected. Each drum is given a name, such as 'The Cock of the North' (with a picture on the frame of a splendid crowing rooster), or 'The Orange Conqueror'. It is usually four feet wide and five feet in diameter, and tattooed with malacca canes bound to the wrists of the drummer by leather straps. When the drumming frenzy heightens, the drummers' hands are often slashed open and blood spatters against the drumhead.

The Belfast parade can take nearly four hours to pass a given point and the marching is exhausting. By the time the brethren reach The Field, they have slowed down to a limp. As they 'fall out', their wives and families arrive with picnic baskets and 'temperance beverages'. A few hundred gather around a platform and listen to their leaders make predictable condemnations of the Irish Republic, and matters such as a visit of a member of the Royal Family to the Vatican. They then spread themselves out on the grass, eat their sandwiches, and watch the young bloods and their paramours coquet behind the bushes. If the weather is warm they will remove their jackets and roll up their sleeves, but the bowler and orange collarette remain 'in situ'. Around 6.00 p.m. they wearily retrace their steps back to their Orange Halls, satisfied that they have done their bit for Queen and country.

Up the Shankill

The Shankill Road in West Belfast is the undisputed epicentre of Orange working-class culture and the place where all the great symbols of Orangeism — the gable-end paintings, the street arches, the bonfires and flags — are regularly found. Orangeism has set this proud, tough and fiercely loyal community apart.

The name Shankill means 'old church', and the first settlement in the area was a religious foundation established in the time of Saint Patrick. Locals refer to the area as 'The Road', which technically starts at Peters Hill and comes to an end below Woodvale Road. But many dispute what the signs say, and insist that the Shankill also takes in North Street, Smithfield, Peters Hill itself and all the small streets along the way. It is a lively place, habitually thronged with shoppers, and receives its flavour from the evangelicals who set up their pitches at various points to let off steam at the ungodly. The Shankill does not, however, lack more worldly entertainments; there are pubs, clubs and entertainment arcades which cater for all the senses. Sitting on a bar stool, one can still hear stories of how Percy Street was bombed in the blitz of 1941, and people will swear that the Catholics in the Falls area guided the Nazi bombers with torchlights over the city. How else, they will say, did the Falls remain unscathed while the rest of Belfast was bombed? And they will give you dark hints that the bombing of Belfast resulted from a secret plot between the Vatican and the Third Reich![6]

The great citadel of Orange life on the Shankill is the West Belfast Orange Hall, situated on the corner with Brookmount Street. Since the early days of the Order in Belfast, this has been the home of lodges in the famous No. 9 District. Old Orangemen tell stories of the lodges and preceptories which have met under its roof, and of the great personalities with whom they marched on 'The Twelfth'.

Away from the Order, many stories are told of how men from 'The Road' went 'over the bridge' (to Harland and Wolff's shipyard on the other side of the River Lagan) to work as joiners, riveters and iron turners and, in the process, build some of the finest ships in the world. But the thesis that the Shankill worker was part of a proletarian elite will be doubted on hearing of the continual round of toil and sweat which he endured. A bitter but poignant poem by Robert Atkinson tells its own story:

> It's right that we should rise at six
> With bleary eyes our porridge mix
> Make a 'piece' of cheese and bread
> Wish that we were still in bed.
>
> It's right that we should daily toil
> Work machines and dig the soil
> Drill the holes, read the gage
> All to get a lowly wage.
>
> It's right that we should know our place
> When learning how to say 'our Grace'
> To touch our caps and bend our knees
> To those who have a life of ease.

It's right that we should be oppressed
Do everything at their behest
Be always humble, keep the rules
For after all, we're bloody fools.

What Price Orangeism?

Being an Orangeman costs money. Although fees differ from lodge to lodge, the average Orangeman pays about £100 a year in dues, sometimes considerably more. This, of course, only gets him inside the lodge door. The cost of regalia has been steadily rising and all the items can come to a princely sum. A basic collarette costs upwards from £30, depending on the level of durability required — those with a leather backing can last for a generation. A decent bowler hat cannot be bought for less than £50. The tradition of wearing a bowler is said to have come from the shipyards, where foremen often wore them as symbols of status. A pair of good white gloves cost around £6; these are a symbol of being well dressed, but have only been worn since the 1950s. A pair of sensible 'marching' shoes is not an optional extra for an Orangeman; given the numerous miles he is expected to tramp each year, they are a pre-requisite. They cost around £50. A reasonable umbrella — a symbol of dignity and style — comes at around £15. Then there are small items like the 'jewels' which are worn on collarettes to designate the number of degrees taken. The cost of these can vary from a few pounds to £60, depending on whether they are hand-painted or not. Some brethren are avid collectors and spend a small fortune acquiring them.

Most of the large lodge banners start at £1,200 and are often renewed to reflect matters of contemporary importance. One example is that of Tullyallen Orange Lodge, near Newtownhamilton in South Armagh; when some of its brethren were killed in 'The Troubles',[7] the lodge commissioned a new banner to commemorate them. Another big expense is the hiring of bands for 'The Twelfth' and other marches. Nowadays a band costs at least £600.

Ireland's Heritage LOL 1303 and 'Tara'

Early in 1970, The Grand Lodge of Ireland wrote to a Belfast private lodge, Saint Mary's Temperance Lodge 1303, giving it permission to change its name to Irish Heritage LOL 1303. The new name was understood to be indicative of the views of the lodge membership, who believed that the entire island should be won back to Protestantism and that the pre-twelfth century Irish Church (which, it felt, had been uncontaminated with popery) should be re-established. These views were part of an assortment of views not generally held by Orangemen. Others included the belief that Irish Protestants had a Gaelic heritage, from which political circumstances had compelled them to retreat, and which they should reclaim. In undertaking the retrieval, the brethren believed that they might go a step further and recover the entire thirty-two counties.

These ideas originated in the mind of William McGrath, the effectual founder of the lodge, who, with his unique communication skills, had persuaded his brethren of their validity. At this time he was in his early fifties and an influential figure in Belfast Orangeism. If his views on Irish history were somewhat odd, so too was his design for the lodge's banner. On one side there were emblems of Ireland's four Provinces, surmounted by a harp and crown; on the reverse were the words 'Oidhreach Éireann' (Ireland's Heritage) and a large map of the thirty-two counties above a quotation from Luke 19: 13, 'Occupy till I come.'

In the mid-1960s, McGrath sensed that the pot in Northern Ireland was about to boil over, and formed a secret loyalist organisation called Tara (after the site of the palace of the old Gaelic kings, in County Meath). This later took on a paramilitary character and attracted a number of figures who became prominent in unionist politics. By 1961 its membership had increased considerably, and it issued a statement urging all loyalists to organise themselves into platoons of twenty under the command of someone capable of acting as sergeant. The organisation saw a 'doomsday' scenario developing, in which British troops would be abruptly withdrawn and the Protestants faced with military invasion from the South. Many Orangemen took this analysis seriously and flocked to Tara. The organisation provided a template for Orange hard-line opinion, and its pronouncements touched a chord in people who were prepared to jump into the trenches. On 20 June 1974 it took a full page advertisement in the *Belfast News Letter* which began:

> Being convinced that darker days than we have yet known still lie ahead for the people of Northern Ireland, we address ourselves to those who wish to preserve for ALL THE PEOPLE OF IRELAND the heritage of faith and freedom that has been almost extinguished in a large part of our land and which is now threatened with extinction in the North-East corner of Ulster. The aim of the enemy is the destruction of our Protestant faith. This they hope to achieve by creating a total war situation in which the Eire army will cross the border and unite with the Provisionals and Regular IRA who are already in our midst . . . What has happened in our Province during the past few years is not just a series of local riot situations, but rather the beginning of the final chapter of an age-long campaign to

subjugate and subdue the Protestant people of Ireland. This is an essential preparation for the campaign against the Protestant character of the British Throne. This situation will continue to grow in intensity until the final battle. . . .

After outlining how Protestants must prepare for combat, the Proclamation continued:

The Roman Catholic Church must be declared an illegal organisation. History proves that it is a conspiracy against the fortunes and liberties of mankind. For generations this evil thing has blighted our land. It must be destroyed so that our fellow countrymen, who have been deceived by it, will have an opportunity of entering into an eternal relationship with God through Christ and of discovering their common identity with us. The indivisible oneness of the Irish people will then become a reality. . . .

It concluded:

The situation is dark. The enemy is strong. Great and grievous difficulties will have to be faced, but all is not lost! Ulster is God's anvil on which is being forged the future not only of Ireland, but of all the British people of which we are proud to form part. Knowing this, we throw down the challenge to a desperate foe — hammer away, ye hostile bands, your hammers break, God's anvil stands.

Underneath was a biblical quotation:

Five of you will chase a hundred, and a hundred of you shall put ten thousand to flight: and your enemies shall fall before you by the sword . . . for I will establish my covenant with you . . . and I will cut off the names of the idols out of the land and they shall no more be remembered . . . for the mouth of the Lord hath spoken it.

It is important to emphasise that Tara was never formally linked with the Orange Order (nor did it ever become a proscribed organisation), but because of the affiliations of its membership, it became associated in the public mind with the Order. Besides, McGrath regularly used Orange Halls when promoting his views, and his lodge regularly met in Clifton Street Orange Hall in Belfast.

In time, whispers spread about McGrath's private life and there were unsubstantiated rumours that he was an M15 agent. The membership of Tara dwindled; a number of the hard-line types drifted towards the UVF and others took up conventional unionist politics. In 1981 McGrath was jailed for sexual offences against boys under his care at the Kincora Boys' Home in East Belfast, and was expelled from the lodge which he founded. In the blaze of adverse publicity which ensued, the remaining members of LOL 1303 found it expedient to wind up the lodge. To McGrath and his brethren, 'doomsday' had arrived, too soon and in unexpected garb.[8]

—30—

International Orangeism

Here I am a loyal Orangeman, just come across the sea
For singin' and for dancin' I hope that I please thee
I can sing and dance like any man, as they did in the days of yore,
And on the 'Twelfth', I'll always wear the Sash My Father Wore.

— second verse of 'The Sash My Father Wore'

Distant Drums

During the nineteenth century, Orangeism spread to many parts of the English-speaking world, transplanted by soldiers, emigrants and missionaries. Its origins in Canada and Australia suggest that it followed in the wake of the army. In New Zealand the first lodge was established by an emigrant from County Wicklow, and missionaries are reputed to have carried it to West Africa in the years before the First World War.

Canada

In Canada its growth was rapid. A military lodge was operating in Halifax, Nova Scotia, as early as 1799, and the following year one was functioning in Montreal. The first Orange marches were held in 1818, but the Canadian Order did not become structured until Ogle Robert Gowan, an illegitimate son of the notorious John Hunter Gowan in Wexford, formed the Grand Lodge of British-America in Brockville, Ontario, in 1830. Gowan held a warrant signed by the Duke of Cumberland and became Deputy Grand Master, as the Duke held the title of Imperial Grand Master.[1]

Orangemen were amongst Canada's foremost pioneers. As the country opened up, lodges could be found from the farmlands of Ontario to the mining regions of Nova Scotia; they appeared in the prairie lands of Alberta, Saskatchewan and Manitoba, and in the fishing grounds of Newfoundland. In Ontario, Orangeism attracted the Mohawk tribes on the Six Nation Indian Reserve at Brantford, and a number of Indian lodges were established, some of which still exist. The tribesmen usually wear their regalia with their traditional Indian headdress and make a colourful sight.

In 1866 a force of Irish-American Fenians invaded Canada, led over the frontier north at Buffalo by the intrepid Colonel John O'Neill. As part of the Canadian militia, Orange lodges marched to meet them at Limestone Ridge on 2 June.[2] The Fenians, cut off from reinforcements and low in ammunition, were forced to retreat. During the emergency the annual meeting of the Grand Lodge of Canada was postponed, because most of its officers and about 1,000 members had responded to the militia call-out.

Historically, Orangeism has been very influential in the public life of Canada; by the 1870s about one-third of the country's male Protestant population were either active or former members of the Order. It built the powerful Protestant machine which shaped Canadian politics for more than a hundred years. In Toronto, for instance, most of the city's mayors during the nineteenth and early twentieth centuries were Orangemen, and elsewhere hundreds of high officials, aldermen, judges and clergymen were members of the Order. It had strong parliamentary muscle, and prime ministers like John A. McDonald and Mackenzie Bowell were leading Orangemen; Bowell was Grand Master of the Canadian Order for many years.

In 1867 the Imperial Grand Orange Council of the World was founded on a Canadian initiative. As early as 1833, Ogle Robert Gowan had proposed the formation of a body to co-ordinate the activities of Orangemen internationally. The Council held its first meeting in London in 1867 and its second in Toronto in 1869. Mackenzie Bowell presided over a meeting of the Council held in Derry in 1876.

In Canada, the lodges work five degrees, the lowest being the 'Orange' and the highest the 'Scarlet', members of which are eligible to become Royal Black Knights of the Camp of Israel, the Canadian equivalent of the Royal Black Preceptory. As in Ireland, the lodge structure is fourfold, though the lowest level, the primary lodge, is sometimes omitted.[3] The Canadian Order runs a well-established membership insurance scheme and maintains homes for necessitous children and senior citizens. Its newspaper, *The Sentinel*, appears ten times a year. The last Canadian Prime Minister to be an Orangeman was John Diefenbaker, leader of the Progressive Conservative Party, who held office between 1958 and 1963.

Australia

Orangeism in Australia dates from 1830, when the 17th Leicestershire Regiment arrived in New South Wales with a warrant (No. 260) granted by the Grand Lodge of England. A number of other regiments with warrants followed, and a small nucleus of lodges developed. Because of regimental comings and goings, roots were not properly set down until the establishment of a Grand Lodge in Sydney in 1845. In 1848 the first 'Twelfth' Orange parades took place in Sydney and Melbourne.

At this time about a quarter of Australia's population were of Irish Catholic descent (they had first arrived as convicts and later as free settlers) and had an abiding hatred of Orangeism. Clashes between the two groupings were frequent, and each 'Twelfth' was an occasion for running battles provoked by either side. In Melbourne the Catholics made a practice of organising hurling matches to coincide with Orange parades, to ensure that enough of their supporters were present to mount attacks. In the 1840s many of the riots went on for several days, and on one occasion a popular Catholic priest, Father Patrick Geoghegan, was fatally shot by an Orangeman. The most notorious incident was in Sydney in 1868 when, in the suburb of Clontarf, a member of the Australian Fenian Brotherhood, called O'Farrell, tried to assassinate the visiting Prince Alfred, Duke of Edinburgh. Feelings ran high among Protestants throughout the country, and the membership of the Order shot up by 30,000 in a single month.[4]

In 1854 the first lodge in South Australia was formed in Port Adelaide, and by 1865 the Order spread to Queensland, where a Grand Lodge was formed two years later. Orangeism took longer to penetrate West Australia, where the first lodges did not appear until 1886, and a Grand Lodge was not established until just before the First World War, in 1913.

Today Orangeism is organised in each Australian state, and in New South Wales and Victoria it runs homes for the elderly and disabled.

New Zealand

Orangeism in New Zealand dates from 1842 when James Carlton Hill, an emigrant from County Wicklow, arrived with a warrant (No. 1707) which had been granted by the Grand Lodge of Ireland ten years earlier. He found Orangemen thin on the ground, and placed an advertisement in an Auckland newspaper stating that he proposed to establish a lodge, inviting eligible Protestants to join him. About a dozen responded, and an induction meeting was held in the Osprey Hotel on High Street. It was successful, and the first lodge was formed a little later in the Masonic Hotel on Princess Street.[5]

Immediately the new lodge ran into trouble. Irish Catholic emigrants got wind of its existence and began intimidating inn-keepers and hoteliers who offered rooms for lodge meetings. Finally, the lodge rented a private house but, after a single meeting, was informed by the landlord that it must leave. He had been told that his property would be burned down if further meetings took place. But the Orangemen were not deterred. The lodge grew and strengthened, notwithstanding occasional ups and downs. It was not until 1867 that a Grand Lodge was formed, by which time the Order had spread to the South Island.

A unique feature of Orangeism in New Zealand is that it is of mixed gender. Male and female lodges developed simultaneously on both the North and South islands. In 1908 the Grand Lodges of both islands amalgamated to form the Grand Lodge of New Zealand. At the time there were sixty male lodges on the North island and eleven female. On the South island there were thirty-three male and fifteen female. Today, lady members hold executive posts at every level. The headquarters are in Christchurch, where the Order runs a Protestant bookshop and publishes its own journal.

The United States

Orangeism appeared in the United States around the time of its advent in Canada (1799). As this was its first showing outside British territory, it had to tread warily and adapt itself to political and constitutional forms which it did not necessarily favour. It was unable to tap into the ruling elite as easily as before, but banged the Protestant drum on numerous issues which made it attractive to social and religious conservatives. In some respects it shared the sentiments of the 'No-Nothing' party, voicing rhetoric which appeared to be white supremacist and excluding from its membership those who were not 'free-born citizens'. Its main focus was on protecting the Protestant values of white, Anglo-Saxon Americans, and in opposing Catholicism and the incoming famine- stricken Irish.

There were a number of lodges in New York by 1820, but the first 'Twelfth' parade did not take place until 1824 when over 200 Orangemen marched in Boston. During the 1860s Orangemen had numerous clashes with Irish immigrants in New York, particularly with members of the Ancient Order of Hibernians. One of the most notorious occurred in 1867 when dozens of Irish workingmen attacked an Orange function in Elm Park. In the resulting riot, nine people were killed and over 100 injured.

These confrontations occurred with regularity on every 'Twelfth'. The one which excited the greatest attention (and resulted in the largest number of fatalities) arose from a wrangle in 1871. The Orangemen were determined to march and the Ancient Order of Hibernians were determined to prevent them. The Mayor of New York, Oakley Hall, came down on the side of the Hibernians and banned the Orange march. There was a great Protestant outcry, and people who were unconnected with either side felt that the Orangemen had been treated unfairly. The mayor was accused of anti-Orange bias (he had in fact marched with the Hibernians on the previous Saint Patrick's Day) and the bickering continued in the press for several days. At the last minute the Mayor's ruling was overturned by Hoffman, the Governor, and the march was permitted. The Orange turnout was relatively small; many Orangemen had gone to a New Jersey march instead, because of the uncertainty. About 500 brethren set off, guarded by a strong force of police, but the march was continually disrupted and had to be abandoned near the Cooper Institute on Fourth Avenue, when a riot ensued. The death toll was almost 60 (including six policemen) and over 300 were injured. Subsequently the police were accused of pro-Irish bias, as charges were not pressed against large numbers of Hibernians who were arrested.

In the United States Orangeism has always played second fiddle to other ultra-conservative organisations, and it never reached anywhere near the influence which it had in Canada. Because of the large Irish Catholic population in the North Eastern conurbations, it came off second best in street brawls and in time became somewhat muted. In 1912 it split into two antagonistic factions — the Lemmonites and the Kirklandites — called after a Past Grand Master, the Reverend George Lemmon, and William Kirkland, the Grand Secretary. This complicated dispute had as much to do with the personalities of the leaders as with the points of policy and principles involved. Some of the issues resulted in legal battles which went on until 1930, when the Lemmonites admitted defeat. The rival Grand Lodges which had sprung up amalgamated later that year, but eighteen years of acrimonious division left its mark and Orangeism in the United States never fully recovered.

Today there are about sixty lodges in twelve states, and the total membership is around 3,000. Most of the lodges celebrate the 'Twelfth' but in a low key. The parades are small and are held in local precincts rather than in downtown areas. The day is seen as an occasion when Orange families picnic in municipal parks under their banners.

West Africa

A familiar sight at the 'Twelfth' celebrations in Belfast each year are Orangemen from West Africa. The history of Orangeism in the region presents a problem, as it is not known when exactly it was introduced. There has been a presumption that its pioneers were missionaries from Ulster, but the information is scanty. The first African lodge appeared in Lagos in 1907 and was called the 'Lagos Fine Blues LOL 801'. It comprised of black Africans, and the warrant number originated in the

Woolwich District Lodge in south London, but that lodge had no connections with Nigeria. It did, however, have associations with military lodges in Egypt, where British servicemen were stationed. Orangeism may have been transplanted to Nigeria from this quarter.

An Orangeman from Lagos, John Amate Atayi, was responsible for taking Orangeism to Togo, when he and a few friends established 'The Lome Defenders of the Truth LOL 867' in 1915. This is the home lodge of the best known of all African Orangemen, Emmanuel Essien, who was elected Imperial President of the Order in 1994.[6]

The first lodge in Ghana, the former Gold Coast, was established when a post office worker at Cape Coast named R.E. Sharley received a copy of the *Orange Standard*. He was so taken by what he read that he contacted the Grand Lodge of England, and arrangements were soon agreed for the formation of a lodge. Today, there are about two dozen lodges in Ghana and church parades are held regularly.

Scotland

Scottish Orangeism can be traced to the Williamite period through organisations like the 'Old Revolutionary Club', which was established to keep the memory of William green. Following the founding of the Order and the advent of military lodges, a number of Scottish regiments were granted warrants. In 1798 the Dumbarton Fusiliers returned from Ireland with warrant No. 573, followed by the Duke of York's Own Highlanders (with warrant No. 841) and the Argyllshire Fusiliers (with warrant No. 915).

For years Orangeism in Scotland came under the jurisdiction of the Grand Lodge of England, but when this was wound up in 1836, Scots brethren refused to quit and founded their own Grand Lodge which met in the King William Tavern in Gallowgate in Glasgow. The Order was later strengthened by the migration of shipyard and engineering workers from Ulster to the Clyde at the end of the nineteenth and early twentieth centuries. The Order put down strong roots in Glasgow, Ayrshire, Renfrewshire and Argyllshire, and in central and eastern Scotland. Today Scotland has about 300 lodges (the largest number outside Ireland) and a membership of about 20,000.[7] It is the only jurisdiction outside of Ulster where the Orange band tradition developed; it has about 150 bands, some of which are of the highest standard, and many of these travel regularly to Northern Ireland to participate in parades, often being hired by Irish lodges. In Scotland, Orangeism is largely a working-class phenomenon and, in politics, many of the brethren are inclined to support the Scottish National Party (which, although not a unionist party, would retain the Queen as head of state in an independent Scotland) and the British Labour Party.

England

In the twentieth century, the great centre of Orangemen in England has been in Liverpool. About two-thirds of the 250 lodges which come under the jurisdiction of the Grand Lodge of England are on Merseyside, particularly in Kirby, Bootle, Birkenhead and the City of Liverpool. The other centres of Orangeism tend to be the large industrial conurbations of the north and Midlands, with the south poorly represented. Few of the lodges outside Merseyside nowadays owe their existence to migrants from Ulster, but to the settled English community.

In Liverpool Orangeism goes back a long way and, in spite of its often tattered reputation, was able for decades to marshal sufficient working-class votes in support of local Tories to keep control of the City Council out of the hands of liberals and socialists. An early triumph came in December 1867 when it successfully put pressure on the Lord Mayor, Edward Whiteley, to ban a march which Fenian sympathisers had planned in protest at the hanging of Allen, Larkin and O'Brien — the Manchester Martyrs — a few months before. The Order later thanked the Lord Mayor for his action.

The Order's influence probably peaked in 1903 when a leading Orangeman, W.W. Rutherford, became Lord Mayor and began to consolidate the Orange-Tory alliance to maximise Protestant working-class support. The alliance was able to exploit the deep prejudices which existed against the large Irish Catholic community, which at that time was living on the poverty line. Among the most prominent was the Reverend George Wise, of the Protestant Reformers Chapel on Netherfold Road. He was a senior Orangeman and, besides hating Catholics, his followers objected to any form of ritualism in the Church of England — even two candles burning on an altar was seen as a popish practice. Protests were held outside Anglican churches, and rallies of thousands of people were organised. The anti-Catholic abuse which poured forth led to Catholic counter-demonstrations, and the police grew alarmed and had Wise bound to the peace. He refused to accept the court's ruling and argued that he was being denied freedom of speech. When he was committed to Walton prison over 5,000 of his followers accompanied him to the prison gates. Rutherford, the Orange Mayor, was among those who organised a petition to the Home Secretary for his release, and the Lady Mayoress and her daughter visited him during his incarceration. Following his release in June 1903, Wise was soon back in action; within weeks he led 2,000 of his followers across the Mersey to Birkenhead, where clashes took place with local Catholics and numerous arrests were made.

Between 1904 and 1909, Liverpool experienced the most bitter sectarian violence in its history, and George Wise and his friends were at the centre of it. The worst clashes took place during the annual marching season, and it was not unusual for the rival sides to use knives, iron piping and even swords in combat. Time and again hundreds of people were intimidated from their homes, and working-class areas were segregated into Protestant and Catholic. The violence continued up to the First World War, when the participants found themselves playing real war games on the Western Front. In the post-war years slum clearances and re-housing, plus the dawning of a more tolerant age, weakened the animosities. After the Second World War, most of the Protestant working-class in Liverpool drifted from Orangeism as matters of religious and ethnic dispute became secondary to other concerns. It is significant that when the brethren in Liverpool objected in December 1995 to the city being twinned with Dublin, they could only muster 373 signatures on the petition of protest which they presented to the Liverpool City Council.[8]

Appendix A

— Maps —

MAP 1: THE ROUTE OF WILLIAM'S FLEET — 1688

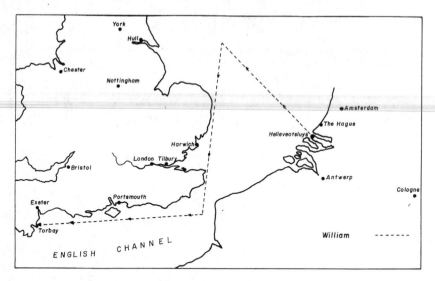

William's fleet left Helleveotsluys on 1 November 1688 and landed in Torbay on 5 November. It initially sailed north but changed course on 2 November when the famous 'Protestant Wind' took it past the Straits of Dover and on to the south-west coast.

MAP 2: THE ROUTE TO LONDON — 1688

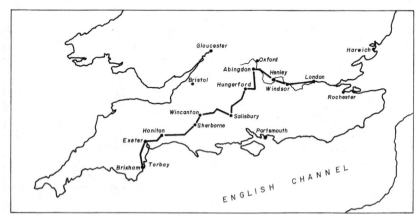

The route that William's army took from Torbay to London — 5 November to 22 December 1688

MAP 3: THE WILLIAMITE CAMPAIGN IN IRELAND — 1689–1691

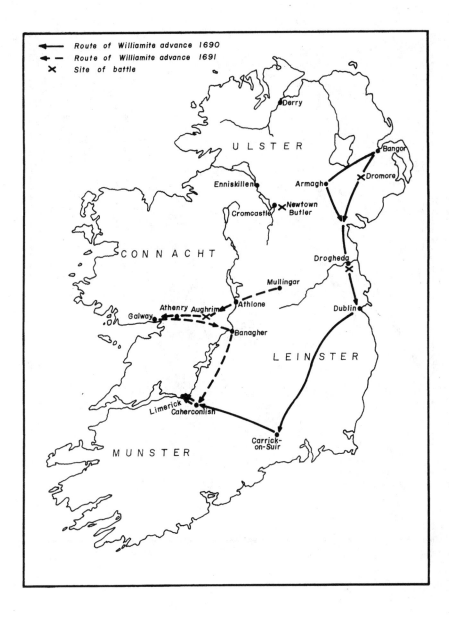

MAP 4: THE SIEGE OF DERRY — 1689

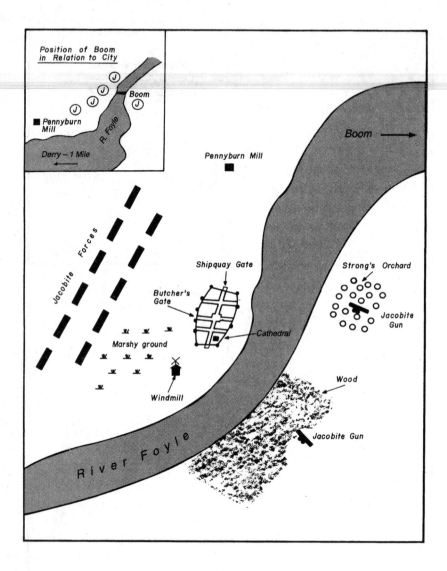

MAP 5: THE BATTLE OF THE BOYNE — 1690

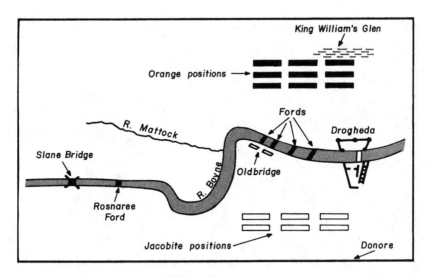

Plan of Battle of the Boyne the original date of which was 1 July 1690. The official anniversary only became 12 July after the Gregorian calendar was introduced to Britain in 1752.

MAP 6: THE SIEGE OF LIMERICK — 1690

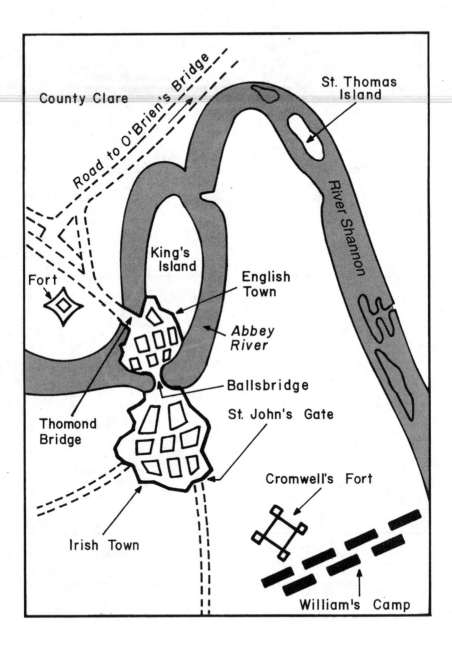

MAP 7: SARSFIELD'S RIDE— 1690

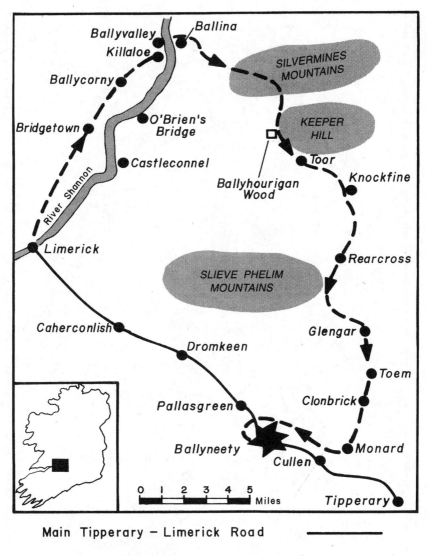

Main Tipperary – Limerick Road ——————

Sarsfield's Ride – – – – – –

MAP 8: PLAN OF ATHLONE — 1691

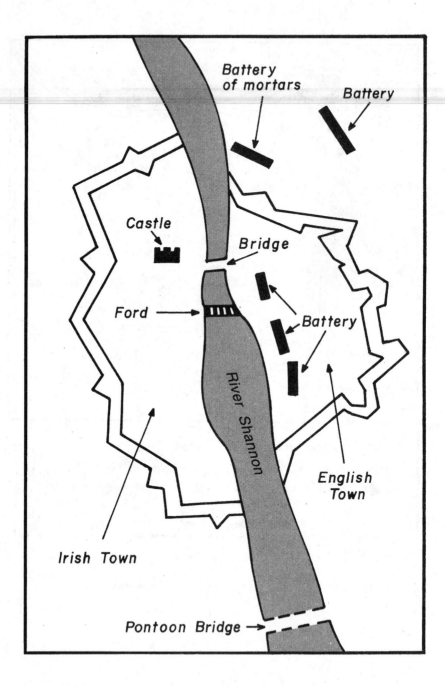

MAP 9: THE BATTLE OF AUGHRIM — 1691

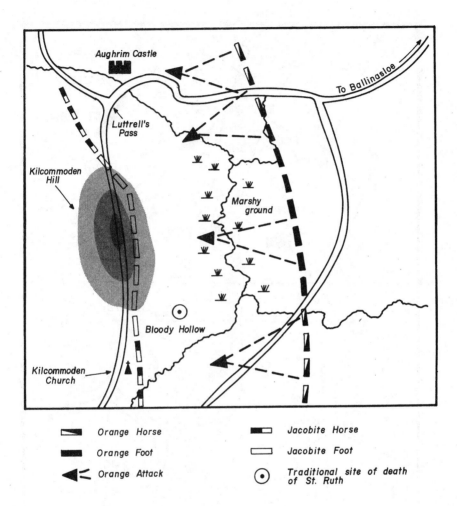

◣ Orange Horse	◆ Jacobite Horse
■ Orange Foot	☐ Jacobite Foot
◀ Orange Attack	⊙ Traditional site of death of St. Ruth

MAP 10: THE BATTLE OF THE DIAMOND — 1795

5.00 am — Monday 21 September

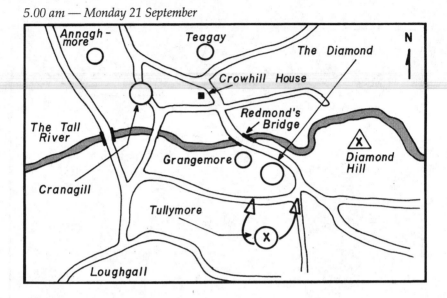

5.00 am — Monday 21 September

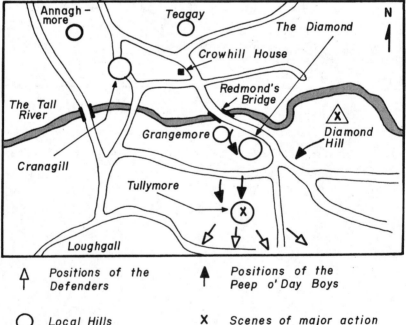

Positions of the Defenders   Positions of the Peep o' Day Boys

Local Hills   X   Scenes of major action

MAP 11: ORANGE LODGES IN IRELAND — 1798

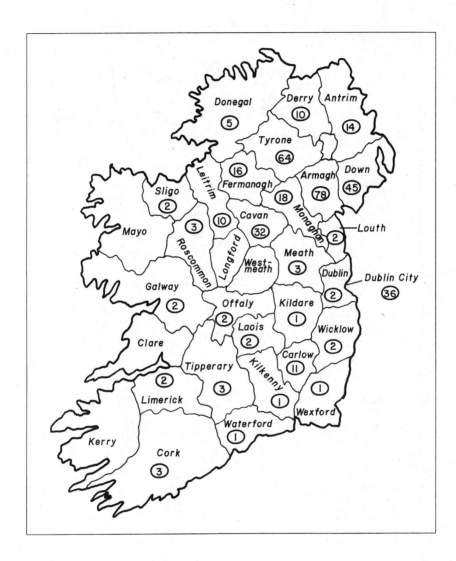

MAP 12: ORANGE LODGES IN IRELAND — 1990

Appendix B

Leaders of Orangeism in Ireland and
Grand Masters of the Grand Lodge of Ireland

Colonel William Blacker (1797)

Colonel Thomas Verner (1798)

Rt. Hon. George Ogle, MP (1801)

Lieutenant General Mervyn Archdall (1819)

Rt. Hon. Charles Henry St John, Earl O'Neill (1821)

HRH Ernest Augustus, Duke of Cumberland (1827)

Rt. Hon. John Willoughby Cole, 2nd Earl of Enniskillen (1828)

Rt. Hon. Robert Jocelyn, Earl of Roden, MP (1836)

Colonel William Willoughby Cole, 3rd Earl of Enniskillen (1846)

Rt. Hon. John H. Crichton, Earl of Erne (1886)

Rt. Hon. James H. Stronge, Bart (1914)

Rt. Hon. William H.H. Lyons (1922)

Rt. Hon. Sir Edward Archdale, Bart, MP (1924)

Rt. Hon. Senator Sir Joseph Davidson (1940)

Rt. Hon. John Miller Andrews (1948)

Rt. Hon. Sir William McCleery (1955)

Captain Sir George Clarke (1958)

John Bryans, J.P. (1969)

Rev. W. Martin Smyth, MP (1972)

Robert S. Saulters (1996)

Appendix C

Grand Lodge of Ireland Office Holders 1998

Grand Master:	Robert S. Saulters
Grand Chaplains:	Reverend Edwin Colvin
	Reverend Canon Dr S. Ernest Long
	Right Reverend D.W. Heavener
	Reverend Dr William Warren Porter
	Reverend Gerald N. Sproule
Grand Secretary:	John McCrea
Grand Treasurer:	Mervyn Bishop
Executive Officer:	George Patton
Grand Lecturer:	John Curry

Appendix D

Addresses of Orange Grand Lodges

Ireland:
House of Orange
65 Dublin Road
Belfast, BT2 7HE
Northern Ireland

England:
c/o Liverpool Provincial Club
108 Everton Road
Liverpool L6 2EP
England

Scotland:
P.O. Box 16190
Glasgow G11 6YD
Scotland

Australia:
P.O. Box 26
Croydon
New South Wales 2132
Australia West

New Zealand:
P.O. Box 6145
Upper Riccarton
Christchurch
New Zealand

USA:
1315 Biggs Road
Oak Hill
Wilmington
Delaware 19805
U.S.A.

Canada (British-America):
House of Orange
94 Sheppard Avenue West
Willowdale
Ontario M2N 1MP
Canada

Togo:
B.P. 204
Lome
Togo
West Africa

Ghana:
P.O. Box 1641
Accra
Ghana
Africa

Appendix E

This lists the major loyalist parades which take place during the 'marching season', which runs from March to August and is resumed for special commemorative parades in October and December. The precise dates vary from year to year, but most are held on the nearest weekend to the commemorative date.

Easter Monday:	Major Apprentice Boys of Derry parade in Derry.
Easter Tuesday:	Junior Loyal Orange Association parades at selected venues throughout Ulster.

June:

10	'Mini-Twelfth' parade by Orange Order in Portadown.
Third Friday	North Belfast 'Mini-Twelfth'.
Fourth Saturday	West Belfast 'Mini-Twelfth'.

July:

1	Battle of the Somme commemorative parades throughout Ulster.
Saturday before the 12th	Donegal lodges parade in seaside village of Rossnowlagh, County Donegal.
Saturday before the 12th	Orangemen in Scotland parade in Glasgow and at various centres throughout the Strathclyde region.
Sunday before the 12th	Orange Order Church parades throughout Ulster.
12	Major Orange Order parades at nineteen venues throughout Ulster.
12	English Orange lodges parade at Stockport near Manchester.
13	Royal Black Preceptory parade preceding sham fight at village of Scarva, County Down.

August

12   Apprentice Boys of Derry parade to commemorate the 'Siege of Derry'.

12   Royal Black Preceptory parade to commemorate the 'Battle of Newtownbutler'.

October

Last Saturday   Royal Black Preceptory holds major parades at six Ulster venues.

Last Sunday   'Reformation Day' church parades by Orange Order throughout Ulster.

18   Apprentice Boys of Derry parade to commemorate the 'Closing of the Gates'.

Appendix F

The House of Orange–Nassau in the Netherlands and Britain

Princes, Stadholders and Kings — 1533–1704

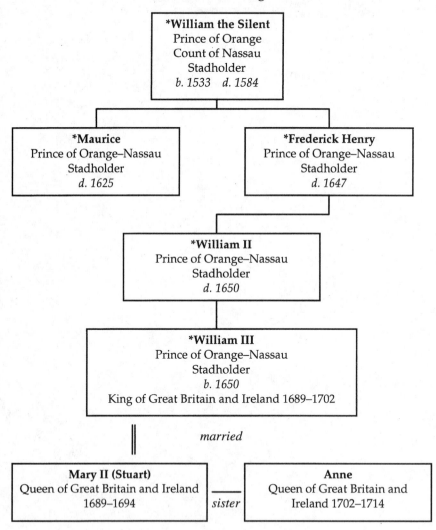

*William the Silent
Prince of Orange
Count of Nassau
Stadholder
b. 1533   d. 1584

*Maurice
Prince of Orange–Nassau
Stadholder
d. 1625

*Frederick Henry
Prince of Orange–Nassau
Stadholder
d. 1647

*William II
Prince of Orange–Nassau
Stadholder
d. 1650

*William III
Prince of Orange–Nassau
Stadholder
b. 1650
King of Great Britain and Ireland 1689–1702

married

Mary II (Stuart)
Queen of Great Britain and Ireland
1689–1694

sister

Anne
Queen of Great Britain and
Ireland 1702–1714

*   These five Princes (William the Silent to William III) were Stadholders of five of the United Provinces — i.e. all but Friesland and Groningen.

Appendix G

Degree Structures in Loyalist Orders

The Royal Black Institution
(meets in 'Preceptories')

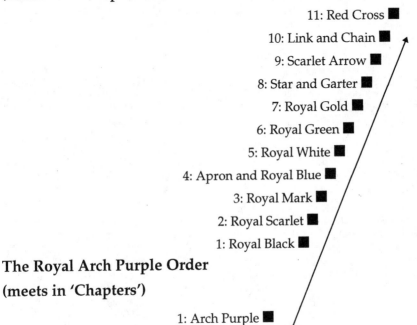

11: Red Cross ■

10: Link and Chain ■

9: Scarlet Arrow ■

8: Star and Garter ■

7: Royal Gold ■

6: Royal Green ■

5: Royal White ■

4: Apron and Royal Blue ■

3: Royal Mark ■

2: Royal Scarlet ■

1: Royal Black ■

The Royal Arch Purple Order
(meets in 'Chapters')

1: Arch Purple ■

The Orange Order
(meets in 'Lodges')

2: The Plain Purple ■

1: The Orange ■

> The Degree Structure begins with 'The Orange' degree in the Orange Order and ascends to the 'Red Cross' degree in the Royal Black Institution. Candidates for the Royal Arch Purple Order degree must be members of the Orange Order. Candidates for the Black degrees must have previously taken the Royal Arch Purple Degree.

Glossary

Apprentice Boys of Derry
The oldest of the loyalist fraternities, based on a group of 'parent clubs' founded to commemorate the 1688-89 Siege of Derry. The first club was founded by Benjamin J. Daris in 1714. Today there are eight 'parent clubs', each of which has numerous branches, with a Central Committee based at the Apprentice Boys Memorial Hall in Derry.

Apprentice Boys do not necessarily have to be Orangemen, but must be Protestants and be initiated into the fraternity in a ceremony held within the Walls of Derry. They wear crimson collarettes to symbolise the crimson banner which flew from Saint Columb's Cathedral during the Siege. The main days of commemoration are 18 December (the Shutting of the Gates) and 12 August (the Relief of the City).

Arch, Orange
Decorative arches are erected annually in Protestant areas of Ulster in celebration of the Orange victory at the Battle of the Boyne. The Roman practice of erecting arches in honour of victorious military commanders lasted in a number of European countries until the late eighteenth century, and the first recorded Orange arch was erected in The Hague in 1691 in honour of King William. Sibbet says that they were erected in Coleraine in 1801, and Gamble mentions one in Tandragee in 1812, which was 'gracefully blended with oak leaves, laurels and roses'. Nowadays Orange arches are a common feature of the 'Twelfth' celebrations and are erected near Orange halls, along processional routes, and in Protestant neighbourhoods. Arches are decorated with symbols from Orange ritual such as the three-runged ladder, the square and compass, the anchor, and the coffin, and are blazoned with such slogans as 'Remember 1690', 'God Save the Queen' and 'This We Will Maintain'.

Banner
The use of large banners in Orange parades dates from the rise of the trade union banner in the mid-nineteenth century; earlier Orangemen paraded behind flags and pennants. Initially, scenes from the Williamite War were the most popular subjects, followed by representations of figures from the Old Testament. Following this, portraits of Protestant divines such as Luther, Latimer and Ridley appeared. In the early twentieth century, portraits of Orange Grand Masters began to be seen, together with depictions of Orange halls, churches and industry-related images. In recent years an innovation is the portrayal of brethren who have lost their lives in the 'Troubles'. For many years the Belfast firm of Bridgett Bros. (founded in 1878) was a prime supplier of banners to lodges in Ulster, as was the English firm of trade union banner makers, Tutill's. A key element in the production of attractive banners was the growing interest of professional painters, and not a few well-known contemporary artists have tried their hands at banner-painting.

Bowler hat
The bowler hat, named after the hatter who developed it, originated in London in the 1850s. In the late nineteenth century it became a symbol of authority in a number of trades and was worn by supervisors, inspectors and foremen in the Belfast shipyards. During the period of the 1912 Home Rule crisis, the brethren frequently paraded before high dignitaries and were anxious to give an air of respectability; the wearing of a bowler was seen as a necessary accompaniment to a smart suit. In recent times this Orange convention has come under threat, as long-haired youths (particularly in Belfast) have been reluctant to undergo the haircutting necessary to look well in a bowler. The wearing of white gloves is of more recent origin, dating from the 1950s and adopted to give added style to the ensemble.

Dan Winter's cottage
A vernacular pre-1760 cottage on the Derryloughlan Road, near the Diamond Crossroad, a few miles from Loughgall, County Armagh, where the decision to establish a defensive society, later called the Orange Order, was made. The cottage and surrounding farmlands are still owned by descendants of Dan Winter. The official Department of Environment

schedule states: 'This house is accepted as the meeting place following the Battle of the Diamond, where the decision to form the Orange Order was made.' The owners were descendants of a John Winter who was recorded in the Ballyhagan Quaker Meeting House records of 1665 as 'a farmer/weaver'. Today the cottage is an Orange museum and contains maps, old family papers, relics of the battle, and other memorabilia.

Dolly's Brae

A narrow roadway between Castlewellan and Ballyward in County Down, which, on 12 July 1849, was the scene of a violent clash between Orangemen and Catholic 'Defenders' in which up to thirty Catholics lost their lives. The affray was the subject of a controversial public enquiry and led to the passing of the Party Processions Act (1850), which banned Orange parades. The sixteen-verse song 'Dolly's Brae' recounts the Orange version of events.

Flute Band

The first Orange flute bands date from the early nineteenth century, among the oldest being Churchill (Londonderry, 1835) and Hamilton (Londonderry, 1850). They copied military bands, at a time when flutes were relatively cheap and easily available. Initially the tunes played were adapted from German, American and British compositions, but soon Orangemen began to compose their own marches. Today there are an estimated 500 flute bands in Ulster. Virtually every street in Protestant working-class areas of Belfast has its own band, and centres like Armagh, Ballymena, Portadown, Lisburn and Lurgan have up to twelve bands each. The average age of band members is between sixteen and twenty, and joining a band is a rite of passage for many working-class Orange children. Nowadays bands are usually hired through advertisements in the Order's newspaper, *The Orange Standard*.

House of Orange

The headquarters of the Loyal Orange Institution of Ireland, at 65 Dublin Road, Belfast.

Independent Orange Order

A breakaway fraternity from the Orange Order, founded in 1903. Initially led by Thomas Sloan, a former shipyard worker who became an MP, and Robert Lindsay Crawford, a Lisburn-born journalist, it grew to fifty-five lodges (most of these were newly formed, rather than having transferred from the old Order). In 1905 the Independents issued the controversial 'Magheramorne Manifesto', which described unionism as a 'discredited creed' and said that it held out the hand of friendship to 'those who worship at different shrines'. In the years prior to the Home Rule crisis of 1912, the leadership split on a number of issues and support declined. The Order still survives, mainly in North Antrim. Among its recent leaders were William Percy, Imperial Grand Master, and George Dawson, Imperial Grand Secretary.

Junior Orange Association

Junior Orange lodges first appeared in Belfast in the 1880s but had a precarious existence until Tommy Henderson, a popular politician from Belfast's Shankill Road, took an interest in them around 1919. They were finally put on a firm footing by Sir George Clark and Walter Williams in the early 1970s, and a Junior Grand Lodge was founded in 1974. Today junior lodges exist in most Orange districts of Northern Ireland, and young Protestant boys are eligible to join between the ages of eight and eighteen. The function of the Junior Order is to inculcate in Protestant youths the principles of the Reformed Faith and to prepare them for membership of the senior Order.

Lambeg Drum

A large cylindrical drum, usually three foot wide and four foot in diameter, made from goatskin stretched over an oak frame. The drum is thought to be descended from the war drums used by King William's Dutch Blue Guard. It is beaten with twelve-inch malacca canes and, when hit strongly at high speed, can reach 120 decibels — the threshold which the human ear can bear without damage. The drums are usually lavishly painted and given such names as 'The Cock of the North', 'The Smasher' or 'The Orange Conqueror'. In rural areas, drum-beating competitions known as 'stick-ins' are a frequent pastime.

'Lilliburlero'

Probably the oldest Orange song in existence, attributed to the Whig politician Thomas, 1st Marquess of Walton (1648-1716). King William's chaplain, Bishop Gilbert Burnet, referred to it in his memoirs, saying: 'It made an impression on the King's army that cannot be imagined . . . . The whole army, and at last the people, both in city and county, were singing it perpetually.' The twelve verses are a biting satire on 'Lying' Dick Talbot, the Lord Deputy, who reinstated Catholics to positions of power prior to the Glorious Revolution of 1688, and who threatened the land settlement which benefited Protestants. The popular nineteenth-century ditty 'The Protestant Boys' is sung to its air.

Last Saturday

The last Saturday in August each year, when members of the Royal Black Preceptory hold their commemorative rallies at different centres throughout Ulster. In the past the rallies were held on 12 August to commemorate the Relief of Derry and the Battle of Newtownbutler, but as the last Saturday in August was a trade holiday in Belfast, a switch was made for the convenience of urban workers. Preceptories in the Republic of Ireland and in County Fermanagh, however, march on the second Saturday in August, as do Scottish preceptories. The Last Saturday marks the end of the loyalist marching season.

Loyal Orangewomen, Association of

A women's fraternity founded in Dublin in the mid-nineteenth century. It became dormant in the 1880s but was revived in 1911, by Mrs R.H. Johnstone of Bawnboy, County Cavan, to oppose the papal decree *Ne Temere*. This was introduced in Ireland in 1908 and required children of mixed Protestant/Catholic marriages to be brought up as Catholics. The first ladies' lodge was formed at the Fowler Memorial Hall, at 12 Rutland Square in Dublin, in 1912. The Association is active in raising funds for the upkeep of Orange halls and for the Lord Enniskillen Memorial Orphan Society. Ladies' lodges only participate in Orange parades when invited to do so by the male lodges. The Orangewomen address one another as 'sisters'.

Lundy

In Orange rhetoric, the name 'Lundy' is synonymous with 'traitor'. It refers to Lieutenant Colonel Robert Lundy, a Scotsman who was appointed Governor of Derry in December 1688. On 27 April 1690, he called a council meeting and recommended immediate surrender to King James, advising English regiments, sent by King William as reinforcements, to return to London. He was deposed by Adam Murray and other advocates of resistance and, after a brief period of house arrest, was allowed to 'escape', fleeing the city. His effigy is burned annually by members of the Apprentice Boys' Association. Macaulay says: 'It is probable that his conduct is to be attributed to faintheartedness and poverty of spirit rather than to zeal for any public cause.'

Orange Card

A term used by Lord Randolph Churchill in a letter to Gerald Fitzgibbon, his Dublin friend, in 1886, when he encouraged Orange extremism against Gladstone's first Home Rule Bill. He said that if the G.O.M. (Grand Old Man — Gladstone) decided to introduce a Home Rule Bill to the House of Commons, the 'Orange Card' would be the one to play.

Orange Lily

The wearing of lilies became customary among King William's Irish supporters in the years following the Williamite Wars (1688-1690) and was seen as an indication of loyalty to the principles of the Glorious Revolution. The introduction of the lily marked a departure from the normal symbol of the House of Orange, which was the orange tree. The popular Orange song 'The Orange Lily O!' poked fun at the anti-Orange Marquis of Wellesley, Lord Lieutenant of Ireland (1821-1827). The wearing of the lily was banned under the Party Processions Act in 1850.

Orange Minstrel, The

Colonel William Blacker of Carrickblacker, Portadown, County Armagh, who was the author of numerous Orange poems and ballads. Three of the former became evergreen: 'No Surrender' (1817), 'Oliver's Advice' (1834) and 'The Battle of the Boyne' (1839).

Blacker (1777-1855) witnessed the Battle of the Diamond and was the first member of the gentry to join the Orange Order. He was a contemporary of Robert Emmet and Thomas Moore in Trinity College, Dublin, and founded the college's first Orange lodge. He was also a founder member of the Grand Lodge of Ireland in Dublin in 1798. Also that year, he was active in the yeomanry in suppressing the rebellion in Wexford. He wrote an important 'Day-Book' on the early days of the Orange Order and was an occasional contributor to the *Dublin University Magazine* under the pen name 'Banville FitzSteward'.

The Orange Standard
The official monthly newspaper of the Grand Lodge of Ireland, founded by the former Imperial Grand Chaplain, Reverend Dr Canon S.E. Long. It is kept at the low cost of fifty pence.

Orange Hall
The focal point of local Orange activity, where lodge meetings are held. The halls frequently double as lodges for the other loyalist Orders, who 'sit' on different dates. There are about 1,000 Orange halls in Ireland, varying in size from large three-storey buildings in cities and towns (where it is usual for several different lodges to have 'lodge rooms' in the same building) to small one-room properties in villages and townlands. Among Ulster's most famous halls are the Charleton Street Orange Hall, Portadown, County Armagh (opened in 1875), and the West Belfast Orange Hall on Belfast's Shankill Road (opened in 1889).

Orange Young Ireland
A label applied to a group of Protestant writers (some of them Orangemen) who contributed to the *Dublin University Magazine* (founded in 1831). They included Isaac Butt, John Anster and Sir Samuel Ferguson. Their articles supported the Protestant Establishment but expressed their frustration with the management of Irish affairs from London, which they frequently felt to be uninformed and incompetent.

Peep O'Day Boys
A Protestant vigilante organisation formed following fisticuffs between a Catholic and a Protestant at a cattle fair in Markethill, County Armagh, in 1874. The organisation's formation marked a resurgence in sectarian violence, attributed to the entry of Catholics to the linen-weaving trade, which threatened the livelihood of Protestant weavers. The vigilantes raided Catholic homes at dawn, on the pretext of searching for arms, and sabotaged their rivals' weaving equipment. The Peep O'Day Boys were a major combative element at the Battle of the Diamond, and it is now well established that the earliest Orangemen were drawn from them.

Royal Arch Purple Order, The
The least well-known of the loyalist Orders, whose single degree occupies an intermediate place between the degrees of the Orange Order and those of the Royal Black Preceptory. The word 'arch' in the Order's name means 'big' or 'chief', and the word 'purple' is used to denote the veil which surrounded the Ark of the Covenant. The Order traces the traditions of its degree back to early Orange ritual ('The Diamond System') and its own origins to a meeting held in Armagh town in July 1820, when Thomas Server, Harry 'The Shaver' Sling and others met to consider ways to preserve the old traditions. The Order was relaunched in Belfast in 1911, when formal structures were adopted and Lieutenant Colonel Sir William Allen was elected the first Grand Master.

Royal Black Preceptory, The
The senior loyalist Order. Its formal title is The Imperial Grand Black Chapter, but it is often referred to simply as 'The Black'. It is the Irish counterpart of an organisation established in Scotland sometime in the eighteenth century, which began to issue warrants in Ireland in 1834. An autonomous Irish body was founded following a meeting in Portadown in 1846, and shortly afterwards the first 'black lodge' was established at Tandragee, County Armagh. The Order is organised as an honorary knighthood, and its members are addressed as 'Sir Knight'. It is less politically oriented than the Orange Order, and its members see themselves as a 'royal priesthood'. It operates an eleven-step degree system, with each degree called after a different colour, culminating in the 'Red Cross'.

Membership of 'The Black' is only open to those who have already taken the two Orange Order degrees and the Royal Arch Purple degree.

Sash, The

Sashes have been common items of military costume for centuries, and King William is reported to have worn an orange-coloured sash 'of the purest watered silk' at the Battle of the Boyne. Orangemen in Ireland did not, however, adopt the practice of wearing sashes until the mid-nineteenth century. Until then, they wore cockades of blue and orange and, occasionally, scarves of similar colours. In recent decades the traditional sash has given way to the more manageable collarette, which was originally intended for lodge use only; these are normally adorned with metal badges detailing the member's lodge and district numbers and showing the emblems of the degrees he has taken. There are numerous references to sashes in Orange poetry and songs, the best-known being 'The Sash My Father Wore'. Georges-Denis Zimmermann, in his *Songs of Irish Rebellion* (Dublin, 1967), says that this song probably dates from the late nineteenth century.

Sham Fight

A larkish re-enactment of the Battle of the Boyne, which was first held in Bandon, County Cork, in the years following the Williamite War, and which became popular for a period in other parts of Ireland before eventually dying out. The only remaining sham fight is held on 13 July each year in the County Down village of Scarva, where up to 30,000 people attend. The 'fight' is held in the demesne of Scarva House, not far from an old Spanish chestnut tree under which King William is reputed to have sheltered during his march to the Boyne. In former times the Scarva 'fight' was held at the nearby Newry canal, and it has been said that participants got so carried away that serious accidents, and even deaths, resulted. For many years the event has been controlled by the Royal Black Preceptory, and it is a major occasion for the rallying of local preceptories.

Somme, Battle of the

An event of sombre mourning for Orangemen, as many of their brethren served in the 36th (Ulster) Division which took part in the Anglo-French offensive of the First World War. This offensive began on 1 July 1916, and nearly half the Division — about 5,500 men — were killed or wounded in the first two days of fighting. Some Orangemen approached the German lines wearing sashes over their uniforms and shouting their defiant slogan 'No Surrender' (the battle, by the Julian calendar, was fought on the anniversary of the Battle of the Boyne). Four posthumous Victoria Crosses were won by the men of the Division — which, although not one hundred per cent Protestant, had overwhelmingly Protestant numbers, mostly drawn from Orange lodges. The Battle continued until mid-November, by which time British forces had suffered approximately 400,000 casualties and advanced a maximum of only eight miles. A strong remembrance of the loss of a generation of manhood is retained by Orangemen who hold annual Somme parades throughout Ulster. It is often incorrectly held that parades on 12 July 1916 were called off because of the tragedy of the Somme. In fact, the Orange Order had previously cancelled 'The Twelfth' so that full concentration could be given to the war effort.

NOTES

Prologue

1. T.B. Macaulay, *History of England* (London, 1855).
2. Eric Hobsbawm, 'Mass producing traditions: Europe 1870-1914' in E. Hobsbawm and T. Ranger, *The Invention of Tradition* (Cambridge, 1983).
3. E.H. Carr, *What Is History* (London, 1961).

Chapter One

1. The Principality of Orange lay 19 km (12 miles) north of Avignon, on the left bank of the Rhône and bordered on the east by Mount Ventoux, centred in a rich wine-growing area. The Counts of Orange, created by Charlemagne, took the title of prince in the thirteenth century. In the early modern period it was a prosperous state and attracted many rich Jewish and Italian merchants who liked the liberality of its laws, although from 1393 it was ruled by absentees. Following the Reformation it became a Protestant bastion. In 1662 Prince Maurice elaborated its fortifications, but these were razed by Louis XIV in 1673 when he overran and annexed the Principality, to put an end to what he called 'that nest of Huguenots'. The various princes of Orange never ceased to let it be known that they were sovereign rulers, deriving their title from an independent state.
2. Philibert de Chavlons, Prince of Orange, was an imperial general in the service of the Holy Roman Emperor Charles V. With Connetable de Burbon, he led the infamous Sack on Rome in May 1527. In eight days hundreds of churches, palaces and houses were pillaged and destroyed. This action, against Pope Clement VII, is sometimes construed, incorrectly, as an early indication of the 'anti-popery' policies of the House of Orange.
3. Rene von Nassau's mother, Claudia, was a sister of the imperial general Prince Philibert. Nassau was a small German duchy on the right bank of the Middle Rhine between the Westerwald forests and the Taunus Mountains in what is today the western part of Hesse. The Duchy was founded in the twelfth century when the Counts of Laurenburg established themselves near the town of Nassau and assumed an additional title. The region contained some of Germany's finest vineyards.
4. A town in north-eastern France. It still has a monument commemorating the heroic resistance of the army of Francis I against the forces of Prince Rene's patron, the Emperor of Charles V.
5. Pieter Geyl, *The Revolt in the Netherlands 1555–1609* (London, 1932), pp. 161-179 and passim.
6. C. V. Wedgwood, *William the Silent* (London 1944), p. 249.
7. John Miller, *The Life and Times of William and Mary* (London, 1974), p. 12.
8. As well as being the 10th Prince William of Orange, he later became William, the 1st of Ireland, 2nd of Scotland, 3rd of England and 4th of Normandy.

Chapter Two

1. Bishop Gilbert Burnet, *History of His Own Times*, published posthumously in 1823 (London), p. 217.
2. R. Latham and W. Matthews (eds.), *Diary of Samuel Pepys* (London, 1989). Entry for March 1668, p. 256.
3. G.M. Trevelyan, *History of England* (London, 1926), p. 559.

Chapter Three

1. Sir William Petty, *The Political Anatomy of Ireland* (written in 1671, published 1691).
2. For an account of the career of Richard Talbot, see the excellent biography by Sir Charles Petrie, *The Great Tyrconnell – a Chapter in Anglo-Irish Relations* (Cork, 1972).
3. S. E. de Beer (ed.), *Evelyn's Diary* (Oxford, 1955).
4. The words 'lilliburlero bullen a la' are a corruption of the Gaelic 'An lile ba léir é ba linn an lá' (the lily was triumphant and we won the day). The lily was the symbol of the early Williamites. The air, once attributed to Purcell, has been traced to a book of psalm-tunes published in Antwerp in 1540.

5. Reputed comments of Oliver St George to the House of Lords Inquiry, 1688, quoted in *Ireland's Fate*, R. Shepherd (London, 1990).

6. Text from the Official Brochure of the Tercentenary Celebrations of the Apprentice Boys of Derry (Londonderry, 1988).

7. Not much is known about Nicholas Brady, save that he attended Westminster School in London and Christ Church, Oxford. His chief claim to fame is his versification of the Psalms and a blank verse translation of Virgil's 'Aeneid'.

Chapter Four

1. The most famous play on the siege, 'Ireland Preserved' was written by one of the siege heroes, Colonel John Mitchelburne (transcript in British Museum, London, Stowe M.S. 977), and was published in 1705. It was staged regularly in Ireland during the eighteenth century.

2. Mrs Cecil Alexander (1818–1895) became well known as a writer of religious poetry for children. Her best known work is the poem/hymn 'All Things Bright and Beautiful'. She was married to William Alexander who, following a period as Bishop of Derry, went on to become Bishop of Armagh and in 1896, Protestant Primate of Ireland.

3. Padraic Colum, *Life of St Columcille* (Dublin, 1935).

4. This was its peacetime population. At the beginning of the siege the population had swollen to 30,000. See E.A. D'Alton, *History of Ireland*, Volume IV, p. 399.

5. The thirteen Apprentice boys were: Henry Campsie, William Crookshanks, Robert and Daniel Sherrard, Alexander Irwin, James Steward, Robert Morrison, Alexander Cunningham, William Cairns, Samuel Hunt, James Pike, John Cunningham, Samuel Harvey. Their English and Scottish surnames will be noted.

6. Reverend George Walker, *A True Account of the Siege of Derry* (London, 1689).

7. 'The Maiden City' by Charlotte Tonna (1790–1846), who also, as Charlotte Elizabeth, wrote *Derry —
a Tale of Revolution* (London 1839).

8. Lieutenant Colonel William Blacker (1777–1855) was a nineteenth-century Orange hero. He was present at the Battle of the Diamond in 1795 (although a little late for the actual fighting!) and was an early member of the Orange Order. Several of his poems and ballads have become part of the Orange canon. He was nicknamed 'The Orange Minstrel' and his family gave significant service to Orangeism during the early years of the Order. See James S. Kane, *For God and the King – the story of the Blackers of Carrickblacker* (Lurgan, 1995).

9. George Chittick, *The Enniskillen Men* (Revised Edition, Belfast, 1994), p. 20.

10. William and Mary were not crowned until April 1689, that is, two months after being offered the crown.

Chapter Five

1. D. C. Boulger, *The Battle of the Boyne* (London, 1911), p. 124.

2. S. McManus, *The Story of the Irish Race* (New York, 1921), p. 441.

3. C.E.J. Caldicott, H. Gough, J.P. Pitton (eds.) *The Huguenots in Ireland* (Dublin, 1987), ch. 11.

4. R.M. Sibbett, *Orangeism in Ireland and Throughout the Empire* (London, 1914), Vol. 1, p. 96.

5. Rev. G. Story, *A True and Impartial History* (London, 1691).

6. A. Hewitson (ed.), *The Diary of Thomas Bellingham, an Officer Under William III* (Preston, 1908). Bellingham later became High Sheriff of County Louth. He built a castle on his estates and changed the name of the locality to Castlebellingham, now the name of an estate village on the main Dublin–Belfast road.

7. This information is based on a lively oral tradition, and was related to the author by an Orange folklorist, but any oral tradition — particularly if over three hundred years old, must be treated with caution. In the author's view this information could well be true. It is known from sundry sources that William spoke with a heavy Dutch accent. To this day, Dutch intonation are not dissimilar to those used in certain varieties of English spoken in Ireland.

8. N.A. Robb, *William of Orange — A Personal Portrait*, Two volumes (London, 1963–1966).

Chapter Six

1. The Duke of Berwick was James' illegitimate son by Arabella Churchill, the sister of the Duke of Marlborough. Following Sarsfield's death at the Battle of Landen (1693) Berwick married Honora,

Sarsfield's widow. Berwick went on to become one of the great soldiers of the age, and a Marshal of France.

2. These are the figures given in an authoritative modern work, *Jacobite Ireland – 1689-91*, J.G. Simms (London, 1969).
3. D. C. Boulger, *The Battle of the Boyne* (London, 1911), p. 149.
4. Ibid.
5. Noel E. French, *The Battle of the Boyne* (Trim, 1989), p. 29.

6.
> Some folk sing of mountains and valleys
> Where wild flowers abundantly grow
> And some of the foam-crested billows
> That surge in the waters below:
> But I am going to sing of a river
> And I hope in the chorus you'll join
> Of the deeds that were done by King William
> On the green grassy slopes of the Boyne.
>
> On the banks of the beautiful river
> Where the bones of our forefathers lie,
> Awaiting the sound of the trumpet
> That call them to glory on high;
> In our hearts we will cherish their memories
> And in one common brotherhood join
> And praise God who sent us King William
> To the green grassy slopes of the Boyne.
>
> And if ever we're called to the service
> And I know like true brethren you'll join
> And fight like our fathers before us
> On the green grassy slopes of the Boyne
> Orangemen remember King William
> And your fathers who with him did join
> And fought for our glorious deliverance
> On the green grassy slopes of the Boyne.

7. The Battle of the Boyne was fought on 1 July. In 1751 the British Isles adopted the Gregorian or New Style calendar to come in line with the rest of Europe, and so the date was brought forward by eleven days; therefore the battle is nowadays commemorated on 12 July, known to Orangemen as the 'Glorious Twelfth'.
8. Pope Innocent XI (1671–1689) had quarrelled with Louis XIV of France, who sought to restrict the rights of the Holy See over the Gallican Church. The Pope, in consequence, became a strong supporter of William's Grand Alliance against Louis. In 1690, the new Pope, Alexander VIII (1689-1691) was less hostile, and was scandalised to learn that Te Deums had been sung in celebration of William's victory at the Boyne.

Chapter Seven

1. Meriol Trevour, *The Shadow of a Crown* (London, 1989), p. 252.
2. Piers Wauchope, *Patrick Sarsfield and the Williamite War* (Dublin, 1992), p. 3.
3. This lively tradition is still found in the villages of Rearcross, Milestone and Holyford. A monument to 'Ned of the Hill' can be found near Holyford village, and nearby in Foilaclog there is a cave which was his reputed hide-out.
4. This point is contradicted in a contemporary account by the Jacobite Officer Charles O'Kelly. In his *Macariae Excidium* (London, 1695), O'Kelly says Theodore (William) resolved to renew the assault the next day but 'could not persuade his men tho' he offered to lead them in person'.
5. Moore, chaplain to Tyrconnell, was appointed Provost during James's dispensation. He has, however, never been included in the official listing. A plaque to his memory in the college's 1937 Reading Room describes him as being 'head of the college' at one time.

6. De Vere exercised poetic licence with the numbers involved.

7. This is a slightly edited version of the speech, which was first quoted by the contemporary Williamite historian Reverend George Story, in his *A True and Impartial History* (London, 1691), pp. 123–5. Its authenticity has been doubted on the grounds that it is unduly pompous and lacks credibility. It should be remembered that St Ruth was addressing men who were unsophisticated and largely illiterate and who may have been impressed by such high-faluting rhetoric.

8. Gordon Lucy (ed.), *Lord Macaulay on Londonderry, Aughrim, Enniskillen and the Boyne* (Lurgan, 1989), p. 82.

9. 'War of Two Kings' by J.G. Simms in *A New History of Ireland,* (Vol. 3), edited by Moody, Martin and Byrne (Oxford, 1976), p. 503.

10. Colonel Charles O'Kelly, *Macariae Excidium or the Destruction of Cyprus* (London, 1695). Three years before his death in 1695, Colonel O'Kelly wrote this history of the war in which he disguised all the names and places with classical allusions as if he were writing about Cyprus. He came from Aughane, County Galway, and was almost eighty-five years old at his death.

11. C. Kilpatrick, *Aughrim – The Last Battle* (Belfast, 1991) p. 21.

12. The Treaty was supposedly signed on the famous Treaty Stone which today rests on a plinth near Thomond Bridge in Limerick. Prior to its being placed there it was, for many years, used as a stepping stone for mounting horses, but small pieces were continually being gouged for souvenirs.

13. Charles O'Brien, the commander of the Irish Brigade at Fontenoy in 1845, leading his men into fire, urged them forward 'against the enemies of France and your own selves'. They responded with cries of 'Cuimhnigí ar Luimneach agus feall na Sasanach' ('Remember Limerick and the treachery of the English'). Quoted in S.J. Connolly, *Religion, Law and Power — The Making of Protestant Ireland* (Oxford, 1992), p. 239.

14. The statue of Sarsfield is by Dublin sculptor John Lawlor, and was erected in 1881. It was cast in Young's Art Foundry in London in 1880.

Chapter Eight

1. Bishop Gilbert Burnet, *History of His Own Times*. Abridged version published by J.M. Dent & Co. (London, 1906), p. 360.

2. David Ogg, *England in the Reigns of James II and William III* (Oxford, 1955), p. 450.

3. Dr Tillotson, an old friend of the King, had endeared himself years before when he lent William money, following his marriage to Mary and prior to his return to Holland from England.

4. After William's death there were several rival claimants for the title Prince of Orange. Eventually John William Firsco of Nassau-Dietz succeeded to the Principality as William IV. In 1815 his son, William VI, became William I, King of the Netherlands. The title is still held in this line.

5. John Millar, *The Life and Times of William and Mary* (London, 1974), p. 195.

6. William King (1650–1729) was imprisoned by the Jacobites, and released following the Battle of the Boyne. He succeeded the Reverend George Walker as Bishop of Derry and later became Archbishop of Dublin. He published in 1691 *The State of the Protestants of Ireland Under the Late King James* — one of the most powerful vindications of the Williamite victory in Ireland.

7. Dr Isaac Watts (1674–1748), clergyman, was one of the most celebrated of hymn writers. Born in Southampton of Nonconformist parents, he wrote between 500 and 600 hymns.

Chapter Nine

1. S.J. Connolly, *Religion, Law and Power — The Making of Protestant Ireland 1660–1769* (Oxford, 1992), p. 81.

2. Robert Shepherd, *Ireland's Fate – the Boyne and After* (London, 1990), p. 201.

3. West's painting 'William Crossing the Boyne' was completed in 1778 for Lord Richard Grosvenor, Duke of Westminster. A copy was made in 1809 and went to America, where it was lost.

4. J.T. Gilbert, *History of Dublin* (Dublin, 1859). Gilbert says that the Boyne Society was formed in Dublin 'in the first half of the last century' (i.e. eighteenth century) (Vol. 3, p. 45). Sibbett, in his *Orangeism in Ireland and Throughout the Empire*, attributes its founding to the 'Island Town' i.e. Enniskillen (Vol. 1, p. 185) and this accords with Orange tradition.

5. Martin Short, *Inside the Brotherhood* (London, 1993), p. 135.

6. Ogle Robert Gowan was a significant figure in nineteenth-century Orangeism in Ireland and Canada. Born in 1803 at Mount Nabo, near Gorey, County Wexford, he was the son of the notorious John Hunter Gowan, a member of the Boyne Society. He was named after George Ogle MP, who became Grand Master of the Grand Orange Lodge of Ireland (elected 1801). Ogle Robert Gowan was initiated at the age of fifteen (although the minimum age was eighteen), emigrated to Canada in 1829 and became the first Canadian Grand Master. He helped to put down a popular rising in Canada in 1837. He died in 1852 and is mentioned in the *Directory of Canadian Biography* as 'the most impressive of all Grand Masters'.

7. William Nolan (ed.), *Tipperary – History and Society* (Dublin, 1985), p. 300.

8. Edward Rogers was a mid-nineteenth century Orange theoretician, who in civilian life was the County Librarian for Armagh. His special contribution to Orangeism lay in relating scriptural history to Orange ritual. He held a number of senior positions and was the first Grand Registrar of the Grand Black Chapter of Ireland (following its 'reconstitution' in 1846). He wrote a number of books including *The Revolution of 1688, Topographical Sketches of Armagh and Tyrone, A Memoir of Armagh Cathedral and an account of the Ancient City*, and a history of the Royal Black Chapter which, though printed, was never published.

9. An official *History of the Royal Arch Purple Order* was produced in 1993, being written by three distinguished members of that Order. It is not available through the regular book trade and much of its material is of little relevance to the general reader.

Chapter Ten

1. Arthur Young, *Tour of Ireland* (London, 1870). Young (1741-1820) was a noted traveller and agriculturist. He traversed the length and breadth of Ireland in 1777-79 and his book was later described by Maria Edgeworth as 'the most faithful portrait of the Irish peasantry which has ever appeared'.

2. The term 'the boys' crops up frequently in Irish history: 'They were those whom the local populace always referred to as "the boys" — Whiteboys, Oakboys, Steelboys . . . the Boys of Wexford (1798 Rebels), Peep O'Day Boys, Orange Boys. To this day in Ireland a local reference to "the boys" will generally be taken to mean the IRA (or whatever terrorist group is supported in the area). The Irish meaning of "boy" thus retained something of its Elizabethan connotation as a swaggerer, a warrior, an armed man. A.T.Q. Stewart, *The Narrow Ground* (London, 1977), p. 116.

3. Richard Madden, *The United Irishmen, Their Lives and Times* (Dublin, 1857), pp. 36–8.

4. W.E.H. Lecky, *A History of Ireland in the Eighteenth Century* (London, 1908), Vol. 2, p. 43.

5. Maldwyn A. Jones, *The Limits of Liberty — American History 1607–1980* (Oxford, 1983), p. 20.

6. W.H.A. Williams, 'Irish Traditional Music in the United States' in *America and Ireland 1776–1976*, Greenwood Press, USA, cited in M. Hall, *Ulster's Scottish Connection* (Newtownabbey, 1993).

7. A.T.Q. Stewart, 'The Mind of Protestant Ulster' in David Watt (ed.), *The Constitution of Northern Ireland – Problems and Prospects* (London, 1981), p. 38.

8. Desmond Bowen, *History and the Shaping of Irish Protestantism* (New York, 1995), p. 151.

9. The American historian, David Miller, as quoted by James Wilson in a video, *The Making of the Orange Order* (Linton Video Production, Garvagh), 1985.

10. Walter Hussey Burgh (1742-1783), MP for Athy (1770) and for Dublin University (1776). Gained fame as an orator.

11. W.E.H. Lecky, *Leaders of Public Opinion in Ireland* (London, 1903), Vol. 1, p. 104.

Chapter Eleven

1. J.A. Froude, *The English in Ireland in the Eighteenth Century* (London, 1874), Vol. 11, pp. 215 & 216.

2. Ibid.

3. Francis Hutcheson (1694-1746). Although associated with the Scottish Enlightenment, Hutcheson was an Irishman (born in Drumalig, near Saintfield, County Down) who spent much of his young life in Dublin where he founded an academy in 1716. He was appointed professor of moral philosophy at Glasgow University in 1729. His moral criteria were based on whether an act tends to promote the general welfare of mankind. He thus anticipated Jeremy Bentham and the Utilitarians, and was the first to use the phrase 'the greatest happiness of the greatest number'.

4. The name 'The Man from God Knows Where' comes from a ballad written by Florence Wilson, which imaginatively outlined Russell's career as a United Irishman during the period 1795–1803. It can be found in a biography of Russell, with the same title, by Denis Carroll (Dublin, 1995), p. 248.

5. Drennan's letter to McTier, dated 2 July 1791, is quoted in A.T.Q. Stewart, *A Deeper Silence – the hidden origins of the United Irishmen* (London, 1993), p. 157.

6. Jonathan Bardon, *A History of Ulster* (Belfast, 1992), p. 47.

7. Harold Nicholson, *A Desire to Please — The Story of Hamilton Rowan and the United Irishmen* (New York, 1943), p. 39.

8. Quoted by James Connolly in *Labour in Irish History* (New Books Publications Edition, Dublin, 1956), p. 47.

9. Froude, op. cit., Vol. 11, p. 161.

10. Jim Smyth, *The Men of No Property* (Dublin, 1992), p. 47.

11. L.M. Cullen, *The Emergence of Modern Ireland 1600-1900* (London, 1991), p. 110.

12. An outline of the political background is given in Kevin Whelan, 'The Origins of the Orange Order', Winter/Spring 1996 issue of the Irish Studies Journal *Bullan*, pp. 19-37.

13. O'Sullivan's evidence is quoted in A.T.Q. Stewart, *The Narrow Ground — Aspects of Ulster 1609-1969*, p. 131.

14. See section on 'The Ancient Order of Hibernians' in A.D. Buckley and K. Andersen in 'Brotherhoods in Ireland', in booklet published by the Ulster Folk and Transport Museum (Cultra, 1988).

Chapter Twelve

1. Fr Quigley (or Coigley) was a native of Mullavilly, County Armagh. He was arrested with United Irish leader Arthur O'Connor and others at Margate, Kent in February 1798 while attempting to escape under false names to France. He was later hanged on Pennington Heath. In *The Diamond in its Historical Setting* (Belfast, 1996) Orange historian Cecil Kilpatrick says: 'As he dropped, an Armagh man in the crowd cried: "There goes Quigley"', p. 14.

2. *William Blacker Manuscripts* quoted in David Miller's *Peep O'Day Boys and Defenders* (Belfast, 1990), pp. 118–119.

3. Atkinson's version of events is quoted in Reverend John Brown in *Orangeism, a New Historical Appreciation* (Belfast, 1867), pp. 93–4.

4. Miller, op. cit., pp. 120–22.

5. Most detailed accounts of the Battle of the Diamond come from Orange sources. One of the best appears in a souvenir booklet published by County Armagh Orange Lodge in 1961.

6. W.J. Fitzpatrick, *The Sham Squire* (Dublin, 1895), pp. 222 & 223. Giffard (1745-1819) later amassed a large fortune and built himself a handsome residence known as Dromartin Castle, at Dundrum, Dublin.

7. This is a reference to Francis Higgins (1746-1802) the owner of *The Freeman's Journal* and one of the most notorious of the informers against the United Irishmen. He became known as 'The Sham Squire' after falsely posing as a gentleman and thereby inducing a lady of means to marry him.

8. R.M. Sibbett, *Orangeism in Ireland and Throughout the Empire* (London, 1914), Vol. 1, p. 287.

9. Sibbett, op. cit., p. 286.

10. Rogers' comments are quoted in *The Formation of the Orange Order 1795-1798 – the edited papers of Colonel William Blacker and Colonel Robert H. Wallace* (Belfast, 1994), p. 27.

11. Sibbett, op. cit., p. 286.

12. Jonathan Bardon, *A History of Ulster* (Belfast, 1992), p. 226.

13. The village of Loughgall is about five miles from the City of Armagh, along the B27 carriageway, and is one of the prettiest villages in Ireland. The surrounding area, noted for its orchards and famous Bramley apples, is often referred to as the 'Garden of Ireland'. The Orange museum is sandwiched between two terraced houses (one of which is 'Sloan's House') at the northern end of the Main Street. Its curator is a remarkable nonagenarian, Mrs Vallery, who has a large fund of stories about early Orangeism. Nowadays the village is quiet; in 1988, however, it was the scene of a British army ambush in which eight IRA men died. At the time of the founding of the Orange Order (1795) its Protestant population was 588, of whom 464 were Anglicans, 110 Presbyterians, and 14 Quakers. Its Catholic population was 469 (see Groves documents in the Public Records Office of Northern Ireland T/808/15264 [i]).

14. Dan Winter's cottage is now a museum. Among the items on display is a seventeenth-century chair known as 'Old Dan's Chair'. Several pieces of ball, which were fired at the cottage during the Battle of the Diamond, may be seen. The cottage is still the property of the Winter family, and the adjacent land is farmed by Geoffrey Daniel Winter. His wife, Mrs Hilda Winter, has recently compiled a historical chart of the family, which is of Huguenot origin.

Chapter Thirteen

1. W.E.H. Lecky, *A History of Ireland in the Eighteenth Century* (London, 1913), Vol. 3, p. 429.
2. Op. cit., pp. 438 & 439.
3. Edited papers of Colonel R.E. Wallace in *The Formation of the Orange Order* (Belfast, 1994), p.43.
4. J.A Froude, *The English in Ireland* (London, 1874), Vol. 3, p. 169.
5. Hereward Senior, *Orangeism in Ireland and Britain 1795–1836* (London, 1966), p. 35.
6. *History of the Royal Arch Purple Order* (Belfast, 1993), p. 36.
7. A.T.Q. Stewart, *The Summer Soldiers — The 1798 Rebellion in Antrim and Down* (Belfast, 1995), p. 44.
8. Wallace, op cit., p. 70.
9. *History of Royal Arch Purple Order*, p. 34.
10. Ibid., p. 35.
11. Senior, op. cit., p. 39.
12. *History of Royal Arch Purple Order*, pp. 33–4.
13. Wallace, op. cit., p. 70.
14. Ibid., p. 134. Reverend Dr Cupples succeeded Reverend Philip Johnson as Grand Chaplain in 1810.
15. *History of Royal Arch Purple Order*, p. 41.
16. Reverend H.W. Cleary, *The Orange Society* (Melbourne, 1897), pp. 64–8.
17. R.M. Sibbett, *Orangeism in Ireland and Throughout the Empire* (London, 1914), Vol. 1, p. 500.
18. In 1964 the United Grand Lodge of England granted Masonic lodges under its authority permission to alter the wording of oaths to make it clear that the penalties mentioned are not always to be taken literally.

Chapter Fourteen

1. Francis Higgins, the 'Sham Squire' (1746–1802), received £1,000 for revealing the hiding place of Fitzgerald.
2. Major Henry Sirr (1764-1841) was among the first to join the Orange Order when it was established in the capital. He was a life-long collector of curiosities, and these are now held in the Royal Irish Academy. His papers, which he intended to destroy, are in Trinity College, Dublin.
3. Father John Murphy (born circa 1753, executed in 1798), was curate at Boulavogue and Monageer in the parish of Kilcormack. He was born at Tinacurry and educated in Saville. Gahan says that he abandoned the Republican cause following the battle of Kilcumney (26 June 1798) — Daniel Gahan, *The People's Rising* (Dublin, 1995), p. 248. He was hanged a few months later at Tullow.
4. *Murder Without Sin* (Goli Publications, Belfast, 1996), p. 59.
5. Sir Richard Musgrave, *Memories of the Different Rebellions in Ireland*, 4th Edition, Fort Wayne, 1995, p. 390.
6. R.M. Sibbett, *Orangeism in Ireland and Throughout the Empire* (London, 1914), p. 389.
7. Reverend Thomas Hamilton, *History of the Irish Presbyterian Church* (Edinburgh, 1887), p. 142.
8. Thomas Pakenham, *The Year of Liberty — The Great Irish Rebellion of 1798* (London, 1969), p. 251.
9. Nationalist accounts query whether these letters stood for Murder Without Sin. In the authoritative book on Irish flags by Hayes-McCoy, *History of Irish Flags* (Dublin, 1970), the author says that 'modern guesswork has suggested Marksmen West Shelmalier (Shelmalier being a district in County Wexford) or Maria Wexfordian Salvet (Mary Save Wexford)'. He dismisses these as fanciful and accepts that many alive at the time held that the letters stood for Murder Without Sin.

Chapter Fifteen

1. *Steadfast for Faith and Freedom — 200 Years of Orangeism* (Belfast, 1995), p. 57.
2. This is the last verse of 'Betsy Gray' as shown in McComb's *Guide to Belfast* (Belfast, 1861), pp. 130–1. It is believed to have been written by William McComb himself.

3.   *The Formation of the Orange Order 1795–1798* (Belfast,1994), p.115.

4.   H. Boylan, *A Dictionary of Irish Biography* (Dublin,1998), p.159.

5.   *History of the Royal Arch Purple Order* (Belfast,1994), pp. 52 & 53.

6.   Ibid., p. 54.

7.   Ibid., p. 52.

8.   John S. Crone, *A Concise Dictionary of Irish Biography* (Dublin, 1937), p. 256.

9.   Sir Jonah Barrington, *The Rise and Fall of the Irish Nation* (Dublin, 1853), pp. 137 & 138.

10. C.A. Read and K.T. Hinkson (eds.), *The Cabinet of Irish Literature*, (London, 1902), p 274.

11. 'The Monks of the Screw' was the name given to a parliamentary social club founded by Lord Avonmore (Barry Yelverton, MP). Its formal name was the 'Order of Saint Patrick'. John Philpott Curran wrote its charter song, which went: 'When Saint Patrick this Order established He called us the "Monks of the Screw"; Good rules he revealed to our Abbot To guide us in what we should do; But first he replenished our fountain with liquor the best in the sky; And he said on the word of a saint; That our fountain would never run dry.'

12. Crone, op. cit., p. 186.

13. When the author visited Saint Patrick's Cathedral in August 1997 he was told by a verger that politicians who visit the Cathedral envy the fulsome tribute given to Ogle. Mr Chris Patten, the last Governor of Hong Kong, had recently remarked that Ogle must have been a remarkable politician to be able to convince his fellows so thoroughly of his virtues.

14. W.J. Fitzpatrick, *The Sham Squire* (Dublin, 1895), p. 201.

15. Sir Jonah Barrington, *Personal Sketches of His Own Times* (Glasgow, 1827), p. 157.

16. Fitzpatrick, op. cit., pp. 202 & 203.

17. Peter Beresford Ellis, *Orangeism — Myth and Reality* (London, 1997), p. 6.

18. Barrington, op. cit., pp.129–30.

19. Sir John Temple, *History of the Irish Rebellion* — subtitled 'together with the barbarous cruelties and bloody massacres which ensued thereupon' (London, 1644) and Archbishop William King, *The State of the Protestants of Ireland under the late King James's Government* (London, 1691).

20. This view is taken by eminent Trinity College, Dublin historian David Dickson in his foreword to the new (4th) edition of Musgrave's book (Fort Wayne, Indiana, 1996).

Chapter Sixteen

1.   Tadeusz Koschiusko was a Polish officer and statesman who fought in the American War of Independence and who later led an uprising in Poland (1794) against occupying powers (Russia, Prussia and Austria).

2.   Quoted in Appendix V of Sir Richard Musgrave's *Memoirs of the Irish Rebellion of 1798*, 4th Edition (Fort Wayne, 1995), pp. 610–11.

3.   Reverend H.W. Cleary, *The Orange Society*, 6th Edition (Melbourne, 1995), pp. 610 & 274.

4.   Ibid., p. 265, footnote 31.

5.   Ibid., p. 269, footnote 52.

6.   Robert Kee, *Ireland — A History* (London, 1980), p. 64.

7.   Cleary, op. cit., pp. 278–80.

8.   W.E.H. Lecky, *Ireland in the Eighteenth Century*, Vol. 5, p. 333, footnote 2.

9.   R.M. Sibbett, *Orangeism in Ireland and Throughout the Empire* (London, 1914), p. 422.

10. Ibid., p. 450.

11. Ibid., p. 454.

12. Kee, op. cit., pp. 412–13.

Chapter Seventeen

1.   R.M. Sibbett, *Orangeism in Ireland and Throughout the Empire*, Vol. 1 (London, 1939) gives Nixon's first name as Robert (p. 481) and later quotes it as Richard (p. 482).

2.   Frank Neal, *Sectarian Violence — The Liverpool Experience 1819–1914* (Manchester, 1988), p. 20.

3.   The 25 July 1807 edition of Cowdrey's *Manchester Gazette and Weekly Advertiser* gives details of 'No Popery' slogans appearing on walls, and of bands playing anti-Catholic tunes.

4.   The arrest and trial of Nixon took place over a period of months. See *Manchester Guardian*, 26 May 1821, and *Manchester Mercury*, 7 August 1821; see also Neal, op. cit., p. 20.

5. Neal, op. cit., p. 20.
6. Neal, op. cit., p. 19. References to Fletcher's anti-Luddite activities are found in E.P. Thompson, *The Making of the English Working Class* (London, 1991 edition), pp. 536, 557, 592, 621 et al.
7. Nixon to Giffard, 11 February 1811 (Report on Orange Lodges IV, H.C. 1835, [605] XVII, app.21, p. 177).
8. W.S. Churchill, *A History of the English-Speaking Peoples*, Vol. IV (London, 1958), p. 32.
9. *The Times*, 22 June 1821.
10. W.E.H. Lecky, *Leaders of Public Opinion in Ireland* (London, 1912), Vol. 2, p. 71.
11. Ibid., p. 71.
12. Sibbett, op. cit., p. 706.

Chapter Eighteen

1. *History of the Royal Arch Purple Order* (Belfast, 1993), p. 74.
2. Peter Dixon, *Canning — Politician and Statesman* (London, 1976), pp. 216–17.
3. Donal McCartney, *The Dawning of Democracy: Ireland 1800–1870* (Dublin, 1987), p. 39.
4. Fergus O'Ferrall, *Catholic Emancipation — Daniel O'Connell and the Birth of Irish Democracy* (Dublin, 1985), p. 10.
5. Edward Brynn, *Crown and Castle — British Rule in Ireland* (Dublin, 1978), p. 99.
6. *Dublin Evening Mail*, 19 October 1825, p. 3, col. 3.
7. Brynn, op. cit., p. 101.
8. R.M. Sibbett, *Orangeism in Ireland and Throughout the Empire* (London, 1939), Vol. 1, p. 580.
9. D. George Boyce, *Nineteenth Century Ireland — The Search for Stability* (Dublin, 1990), p. 40.
10. Charles Chenevix Trench, *The Great Dan* (London, 1984), p. 85.
11. Ibid., p. 85.
12. Ibid., p. 86.
13. Seán O'Faoláin, *King of the Beggars* (Dublin, 1980 edition), p. 157.
14. Ibid., p. 163.
15. Sibbett, op. cit., Vol. 1, p. 686.

Chapter Nineteen

1. Norman Lowe, *Mastering Modern British History* (London, 1984), p. 24.
2. R.M. Sibbett, *Orangeism in Ireland and throughout the Empire* London, 1939), Vol. I, p. 695.
3. Justin McCarthy, *History of Our Own Times* (London, 1908), pp. 6 & 7.
4. Anthony Bird, *The Damnable Duke of Cumberland* (London, 1966), p. 9.
5. Ibid., pp. 9 & 10.
6. Ibid., p. 174.
7. Sibbett, op. cit., Vol. 2, p. 11.
8. Fergus O'Ferrall, *Catholic Emancipation — Daniel O'Connell and the Birth of Irish Democracy 1820-70* (Dublin, 1985), p. 208.
9. Ibid., p. 208.
10. Ibid., p. 211.
11. Ibid., p. 213.
12. J.C. Beckett, *The Making of Modern Ireland* (London, 1966), p. 304.
13. O'Neill died in 1841 and was succeeded in the Viscountcy by his brother who died without issue in 1855. The Reverend William Chichester then assumed the O'Neill surname and succeeded to the inheritance at Shane's Castle.
14. T.W. Latimer, *A History of Irish Presbyterianism* (Belfast, 1893), p. 57.
15. Jonathan Bardon and David Burnett, *Belfast — a Pocket History* (Belfast, 1996), p. 46.
16. Constantine Fitzgibbon, *The Red Hand — The Ulster Colony* (London, 1971), p. 197.
17. W.E. Vaughan (ed.), *A New History of Ireland* (New York, 1989), p. 80, Vol. V. p. 387
18. Mortimer O'Sullivan, *Captain Rock Detected* (London, 1824), p. 284.
19. Donal McCartney, *The Dawning of Democracy in Ireland 1800–1870* (Dublin, 1987), p. 101.
20. The name Ribbonmen appears to have come from the movement's enemies. At different times they called themselves names like 'The Knights of Saint Patrick' and 'The Sons of the Shamrock'.
21. McCartney, op. cit., p. 83.

Chapter Twenty

1. D. Harman Akenson (ed.), *Conor — A Biography of Conor Cruise O'Brien* Vol. II, (Montreal, 1994), p. 186.
2. Hereward Senior, *Orangeism in Ireland and Britain 1796–1836* (London, 1966), p. 239.
3. Tony Gray, *The Orange Order* (London, 1972), p. 113.
4. M. Tierney and M. MacCurtain, *The Birth of Modern Ireland* (Dublin, 1969), p. 34.
5. Brian Inglis, *The Story of Ireland* (London, 1956), p. 134.
6. R.B. O'Brien, *Thomas Drummond: His Life and Letters* (London, 1889), pp. 289–314.
7. See preface to Shaw's play *John Bull's Other Island* (1904).
8. Robert Kee, *The Green Flag* (London, 1972), p. 209.
9. R.M. Sibbett, *Orangeism in Ireland and Throughout the Empire* (London, 1939), Vol. II, p. 83.
10. Ibid., p. 86–7.
11. *Blackwoods Magazine*, (1838) XLIV, p. 730.
12. F.S.L. Lyons and A.J. Hawkins (eds.), *Ireland Under the Union* (Oxford, 1980), p. 64.
13. D.J. Hickey and E.J. Doherty, *A Dictionary of Irish History since 1800* (Dublin, 1980), p. 456.
14. Katharine Tynan Hickson (ed.), *The Cabinet of Irish Literature* (London, 1902), Vol. II, pp. 304–5.
15. Malcolm Brown, *Sir Samuel Ferguson* (New Jersey, 1972), pp. 40–41.

Chapter Twenty-One

1. Robert Johnston, *Belfast — Portraits of a City* (London, 1990), p. 82.
2. Flann Campbell, *The Dissenting Voice* (Belfast, 1991), p. 205.
3. Jonathan Bardon, *A History of Ulster* (Belfast, 1992), p. 250. A thumbnail entry on Bishop Jocelyn (1764–1843) in the *Concise Dictionary of National Biography* (Oxford, 1961), p. 692, says: 'Bishop of Clogher, son of Robert, 1st Earl of Roden, BA Trinity College, Dublin, Bishop of Ferns and Leighlin 1809, Clogher, 1850. Deposed for scandalous crime.'
4. *Steadfast for Faith and Freedom — 200 Years of Orangeism*, published by Grand Orange Lodge of Ireland (Belfast, 1995), p. 25.
5. Johnston, op. cit., p. 101.
6. Reverend H.W. Cleary, *The Orange Society* (Melbourne, 1897), p. 365.
7. Hereward Senior, *Orangeism in Ireland and Britain 1795–1836* (London, 1966), p. 257.
8. Fairman's letters and those of other members of the Imperial Grand Lodge are found in the Appendix to the Report of the Select Parliamentary Committee (English) of 1835. See also: Barry O'Brien, *Thomas Drummond* (London, 1889).
9. Norman Wilding and Philip Lundy, *An Encyclopaedia of Parliament* (London, 1958), pp. 520 & 521.
10. *History of the Royal Arch Purple Order* (Belfast), p. 83. The English branch of the Order appears to have co-operated less fully with the Select Committee than the Irish one. The Report of the Committee on English Orangeism says that, with one exception, all the Orange leaders declined to give information on oaths, secret signs and passwords.
11. Ibid., p. 9.
12 Cleary, op. cit., p. 352.
13. Elie Halévy, *A History of the English People in the Nineteenth Century* (Paris, 1945).
14. Claire Jerrold, *The Early Court of Queen Victoria* (London, 1912).
15. Harriet Martineau, *The Thirty Years' Peace* (London, 1849).
16. M.W. Dewar, J. Brown and S.E. Long, *Orangeism — A New Historical Appreciation* (Belfast, 1967), p. 130.
17. Cleary, op. cit., p. 381.

Chapter Twenty-Two

1. R.M. Sibbett, *Orangeism in Ireland and Throughout the Empire* (London, 1939), Vol. 2, p. 215.
2. J.W. Good, *Irish Unionism* (Dublin, 1920), p. 107.
3. Lord Roden's speech constitutes Appendix 'F' of the 'Berwick Report' dated 22 September 1849.
4. Different sources give different numbers for those killed: Stewart in *The Narrow Ground* (1977, p. 8) says 6; Jarman in *Material Conflicts: Parades and Visual Displays in Northern Ireland* (1997, p. 55) says 8; Campbell in *The Dissenting Voice* (1991, p. 55) says 30. The writer's view is that the figure given by *The Newry Telegraph* (a local contemporary source) is probably nearest to the truth.

5. Richard Niven, *Orangeism – As It Was And Is* (1910), pp. 69 & 70.
6. William Beers' speech constitutes Appendix 'D' of the 'Berwick Report'.
7. W.J. Martin, *The Battle of Dolly's Brae – 12th July 1849* published by the Grand Lodge of Ireland's Educational Committee (undated).
8. Niven, op. cit., pp. 44 & 45.
9. Aiken McClelland, *William Johnston of Ballykilbeg* (Lurgan, 1990), p. 52.
10. T. Desmond Williams (ed.), *Secret Societies in Ireland* (Dublin, 1973), p. 128.
11. McClelland, op. cit. This is the only full-length biography of Johnston to date. A useful booklet on his career is 'William Johnston of Ballykilbeg and the Right to March', published by The Ulster Society, Lurgan (undated).
12. Philip Magnus, *Gladstone — A Biography* (London, 1954), p. 198.
13. Desmond Bowen, *History and the Shaping of Irish Protestantism* (New York, 1995), p. 309. Robert Lowe (afterwards Viscount Sherbrook) was the leader of a breakaway Liberal faction called the Adullamites.
14. Williams, op. cit., p. 129.

Chapter Twenty-Three

1. M. Tierney, *Ireland Since 1870* (Dublin, 1988), p. 39.
2. M. Pearce and G. Stewart, *British Political History 1867–1990* (London, 1992).
3. T.W. Moody, *Davitt and the Irish Revolution 1846–1882* (Oxford, 1982), p. 447.
4. F. Campbell, *The Dissenting Voice* (Belfast, 1991), p. 287.
5. Joyce Marlow, *Captain Boycott and the Irish* (London, 1972), p. 146.
6. D.J. Hickey and J.E. Doherty, *A Dictionary of Irish History 1800 to 1980* (Dublin, 1980), p. 42.
7. Selected verses from the poem 'Bycutt's Volunteers' which appeared in *The Nation* on 21 November 1880.

Chapter Twenty-Four

1. Patrick Buckland, *Irish Unionism* (London, 1973), p. 5.
2. John Morley, *The Life of William Ewart Gladstone* (London, 1907), Vol. 2, pp. 484 & 485.
3. Robert Rhodes James, *Lord Randolph Churchill* (London, 1959), p. 224.
4. Ibid., p. 226.
5. F.S.L. Lyons, *Parnell* (Dublin, 1963), p. 18.
6. J.E. Doherty and D.J. Hickey, *A Chronology of Irish History since 1500* (Dublin, 1989), p. 160.
7. Alwin Jackson, *Colonel Edward Saunderson* (Oxford, 1995), p. 27.
8. *Belfast News Letter*, 14 July 1882.
9. R.F. Foster, *Lord Randolph Churchill — A Political Life* (Oxford, 1981), p. 40.
10. Taylor Downing (ed.), *The Troubles* (London, 1980), p. 68.
11. R.F. Foster, *Paddy and Mr Punch* (London, 1993), p. 251.
12. Liz Curtis, *The Cause of Ireland* (Belfast, 1994), p. 131.
13. Peter Gibbon, *The Origins of Ulster Unionism* (London, 1975), p. 126. (Dublin, 1973), p. 12.
14. Patrick Buckland, *Ulster Unionism and the Origins of Northern Ireland* (Dublin 1973), p. 12.
15. Winston S. Churchill, *Lord Randolph Churchill* (London, 1906), pp. 62 & 63.
16. James, op. cit., p. 234.
17. Aiken McClelland, *William Johnston of Ballykilbeg* (Lurgan, 1990), p. 97.
18. James, op. cit., pp. 97 & 98.
19. Stephen J. Lee, *Aspects of British Political History 1815–1914* (London, 1994), p. 167.
20. David Williamson (ed.), *Gladstone — Statesman and Scholar* (London, 1898), p. 839.
21. Philip Magnus, *Gladstone — A Biography* (London, 1954), p. 357.

Chapter Twenty-Five

1. Andrew Boyd, *Holy War in Belfast* (Tralee, 1969), p. 38.
2. Ibid., p. 39.
3. Ibid., p. 43.
4. A.C. Hepburn, *The Conflict of Nationality in Modern Ireland* (London, 1980), p. 23.
5. Austen Morgan, *Labour and Partition — The Belfast Working Class* (London, 1991), p. 45.

6. John Boyle, 'The Belfast Protestant Association and the Independent Orange Order' in *Irish Historical Studies*, September 1962, p. 119.
7. Ibid., p. 146.
8. Lord Cushenden (formerly Ronald McNeill) was an Ulster Unionist who, during the Home Rule debates, caused a sensation by hurling a book at the head of Winston Churchill. His work, *Ulster's Stand for the Union* (London, 1922), contains an important account of the struggle against Home Rule, from a Unionist viewpoint.
9. H. Montgomery Hyde, *Carson* (London, 1953), p. 258.
10. A.T.Q. Stewart, *Edward Carson* (Dublin, 1981), p. 73.
11. Patrick Riddle, *Fire Over Ulster* (London, 1970), pp. 16 & 17.
12. These are selected verses quoted from the fuller version given in A.T.Q. Stewart, *The Ulster Crisis* (London, 1967), pp. 55 & 56.
13. W.E. Vaughan (ed.), *A New History of Ireland*, Vol. VI (Oxford, 1996), p. 133.

Chapter Twenty-Six

1. Patrick Riddell, *Fire Over Ulster* (London, 1970), p. 20.
2. T. Bartlett and K. Jeffries (eds.), *A Military History of Ireland* (Cambridge, 1996), p. 392.
3. D.J. Owen, *History of Belfast* (Belfast and London, 1921), p. 346.
4. Brian Barton, *A Pocket History of Ulster* (Dublin, 1966), p. 33.
5. Sir Douglas Savory, *The Origin of the Constitution of Northern Ireland* (Belfast, 1959), p. 10.
6. Ibid.
7. Ibid.
8. The Minutes are of a summary nature and not very revealing. The account of the Grand Lodge meeting held on 8 March 1798, given in Chapter 15, is based on oral tradition.
9. *The Irish Times*, 13 July 1995, p. 13.
10. B. O'Leary and J.M. McGarry, *The Politics of Antagonism — Understanding Northern Ireland* (London, 1996), p. 107.
11. Tony Gray, *The Orange Order* (London, 1972), p. 227.
12. Thomas Hennessy, *A History of Northern Ireland 1920–1966* (Basingstoke and London, 1997), p. 114.
13. Dr Verwoerd's views were expressed in one of his replies to Harold Macmillan's famous 'Wind of Change' speech delivered in Cape Town in February 1960.
14. David Fitzpatrick, *The Two Irelands 1912–1939* (Oxford, 1998), p. 161.
15. William A. Carson, *Ulster and the Irish Republic* (Belfast, 1956), p. 21.

Chapter Twenty-Seven

1. Freddie Hall was the senior police officer in charge of the police operation at Drumcree in 1995.
2. Paul Arthur and Keith Jeffrey, *Northern Ireland Since 1968* (London, 1988), p. 18.
3. *Orange Standard*, February issue 1997, p. 4.
4. *Orange Standard*, August issue 1995, p. 1.
5. *For God and Ulster — An Alternative Guide to the Loyal Orders*, published by the Pat Finucane Centre (Derry, 1997), p. 41.
6. *The Times*, 27 July 1998, p. 4.
7. John McGarry and Brendan O'Leary, *Understanding Northern Ireland* (London, 1995), p. 418.
8. *Orange Standard*, June issue 1995, p. 1.
9. Graham G.W. Montgomery and J. Richard Whitten, *The Order on the March* (Belfast, 1995), p. 36.
10. *The Irish Times*, 7 July 1996, p. 10.
11. Montgomery and Whitten, op. cit., p. 39.
12. *Belfast News Letter*, 11 July 1995, p. 3.
13. Denis Cook, *Persecuting Zeal — A Portrait of Ian Paisley* (Dingle, 1996), p. 213.
14. *Sunday Times*, 14 July 1996, p. 15 (Focus section).
15. *The Irish Times*, 13 July 1996, p. 9 (article by Suzanne Breen).
16. *The Irish Times*, 13 July 1996, p. 9 (article by Jim Cusack).
17. David Sharrock and Nigel Davenport, *Man of War/Man of Peace — An Unauthorised Biography of Gerry Adams* (London, 1997), p. 413.

18. *The Irish Times*, 14 July 1998, p. 6.
19. *Irish Post*, 6 July 1997, p. 4.
20. Editorial, *The Irish Times*, 'The Shadow of Drumcree', 4 July 1998, p. 15.
21. *The Irish Times*, 13 July 1998, p. 2.
22. *The Irish Times*, 18 July 1998, p. 2.
23. *The Irish Times*, 19 July 1998, p. 6.
24. *The Irish Times*, 11 July 1998, p. 11.
25. *The Irish Times*, 13 July 1998.

Chapter Twenty-Eight

1. *The Irish Times*, 13 August 1996, p. 9.
2. Letter, 17 October 1996, from Dr Buckley to the author.
3. Aiken McClelland, 'The Origin of the Imperial Grand Black Chapter of the British Commonwealth' in *Journal of the Royal Society of Antiquaries of Ireland* (Dublin, 1968), Vol. 98, p. 191.
4. Ibid., p. 194.
5. *The Irish Times*, 12 April 1997, Weekend Supplement, p. 1.
6. Tony Gray, *The Orange Order* (London, 1972), p. 210.
7. 'Manual with Opening Ceremony and Ceremony of Installation for the Working of the Royal Arch Purple Degree of Ireland' (1956), p. 1.
8. *Orange Standard*, June 1998, p. 13.
9. Official Brochure of the Tercentenary Celebrations of the Apprentice Boys of Derry, p. 13.
10. Derek Miller, *Still Under Siege*, (Lurgan, 1989), pp. 66 and 67.

Chapter Twenty-Nine

1. H.W. Cleary, *The Orange Society* (Melbourne, 1897), pp. 400 & 406.
2. Fergal Tobin, *The Best of Decades — Ireland in the 1960s* (Dublin, 1996), pp. 201–2.
3. The term 'ridden the goat' means having conquered the devil, who traditionally is depicted with the horns and hooves of a goat. The term is used in reference to a burlesque associated with the initiation ceremony of the Royal Arch Purple degree. Critics insist that an actual goat is present in the lodge and that initiates are required to sit on its back. The author is assured, however, that this does not happen.
4. Fred L. Pick and G. Norman Knight, *The Freemason's Pocket Reference Book* (London, 1963), 4th edition, p. 198. An Orange Order denial of any association with Freemasonry is given in *The Orange Order — An Evangelical Perspective* by Reverend I. Meredith (Grand Chaplain, Grand Orange Lodge of Scotland) and Reverend B. Kennaway (Deputy Grand Chaplain, Grand Lodge of Ireland), (Belfast, 1993).
5. Pride of place in the parade is given to a different District each year. The only parade which nowadays takes place in the Irish Republic is at Rossnowlagh, County Donegal, where up to 6,000 Orangemen and women march on 'The Twelfth'. Orangeism flourishes in Raphoe, Saint Johnston, Manorcunningham and other areas of County Donegal. Lodges from counties Cavan and Monaghan normally participate in the Loughgall, County Armagh parade; those in Leitrim join the Lisbellaw, County Fermanagh parade. There are 43 lodges in the Republic: Leitrim 2; Cavan 18; Monaghan 22; Dublin and Wicklow 1.
6. An excellent account of life on the Shankill Road is given in Paul Hamilton, *Up the Shankill* (Belfast, 1979).
7. *The Irish Times* article by Carmel Robinson, 14 June 1997.
8. A detailed account of the political career of William McGrath is found in Chris Moore, *The Kincora Scandal* (Dublin, 1996).

Chapter Thirty

1. A biographical sketch of Ogle Gowan appears in *Murder Without Sin*, a book published by the Grand Lodge of Ireland in 1966, containing edited extracts from Gowan's own book *Orangeism — Its Origin and History* (Toronto, 1859). A full-length biography of Gowan is *The Orangeman* by Don Akeson (Toronto, 1986).
2. Michael Kenny, *The Fenians* (Dublin, 1997), p. 36.

3. Alan Axelrod, *The International Encyclopaedia of Secret Societies and Fraternal Orders* (New York, 1996), p. 190.

4. Tony Gray, *The Orange Order* (London, 1972), p. 261.

5. *Steadfast for Faith and Freedom — 200 Years of Orangeism*, published by the Grand Lodge of Ireland (Belfast, 1995), p. 75.

6. Ibid., p. 73.

7. *A Celebration: 1690–1990, The Orange Institution*, published by the Grand Lodge of Ireland (Belfast, 1990), p. 93.

8. *Irish Post*, 27 January 1996, p. 12.

Bibliography

This bibliography includes details of author, title and year of publication. It does not follow the convention of supplying place and publisher, since neither is necessary for locating books in libraries and bookshops.

Akenson, Don, *The Orangeman* (1986)

Arthur, Paul and Jeffrey, K., *Northern Ireland Since 1986* (1988)

Axelrod, Alan, *The International Encyclopaedia of Secret Societies and Fraternal Orders* (1997)

Ball, J.T., *The Reformed Church in Ireland* (1886)

Bardon, Jonathan, *A History of Ulster* (1992)

Barrington, Sir Jonah, *Personal Sketches of His Own Times* (1827)

Barrington, Sir Jonah, *The Rise and Fall of the Irish Nation* (1858)

Bartlett, C.J., *Castlereagh* (1966)

Bartlett, T. and Jeffries, K., *A Military History of Ireland* (1996)

Barton, Brian, *A Pocket History of Ulster* (1966)

Barton, Brian, *Brookeborough – The Making of a Prime Minister* (1986)

Bellingham, Thomas, *Diary of Thomas Bellingham – An Officer under William III* (1908)

Beresford Ellis, Peter, *The Boyne Water* (1976)

Bird, Anthony, *The Damnable Duke of Cumberland* (1966)

Blacker, William, *The Formation of the Orange Order – the edited papers of Col. Wm. Blacker and Col. R.H. Wallace* (1994)

Boulger, D.C., *The Battle of the Boyne* (1911)

Bowen, Desmond, *History and the Shaping of Irish Protestantism* (1995)

Boyce, D. George, *Nineteenth Century Ireland – The Search for Stability* (1990)

Boyd, Andrew, *Holy War in Belfast* (1969)

Brown, Malcolm, *Sir Samuel Ferguson* (1972)

Brynn, Edward, *Crown and Castle – British Rule in Ireland* (1978)

Buckland, Patrick, *Irish Unionism* (1973)

Burnet, David and Bardon, Jonathan, *A Pocket History of Belfast* (1996)

Burnet, Gilbert, *History of His Own Times* (1823)

Caldicott, C.E.J. et al, *The Huguenots in Ireland* (1997)

Campbell, Flann, *The Dissenting Voice* (1991)

Carroll, Denis, *The Man From God Knows Where* (1995)

Carson, William A., *Ulster and the Irish Republic* (1956)

Churchill, Winston S., *Lord Randolph Churchill* (1906)

Cleary, S.J., *The Orange Society* (1897)

Cochrane, Fergal, *Unionist Politics* (1997)

Connolly, S.J., *Religion, Law and Power – The Making of Protestant Ireland 1600-1760* (1992)

Cook, Denis, *Persecuting Zeal – A Portrait of Ian Paisley* (1996)

Crawford, Robert, *Loyal to King Billy* (1987)

Cullen, L.M., *The Emergence of Modern Ireland 1600-1900* (1991)

Curtayne, Alice, *Patrick Sarsfield* (1934)

Curtis, Liz, *The Cause of Ireland* (1994)

de Paor, Liam, *Divided Ulster* (1970).

Dewar, M. et al, *Orangeism – A New Historical Appreciation* (1967)

Donnelly, S. James & Clark, Samuel, *Irish Peasants – Violence and Political Unrest 1780-1914* (1993)

Downing, Taylor, *The Troubles* (1980)

Dunlop, John, *A Precarious Belonging* (1995)

Elliott, Marianne, *Partners in Revolution* (1982)

Elliott, Marianne, *Wolfe Tone – Prophet of Irish Independence* (1989)

Elizabeth, Charlotte (Tonna), *Derry – A Tale of Revolution* (1839)

Falkiner, C. Litton, *Studies in Irish History and Biography* (1902)

Fitzgibbon, Constantine, *The Red Hand – The Ulster Colony* (1971)

Fitzpatrick, David, *The Two Irelands* (1998)

Fitzpatrick, W.J., *The Sham Squire* (1895)

Foster, R.F., *Lord Randolph Churchill – A Political Life* (1981)

Foster, R.F., *Paddy and Mr Punch* (1993)

Froude, J.A., *The English in Ireland in the Eighteenth Century* (1879)

Gahan, Daniel, *The People's Rising* (1995)

Gerrold, Claire, *The Early Court of Queen Victoria* (1912)

Geyl, Pieter, *The Revolt in the Netherlands 1555-1609* (1932)

Gilbert, J.A., *A History of Dublin* (1859)

Good, J.W., *Irish Unionism* (1920)

Gould, Robert Freke, *A Concise History of Freemasonry* (1903)

Grew, Marion E., *The House of Orange* (1947)

Gray, Tony, *The Orange Order* (1972)

Halévy, Elie, *A History of the English People in the Nineteenth Century* (1945)

Hall, M., *Ulster's Scottish Connection* (1993)

Hamill, John, *The Craft* (1986)

Hamilton, Paul, *Up The Shankill* (1994)

Hamilton, Thomas, *History of the Irish Presbyterian Church* (1887)

Hammond, J.L., *Gladstone and the Irish Nation* (1964)

Hennessy, Thomas, *A History of Northern Ireland* (1997)

Hepburn, A.C., *The Conflict of Nationality in Modern Ireland* (1980)

Hickey, D.J. and Doherty, E.J., *A Dictionary of Irish History 1800-1980* (1980)

Hobsbawm, Eric and Ranger, T., *The Making of Tradition* (1983)

Hyde, Montgomery H., *Carson* (1981)

Inglis, Brian, *The Story of Ireland* (1956)

Jackson, Alwin, *Colonel Edward Saunderson* (1995)

James, Rhodes Robert, *Lord Randolph Churchill* (1959)

Jarman, Neil, *Material Conflicts* (1997)

Jenkins, Roy, *Asquith* (1964)

Jenkins, Roy, *Gladstone* (1995)

Johnston, Robert, *Belfast – Portraits of a City* (1990)

Jones, Maldwyn A., *The Limits of Liberty – American History 1607-1980* (1983)

Kane, James S., *For God and King – The Story of the Blackers of Carrickblacker* (1995)

Kee, Robert, *Ireland – A History* (1980)

Kee, Robert, *The Green Flag* (1972)

Kilpatrick, Cecil et al, *History of the Royal Arch Purple Order* (1993)

King, William, *The State of the Protestants of Ireland under the late King James's Government* (1691)

Kishlansky, Mark, *A Monarchy Transformed* (1996)

Latimer, T. W., *A History of Irish Presbyterianism* (1893)

Lecky, W.E.H., *History of Ireland in the Eighteenth Century* (1908)

Lecky, W.E.H., *Leaders of Public Opinion in Ireland* (1903)

Lee, Stephen J., *Aspects of British Political History* (1994)

Lowe, Worman, *Mastering Modern British History* (1984)

Lucy, Gordon, *Lord Macaulay on Londonderry, Aughrim, Enniskillen and the Boyne* (1989)

Lyons, F.S.L., *Parnell* (1963)

Lyons, F.S.L. and Hawkings, A.J., *Ireland Under the Union* (1980)

Macaulay, T.B., *A History of England* (1849)

McBride, Ian, *The Siege of Derry in Ulster Protestant Mythology* (1997)

McCartney, Donal, *The Dawning of Democracy: Ireland 1800-1870* (1987)

McCarthy, Justin, *History of Our Own Times* (1908)

McClelland, Aiken, *William Johnston of Ballykilbeg* (1990)

McGarry, John and O'Leary, Brendan, *Understanding Northern Ireland* (1995)

McGarry, John and O'Leary, Brendan, *The Politics of Antagonism* (1996)

McManus, Seamus, *The Story of the Irish Race* (1921)

McNeill, Ronald, *Ulster's Stand for the Union* (1992)

Madden, Richard, *The United Irishmen, Their Lives and Times* (1857)

Marlow, Joyce, *Captain Boycott and the Irish* (1972)

Marshall, William S., *The Billy Boys* (1996)

Martineau, Harriet, *The Thirty Years' Peace* (1849)

Miller, D.W., *Queen's Rebels* (1997)

Miller, David, *Peep O'Day Boys and Defenders* (1990)

Miller, Derek, *Still Under Siege* (1989)

Miller, John, *James II – A Study of Kingship* (1978)

Miller, John, *The Life and Times of William and Mary* (1974)

Moody, T.W., *Davitt and the Irish Revolution 1846-1882* (1982)

Moore, Chris, *The Kincora Scandal* (1996)

Morgan, Austin, *Labour and Partition – The Belfast Working Class* (1990)

Murphy, Dervla, *A Place Apart* (1978)

Musgrave, Sir Richard, *Memories of the Different Rebellions in Ireland* (1802)

Neal, Frank, *Sectarian Violence – The Liverpool Experience 1819-1914* (1988)

Niven, Richard, *Orangeism – As It Was And Is* (1910)

O'Brien, R. Barry, *Thomas Drummond, His Life and Letters* (1889)

O'Faoláin, Seán, *King of the Beggars* (1980)

O'Ferrall, Fergus, *Catholic Emancipation – Daniel O'Connell and the Birth of Irish Democracy 1820-1870* (1985)

Ogg, David, *England in the Reign of James II and William III* (1955)

O'Kelly, Charles, *Macariae Exciduum* (1695)

O'Sullivan, Mortimer, *Captain Rock Detected* (1824)

Owen, D.J., *History of Belfast* (1921)

Pakenham, Thomas, *The Year of Liberty – The Great Irish Rebellion of 1798* (1969)

Pearce, M. and Stewart, G., *British Political History 1867-1990* (1992)

Petrie, Sir Charles, *The Great Tyrconnell* (1972)

Petty, William, *The Political Anatomy of Ireland* (1691)

Piatogorsky, Alexander, *Who's Afraid of Freemasons?* (1997)

Pick, Fred & Knight, Norman G., *The Freemason's Handbook* (1963)

Riddell, Patrick, *Fire Over Ulster* (1970)

Robb, Nessa A., *William of Orange – A Personal Portrait* (1966)

Senior, Hereward, *Orangeism in Ireland and Britain 1795-1836* (1996)

Sharrock, David and Davenport, Nigel, *Man of War/Man of Peace – An Unauthorised Biography of Gerry Adams* (1997)

Shephard, Robert, *Ireland's Fate* (1990).

Short, Martin, *Inside the Brotherhood* (1993)

Sibbett, R.M., *Orangeism in Ireland and Throughout the Empire* (1914).

Simms, J.G., *Jacobite Ireland 1689-91* (1969)

Smyth, Jim, *Men of No Property* (1992)

Stewart, A.T.Q., *A Deeper Silence – The Hidden Origins of the United Irishmen* (1993)

Stewart, A.T.Q., *Edward Carson* (1981)

Stewart, A.T.Q., *The Narrow Ground* (1977)

Stewart, A.T.Q., *The Summer Soldiers* (1995)

Stewart, A.T.Q., *The Ulster Crisis* (1967)

Story, George, *A True and Impartial History of the Affairs of Ireland During the Last Two Years* (1691)

Temple, John, *History of the Irish Rebellion* (1644)

Thompson, E.P., *The Making of the English Working Class* (1963)

Thornley, David, *Isaac Butt and Home Rule* (1964)

Tierney, M., *Ireland Since 1870* (1988)

Tillyard, Stella, *Citizen Lord – Edward Fitzgerald 1763-1798* (1997)

Tonna, Charlotte Elizabeth, *see* Elizabeth, Charlotte
Trench, Charles Chenevix, *The Great Dan* (1984)
Walker, George, *A True Account of the Siege of Derry* (1689)
Waucope, Piers, *Patrick Sarsfield and the Williamite Wars* (1944)
Wedgwood, C.V., *William the Silent* (1944)
Whelan, Kevin, *The Tree of Liberty* (1996)
Williams, T. Desmond, *Secret Societies in Ireland* (1973)

Pamphlets and Booklets

Apprentice Boys of Derry, 'Official Brochure of Tercentenary Celebrations of Apprentice Boys of Derry' (Londonderry, 1989)
Beresford Ellis, Peter, 'Orangeism – Myth or Reality' (London, 1997)
Buckland, Patrick, 'Irish Unionism' (Historical Society, London, 1973)
Buckley, A.D. and Anderson, Kenneth, 'Brotherhoods in Ireland' (Belfast, 1988)
Campbell, Alan, 'The Scarlet Woman of the Apocalypse' (Belfast, 1997)
Chittick, George, 'The Enniskillen Men' (Belfast, 1994)
Clifford, Brendan, 'Freemasonry and the United Irishmen' (Belfast, 1996)
Cordner, William, 'Brownlow House – A Short Guide' (Lurgan, 1993)
Dewar, M.W., 'Why Orangeism?' (Belfast, 1959)
Fitzpatrick, Michael, 'Historic Gorey – Reflections on 1798' (Gorey, 1998)
French, Noel E., 'The Battle of the Boyne' (Trim, 1998)
GOLI – Grand Orange Lodge of Ireland, 'A Celebration: 1690-1990 – The Orange Institution' (Belfast, 1990)
GOLI – Grand Orange Lodge of Ireland, 'Murder Without Sin' (Belfast 1990)
GOLI – Grand Orange Lodge of Ireland, 'Steadfast for Faith and Freedom: 200 Years of Orangeism' (Belfast 1995)
Holmes, Finley, 'Presbyterians and Orangeism 1795-1995' (Belfast, 1996)
Kenny, Michael, 'The Fenians' (Dublin, 1997)
Kilpatrick, Cecil, 'Aughrim – The Last Battle' (Belfast, 1991)
Kilpatrick, Cecil, 'The Diamond in its Historical Setting' (Belfast, 1996)
McClelland, Aiken, 'The Formation of the Orange Order' (no publisher or date)
Martin, W.J., 'The Battle of Dolly's Brae – 12 July 1849' (Belfast, n.d.)
Meredith, Ian and Kenneway, Brian, 'The Orange Order – An Evangelical Perspective' (Belfast, 1993)
Montgomery, G.G.W. and Whitton, R., 'The Order on the March' (Belfast, 1995)
O'Boyle, Enda, 'Battle of the Boyne' (Duleek Historical Society, n.d.)
Pat Finucane Centre, 'Londonderry, For God and Ulster' (Londonderry, 1997)
Ulster Society, Lurgan, 'The Orange Lark and Other Songs in the Orange Tradition' (1987)
Ulster Society, Lurgan, 'William Johnston of Ballykilbeg' (n.d.)

Reports

Select Committee (1835)
Report from the Select Committee appointed to 'Inquire into the Nature, Character, Extent and Tendency of Orange Associations in Ireland' (London, House of Commons)
Dolly's Brae Report (1849)
Papers relating to an investigation held at Castlewellan, County Down, into occurrences at Dolly's Brae on 12 July 1849 (London, House of Commons)

Index

Act of Settlement, 10, 36
Adair, Rev Patrick, 58
Adams, Gerry, 341, 347-8
Africa, Orangeism in, 397-8, 415
Aghaderg, 131
Aldermen of Skinners Alley, 10, 74, 93-4, 178-9, 183, 187
Allen, Sir William, 361, 364-5, 423
American War of Independence, 116, 118-9
'Ancient Britons', 194-5
Ancient Order of Hibernians, 130
Anglican Church, 88, 109, 114, 128, 203-4
Anglo-Irish Agreement (1985), 337-8, 341
Anglo-Irish Treaty (1921), 329-30
Annesley, Hugh, 346
Anti-Union (newspaper), 197
Antrim, Earl of, 39, 44-5, 46, 65
Antrim
    Grand Lodge, 199
    rebellion of 1798, 175-6
Antrim (North East) Association, 37
Apprentice Boys, 45, 342, 343, 368-74, 416-17, 420
Archdale, Mervyn, 236
Armagh
    County Museum, 104-7
    Grand Lodge, 165, 180, 341, 383
    Orange Order in, 11, 216-17, 273
    'Outrages', 147-50
    rural conflict in, 129-130
Athlone, Earl of, 178-9
Athlone
    battle of, 75-7, 98, 408
    siege of, 70
Atkinson, Joseph, 136-7
Atkinson, Wolsey, 11, 142, 145, 165, 180
Aughrim, battle of, 78-81, 409
Australia, Orangeism in, 394-5, 415

Bagwell, John, 110
Baker, Major Henry, 47, 49
Ballyholand, massacre at, 194
Ballymena, 1798 rebellion, 175
Ballymoney (Country Antrim), 351-2
Bandon (County Cork), 40-1, 42, 99-100, 102
Bangor, Johnston's march to, 282-3

Bantry Bay, French fleet in, 162-3
Barclay, Alexander, 130-1
Barrington, Sir Jonah, 184, 187-8, 199-200, 201
Barry-Maxwell, John, 178
Becker, Bernard, 293-4
Beers, Francis, 275, 278-9
Beers, William, 275, 276, 278-9
Belfast
    Academical Institute, 258
    evangelicalism in, 312-16
    Falls Road, 238, 309-10, 388
    industrial growth, 238
    O'Connell's visit to, 262
    Orange halls attacked, 339
    Ormeau Road marches, 343, 347, 352, 385-7
    Randolph Churchill's visit to, 306-7
    reaction to Home Rule, 304-10
    sectarianism, 238-9, 310, 329
    Shankhill Road, 238, 387-8
    and Solemn League & Covenant, 320-22
    William III's visit to, 57-9
Belfast Election Circular, The, 283
Belfast Evening Telegraph, 324
Belfast News Letter, 305, 313, 318, 338, 357, 390-1
Belfast Protestant Association, 321-2
Benevolent and Loyal Orange Institution, 237
Bentinck, Hans Willem, 25, 89
Beresford, Lord George, 226, 235
Beresford, John Claudius, 178-9, 186-7, 194, 195, 199, 201
Beresford, John Lucius, 123, 186, 199
Beresford, Willie, 139
Berwick, Walter, 277-9
Bingham, Rev William, 351, 353
Blacker, Rev Stewart, 136, 149, 267-8, 273, 357
Blacker, William, 51, 136, 137-8, 145, 154, 165, 178-9, 236, 237, 243, 248, 253-4, 267, 273, 422-3
Blaney, Lord, 37
Boycott, Charles, 292-5
Boyd, Alex, 323
Boyne, Battle of the, 55, 61-8, 98-9, 405
Boyne Obelisk, 98-9
Boyne Society, 100-7, 110, 185
Brady, Nicholas, 40

Braithwaite, Richard, 321
Breughel, Pieter, the Elder, 18-19
Bridge, John, 111-13,
Britain, Orangeism in, 10, 30, 203-11, 212-14, 237, 262-70, 398-400, 415, 416
Brougham, Henry, 220
Browning, Captain Micriah, 50
Brownlow, Sir William, 128, 149, 154, 164, 199-200, 268
Brownlow House (Lurgan), 359-60, 364
Brunswick Clubs, 231-3, 235
Buckley, Dr Anthony, 356-7
Burke, Walter, 78, 80
Burnet, Bishop Gilbert, 24, 25, 30, 88, 90, 422
Butler, Mary, 111
Butt, Isaac, 253, 287, 423
Byrne, Terence, 131

Cairns, David, 46, 47
Campsie, Henry, 45-6
Canada, Orangeism in, 393-4, 415
Carhampton, Lord, 151, 164
Carnarvon, Lord, 299
Carrick-on-Suir, 87
Carrickfergus, 54, 56, 116, 306
Carron, Peter, 155
Carson, Sir Edward, 319-23 325-6, 328
Castlereagh, Lord, 196-7, 200-1, 202, 213
Catholic Association, 221-2, 226-7, 228, 236
Catholic Committee, 116, 122-3
Catholic Emancipation, 219, 221-2, 227, 228, 231-2, 233, 234-6, 299-301
Catholic Relief Acts, 121-3, 128, 185, 198
'Catholic Rent', 222
Charlemont, Earl of, 115, 119, 128
Charles II, King of England, 21, 23, 26-7, 35
Chetwoode, C. Eustace, 210-11, 214, 236, 263-4, 267
Church of Ireland, disestablishment, 285-6, 298
Churchill, J., *see* Marlborough, Duke of
Churchill, Lord Randolph, 298, 303-4, 306-7, 422
civil rights movement, 335
Clare, Lord, 196, 200
Clarendon, Lord Lieutenant, 35-6
Clark, Sir George, 332-3

Clogheen (County Tipperary), 110
Cloncurry, Lord, 233
Cole, Lord, 201
Comber Letter, 38-9, 45
'Constitution of 1782', 118
Cooke, Edward, 194
Cooke, Rev Henry, 258-60, 261-2
Cookstown (County Tyrone), 345
Costello, James, 249-50
Craig, Sir James, 320, 326, 329, 331-2, 376
Crammie, Col, 382
Crawford, Robert, 317-18, 421
Cromwell, Oliver, 34, 35, 40
Cumberland, Duke of, 211, 229-31, 235, 237, 243, 263, 264, 266, 268-70
Cupples, Rev Snowden, 10, 158
'Curragh Incident', 331
Curran, Philpott, 149, 150, 151
Cuthbert, Joseph, 155

Dalrymple, Sir John, 86
Dalrymple, William, 156
Danby, Earl of, 29
Daris, Benjamin J., 297, 420
Davidson, Sir Joseph, 331-2
Davis, Thomas, 248, 254
Davitt, Michael, 289-291, 295
Dawson, Arthur, 199, 201
de Valera, Eamon, 329-30
'Defenders, 10, 129, 130-1, 132-3, 135-8, 140, 152, 166, 360, 421
Democratic Unionist Party (DUP), 340
Derry
    Apprentice Boys, 368-74, 416-17, 420
    'Battle of the Bogside', 342
    gerrymandering, 340
    riots in, 371-2
    Saint Columb's Cathedral, 370, 373, 420
    siege of, 12, 42, 43-51, 102, 297, 404
Diamond, Battle of the, 11, 134-8, 247, 343, 410, 420-1
Dickson, William Steel, 116-17
Dill, Rev Samuel, 273-4
Dillon, John, 291
Dillon, John Blake, 248
Dilly, John and Abraham, 133, 139
disestablishment, 285-6, 298
Dixon, Margery, 172
Dixon, Thomas, 172
'Dolly's Brae', 275-8, 421
Donegal, Orangeism in, 216
Donegall, Lord, 113, 238
Douglas, General James, 70

Down Protestant Association, 281
Down Recorder, The, 279
'Down Survey', 34-5
Downing Street Declaration (1993), 340
Downshire Protestant, The, 281
Drennan, Dr William, 126, 127
Drew, Thomas, 314-5
Drogheda, Marquis of, 178-9
Dromore, the 'Break' of, 41
Drumcree, 343-53
Drummond, Thomas, 246-8
Dublin
    Aldermen, 93-4
    'Bottle riot', 220-1
    City Hall, 94-5
    College Green Tapestries, 98
    first Orange Lodge, 164-5
    first Orange Parade, 74
    Protestant Association, 261
    statue to William III, 95-7, 219-20
Dublin Evening Mail, 219
Dublin Protestant Operatives Association (DPOA), 252-3
Dublin University Magazine, 253-6, 423
Duffy, Charles Gavan, 247, 248
Duigenan, Dr Patrick ('Paddy'), 178, 181, 182-4, 187, 200, 201, 218

Easter Rising (1916), 328
Education Acts, 337-8
Egan, William, 112
Eldon, Lord, 231, 232
emigration, 114-15, 252, 398
Emmet, Robert, 218, 222
Enniskillen, Lord, 178, 237, 243, 273, 280, 305
Enniskillen, 51-2, 345
Erne, Earl of, 292-3
Evangelicalism, 312-16, 386, 388
Eyre, Robert Hedges, 237

Fairman, William, 263-5, 267, 268-9, 270
Famine, the, 273
Ferguson, John Guy, 268-9
Ferguson, Samuel, 254-6, 423
Fitzgerald, Lord Edward, 162, 166
FitzGerald, Garret, 337
Fitzgerald, Nicholas, 75
Fitzgibbon, Gerald, 310
Fitzwilliam, Lord, 122, 126
Flanagan, Rev John, 286
Flanagan, Ronnie, 339-40, 351
Fletcher, Ralph, 207, 208, 210, 212
'Flight of the Earls', 32, 44
Flood, Henry, 115, 117, 118, 119, 121

Forkhill, 130-1
Forty-Shilling Freeholders, 123, 124
Foster, Sir John, 199, 201
Foster, W.E. 'Buckshot', 290, 294, 295, 298, 304
Framework Document (1995), 341
Frederick Henry, Prince of Orange, 20-1, 53
Freemasonry, 100-1, 104, 132, 140, 152-4, 161, 339-40, 356, 362, 365, 376, 384-5
French expeditions, 162-3, 191-2
French Revolution, 124

Galbraith, Thomas, 322
George III, King of England, 202, 212
George IV, King of England, 229, 231, 235
Gerard, Balthazar, 17-18
German Hessian Dragoons, 195
gerrymandering, 334
Gibbons, Grinling, 95
Giffard, Harding, 179
Giffard, John, 11, 139-40, 152, 164, 179, 194-5, 209, 216
Gillan, Daniel, 155
Ginkel, Godard, 57, 60, 74, 75-80, 82-4, 89
Gladstone, William, 285-6, 297-9, 301, 304, 308-9, 310-11
Glencoe (Scotland), 85-6
'Good Friday Agreement' (1998), 350
Gordon, Duke of, 229
Gosford, Earl of, 149-50, 151, 156
Government of Ireland Act (1920), 328-9, 331-2
Gowan, John Hunter, 166-7, 172, 178, 189-90
Gowan, Robert Ogle, 102-4, 174-5
Grace, Richard, 70, 75
Gracey, Harold, 344
Graham, Rev John, 369, 370
Grattan, Henry, 115, 119, 149, 150, 151, 200
Gray, Betsy, 176-7
Gray, Sam, 234
Gregg, Rev Tresham, 251-2
Grevell, Charles, 230
Guiness, Arthur, 179-80

Hall, William, 209
Hamilton, Rev Andrew, 101-2
Hamilton, Gustavus, 51, 57
Hamilton, Richard, 38, 41, 49, 63, 64, 67
Hammer, Sir John, 65-6
Hanna, Rev Hugh 'Roaring', 305, 313-4

Hare, Richard, 104
Harland and Wolff, 310-11, 315-16, 334, 388
Hart, James, 154-5
Harvey, Beauchamp Bagenel, 169
'Hawarden Kite', 300, 301
Haywood, Joseph, 265, 269
Healy, Timothy, 160-1
'Hearts of Oak', 113
'Hearts of Steel', 113-14
Hely-Hutchinson, John, 183
Henderson, Tommy, 373
Higgins, Francis, 166
Hillsborough, 38, 109, 261-2, 337
Hoche, General Lazare, 162-3, 165
Home Government Association, 287
Home Rule, 297-311, 319, 320-22, 324
Home Rule Act (1914), 328
Hope, Jemmy, 127
Hopkins, Dr Ezekiel, 45
House of Orange, 9-10, 13-14, 15-25, 418
'Howth Set', 304
Hudson, Rev Edward, 131
Huguenots, persecution of, 18, 28, 75, 87
Humbert, Jean Joseph, 191-2
Hume, Joseph, 264, 266, 268, 270

Irish Loyal and Patriotic Union, 99, 299
Irish Protestant, The, 317
Irish Republican Army (IRA), 97, 229, 335, 339, 341, 347
Irish Tenant Protection Association, 247
Irish Volunteers, 102
Irwin, Robert, 139, 145

Jackson, Richard, 130
James II, King of England, 26, 35, 39-40, 87, 89
  overthrown, 27-31, 37
  campaign in Ireland, 42, 46-7, 54-5, 61-9
Jeffreys, Judge, 27, 30
Jeffs, Isaac, 133
Johnson, Henry, 169-70
Johnson, Rev Philip, 157-8, 199, 212
Johnston, William, 280-5, 372, 306-7, 315-16
Johnstone, Mrs R.H., 366, 422

Keating, Rev. Dean, 179
Keating, Robert, 112

Kelly, John, 170
Kenyon, Lord George, 210, 212, 213, 214, 231, 232, 263, 267, 270
Keogh, Matthew, 171
Killala, French fleet at, 191-2
Killeavy Volunteers, 107
Kingsborough, Lord, 195
Kipling, Rudyard, 323-4
Knox, Francis, 201

Lake, Gerard, 164, 173, 175
Land Acts, 304
Land League, 289-96, 298-303
Land War, 288-96
landlordism, 108-9, 113, 247, 288-93
Larne
  gunrunning, 322-3, 324, 326
  rebellion (1798), 175
Lauzun, Comte de, 56, 59, 61, 62, 63, 65, 66, 67, 70, 71
Law, Andrew Bonar, 324-5
Lawless, Jack, 233-4, 242
le Froy, Thomas Langlois, 232-3
Lecky, Thomas, 112, 145, 147-8, 213
Lees, Harcourt, 226, 229
Leighton, Captain Baldwin, 38
Leinster, rebellion in, 166, 174-5
  see also Wexford, rebellion in
Leitrim, Earl of, 288
Lichfield House Compact, 246
Limerick
  siege of, 70-3, 82-3, 406
  Treaty of, 83, 86
Lisburn, 158
Lisnagraed, 131
Lloyd George, David, 319, 328
Londonderry, Marquess of, 331
Loughgall (County Armagh), 134-5,
  founding of Orange Order, 139-40
  Land League, 290
Louis XIV, King of France, 23-4, 26, 28, 29, 69, 89, 92
Loyal and Friendly Society of Blue and Orange, 10
Luddites, 204-5, 208
Lundy, Colonel Robert, 37-8, 47, 370-1, 422
Luttrell, Henry, 78, 80-1, 82, 83, 84

Macan, A.J., 149
McAteer, Eddie, 382
McCarthy, Lt Colonel Justin, 40-1, 42
McCarthy, General Mor, 54, 62
McCelland, Aiken, 363
MacCionnaith, Breandan, 343, 349, 350

McCracken, Henry Joy, 175-6
MacDonald, Alexander, 85-6
McGrath, William, 390, 392
Mackay, Hugh, 75, 77, 78-80
McKenna, Owen, 155
McKenna, William, 155
McNally, Leonard, 165
McTier, Samuel, 126
Magee, John, 223-5
Magheramorne Manifesto, 317-8, 421
Makemie, Rev Francis, 114
'Marksmen', 152-3
Marlborough, John Churchill, Duke of, 27, 30, 31, 74
Mary II, Queen of England (Mary of Orange), 52, 88-9
Mary Stuart (William III's mother), 21-2
Masonic Order *see* Freemasonry
'Massacre of Rathcormac', 244
Massacre of St Bartholomew, 18
Maurice of Nassau, Prince of Orange, 19-20
Meredith, Sir William, 279
Minford, Nat, 382
Mitchel, John, 274
Mitchelburne, Colonel John, 49, 50, 287
Mitchell, George, 341
Moira, Earl of, 148-9
Molesworth, Sir William, 264, 269
Molyneaux, James, 338
Monaghan Militia, 155
Monmouth, Duke of, 27
Montgomery, Henry, 259-60
Montgomery, Samuel, 179
Monthly Magazine, The, 160
Moore, John, 81
Morrison, James, 46
Mountalexander, Earl of, 37, 38, 41
Mountcashel, Lord, 52
Mountjoy, Lord, 44, 46, 122, 170
Mullaghbawn, 130
Mulgrave, Lord, 246
Murphy, John, 170
Murphy, Fr John, 167-8
Murphy, Fr Michael, 171
Murray, Adam, 47
Musgrave, Sir Richard, 10, 181, 178-9, 188-9, 200, 201, 218, 246

Nation (newspaper), 248, 253, 274, 295-6
Nationalist demonstrations, 281
Netherlands (House of Orange), 9-10, 15-25
New Ross, battle of, 169-70
New Zealand, Orangeism in, 393, 395-6, 415

Newport, Sir John, 213, 230
Newry Telegraph, 278
Newtownbarry, (County Wexford)
   244
Nixon, John, 333
Nixon, Ralph, 205-7, 209
North, Lord, 118, 121-2, 183
North Cork Militia, 194
Northern Ireland, established,
   328-9, 333
Northern Star, The, 127, 151,
   155, 156-7
Northern Whig, 239, 313, 318
Nugent, George, 176

'Oakboys', 113
O'Connell, Daniel, 101, 197, 218,
   219, 221-7, 228, 232-3, 236,
   241, 245-6, 248-9, 262
O'Connor, Arthur, 162
O'Connor, Charles, 116, 237
O'Doherty, Sir Cahir, 32
Ogle, George, 78-9, 184-6, 199,
   201, 216
O'Moore family (County Laois), 71
O'Kelly, Charles, 81
Oldenbarneveldt, Johan van, 19,
   86
O'Leary, Fr Arthur, 218
O'Neill, Hugh, Earl of Tyrone, 32
O'Neill, Sir Neil, 64-5
O'Neill, Sir Phelim, 33, 44
O'Neill, Phelim (Stormont MP),
   382
O'Sullivan, Rev Mortimer, 130-1
'Orange Boys', 132-8, 143, 148
'Orangemen', 131
Orange, House of, 9-10, 13-14,
   15-25, 418
Orange Order
   origins, 10-12
   founding of, 138-46
   first public appearance,
     156
   and Act of Union, 197-9
   reformed (1800), 215-7
   parliamentary enquiry into,
     266-70
   dissolved temporarily, 270-
     1, 272-3
   suppressed under Unlawful
     Societies Act, 225-6, 237
   revived, 236-8
   and Land League, 290-6
   growth of, 316
   and Home Rule, 301-308,
     309-311, 319-322
   and First World War, 326-8,
     349, 364, 424
   and Stormont, 330-31, 340
   and the Ulster Unionist
     Council, 332-3

and the 'Troubles', 339-41
and Drumcree, 343-54
abuse of power, 247, 334
links with freemasonry,
   100-1, 384-5
organisation of, 216, 357-8,
   382-3, 411-12, 419
membership, 375-6
membership qualifications,
   381-2
revenue, 389-90
reputation of, 353-4
rituals, 102, 107, 215-6,
   361-4, 376-82
'Romish Rigmarole', 383-4
and RUC, 333, 339, 40
women in, 365-7, 422
Benevolent and Loyal
   Orange Institution, 229

Grand Lodge of Ireland,
   177-82, 198-9, 215, 220,
   234-4, 267-8, 270-1,
   286, 291, 305, 345-6, 349,
   353, 375, 390, 413
Grand Masters, 413
Imperial Grand Orange
   Council of the World,
   284
Independent Orange Order
   ('I Double O'), 213, 323-5,
   421
Junior Orange Association,
   367-8, 416, 421
Loyal Orangewomen, Asso-
   ciation of, 365-7, 422
see also Orange parades;
   Orange societies;
   Orangeism; Royal Arch
   Purple Order; Royal
   Black Institution
Orange parades
   Bellaghy, 355-6
   Drumcree, 339, 343-53
   first parades, 74, 156
   marching season, 416-17
   militancy of, 242-4, 342-3
   Ormeau Road, 343, 347,
     352, 385-7
   prohibited, 278-81
   regalia and format, 356,
     361, 385-7, 389, 420-2
   Scarva, 360-1
Orange societies
   growth of 100-7, 140-1
   role of, 193-5
   Aldermen of Skinners Alley,
     10, 74, 93-4, 178-9, 183,
     187
   Boyne Society, 100-7, 111,
     185
   Brunswick Clubs, 231-3

Constitution Club of the
   Gentlemen of Kerry, 10
'Orange Boys', 132-8, 143,
   148
'Orange Young Ireland',
   253-6, 423
Protestant Association, 250
see also Orange Order
Orange Standard (newspaper),
   339, 423
Orangeism
   origins, 9-10
   growth of, 140-1, 154-5,
     164, 257, 261-2
   in Britain, 10, 30, 203-11,
     212-14, 237, 262-70,
     398-400, 415, 416
   internationally, 393-8, 415
   William III, symbol of, 12,
     13-14, 97-100, 361, 385
   see also Orange parades;
     Orange Order; Orange
     societies
'Order of Liberators', 233
Ormond, Duke of, 35, 87
Osborne, Alexander, 41
Overend, Robert 'Black Bob',
   355-6

Paisley, Rev Ian, 338, 340, 345,
   351
Parades Commission, 349-50
paramilitary violence, 335, 338
parliamentary reform, 114-116,
   117-119, 120
Parnell, Charles Stewart, 201,
   289-90, 295, 299-300
Parnell, Sir John, 199
Party Emblems Act (1860), 280-1,
   371
Party Processions Act (1850),
   248, 279-80, 282, 284, 371-
   2, 421, 422
Patten, Joel, 353
Patton, George, 349-50
'Pedlar's Wallet', 160
Peel, Sir Robert, 222-3, 225,
   229, 231, 232, 234-4
'Peep O'Day Boys', 10, 129, 130-
   1, 134-8, 142, 148, 182, 366,
   423
'Peterloo Massacre', 208
Petty, Sir William, 34, 36
Phillips, George, 45
Phoenix Park murders, 302
Pirrie, Lord, 316
Pitt, William (the Younger),
   123, 125, 195, 202-3
plantations, 32-5, 85, 87
Plowden, Francis, 11, 218
Plunket, William Conyngham,
   213, 221

Plunkett, Sir Horace, 328
Pontis, Marquis de, 39-40
Portadown, 11, 153, 248
  first Grand Lodge, 165
  Garvaghy Road, 339, 343-4,
    346, 348-9, 350
  rebellion (1641), 34
Presbyterians, 10, 88, 114, 123-4,
  128-9, 130, 141, 257-8, 262

Quigley, 'Captain', 135-6, 137, 146

Randalstown, 1798 rebellion, 175
'Rapparees', 87
Rawden, Sir Arthur 'The
  Fighting Cock', 38, 41
rebellion (1641), 33, 343
rebellion (1798), 166-73, 174-7
Redmond, John, 319, 326
Redpath, James, 295
'Redshanks', 39, 45-6
religious education, 331-2
Rene, Prince of Orange, 16
Reynolds, Thomas, 166
'Ribbonmen', 225, 239, 240-1,
  243, 274-8
Richardson, Sir George, 322
Robinson, Richard, 145
Roche, Fr Philip, 173
Rochford, Gustave, 199, 201
'Rockites', 239-41
Roden, Lord, 260-1, 273, 274-5,
  275-6, 278, 279-80
Roe, Thomas, 312-13
Rogers, Edward, 143
Rosen, Conrad van, 42, 49
Rossmore, Lord, 303-4, 306
Roth, Michael, 39
Rowan, Hamilton, 126
Royal Arch Purple Order, 105,
  181, 216-17, 356-8, 361-4,
  371, 419, 423
Royal Black Institution, 284,
  338, 342, 355-61, 382, 416-
  17, 419, 423-4
Royal Boyne Society, 10
Royal Ulster Constabulary
  (RUC), 329, 333, 338, , 343-
  4, 349
  and Orange marches, 343,
    346-8
  and Orange Order, 333,
    339-40
Royal Irish Constabulary (RIC)
  335
Russell, Lord John, 270
Russell, Thomas, 125-6
Rutherford, W.W., 399
Ryan, Daniel, 164-5, 166
Ryder, Rev William, 244-5

St Ruth, Marquis de, 74-82

Sandyes, Charles, 166
Sarsfield, Patrick, 27, 42, 55, 62,
  65, 70-3, 75, 78, 81, 82, 83,
  84, 86-7, 407
Saulters, Robert, 347, 353
Saunderson, Edward, 302-4,
  306-9, 315-16, 320, 343
Saurin, William, 197, 199, 218,
  223-4
Scarva (County Down), 360-1,
  424
Schomberg, Duke of, 53-6, 57,
  64-5, 66
Scotland
  Glencoe, 85-6
  Jacobites, 108
  Loyal Black Association of
    Scotland, 358
  Orangeism in, 398, 415,
    416
  sectarianism, 10, 129-30, 329,
    332, 338-9
Sellis, Joseph, 231
Server, Thomas, 216-17, 367
Shanahan, Daniel, 155
Sheehy, Fr Nicholas, 111-13
Sheil, Richard Lalor, 221
Sheldon, Dominic, 78, 82
Sidmouth, Lord, 210-11
Simms, Robert, 125
Sinclair, Thomas, 139, 144
Sinn Féin, 340-3, 347-8, 365
Sirr, Henry, 112, 166, 178-9, 186
Sling, Henry 'The Shaver', 216-7,
  367
Sloan, James, 11, 139-42, 143-6,
  152-3, 154, 178, 182
Sloan, Thomas, 315-16, 421
Smith, Richard Carpenter, 180
Smyth, Rev Martin, 346
Solemn League and Covenant,
  143, 320-22, 324
Special Powers Act (1922), 333-4
Star of Brunswick, The, 233
Staunton, Henry, 206
'Steelboys', 113-14
Stone, Archbishop George, 115
Stormont, 330-31, 334-5, 382
Story, George, 98
Stronge, Sir Norman, 382
Stuarts, flag of, 131
Sunningdale agreement, 335-6

Tandy, James Napper, 127
'TARA', 389, 392
Taylor, Samuel, 206, 212
Templepatrick, 113
Templeton, George, 145
Templeton, John, 153, 154
Thatcher, Margaret, 337-8
Thurot, Admiral, 116
Tithe War (1830-3), 244-5

tithes, 109-10
Tollymore, 274-7
Tone, Theobald Wolfe, 121-2, 125-
  7, 138, 162-3, 165, 192-3
Tonna, Charlotte, 365
Trew, Arthur, 321
Trimble, David, 345-6, 351
Trinity College Dublin, 39, 74,
  96, 101, 183, 253, 423
Tyrconnell, Richard Talbot, Earl
  of, 35-42, 44, 46, 61, 62, 63,
  67, 70, 71, 75
Ulster Defence Association
  (UDA), 353
Ulster Defence Regiment
  (UDR), 339
Ulster Freedom Fighters (UFF),
  339
Ulster Guardian, The, 317
Ulster Unionist Party (UUP),
  338-340
Ulster Volunteer Force (UVF),
  322-24, 326, 342, 353, 364,
  388
Union, Act of (1801), 195-201
  Catholic response to, 197,
    249
  Orange response to, 197-8
Unionish Party, 320, 332
United Irishman (newspaper),
  125-8, 138, 274
United Irishmen, 125-7, 140,
  151, 152, 154, 155, 162, 165-
  6, 168, 222, 384
United States of America,
  Orangeism in, 114-15, 316,
  396-7, 415
Unlawful Societies Act (1825),
  225-6, 229, 237

Verner Hart, James, 11, 135,
  144-5, 149, 150-1, 154,
Verner, Thomas, 164, 178-9,
  180, 181, 194, 198-9, 206,
  215-16, 236
Verner, William, 181, 243, 247,
  267
Verwoerd, Dr Hendrik, 333
Vinegar Hill, 168, 171, 173
Volunteers, 116-119, 124, 126,
  127

Walker, Rev George, 47-8, 50,
  57, 58, 66, 101-2, 307, 313
Walker, Thomas, 160
Wallace, Robert, 322
Waring, Rev Holt, 180, 250-1, 267
Watts, Isaac, 91
Wellesley, Richard Colley, 218-
  21
Wellington, Duke of, 228-9, 231,
  234-5

Wexford
    first Orange Lodge, 167
    rebellion in, 166-73, 195
'Wexford True Blues', 102
White, Hawtrey, 172
White, Henry, 231
'Whiteboys', 110-13, 121
'Wicklow Orange Blazers', 102
'wild geese', 84, 87
William I (the Silent), Prince of
    Orange, 16-19
William II, Prince of Orange, 20,
    21-2, 47
William III, King of England
    (William of Orange)
    as Prince of Orange, 13, 24-5
    early life, 22, 23
    character of, 25, 86

'Glorious Revolution', 10,
    26-31, 52, 402
campaign in Ireland, 10,
    38, 53, 55, 56-73, 403
at Battle of the Boyne, 62-8
at siege of Limerick, 70-3
and Scottish Jacobites, 85-6
and Ascendancy, 86-8
death, 90-1
statue in Dublin, 95-7, 219-20
'William's Men', 131
symbol of Orangeism, 12,
    13-14, 97-100, 361, 385
William IV, King of England, 270
Williamite Wars, 10, 14, 37-68,
    131
Wilson, Sir Henry, 325
Wilson, James 'Buddra', 132-4, 137-

140, 142-3, 145, 152-3, 154
Winter, Dan, 10, 134-5, 137-141,
    144, 145, 146, 152-3, 154,
    182, 420-1
Wise, Rev George, 399-400
Witt, Johan de, 23-4, 86
Wolfe, John, 151
women and Orange Order, 365-7
Wright, Billy, 350
Württemburg, Duke of, 55, 57,
    65, 74, 79
Wyse, Thomas, 116

York, the 'Grand old Duke' of,
    211-14, 230
Young, Arthur, 109
'Young Ireland', 254
'Young Ulster', 310-11